GROWING DEMANDS ON A SHRINKING HERITAGE: MANAGING RESOURCE-USE CONFLICTS

ESSAYS FROM THE FIFTH INSTITUTE
CONFERENCE ON NATURAL RESOURCES LAW

Edited by

MONIQUE ROSS
J. OWEN SAUNDERS

Canadian Institute of Resources Law
Institut canadien du droit des ressources

Calgary
1992

Canadian Cataloguing in Publication Data

Institute Conference on Natural Resources Law
    (5th : 1991 : Ottawa, Ont.)
        Growing demands on a shrinking heritage

    Conference held in Ontario, May 9-11, 1991.
    Includes bibliographical references.
    ISBN 0-919269-35-4

    1. Natural resources — Law and legislation — Canada
— Congresses. 2. Natural resources — Canada — Management
— Congresses. 3. Nature conservation — Law and
legislation — Canada — Congresses. I. Ross, Monique,
1949- II. Saunders, J. Owen (John Owen), 1948-
III. Canadian Institute of Resources Law. IV. Title.
KE5110.A66 1991   346.7104'4   C92-091429-2
KF5505.A17 1991   73/30

Printed in Canada

CONTRIBUTORS

Michel Bélanger, Président, Membre Associé, Centre de Médecine, Éthique et Droit, Université McGill, Montréal, Québec.

Jamie Benidickson, Faculty of Law, Common Law Section, University of Ottawa, Ottawa, Ontario.

Lloyd Binder, Research Associate, Arctic Institute of North America, The University of Calgary, Calgary, Alberta.

Adrian J. Bradbrook, Dean, Faculty of Law, University of Adelaide, Adelaide, Australia; and 1991 Chair of Natural Resources Law, The University of Calgary, Calgary, Alberta.

Robert B. Gibson, Associate Professor, Environment and Resource Studies, University of Waterloo, Waterloo, Ontario.

John Girt, Girt and Associates, Consultants in Environmental Management and Economic Development, Aylmer, Québec.

Jack Knetsch, Professor of Economics, School of Resource and Environmental Management, Simon Fraser University, Burnaby, British Columbia.

Nikita Lopoukhine, Acting Director, Natural Resources Branch, Canadian Parks Service, Environment Canada, Hull, Québec.

Alastair R. Lucas, Professor, Faculty of Law, The University of Calgary, Calgary, Alberta.

Martin K. Luckert, Assistant Professor, Department of Rural Economy, The University of Alberta, Edmonton, Alberta.

Robert Mainville, Partner, O'Reilly Mainville, Montréal, Québec.

J. Michael M'Gonigle, Associate Professor, School of Resource and Environmental Management, Simon Fraser University, Burnaby, British Columbia.

Gerald McKeating, Director, Canadian Wildlife Service, Conservation and Protection, Western and Northern Region, Edmonton, Alberta.

David McRobert, Program Coordinator, Pollution Probe, Toronto, Ontario; now serving as Policy Coordinator, Waste Reduction Office, Ontario Ministry of the Environment in Toronto, Ontario.

Paul Muldoon, Program Director and Counsel, Pollution Probe, Toronto, Ontario.

David Neave, Executive Director, Wildlife Habitat Canada, Ottawa, Ontario.

J. Gordon Nelson, Professor of Geography and Urban and Regional Planning, Faculty of Environmental Studies; and Chairperson, Heritage Resources Centre, The University of Waterloo, Waterloo, Ontario.

The Right Hon. Sir Geoffrey Palmer, Professor of Law, Victoria University of Wellington; Ida Beam Distinguished Visiting Professor, University of Iowa; and former Prime Minister of New Zealand, Wellington, New Zealand.

Evelyn W. Pinkerton, Research Associate, School of Community and Regional Planning, University of British Columbia, Vancouver, British Columbia.

Michael Robinson, Executive Director and Adjunct Professor, Arctic Institute of North America, The University of Calgary, Calgary, Alberta.

Monique Ross, Research Associate, Canadian Institute of Resources Law, The University of Calgary, Calgary, Alberta.

H. Ian Rounthwaite, Professor, Faculty of Law, The University of Calgary, Calgary, Alberta.

J. Owen Saunders, Executive Director, Canadian Institute of Resources Law; and Adjunct Professor, Faculty of Law, The University of Calgary, Calgary, Alberta.

Barry Stuart, Chief Land Claims Negotiator, Yukon Territorial Government; now serving as Yukon Territorial Court Judge, Whitehorse, Yukon.

Judith Swan, Executive Director, Oceans Institute of Canada, Halifax, Nova Scotia.

PREFACE

Conflict has always been an underlying theme in the management of natural resources, whether between specific uses of the resource (for example, forestry versus fisheries) or, as has been more recently the case, between philosophies of resource management. But while such conflicts are not new, recent disputes have arguably taken on a significantly different character than past ones.

The most obvious change in the nature of resource-use conflicts in recent years is the growth in the number of competing users. Aboriginal groups, for example, are more and more frequently involved in such conflicts, asserting traditional hunting, fishing, and trapping rights against industrial, recreational, or other users. Similarly, a flourishing recreation industry is now competing for space with traditional users. More generally, it is trite to observe that the public at large has taken a significantly greater interest in how resources are used; concern over threatened species and habitat, for example, is no longer limited to a handful of environmentalists, but is shared by a large segment of the population.

As the range of interests has expanded, the mechanisms that once served to address these conflicts have increasingly proven incapable of dealing with a new agenda and new actors. This is especially true with respect to legal mechanisms. Most obviously, the tools created by the common law for resolving resource-use conflicts are in many respects inadequate for coming to grips with new and different property interests. If we are to manage such conflicts successfully in the future, new mechanisms for dispute resolution must be created or old mechanisms must be given new life.

The goal of this volume of essays is to provide a greater understanding of the nature of resource-use rights and resource-use conflicts, with special emphasis on existing legal, economic, and institutional barriers to their resolution, and to explore ways in which conflicts have been or might best be addressed, in both the Canadian and international context. To this end, the volume brings together legal and non-legal voices in order to provide cross-disciplinary and cross-sectoral perspectives on problems and solutions associated with conflicting resource uses.

The essays in this volume fall thematically into five major groupings, with a final essay summarizing a major initiative to recast New Zealand's resources management regime, an initiative which should prove of interest to natural resources managers in general.

The first section deals in a general way with the problem of resource-use rights and conflicts from the perspective of both law and economics, although none of the three papers can be considered as presenting the "traditional" approach to the subject. Indeed, in many respects they represent a critique of the way both those disciplines have looked at environmental issues in the past.

The second group of essays is devoted to what has arguably become the underlying cause of most resource-use conflicts over the past decade, that is, the issue of wilderness preservation. The wilderness concept is important not only because of the deep and strongly felt feelings that it engenders in a large number of environmental advocates, but also for the special problems that it poses for policy makers. Specifically, much of the wilderness debate is predicated on the supposition that there are no trade-offs to be made, no compromises possible. One either has wilderness or has something else; real wilderness preservation in this view does not admit of any resource exploitation. Given such positions, it is not surprising that many writers believe that wilderness preservation will be one of the major issues of debate on the environmental agenda of the next decade.

A third group of essays deals with an issue that has been in the forefront of Canadian public policy concerns for the past decade — land claims. The papers in this section, however, are not directed at describing either generally or specifically the process and substance of land claims as such. Rather, they attempt to analyze land claims agreements as yet another mechanism for addressing resource-use conflicts; and certainly much of the core of land claims involves precisely a conflict among different potential users and uses of natural resources.

The fourth section addresses what is fast becoming one of the most pressing areas of conflict in natural resources management — the international arena. Clearly, this topic could easily fill a volume in its own right; the attempt here, however, is to give a sense of the scope of resource conflicts and of the mechanisms — both bilateral and multilateral — that are now being developed to deal with them.

A final group of essays looks at the potential of a range of mechanisms — co-management, environmental impact assessment, and "non-traditional" legal techniques — that might be considered as alternative routes for dispute resolution with respect to natural resources management. It is perhaps appropriate that these papers should lead into the final essay by Sir Geoffrey Palmer, which not only in itself suggests an alternative approach, but also illustrates the political possibility of radical transformation in the way resources are managed.

These essays arise out of the fifth biennial conference on natural resources law sponsored by the Canadian Institute of Resources Law, held in Ottawa, 9-11 May 1991. The conference was co-sponsored by the Faculty of Law (Common Law Section) of the University of Ottawa. In chairing the Conference Planning Committee, we benefited greatly from the advice provided by the other Committee members: Dean Donald McRae and Professor Jamie Benedickson of the Faculty of Law, University of Ottawa;

Susan Blackman and Janet Keeping, our colleagues at the Institute; and Barry Barton, then with the Institute and now with the Faculty of Law, University of Waikato, Hamilton, New Zealand.

Financial support for the Conference was provided by Alberta Forestry Lands and Wildlife, Ontario Ministry of Northern Development and Mines, the Department of the Secretary of State of Canada, Petro-Canada, Gulf Canada Resources Ltd., MacMillan Bloedel, the Walter and Duncan Gordon Foundation, the Helen McCrea Peacock Foundation, and an anonymous donor. The Alberta Law Foundation generously provided a grant to assist with the publication of this volume of essays.

During the editing of the papers we were assisted on the footnoting by Evangeline Case, the Institute's Publications Officer, and by Ingrid Liepa, Scott Paul, and Jane Sidnell, students in the Faculty of Law at the University of Calgary, then serving as summer Research Assistants in the Institute.

Nancy Money of the Institute coordinated the production of this volume; Patricia Albrecht, also of the Institute, assisted with the typing of a number of the papers. Finally, we owe special thanks to Terry Teskey for her technical editing of the essays and to Susan Parsons of the Institute for her contributions to layout, typing, and production of the volume.

Monique Ross
J. Owen Saunders
Calgary, Alberta
9 September 1992

TABLE OF CONTENTS

1

RESOURCE-USE RIGHTS AND RESOURCE-USE CONFLICTS

NATURAL RESOURCE USE CONFLICTS: "HARD vs. SOFT" RIGHTS

Alastair R. Lucas

A significant trend of the 1980s that shows few signs of abating is the proliferation of increasingly stringent environmental regulatory laws. The public rights established by these measures have had a major impact upon traditional natural resource property rights. Resource-use conflicts have often pitted "hard" natural resource rights, such as metallic-mineral rights, which are exclusive and virtually without qualification, against "soft" rights, such as water-use rights, which are considered to be stamped with a public interest that often requires them to give way. Today, however, natural resource-use rights, whether hard or soft, must contend with new environmental integrity rights. Certain natural resource-use rights, such as rights to the natural flow of water, are also consistent with environmental protection, but these are not well developed in Canada.

Public perceptions that in the past have attached relatively minor economic and social value to the natural environment are rapidly changing. The importance of quality of life, in which a healthy environment plays a significant role, has been recognized.[1] Scientific evidence has shown the public health dangers of toxic substances in the environment. There is also strong evidence, now largely accepted by the public and by governments, that transnational and even global ecosystems are in danger as a result of human activities, notably natural resource exploitation. The best example is the

---

1   Canada. Department of the Environment, *Environment and Development: A Canadian Perspective* (Ottawa: Supply and Services, 1987) at 7.

greenhouse effect, which appears to be causing a potentially disastrous global warming, to which the combustion of energy resources makes the largest contribution.[2] The result is that governments have shown an unprecedented seriousness about environmental protection. More stringent regulatory standards have been established, and there are signs that enforcement is becoming more vigorous.[3]

In the following sections it is argued that these public environmental integrity rights, particularly those recently established or proposed under federal and provincial legislation, significantly affect statutory rights to natural resource use. So far, these effects have mainly taken the form of regulation of the manner in which natural resource rights may be exercised, with a view to protecting these emergent environmental integrity rights. The natural resource rights themselves are at the point of being redefined by these environmental laws to make it a condition of their exercise that the natural environment not be significantly damaged.

The nature of hard mineral resource rights and soft water use rights is discussed in the first section. The focus then shifts to the emergence of public environmental integrity rights, the nature of these rights, and their effects on statutory natural resource use rights. Laws concerning nature protection, contaminant control, and environmental impact assessment are analyzed. The case of mineral rights versus natural area protection is examined through an analysis of the Supreme Court of Canada's decision in the *Tener* case.[4] Rationales for environmental integrity rights are then considered.

"HARD" MINERAL RESOURCE RIGHTS

Production of mineral resources in Canada has been carried out under reasonably full and secure rights that often amount to the complete mineral portion of fee simple property interests.[5] The mineral estate, as an element of the bundle of rights making up the fee simple interest in land, could be severed by sale and grant. It also became common for mineral rights owners to grant lesser interests involving rights to enter, explore for, and — if found — to produce and remove certain mineral resources. This type of property

---

2   See B. Bolin *et al.*, eds., *The Greenhouse Effect, Climatic Change and Ecosystems* (IUCN, Scientific Committee on Problems of the Environment, 1986); S. Schneider, *The Green House Effect* (1990).

3   See, for example, Canada. Department of the Environment, *Canadian Environmental Protection Act: Enforcement and Compliance Policy* (Ottawa: Supply and Services, 1988).

4   *R.* v. *Tener*, [1985] 3 W.W.R. 673 (S.C.C.).

5   For example, the British Columbia mineral claims in issue in the *Tener, id.*, were Crown-granted mineral claims.

interest is ideally suited to petroleum and natural gas resources, whose existence under particular land is uncertain and which require exploration and discovery before production can even be contemplated.[6]

Originally, mineral rights were obtained as part of full fee simple land grants from the Crown or, where there was already a Crown grant, through grants from the owner, as described, of either severed interests in mines and minerals or lesser property interests such as *profits à prendre*. The real-property nature of these interests was considered to be important. They were exclusive; contained no inherent qualifications; could be sold, bequeathed, or otherwise dealt with by the owner; and could be protected, if necessary, through legal action. The contractual character of the acquisition also provided a possible basis for legal action. Because of the importance of mineral development on Crown lands, modern Canadian mineral rights are more likely to be statutory, with exploration tenures leading to leases for defined periods at the development and production stage. Thus, a relatively high order of security remains whether one looks at metallic minerals or at oil and gas. An example of a grant that conveys such a full and secure right is that construed by the Supreme Court of Canada in *R. v. Tener*[7]:

> Know ye that we do by these presents ... in consideration of the fulfilment of the conditions of the laws providing for the acquisition of minerals ... give and grant unto WESTERN INVESTMENTS LIMITED [predecessor in title to the respondents] its successors and assigns, all minerals ... and the right to the use and possession of the surface of such mineral claim ... for the purpose of winning and getting from and out of such claim the minerals contained therein, including all operations connected therewith or with the business of mining.
>
> [The grant included a version of the habendum clause]:
>
> > To have and to hold the same unto the said WESTERN INVESTMENTS LIMITED its successors and assigns for ever ....

On the strength of these rights, the investment required to efficiently explore for, produce, and market the mineral resources could be confidently made.

At an early stage in the settlement of the Canadian west, the federal government recognized the value of these mineral resources and began to reserve them from original grants of land.[8] These mineral rights were then allocated, first by the federal government, and later, after the Natural

---

6   Though the specific granting language must be carefully examined, both freehold and Alberta Crown oil and gas leases are generally considered to grant *profit à prendre* interests. See *Berkheiser* v. *Berkheiser*, [1957] S.C.R. 387 (S.C.C.).

7   *Tener, supra,* note 4.

8   See David E. Lewis & Andrew R. Thompson, *Canadian Oil and Gas* (Toronto: Butterworths, Cont. Service) vol.1, div.A, para.27.

Resources Transfer Agreements,[9] by provincial governments, under disposition systems that established allocation procedures and defined the rights and obligations of the holders of the statutory tenures. Today, the bulk of mineral development occurs under these statutory tenures, which include Crown petroleum and natural gas leases, as well as metallic-mineral claims and leases.

Most varieties of these statutory mineral rights have been recognized as conveying, through contractual means, rights of a real-property nature.[10] It is highly likely, for example, that Alberta Crown petroleum and natural gas leases convey vested rights of a real-property character. Similarly, while certain mineral claims have been legislatively downgraded from real-property to chattel (personal property) interests,[11] even the latter are more ample and secure than mere regulatory permissions. Statutory mineral rights of a real-property character fall within the ambit of expropriation legislation, so that if taken by governmental authorities, there are clear rights to compensation.[12] Even in the absence of expropriation statutes, there is an ill-defined, but judicially recognized, implied right to compensation for government taking.[13]

When necessary, courts have determined the legal character of these mineral resource interests by carefully scrutinizing the statutory language that authorizes their creation and defines them, the language of the granting instruments, and the process of interest allocation. This inquiry determines whether or not the legislature intended to grant vested contractual or property interests or whether its intention was merely to grant revocable permission to exploit Crown mineral resources.[14] This interpretive process normally requires consideration of the social, economic, and political context of the legislation, an analysis that has the effect of factoring in societal purposes and objectives. Some courts, however, adopted the approach of using traditional property-interest categories as guides, along with certain basic distinguishing

---

9   The Natural Resources Transfer Agreements, 1929, confirmed by the *British North America Act*, 1930, 20-21 Geo. V, c.26 (U.K.), transferred to the western provinces natural resources that had been retained by the federal government when the provinces were originally created.

10   Rowland J. Harrison, "The Legal Character of Petroleum Licences" (1980) 58 Can. Bar Rev. 483; Alastair Lucas, "Acquisition of Natural Resource Interests by the State: Canada" (1987) J. Energy and Nat. Res. L. (December 1987 Supp.) 27.

11   *Cream Silver Mines Ltd. (NPL)* v. *R.*, [1986] 4 W.W.R. 328 (B.C.S.C.), concerning claims under the B.C. *Mineral Act*.

12   *Tener, supra*, note 4.

13   *Manitoba Fisheries Ltd.* v. *R.* (1978), 88 D.L.R. (3d) 462 (S.C.C.).

14   Lucas, *supra*, note 10.

criteria such as exclusivity of interests, transferability, and defeasibility, so that the process became one of highly conceptual classification.[15]

The result is that these statutory mineral rights have generally been recognized as rights of the highest order. They are hard rights in the sense that they are exclusive and reasonably secure, free in their essential elements from qualification by government except upon payment of fair compensation. Like any other property right they are subject to reasonable regulation, particularly regarding technical requirements for exploration and production, and environmental and public health regulations.[16]

When these statutory mineral rights conflict or threaten to conflict with other natural resource rights, the law provides regulatory or judicial means to weigh and accommodate the respective rights with a view to facilitating development. Alberta oil and gas leaseholders can, for example, apply for and obtain permission from the Energy Resources Conservation Board to drill through seams of coal.[17] In the case of conflict between mineral owners and holders of water rights, mineral development can normally proceed in the absence of unreasonable interference with water quantity or quality.

"SOFT" WATER RESOURCE RIGHTS

Though water quantity and quality rights have a clear and apparently secure foundation in riparian law, and latterly in western Canada under water rights statutes, they have proven weak when pitted against mineral resource rights. This is especially true for water quality rights. In earlier times, when development was sparse, mineral activity simply proceeded and contaminants were discharged into streams. Only if this pollution directly and seriously affected water rights holders would legal action be taken. This was largely a consequence of practical problems of cost and proof. While riparian owners could in theory sue for injunctions to protect their riparian rights, even in the absence of damage, the reasonable use standard made it difficult to establish interference with the rights.[18] And if interference were shown, the right could be qualified by judicial reluctance to award injunctive relief in the

---

15   See *Re Timber Regulations; A.G. Man.* v. *A.G. Can.*, [1933] S.C.R. 616 (S.C.C.), aff'd [1935] A.C. 184.

16   *Tener, supra*, note 4, *per* Estey J at 685-686.

17   Alberta. Energy Resources Conservation Board, Application by Gulf Canada Resources Inc. for a Gas Processing Plant in the Robb-Hanlan Area. ERCB Decision 81-1, 22 January 1981.

18   *Lockwood* v. *Brentwood Park Investments Ltd.* (1967), 64 D.L.R. (2d) 212 (N.S.S.C.), aff'd with a variation, (1970), 1 N.S.R. (2d) 669 (N.S.C.A.) [hereinafter *Lockwood* cited to D.L.R.].

absence of a strong likelihood of serious harm.[19]

While some nineteenth-century English courts were prepared to give water rights a higher status by characterizing them as including the right to receive water flowing in a natural stream without sensible diminution in quantity or quality,[20] this standard gave way, particularly in Canada, to the reasonable use criterion.[21] This rationality standard provided the flexibility necessary to permit industrial development, including mineral exploitation, that required substantial water withdrawal for processing activities and the subsequent discharge of waste into streams.

As Joseph Sax put it in the U.S. context, there was effective judicial recognition of a right to pollute, though not a property right to pollute.[22] This reflected the fact that in the United States water was viewed as a public resource to be allocated to those activities that advanced the contemporary public interest. Originally this U.S. public interest was seen as primarily developmental, so that natural flow water rights yielded to more intensive agricultural, municipal, and industrial uses.

Similarly in Canada, the public interest required that soft water rights yield to more withdrawal-intensive uses — mainly agricultural, but including industrial water uses based on exercise of mineral resource rights.[23] So long as water was in relatively abundant supply, as it has been until recently, there were few serious conflicts. But when conflicts did arise, the weakness of both riparian water rights and statutory prior-allocation water rights was abundantly clear, whether the competing interests were statutory mineral rights, timber rights,[24] or developmental land rights.[25]

The western Canadian statutory water rights may be even softer in this sense than the riparian rights that they largely replaced. Analysis of the statutory rights-granting provisions, the granting instruments (water licences), and the various defeasibility provisions under which the rights may be

---

19   *Id.*, at 236.

20   *John Young & Co.* v. *Bankier Distillery*, [1893] A.C. 691 (H.L.).

21   *Lockwood, supra*, note 18.

22   Joseph L. Sax, "The Limits of Private Rights in Public Waters" (1989) 19 Envir. L. 473, 476.

23   Riparian rights were replaced in western Canada by statutory prior-allocation systems in order to facilitate irrigation developments and other more intensive beneficial water uses. See Alastair R. Lucas, *Security of Title in Canadian Water Rights* (Calgary: Canadian Institute of Resources Law, 1990) at 17-18.

24   *Palmer* v. *Nova Scotia Forest Industries* (1983), 2 D.L.R. (4th) 397 (N.S.T.D.).

25   *Lockwood, supra*, note 18.

modified or even abrogated, suggests that there is at least serious doubt whether water licence rights are property rights or even vested rights arising under contract.[26] Rather, they appear to be mere regulatory permissions, subject to modification by the water resources authorities so long as statutory powers are not exceeded and fair procedures are used. Moreover, water quality rights suffer simply because new withdrawal rights continue to be granted while doubt remains about what the statutes provide — particularly in relation to water quality[27] — and management policies often diverge from the apparent requirements of statutes.

A class of water rights that may be regarded as particularly soft, even within the category of statutory rights, is rights to the natural flow of water, for fish conservation, wetland protection, or other like purposes. These "in-stream" rights have received considerable recent attention in U.S. prior-appropriation water law.[28]

In Canada, the existence in most jurisdictions of natural flow water rights is not even certain. Alberta's *Water Resources Act* does provide for natural licences,[29] and a licence has been granted to a society formed to protect water levels in a wetland nature preserve.[30] Even in Alberta, however, the future of natural flow rights is uncertain, since they create difficult management problems where stream flows are highly variable. Such rights rank below withdrawal uses in the Alberta statutory purpose ranking[31] so that they may (subject to compensation) be reallocated to "higher" developmental uses.

The result is that while water rights apparently enjoy a legal status similar to that of mineral resource rights, in practice the legal system has not been effective in protecting, and to a degree in even recognizing, these rights. Water quality rights and natural flow rights have proven to be particularly soft in this sense, and have suffered an incremental but steady weakening as the exercise of mineral rights increases the disposal of contaminants into water.

---

26 Lucas, *supra*, note 23, at 31-32.

27 *Id.*, at 96; David R. Percy, *The Regulation of Ground Water in Alberta* (Edmonton: Environmental Law Centre, 1987) at 7-16.

28 Sax, *supra*, note 22.

29 *Water Resources Act*, R.S.A. 1980, c.W-5, s.11(1)(c): "[U]se water in its natural state for conservation, recreation or propagation of fish or wildlife or any like purpose."

30 Interim Water Licence No.14086 granted to Wagner Bog Natural Area Society, 20 December 1985; see Donna Tingley, "Natural State Water Licensing" (1986) 16 Resources 4.

31 *Water Resources Act, supra*, note 29.

THE EMERGENCE OF ENVIRONMENTAL
INTEGRITY RIGHTS

Today there is an analogous softening trend that is affecting traditional hard mineral rights such as metallic minerals and oil and gas. The competition and conflict are provided by environmental quality rights — rights heretofore considered to be decidedly soft rights, that, in the form of water quality rights, could not hold their own against the exercise of polluting agricultural and industrial water-use rights.

The public interest that underlies the distinction between hard and soft natural resource rights has begun to change. Exploitive natural resource development is still viewed as an important economic activity, but one whose benefits must be carefully weighed against environment, safety, and regional economic detriments.[32] Mineral resource development must be assessed and regulated to mitigate these adverse impacts.

A high level of public consciousness about environmental protection has developed, particularly since the mid-1980s. This perspective differs fundamentally from the environmental concerns of the 1970s, which focused largely on local environmental issues — primarily aesthetics and natural area protection.[33] Now, improved scientific information that more clearly shows threats to ecological systems, and improved public education and information, have brought these threats to the attention of individual Canadians. They consider that their health, personal enjoyment, and even personal freedoms are in danger. Moreover, they are increasingly aware that these problems are global in scale. Notwithstanding lingering scientific doubts, a significant majority of Canadians agree that issues such as global warming caused by a greenhouse effect, and ocean pollution, are serious environmental problems that must be addressed nationally and internationally.[34]

The preeminence of natural resource development in the national economy is being seriously questioned. When asked in 1989 whether they think economic or environmental priorities should most influence land-use decisions, Canadians responded that environmental priorities should prevail, by a margin of 63 percent to 18 percent.[35] Even in resource-dependent

---

32   See Canada. Department of the Environment, *A Framework for Discussion on the Environment* (Ottawa: Supply and Services, 1990) at 3-6.

33   Keith Neuman, "Public Opinion on the Environment: Trends and Implications for Law and Public Policy in the 1990's" *in* Donna Tingley, ed., *Into the Future: Environmental Law and Policy for the 1990's* (Edmonton: Environmental Law Centre, 1990) at 4.

34   *Id.*, at 20.

35   *Id.*, at 5.

Alberta, the margin was 61 percent to 18 percent.

The perceived strategic and political significance of energy resources no longer secures this industry against stringent environmental measures. This is reflected, for example, in air pollution measures aimed at reduction of SO_2 and NO_x emissions, to which the energy sector is a major contributor.[36] Even more serious are proposals to reduce emissions of CO_2, a contaminant that contributes significantly to the greenhouse effect.[37] The ground for these measures was prepared by the de-linking of growth in energy use and general economic growth that occurred after the first oil price shock in 1973.[38] It became apparent to governments, regulators, and the public that healthy economies could be maintained using less energy and emphasizing less environmentally damaging energy sources.

STATUTORY ENVIRONMENTAL RIGHTS

These changes in the public interest that underlies Canadian natural resources law resulted in a series of legal developments that have had the effect of "hardening" renewable resource and environmental quality rights, and correspondingly "softening" mineral resource rights. It must be emphasized that we are dealing with statutory public environmental rights here. The common law has contributed little in Canada to the development of rights to maintain the integrity of the natural environment. There has, for example, been no Canadian recognition of a public trust concept to parallel doctrinal advances in the United States.[39]

These environmental rights are directed, at least in part, towards maintenance and protection of the environment as such, and not merely towards ensuring its availability for human exploitation. They are essentially

---

36   See, for example, the agreements signed between the federal government and the provinces following the announcement of the Federal-provincial Acid Rain Control Program in 1985. The Canada-Newfoundland Agreement Respecting a Sulphur Dioxide Reduction Program, 9 March 1987, is typical of those agreements. See also Alberta. Energy Resources Conservation Board, Informational Letter, IL 88-13, Sulphur Recovery Guidelines For Sour Gas Plants in Alberta, August 1988; and Canadian Council of Ministers of the Environment, Federal-provincial L.R.T.A.P. Steering Committee, *Management Plan for Nitrogen Oxides (NO_x) and Volatile Organic Compounds (VOCs): Final Draft* (Winnipeg: Canadian Council of Ministers, 4 October 1990).

37   The 1991 Federal Green Plan commits the government to stabilize emissions of CO_2 and other greenhouse gases at 1990 levels by 2000.

38   Personal communication with Peter O'Dell, Energy Institute, University of Rotterdam, 1990, citing O.E.C.D. report statistics.

39   *Green* v. *The Queen in Right of Ontario*, [1973] 2 O.R. 396 (Ont. H.C.). See Constance D. Hunt, "The Public Trust Doctrine in Canada" in John Swaigen, ed., *Environmental Rights in Canada* (Toronto: Butterworths, 1981) at 151.

public rights that must be enforced by responsible public authorities, though there is the possibility of privately initiated judicial review to ensure that the public environmental protection duties are carried out.[40] Under recent advances in the law of standing, private persons and interest groups able to demonstrate through their activities and involvement a genuine interest in the enforcement of these rights are likely to be permitted standing to obtain judicial review.[41]

Mineral Rights vs. Natural Area Protection

The intention to safeguard nature is apparent in statutes such as the federal *Fisheries Act*,[42] which protects fish and fish habitat, and has been held not to be limited to conservation of commercially valuable fish species.[43] This Act is the authority for a series of industry-specific water contaminant discharge limits. The *Migratory Birds Convention Act*[44] is specifically designed to protect waterfowl and other migratory bird species. Wildlife protection measures, including establishment of sanctuaries, are authorized under the *Canada Wildlife Act*.[45] National parks are preserved for the enjoyment of present and future generations of Canadians under the *National Parks Act*.[46] These parks and wildlife statutes have counterparts in the provinces, and it was under one of these provincial park acts that a classic legal confrontation arose between mineral rights and park protection provisions.

The Supreme Court of Canada held in the *Tener* case[47] that Crown-granted mineral claims, for which the owners were denied exploration and work permits under subsequently enacted legislation that established the area as a provincial park, had been taken by the Crown, so that compensation was

---

40   Such as the EARP cases, *Canadian Wildlife Federation* v. *Canada (Minister of the Environment)*, [1990] 2 W.W.R. 69 (F.C.A.), and *Friends of the Oldman River Society* v. *Canada (Minister of Transport)* (1990) 5 C.E.L.R. (N.S.) 1 (F.C.A.), in which duties to carry out environmental impact assessment under the Federal Environmental Assessment and Review Process Guidelines Order, S.O.R./84-467, were enforced in actions by environmental groups.

41   *Minister of Finance* v. *Finlay*, [1986] 2 S.C.R. 607; Andrew J. Roman & Mart Pikkov, "Public Interest Litigation in Canada" *in* Tingley, *supra*, note 33, at 165.

42   *Fisheries Act*, R.S.C. 1985, c.F-14, ss.34-37.

43   See *R.* v. *Jordan River Mines Ltd.*, [1974] 4 W.W.R. 337, 339-340 (B.C. Prov. Ct.).

44   *Migratory Birds Convention Act*, R.S.C. 1985, c.M-7.

45   *Canada Wildlife Act*, R.S.C. 1985, c.W-9.

46   *National Parks Act*, R.S.C. 1985, c.N-14.

47   *Tener, supra*, note 4.

payable under relevant expropriation laws. The result seems to confirm the preeminent character of natural resource property rights in the event of conflict with statutory nature protection laws. Yet closer examination reveals considerable strength in these public nature preservation rights and corresponding weakness in the mineral rights.

First, while the mineral rights prevailed in *Tener*, the result was an expropriation for public purposes under the park legislation, and the conversion to a right to fair compensation. The problem is that the notorious difficulty in valuing undeveloped mineral interests creates a large measure of insecurity for the mineral rights holder.

Secondly, and more seriously, the conceptual tests developed by the Court to determine when a taking for park use occurred leave considerable scope for regulatory restrictions on mineral property rights. According to the majority decision, regulatory constraints on natural resource rights can amount to expropriation when there is effective denial of the right to exploit the minerals that has the effect of enhancing the value of public property. Thus, in *Tener*, denial of the park use permits meant denial of access to the mineral claims, and consequently removal of the very essence of this form of property right, namely the right to explore for and exploit the minerals. Estey J distinguished this enhancement of the value of public property from zoning, regulation of specific activity on land, and protective regulation such as fire protection. He might have added environmental protection.[48] All these forms of regulation were considered to add nothing to the value of public property, and so involve no taking of property rights.

Thus, there is considerable room for environmental and public safety regulation that has the effect of limiting hard mineral resource rights and preserving nature. These regulations could include park or other land-use measures that limit the scale, manner, and timing of mineral development. Regulation could conceivably mean limitation to small-scale or seasonal development that could make the economics of mineral exploitation questionable.

Clearly, to a degree these measures would enhance the value of adjacent public park or nature reserve property. They help to protect and sustain the integrity of the natural environment, and thus support the public rights created by the nature protection and contaminant control statutes. The legal standard laid down in the *Tener* case is difficult to apply in practice, and if it does permit mineral rights to be seriously affected it weakens the private mineral property rights at the expense of public environmental integrity rights.

---

48   *Id.*, at 686.

While all of these parks and wildlife statutes may be viewed (sometimes tenuously) as maintaining ecological integrity rather than fostering human exploitation of nature, they are all relatively well established measures. Some, like the *Fisheries Act*, date from the nineteenth century.[49] They are an important part of the legislative fabric that establishes environmental quality rights. But it is in a series of more recent statutes that one discerns most clearly the trend towards hardening of environmental rights into rights to maintenance of ecological integrity.

Protection of Ecological Systems Against Contamination

The most important of these recent statutes is the *Canadian Environmental Protection Act* (CEPA).[50] Even in the long title of the Act — "An Act Respecting the Protection of the Environment and of Human Life and Health" — the environment itself is distinguished from humans and their dependence upon the natural environment. It is declared in the Preamble that: "the protection of the environment is essential to the well-being of Canada ...." "Environment" means the components of the Earth and includes:

(a)   air, land and water,

(b)   all layers of the atmosphere,

(c)   all organic and inorganic matter and living organisms, and

(d)   the interacting natural systems that include components referred to in paragraphs (a) to (c).[51]

The critical concept of toxicity — the criterion for regulation or prohibition of environmentally damaging substances — is defined as a substance that is entering or may enter the environment in a quantity or concentration, or under conditions:

(a)   having or that may have an immediate or long-term harmful effect on the environment;

(b)   constituting or that may constitute a danger to the environment on which human life depends; or

(c)   constituting or that may constitute a danger in Canada to human life or health.[52]

It is again significant that the environment as a natural system is singled out in its own right, apart from any effects on human health and independent of any economic utility. This is the result of a change made in the definition

---

49   See Kernaghan Webb, *Pollution Control in Canada: The Regulatory Approach in the 1980's* (Ottawa: Law Reform Commission of Canada, 1988) at 11.

50   *Canadian Environmental Protection Act*, S.C. 1988, c.22.

51   *Id.*, s.3.

52   *Id.*, s.11.

included in the original draft Bill that was circulated for public comment. Specification of the natural environment was urged by public groups and by the Canadian Environmental Advisory Council.[53] This change was even clearer in the CEPA Bill before the following words were removed from the end of clause 11(a), following the second-reading stage review by the Parliamentary Committee: "that is likely to interfere with important biological processes."[54]

Failure to comply with requirements under the Act, and thus interference with these ecological integrity rights, may result in enforcement actions either by the governmental authorities or, less directly, by citizens themselves. Quasi-criminal prosecutions may be launched and actions for injunction may be initiated by the Minister.[55] "Any person" who has suffered loss as a result of conduct contrary to the Act may sue to recover damages.[56] This latter right has the indirect effect of promoting conduct consistent with ecological integrity. Individuals also have process rights to initiate and to be informed about toxicity regulation,[57] as well as to require that alleged contraventions of the Act be investigated.[58]

Environmental Impact Assessment

The proposed *Canadian Environmental Assessment Act*[59] also fosters ecological integrity rights. Its purpose is to "encourage actions that promote sustainable development and thereby achieve or maintain a healthy environment" (as well as a healthy economy), and consequently to ensure that environmental effects of proposed projects receive careful consideration before decisions are made.[60] Sustainable development is to be promoted, a concept

---

53   Canadian Environmental Advisory Council, *Review of the Proposed Environmental Protection Act* (Ottawa: Supply and Services, 1987).

54   See Canada. House of Commons. Legislative Committee on Bill C-74, "Report to the House" in *Minutes of Proceedings and Evidence of the Legislative Committee on Bill C-74* (Ottawa: Queen's Printer, 23 March 1988) at 26:3.

55   CEPA, *supra*, note 50, ss.111-133 (offences and punishment), s.134 (ticketing), s.135 (injunction). Private prosecutions may also be brought by individual citizens.

56   *Id.*, s.136.

57   *Id.*, ss.12(4)-12(5) (request that substance be added to Priority Substances List); ss.13(2), 48(2), 86(4) (notice of objection requesting establishment of board of review).

58   *Id.*, ss.108-110. The Minister must inform the applicants on the progress of the investigation and provide written reasons if the investigation is discontinued.

59   Bill C-13, *Canadian Environmental Assessment Act, 1992*, passed by the House of Commons, 19 March 1992.

60   *Id.*, s.4.

that appears to demand preservation of ecological integrity.[61] The definition of "environment" is the same as in CEPA.[62]

Ultimately, following environmental assessment and review, projects may proceed only where the responsible governmental authority concludes that "the project is not likely to cause significant adverse environmental effects, or ... is likely to cause significant adverse environmental effects that can be mitigated or justified in the circumstances."[63] While these requirements are to be enforced by a special government agency, there is a role in their enforcement for members of the public. Assessment information relevant to proposed projects must be available to the public,[64] and members of the public must be given an opportunity to participate in the assessment at the panel review stage.[65]

Proposed Alberta environmental impact assessment provisions[66] require, in the case of natural resource projects, that environmental assessment and review be carried out either by the Energy Resources Conservation Board or the new Natural Resources Conservation Board.[67] Approval decisions, following assessment and review, would also be made by the appropriate Board, with the prior authorization of the provincial cabinet.[68] In such decisions, environmental effects would be only one set of factors to be considered.

The *Environmental Protection and Enhancement Act*, in which these environmental assessment provisions are included, requires that all decisions under the Act be made to support and promote the protection, enhancement, and wise use of the environment while recognizing the following:

(a) the protection of the environment is essential to the integrity of ecosystems and human health and to well-being of society ...

(c) the principle of sustainable development which ensures that the use of resources and environment today does not impair prospects for their use by future generations ...

---

61   *Id.*, Preamble.

62   *Id.*, s.2.

63   *Id.*, s.37(1).

64   *Id.*, s.34(a).

65   *Id.*, s.34(b).

66   *Alberta Environmental Protection and Enhancement Act*, Bill 23, 1992, ss.38-57.

67   By the ERCB under the *Energy Resources Conservation Act*, R.S.A. 1980, c.E-11 and the relevant energy resource statute, or by the NRCB under the *Natural Resources Conservation Board Act*, S.A. 1990, c.N-5.5.

68   *Supra*, note 66, s.51; *Natural Resources Conservation Board Act*, id., s.9.

(d) the interrelated factors associated with the environment should be recognized ....[69]

Arguably, the overall intention of both Acts is preservation of ecological integrity. While inclusion in the federal bill of the "or justified in the circumstances" exception suggests lingering legislative uncertainty about the hardening of ecological integrity rights in the event of direct conflict with developmental rights such as mineral resource rights, the direction of movement seems clear. Even the "justification" may, as a matter of interpretation, be read as not seriously inconsistent with preservation of ecological integrity, and, consequently, with the ability to meet the needs of future generations. The Alberta Act also requires recognition of "the need for Alberta's economic growth and prosperity in an environmentally responsible manner and the need to integrate environmental protection and economic decisions in the earliest stages of planning."[70] Significantly, the economic objective is qualified not only by environmental planning and protection goals, but also by the broader sustainable development and ecological integrity objectives.

This interpretive question is important, in considering the "significant adverse effects" (in the federal Act) or "public interest" acceptability (in the Alberta legislation) standards. If there is a duty to determine on the basis of the environmental assessment information not merely the regulatory conditions on which natural resource rights may be exercised, but whether ultimately such rights may be exercised at all, then the natural resource rights themselves are seriously weakened. At some point the line is crossed between mere regulation and actual redefinition of the natural resource rights by attaching the qualification that such rights cannot be exercised to cause ecologically significant adverse or unacceptable environmental damage. This would be analogous to the qualification built into riparian water rights that such rights must be used so as to avoid unreasonable interference with the rights of downstream riparian owners.

The proposed *Canadian Environmental Assessment Act*, as well as the proposed Alberta environmental assessment provisions, suggest governmental caution and uncertainty about taking this critical step of clearly embedding ecological integrity qualifications in natural resource rights. In both Acts, emphasis is on the environmental impact assessment process, so that this rights qualification issue is obscured by a haze of EIA process and procedure.

Environmental Bills of Rights

Another legal technique for creating and enforcing ecological integrity

---

69   *Supra*, note 66, s.2.

70   *Id.*, s.2(b).

rights that has been the subject of much discussion[71] but, until recently, of very little action, is the "Environmental Bill of Rights". This idea is often linked to the common law public trust concept, which confers public rights to maintenance of the integrity of the natural environment as a public heritage.[72] Typically, proposed environmental bills of rights have, like Michigan's pioneering 1970 *Environmental Protection Act*,[73] given citizens standing to sue to protect the public rights and, at least partially, have shifted the burden of proof to the alleged polluter.

Quebec's *Environment Quality Act*[74] establishes a right in any person to sue for injunctive relief as a consequence of environmentally damaging action contrary to the Act. The substantive standards in such actions are thus linked to the contaminant limits fixed under the statute. An Environmental Bill of Rights that permits citizen legal actions against polluters was adopted by the Northwest Territories legislature in 1990.[75] In late 1990 Ontario initiated a consultative process designed to develop an Environmental Bill of Rights.

RATIONALES FOR ECOLOGICAL INTEGRITY RIGHTS

Utilitarian Rationales

It must be emphasized that these statutory ecological integrity rights are vested in humans. At present, protection of the environment as such in statutes such as CEPA is most appropriately justified on the utilitarian basis that ecological system breakdown is likely ultimately to have adverse effects on humans. These may, for example, be direct dangers to health, such as increased incidence of cancers caused by serious deterioration of the ozone layer, or a more general deterioration in the quality of life and the possibility of property damage resulting from global warming and a consequential rise in sea levels.

It may be possible to factor in an element of altruistic justification for these rights, based on an ethical duty such as that proposed by Tribe.[76]

---

71   See Law Reform Commission of Canada, *Crimes Against the Environment: Working Paper No.44* (Ottawa: Law Reform Commission, 1985) at 12-13; Joseph Sax, *Defending the Environment: A Strategy for Citizen Action* (New York: Knopf, 1971).

72   *Id.*; see *supra*, note 39.

73   *Environmental Protection Act*, Mich. Pub. L. §127 (1970).

74   *Environment Quality Act*, R.S.Q. 1977, c.Q-2, ss.19.1-19.7.

75   *The Environmental Rights Act*, S.N.W.T., 1990, c.38.

76   L. Tribe, "Ways Not to Think About Plastic Trees: New Foundations for Environmental Law" (1974) 83 Yale L.J. 1315.

Indeed, there has been a renewed interest in the idea of environmental stewardship. The "Land Ethic" of U.S. naturalist Aldo Leopold has been the subject of new attention by U.S. natural resources lawyers and policy makers.[77] Leopold's ethical attitude toward land involved recognition of intrinsic moral worth at the biotic community level, though he also believed that this ethic furthered human utility.

Protecting Nature for Its Own Sake

This nature-centred approach requires a radically different view of environmental rights. A purely biocentric rational for protecting the environment leads directly to vesting rights in the environment itself.[78] If the value of nature derives from its inherent qualities rather than its usefulness in serving human values, then it should have a right to exist entirely independent of humanity. Thus, Stone in a well-known article asked, "Should trees have standing?"[79]

In Canada at present, the answer to Stone's question appears to be no. It is doubtful whether politicians, policy makers, judges, or the public are ready for legal actions by or on behalf of trees or wild animals. In its report, *Crimes Against the Environment*, the Law Reform Commission of Canada stated that "for criminal law, or law generally for that matter, to acknowledge [this category of right] in the strict and literal sense would be truly *revolutionary* [emphasis in original]."[80] The Commission noted that efforts to argue the case have received meagre support, whether in philosophical or legal terms, and that serious conceptual difficulties exist. It concluded, "In our view, there are more than adequate grounds for more rigorous environmental protection right now, whether or not nonhuman entities are granted legal rights at some future date."[81] Even public environmental organizations have eschewed biocentric rationales for environmental law reform.

The new statutory environmental rights, though at first impression based at least in part on protecting nature for its own sake, are consistent with this view. Their rationale remains essentially ethnocentric, that is, utilitarian. What is different is the greater importance given to the welfare and integrity of

---

77   See Eric T. Freyfogle, "The Land Ethic and Pilgrim Leopold" (1990) 61 U. Colo. L. Rev. 217; Aldo Leopold, *A Sand County Almanac: And Sketches Here and There* (New York: Oxford University Press, 1960).

78   Law Reform Commission of Canada, *supra*, note 71, at 10.

79   Christopher D. Stone, "Should Trees Have Standing? — Toward Legal Rights for Natural Objects" (1972) 45 S. Cal. L. Rev. 450.

80   Law Reform Commission of Canada, *supra*, note 71, at 10.

81   *Id.*

ecological systems, including transnational and even global systems, in protecting human welfare. This is a step beyond human-environment linkage based merely on human exploitation of natural resources. It is a significant step because it confirms a utilitarian basis for international action and the support of national measures on such global ecosystem problems as the greenhouse effect and ocean pollution.

There is no Canadian legislation yet that grants virtually unqualified protection to species in the manner of U.S. laws such as the *Endangered Species Act*.[82] Such laws, which provide hard protection for nature, occupy a special place. The statutory environmental rights that they create differ fundamentally from traditional property rights. Species protection rights, according to Rolston, have their roots in evolutionary natural history. Property rights, he says, "are a cultural phenomenon, embodied in civic laws. Evolutionary history is a natural phenomenon, following natural laws."[83] The respective underlying values may be seen as respect for property versus respect for life.[84]

In this context of species protection, the Canadian system would apply risk analysis with a rationality standard under environmental assessment and contaminant-control regulatory provisions. For example, potential harm to fish as a result of the development of mineral rights would be evaluated on this basis under the ministerial review provisions of the *Fisheries Act*.[85]

CONCLUSION

Public environmental integrity rights under recently enacted and currently proposed Canadian statutes place increasingly severe restrictions on developmental natural resource rights. Environmental rights no longer share the "softness" associated with certain renewable resource rights, such as water quality rights, that permit them to be weakened through implicit risk assessment based on rationality standards. There are signs that the relative ineffectiveness of the legal system in recognizing and protecting water quality rights will not be repeated in the case of the new environmental integrity rights. Environmental assessment statutes, park and nature reserve statutes, and proposed environmental bills of rights are poised to go beyond merely restricting the exercise of natural resource-use rights. At present, they come

---

82   *Endangered Species Act of 1973*, 16 U.S.C., para.1531.

83   Holmes Rolston, "Property Rights and Endangered Species" (1990) 61 U. Colo. L. Rev., 283-284.

84   *Id.*, at 302.

85   *Supra*, note 42, ss.35, 37, in the absence of specific protective provisions under park or reserve legislation.

close to redefining the natural resource-use rights themselves, so as to exclude any use that causes ecologically significant impacts. This redefinition has not yet been fully accomplished, but strong public pressure towards this end is likely to continue.

ECONOMICS, LOSSES, FAIRNESS AND RESOURCE-USE CONFLICTS

Jack L. Knetsch[*]

One major reason why it has proven difficult to accommodate conflicts among users of natural resources is that in large part, voluntary economic market exchanges are either not feasible or are an inefficient, inequitable, unfair, and otherwise inappropriate means of allocating among competing demands. Moreover, there is growing recognition that regulatory and other non-market means of allocation often fail to take proper account of the full range of interests, frequently lack predictability, and are slow to respond to changing values.

While present economic and legal institutions may appear to successfully resolve competing demands with a large measure of efficiency, equity, and acceptance in the majority of cases, there is also increasing awareness that these institutions fail to provide satisfactory results in many specific, often highly visible and important, instances. And this is increasingly being interpreted as a signal that the system may be systematically failing to provide socially desired allocations of entitlements in many other cases as well.

Economic issues are the source of many of the difficulties. Yet, many economic analyses of resource conflicts have not made resolutions easier; in part, this may be due to their having provided misleading information.

The focus of this review is less on the better-known sources of allocation problems, and more on recent findings of people's valuations of losses relative to gains, and on reasons why individuals find some changes fair and acceptable and others unfair and unacceptable. The disparity between the importance of gains and losses to people and the "rules" of acceptable actions appears both to add to the sense of unresolved conflict and to frustrate many conventional approaches to resolving conflict. A greater awareness and understanding of the gain/loss valuation differences and their impacts on fairness judgments might, however, lead to more useful institutional reform.

FAILURES AND REJECTIONS OF MARKETS

Many natural resource commodities and services commonly trade in markets and have economic values assessed in market prices, with supplies distributed accordingly. Timber, minerals, and fish are among those for which

* Much of this discussion is based on findings from research supported by Fisheries and Oceans Canada and the Ontario Ministry of the Environment, and the Social Sciences and Humanities Research Council of Canada.

commercial dealings provide useful investment incentives and allocation guidance.

Other natural resource outputs are not traded in markets or do so in sufficiently small degree that economic exchange yields little or no useful indication of social worth, and allocations may not correlate very well with wants and needs. Wilderness reservation, traditional hunting, outdoor recreation, and wildlife are prominent examples.

The specific causes of particular conflicts and allocation problems vary. Most, however, have in common a failure of legal and economic institutions to assure that all values, pecuniary and non-pecuniary alike, receive commensurate weight in allocation decisions or to provide any serious incentive for people to consider the possible harmful impacts of their decisions on other parties or on the long-term productivity of many resources. Efficient and acceptable allocations are often precluded, for example, by the lack of incentive to take account of external costs imposed on others, the motivation to overuse open-access common property, the lack of any private return to providing public goods, the distortions fostered by monopoly control, and outcomes that do not provide a satisfactory range of opportunities for various population groups to benefit from the use of resources.

When individuals, households, private businesses, statutory authorities, and government agencies responsible for environmental degradation are not required to bear these costs, they then do not pay the full costs of their activities, and have a perverse incentive to pursue activities that generate such losses and to impose them on others. The absence of an economic or legal need to fully weigh environmental or other such "third-party" costs contrasts sharply with the incentive to economize on the use of other goods or production inputs, and is a pervasive cause of resource conflicts.

Garrett Hardin characterized the misdirected incentives leading to environmental disruptions and depletion of unrestricted, or open, access common property as "the tragedy of the commons":[1]

> The tragedy of the commons develops in this way. Picture a pasture open to all. It is to be expected that each herdsman will try to keep as many cattle as possible on the commons. Such an arrangement may work reasonably satisfactorily for centuries because tribal wars, poaching and disease keep the numbers of both man and beast well below the carrying capacity of the land. Finally, however, comes the day of reckoning, that is, the day when the long-desired goal of social stability becomes a reality. At this point, the inherent logic of the commons remorselessly generates tragedy ....
>
> Adding together the component partial utilities, the rational herdsman concludes that the only sensible course for him to pursue is to add another animal to his herd. And

---

1   Garrett Hardin, "The Tragedy of the Commons" (1968) 162 Science 1243 at 1244.

another .... But this is the conclusion reached by each and every rational herdsman sharing a commons. Therein is the tragedy. Each man is locked into a system that compels him to increase his herd without limit — in a world that is limited. Ruin is the destination toward which all men rush, each pursuing his own best interest in a society that believes in the freedom of the commons.

Destructive over-exploitation of fish stocks is but one illustration of conflict primarily due to the common-property nature of free access, which in this case gives little incentive for any one individual to conserve if this person knows that others can and will take any fish that he or she might leave for the purpose of maintaining future stocks.

Some commodities need not be consumed, or even seen, to be enjoyed and valued. Wilderness areas and habitat for rare species of wildlife, for example, derive much of their value from people's knowledge that they exist and have been set aside for long-term protection. Indeed, in some cases extensive use of the areas may degrade the resource and reduce its value. Given the inability to exclude non-contributors from benefiting from such resources and the incentive of beneficiaries to free-ride on the contributions of others, non-market provisions are usually necessary — provisions that often must come at the expense of uses with more conspicuous economic worth.

A further, and generally much less appreciated, cause of resource conflict and impediment to its resolution stems from people's varying perceptions of risks and their consequences. It is common to presume that people weigh only the size of the expected loss when considering the adverse impacts that may result from a risky choice — that is, that they frame possible losses solely in terms of the magnitude of any loss multiplied by the probability of its occurrence. However, recent research has found that people's aversion to possible losses varies greatly depending on the nature of the risk and the particular circumstances of their exposure. For example, even if all other things are equal, most people react far more negatively to a risk imposed on them by others than to one they assume voluntarily. They would also sacrifice much less to avoid a risk over which they feel they have some control compared to ones in which they feel a lack of influence; and they find risks that are more uncertain, are less familiar, and have delayed consequences much more aversive than ones of similar but familiar and more immediate impact.[2] Introduction of risks from chemical discharges from a new processing plant can, therefore, be fully expected to cause great anxiety and resistance from a resident population even if they can be shown that they have undertaken even greater risks to themselves by increasing use of their automobiles.

---

2   Paul Slovic, "Perception of Risk" (1987) 236 Science 280.

For these and other reasons, many values associated with natural resources and resource uses do not find ready expression in market prices. The non-pecuniary nature of these values does not mean that they are not important contributors to economic welfare. Nor does it suggest that such resources or resource uses are any less economically valuable than other resources or goods that are provided and traded at market-established prices. The difference is only that a market is possible and desired in some cases, and is impossible or rejected in others. It is not that one class or the other is economically more valuable because of the circumstances under which it is made available and allocated.

While this continues to be the source of some confusion and continuing bias, market and non-market or non-pecuniary values are equally *economic* values. In both cases people are willing to give up other things and other resources in order to make them available or to prevent their destruction. It is this willingness to sacrifice that expresses or measures economic worth. The conversion of a plot of agricultural or timber land to a public park or a wildlife reserve, for example, may well increase the economic value of the resource even though the cash flow from the previous use of the land is not replaced by any cash or commercial transaction associated with the new use.

The non-pecuniary nature of many resource values — including the existence value or option value of having certain amenities available even if no present use is anticipated, the satisfaction of maintaining traditional entitlements, and freedom from fear of exposure to substances with uncertain consequences — does, however, make comparisons with other competing allocations more difficult.

ECONOMIC VALUES AND THEIR ASSESSMENT

The economic — pecuniary and non-pecuniary — importance of conflicting uses remains central to how resource use is allocated among competing claimants. However, given the uncertainties and lack of ready means of measurement, and the often-misunderstood nature of what is to be measured, many assessments have not necessarily raised the level of informed debate or improved proposed resolutions of resource conflicts. Quite apart from the obvious, and expected, self-serving exaggerations and biased assertions of interested parties, there are other more systematic worries about valuations and their use in judgments, allocation decisions, and regulatory reform.

The first is the fairly obvious discounting of less easily assessed non-pecuniary values in planning decisions, in litigation, and in reform proposals, relative to more easily appreciated — and more easily measured — financial data. Although there are numerous exceptions, courts, for example, still often treat some amenity values as "mere delights" and not the equal of commercial returns.

A second source of potential malassessment is the practice of taking various expenditures, or cost outlays, associated with the use or development of a resource to represent the value of the resource itself — a feature of what Tom Power has aptly called "folk economics".[3] The usual accountings include such analysts' employment-generating activities as estimating tourist expenditures, studying local economic impacts, and using multipliers to determine so-called spin-offs. Although these are frequently done with great technical competence, this is not uniformly the case, and in nearly all cases they reflect narrow interests of local boosterism rather than resource values.

The common attribution of associated spending and secondary or spin-off impacts to the value of the resource prompting the expenditures leads to a nonsensical conclusion that a recreation facility located in some remote area is more valuable than an equally attractive one located close to users because it requires greater effort and cost to get to the more distant site. It is to say that a mineral deposit deeper in the earth is more valuable than one closer to the surface because more wage income will be generated in bringing the ore up to the processing facility. Such accountings give rise to poor decisions and to the spectacle of officials solemnly attempting to construct an economic justification for preserving an important historical, cultural, or environmental site by calling attention to the largely irrelevant spending by a few visitors, while totally ignoring large real losses in economic welfare that would accompany demise of the asset.

A further, related problem with the counting of expenditure impacts is that if these associated benefits are to be credited as part of the gains attributable to a particular project, then the expenditures, jobs, and income that are not realized because of the spending that is displaced by this use must surely be debited as part of the costs. It is clearly misleading to count the secondary gains without counting the secondary costs. While there may be an interest in increasing or maintaining economic activity in a particular area, the justification for projects contributing to this turns on the added value of having employment and income accruing in one area rather than in another region; the justification of economic feasibility or efficiency is not demonstrated by such one-sided accounting. The practice of crediting spin-off gains and ignoring commensurate losses resulting from the displaced spending leads not only to a further over-supply of wasteful projects, but blunts the search for ones that will more nearly satisfy both objectives of more productive use of economic resources and maintenance of activity in areas of deserving concern.

---

3   Thomas Michael Power, *The Economic Pursuit of Quality* (Armonk, N.Y.: M.E. Sharp, 1988).

The pervasiveness of using local impacts as measures of resource values is in part attributable to another difficulty in sorting out more reasonable responses to a wide array of policy issues: the asymmetry of interests and incentives between parties having a large but diffuse interest in the results and those having a smaller but concentrated interest. Small groups representing specific interests are often able to impose costs of uneconomic alternatives on another group because these costs are spread among a larger number of individuals. As the loss to any single member of the larger group may be relatively small, there is little incentive for any single person to be too offended, to become very interested in the issue, to protest, or to attempt to persuade others of the wastefulness of the proposal. The larger returns to each in the small group provide quite the opposite incentive.[4] This asymmetry often results in unbalanced information, a lack of critical review, and biased treatments of gains and losses.

There is also a too-easy assumption that market prices, which may adequately measure the value of a substitute, also measure the value to people who consider alternatives as being inferior to a particular holding to which they have a particular attachment. A compensation payment of the market price of another house, for example, is unlikely to leave a long-term resident as well off as before the taking of the person's home.[5]

GAINS AND LOSSES

A further asymmetry that may often seriously compromise efficient and equitable choices of entitlements is the commonly unappreciated disparity between measures of positive and negative changes in economic well-being.

Something has economic worth only to the extent that people are willing to give up something else in order to acquire or keep it. The usual textbook suggestion is, for example, "The economic value of something is how much someone is willing to pay for it or, if he [or she] has it already, how much money he [or she] demands to part with it."[6] There is little disagreement on this — welfare gains are correctly measured by the maximum sums that gainers would pay to obtain them and losses "are measured by the total number of dollars which prospective losers would insist on as the price of agreeing to adoption."[7]

---

4   Randall Bartlett, *Economic Foundation of Political Power* (New York: Free Press, 1973).

5   Jack L. Knetsch, *Property Rights and Compensation: Compulsory Acquisition and Other Losses* (Toronto: Butterworths, 1983).

6   Richard A. Posner, *Economic Analysis of Law*, 3rd ed. (Boston: Little, Brown, 1986) at 11.

7   Frank I. Michelman, "Property, Utility and Fairness: Comments on the Ethical Foundations of 'Just Compensation' Law" (1967) 80 Harvard L.R. 1165 at 1214.

However, rather than the compensation measure, a second measure of loss is commonly used to weigh adverse impacts and assign entitlements: the maximum willingness of an individual to pay to avoid giving something up. The reasons for the common use of this second, and usually inappropriate, measure, are:

1. that its calculation is often more convenient than the correct compensation measure, and

2. that it is widely assumed that for all practical purposes the two measures will result in fully equivalent assessments.

Any disparity between the willingness-to-pay (WTP) and the compensation-demanded (willingness to accept, or WTA) measures is confidently expected to be negligibly small and of no practical importance: "the differences between compensating and equivalent measures are trivial",[8] and "[a]s a practical matter it usually does not make much difference which of these two approaches ... is adopted."[9]

As a result, it has become common practice to base assessments for all manner of policy and planning purposes on this presumption of evaluation equivalence. No reckoning of any difference is made, or thought to be necessary. The possibility of differing values is generally ignored in proposals to resolve resource-use conflicts and deliberations leading to the assignment of property entitlements, as well as in benefit-cost analyses, assessments of damages, and the setting of health, safety, and environmental standards.

There is, however, little evidence to support this traditional view of equivalence. Instead, the available evidence — which has been accumulating for a dozen or so years — supports an alternative view of large and systematic disparities. People value losses much more than they do commensurate gains.

The recent research studies are consistent in finding that people require payments to give up entitlements that are from about two or three to well over five times larger than the maximum sums they would agree to pay to retain the same rights. The differences are not trivial, and attempts to understand and deal with resource conflicts will be severely hindered by continuing to ignore them.

A useful summary of the findings from the research on gains and losses is provided by the choices made by two comparable groups of individuals

---

8   Alan Randall, *Resource Economics: An Economic Approach to Natural Resource and Environmental Policy* (Columbus, Ohio: Grid, 1987) at 244.

9   Steven E. Rhoads, *The Economists' View of the World: Government, Markets, and Public Policy* (Cambridge: Cambridge University Press, 1985) at 125.

participating in a simple experiment.[10] Each individual in the first group was given a coffee mug and all were told that the mug was theirs to keep. They were then offered a four-hundred-gram Swiss chocolate bar of roughly comparable price in exchange for their mug.

The participants in the second group were offered the opposite choice. They were each initially given one of the large chocolate bars and then offered a mug in exchange for their chocolate bar. All other conditions were identical to those of the first group.

The participants in both groups had the identical opportunity of ending up with a coffee mug or a chocolate bar; there was no effort required to make any necessary trade and no uncertainty concerning the validity of the exchange offers.

Conventional economic assumptions about how people value gains and losses, which are the presumptions used in most economic analyses, including valuations of competing resource uses, offer a strong prediction of what should occur. The relative numbers of individuals preferring mugs to chocolate bars should be roughly equal in the two groups, as the relative preferences are not expected to be affected by which initial entitlement is awarded or by any difference in the value of gains and losses.

The results of the experiment showed a very different pattern of preferences from the one predicted by traditional economic principles. Rather than roughly equal proportions in each group preferring the chocolate bar and the mug, the numbers varied widely and systematically in accord with the direction of the necessary exchange.

Group	Prefer Mug	Prefer Chocolate
1. Give up mug for chocolate	89 percent	11 percent
2. Give up chocolate for mug	10 percent	90 percent

Nearly nine out of every ten (89 percent) of those individuals required to lose their mug in order to gain a chocolate bar (Group 1) indicated that they valued a mug more than the chocolate. Only one in ten favoured a loss of their chocolate bar to gain a mug (Group 2).

Participants' preferences were clearly not independent of the initial entitlement or the direction of trade offers, as is commonly assumed. The individuals taking part in this exercise valued a mug more than a chocolate bar when facing the prospect of losing the mug, but valued a mug less than

---

10   Further details are provided in Jack L. Knetsch, "The Endowment Effect and Evidence of Nonreversible Indifference Curves" (1989) 79 The American Economic Rev. 1277.

the chocolate when given the choice of gaining a mug at the cost of giving up the chocolate.

The reference position of people in the experiment mattered very much in terms of whether the good was valued as a potential loss or as giving up a possible gain. In common with most experience, but in contrast with much of conventional economics, losses were worth more than fully commensurate gains.

The results of the simple coffee mug and chocolate bar exchange exercise are representative of a general finding from essentially all controlled tests of the equivalence proposition. An early example is the response of a sample of duck hunters in the United States who indicated that, on average, they would pay $247 each to maintain a wetland necessary to support present duck populations, but would demand a minimum compensation of $1044 to agree to its demise — a bit over a four-fold difference.[11] In another early study, Thaler[12] found that people placed very different values on a .001 change in risk to their life depending on the direction of the change. The compensation they demanded was one or two orders of magnitude greater to accept the risk (a loss) than the largest amount they were prepared to pay to eliminate an identical risk (a gain).

Similar disparities have now been reported by many investigators using a variety of methods to evaluate widely varied assets, and differences have been shown to be independent of transaction costs, repetition of trade offers, income effects, or wealth constraints.[13] The results of the many tests and studies are consistent in showing that losses matter much more to people than commensurate gains, and that reductions in losses are more valuable than forgone gains.

While these findings have until recently not proven popular with many economic practitioners — an unfortunate social cost of their reluctance to give up conventional assertions — they seem in accord with the strong intuitions of most people. Oliver Wendell Holmes summarized this intuition many years before the recent studies were undertaken in these terms:

> It is in the nature of man's mind. A thing which you have enjoyed and used as your own for a long time, whether property or an opinion, takes root in your being and cannot be torn away without your resenting the act and trying to defend yourself, however you came by it.

---

11   Judd Hammack & Gardner Mallard Brown, *Waterfowl and Wetlands: Toward Bioeconomic Analysis* (Baltimore: Resources for the Future, 1974).

12   Richard Thaler, "Toward a Positive Theory of Consumer Choice" (1980) 1 J. of Economic Behavior and Organization 39.

13   Daniel Kahneman, Jack L. Knetsch & Richard Thaler, "Experimental Tests of the Endowment Effect and the Coase Theorem" (1990) 98 J. of Political Economy 1325.

The law can ask no better justification than the deepest instincts of man.[14]

The empirical evidence seems to be consistent with Holmes' statement; it differs only in the finding that the reluctance to give something up does not necessarily occur only after "a long time." Once a reference position is perceived, people value gains and losses as departures from this neutral point, and motivations respond accordingly.[15]

Further, while individuals exhibit disparities between gain and loss values, or endowment effects as they are often called, it also appears that groups respond in similar fashion. Frey and Pommerehne note that collective endowment effects motivate many public efforts to protect groups against losses. An example is the restrictions many countries impose on the export of national art treasures, and the notable ease of raising funds to prevent the loss of such an object relative to the difficulty of securing support when "undertaken in order to buy some art object deemed worthwhile."[16]

If the valuation differences represent the general case, as the evidence now suggests, then people will react very differently to actions and policies than might be expected on the basis of the usual assumption of equivalence between gains and losses. The conventional assertion may prove to be a poor basis for predicting behaviour, and its continued use is likely giving rise to misleading assessments of changes in people's economic welfare and poor predictions of their acceptance of policy decisions.

FAIRNESS AND ACCEPTANCE OF ALLOCATIONS

The disparate valuations of gains and losses influences many choices, including people's judgments of which economic changes or policies are more acceptable to them and which are less so. Actions that impose losses on particular parties or groups are typically viewed as being more onerous and are consequently judged unfair.

Strong evidence reflecting such patterns has been found among both survey respondents and groups participating in real money exchange experiments.[17] Differing valuations of losses and forgone gains were clearly

---

14   Oliver W. Holmes, "The Path of the Law" (1897) 10 Harvard L. Rev. 457 at 477.

15   Daniel Kahneman & Amos Tversky, "Prospect Theory: An Analysis of Decision Under Risk" (1979) 47 Econometrica 263.

16   Bruno S. Frey & Werner W. Pommerehne, "International Trade in Art: Attitudes and Behaviour" (1987) 34 Rivista Internaxionale di Scienze Economiche e Commerciali 465 at 474.

17   See Daniel Kahneman, Jack L. Knetsch & Richard Thaler, "Fairness as a Constraint on Profit Seeking: Entitlements in the Market" (1986) 76 The American Economic Review 728; and Daniel Kahneman, Jack L. Knetsch & Richard H. Thaler, "Fairness and the

evident in the responses, for example, of two groups who were asked to judge the fairness of reducing workers' incomes in particular circumstances. One group was told that the employer reduced wages by 10 percent. The other group was told that the employer accomplished the same dollar reduction by eliminating the workers' bonuses. Nearly two-thirds thought the wage cut unfair, but only 20 percent had a similar view of an equal loss in the form of foregoing a bonus. The wage cut was seen as a loss whereas the elimination of the bonus was viewed as a much less aversive forgone gain.

The primary "rule" that motivated most judgments was that it is unfair for one party to suffer a loss for the direct benefit of another party. Such "zero-sum" games were widely seen as unfair in all of the different contexts used, including employee-employer relations, landlord-tenant dealings, and buyer-seller exchanges.

For example, in responding to the following vignette, over 80 percent viewed the action of the store manager as unfair: "A hardware store has been selling snow shovels for fifteen dollars. The morning after a large snowstorm, the store raises the price to twenty." Even though the heavy snowfall made the shovels more desirable and valuable, raising the price was apparently seen by the overwhelming majority of people as imposing an unjustified loss on the consumer for the benefit of the store owner. The price change was, therefore, not considered acceptable.

Cutting wages to a current employee in the face of other workers willing to work for less was similarly viewed as one party's suffering a loss for the benefit of another, and was therefore thought to be unfair. And raising rents to a sitting tenant, even when other housing prices had gone up, was widely seen as unfair for the same reason.

Factors that divert the gain from the party initiating the change have a dramatic effect on the perceived fairness of the actions. If one of the parties changes, or if one party is not seen to gain at the other's expense, an action such as raising prices, which would normally be considered unfair, becomes acceptable to most people.

When respondents were asked, for instance, if they thought it was fair for a store to ration a single remaining toy by selling it to the highest bidder, three-quarters indicated that this was not acceptable. However, when the information that "the proceeds will go to UNICEF" was added, indicating that the gain would go to a charity rather than to the store owner, the same auction became acceptable to four out of five respondents. When the store was seen to benefit at the expense of the customer, it was judged to be unfair, but when

---

the store was seen not to profit from the added outlay of the customer, then it became fair in the judgments of the respondents.

Similarly, even though raising rents to a sitting tenant was widely felt to be unfair, it became acceptable to impose the same increase on a new tenant. A new employee's receiving a lower wage is considered fair because there is little or no notion of a higher reference wage; but reducing the wage of a current employee imposes such a loss from the reference position of the former, higher wage, and is therefore thought to be unfair.

Raising prices to pass on costs is another important class of cases where one party is not seen to benefit from the imposition of losses on the other. Such actions are widely seen to be fair, even when losers are put to considerable inconvenience. In one case, respondents were asked about raising rents to "a tenant living on a fixed income" where an increase would mean "the tenant would have to move." However, because "the landlord's costs have increased substantially ... and the landlord raises the rent to cover the cost increases", the increased rent was viewed as fair by a ratio of three to one.

There seems to be great sympathy for allowing firms to maintain their reference level of return. Thus, passing on costs is widely seen as permissible quite independent of market conditions. And while cutting wages of current employees was judged unfair by most respondents, an exception was normally made in cases where the employer was said to be losing money. It then became acceptable to most people to cut even nominal wages. A limitation exists, however: that any losses must be seen to pertain directly to the transaction at hand. It was not considered fair for a landlord to raise rents to make up for the loss of another source of income.

Again, contrary to common views of economic behaviour, people appear to be strongly motivated by quite clear notions of fairness. Actions were judged to be fair or unfair in particular patterns, and people indicated a willingness to modify their behaviour accordingly, even at some cost to themselves and when there was little chance that others could retaliate and discipline their unfair behaviour.

LOSSES AND RESOLVING CONFLICTS

The apparent disparity between people's valuations of losses relative to gains and the related perceptions of what actions are likely to be considered as fair or unfair, do not come readily from standard views of economic behaviour. The disparity and fairness criteria are, however, likely to influence people's reactions to the behaviour of others and to public policies and actions, and will therefore have direct implications for the acceptance of new competing resource uses and the ways in which conflicts are resolved.

Although most policy decisions are not based on explicit estimates of economic costs and benefits, awareness and appreciation of the economic consequences of alternative actions usually play a significant role in formulating options and choosing among them. However, losses resulting from an action or policy are likely to be understated in deliberations based on the conventional view of losses being weighed equally with gains. Consequently, changes having actual net negative impacts will be unduly encouraged, damages will be under-assessed, compensation awards may be too small, inappropriate standards of protection against injuries will likely be set, inadequate mitigation measures will be undertaken, and choices of preferred legal entitlements will be biased.[18]

The extent to which disparities between valuation of gains and losses can influence policy preferences is illustrated by the choice between mitigation and cash compensation remedies. Convention suggests that, other things equal, it is always better, or more efficient, to choose monetary awards over mitigation. Such payments allow recipients to purchase whatever they value most, whereas mitigating works limit the remedy to whatever value is attached to reducing a particular harm, and this may be of less consequence to the affected parties. In other words, it is presumed to be better to give people money that they can use for food or holidays, or whatever they want, than to spend a like sum on restoring habitat for a species they may care little about or which they consider to be in ample supply.

The findings of large disparities between gains and losses suggest an alternative view of the relative merits of the options. Mitigation may be treated by people as reducing a loss, and worth correspondingly more because of this; compensation may be viewed as leaving the aversive loss intact in return for a monetary gain, which, by being a gain, is worth correspondingly less.

The strength of this intuition has been borne out in survey studies in which respondents indicated, for example, that they greatly preferred having a large sum of money spent on reducing — but not eliminating — even a minor harm to having an equal or greater sum spent on an alternative of direct benefit to them. For example, they preferred having money spent reducing stream sediment that only brought back fish numbers by 5 percent to having the funds spent on local park and recreation facilities. Further, when the alternative to reducing the sediment was putting the damage award into a

---

18   See Duncan Kennedy, "Cost-Benefit Analysis of Entitlement: A Critique" (1981) 33 Stanford L. Rev. 387; and Jack L. Knetsch, "Environmental Policy Implications of Disparities Between Willingness to Pay and Compensation Demanded Measures of Values" (1990) 18 J. of Environmental Economics and Management 227.

general fund to be used, presumably, on whatever was most urgently needed by the community — allegedly the most efficient solution possible — it was viewed even more unfavourably.[19]

The evidence suggests that the form of remedial action probably has a large influence on its acceptability. It seems likely, for example, that replacing losses with close substitutes would be favoured over less closely related measures. Activities that promote notions of participation, and those that provide benefits for more members of the community who are seen to have suffered losses, are similarly likely to be better received.

More generally, an appreciation of the intuition that losses are far more aversive than forgone gains, and that people have quite definite notions of fairness, can lead to a better understanding of reactions and can suggest alternative means of dealing with resource conflicts, ways that will probably be more acceptable and effective.

Negotiating resolutions of conflicts will, for example, be more effective to the extent that parties are asked to forgo gains rather than accept a far more aversive loss. A reduced salary bonus is easier to accept than a wage cut; ending a discount is less aversive than raising prices; and sharing profits of a development may be preferred to paying increased costs.

In a similar way, conversion of an environmentally valuable asset to another use that would yield benefits to others might well be seen to be unfair even though it may be thought efficient. Like imposing a wage cut on a worker because another is willing to work for less, converting a local park to a valuable office block is probably seen as unfair. The gain would likely be seen as obtained directly as a result of losses to prior users of the resource. Also, compensation for pollution abatement activities may be popular, not because it adds to efficient production — it usually does not — but because a reduction of the costs imposed is seen to be fair. And imposing a loss is regarded as far more unfair than denial of an equivalent forgone gain. Thus, prohibitions that preclude potential profits are widely sanctioned as acceptable, whereas restrictions that impose out-of-pocket costs are as often agreed to be unfair. Findings of liability and compensation rules are often compatible with this distinction and enjoy a large measure of community support as a result.[20]

---

19   Jack L. Knetsch, *The Relative Values of Mitigation and Compensation Remedies* (Working Paper) (Vancouver: Simon Fraser University, 1991).

20   See Frank H. Stephen & Eric Young, "An Economic Insight on the Judicial Control of Planning Authorities' Discretion" (1985) 7 Urban Law and Policy 133; and David Cohen & Jack L. Knetsch, "Judicial Choice and Disparities Between Measures of Economic Value" Univ. of Toronto Law J. (in press).

For many of the same reasons, disruptive changes that are seen to reduce losses are more acceptable than ones that offer less valued gains. A waste storage and treatment facility that will effectively rid a community of current accumulations of inadequately treated materials will be favoured over a more efficient one that will also deal with wastes generated in other jurisdictions.

Just as passing on costs was generally accepted regardless of market demand and supply conditions, policies that use fees to recover costs are likely to be more acceptable than ones that appear only to add to the returns of the taxing jurisdiction. And, contrary to the conventional dictates of public finance counsellors, collections of funds diverted to "general revenue" accounts will be much less acceptable than ones "earmarked" for a specific, announced purpose related to the levy.

Similarly, redistribution of resource earning or use entitlements may be less disruptive if it is designed to be less than permanent in nature, rather than shifting the resource from one party to the direct benefit of another. For example, while the international sale of national art treasures is widely resisted, their loan to other countries is not — even if the loans are widely known to be permanent.[21] Similarly, payments to equalization funds could be limited to periods when specified inequalities existed — even though it might be widely appreciated that such inequalities will almost certainly persist for very long periods, even exceeding present lifespans.

While transfers from one party to the benefit of another are generally judged harshly, the research findings suggest that perhaps a large portion of the usual resistance might be overcome with the use of an acceptable standard to induce a reference level from which changes are framed by people as gains or losses. For example, payments into an equalization fund could be made more acceptable if the funds were distributed to regions recognized as being below some norm. Communities below this reference position would be seen as being in a loss position, and the redistribution payments would then be taken as reducing losses rather than as a less acceptable bestowing of benefits. The contributors might then also see their payments somewhat less as losses, and somewhat more as reductions to their gains and as payments to a fund that could also benefit them in the future. The use of "poverty lines" in jurisdictions throughout the world is a notable example of the success of such a strategy even though the poverty levels are widely known to be little more than arbitrary designations.

Distinctions between gains and losses — and as to whether a positive change is taken as reduction of a loss or a gain, while a negative change is

---

21   Frey & Pommerehne, *supra*, note 16.

perceived as a loss or a forgone gain, which to a large extent determines the desirability of changes or the acceptability of a proposed resolution of conflicts — are not necessarily determined by either the *status quo* or extant legal entitlements. Reference positions may well be based instead on an expected or normal condition, which may differ from the present and from legally enforceable rights. Reducing current pollution levels, for example, may be viewed as a reduction of a loss from the referent of a clean environment and therefore worth more than when viewed as an improvement from present levels of degradation.

And, contrary to common presumptions, extant legal entitlements do not appear to be a useful predictor of people's reference levels or determinant of the appropriate basis to be used to measure losses. The monetary measure of a welfare loss associated with the harmful action of a neighbour remains the sum of money that would just maintain the welfare of the individual at the level existing prior to the loss. The existing property rights determine whether or not an injured party has a cause of action against the neighbour, and therefore can or cannot obtain injunctive relief or receive compensation for the damage. The assignment of rights may influence the extent of the welfare loss felt by the injured party — violations of known rights may well prompt greater outrage than lawful changes — but the basis for assessing the loss is not determined by the entitlement.[22]

CONCLUSIONS

There seems to be little empirical evidence to support the conventional view that people weigh gains and losses equally. Losses appear to be a much greater concern to people, but this is often not reflected in the usual assessments or in many policy proposals. Recent findings also suggest that perceptions of fairness and related acceptance of changes are related to similar patterns.

On present evidence, some policy choices appear unnecessarily costly and generate acrimony that might be avoided; that is, ignoring the differential weighting of the gains and losses is likely to exacerbate the difficulty of resolving conflicts in resource use and make reasonable choices less certain. Improvements that take greater account of actual behaviour and reactions may well provide greater opportunities for more productive negotiations and eventual resolutions.

---

22 Knetsch, *supra*, note 18.

LAW REFORM IN THE AGE OF ECOLOGY: ON THE NEED FOR AN "ECO-CONSTITUTION" IN CANADA

J. Michael M'Gonigle

The theme of this volume of essays is two-sided, as it concerns both the growth in resource demands on a shrinking heritage and the management of the conflicts that ensue. This is one of the most critical issues on the political agenda anywhere in the world, but it is especially topical in Canada today. While technical economic or legal proposals are important, the topic ultimately poses a profoundly political, even cultural, challenge to Canadian society.

From this larger perspective, assumptions subsumed in the theme itself become apparent. First, we accept that demands on our natural (and indeed social) heritage will inevitably grow, but without any attention to how long this very process itself can continue, or how, on the contrary, it might be brought to an end. Second, it is similarly assumed that the conflicts that inevitably follow can, in some significant way, be "managed". Such optimism is similar to that evident in the popular phrase "sustainable development", a phrase rooted in another assumption that existing patterns of development can, in fact, be modified to be made sustainable.

When one questions these assumptions, one is led in dramatically new directions, both intellectually and in the practical search for "sustainable" resource policies. Indeed, if one maintains an imaginative and open frame of mind, one may well be led into another Canadian debate, which is also replete with assumptions about what is wrong with the country, and what is possible. This is, of course, the debate about our national constitution.

These debates and assumptions are related. I will argue that at stake in economic growth, escalating resource demands, diminishing environmental sustainability, and even the future of the constitution is the need not only for law reform, but for a more fundamental transformation in our institutions. The title of this paper refers to our being in an "age of ecology". Activists talk even more urgently than that, referring to the 1990s as the "turnaround decade". This seeming hyperbole stems from the widespread fear that our planet, our country, and our local environments are in terrible shape, and getting worse. In this light, to speak of "managing" growing resource-use "conflicts" may seem almost oxymoronic.

The call for a more radical approach to our resource and ecological problems is not new. The political economy, and especially political ecology, literatures are replete with it,[1] although these literatures make only the smallest inroads into discourse within academic or practical resource management. In the area of law reform, as well, the need for more basic approaches is evident to those who have watched or participated in the frustrations and failed promise of the public participation movement, now over twenty years old. For example, it has taken two full decades after the passage in the United States of the *National Environmental Policy Act* of 1969 for Canada even to introduce a comparable piece of legislation into Parliament. Over that time, the prospects for global survival have certainly not improved, with all manner of global environmental problems and pressures facing us today that were unimagined in the 1960s.

The economics of growth has long been targeted as the source of many of our environmental woes, analysis which is outside the major focus of this paper.[2] However, parallel to the rise of modern market institutions over the past few centuries has been the rise of the state and, with it, the dominance of a peculiarly western concept of constitutionalism. Its ideological roots are the same as those of the market economy with which it grew up — society defined as an aggregation of competitive individuals.

I will argue that this view, which I call "liberal constitutionalism", is too narrow for the world that we confront today. As the ozone layer thins, as the planet heats up, as whole species die out at a rate now measured not in years but in minutes — and as we slowly ponder our responses — it is becoming increasingly apparent that the way in which human affairs are presently conducted and controlled requires basic reappraisal. To the degree to which our constitution defines us in Canada, and this definition has permitted, or encouraged, the erosion of our sustainability, it follows that we should rethink our constitutionalism to be responsive not just to political but to ecological factors.

Resolving resource conflicts in order to achieve sustainability demands that, as a society, we be able to ask radical questions and engage in an open-minded debate on fundamentals. We must be able to confront our understanding of the role and structure of the state. But, because our economic assumptions and structures are also in question, the ability to carry

---

1   For one particular merging of these literatures, see Martin Tyle, *Ecology and Socialism* (London: Radius, 1988).

2   See, however, the recent book by Herman E. Daly & John B. Cobb, Jr., *For the Common Good: Redirecting the Economy Toward Community, the Environment, and a Sustainable Future* (Boston: Beacon, 1989), which sets out the premises and possibilities of a new thermodynamically based ecological economics. See also the new journal, *Ecological Economics*.

on an open discourse remains problematic. Unfortunately, a larger vision of reform may only be achieved when there is a shared realization that our survival is truly at stake.

THE FUTURE OF THE CANADIAN STATE: TWO COMPETING VISIONS

Canada's present constitutional turmoil has thrust us into a unique position in the industrialized democratic world. Fundamental debate about the structure and future of the state is now the order of the day, whether one is a Quebec separatist, a native lands claimant, a radical ecologist, or just someone who reads the daily paper. For most nations, such debate remains unthinkable. In Canada, what at another time might even be considered subversive is now legitimate discourse.[3]

To talk of community control or of an eco-constitution is, however, to challenge the direction of modern history. Indeed, liberal democracy (and the free-market economics of globalization that accompanies it) has achieved such success in recent decades that it has gained the status of an almost final social truth. We are, it is said, at the end of history: we are witnessing "the end point of mankind's [sic] ideological evolution and the emergence of Western liberal democracy as the final form of human government."[4]

In this light, it is ironic that, at the supposed end of history, Canada is redefining itself. But even more significant is that everywhere what that "final" form of liberal democracy will look like in the years ahead is being questioned by its supposed supporters. I refer, in particular, to the so-called minimalist perspective that would reduce the state's role to that of a market referee and protector of the rights of individual freedom and private property.[5] This neo-conservative strategy has been politically dominant in the West for over a decade now. It is evident, for example, in the Canadian/American Free Trade Agreement, which in effect declares illegal an array of economic and regulatory tools that might be used to protect the

---

3   In Keith G. Banting & Richard Simeon, "Introduction: The Politics of Constitutional Change" in Banting & Simeon, eds., *Redesigning the State: The Politics of Constitutional Change in Industrial Nations* (Toronto: University of Toronto Press, 1985) at 12, it is contended that the conditions for constitutional change depend, in part, on a sense that the "rules of the game are systematically and unfairly biased against the group, or that they frustrate the group in pursuit of its collective goals", and the increased salience of regional and ethnic conflict. These conditions might as easily apply to native groups and even ecological activists in Canada today as to separatists in Quebec.

4   Francis Fukuyama, "Are We at the End of History?" (1990) 121:2 Fortune 75.

5   For a classical theoretical work from this perspective, see Robert Nozick, *Anarchy, State and Utopia* (New York: Basic, 1974).

Canadian environment, its resource base, and its economy. In practice, this belief in the ultimate triumph of "liberal" democracy also entails acceptance of an expansionist market ideology on a global scale, the antithesis of the ecologist's locally self-reliant, decentralist vision for the future.

In looking to constitutional reform as a basis for resolving the escalating problems of resource conflict and declining sustainability, it is important to keep distinct these two underlying political visions — the liberal/corporatist and the ecological/communitarian. The two are fundamentally at odds, on opposite sides of the most basic choice confronting both our growth economy and our political life today: whether to continue on our inherited path of external expansionism or, finally, to initiate meaningful internal reform.

In this vein, political ecologists have long argued that we must "decentralize" society to a community level in order to survive.[6] What this means for the structure of governance has, however, been little considered; a unifying vision of how an ecologically based decentralist constitution might work is lacking. The constitutional crisis in Canada offers an unexpected historical opportunity for ecologists to put this situation right by beginning to develop a new conception of the state and its constitution — an "eco-constitution" — and by translating that vision into debate and action.

THE FALLACY OF THE
LIBERAL CONSTITUTION?

Historically, the liberal constitution of the western democracies was designed primarily to regulate political relations between the state and its individual citizens. A constitution is deemed successful to the extent that it safeguards property and individual rights. Economic relations of the "free market" are on principle outside politics, an area where the state should not intrude. The American constitution, for example, is admired for the lack of constraints it places on individual freedom and for its equality of opportunity. The Lockean spirit that animates both the Canadian and the American constitution embodies the competitive market ideology that permits the individual to claim anything as long as someone else does not posit a counterclaim.[7] Thus, the free individual, not the "community", is the focus

---

6   It is again beyond the scope of this paper to review this well-worn argument in detail. However, for a recent discussion of this perspective, see Chris Plant & Judith Plant, eds., *Putting Power in Its Place: Create Community Control!* (Gabriola Island: New Society, 1991). It is noteworthy that the sort of arguments being made in the present paper find receptive audiences through alternative presses (such as the North American-wide cooperative New Society Publishers) but rarely make it into mainstream policy debates. The Plants' book contains an earlier formation of the present analysis, "Our Home and Native Land? Creating an Eco-constitution in Canada".

7   See, for example, Leslie Armour, "John Locke and American Constitutionalism" *in* Alan S.

for constitutional consideration. And, of course, the natural environment that surrounds and pervades the whole structure is not considered at all.

In contrast to this narrow focus, the historical reality is that society is "self-constituted" by the workings of the whole — of economic forces acting on individuals, of central government on communities, of society on nature. Our legal constitution is, however, confined to a small part of that whole, essentially to the structure of central political administration. But its assumptions are so powerful that enshrining them into the new creature called the "state" has dramatically shaped the evolution of western society over the past three or four centuries.

In the western world, sovereignty, by definition, emanates from the top. Politically, our national constitutions simply assume that power is to be centralized, and then seek to "balance" centralized powers by keeping them apart. This is the implication of the "separation of powers" between the executive, legislative, and judicial branches of government, all top-down centralized institutions.[8] Whether or not there is a need for limits on centralized power itself is not asked.

This description applies even in federal states such as Canada. Although the early provincial autonomists articulated anti-centralist sentiments from the beginning of Canada's history, their claims were still rooted in the rights-based liberal tradition, with the provincial governments seen as all powerful "individuals" in their particular jurisdictional spheres. An alternative view of politics as a participatory endeavour, and of provinces as participatory communitarian structures, was absent.[9]

The signal achievement of the liberal constitution has been to confer political rights on individuals within this structure of centralized power. Our constitution does not, however, recognize the concept of, nor confer specific rights on, territorial community, let alone ask the question of how much social

---

Rosenbaum, ed., *Constitutionalism: The Philosophical Dimension, Contributions in Legal Studies,* No.46 (New York: Greenwood, 1988) at 9.

8   It could well be argued that the most enduring American constitutional contribution is not the maximization of individual freedom, but the greater division of centralized governmental power that it achieves through its particular process of separating the executive and legislative branches.

9   For an extensive discussion of this, see Robert C. Vipond, *Liberty and Community: Canadian Federalism and the Failure of the Constitution* (Albany: State University of New York Press, 1991). The Meech Lake Accord, a product of secret negotiations involving eleven men, the Prime Minister and ten Premiers, exemplifies the dominance in the Canadian state as a whole of a centralized hierarchical model of political life. That it was toppled by a native leader, Elijah Harper, on the floor of a provincial legislature is itself a telling anomaly.

power should remain embedded at that level. Instead, protecting community interests is often even delegitimized, dismissed as just the NIMBY syndrome. Yet to isolate the individual as the ultimate social actor is clearly incorrect — after all, the community was there first, and individuals are born into and moulded by it. A philosophical rethinking is called for.[10]

In short, it can be argued that our constitution — that is, the fundamental political basis for the treatment of our resources and environment — is founded on several false assumptions about the nature of the individual, the irrevelance of community, and the neutrality (and manageability) of central power. Our constitutional premises are questionable on another important fundamental as well — the belief that the competitive market is an objective mechanism where politics is unwelcome, where the market could be "free". In fact, the competitive market mechanism is not merely a mechanism for apolitical exchange but has its own rules, its own internal "constitution" if you like. Such rules might, for example, include its inherent need to grow and expand and its tendency to increase its levels of resource throughput and consumption.

These unstated philosophical assumptions have had profound consequences for how Canada has evolved, and they continue to limit our future possibilities. Simply put, with territorial community and the natural environment politically unrepresented, and with individuals fragmented into little social atoms, the expansionist tendencies of the market have been overpowering, successfully able to overwhelm myriad local resistances, so as to become the central driving force of Canadian and, indeed, of global history.

Ultimately the purpose of any constitution, however defined, is to "constitute" the social collective over time. If so, any debate that takes ecological and cultural sustainability seriously must begin by questioning the liberal conception of the constitution itself. As Quebeckers realize, we are engaged in a collective process of "social self-constitution", of defining how we actually evolve as a culture. But by setting economic power free to pursue its own ends, the liberal constitution, including Canada's, allows society itself to be created as a mere side-effect of the pursuit of economic growth and power. We are, in short, a product both of a "formal" constitution — the legal

---

10   In this light, it is interesting that, in recent years, an extensive academic literature has built up around the communitarian critique of liberalism. See, for example, Richard A. Rodewald, "Does Liberalism Rest on a Mistake?" (1985) 15:2 Canadian Journal of Philosophy 231; H.N. Hirsch, "The Threnody of Liberalism: Constitutional Liberty and the Renewal of Community" (1986) 14:3 Political Theory 423; M. Sandel, *Liberalism and the Limits of Political Theory* (New York: Cambridge University Press, 1987); Patrick Neal & David Paris, "Liberalism and the Communitarian Critique: A Guide for the Perplexed" (1990) 23:3 Canadian Journal of Political Science 419.

rules of state — and especially of an "informal" constitution — the operational rules of the competitive market. This understanding begins to open a new vista on resource conflicts and constitutional change.

In Canada, dependency theorists from Harold Innis to Mel Watkins have long pointed out how our role as a raw resource supplier to the international market has moulded the economic, political, and cultural fabric of the country. Take, for example, forestry conflicts in British Columbia. Forestry is the province's number one industry, and governmental policy there is driven by a fear of job loss and potential disinvestment by an industry that is cutting at 50 percent above the long-run sustained yield and that has long been shedding labour to remain internationally competitive. Although "community forestry" options are often touted as having the potential to create meaningful local control and allow for sustainable forestry,[11] they are essentially prohibited by the informal constitution — all the forest land is contractually "owned" by a handful of multinational forest giants through long-term "tenure" rights.

Thus does the informal (corporate) constitution dominate the formal (governmental) one, and shape our future self-constitution as a society. The implications for resource conflicts and management are apparent. For example, forest resource management in British Columbia is at a stalemate, and democratic politics has been reduced to almost continuous protest. As the cut goes up year by year, the very legitimacy of alternative uses of the forest is challenged as emanating from "single-interest groups", "protesters", and "preservationists". Meanwhile native activists whose millennia-old community land base has, through tenure contracts, been removed from their control without their participation or agreement, take to the barricades and are criminalized. A similar story of the loss of formal and informal community control and of resource mismanagement, in Nova Scotia's fisheries, was told in a previous volume of essays from this Institute.[12] Such examples abound.

IS THERE AN ALTERNATIVE?
EXPLORING THE ECO-CONSTITUTION

As discussed above, a major concern of both political ecologists and political economists has been the "centralization" of social power. Descriptions of our economy in geographical terms like "core and periphery" or in power terms of "hegemony" and "domination" abound in the literature. When a state's constitution is questioned, however, these structural concerns

---

11   For example, this perspective on Canadian forestry issues infuses the new journal *Forest Planning in Canada*, Victoria, B.C.

12   See David VanderZwagg *et al.*, "In Search of Sustainable Development in Nova Scotia's Fisheries" *in* J. Owen Saunders, ed., *The Legal Challenge of Sustainable Development* (Calgary: Canadian Institute of Resources Law, 1990) at 94.

take on even greater moment, although the real object of concern is not the state alone, but the structure of centralized society as a cultural whole.

A fundamental belief of western society is that power does, and more importantly should, reside at the top — in parliaments and cathedrals, in the corporate boardroom, in the Crown. Institutional authority displaces authority emanating from the "locale", from territorial communities. If one is to start with the fundamentals in rooting out the problems of growing demands on and conflicts over resources, this is a promising place to begin.

In essence, the basis of the eco-constitution is to seek to re-root social power in territorial community. The motivating factor here is the belief that all our social institutions grow out of those roots and, in the end, survive only by keeping them strong and by themselves not growing too tall. If we grow too tall and proud, we will crash. In short, to maintain stability, power must be delegated not from the Crown down, but from the community up.

How would such a radically different perspective change the way in which we deal with constitutional questions, and what might its implications be for specific resource conflicts? For one thing, it would give a far higher priority not just to the "settlement" of native land claims but to the basic reorganization of our national fabric around a decentralist vision. In Canada, native cultures have traditionally embodied a perspective that is especially appropriate to an era of shrinking resources — the knowledge of how to live in place. This is not just romantic philosophy but has practical significance. For example, native people are the clearest articulators of the foundation of the eco-constitution — through their claim to "title" to their ancestral land. In making this claim, they deny that sovereignty emanates from the legislative buildings in Toronto or Victoria, from Parliament in Ottawa, or from the Queen at Westminster. It emanates from the spirit of the land itself, and is expressed through their community on that land.

In contrast, in the western view, we set out no ultimate justification for the authority of central government, other than that history has made it so. The Queen does not rule by divine decree, but by accident of birth. Neither does Parliament turn to religious texts to justify its existence; it is there by historical accident. But the Crown through its ministers has a historical monopoly on the use of legitimate force. It is the sovereign, and that is enough to justify its position.

Native cultures, however, tell us that human laws must reflect natural laws, that there is a larger order to which human society must conform. In this light, to recognize that modernity has lost contact with the experience of nature, and of a level of community that works with nature, is not something to toss off lightly. It has left us dependent, and vulnerable. To talk of natural law is radical, because it means that, as a society, we are accountable.

This perspective can be translated into practical constitutional reform, in particular through the vehicle of a local veto in a new third level of government. In our present debate, we assume that only two levels of constitutional authority are possible, the federal and provincial governments. These are, however, both manifestations of the same centralist state. In the eco-constitution, a counterbalancing decentralist level of government is necessary. If one were to recover a truer philosophical foundation for this constitution, this level would even be recognized as the ultimate source of sovereignty (in contemporary native parlance, "title"), with limited jurisdictional authority delegated up to other levels.

This change would instill a whole new dynamic in our political and economic decision making. It would, above all, transform the role of provinces, because natural resources are presently vested in the Crown in right of the province. This is the source of so much of Canada's economic wealth—from the forests and mines to hydroelectricity and water. Who controls it, and for what purpose, is key to resolving conflicts and achieving sustainability.

From this perspective, new approaches emerge on a range of specifics. For example, if rural areas are not to continue subsidizing urban ones with underpriced resources, perhaps resource rents from the sale of "Crown" forests and minerals should stay at the local level, rather than going into provincial coffers. If, in Canada, over half the national population is contained within a few metropolitan areas (which are incredibly profligate with imported resources), what special constitutional role should be assigned to cities, and how should rural/urban relations be mediated? There are no definitive answers to such questions because, for one thing, they simply have not been considered. As with any "paradigm shift", many puzzles remain to be worked out, and they can be done so only by open and informed democratic debate.

As presently proposed, however, constitutional change would lead to an accelerated attack on the "peripheral" resource base, and on the native communities who live there. In Quebec after separation, for example, counterbalancing federal jurisdiction over the environment and native rights would likely be lost. In contrast, if the local native nations who presently live there had a political veto over such developments, an eco-constitution would not only shift political decision making but, even more importantly, it could begin a *fundamental economic reorientation as well*,[13] the key to resolving

---

13   For example, creating a local territorial veto might be analogized into terms discussed by my colleague and co-panelist, Jack Knetsch, that is, as a vehicle for shifting not just legal, but constitutional, entitlements. This would then alter the bargaining position of local inhabitants (on the impacts of resource extraction by outside interests) from their "willingness to pay" to avoid such impacts to their "compensation demanded". By this shift

resource conflicts over the long term. Thus does the eco-constitution merge the informal into the formal constitution.

Despite the fears that such a grand redesign will generate, such political restructuring could lead to much greater resource efficiencies, and much-reduced conflict. For example, if the Quebec Cree, or the small northern communities of any province, could block a hydro project on a local river, Montreal and other urban areas would, at a political stroke, be pressed to do what economists and energy experts have long been advising — internalize the full costs and, in the process, become more resource efficient: conserve, reduce demand rather than increase supply, recycle.[14] Whether it is energy, agriculture, fisheries, or a range of resource and social objectives, a third-level veto would inherently tend to move us towards internal social reform at the core, not further expansionism at the periphery. Other issues being addressed in this volume — such as wilderness preservation, co-management, and land claims settlements — take on larger significance from the perspective advocated here.

Above all, then, eco-constitutionalism reasserts the primacy of political structure over economic decision. Re-embedding the economy within the community turns our economically driven modern history on its head; the eco-constitution is the foundation for the transformative economy, not the reverse.[15] By reversing the traditional core-periphery relationship politically, the eco-constitution should tend to change the relationship economically as well; that is, it will tend to create a new, more sustainable infrastructure, to "develop sustainability", and not just promote "sustainable development".[16]

---

in bargaining power, the costs of such extraction would be increased, and made less attractive.

14   It is beyond the scope of this paper to review the state of so-called least-cost energy planning, nor the burgeoning literature on the "eco-city". For introductory references, however, see Jose Goldemberg et al., Energy for a Sustainable World (New Delhi: Wiley, 1988); and David Morris, Self-Reliant Cities: Energy and the Transformation of Urban America (San Francisco: Sierra Club Books, 1982).

15   I appreciate the complicated philosophical arguments that this perspective raises, and the charges of naïveté that inevitably follow. It is not possible to consider this matter in detail. In sum, however, the thrust of the argument here is to recognize that the important tension in contemporary social structures is not between political and economic power (which are largely mirror images of each other), but between institutionally centralized and territorially based power of all kinds.

16   The reversal in phrasing is significant. Among environmentalists, the phrase "sustainable development" has often been lightly dismissed with the incisive statement that "they got the noun, we got the adjective". "Developing sustainability" changes this to give "them" the verb (economic growth), and give "us" (ecologists) the noun (a no-growth society). This radical economic analysis fulfills the status quo dependence on economic growth and yet

To ensure this, the central state remains important. Indeed, by reasserting political over economic decision at a community level, the eco-constitution should reinvigorate politics to overcome the lassitude that, in this century, has settled over western democracies.[17] In Canada, many familiar roles would remain for a reorganized federal government. For example, maintenance of "national standards" in areas such as human and democratic rights, environmental protection, protection of minorities, and social welfare would be within the jurisdiction of a federal authority, or of a transformed Charter of Rights and Obligations. Equitable relations between third-level communities must be maintained within some overall "confederation" (to resurrect an old Canadian term), and the common interests of this confederation represented abroad.

Other roles would, however, change dramatically, especially as the other side of a decentralized polity is a decentralized economy. Protection of the communitarian base from external aggression, including regulation of inter-community trade (at various levels) to protect and encourage the community economy, would also be a dominant central function, something which entails a very different direction than occurs today with the surrender of authority under the Canada-U.S. Free Trade Agreement or the GATT rules.

By having protective jurisdictional powers held within a coordinating confederation, the eco-constitution would build in a "double veto" — the local community restraining economic exploitation by outside interests, the confederal authority constraining local abuse. Over the past several hundred years the absence of a local veto, combined with the ability of central political power to exploit (rather than to protect) local territories, has led us to erode ecological and cultural structures. By creating a double veto our constitution would turn this around, tending to seek a higher, rather than a lower, common denominator.

CONCLUSION: A NEW SOCIAL MOVEMENT

This is, many will say, simply utopian. But in the face of growing environmental threats of a global scale, maintaining the *status quo* may be even more so. Certainly, the changes envisioned here cannot ultimately be

---

meets the need for gradual social transformation. As is discussed below, this gradualism provides the basis for a redefined liberalism. For further discussion of some of these issues, see J. Michael M'Gonigle, "Developing Sustainability: A Native/Environmentalist Prescription for Third-Level Government (1989-90) 84 B.C. Studies 65.

17   In the face of concentrated informal (i.e., corporate) constitutional power, formal democratic politics, especially at the central but also at the community level, has been seen to be increasingly irrelevant. This has undermined the state's legitimacy, so that popular participation has plummeted.

carried out in Canada alone, but with the cultural traditions emanating from the country's First Nations, its still-rich resource base, its diverse rural and cultural roots, and the unique historical opportunity brought on by the constitutional impasse, Canada may well be the country that could lead a far larger international debate in the years ahead.

In the literature on political change, it is often stated that basic policy directions in opposition to established economic interests (e.g., environmentalism, feminism) emanate not from government, but from the so-called new social movements. Most assuredly, advocacy for such a fundamental restructuring will not come from the corridors of power, but from the communities who feel most directly the pressures of growing demands on their shrinking resource base, and from those who seek to reduce conflicts at their roots. Strategically, natives, ecologists, progressive Québécois nationalists, feminists, labour, and the "alternatives" movement provide the core constituency for the movement, but the movement is potentially far wider.

In the age of ecology, instead of a class or special-interest movement, what is possible is a new, more broadly based "social" liberalism. Aware of the profound contradictions and limitations of our modern centralist politics when confronted by trans-systemic economic and ecological forces, such a new social liberalism might seek a transformative institutional design that builds on the legacy of our history of material progress but reshapes our future endeavours to the needs of real resource limits. But we could do so gradually, not by trying to manage still more conflict, but by ending the continuous expansion of our human systems into an already seriously diminished resource base.

2

PRESERVING WILDERNESS

CANADA'S WILDLANDS: THREE TRADITIONS IN CONFLICT FROM A SUSTAINABLE DEVELOPMENT PERSPECTIVE

J. Gordon Nelson

Conflict is a fundamental characteristic of wildlands. Conflicting changes in geologic, biologic, or other natural or biophysical processes have been commonplace in and among forests, grasslands, river channels, shorelines, sand dunes, and other features of wildlands. The form or state of such landscape features is in constant flux. Change is endemic in the system, its rate and extent varying with the differing effects through space and time of agencies such as wind, waves, vulcanism, earthquakes, disease, and fire. Although the foregoing natural agencies can act more or less independently of humans, this has been less and less the case over the last ten thousand years, and particularly over the last century, as a result of the increasing impact of human activities on ecosystem processes.

Some observers see the interweaving of culture and nature as having led to "the death of nature" as an overriding force independent of human activities and impacts.[1] In this sense, the final nail in the coffin of nature has been the changes in atmospheric chemistry induced by SO_2, NOx, CO_2, methane, and other emissions from coal-burning power plants, autos, domesticated livestock, sprays and aerosols, and other products of expanding urban and industrial enterprises. The pervasiveness of these effects in the form of acid rain, Arctic haze, widespread global warming, rising sea levels, and other changes makes it increasingly difficult to retain the notion of a nature substantially independent of humans and their works. Historically, such a view

---

1   Bill McKibben, *The End of Nature* (New York: Anchor, 1990).

can be seen as essentially an American one, with thinkers from Europe and other parts of the world being less concerned with the separation of nature from humans and with the struggle with nature and wilderness as part of the national experience and purpose.[2]

Even so, the pervasiveness, intensity, and impacts of acid rain and other global changes are working to bring different peoples and nations together in the common interest. Of special significance in this regard are the losses of wetlands and wildlife, destruction of rain forests and genetic diversity, pollution of oceans, lakes, streams, and groundwater, soil erosion and exhaustion, and desertification. All of these human-induced changes affect tens, if not hundreds, of millions of people over tens of thousands of square kilometres. They transcend ethnic and cultural as well as state and national boundaries.

It is such changes and their implications for human and other life on this planet that led hundreds of scientists, scholars, professionals, and managers to participate with the International Union for the Conservation of Nature and Natural Resources (IUCN) and other international organizations in the preparation of the 1980 World Conservation Strategy (WCS), intended to bring peoples and nations together to deal with global change.[3] The WCS focused on the idea of "living resource conservation" and sustainable development. Three elements were seen as crucial in this regard:

1. the maintenance of natural diversity, for example, in the tropical rain forests or North American grasslands;

2. the preservation of essential ecological processes, for example, the rise and fall of Great Lakes water levels; and

3. the protection of resource productivity, for example, of Canadian west or east coast fisheries or of prairie potholes for waterfowl and other life.

Nearly a decade later, the World Commission on Environment and Development, the so-called Brundtland Commission, strongly supported the idea of sustainable development but in a more humanistic way, with concern for conservation as a form of equity within and among generations.[4]

---

2   R.J. Forbes, *The Conquest of Nature: Technology and Its Consequences* (New York: Praeger, 1968); Hans Huth, *Nature and the American: Three Centuries of Changing Attitudes* (Berkeley: University of California Press, 1957).

3   International Union for the Conservation of Nature and Natural Resources (IUCN), United Nations Environment Programme (UNEP), and World Wildlife Fund (WWF), *World Conservation Strategy: Living Resource Conservation for Sustainable Development* (Gland, Switzerland: IUCN, 1980).

4   World Commission on Environment and Development, *Our Common Future* (Oxford: Oxford University Press, 1987) (Chair: G.H. Brundtland).

Conservation and development were seen as opposite sides of the same coin, dependent on one another. Economic development was not seen as possible without conservation of soil, water, and other resources. Conservation also was not seen as possible without economic growth to provide the basic necessities of life to poverty-stricken people in developing countries in Africa, Asia, and South America. Without such growth, it was thought to be impossible for the growing farming and fishing populations to reduce their pressure on soil, fish, and other resources and to escape the vicious cycle of poverty and environmental degradation.

It has also been pointed out that the extraordinarily high rates of per capita consumption by the approximately one billion wealthier North American and European members of the six-billion-person global community is a principal cause of many environmental problems.[5] The effects of the wealthier population are thirty or forty times what their numbers alone would suggest. It has also been noted that the standards of living of the wealthier humans are so high as to be unattainable by the remaining members of the global family without disastrous environmental consequences. In other words, the trickle-down theory that has been a principal justification of the post-World War II uneven economic growth in different places and countries can no longer be held out as the way to future equity among peoples. The old development model is dead — although this has yet to be widely recognized in Canada and the United States — and a new model must be found. Hence the interest of many people in the notion of sustainable development and the growing debate, in Canada and other parts of the world, about what it means.

To many, the foregoing remarks may seem to have little to do with wildlands and wilderness. However, they set a broad and pressing context in which the role and future of wildlands must be considered. The context is one of increasingly high pressure on resources and environment, of rising economic and other disparities among peoples and nations, of increasing inter-regional and international interactions and dependencies, and of the clear need for new approaches to resolve problems.

One basic concern is the protection and use of wildlands, which are viewed as important for many natural, social, cultural, recreational, economic, and other reasons. Such broad uses are often not compatible with one another, and this is becoming truer with each passing decade, as a brief review of wildlands history in Canada will demonstrate.

---

5   Ted Trainer, *Developed to Death: Rethinking Third World Development* (London: Greenprint, 1989).

THE INDIGENOUS OR NATIVE TRADITION

At least three basic traditions of wildland use and protection exist in Canada. Each of these traditions — the indigenous, the bush, and the wilderness — measures its development in centuries. The indigenous or native tradition is the oldest and most complex of the three. Its origins are obscure but can be thought of as commencing many millennia ago in North America, following the migration of Asian peoples across a land-bridge at the Bering Strait. More than ten thousand years ago, indigenous people were hunting bison and other animals in many parts of what is now North America. At about the time of Christ, native people were growing corn and beans in the southern parts of North America. By the year 1000, native people had created very successful agricultural societies and were living in villages and towns in, for example, present-day Ontario, New York, and New Mexico. The level of civilization in these societies was high. Towns in New Mexico as well as in Huronia, Ontario, are said to have had thousands of residents. The Anasazi or the Basketmaker and Pueblo peoples of New Mexico and the U.S. Southwest created large plazas, with hundreds of homes and many ceremonial buildings or *kivas*, as well as colourful pottery, jewellery, petroglyphs, and other art. Populations in the southwestern villages and in longhouse counterparts in eastern Canada and the U.S. often were quite high.[6]

Some indigenous societies remained basically hunting and gathering economies until crushed by European invasion in the eighteenth and nineteenth centuries. Examples are the Blackfeet and Assiniboine of the Canadian plains. Some native people have continued to hunt and fish for much of their livelihood up to the present time, adapting to the European commercial economy by becoming trappers and part-or full-time workers in various kinds of natural-resource-based industries. Examples are the present-day Cree, Dene, and Inuit. In an attempt to secure land to which they think they are entitled by earlier treaties, or to obtain lands for which unclear or no agreements were concluded with the invaders, many of the native people are in the process of negotiating land claims. A number of the lands in contention are of interest to members of the other wildland traditions. For example, some are in national parks, forests, or other holdings.

In the course of their land-use history, native people have changed the wildlife, vegetation, soil, and other elements of the environment in ways that are sometimes obvious and sometimes not. The plazas, irrigation structures, and other technology of the southwest Basketmaker or Pueblo peoples are still

---

6   Conrad Heidenreich, *Huronia: A History and Geography of the Huron Indians 1600-1650* (Toronto: McClelland & Stewart, 1971); Robert H. Lister & Florence C. Lister, *Those Who Came Before* (Tucson: University of Arizona Press, 1983).

very apparent. The erosion and alkalization of soils through irrigation are not so obvious, although these are thought by some to have been a major reason for the fourteenth- and fifteenth-century abandonment of towns and villages in the U.S. Southwest.[7]

The former villages of the Hurons or the Neutrals of southern Ontario are usually not discernable, except to expert eyes, partly because of the transitory and shifting nature of their settlement, and partly because of the destructive and enduring influence of more recent activities of the European invaders. Yet nineteenth-century European observations of Indian villages show that erosion was occurring from cultivated fields. Such observations also show that large areas were cleared for agriculture by native people, who were productive enough to support a relatively sophisticated political system that controlled large amounts of land. These people also hunted in large surrounding forested areas and traded goods from hundreds of miles away.[8]

Forests and other vegetation must have been cleared and altered on numerous occasions by native activities, raising the question of how far back in history we would have to go to find lands and waters natural or wild in the sense of having been little disturbed by humans. Indeed, many of the forests viewed by early settlers as wild and natural in the foregoing sense may have been fundamentally influenced by native people. An outstanding example is that part of southern Ontario located one hundred to two hundred miles north of the Lake Erie shore. This was the territory of the Neutrals, practitioners of shifting cultivation in a village system. Numerous remains of settlements have been found in this area. These predate 1644, the year when the Neutrals were defeated by the Iroquois and left their cultivated lands to the hunting and gathering activities of other tribes. Subsequently, an unknown amount of cleared agricultural land succeeded to the maple forests and oak savannahs seen by the early Caucasian settlers 150 years later, around 1800.

Not much is known about the conservation activities of the native people, whether they were agriculturalists, hunters, fishers, gatherers, or a mixture thereof, as for example were the Mandan people who lived in the upper Missouri Valley in the present-day North Dakota area. Little in the literature suggests that official conservation policies or rules of the type favoured by later Caucasian peoples were in vogue. Native people are thought to have respected and protected wildlife through animistic beliefs, taboos, and other social practices. Respect for other life is thought to have been high, and ceremonies were held before and after the taking of deer, fish, and other animals.

---

7   Lister & Lister, *supra*, note 6.

8   Heidenreich, *supra*, note 6.

However, native people are known to have killed animals in large numbers, as did for example the Plains Indians with the bison.[9] Much of this killing occurred after the arrival of the Europeans and was influenced by their technology and commercial system. The introduction of the horse and of firearms allowed far more killing and wasting than had been possible with the pre-European pedestrian technology of wood, bone, and stone.

Aspects of the native belief system may have allowed for large-scale killing. Some Plains Indians are said to have thought the bison came from the ground, and could have thought of them as inexhaustible. The great open spaces in which relatively small numbers of native people hunted large pre-European animal populations undoubtedly lessened indigenous impacts on wildlife. Under such circumstances, it would be difficult to hunt down numerous animals over a large area and reduce their populations significantly. Modern studies of Inuit hunting indicate that relatively large areas remote from more frequently hunted sites would harbour wildlife and would be hunted only occasionally, in times of need.

On the other hand, some scholars have suggested that pedestrian spear-wielding native peoples of approximately ten thousand years ago had a major role in the extinction of the giant bison and other Pleistocene or Ice Age fauna.[10] There is little to suggest that native people deliberately set aside areas or reserves in which hunting was prohibited. Rather, the general practice seems to have been to hunt as location, time, knowledge, and other circumstances allowed. Wildlife numbers do appear to have been unusually high in the transition zones between the general localities or territories preferred by different groups or tribes of native people. The dangers of attack by other tribes were greater in these intertribal transition areas. They were therefore less frequently hunted, and deer, bison, and other animals reportedly were more numerous within them.[11]

Today, native people are working hard not only to retain access or rights to lands traditionally used by them, but also to lands and waters lost or surrendered through treaties or sales, encroachments, or other means in the last century or so. In many cases, Canadians, including members of the bush and wilderness tradition, are sympathetic to the native claims and to their goal of greater control over their way of life and the wildlife and wildland resources essential thereto. However, the majority of additional land and water

---

9   J.G. Nelson, *The Last Refuge* (Montreal: Harvest House, 1973).

10   P.S. Martin & H.E. Wright, Jr., eds., *Pleistocene Extinctions: The Search for a Cause*, vol.6 of the Proceedings of the 7th Congress of the International Association for Quaternary Research (New Haven & London: Yale University Press, 1967).

11   *Supra*, note 9.

must necessarily come from lands used for parks, wildlife reserves, or wilderness, or for trapping, recreational hunting and fishing, forestry, or other bush uses. The members of the bush or wilderness traditions therefore are concerned that what they see as their access and rights will be adversely affected by additional allocations to native people.

THE BUSH TRADITION

In the context of this paper, the term "backcountry or bush uses" refers to the mix of subsistence, recreational, and extractive activities that have been pursued in wildlands or hinterlands outside urban settlements since the Caucasians arrived in North America about four centuries ago. Scientific activities may be marginal in this regard, but they are not treated separately here, partly because they exhibit some of the impermanence typical of the bush tradition.

The original bush image is probably best exemplified by the *coureurs des bois*, the French Canadian hunters, trappers, and backcountry people. Other manifestations are the traders or other members of the fur-trade enterprise.[12] Prospectors, miners, lumbermen, railroad and other surveyors all opened up and exploited the minerals, forests, wildlife, and other resources of the wildlands.[13] In general, their subsistence upon and exploitation of the land has been shortlived and ephemeral, lasting from a few days to a few decades.

The bush typically has been seen not as a homeland — as with the native people — but as a new frontier to be discovered, explored, and used for the benefit of the metropole and the frontiersmen, who would often leave after striking it rich or spending some time in the bush, or the outback, as it is known in Australia and New Zealand. Although the bush people or frontiersmen sometimes operated as individuals or in small groups, they typically were linked economically to corporate enterprises such as the North West and Hudson's Bay companies and the Canadian Pacific Railway. The companies were generally headquartered in large settlements or urban areas such as Montreal, Toronto, and Winnipeg, where they kept in close touch with supportive government officials.

The impact of the bush tradition on the environment has been very extensive, intensive, and complex, and continues to accelerate today. Beaver and other fur-bearers were by the 1820s reduced substantially by heavy trapping, leading to the integration of many small enterprises and the

---

12   *Id.*

13   J.G. Nelson & R.C. Scace, eds., *Canadian Parks in Perspective*, based on the conference "Canadian National Parks Today and Tomorrow", Calgary, October 1968 (Montreal: Harvest House, 1970).

amalgamation of the North West and Hudson's Bay companies in 1821. Fires frequently caused by prospectors, miners, and surveyors destroyed thousands of acres of boreal and mountain forests by the early 1900s. Careless railroad, mining, and other frontier activities as well as tourists and recreationists continued the carnage well into the twentieth century. Hunting of bison, elk, caribou, and other wildlife for food for traders, prospectors, miners, and other bush people, as well as for sport and adventure, all but eliminated the plains bison by 1880 and led to sharp reductions in musk-ox, elk, deer, caribou, waterfowl, and other populations in the west and the far north. Typically, the native people were drawn into bush activities, trapping for the Hudson's Bay Company and working for hunting camps and tourist lodges as well as for many other back-country enterprises.[14]

Bush mentality and uses continue to manifest themselves today in the form of massive lumber operations in B.C. or Alberta, producing largely for export to overseas markets. Other examples include energy projects such as the Peace River dam, which lowered flows and damaged wetlands, marshlands, and meadows providing habitat for bison and other animals of Wood Buffalo National Park, hundreds of miles downstream from the reservoir.

Conservation programs have long been part of the bush tradition, but have generally proven to be uneven, insufficiently comprehensive, and ineffective. In the early 1920s, for example, following the amalgamation of the highly competitive North West and Hudson's Bay companies, the new Governor, George Simpson, led in the establishment of policies and practices designed to cause the beaver to "recruit" on "exhausted ground". Certain areas were set aside from trapping to provide for recovery over the years. Trapping quotas or guidelines were set and a management system was created to provide for sustained production of beaver and other animals. Competition from "free" and Missouri River traders ultimately made it impossible for the Hudson's Bay Company to leave unharvested beaver, and led to the demise of the conservation system.

The introduction of coal-burning engines and other technology led to reductions in forest and grass fires, but some continue to the present day. Bag limits, hunting seasons, quota systems, and other methods reduced the toll in wildlife and brought recovery of waterfowl, migratory bird, elk, antelope, and other populations. The creation of waterfowl and other wildlife reserves offering some habitat protection has greatly enhanced conservation efforts. More recently, habitat protection has been extended to private land through stewardship programs encouraged by agencies such as Wildlife Habitat

---

14   *Supra*, note 9.

Canada and Ducks Unlimited.[15] These programs do, however, focus on game species such as ducks and geese, valued by sportsmen to a much greater degree, to the neglect of protection of non-game birds and other life.

Efforts to control the effects of lumbering and energy projects have probably been least effective. Vast areas in northern Ontario, for example, have been clear-cut. While reforestation has been attempted, it often has had limited success. The situation is similar in other provinces.

One method developed in the 1960s to control large energy or megaprojects, such as those proposed for the Mackenzie Valley and the western Arctic, was environmental impact assessment, latterly known as EIA. The Berger report[16] and other public inquiries of the 1970s were reflections of this approach and had useful but controversial results. Many people would agree that the ten-year delay caused in part by the Berger inquiry led to an avoidance of largely unwanted impacts on the environment and the way of life and destiny of native people. On the other hand, some have argued that the result was a lost opportunity for development and economic gain that may not come again. Similar arguments are being made now about James Bay II. In any event, the bush tradition is still alive and well in Canada and competing for even greater amounts of wildland resources, while still offering ineffective conservation and limited benefits to local and native people.

THE WILDERNESS TRADITION

The wilderness tradition appeared at about the turn of the twentieth century.[17] Very little evidence exists of wilderness thinking prior to that time in what is now Canada, the native and bush traditions being dominant. The wilderness idea seems to have spread to Canada principally from the United States, where it began to assume icon status in the middle to late nineteenth century. The U.S. was also the hearth of the evolving idea of the national park — the institutional handmaiden of wilderness. In the 1830s George Catlin, a Philadelphia lawyer, advanced the notion that the northern Great Plains and

---

15   Oriana Trombetti & Kenneth W. Cox, eds., *Land, Law and Wildlife Conservation: The Role and Use of Conservation Easements and Covenants in Canada*, Reference Paper 3 (Ottawa: Wildlife Habitat Canada, 1990); J.G. Nelson & Stephen Woodley, eds., *Heritage Conservation and Sustainable Development: From Parks and Protected Areas to Private Stewardship and Conservation Strategies*, Conference Proceedings, 14-20 May 1989, Ottawa-Quebec City-Tadoussac (Waterloo: Heritage Resources Centre, University of Waterloo, 1990).

16   Thomas R. Berger, *Northern Frontier, Northern Homeland: The Report of the Mackenzie Valley Pipeline Inquiry* (Toronto: Lorimer, 1977).

17   Huth, *supra*, note 2; Roderick Nash, *Wilderness and the American Mind* (New Haven & London: Yale University Press, 1967).

their nomadic native people should be forever protected in an American national park. But the idea of including native people in publicly owned lands and waters set aside as national parks was soon abandoned, as it was incompatible with agricultural settlement on nearby lands or with forestry, mining, and other activities in the bush tradition.

John Muir and others in the late nineteenth and early twentieth centuries promoted the idea of protecting wilderness as land largely unaffected by humans within national parks and similar reserves. Muir and others were also instrumental in the creation of the Sierra Club, the Wilderness Society, and the National Parks and Conservation Association. Today, these citizen groups have large memberships and work to promote the wilderness idea and the setting up of national parks and related reserves, not only in the U.S. but around the world.

James Harkin, an early director of the Canadian National Park Service, also was a promoter of the wilderness idea and the establishment of national parks in Canada. But in Canada the concept was more compromised from the beginning. For example, tourists were allowed in Canadian national parks such as Banff, with resident populations reaching several thousand people. Harkin and others also seem to have been more supportive of road systems for recreation and tourism than were U.S. authorities. In Canada, tourism and its infrastructure were more often seen as necessary to secure citizen and government support for national parks as well as wilderness, wildlife, and other conservation generally.

The wilderness tradition has established roots more unevenly in Canadian than in U.S. soil. It appears to be strongest in the West and increasingly so in Ontario, as is evidenced in the proceedings of the National Assembly held in Banff on the occasion of the National Park Centennial in 1985.[18] In eastern Canada, including Quebec, as well as in the North, the bush and native traditions are generally dominant.

In general, the idea and expression of wilderness in the form of large national and provincial parks and relatively undisturbed remote hinterlands is under pressure throughout the country. Examples include struggles over forestry, water power, and other projects in parts of Alberta, British Columbia, and Quebec, as well as conflicts about logging, bison hunting, and other activities in Wood Buffalo National Park in Alberta and the Northwest Territories.

---

18   R.C. Scace & J.G. Nelson, eds., *Heritage for Tomorrow*, Proceedings of the Canadian Assembly on National Parks and Protected Areas, vol.1 (Ottawa: Supply and Services, 1986).

What effects have the wilderness idea and associated institutions, such as national and provincial parks, had on forests, grasslands, wildlife, and other aspects of environment and society in Canada over the decades? It must be said at the outset that a detailed answer cannot be given because careful monitoring of changes in kind and number has not been carried out. State-of-the-park reporting and monitoring systems have been stipulated in a recent amendment to the *National Parks Act*[19] and are now being developed and incorporated into state-of-the-environment reporting in Canada. Records of land use and environmental change on public land are uneven and incomplete in Canada generally.

Historical and observational evidence does show that national parks such as Banff, Waterton, Glacier, Wood Buffalo, Point Pelee, and Fundy have led to much afforestation, to increases in wildlife from low ebbs at the turn of the nineteenth century, and to protection and improvement of soils and water. Similar statements can be made about some large provincial parks, such as Quetico in northwest Ontario. But other provincial parks, such as Algonquin in southern Ontario or Strathcona in British Columbia, are subject to forestry and mining pressures and have consequently lost some of their wilderness character and resources.

Without the wilderness and wildlife protection concepts as well as associated institutions such as national and provincial parks — especially where the latter provide for large wilderness zones — many areas where forests or wildlife were removed or altered by fire, clearing, lumbering, or other human activities in the nineteenth and twentieth centuries would not have recovered as well in terms of flora and fauna and condition of soils and waters. They would not exist in their present relatively wild state. Equally, the recreation, tourism, forest, wildlife, water, and other resource values, as well as more recently recognized educational, research, environmental monitoring, and "gene pool" uses, would be much reduced or forgone. More detailed information on the current state of ecosystems in national parks and related management arrangements is urgently needed in order to better understand their character, changes, and uses as a basis for improved planning and management in the future.[20] In this sense, it is clear that wilderness areas and national parks and other institutions are not single-purpose areas, "frills", or "luxuries", but rather perform many fundamental roles of value to

---

19   *National Parks Act*, R.S.C. 1985, c.N-14, s.5(1.5), as am. by S.C. 1988, c.48.

20   J.G. Nelson *et al.*, "The ABC Resource Survey Method, the ESA Concept and Comprehensive Land Use Planning and Management" *in* Michael R. Moss, ed., *Landscape Ecology and Management: Proceedings of the First Symposium of the Canadian Society for Landscape Ecology and Management*, University of Guelph, May 1987 (Montreal: Polyscience Publications, 1988) at 143.

development and conservation in Canada.

In this sense also, it is important to recognize that the foregoing changes or achievements in wilderness conservation have been gained by a protectionist rather than a management approach. The basic policy has been to prohibit certain exploitive activities, such as lumbering and mining, and to prevent or control certain processes, such as fire, insect outbreaks, and disease, in the name of conservation. This protectionist policy has had the valuable effects described previously on wildlife, vegetation, and landscape. However, it has also had many unanticipated effects or "surprises".

For example, very large areas in many national parks such as Banff and Waterton are now covered with even-age lodgepole pine, which develops after burning. Control of fire in the name of conservation has prevented openings in this forest for aspen, low shrubs, grass, or other vegetation, as well as for the animals associated with these missing habitats. Disease control has had a similar effect, even contributing to the reduction or elimination of wildlife populations in national parks, for example wolves in Banff because of the fear of rabies. The current plan to kill thousands of bison in Wood Buffalo National Park originated largely from a desire to control diseases such as brucellosis, which are considered threats to domestic stock. For such reasons, concerned persons in the Canadian Parks Service as well as academics and citizen groups are beginning to advocate increased active planning and management, as compared to the previous protectionist philosophy. For example, attempts are being made to use controlled burning to open forests and create more diverse ecosystems.

Efforts are also being made to manage processes and effects ensuing from attempts to promote recreational and tourist uses of wildlands in national and provincial parks.[21] An example is the elimination of animals such as exotic trout for sport fishing or plants such as exotic roadside grasses, in order to maintain the parks as close as possible to the ecosystem prevalent in Indian days. The aim is to enhance wild, scientific, educational, and gene pool values.

A major difficulty with the introduction of such active management is that it brings values to the fore more than the protectionist model of management. In this sense, the management approach highlights the controversial relationship between technical or scientific and lay or political input into decisions. It does not seem unfair to say that many wilderness or park managers tend to see park management as largely a technical problem,

---

21   J. Gordon Nelson, "Wilderness in Canada: Past, Present, Future" (1989) 29:1 Natural
      Resources Journal 83.

whereas other people see the issues as value-laden and as requiring citizen involvement in a regular and more detailed way. The latter consider that public involvement is needed more frequently than, for example, at the five-year intervals stipulated for review of park management plans. Environmental assessments are now undertaken more regularly in the planning and management of road improvements, ski expansion, or other activities. Such assessments will have to extend to other concerns, for example, to policies and practices bearing on the desired state of park or wilderness ecosystems. Such assessments will involve more lay or citizen input.

To more fully appreciate the above, it should be noted that scientists are hardly a uniform group with regard to expertise. Rather, they vary in their special knowledge and preferences, so that they exhibit the qualities of both the scientist or professional and the lay person. Some scientists have special knowledge of bison, deer, or other large mammals whereas others specialize in plants rather than animals.

E.O. Wilson, the famous proponent of social biology, has recognized this variety or pluralism in science in some of his recent writing.[22] In fact, he has encouraged more specialization in certain fields or grouping of plants and animals, be they butterflies, fish, or birds. He justifies this, in part, on the grounds that such concentration of knowledge is needed at a time when many species about which we have good understanding are threatened by development and, in part, because many species that we need to know more about are disappearing from rainforests and other ecosystems before we have the chance to study, understand, and defend them.

Such a pluralist view portrays science in political terms as a field marked by different understandings and values, and by the need to make compromises and trade-offs among natural phenomena on scientific or professional grounds. For example, scientists knowledgeable about either the deer or the Carolinian vegetation of Rondeau Provincial Park, Ontario, do not have any special claim to the values that would decide between deer or plants in the event that excessive deer grazing threatened to destroy the Carolinian vegetation. In this sense, whether or not to cull the deer is basically a political or citizen's and not a scientific decision.

A final effect of the development of the wilderness idea and associated institutions is, briefly, the displacement of native and local people and their socio-economic and cultural activities. So that a strict protectionist regime could be set up in the national parks in the late nineteenth and early twentieth

---

22   E.O. Wilson, "The Coming Pluralization of Biology and the Stewardship of Systematics" (1989) 39:4 BioScience 242.

centuries, native people who had lived or hunted in these areas for centuries or millennia were excluded along with the lumbermen, miners, and other members of the bush and development traditions who had invaded these areas in European times. More recently, in national parks set aside in the 1960s, such as Konchibougac in New Brunswick or Kluane in the Yukon, similar displacements took place. The result was to alienate the people directly affected, as well as members of the native and bush tradition more generally. Conflict in some of these cases has been enduring, for example in the Maritimes.

CONCLUSION

What can we conclude from the foregoing brief and general analysis of a complex problem? First, conflict is endemic within wildlands and has been constant for more than a century in Canada. Second, conflict is increasing among the native, bush, and wilderness traditions because of the growing pace and scale of development; the undertaking of more wide-ranging and intense mining, lumbering, dam construction, and other bush activities; and the increasing demands of native peoples for settlement of land claims and greater control over their future. Newer problems are created by the use of wilderness and lands traditionally occupied by native people for military purposes. These activities may or may not be seen as part of the bush tradition, but they are very disturbing and much objected to by native people.

Many cases involve demands for more use of lands for native and bush purposes. They also often involve proposals for change in land use or for surrender of part or all of national parks or other areas important for wilderness. Currently in Ontario, for example, the provincial government is allowing native people to hunt in some or all of the wilderness areas located in provincial parks. The reaction of the wilderness and nature conservation community against this initiative has been quite strong.

The third basic conclusion is that we are not clear on what should be done under these increasingly stressful circumstances. It seems that as a first step, one has to decide whether or not one accepts all three of the wildland traditions as having a valid claim to use and conservation of land and waters. This is especially the case with the wilderness tradition, because it is under the greatest pressure for change. Lands and waters where the human presence can be seen as transitory, and where little sign of human activity can be found, are disappearing rapidly in Canada.

All three traditions can be viewed as having historic validity and considerable economic and social value, providing that conservation safeguards are present against unwanted and costly resource and environmental degradation. Many of the proposals in the bush tradition, such as lumbering at the boreal forest/tundra fringe in the north, or building James

Bay Phase II, are questionable in this regard. They also are in conflict with native ways of life and with wilderness more generally. It is, however, inappropriate to think of the native and wilderness traditions as being consistently linked against bush activities, because the native and wilderness traditions are not always compatible, as we have seen earlier in regard to hunting in wilderness areas in provincial parks.

Practices of questionable conservational or wilderness value are also occurring in many national parks; a good example is the proposed bison slaughter in Wood Buffalo National Park. This very complex case cannot be discussed in detail here. Suffice it to say that its origins lie in pressures from ranchers and agricultural interests to control the bison in order to reduce the risk to nearby commercial cattle of infection with brucellosis or other diseases. The lands in question are low in carrying capacity, and the economic value of the whole frontier enterprise is questionable, especially in circumstances where cattle and other agricultural prices are low and frequently subsidized in North America.

The elimination of the park bison is also an attempt to remove what are termed plains bison and replace them with what are termed wood bison, from the Mackenzie Wildlife Reserve north of Wood Buffalo. This effort to recreate pre-European conditions and increase diversity is controversial from a genetic standpoint, as there has been much intermixing among animals over the decades and, in all cases, they have recovered from small populations surviving the slaughter at the end of the nineteenth century. In the search for an acceptable way of conducting the slaughter, the federal government has apparently decided to give the native people a chance to conduct a controlled kill of the Wood Buffalo herd over a number of years. The kill is to be under the general direction of a board or committee on which national park personnel and citizen conservation representation is very low in comparison to representation from Agriculture, Indian and Northern Affairs, and other government agencies. As a result of this process, the National Park Service has lost control of the bison, and indeed of Wood Buffalo National Park, to other interests. Any wilderness image that the park can be claimed to have must endure the elimination of thousands of plains bison — a very costly and difficult venture because of the large park size — as well as the various effects that the slaughter of the main park herbivore will have on the rest of the Wood Buffalo ecosystem.

Ultimately, it must be asked whether the goal of eliminating diseased bison to protect cattle and other stock against brucellosis and other diseases is attainable, even if, after costs of millions of dollars, the proposed eradication program in Wood Buffalo National Park is judged to be successful. The disease is known to occur in many other wild animals such as caribou in the Canadian and Alaskan north as well as, for example, in many African ungulates, including the African buffalo, the eland, and the hippopotamus. Any eradication in Wood Buffalo National Park may not, therefore, be a long-term success.

One matter of much concern among members of the wilderness tradition, and many citizens and observers generally, is that the decision to recommend a bison slaughter to the federal Minister of the Environment was made by an environmental impact assessment panel on the basis of limited consultation with people in the country at large. Public meetings under the auspices of the panel and the Federal Environmental Assessment Review Office (FEARO) were held in the vicinity of Wood Buffalo National Park, to provide opportunity for local people to comment. But no public hearings were held to secure views in, for example, Vancouver, Toronto, or Ottawa. Such widespread consultation would have been appropriate for a major national park that has received international recognition as a World Heritage Area. Such consultation would have given many Canadians who supported the wilderness tradition, or who had other concerns, an opportunity to express their values and views. In the 1960s and 1970s, national hearings would have been held more or less as a matter of course on such an important question for Canadians generally. The federal government and other agencies have been shy of such national hearings since that time, in part because local concerns have been seen as paramount, and in part because nation-wide participation did cause unanticipated problems, for example, the cancellation of the Lake Louise ski development in Banff National Park in the early 1970s.

In light of the foregoing, it seems to me, and given the nature of the issues it is important to stress the personal perspective, that a very different approach needs to be taken to wildlands management in Canada. The three major reasons for this conclusion are, first, the inevitability of conflict about changes in wildlands among members of the three traditions; second, the steady degradation and loss of areas that could be viewed as wilderness in the classical sense; and third, the increasingly evident failure of governments to deal consistently, equitably, and effectively with this situation. Appeals to the historic or other precedence of one tradition over another will not solve this conflict, as all three traditions have historic and other validity in the minds of their proponents. Appeals for equity, especially for native people, will have considerable support among members of all three traditions, as well as citizens generally, but not, for example, to the point of seriously reducing or eliminating areas viewed as wilderness. In this context, the large and growing number of urbanites with a strong interest in wilderness should be kept in mind.

In recent years, conflict over wildlands has reached the threshold of violence, for example in the case of Moresby, British Columbia, or Temagami, Ontario. In my view, it is very likely that such thresholds will be reached and breached in the future if present land-use expansion and management approaches continue. The chances for major conflict accelerate as governments take decisions after consulting only one group or tradition, and not all interested parties, including the general citizenry. Much anger was generated in the past among native and wilderness proponents when government met and made arrangements behind closed doors with companies and interests supportive of the bush tradition. Much anger has been generated recently by the Ontario government's decision to consider allowing hunting in provincial parks, after meetings with native people and not with members of the wilderness tradition or other interested parties. There appears, for example, to have been no assessment or consultation with scientists about the effects that the hunting would have upon the moose or other large mammal populations or, indeed, upon scientific research. One would hope that such situations would not become more common if native people secure a status as a separate or fourth level of government, which they are now generally seeking.

What kinds of changes are desirable? Space is not sufficient to consider these in any detail. Scientific and technical information and research continue to be necessary, but much more attention should be paid to regular public involvement at the local, provincial, national and, indeed, international level. Scientific input will continue to be invaluable in promoting understanding of change and its implications. In this context, the concept of ecological integrity or ecological health may hold considerable promise as a fundamental guideline for planning and management of wildlands.

In any event, information will have to be more pluralistic. It will have to cut across traditions and involve more groups in systematic and regular ways, because of the growing recognition of values that lie beyond science as well as the incompleteness and uncertainty of any human ways of knowing, whether they be scientific, indigenous, or otherwise.

Much more attention will have to be paid to what Serafin calls "the politics of communication".[23] The decision-making system will have to be more open, even to the extent that this results in the open disagreements and the messy, uneven planning procedures so disliked by many government and corporate people. Efficiency in the economic, technical, and bureaucratic senses probably will not be well served by involving all major parties from the earliest stage in an interactive and evolving search for solutions to wildlands issues. But in the end, such a process will likely be more effective.

---

23   R. Serafin, *Institutions, Environment, Development: The Politics of Communication in Three Environmental Programs in the Great Lakes Region* (Ph.D. diss., University of Waterloo, 1991).

In this context also, more attention will have to be given to providing citizens with the information and skills needed to become effectively involved in such issues; citizens need preparation for a civics approach.

Without long-term dialogue and efforts at understanding and compromise on the part of the native and bush traditions in particular, the wilderness perceived and valued by so many people will disappear. With this observation we are drawn back to the major issues of climatic and other global changes and of sustainable development that were discussed at the outset. Wilderness areas and uses are a key part of any efforts to understand and adapt to global change as well as to follow a path of sustainable development. Wilderness areas provide for research and monitoring of environmental changes, for education and understanding. The relatively new concept of biosphere reserves, which stresses protection, use, monitoring, and research, is especially promising in this regard, with several such areas now having been created in Canada, for example, at Waterton, Alberta; Riding Mountain, Manitoba; and Long Point, Ontario. More can be done in the management of wildlands for research and monitoring as a basis for overall understanding. National and provincial parks and other reserves managers have generally not favoured such activities as land uses in the past; often, environmental learning activities are the first to be curtailed during periods of budgetary constraint.

Wilderness and related areas such as biosphere reserves, national and provincial parks, and local environmentally significant areas like those in Ontario, are multipurpose in that they offer uses of value to sustainable development, including protection of wetlands and water supply for domestic, irrigation, flood control, and industrial purposes. In this sense, many small wilderness or wildland areas need to be thought of and planned not so much as isolated "islands of green", but as interconnected nodes and corridors that, through cooperation among various public agencies and private landowners, can form linked networks for movement of water, animals, and plants as well as frequently serving as trails for hiking and other human uses.

In this sense also, wilderness areas and national parks and other reserves are increasingly recognized as part of a coordinated approach to land-use or to integrated landscape planning and management.[24] Intensive use of lands for industrial, agricultural, or urban purposes depends for sustainability on management of nearby as well as distant lands for wilderness, wildland, and nature conservation purposes. The pressures on wilderness and wildlands through population growth, expansion of exploitive activities, and the rising demands of a highly consumerist Canadian society require more than the

---

24   J.G. Nelson, "Beyond National Parks and Protected Areas: From Public and Private Stewardship to Landscape Planning and Management" (1991) 21:1 Environments 23.

modulation of growth. These pressures also require the setting aside of certain areas to protect them from exploitive activities and their effects in a way that was not so necessary in earlier times, when relatively small populations with less powerful economies and technologies could use resources without major concern about depletion and degradation. Safeguards were involuntarily provided by the large wild spaces that residents of Canada collectively no longer have, particularly in more settled areas in the south.

Wilderness areas, national parks, and related reserves — indeed wildlands generally — would benefit from more frequent, regular, and comprehensive assessments of proposals for land-use changes of various kinds and scales. Such assessments should be comprehensive in the sense of considering all the so-called environmental (natural), social, and economic aspects in one review, in the spirit of sustainable development. In the comprehensive sense also, assessments and associated monitoring of change should be linked to more widespread participation and communication in the pluralistic spirit. Such assessments and monitoring can be more frequent and regular through the use of practices such as class assessments — essentially guidelines for practice — by responsible agencies, as well as by more continuous interaction with concerned groups and persons through the use of round tables or fora, annual reports, state-of-the-park reports, and the like.

The opinions expressed in this paper about wildlands and wilderness are still not widely recognized and accepted. Many Canadians persist in the belief that a lot of relatively untouched wilderness remains. Politicians appear to be inadequately informed about either the size of the remaining wilderness or the significance of its loss to other uses, as indeed do many senior bureaucrats, including members of Environment Canada. This Department remains organized largely along sectoral or systematic lines, and there is little concrete evidence of cross-sectoral or holistic thinking in the land use, ecological, or landscape sense.

The idea of cross-sectoral thinking and practice is a basic part of the concept of sustainable development and has been strongly supported in the IUCN World Conservation Strategy and the Brundtland Report. But it is still largely unaccepted and unimplemented in Canada, along with its counterpart, the assessment of the interactive and cumulative effects of developments not only at the project but also at the program and policy stages. Public and private agencies, while cooperating in some ways in some situations — for example, the increasingly active federal and provincial Round Tables on Environment and Development — are still largely ineffective in dealing with the large-scale and cumulative impacts of development on the resources and environment so important to Canadian ways of life in the future. Amid this generally dismal picture, there is little that receives less attention than the future of wildlands, and especially the disappearing wilderness that many people perceive and rightly value so highly for utilitarian and emotional reasons.

THE IMPACT OF WILDERNESS PRESERVATION ON RESOURCE DEVELOPMENT RIGHTS: EXPROPRIATION AND COMPENSATION ISSUES

H. Ian Rounthwaite

In an article written in 1983 for the First Banff Conference on Natural Resources Law,[1] Sheilah Martin pointed out that land withdrawn for wilderness preservation and similar purposes is an illustration of "the conflicting interests between the Crown, as the grantor of resource rights, and industry, as the holder of those rights."[2] Professor Martin argued that the security of tenure of the holder of resource rights is threatened by government on two fronts: by its legislative powers and by its contractual capacity, as owner of the resource, to alter the terms and conditions on which the resource rights may be held. Where vested resource rights are adversely affected by the Crown's acting in its contractual capacity, no compensation need be paid to the holder of the resource rights, provided that the original instrument under which the resource rights are held contains a suitable "compliance with laws" clause.[3] Compensation need only be paid when the Crown exercises its legislative powers to adversely affect contractual or proprietary rights.[4] A number of significant events have occurred since 1983 that make it timely to reconsider some of the issues raised by Professor Martin.

First, on 9 May 1985, the Supreme Court handed down its decision in *R. v. Tener*,[5] which was based on a significantly different analysis than the decision of the B.C. Court of Appeal that formed the basis of Professor Martin's essay. This decision, when read with the Court's decision in the *Manitoba Fisheries* case,[6] may be an indication that the Supreme Court is taking a broad approach to the question of whether there has been a compulsory taking or acquisition requiring the payment of compensation. If

---

1   Sheilah L. Martin, "Land Withdrawals: Government Needs Versus Vested Rights" *in* Nigel Bankes & J. Owen Saunders, eds., *Public Disposition of Natural Resources: Essays from the First Banff Conference on Natural Resources Law* (Calgary: Canadian Institute of Resources Law, 1984).

2   *Id.*, at 129.

3   *Id.*, at 130-131.

4   *Id.*, at 131.

5   *R. v. Tener*, [1985] 3 W.W.R. 673, 32 L.C.R. 340 (S.C.C.).

6   *Manitoba Fisheries Ltd. v. R.*, [1979] 1 S.C.R. 101, [1978] 6 W.W.R. 496 (S.C.C.).

the Court is expanding the legal definition of "compulsory taking", there will be significant financial implications for governments contemplating the withdrawal of land for wilderness preservation.

Second, it can be argued that there has been a noticeable shift in the public, and consequently the political, attitude towards wilderness preservation during the last decade at the international, national, and provincial levels. In 1980, the International Union for the Conservation of Nature and Natural Resources (IUCN) brought the concept of "sustainable development" to the notice of the world.[7] The Brundtland Commission adopted "sustainable development" as the central theme of its report in 1987.[8] On a national level, Canada's recently released Green Plan[9] pledges $350 million in order to achieve sustainable development of the country's renewable resources. The goals of sustainable development promoted by the Green Plan include shifting management strategies for forestry development from sustained yield to sustainable development and promoting the long-term sustainability of the fisheries resource. A further $175 million is dedicated to protecting unique ecological areas. Provincially, the Alberta Conservation Strategy also adopts "sustainable development" as its central theme.[10]

Third, recent amendments to the *National Parks Act*,[11] as confirmed by policy pronouncements with respect to wilderness preservation in the Green Plan, seem to reaffirm the traditional role of the national parks as the federal government's primary tool for preserving wilderness values for future generations.[12] For example, the Green Plan adopts a goal of setting aside as

---

7   International Union for Conservation of Nature and Natural Resources (IUCN), United Nations Environment Programme (UNEP) and World Wildlife Fund (WWF), *World Conservation Strategy Living Resource Conservation for Sustainable Development* (Gland, Switzerland: IUCN, 1980).

8   World Commission on Environment and Development, *Our Common Future* (Oxford: Oxford University Press, 1987) (Chair: G.H. Brundtland).

9   Canada. Dept. of Environment, *Canada's Green Plan: Canada's Green Plan for a Healthy Environment* (Ottawa: Supply and Services, 1990).

10   Public Advisory Committees to the Environment Council of Alberta, *Alberta Conservation Strategy: Framework for Action; A Draft for Public Discussion* (Edmonton: Environment Council of Alberta, 1990).

11   *National Parks Act*, R.S.C. 1985, c.N-14, as am. by R.S.C. 1985 (1st Supp.), c.31; R.S.C. 1985 (4th Supp.), c.39.

12   Parks Canada employs a five-class system of zoning that includes Special Preservation (Zone I), Wilderness (Zone II), and Natural Areas (Zone III). Canada. Dept. of Environment, *A Planning Scenario for the Four Mountain Parks Block* (Draft) (Calgary: Parks Canada Western Region, 1984). Additionally, under s.5(8) of the Act, Cabinet may declare by regulation any region of a park that exists in a natural state or that is capable of returning to a natural state to be wilderness area.

protected space 12 percent of Canada, which is to be accomplished through the establishment of five new national parks and six new national marine parks, as well as completion of the terrestrial parks system by the year 2000.[13] As noted above, the Green Plan suggests that this can be accomplished for $175 million.

In order to focus the analysis, I have assumed that the decision has been made to establish a new national park in northeastern British Columbia and northwestern Alberta. The land is subject to two outstanding natural resource interests, the first under the British Columbia *Mineral Tenure Act*[14] and the second under the Alberta *Forests Act*.[15]

The purpose of this paper is to consider the implications of recent case law on the entitlement of holders of natural resource rights to compensation where government policy limits or restricts the full development of vested natural resource rights.[16] In the event that compensation must be paid in order to promote a policy of wilderness preservation, the paper also attempts to suggest the measure of compensation payable and the kinds of losses for which compensation is recoverable.

The first section explores the withdrawal process itself. What is the legislative mandate to withdraw land for park purposes and how is it implemented? Although there may be a potential constitutional problem should the province decline to participate in the process, its resolution is beyond the scope of the paper.

The second section considers the nature of the interest or interests that may be affected when land is set aside for wilderness preservation. The land may have been subject to a wide range of mineral, timber, water, and other resource uses that can no longer be developed. Whether compensation is payable, and its measure, will be determined by a complex analysis of the statutory regime under which the interest was obtained, as well as by a consideration of whether the interest can be classified as statutory, proprietary, or contractual. This classification may vary with the kind of resource interest involved and the jurisdiction in which it is found. Special attention must be given to the precise wording of the legislation under which the interest was

---

13 The goals and initiatives of the Green Plan for Special Spaces and Species, as set out in Canada. Dept. of Environment, *Canada's Green Plan: Summary of Goals and Key Initiatives* (Ottawa: Supply and Services, 1990) at 11-14.

14 *Mineral Tenure Act*, R.S.B.C. 1979, c.263.3.

15 *Forests Act*, R.S.A. 1980, c.F-16.

16 "Full development" is used to mean the ability of the interest holder to exploit the natural resource for its full economic value.

obtained and the withdrawal accomplished, as well as the terms and conditions of the lease, licence, or permit under which the affected resource development rights are held.

Finally, the paper turns to consider whether compensation must be paid to the holders of mineral and timber interests, and if so, what is the appropriate measure of compensation. A close examination of the *Manitoba Fisheries* case[17] and the *Tener*[18] decision may provide support for an argument that the Supreme Court is prepared to expand the ambit of what constitutes a compulsory taking or acquisition beyond the traditional proprietary or contractual analysis when the legislation is silent with respect to the payment of compensation.

WITHDRAWAL PROCESS

The *National Parks Act*[19] authorizes the establishment or enlargement of a national park in two ways: where title to the land is unencumbered and vested in the Crown in right of Canada,[20] and where the Minister[21] is authorized by Cabinet "to purchase, expropriate or otherwise acquire any lands or interests therein for the purposes of a park."[22] Subsection 4(5) of the Act provides that the *Expropriation Act*[23] applies to any expropriation proceedings under s.4. The scope of the application of the federal *Expropriation Act* to land withdrawals and acquisitions is consequently limited to withdrawals and acquisitions of land or interests in land presently within the boundaries of an existing national park or in land already under federal control. Where the land or interest to be acquired for national park purposes is owned privately by the provincial Crown, acquisition must occur under provincial legislation relevant to the nature of the outstanding interests.[24] For

---

17 *Supra*, note 6.

18 *Supra*, note 5.

19 *Supra*, note 11.

20 *Id.*, s.3(2)-(6). In addition to "clear" title, the section requires that an agreement has been reached with the appropriate province in addition to notice and form requirements.

21 The *National Parks Act* is under the administration of the Minister of the Environment, SI/84-176.

22 *Supra*, note 11, s.4(4).

23 *Expropriation Act*, R.S.C. 1985, c.E-21.

24 The procedure for the transfer of land from the provincial Crown to the federal Crown is canvassed in *Shaw v. R.*, [1980] 2 F.C. 608 (T.D.) at 632-633 and *A.G. of Can.* v. *Higbie*, [1945] S.C.R. (S.C.C.) 385 *per* Rinfret CJ at 404. Briefly, since there is only one Crown on a theory of indivisibility, the land, if not vested in the provincial Crown, is acquired by the province, which then transfers the beneficial interest to the federal Crown. The underlying

example, the Alberta *Public Lands Act* authorizes the Minister of Forestry, Lands and Wildlife to reserve public lands for any reason and to permit its use by the Crown in right of Canada.[25] Further, once the land is acquired by the provincial Crown, administrative control, rather than the underlying fee simple, may be transferred to the federal Crown. If the federal expropriation power extended to permit the compulsory taking of private interests in land under the legislative control of the province, such power would likely be beyond the constitutional competence of Parliament.[26] Consequently, if land and interests therein in northwestern Alberta and northeastern British Columbia are to be set aside for national park purposes, resort must be had to provincial and not federal legislation.

THE NATURE OF THE INTEREST(S)

The two resource interests to be examined include a mineral interest located and recorded under the British Columbia *Mineral Tenure Act*[27] and a forest management agreement entered into pursuant to the Alberta *Forests Act*.[28] Classification of the legal nature of these interests depends, in part, upon whether the focus is on the statutory provisions under which they are granted or whether classical principles of real property law are applied to them.

At common law, mineral interests and timber interests could be disposed of by the Crown in several ways.[29] First, a transfer of the corporeal fee in the land would include both the timber growing upon it and the minerals within it. Second, a corporeal fee interest in trees or minerals can be carved out of the fee simple estate and conveyed separately.[30] Third, there is a long line of authority for the classification of the nature of a mineral claim or timber interest as an incorporeal hereditament in the nature of a *profit à prendre*.[31] Finally, mineral and timber interests may be construed as being

---

title remains in the province with administrative control passing to the federal Crown.

25   *Public Lands Act*, R.S.A. 1980, c.P-30, s.17(d).

26   The taking would have to be declared to be for the general benefit and advantage of the Dominion, a declaration that may be politically unpalatable.

27   *Supra*, note 14.

28   *Supra*, note 15.

29   For a discussion of techniques for disposing of timber rights in Alberta and at common law, see N.D. Bankes, *Crown Timber Rights in Alberta* (Calgary: Canadian Institute of Resources Law, 1986).

30   *Liford's Case*, 11 Co. Rep. 466; *Smith* v. *Daly*, [1949] O.R. 601, [1949] 4 D.L.R. 45 (Ont. H.C.); *Re Newsome and Masters* (1984), 60 B.C.L.R. 121 (B.C.S.C.).

31   Mineral: *Duke of Portland* v. *Hill* (1866), L.R. 2 Eq. 765; *Duke of Sutherland* v. *Heathcote*,

only a chattel interest, in the nature of a personal licence.[32]

The classification of the nature of the interest may, however, turn on the specific language of the legislation in question. The statutory language may affect the classification of the nature of the interest in either of two ways. The statute may confer any number of proprietary-type "rights" on the holder of the resource interest. These rights, such as the right to enter, possess, exclude, and remove, invite an analogy to classical principles of real property law and the labelling of the interest according to the extent to which the rights mirror property interests recognized by the general law.[33] Alternatively, the statute itself may declare that the resource interest is of a particular kind. This latter possibility is graphically illustrated in the British Columbia Supreme Court decision in *Cream Silver Mines Ltd.* v. *B.C.*[34]

Cream Silver Mines involved the question whether a mineral claim located and recorded under the *Mineral Act*[35] of British Columbia was "land" within s.11(c) of the *Park Act*.[36] The plaintiff had established its mineral claims in 1966. Prior to 1977, there was no doubt that the interest of a free miner in his or her mineral claim constituted an interest in land.[37] However, in 1977, the province enacted a new *Mineral Act*[38] that provided that the interest of the holder of a mineral claim was deemed to be a "chattel

---

[1892] 1 Ch. 475 at 483 (C.A.). Timber: *Vaughan-Rys* v. *Clary* (1910), 15 B.C.R. 9 (S.C.); *Anderson* v. *Rolandi Brothers Logging Co.* (1955), 17 W.W.R. (N.S.) 119 (B.C.S.C.).

32 The cases that classify a contract to cut and remove timber from the land of another as a mere chattel or licence interest are reviewed by Bankes, *supra*, note 29, at 6-10. At page 10, Professor Bankes rightly concludes that "it seems difficult to deny that the interest granted will ordinarily be construed as a type of profit — a right to go on the lands, cut and remove the timber."

33 This was the approach taken by Mr. Justice Rand in *Berkheiser* v. *Berkheiser*, [1957] S.C.R. 387, 7 D.L.R. (2d) 721 (S.C.C.) in characterizing the nature of an oil and gas lease. "The word 'grant', then, not being significant of title and the word 'lease' not carrying with it the possession with which it is ordinarily associated, we look to the detailed description of the acts authorized for the true intendment of the instrument" at S.C.R. 392.

34 *Cream Silver Mines Ltd.* v. *B.C.*, [1986] 4 W.W.R. 328 (B.C.S.C.).

35 *Supra*, note 14.

36 *Park Act*, R.S.B.C. 1979, c.309.

37 Prior to 1977, the legislation described the interest of a free miner in a mineral claim as "a chattel interest, equivalent to a lease, for one year, and thence from year to year". R.S.B.C. 1960, c.244. See also *Stussi* v. *Brown* (1897), 5 B.C.R. 380, 1 M.M.C. 195 (B.C.C.A.); *Chassy* v. *May*, [1921] 1 W.W.R. 69 (B.C.C.A.); *A.G. B.C.* v. *Westgarde*, [1971] 5 W.W.R. 154 (B.C.S.C.).

38 *Mineral Act*, S.B.C. 1977, c.54.

interest".[39] If the nature of this chattel interest was a chattel personal rather than a chattel real, it was arguable that it could not be expropriated by the Crown under the *Park Act*, which authorized the expropriation of land only.

Southin J held that the change in the legislation resulted in a mineral claim being classified as a chattel personal rather than a chattel real. Consequently, not only was the mineral claim not an interest in land, it was not land. The court noted the principle of statutory interpretation that the legislature must be taken to be aware of judicial interpretations of statutory provisions, and when it changes the wording of a statute it must intend also to change the meaning.

> If the legislature did not intend to change the law, there was no purpose to the change made in 1977. It would be wrong of me to assume that the legislature was unaware of the long standing significance to the words "equivalent to a lease, for one year" when it omitted them in 1977.[40]

The court also found that since a chattel real at common law only encompassed a leasehold interest, and since a free miners interest could no longer be considered the "equivalent of a lease", it could only be a chattel personal after the 1977 amendment.

There may be great danger in the court's basing its decision primarily on a principle of statutory interpretation. Principles of statutory interpretation are notoriously fickle creatures of judicial creation, in that for each "principle" that supports a particular result there is an alternative principle supporting the opposite result. While Madame Justice Southin is correct in stating that a change in legislative language may mean the legislature intended to change the meaning of the enactment, it is also true that this is only a presumption that may be rebutted by other factors, such as careless drafting or the possibility that the change was to modernize the language or style of the legislation.[41] A strong argument can be made that the 1977 amendments were purely for housekeeping reasons and were not intended by the legislature to lead to the classification of a mineral claim as a species of personal property.

This argument is strengthened if the *Mineral Tenure Act*[42] is read as a whole in an attempt to identify the types of rights that are acquired under a mineral claim. It will be seen that the rights conferred by the Act are more

---

39   *Id.*, s.21(1).

40   *Supra*, note 34, at 331.

41   P.J. Langan, ed., *Maxwell On the Interpretation of Statutes*, 12th ed. (London: Sweet & Maxwell, 1969) at 282.

42   *Supra*, note 14.

consistent with the kinds of rights and interests in land recognized by the law of real property than with those recognized by the law of personal property. Mineral title under the Act means a claim or a lease[43] and is considered to be an individual and distinct mineral title.[44] The holder of a mineral claim may acquire the surface rights of unreserved Crown lands for the purpose of developing and producing the minerals[45] and "is entitled to those minerals ... that are situated vertically downward from and inside the boundaries of his claim."[46]

Perhaps the most telling provisions of the Act for classification purposes are those dealing with the priority of claims and forfeiture for non-compliance with exploration and development performance requirements.[47] Clearly, the language of these sections of the Act envisions that the rights of a holder of a mining claim are vested rights to the mineral title covered by the claim. It seems strange indeed to speak of personal property rights as being interests that upon forfeiture will vest in the Crown. The chattel interest referred to under s.24(2) may mean no more than a statutory interest in mineral title that is a statutory chattel in the nature of a chattel real, albeit a new form of real property created by the *Mineral Tenure Act.*

The essence of the argument is that the classification of the nature of a mining claim interest should be determined according to the rights obtained under the statute. It should be a matter of substance rather than merely one of form. It should not be forgotten that leasehold interests were at one time considered to be purely personal interests until they evolved into an interest in land in the nature of a chattel real. In determining whether an agreement constitutes a leasehold interest or a personal licence of occupation, the courts have not hesitated to go beyond the form of the agreement and classify the interest according to its substance.[48] As a matter of substance, the holder of a mining claim is entitled to have a mining lease issued upon compliance with the Act.[49] A mining lease is without doubt an interest in land, and in this respect a mineral claim is analogous to an option to acquire the fee simple in a land transaction, which upon its exercise constitutes an equitable interest in

---

43 *Id.,* s.1.

44 *Id.,* s.10(1).

45 *Id.,* s.13(1).

46 *Id.,* s.24(1).

47 *Id.,* ss.14, 25, 29(1), 31, 36.

48 See discussion at *supra,* note 33.

49 *Mineral Tenure Act, supra,* note 14, s.37(1).

land.[50] It may be useful to conclude the discussion of the *Cream Silver Mines* case by asking a rhetorical question: If Southin J is correct that a mining licence is a personal chattel and not an interest in land, what form of personal chattel is it? Is it a chose in possession or a chose in action? Is it moveable or immoveable, tangible or intangible? The difficulty of classifying a mining licence as a particular form of personal property indicates that the better view is that it is an interest in land.

The classification of the nature of timber interests under the Alberta *Forests Act* has been discussed at length by Professor Bankes.[51] Consequently, only a brief account is required for the purpose of this essay.

The Act authorizes the disposition of Crown timber in three ways; by a Forest Management Agreement (FMA), by the sale of timber quota certificates and the issuance of timber licences to timber quota holders, and by the issuance of timber permits.[52] The purpose of an FMA is to enable its holder to enter on forest land for the purpose of establishing, growing, and harvesting timber "in a manner designed to provide a perpetual sustained yield."[53] Consequently, the FMA's purpose is clear: to provide a perpetual sustained yield. The holder of a FMA, except as against the Crown and subject to the terms of the FMA, has a vested ownership interest in all Crown timber on the land that is subject to the FMA and "is entitled to reasonable compensation from any person who causes loss of or damage to any of the timber or any improvements created by the holder."[54] The legal nature of the interest obtained by the holder of a FMA is likely a corporeal interest in land that includes the right to manage the land for perpetual sustained yield purposes. Although less clear, it is also likely that timber quotas and timber licences also amount to interests in land in the nature of a *profit à prendre*. The difficulty arises owing to s.28(1) of the Act.

> A timber quota holder, whether or not he holds a timber licence, and a holder of a timber permit do not acquire any right or interest in the forest land that is the subject of the quota, licence or permit, but may enter on the land for the purpose of doing or complying with those things specified in the licence or permit or in this Act or the regulations.

This section does not necessarily lead to the conclusion that the holder does not acquire an interest in land recognized by the general law. It may be read as limiting the corporeal rights of the interest holder, in that it provides

---

50   *Can. Long Island Petroleums Ltd.* v. *Irving Indust. Ltd.*, [1975] 2 S.C.R. 715 (S.C.C.).

51   *Supra*, note 29.

52   *Supra*, note 15.

53   *Id.*, s.16(1).

54   *Id.*, s.16(2).

that the holder does not acquire any right or interest in the forest land itself, the corporeal hereditament. However, a *profit à prendre*, an incorporeal hereditament, is the right to enter the land of another to cut and remove timber. It does not give the holder of the profit a corporeal interest in the land, but an incorporeal interest with respect to another's land. A *profit à prendre* has long been recognized as an incorporeal hereditament amounting to a real property interest.[55]

Finally, the *Forests Act* makes it clear that a timber quota holder, a timber licensee, and a timber permittee may be paid compensation if the quota, licence, or permit is altered, varied, or cancelled through no fault of the holder.[56] The Act gives very little guidance, however, as to the way in which compensation is to be quantified.[57]

COMPULSORY TAKING AND COMPENSATION

Land may be set aside for wilderness preservation through government acquisition, expropriation, or the exercise of its regulatory powers. If land or an interest in land is acquired by expropriation, compensation will be payable only where the statute authorizing the expropriation contemplates, either expressly or by implication, such payment.[58] Where land or an interest in land is actually taken, however, the authorizing legislation will be construed by the courts in light of a presumption in favour of the payment of compensation.[59] Thus the question of what amounts to a "taking" of land or an interest therein, as opposed to the exercise of regulatory powers in the public interest, must be considered. At what point does regulation in the

---

55   Robert Megarry & H.W.R. Wade, eds., *The Law of Real Property*, 5th ed. (London: Stevens & Sons, 1984) c.15 at 834.

56   *Supra*, note 52, s.27.

57   Bankes, *supra*, note 29, at 94, indicates that compensation issues are usually negotiated and included as terms of FMAs. In addition, the Department of Energy, Mines and Natural Resources has issued Information Letters 80-8 and 85-17, which provide a table of compensation that would be applied in calculating the compensation due to Crown timber outside FMA areas.

58   This is subject to Professor Martin's argument, *supra*, note 1, that the *Manitoba Fisheries* case may provide support for a common law principle of no expropriation without compensation. See the judgment of Wilson J in *R. v. Tener*, [1985] 3 W.W.R. 673, 32 L.C.R. 340 at 696 citing Lord Parmoor in *Rockingham Sisters of Charity v. R.*, [1922] 2 A.C. 315 at 322 (P.C.): "No owner of lands expropriated by statute for public purposes is entitled to compensation, either for the value of land taken, or for damage on the ground that his land is injuriously affected, unless he can establish a statutory right." See also *A.G. v. De Keyser's Royal Hotel Ltd.*, [1920] A.C. 508 at 542 (H.L.) *per Lord Atkinson and Belfast Corp. v. O.D. Cars Ltd.*, [1960] A.C. 490 at 523 (H.L.) *per* Lord Radcliffe.

59   *R. v. Loiselle*, [1962] S.C.R. 624, 35 D.L.R. (2d) 274 (S.C.C.).

public interest cross the line and become a taking requiring the payment of compensation?

The taking/regulation dichotomy has been considered recently in two important cases. In the *Manitoba Fisheries* case[60] and the more recent *Tener*[61] decision, the Supreme Court of Canada gave several important insights into when government regulation amounted to a taking requiring the payment of compensation.

The conventional analytical approach to expropriation cases requires the court to identify the nature of the plaintiff's interest that is adversely affected by governmental regulation and then to ask whether the regulation constitutes a taking of that interest. Difficulties often arise, however, where the regulatory action of government adversely affects the economic value of the plaintiff's interest but the Crown does not acquire either the legal or beneficial interests held by the plaintiff. In the *Manitoba Fisheries* case, federal legislation prohibited the exportation of freshwater fish from Manitoba unless the exporter obtained a licence from the marketing authority set up under the legislation. The plaintiff, who had been exporting freshwater fish for decades, failed to obtain a licence and was effectively put out of business. At trial and in the Manitoba Court of Appeal, it was held that although the *Freshwater Fish Marketing Act* created a monopoly over the exportation of freshwater fish in favour of the Marketing Corporation, the effect of the legislation could not be regarded as a taking or acquisition of the plaintiff's business. In the Supreme Court, Mr. Justice Ritchie disagreed. The function and effect of the exercise of the regulatory powers of government was to put the plaintiff out of business. In effect, the Marketing Corporation took the plaintiff's business by conferring upon itself the ability to control access to the freshwater fish market.[62]

It has been argued that the *Manitoba Fisheries* case indicates a willingness on the part of the Supreme Court of Canada to recognize a common law principle requiring the payment of compensation, notwithstanding that the authorizing legislation may be silent on the point.[63]

---

60   *Supra*, note 6.

61   *Supra*, note 5.

62   The *Manitoba Fisheries* case, *supra*, note 6, may also be read as support for the conventional approach to the question of what constitutes a taking. At 502, Ritchie J states, "[G]oodwill, although intangible in character, is part of the property of a business just as much as the premises, machinery and equipment employed in the production of the product whose quality engenders that goodwill." The Marketing Corporation therefore acquired the plaintiff's "goodwill", a valuable property right recognized by the general law.

63   See Martin, *supra*, note 1.

Although the decision may be read in this way, the Court's decision in the *Tener* case provides an explanation for the *Manitoba Fisheries* case that does not go so far. In *Tener*, a series of amendments to the British Columbia *Park Act*[64] effectively prevented the plaintiff from developing its mineral claim in Wells Grey Provincial Park. The plaintiff had acquired its mineral interests in 1937 from the province, which granted the minerals to the plaintiff in fee simple together with the right to use and possess the surface for the purpose of winning the minerals. In 1982, the Crown notified the plaintiff that it would not, as a matter of policy, issue the plaintiff a permit that it required to gain access to its mineral claim.

Both Mr. Justice Estey,[65] who delivered the leading opinion, and Madame Justice Wilson[66] agreed that the province's regulatory activity amounted to a "taking", requiring the payment of compensation. Estey J stated the principle to be applied to determine whether regulatory action constitutes an expropriation: An expropriation or compulsory taking occurs if the Crown or a public authority acquires from the owner an interest in property. Difficulties in computing the value or the nature of the interest taken are not relevant to either the determination of the interest taken or to the question whether compensation must be paid.[67] He went on to distinguish between "zoning" of land, which does not amount to a taking, and regulation of specific activity on land, which may amount to a taking.

> The imposition of zoning regulation and the regulation of activities on lands, fire regulation limits and so on add nothing to the value of public property .... The notice of 1978 [*sic*] took value from the respondents and added value to the park. The taker, the government of the province, clearly did so in exercise of its valid authority to govern. It clearly enhanced the value of its asset, the park.[68]

In order for regulatory activity to amount to a taking, it appears that the regulation must affect the plaintiff's property interests specifically in such a way that value is taken from the plaintiff and with the effect of enhancing the value of Crown property. If these criteria are applied to the situation in *Manitoba Fisheries*, it can be argued that giving the Fish Marketing Corporation the exclusive right to licence the export of freshwater fish diminishes the economic power of the plaintiff by enhancing the economic power of the Corporation. If this interpretation of *Manitoba Fisheries* and

---

64 *Park Act*, R.S.B.C. 1979, c.309, s.18.

65 Mr. Justice Estey wrote on behalf of himself and Beetz, McIntyre, Chouinard, and LeDain JJ.

66 Madame Justice Wilson wrote on behalf of herself and Chief Justice Dickson.

67 *Supra*, note 5, at 678-679.

68 *Id.*, at 686.

Tener is correct, support is found for a cause-and-effect analysis to determine whether governmental regulatory activity constitutes a taking. Where the effect of the regulatory activity is to cause a serious derogation of the exercise of private rights, the government will have crossed over the line from regulation in the public interest to an expropriation or taking of those private interests. The question whether compensation must be paid is an entirely different question, to be determined by the application of common law presumptions well established by the jurisprudence of expropriation law.

Before leaving this discussion, it should be noted that Wilson J's judgment provides strong support for a cause-and-effect analysis of the takings issue. According to her, the case should be divided into three parts. First, what was the nature of the respondent's mineral interest? Second, did the Crown's refusal to issue a park use permit amount to an expropriation or injurious affection of the respondent's mineral interest? Third, if so, did the respondent have a statutory right to compensation?[69] For the purposes of this paper, the first and second parts of the decision are particularly interesting.

Madame Justice Wilson had no doubt that the respondent's interest should be classified as a *profit à prendre*, and the essential function of a profit is the right to enter upon the land of another for the purpose of severing the thing that is the subject of the *profit*. Whether the refusal to issue a park use permit amounted to a taking should be determined by the effect of the refusal on the ability of the respondent to exercise its rights as the holder of a *profit à prendre*. Throughout her opinion, Wilson J lays great emphasis on how the government's regulatory power affects the respondent's ability to exercise its private rights.

> While the grant or refusal of a licence or permit may constitute mere regulation in some instances, it cannot be viewed as mere regulation when it has the effect of defeating the respondent's entire interest in the land .... The reality is that the respondents now have no access to their claims, no ability to develop them and realize on them and no ability to sell them to anyone else. They are effectively beyond their reach .... By depriving the holder of the profit of his interest — his right to go on the land for the purpose of severing the minerals and making them his own — the owner of the fee has effectively removed the encumbrance from his land. It would, in my view, be quite unconscionable to say that this cannot constitute an expropriation in some technical, legalistic sense .... Moreover, what in effect has happened here is the derogation by the Crown from its grant of the mineral claims to the respondents predecessors in title.[70]

It seems clear that, in order to decide the question whether there has been a taking of the resource interest, Wilson J is prepared to look at the function of the nature of the resource interest affected by government regulation and

---

69   *Id.*, at 689.

70   *Id.*, at 699-700.

the effect of the regulation on the ability of the holder of the resource interest to develop it. Focusing on the inter-relationship of the nature of the resource interest held and the effect of government regulation on the exercise of property rights that accompany the resource interest will yield significant economic considerations for policy makers who wish to use governments' regulatory powers to preserve wilderness. Setting aside wilderness areas that are subject to existing resource interests may now be classified as an expropriation or taking rather than mere regulation in the public interest.

In the event that a land withdrawal is construed to amount to an expropriation or taking requiring the payment of compensation, some consideration should be given to the way in which such compensation is to be calculated where the affected interest is a mineral claim in British Columbia or a forest interest in Alberta. In both cases, where the interest taken amounts to an interest in land, it appears that compensation issues must be quantified under the applicable expropriation legislation of the province.[71] Although there are minor differences in the two Acts, for the purposes of this paper they may be considered together.

The leading writer on the subject of expropriation and compensation in Canada has noted a trend since the early 1970s to bring expropriation legislation across the country into some degree of conformity, based on the Ontario and federal statutes.[72] Both the Alberta statute and the British Columbia statute adopt what Professor Todd calls the "market value plus" check list of compensable items.[73] This should be contrasted with the common law measure, which required that the appropriate compensation be based on the "value to the owner" test as explained in *Diggon-Hibben Ltd.* v. *R.*[74] and adopted by Spence J in *Kramer* v. *Wascana Centre Authority.*[75] In essence, both the market-value-plus approach and the value-to-the-owner method of assessment should provide the same measure of compensation. Each is predicated on a basic formula that begins with the "market value" of the interest taken and then makes adjustments based on factors such as special

---

71 In British Columbia, the *Expropriation Act*, S.B.C. 1987, c.23 [hereinafter the B.C. statute]; in Alberta, the *Expropriation Act*, R.S.A. 1980, c.E-16 [hereinafter the Alberta statute].

72 Eric C.E. Todd, *The Law of Expropriation and Compensation in Canada* (Toronto: Carswell, 1976).

73 *Id.*, at 117.

74 *Diggon-Hibben Ltd.* v. *R.*, [1949] S.C.R. 712 at 715 (S.C.C.): "the owner at the moment of expropriation is to be deemed as without title, but all else remaining the same, and the question is what would he, as a prudent man, at that moment, pay for the property rather than be ejected from it."

75 *Kramer* v. *Wascana Centre Authority*, [1967] S.C.R. 237, at 242 (S.C.C.).

value to the owner, disturbance damages, severance damage, and injurious affection, mitigation, and abandonment.

For example, both expropriation statutes provide that the basic formula is to be the market value of the estate or interest taken plus reasonable disturbance damages.[76] Where the interest is that of a lessee, the disturbance damages are to be based on the length of the term, its unexpired duration, the right of renewal if any, and the reasonable prospect of renewal, as well as the nature of the lessee's business and the extent of the lessee's investment that cannot reasonably be expected to be recovered.[77]

Unfortunately, there are very few cases in which the courts or an expropriation compensation board has been called upon to quantify the appropriate measure of compensation where a resource interest has been taken. It may be particularly difficult to establish market value for a resource interest that is of limited duration and where it is difficult to classify the proprietary nature of the interest. This problem is exacerbated where the resource itself is subject to large fluctuations in price.

Two methods of establishing market value that may be useful are the comparative, or market data, method and the income, or economic, approach. The comparative approach requires a comparison of the expropriated resource interest with other, similarly situated resource interests that have recently been sold on the open market. The difficulty, of course, will be to establish a sufficiently reliable pool of recent sales for comparison. This problem was recognized by Rand J in *Gagetown Lumber Co. v. R.*[78] when he discussed the difficulty of establishing the relationship of market value and value to the owner.

> Where the position of the owner *vis-à-vis* the land is not different from that of any purchaser, that value is the measure; where the owner is in special relations to the land, as in the case of an established business, the measure is the value to him as a prudent man, what he would pay, as the price of the land, rather than be dispossessed, that price thereafter, in effect, representing the capital cost of the business to which the profits would be related. But evidence of those relations issuing in special injury upon extrusion and their value in terms of money must be adduced.[79]

In the absence of sufficient comparative data, resort may be had to the income approach. This approach attempts to quantify what a prudent purchaser would pay based on the capitalized value of a stream of income

---

76   *Expropriation Act*, S.B.C. 1987, c.23.

77   *Id.*, s.38.

78   *Gagetown Lumber Co. v. R.*, [1957] S.C.R. 44 (S.C.C.).

79   *Id.*, at 51.

from the property. An attempt was made at trial in the *Gagetown Lumber* case to introduce evidence of the capitalized value of the expropriated forest resource interest, which illustrates vividly the difficulties inherent in capitalizing the value of a resource interest. An attempt must be made to establish market value taking into account projected price fluctuations and deducting an appropriate amount for variables such as royalties, production and processing costs, environmental mitigation and reclamation costs, and the risks of natural hazards, to list but a few of the variables that must be worked into the equation. It is unlikely that a court or arbitration board would embrace this method of computation given the uncertainties. Unfortunately, the alternatives may be equally problematic.

Regardless of the approach taken to establishing market value and value to the owner, both the legislation and common law provide for compensation for disturbance damages and damages for severance and injurious affection. Again, however, quantification of these kinds of loss will prove to be extremely difficult in many resource interest expropriation cases.[80]

CONCLUSIONS AND RECOMMENDATIONS

The goal of this paper was to raise and consider some of the difficult legal questions that will arise when public policies designed to preserve wilderness clash with the proprietary interests of holders of resource rights and interests. The jurisprudence of expropriation law requires that the nature of the resource interest be classified according to traditional proprietary rights recognized by the common law. It also suggests that the effect of regulations implementing preservationist policies on the exercise of vested common law proprietary rights may be determinative of the question of whether the regulations amount to an expropriation or taking of an interest in land. If this is indeed correct, it may be financially prohibitive to set aside large tracts of Crown land for wilderness preservation if the property is subject to pre-existing resource development rights. Furthermore, the difficulty in determining the legal nature of many resource interests and the complexity of calculating the measure of compensation payable in the event of an expropriation or taking may act as a strong disincentive for the resource sector to invest the large sums of money necessary to develop forest and mining resources.

The fact of the matter is that wilderness preservation as a matter of public policy in the 1990s will conflict with resource development founded on public

---

80   I would be remiss if I did not confess to feelings of inadequacy in attempting to quantify compensation in any given case. My purpose is not to establish compensation but to provide a brief description of the methods of calculating compensation that the courts have considered in the past.

policy formulated in the 1970s and 1980s. Security of tenure, a prime concern of holders of resource development rights, may often be negated by preserving wilderness unless the resource sector is confident that adequate compensation will be paid when natural resources cannot be developed.

Unfortunately, recent legislation and case law is confusing and is not likely to lead to the degree of confidence required to encourage sustainable development of our natural resources. It may be that classifying the nature of natural resource interests according to traditional categories of property law estates and interests is no longer a useful way to resolve the conflict between regulation in the public interest and private property rights. An analysis based on common law proprietary rights fails to recognize that these rights were protected by the common law in order to promote policies that may have been suitable for society in the past but are now inappropriate.

One response to this impasse is through the enactment of compensation legislation that deals specifically with the payment of compensation when resource development rights are adversely affected by land withdrawals. Although there are several examples of resource allocation legislation that requires the payment of compensation when land is withdrawn from development, little is said concerning the resource holder's entitlement to compensation or the measure of compensation that will be paid. Of course, this may prove to be an exceedingly difficult, but not impossible, task and would at least provide a degree of certainty for potential resource interest investors. Alternatively, compensation issues could be negotiated as part of the resource allocation process and incorporated into the licensing and permitting process. Again, greater certainty would be the result. Security (or insecurity) of tenure would be offset by security of compensation.

CHANGING VALUES OF NATURAL RESOURCES AND THE EVOLUTION OF PROPERTY RIGHTS: THE CASE OF WILDERNESS

Martin K. Luckert

The evolution of societies is accompanied, or perhaps caused, by changing values. Changes in values have become increasingly evident in the management of natural resources in Canada. Whereas management strategies have historically been based on the extraction and processing of natural resources, today's resource managers must seek to accommodate society's increasing demands for values associated with non-consumptive uses.

The new types of natural resource value that have emerged are quite different from traditional valuations of resources. While previous uses of resources were primarily dependent on natural features of the resource, which influenced costs of extraction and production, new resource values depend on how members of societies perceive natural features.

The importance of society's perceptions in defining resource values is, perhaps, nowhere more evident than in the case of wilderness. Members of society have vastly different perceptions of what wilderness areas and experiences entail. These differences have caused the mere definition of the concept of wilderness to be elusive. As a consequence, the definition of wilderness has been relegated to political processes, wherein varying definitions have arisen as governments have attempted to reflect the perceptions of their populaces.

An important factor in influencing societies' perceptions of natural resources is property rights. Property rights play a prominent role in defining concepts of resources by influencing the context in which values may be experienced. As an integral part of resource values, institutional systems of property rights must evolve as social values change. Therefore, governments have had to adopt various property-right solutions to facilitate the emergence of non-consumptive resource values.

Dales has described property rights as the interface between law and economics.[1] By defining the rules that individuals, or firms, must follow in using natural resources, property rights provide a framework within which the economic transactions of firms may take place. In market economies, transactions between individuals or firms consist of the buying, selling, and

---

1   J.H. Dales, *Pollution, Property and Prices: An Essay in Policy Making and Economics* (Toronto: University of Toronto Press, 1968).

leasing of property rights. Indeed, the efficiency with which an economy performs, and the distributions of wealth that result, are largely dependent upon the conditions under which property rights may be held and traded.[2]

The realization that property rights are of importance in analyzing resource values has generated a relatively new field of research known as the property-rights approach to economics. This area of study has been concerned with the different ways in which property rights have evolved, and may evolve, to accommodate the changing values of society.

As property rights have evolved to accommodate wilderness values, governments in North America have largely retained public ownership of wilderness areas and thereby controlled the allocation of wilderness resources and the distribution of wilderness values. Some writers have disagreed with public ownership of natural resources, claiming that public managers, insulated from market incentives, make inappropriate management decisions.[3] This group of theorists favours the establishment of private property rights in order to allow economic transactions between private individuals to allocate resources and distribute wealth.

The purpose of this paper is to investigate what types of property rights might evolve to facilitate emerging wilderness values. I will first explore theories describing the evolution of property rights to natural resources. Investigating the process of property-right evolution provides insights into the types of property rights to natural resources that may evolve, and into whether such systems are likely to further the interests of society. In sum, these theories may be used to assess the strengths and weaknesses of alternative types of property rights that may emerge to accommodate the rise of wilderness values.

THE EVOLUTION OF PROPERTY RIGHTS

Property rights have been described as evolving through various channels by differing processes, but a common element of these evolutionary theories is the recognition that the emergence of new resource values causes institutions to change in order to accommodate new values.[4] If new forms of

---

2   For a description of the effect of property rights on resource allocations and income distributions, see Alan Randall, *Resource Economics: An Economic Approach to Natural Resource and Environmental Policy*, 2nd ed. (Toronto: Wiley, 1987).

3   For a collection of essays representing this school of thought, see Walter E. Block, ed., *Economics and the Environment: A Reconciliation* (Vancouver: Fraser Institute, 1990).

4   See, for example, Harold Demsetz, "Toward a Theory of Property Rights" (1967) 57:2 American Economic Rev. 347; Peter H. Pearse, "Property Rights and the Development of Natural Resource Policies in Canada" (1988) 14:3 Canadian Public Policy 307.

property rights are not forthcoming, then natural resources management may suffer from problems of open access, where no individual has a stake in managing the resource, and, as a result, resource values may be dissipated.[5]

Another common feature among such theories is that they attempt to assess those conditions that will influence how and whether property rights evolve. The descriptions that follow will concentrate on such conditions in order to assess, in a later section, what types of property rights may evolve to facilitate emerging wilderness values.

The Evolution of Private Property Rights through Private Negotiations: The Coase Theorem

A cornerstone of the property-rights approach to economics is an article written by Coase.[6] In his seminal work, Coase analyzed a situation in which the actions of one firm were having deleterious affects on the production of another. That is, Coase concentrated on the problem of negative externalities.[7] In such situations, Coase showed that firms may have incentives to negotiate a solution by buying and selling property rights.

For example, assume that a pulp mill is emitting residues into a lake.[8] A local fishing club discovers the lake's potential for angling, but believes that the pulp mill's emissions are too high to allow the lake to sustain a healthy fish population. Since the pulp mill has the prior right to pollute, the fishing club must negotiate with it to reduce emissions.

Coase showed that under certain conditions, the two parties could negotiate a solution that would increase the overall welfare of both. Furthermore, such a solution does not depend upon whether the pulp company has the prior right to pollute. That is, if the fishing club has the prior rights to the lake, and the pulp company is negotiating with the fishing club to allow pulp production, and accompanying emissions, the solution will be identical.[9]

---

5   See, for example, Steven N.S. Cheung, "The Structure of a Contract and the Theory of a Non-Exclusive Resource" (1970) 13:1 J. of Law and Economics 49.

6   R.H. Coase, "The Problem of Social Cost" (1960) 3 J. of Law and Economics 1.

7   Although Coase addressed the problem of negative externalities, the same arguments may be applied to positive externalities. Thus, Coasian theory may be used to assess how and whether private property rights may evolve to internalize emerging resource values, such as those associated with wilderness areas.

8   Wilderness is not used as an example because, as a later section of this paper will show characteristics of wilderness create special considerations in assessing how property rights may emerge.

9   An alternative scenario would be for neither party to have prior rights to the lake. For a discussion of how property rights may evolve spontaneously in such a case, see Carl J.

An integral part of the Coase solution is the concept of the "reciprocal nature of externalities".[10] This concept recognizes that there are two sides to every externality problem. On one side, there are costs born as a result of the externality, while on the other side, benefits are being reaped by causing damage. That is, there is a demand for pollution abatement from the fishing club; however, there are also costs incurred by the pulp company in supplying such abatement. Thus, the optimal solution to the damage problem must seek to maximize the total welfare obtainable from the situation by considering values to both parties. That is, the solution must seek to determine how much damage is optimal.[11]

By showing how negotiations between private parties may result in optimum solutions, Coase identified a means for private property rights to evolve without the guidance of governments. However, as with most models, it is the assumptions behind the model's proofs that are of interest in considering the real-world applicability of Coase's theorem. Several conditions may prevent negotiations from producing optimum property-right solutions.

First, as Coase recognized, transactions costs may prevent negotiations from yielding optimal solutions, or in some cases, completely preclude negotiations. Transactions costs arise from the processes of negotiating, policing, and enforcing agreements.[12] In the presence of transactions costs, Randall has shown how the negotiated solution will tend to be biased.[13] For example, if the pulp mill has the right to pollute the lake, in the presence of transactions costs the lake will become too polluted. Likewise, if the fishing club has the right to prevent the pulp company from polluting, then transactions costs will not allow the pulp mill to produce enough emissions. In the extreme, if transactions costs are severe enough, negotiations are precluded and the original disposition of rights determines whether fishing or pulp production takes place. Thus, under such conditions, externalities may persist.[14]

Dahlman, *The Open Field System and Beyond: A Property Rights Analysis of an Economic Institution* (Cambridge: Cambridge University Press, 1980).

10   Coase, *supra*, note 6.

11   It may seem odd to speak of optimum levels of damage. However, Dales, *supra*, note 1, reminds us that "to live is to pollute." Thus, finding a solution to pollution problems requires weighing the benefits of polluting against the costs of pollution.

12   The processes of negotiating, policing, and enforcing agreements may require firms to undertake the costly activity of gathering information. Therefore, a portion of the transactions costs associated with these processes may arise as firms attempt to educate themselves in order to make the best possible decisions.

13   Randall, *supra*, note 2.

14   Transactions costs may also preclude the initial establishment of property rights to either

Negotiations may also bias the internalization of externalities because of differences in bargaining power between parties. Bargaining power may differ because of differing amounts of income available for negotiations, or because one party may be able to exert monopoly power in negotiations. In cases where parties must negotiate under income constraints, true costs and benefits incurred by firms may not be adequately expressed in negotiations conducted with dollars.[15] Furthermore, negotiations may be biased if the party who does not hold prior rights is dependent on the other for the sole supply of fishing or pulping opportunities. In such situations, parties with market power could bias negotiations in their favour. Both of these sources of imbalanced bargaining power cause negotiated solutions to be biased towards the rights held by the stronger negotiator.

A further problem with the Coase solution is that the transferability of property rights may be restricted by indivisible goods. If the fishing club wishes to purchase only half of the fishing potential of the lake, then it will not be able to bid effectively to buy rights to the whole lake, which is being polluted.

A final criticism of the Coase solution is that it ignores distributive justice.[16] By attempting to maximize the overall welfare of the two parties, the solution ignores the distribution of that welfare between the individual firms. Thus, in our example above, the fishing club could be forced to pay the pulp company to not pollute, despite the possibility of public sentiment that it is the obligation of the pulp mill to reduce pollutants to accommodate the fishing values.

Despite these limitations, the Coasian model has proven valuable for many uses. First, there is evidence that such solutions can effectively facilitate the evolution of new types of property rights to deal with emerging resource values and resulting externality problems. Luckert reports that such has been the case in Canada, where new wood-processing technology has caused several wood species to emerge as valuable resources.[17] In administering mixed

---

party. See Peter H. Pearse, "Property Rights and the Regulation of Commercial Fisheries" (1980) 11 J. of Business Administration 185, for a discussion of how transactions costs have played an important role in preventing property-right solutions to fisheries problems.

15   See, for example, John V. Krutilla & Anthony C. Fisher, *The Economics of Natural Environments: Studies in the Valuation of Commodity and Amenity Resources*, 2nd ed. (Washington, D.C.: Resources for the Future, 1985); Randall, *supra*, note 2.

16   See, for example, Murray N. Rothbard, "Law, Property Rights, and Air Pollution" *in* Block, *supra*, note 3, at 233.

17   M.K. Luckert, *Tenures for Mixed Wood Management: A Framework for Policy Analysis* (Forestry Economics and Policy Analysis Project) (Working Paper 164) (Vancouver: University of British Columbia, 1991).

wood stands with provincial tenure agreements, governments have frequently relied on private negotiations to coordinate the orderly harvesting and processing of these newly valued wood species.

Second, the Coasian framework has led to a more comprehensive understanding of externalities. Externalities exist because of the absence of property rights. The logical extension of this realization is that externalities may be internalized by creating property rights. This has been the thrust behind recent work calling for the creation of private property rights.[18]

However, as discussed above, perhaps the most important contributions of the Coase theorem have been the subsequent debates regarding the assumptions behind the model. These assumptions identify conditions wherein private negotiations may fail to establish property rights that are capable of internalizing external values.

The Evolution of Property Rights through Judicial and Legislative Processes

Although the Coasè theorem is valuable in understanding the evolution of private property rights, it may not be directly applied to natural resources values in Canada because of the predominance of publicly owned natural resources.[19] Because natural resources in Canada were originally publicly held, the evolution of property rights to natural resources has largely been a process whereby various forms of usufructuary rights have been transferred to the private sector.[20] Owing to the large role that governments have played in the evolution of property rights to natural resources, other theories have arisen wherein regulatory bodies guide changes in property rights through channels other than private market negotiations.

Scott has reviewed theories wherein property rights are described as evolving through legislative and judicial channels.[21] The legislative theory assumes that governments are in a position to act on behalf of the people to reform property rights. Applied to the case of wilderness, this theory would have governments responding to social demands for change by legislating the creation of new wilderness areas. The judicial theory assumes that property

---

18   Block, *supra*, note 3.

19   In 1867, jurisdiction over most natural resources was passed to the newly created Canadian provinces.

20   For a description of this process in Ontario, see H.V. Nelles, *The Politics of Development: Forests, Mines, and Hydroelectric Power in Ontario, 1849-1941* (Toronto: Macmillan, 1974).

21   Anthony Scott, "Property Rights and Property Wrongs" (1983) 16:4 Canadian J. of Economics 555.

rights evolve in response to demanding litigants, and would describe property rights to wilderness values as evolving in response to litigative disputes that would arise and be settled in courts.

Although these theories of change differ considerably, they are similar, to each other and to the Coase theorem, in that the evolution of property rights is driven by the demand for, and supply of, changes to property-rights structures. While all theories tend to agree that the demand for change in property rights usually comes from parties dissatisfied with the *status quo*, theories differ with respect to the source of the supply for changes. Proponents of the legislative theory assert that the source of these changes is new developments in government policy. While this may be the predominant view of economists wishing to provide recommendations to policy makers, Scott argues that in the case of natural resources the supply is more often from courts, which reinterpret, and thereby redefine, laws governing property rights.[22]

An integral part of the development of these theories has been analyses of whether property regimes evolve towards greater heights of social efficiency. Some writers claim that property rights structures that are not in the best interests of society are weeded out as they evolve.[23] Others have reservations about such optimism, which parallel the concerns raised regarding the Coase solution. Scott poses several questions regarding the efficient operation of the market for litigative changes in property rights — questions that are also applicable to the market for legislative changes.[24] First, he proposes that wealth constraints result in fewer cases by poor litigants coming to court. Likewise, wealth constraints may prevent members of the general populace, or lobbying groups, from adequately expressing their concerns to legislators. Second, Scott points out that the lack of competition in the demand for judicial change may lead to biased determinations. Similarly, if competition is lacking among lobbying groups, then government decisions may be biased. Lastly, he notes that judicial procedures, constrained by transactions costs of trials, may not allow standing in court to parties who are modestly affected by policy changes. In lobbying for changes in legislation, it is also probable that transactions costs will preclude parties that are only moderately interested in changing property rights.

---

22   See, for example, Anthony D. Scott, *Does Government Create Real Property Rights? Private Interests in Natural Resources* (Discussion Paper No.84-26) (Vancouver: Dept. of Economics, University of British Columbia, 1990).

23   Lance E. Davis & Douglas C. North with the assistance of Calla Smorodin, *Institutional Change and American Economic Growth* (London: Cambridge University Press, 1971); Richard A. Posner, *Economic Analysis of Law* (Toronto: Little, Brown, 1972).

24   Scott, *supra*, note 21.

A further common feature among property-right theories is the need for perfect transferability of resource rights. Since all theories depend on the trade of resource rights, within various forms of supply and demand, any restrictions on transferability may preclude optimum solutions. One example of restricted transferability arises if resources are not perfectly divisible, as discussed above in the example of the lake.

Finally, distributional problems may also be encountered in judicial and litigative arenas. Concerns over "the squeaky wheel getting the grease" raise questions about whether society at large is fairly represented by groups seeking legislative or litigative changes.

The above list of difficulties parallels that of the Coasian problem in that concerns arise because of transactions costs, market power, income constraints, resource indivisibility, and wealth distributions. However, as will be discussed below, the implications of these problems for the facilitation of emerging wideness values differ considerably between private markets, and litigative and judicial arenas.

THE CASE OF WILDERNESS

In applying these models of the evolution of property rights to the case of wilderness, the objective of this analysis is to identify consequences of alternative forms of property rights that may evolve to facilitate society's demands for wilderness values. As a starting point to this analysis, I will first describe the values associated with wilderness areas.

Values of Wilderness

Writers have long been preoccupied with values associated with natural systems, such as wilderness areas. The values associated with wilderness may be classified into two general categories. The first may be referred to as natural values, which are defined as intrinsic to resources and may therefore exist in the absence of humankind. The second type of values is a consequence of human perception of natural resources.

Intrinsic Natural Resources

Natural systems existed long before humans became an integral, and frequently dominating, element of ecosystems. Thus, it has been argued, values associated with such systems may exist independently of humankind.[25] By contrast, others have claimed that values are strictly human concepts that cannot exist independently of people. That is, it is people's perceptions of natural resources that create values. Therefore, natural systems

---

25 See, for example, H. Rolston, "Human Values and Natural Systems" (1988) 1 Society and Natural Resources 271.

must provide some benefit to humans if they are to be relevant to decision making.[26] Economists, in attempting to define non-marketed resource values, have largely adopted this ethnocentric approach and have therefore concentrated on values that may be identified as accruing to members of society.

Social Values

Economists have generally classified values of natural resources as use and non-use values.[27] Use values may be further subdivided according to whether they are derived from direct or indirect uses of natural resources. Direct use values arise from consumptive activities such as mining, timber harvesting, and hunting, and from non-consumptive uses such as bird watching. Indirect uses occur where people do not come in direct contact with the resource, such as when viewing wildlife in books or on television.

Non-use values arise because people derive value from preserving natural resources. These values may emerge because people like the notion of maintaining a resource, even if they have no plans to use it. That is, people enjoy vicarious experiences from the existence of the resource, or derive pleasure from the prospect of leaving the resource to future generations. In the presence of future uncertainty, non-use values may include elements of option value. Such values arise if individuals believe that preserving a resource leaves open options that will enhance opportunities in the future.[28]

Social Values and the Definition of Wilderness Concepts

Concepts of wilderness are created when people, with their social values, perceive natural physical features. Although such a process has resulted in numerous concepts of wilderness, characteristics have emerged that are

---

26   See, for example, R.B. Riley, "Human Values and Natural Systems: Fragments From a Designer's Response" (1988) 1 Society and Natural Resources 291; M.K. Luckert & W.L. Adamowicz, *On Empirical Measures of the Social Rate of Discount* (Staff Paper No.90-01) (Edmonton: Department of Rural Economy, University of Alberta, 1990).

27   For a description of such values associated with wildlife resources, see J. Asafu-Adjaye, W. Phillips & W.L. Adamowicz, *Towards the Measurement of Total Economic Value: The Case of Wildlife Resources in Alberta* (Staff Paper No.89-16) (Edmonton: Department of Rural Economy, University of Alberta, 1989); W.L. Adamowicz & P.C. Boxall, "Economic Aspects of Hoofed Mammals in Alberta" in *The Hoofed Mammals of Alberta* (Edmonton: University of Alberta Press, 1992) [in press].

28   Option values may vary between individuals because of differing risk preferences. In cases where individuals are neutral or averse to risk, option values are positive. For a more technical definition of option value, see A.C. Fisher & C.E. Ferguson, "Environmental Damages and Option Values" (1986) 1 Natural Resources Modelling 111.

common to most definitions of wilderness.

Use values of wilderness areas, associated with extensive recreational activities such as backpacking, have led to the view that wilderness areas should be large and relatively pristine. These characteristics have been further emphasized by non-use values associated with preserving complete ecosystems.

Additional non-use values are derived because wilderness areas are thought of as being an important part of the public heritage, to be passed on to future generations. These desires have led to heightened valuations of wilderness areas perceived as being unique. Uniqueness may create option values if the populace fears the possibility of irreversibly losing natural systems to consumptive resource uses.

Private Property Rights and Wilderness Values

Given the diverse assortment of wilderness values, how might private property rights evolve to facilitate the demands of society? Starting with the current disposition of property rights to natural resources in Canada, such an approach would have governments selling wilderness areas to private individuals or groups.[29] This approach would allow those interested in preserving wilderness to bid against groups interested in alternative, perhaps consumptive, resource uses.

With property rights to natural resources currently in government ownership, the initial demand for such a proposal would have to come from dissatisfied members of society. Depending on the course of action chosen, the demand for new forms of property rights could take the form of lobbying or litigation (or both). If the government or the courts were in a position to supply changes in property rights, then the process could begin and private parties would bid for resource rights.

An initial problem that the government would have to face would be to determine the size of parcels to be auctioned. In putting together parcels for sale, the government would likely run into indivisibility problems. If it decided to sell relatively small blocks, the potential for maintaining wilderness values could be destroyed. Groups interested in preserving wilderness would have to offer the highest bid on all plots within a potential wilderness area. If wilderness groups failed to acquire one small plot, then the wilderness values associated with an area could be ruined.[30]

---

29   For examples of such proposals, see Marion Clawson, *The Federal Lands Revisited* (Washington, D.C.: Resources for the Future, 1983) at 170; Walter E. Block, "Environmental Problems, Private Property Right Solutions" *in* Block, *supra*, note 3, at 281.

30   From this example, it is evident that indivisibility of wilderness may have two dimensions.

In order to accommodate the indivisibility of wilderness values, governments could choose to offer large areas for sale, However, in such situations, income constraints of competing buyers would likely prevent many groups from participating in auctions, reducing competition among potential buyers. Even in cases where groups were able to raise sufficient capital to submit bids, income constraints would likely cause bids to under-represent the true values associated with the resource. Furthermore, if large areas of land were sold, groups that successfully bid for property rights might be able to exert monopoly power in selling the values of their acquired resources, especially in cases where resource areas sold had unique characteristics.[31]

However, such market failures would likely pale in comparison to problems associated with transactions costs. Wilderness groups would likely be outbid by competing interests, because transactions costs would prevent owners of wilderness areas from gaining exclusive rights to their purchased resource. To begin with, the vast nature of wilderness areas would make it difficult for administrators to charge fees and/or protect wilderness values from other users.[32] However, problems associated with charging wilderness users are likely to be small when compared to transactions costs problems associated with non-use values. If wilderness groups were to acquire resource rights, it would be virtually impossible for such groups to collect fees from all of the people enjoying preservation benefits, including existence and heritage values.[33]

In the presence of so many biases, economists have frequently encountered difficulties in predicting whether a good or service is being over- or under-provided.[34] However, in sorting through the biases associated with

---

Besides the indivisibility problems associated with large areas, there are also problems that arise because of the unique and pristine characteristics of wilderness, which prevent multiple resource uses within wilderness areas.

31   In economic theory, one cause for deviations from perfect competition is the presence of product differentiation. Wilderness areas, if they contain unique features, may be viewed as being extremely differentiated products.

32   In cases where road access is limited and is the only means of approaching a wilderness area, such problems may be minimal.

33   Wilderness owners would run into severe transactions costs in attempting to identify those individuals who are benefitting from non-use values, in order to collect "non-use fees". Beneficiaries would have incentives to conceal the fact that they value wilderness areas, if disclosing such information meant that they would have to pay fees for benefits that could be derived from other people's expenditures. That is, because wilderness owners would not be able to sell exclusive rights to non-use values, individuals would have incentives to become "free-riders".

34   This dilemma is referred to as "the problem of the second best" by R.G. Lipsey & Kevin Lancaster, "The General Theory of Second Best" (1956) 24 Rev. of Economic Studies 11.

wilderness, the results are fairly straightforward.

In cases where the government would sell parcels smaller than needed for wilderness areas, the indivisibility of wilderness areas would put wilderness groups at a disadvantage compared to competing bidders with other, more divisible interests, because they would have to successfully bid for numerous plots.[35] This disadvantage would prevent creation of sufficient numbers of wilderness areas.

If the government offered large parcels for sale, then income constraints may, or may not, cause wilderness areas to be under-provided, depending on the relative income constraints of competing groups. Groups with more constrained incomes would be at a disadvantage in bidding. Therefore, if wilderness groups were among those bidders with severe income constraints, then, once again, too few wilderness areas would be created. Furthermore, the groups that did successfully gain control of these large areas might be in a position to exert monopoly power. That is, no matter what kind of good or service was produced on the newly purchased area, it is possible that the private owner would limit the supply of goods or services, in order to elevate prices.[36] Thus, even if wilderness groups were not income constrained, and sufficient numbers of areas were purchased, the large and unique characteristics associated with wilderness areas would create opportunities for owners of these areas to suppress the supply of these values to the public.

A final, and perhaps most important, problem is that there would be high transactions costs associated with internalizing the numerous types of wilderness values. Even if transactions costs associated with charging user fees were not prohibitive, it would be virtually impossible for wilderness owners to collect fees associated with non-use values. The difficulties wilderness owners would have in trying to collect returns on their investments would cause insufficient numbers of wilderness areas to be created.

Besides problems associated with the under-provision of wilderness values, there would also likely be distributional problems. If wilderness areas were offered for sale, it would be possible for wealthy individuals or groups to buy entire wilderness areas for their exclusive use. It is unlikely that society would stand for such a distribution of wilderness values, given that such areas are frequently perceived to be part of the public heritage.

---

35   While it is possible that other competing uses could also suffer from indivisibility problems, it is difficult to imagine another use that is as indivisible as wilderness.

36   For a discussion of monopoly behaviour, see J.P. Gould & C.E. Ferguson, *Microeconomic Theory*, 5th ed. (Homewood, Ill.: Richard D. Irwin, 1980).

Public Property Rights and Wilderness Values

An alternative to private property rights to wilderness values would be to retain such areas in the hands of governments. In such cases, property rights would not suffer from problems associated with private bidding. Instead, they would evolve according to the forces of supply and demand within judicial and legislative arenas. However, as discussed above, many of the same types of problem would exist under such a scenario. That is, these procedures are also confounded by problems associated with indivisibilities, income constraints, market power, transactions costs, and wealth distributions.

Although the problems associated with forming private and public property rights may be similar, their implications for the facilitation of emerging resource values are different. These differences occur because of the different nature of the demand and supplies of private, versus public, property rights. Whereas money is the driving force in establishing private property rights, words are the primary currency in judicial and litigative arenas that affect public property rights.

As a result of these different types of markets, problems associated with income constraints and monopoly power, caused by indivisibilities, may be alleviated. The indirect role of money in judicial and legislative markets alleviates income constraint problems. Although litigants and lobbying groups with fewer income constraints are still likely to have more influence in these arenas, the biases will probably be lessened because dollars are not the sole means of expressing values. With income constraints posing a lesser problem, competing groups would be on more equal footing.

Public property rights may also alleviate monopoly problems. If governments control the supply of wilderness areas, they may determine whether and how much to charge for user fees. On the demand side, the reduced importance of income constraints may allow more groups and individuals to participate in demanding changes in policies, thereby increasing competition.

Problems associated with transactions costs may also be alleviated by legislative and judicial markets. With the supply for changes being influenced by words, values associated with non-use values derived by the general populace may be expressed by parties demanding change. Therefore, such values may be internalized into the considerations of the supplying decision makers.

Furthermore, legislative and judicial arenas may be best equipped to handle distributional questions associated with wilderness values. With wilderness areas perceived as being part of the public heritage, the distribution of wilderness benefits among present and future members of society plays an integral role in defining wilderness values. It is doubtful that society would allow values associated with a public heritage to be subject to distributional patterns that result from private property rights, where distributional concerns are external to the decision making of private firms. In contrast, distributional concerns are frequently central to public decision making.[37]

Finally, despite distortions present in legislative and judicial arenas, the governmental processes themselves are a source of value to society. As Leman points out, "The political process is often messy, biased, and inconclusive, but the public revels in it and would not accept any outcome that did not run this gauntlet."[38]

CONCLUSIONS

Property rights to natural resource values in Canada may evolve according to differing processes depending on whether such values are facilitated by private or public property rights. Theories on the evolution of property rights have shown us that the solution to accommodating such external values is, where possible, to establish property rights. But the question remains, What type of property rights?

As new values to resources arise, they must be assessed according to characteristics that determine whether they are marketable. Some goods and services many prove to be marketable, in that they may be internalized with private property rights. However, there are also values that are non-marketable. That is, resources may contain values that remain external to market considerations under systems of private property rights. In such cases, public property rights may be more suitable.

The nature of wilderness values implies that private property rights would result in the under-provision of such values, and that the resulting distribution of wilderness values would probably be unacceptable to society. Analysis suggests that public ownership, while likely to suffer from some of the same problems as private property rights, could alleviate many of the biases present in the trade of private property rights. That is, judicial and political processes may better allow for the representation of the vast assortment of values associated with wilderness areas. Furthermore, such processes explicitly take account of distributional concerns and are in themselves valued by society.

If property rights to emerging resource values are to remain in public hands, a great deal of responsibility will be placed on public resource

---

37   See, for example, C.K. Leman, "The Revolution of Saints: The Ideology of Privatization and its Consequences for the Public Lands" *in* Adrien E. Gamache, ed., *Selling the Federal Forests* (Seattle: College of Forest Resources, University of Washington, 1984) at 93.

38   *Id.*, at 128.

managers. However, this responsibility can, and should, be shared with members of society. As resource managers are rapidly discovering, natural resources may no longer merely be managed for the people — they must be managed with the people. Therefore, it will be up to public managers to provide opportunities for members of society to participate in decision-making processes. The more that such participation is facilitated, the more competitive the decision-making process will become, and the less severe will be the biases associated with public decision-making arenas.

Another source of aid to resource managers lies in new developments in economics. Although economists have historically been largely content with describing opportunity costs associated with preserving wilderness areas, methodology is rapidly being developed to directly assess wilderness values. While some of these methods attempt to mimic market processes, others are adopting psychological approaches that seek to gain a better understanding of resource values by studying human perceptions.

Another area of economic research that will prove helpful to resource managers is further exploration into alternative types of property rights to wilderness values. This paper has only considered strengths and weaknesses of public versus private property rights. However, there are numerous possibilities that lie between these two extremes. For example, further research should consider the appropriateness of establishing Crown corporations, or schemes whereby wilderness areas are leased to managing companies.

Natural resource management in Canada is undergoing rapid change as new resource values emerge. How well resources are managed in the future will be greatly influenced by the types of property rights to evolve in the coming decades. With more study into the values associated with natural resources, and the appropriateness of alternative property-right structures in accommodating these values, the evolution of property rights may take a more efficient path in accommodating the changing needs of society.

WILDLIFE STEWARDSHIP
ON FARM LAND

John Girt and David Neave

Appreciation of the importance of wildlife within Canadian agricultural landscapes is growing. Wildlife fulfills a number of crucial functions, ranging from providing sources of recreation and food to supporting ecosystems upon which farming is heavily dependent. However, the protection and management of wildlife within agricultural landscapes as private and public assets is not a well-developed part of farm or rural planning. Farmers sometimes treat wildlife with hostility. In some cases, this is due to the crop damage that they cause, in others because of the financial returns associated with destruction and pollution of their habitat. Generally, however, indifference towards wildlife seems best to capture the dominant management practice. As a result, populations of a number of important wildlife species have been declining significantly over large areas of Canada, while other species have been increasing. Most of these changes have not been deliberate. The management of wildlife has tended to become an issue only when desirable species have been threatened, resulting in efforts to restock populations or set up habitat reservations. The former approach is particularly popular with respect to fish, and will be largely ignored in this paper. Rather, we will concentrate on approaches to the management of land-based animals in areas dominated by farms.

This paper will examine the reasons why it is preferable to view and manage wildlife as an integral part of farming systems, rather than to place undue reliance on wildlife reservations in farming areas for protection and conservation. There are many situations where providing improved habitat on farms will realize other significant benefits to farmers and society at large, including reduced rates of soil and water degradation, that are not available to the same extent by using the alternative approach. However, the promotion of wildlife management on private lands, particularly lands for farming, faces a number of legal, financial, policy, and institutional constraints. The paper will conclude with a review of existing and proposed schemes for encouraging the private stewardship of wildlife on farms and for the promotion of more-sustainable agriculture.

A FARMING PERSPECTIVE

Farming has shaped wide expanses of Canada's southern and most inhabited areas. Although in many parts farming has been the dominant activity for no more than a century, it has brought profound changes to our landscapes. The full impact of these changes on wildlife populations will never be known with any accuracy, but they will have been profound, in terms not only of numbers but also of the mix of species. Some of the changes will have occurred simply because trees were replaced with fields, others as a result of the use of chemicals, monoculture, and increased field sizes so typical of Canadian agriculture today.

At the risk of overgeneralization, one can propose that from a wildlife point of view Canadian agriculture has gone through two phases. The first was an expansionary one, during which time most land was cleared. Since then, in the second phase, there has been a retraction, and some fields have reverted back to native bush. At the same time the intensity of use, including the application of chemicals, has increased in the fields remaining in agriculture.

The two phases have been more or less distinct in the centres of agriculture located in the eastern parts of the country, but in the Prairies the end of the first phase occurred after the second phase had begun. During the 1970s Prairie farmers were encouraged to produce more grains. The 1980s have seen these hopes dashed, so that the abandonment of phase one in this region has only just begun. Unfortunately, in the opinion of most wildlife biologists this change has come too late, and the recent land clearance and draining of wetlands in the Prairies is jeopardizing the viability of many of the indigenous species, particularly waterfowl.

When driving or flying over the Prairies today, it is hard to realize what a complex and rich ecosystem once existed in this area. Further, the landscape that has replaced it is not ecologically stable and is showing distinct and troublesome signs of degradation.[1] The entire soil and water base that provides farming in the Prairies with its production advantages in grains and oilseeds is being degraded by farm practices. The current landscape does not seem to support sustainable farming any more than it supports sustainable waterfowl populations, and a similar situation is found in other parts of Canada.[2] This observation will be developed below.

During both of these phases, farmers' attitudes towards wildlife can only be described as "exotic". The farmer still does not consider wildlife as a positive element in the production of food. In relatively few cases, it is a hindrance to be eliminated; sometimes wildlife is viewed as an added benefit of the landscape. Some animals are labelled as pests to be eradicated. Most species, however, probably do not fit into either category. Farming families do

---

1   Canada. Dept. of the Environment, *Agricultural Soil and Water Resources in Canada: Situation and Outlook* (Ottawa: Supply and Services, 1985); Prairie Habitat Joint Venture, *Prairie Habitat: A Prospectus* (Winnipeg, 1988); Science Council of Canada, *A Growing Concern: Soil Degradation in Canada* (Ottawa: Science Council of Canada, 1986).

2   See, for example, *Agricultural Soil and Water Resources in Canada, id.*; *A Growing Concern: Soil Degradation in Canada, id.*

become attached to a few species, particularly the birds and deer that use their farms, though deer, in particular, can cause frustration when they damage or eat crops, or when deer hunters occasion damage.

Except as they call for methods of control, animals generally are not considered in information and advice on farming practices. The impacts on wildlife of removing trees, fence lines, ponds, or wetlands in order to extend the area of cropland have not been significant factors in farmers' decision making.

Generally, in rural areas wildlife populations survive in increasingly isolated islands in a sea of fields and highways. Their long-run viability is threatened by the declining biodiversity of their habitat and by their own inbreeding. The outlook for some species is now causing concern and requiring action. The loss of wildlife habitat on farms has threatened the long-term viability of a wide range of migratory birds to such an extent that, to offset these effects, Canada and the United States have combined their efforts under the 1.5-billion-dollar North American Waterfowl Management Plan to design and deliver programs (valued at one billion dollars in Canada alone) over the next ten years.[3]

Agricultural fertilizers and pesticides are also endangering wildlife populations. In the case of pesticides, although certain species undoubtedly need to be controlled, the impact of the chemicals that are used frequently extends beyond targeted species. Agricultural pollution of surface waters from field run-off containing chemicals is also a threat. For example, the detrimental effects on birds and fish of agricultural chemicals in the Great Lakes are becoming well known.[4]

But paradigms are changing in farm production. The focus in the past has been on the maximization of yields through the use of chemicals and the unintentional consumption of organic matter in soils. Now there is growing pressure to move farming away from a reliance on the unbridled consumption of soil nutrients and the chemicals used to replace them, to a situation where more use is made of the naturally occurring biological and mechanical processes to produce crops. This type of farming, which is known under a variety of names, including alternative agriculture, conservation agriculture, low-input agriculture, ecological farming, and organic farming, stresses the replacement of non-renewable inputs with organic inputs continuously

---

3   Canada. Dept. of the Environment, Canadian Wildlife Service and United States. Dept. of the Interior, Fish and Wildlife Service, *North American Waterfowl Management Plan: A Strategy of Cooperation* (Ottawa: Supply and Services, 1986).

4   Canada. Dept of the Environment *et al.*, *Toxic Chemicals in the Great Lakes and Associated Effects* (Synopsis) (Ottawa: Supplies and Services, 1991).

produced on the farm.

On the farm itself these "alternative" approaches to crop and livestock production are being encouraged as a means of stemming potentially substantial economic losses that result from continuing soil degradation and increasing energy costs, and increasing public concerns about the use of chemicals in the production of food. These approaches also offer the prospect of a less environmentally damaging agriculture by reducing its off-farm effects on water quality and the supply of habitat.[5]

In Canada, as in the United States and most of Europe, widespread adoption of these more sustainable farm practices is severely constrained by current farm programs. In financial terms, these programs now provide incentives equivalent to more than half the net farm income of most farmers in Canada, and they are structured to sustain the types of production that cause environmental problems on and off the farm rather than those that are part of the solutions. It is true that governments in Canada do support much of the research and on-farm trials of new approaches to production, including sustainable agriculture, but most of the programs providing immediate protection of farm incomes from the effect of natural and market hazards, as well as some of the marketing frameworks that they provide for farm produce, are at best neutral if not hostile to the encouragement of new approaches to production.[6]

Van Kooten provided a demonstration of this point by applying rational economic modelling techniques to the balance sheet of a typical grain farm in southeastern Saskatchewan.[7] Using current world grain prices, if governments did not provide some kind of income support, farmers would leave in an unimproved state over 500 of 1,200 farm acres, some or all of which would offer potential habitat for wildlife. With the 1990 levels of government

---

5   See, for example, Pierre R. Crosson, "Supplying the Environmental Values of Agriculture" (1990) 98 Resources 4; Pierre R. Crosson & Janet Ekey Ostrov, "Alternative Agriculture: Sorting Out its Environmental Benefits" (1988) 92 Resources 13; Federal-provincial Committee on Environmental Sustainability, *Growing Together: Report to the Ministers of Agriculture: Federal-provincial Agriculture Committee on Environmental Sustainability 30 June 1990* (Ottawa: Agriculture Canada, 1990); National Research Council, Committee on the Role of Alternative Farming Methods in Modern Production Agriculture & Board of Agriculture, *Alternative Agriculture* (Washington D.C.: National Academy Press, 1989).

6   Federal-provincial Committee on Environmental Sustainability, *id.*; John Girt, *Common Ground: Recommendations for Policy Reform to Integrate Wildlife Habitat, Environmental and Agricultural Objectives on the Farm* (Ottawa: Wildlife Habitat Canada, 1990).

7   G.C. van Kooten, *Policy Directions for Sustainable Agriculture* (Paper presented at the Science Council of Canada/Canadian Agricultural Economics and Farm Management Society Workshop on Sustainable Agriculture, Winnipeg, 5-7 May 1991).

support, it would be economically viable to cultivate half of this area, leaving 230 unimproved acres. However, the recently announced Gross Revenue Insurance Program (GRIP)[8] will provide an even greater incentive to sow crops, reducing the unimproved area to less than 200 acres.

In other words, providing a farmer had adjusted his farm land use accordingly, the opportunity cost of an additional acre of habitat (the income loss from having this acre in habitat rather than crops) would be ten dollars with no government support, fifty-five dollars with 1990 levels of government support, and ninety dollars with GRIP. Not only does this indicate the economic power of government programs, but also, if the trade war in agricultural commodities were ended, the need for consumers of wildlife to be prepared to pay for their commodity at rates reflecting general economic conditions.

In the meantime, there seems to be no legitimate reason why some of the government income support to farmers could not be directed through payments for habitat that would bring other environmental benefits as well. Alternatively, and in the long run preferably, a solution would be to decouple farm income support from actual use of the land, for example, acres in a crop, so that habitat and cropland would not compete directly in a farmer's decision making. At present, the more extensively an area is sown with crops, the more support is received, irrespective of whether the same quantity of production could be achieved on a smaller land base or of the productivity of the last acre of cropland.[9] The other income support program — the Net Income Stabilization Account — announced by the Minister of Agriculture along with GRIP[10] — is decoupled and preferable in this regard.

WILDLIFE MANAGERS' PERSPECTIVES

What of the situation with respect to the management of wildlife in Canada? Here, as in most economically developed countries, attention has tended to focus on three issues: the protection and management of species for subsistence and recreational hunting and fishing; the protection of endangered species (almost exclusively a few birds, mammals, and reptiles); and the identification, protection, and management of reservations or natural parks. The issue of farmland management for the protection of wildlife has until recently received very little attention.

The attention and the priority given to wildlife issues in general are well represented by the place of wildlife in the World Conservation Strategy. The

---

8   Canada. Dept. of Agriculture, Release, "Farm Income Enabling Legislation" (4 March 1991).

9   Girt, *supra*, note 6.

10   *Supra*, note 8.

Strategy,[11] while making the maintenance "of essential ecological processes and life-support systems" its first priority, interprets this to mean, in the case of agricultural areas, soil and water protection and the recycling of nutrients in support of food production for humans. This food production focus is continued in its second priority — "to preserve genetic diversity" — and in its last — "to ensure the sustainable utilization of species and ecosystems ... which support millions of rural communities ...."[12] Preservation of species receives only passing mention at the end of the section on genetic diversity, where the possible detrimental effects of farming are noted with no further comment. In the section on the sustainable utilization of species and ecosystems, wildlife is examined as a subsistence resource and as a source of income through trapping and recreation. Potential and real conflicts with farming are ignored apart from the impact of overgrazing of domesticated livestock.

The Canadian response to the IUCN document goes somewhat further.[13] In the section on the preservation of genetic diversity, the document recognizes that species have a right to exist by themselves without having any obvious or direct link to human survival. It provides a description of initiatives to protect and increase the numbers of certain endangered species, as well as a description of Canada's system of protected areas. There is no mention of stewardship on private lands that are not protected as ecological preserves. Further on, in the section on the sustainable utilization of species and ecosystems, the document describes stewardship programs, stressing, however, that such initiatives are applied to "special" ecological areas, rather than to general classes such as farms. The management on private lands of habitat for utilized species, particularly for game birds and mammals, is mentioned. Other sections dealing with institutional procedures that are designed to strengthen the management of living resources and ecosystems, review Canadian legislation for environmental assessment and environmental contamination as ways of preventing problems. They also mention the initial efforts made at that time to address the fact that certain non-wildlife programs inadvertently encourage the destruction of wildlife habitat.

---

11   International Union for Conservation of Nature and Natural Resources (IUCN), United Nations Environment Programme (UNEP) & World Wildlife Fund (WWF), *World Conservation Strategy: Living Resource Conservation for Sustainable Development* (Gland, Switzerland: IUCN, 1980).

12   *Id.*, at VI.

13   Canada. Dept. of the Environment, D.F.W. Pollard & M.R. McKechnie, *World Conservation Strategy — Canada: A Report on Achievements in Conservation* (Ottawa: Supply and Services, 1986).

This latter initiative is one of the first, formal recognitions that wildlife should perhaps not be treated as "exotic", but rather that humans, in wildlife management, should be treated as "aliens". The importance of improving the prospects for wildlife surviving on private lands receives more attention in later policy statements, such as that entitled *A Wildlife Policy for Canada*, published in 1990[14] and supported by all provincial governments as well as the federal government. Generally speaking, though, wildlife managers have opted for concentrating on the establishment and management of reserves to protect Canada's heritage of land-based wildlife at the expense of the integrity of the rest of the landscape. This policy not only artificially isolates wildlife in a geographic sense and separates many from the full range of their normal habitats, but is, particularly in a large and ecologically diverse country, very expensive and, more likely than not, incapable of providing sufficient protection to all species. At the same time, support to private land owners and operators of other public spaces, such as city parks and harvested forests, to provide habitat on their lands has been a lower priority. Those lands are geographically more dispersed and are essentially almost a free good for wildlife agencies. They do not have to be purchased and have lower operating costs for the management of wildlife, as the additional operations that are necessary to support wildlife can be integrated with normal day-to-day operations of the land user. Of course, the same can be said about the use of farm land for wildlife preservation and enhancement.

One must also question the isolationist approach to wildlife management from the point of view of:

1. whether sufficient habitat can ever be protected by this method;

2. whether private landowners can gain in more than a self-centred aesthetic sense from the enhanced presence of wildlife;

3. whether there are additional public benefits from private stewardship that have not as yet been considered.

In each case, the answer indicates the need for a supplementary, alternative approach to wildlife management based on privately owned land. The most powerful reason for this is that wildlife is part of an ecosystem, and if this ecosystem is being degraded and used in an unsustainable manner, wildlife suffers. The corollary is, of course, that improvements to the way in which ecosystems are used, no matter what the cause of this change, will tend to benefit all of its components to some degree. This means that wildlife habitat, for example, can provide control of water run-off, thus alleviating soil

---

14   Canada. Dept. of the Environment, Canadian Wildlife Service & Wildlife Minister's Council of Canada, *A Wildlife Policy for Canada* (Ottawa: Environment Canada, 1990).

degradation and water pollution on farms. Alternatively, introducing methods to control soil degradation will also provide more habitat. Conservation tillage techniques provide a more stable, more organically rich, and less chemically polluted field environment for small animals, including invertebrates. Not only will more of these species survive but, because they will enrich the food chain, other species will increase in numbers as well, including those that are more mobile.

Our somewhat limited views concerning the environment have tended to focus on simple relationships. We have been inclined to undervalue the full impact of the changes and to focus on one issue at a time. Consequently, the benefits of acts aimed at preventing and improving the environment in a comprehensive manner have been ignored. When a systems approach to the management of ecosystems is adopted, no single component can be treated as exotic or alien.

Ideally, therefore, wildlife, particularly if the whole spectrum of possible species is focused upon, becomes an integral part of a sustainable agricultural landscape. Sustainable agriculture will have more crop rotations in each field, more wind barriers, more grassed or vegetated waterways to control run-off of rain and snow melt. It will use plant and animal residues as a resource, and favour biological over chemical controls of pests wherever possible. All of these tendencies will benefit larger and more diverse wildlife populations, many of which will become an integral part of the biological production system that the farmer relies on to provide crops and a favourable environment in which animals may be raised.

In addition to these benefits to the farmer, one must not lose sight of the fact that wildlife itself has considerable consumer value, particularly in key environments. City dwellers value the ability to observe wildlife in rural areas. Likewise, many farmers welcome the opportunity to fish in a river that is not ecologically devastated. Wildlife habitats provide the means to cleaner, less polluted tap water in towns and cities, and lower maintenance costs for the countryside. If wildlife forms part of a more diversified system of farm production, the farm system will have less variable income streams and less need of short-term income assistance. Wildlife can also provide us with indicators that are needed to gauge the success or failure to develop sustainably. Because of their shorter life cycles, and in some cases restricted living spaces, as well as their sensitivity to environmental factors, tracking the health and population dynamics of wildlife species can provide humankind with useful indicators not only of the presence or absence of pollutants, but of the viability of ecosystems themselves, which are the basic building blocks for a sustainable existence.

People benefit from studying how natural systems function and from trying to imitate them, even when they are being changed. We must learn to seek the benefits of agglomeration rather than focus on one issue at a time and try to remedy problems caused by an approach that tends to treat individual "symptoms" as discrete problems. Farmers and wildlife managers must together realize that wildlife is being treated as exotic and work together to improve the situation. Of course, moves in this direction are underway, and the balance of this paper will review some of the more relevant developments as well as set out priorities to be maintained in order to accelerate the momentum for change.

Members of the wildlife community have begun to establish contacts with the farming community through stewardship programs designed to provide support to farmers who operate their farms so as to provide habitat for wildlife as well as traditional farm products. Most provincial governments, along with private agencies such as Wildlife Habitat Canada, now offer some form of land stewardship programs to farmers who provide habitat.[15] Such programs exist in all provinces; however, it is also true that in each province they are not considered part of the central focus of public support for farming, and they are also delivered by wildlife bureaucracies and non-government organizations with only minimal input from farm advisory agencies.

Generally speaking, Departments of Agriculture have close contact with wildlife issues only through the delivery of wildlife damage programs, which compensate farmers for damage caused by livestock predation or crop destruction. However, such programs treat wildlife as alien and fail to provide a basis for the approach suggested here. Damage compensation is provided only for specific species, and when these programs were designed, no consideration was given to the net benefit and cost to farmers and society of maintaining a whole and viable wildlife population living off farm land.

Recently, however, there have been signs of growing cooperation between agricultural and wildlife agencies in support of these desirable changes,[16] most notably in the Prairie provinces under the Prairie Habitat Joint Venture of the North American Waterfowl Management Plan.[17] Moreover, wildlife agencies are tending to rely more heavily on private stewardship rather than on land purchase programs that typified the operations of agencies such as Ducks Unlimited. The case of the North American Waterfowl Management

---

15   Wildlife Habitat Canada, *Wildlife Conservation on Private Lands. Proceedings of the Private Stewardship/Landowner Contract Workshop* (Ottawa, 1987).

16   Canada. Dept. of Agriculture, *The Agriculture/Wildlife Interface in Alberta* (Edmonton: Agriculture Canada, 1990) (mimeograph); Federal-provincial Committee on Environmental Sustainability, *supra*, note 5.

17   *Supra*, note 3.

Plan is particularly interesting, since the focus of these recent initiatives is to support the supply of habitat for waterfowl through a combination of incentive programs and initiatives designed to lead to the reform of policies, particularly agricultural in the case of the Prairies, that inadvertently encourage the destruction of habitat.

Members of the wildlife community have also begun to lobby agricultural agencies to remove aspects of their programs that discourage the protection and improvement of habitat on farms. The process is complicated by:

1. the shared federal-provincial jurisdiction over agriculture;

2. the rivalries between farmers in the East and West over their varying governmental programs that, for political reasons, make economically powerful federal farm programs in the West particularly difficult to adjust;

3. the strong tendency to examine the individual rather than the cumulative effect of programs; and

4. the competing agricultural priorities and lack of clear vision for agriculture from a wildlife point of view, and for wildlife from an agricultural point of view.

THE BASIS FOR AN IMPROVED PARTNERSHIP

A future vision for agriculture provides a convenient point to turn our focus back to agriculture. A collective vision for the farming of the future is beginning to emerge from numerous industry and government consultations, as well as the efforts of a number of individuals and non-agricultural organizations concerned with agriculture's environmental impact. Its imperatives include: the reduction of farm-sourced pollution of surface and ground waters;[18] more habitat for wildlife;[19] less on-farm degradation of soils;[20] and the reduction of chemical consumption on farms.[21] Its

---

18 Federal-provincial Committee on Environmental Sustainability, *supra*, note 5; International Joint Commission, *Pollution in the Great Lakes Basin from Land Use Activities* (Windsor: International Joint Commission, 1980); *Canada-Ontario Soil and Water Environmental Enhancement Program* [a federal-provincial agreement] (1990).

19 Federal-provincial Committee on Environmental Sustainability, *supra*, note 5; Canada. Dept. of the Environment, Canadian Wildlife Service & United States. Dept. of the Interior, Fish and Wildlife Service, *supra*, note 3.

20 Federal-provincial Committee on Environmental Sustainability, *supra*, note 5; Canada. Standing Senate Committee on Agriculture, Fisheries and Forestry, *Soil at Risk: Canada's Eroding Future* (Ottawa: Senate, 1984); Canada. Dept. of the Environment, Canadian Wildlife Service & United States. Dept. of the Interior, Fish and Wildlife Service, *supra*, note 3; and Federal-provincial Agricultural Soil and Water Accords that have been signed over the past few years with all ten provinces.

implementation will necessitate:

1. Federal-provincial agreements to coordinate new and existing initiatives in soil and water conservation;[22]

2. Commitments to review and adjust all policies and programs to ensure that they are consistent with the vision:

   (a) This was recommended by the Federal-provincial Committee on Environmental Sustainability[23] to the federal and provincial Ministers of Agriculture and accepted by all, although no tangible results are apparent at this time; and

   (b) A working group has been established under the Prairie Habitat Joint Venture of the North American Waterfowl Management Plan to make recommendations on ways of ensuring that agricultural policies are supportive of habitat objectives;

3. Land stewardship programs — for example, initiatives under the North American Waterfowl Management Plan;

4. Recommendations for a new pesticide regulatory regime designed, among other things, to minimize the consumption of pesticides in view of private and public benefits and costs;[24]

5. The incorporation of wildlife and agricultural issues into the deliberations of national and provincial Round Tables on the Economy;

6. The design of comprehensive conservation plans, for example, for the Niagara Peninsula.[25]

The following is still lacking:

1. A vision as to how the rural landscape should be structured and the uses and species it should support, which can provide the substantiation for specific goals or targets, not just in terms of timelines but in terms of specific land use or environmental changes, for the concerned sectors. At present, not only is the vision very unclear, but wildlife managers also

---

21   Federal-provincial Committee on Environmental Sustainability, *supra*, note 5; International Joint Commission, *supra*, note 18; Pesticide Registration Review Team, *Recommendations for a Revised Federal Pest Management Regulatory System* (Final Report) (Ottawa, 1990).

22   The federal government has announced its intention of expanding these agreements.

23   Federal-provincial Committee on Environmental Sustainability, *supra*, note 5.

24   *Recommendations for a Revised Federal Pest Management Regulatory System*, Final Report, *supra*, note 21.

25   The Preservation of Rural Lands Society, *The Niagara Conservation Strategy* (St. Catherines, Ont., 1988).

tend to operate at arm's length from, and frequently at cross-purposes with, sectoral managers, who play a far more significant role in moulding the landscape, however inadvertently. This tends to result in programs being poorly focused — much activity is occurring, but in the absence of clear goals, the direction is difficult to determine.

2. Financing commensurate with the commitment and consistent with the general level of public support provided to agriculture. In recent years, public support to agriculture has amounted to over four billion dollars per year, much of it for income support for some of the very programs that are of concern. In contrast, expenditures on wildlife and environmental issues amount to only a few million dollars each year.

    On the other hand, agricultural expenditures by wildlife bureaucracies amount to a greater proportion of their funds. For example, the North American Waterfowl Management Plan alone is scheduled to disperse one billion dollars in little more than ten years in Canada, much of it to farm land.[26] By way of contrast, federal expenditures on agricultural soil and water accords with the provinces are planned to total no more than two hundred million dollars annually over the next six years.[27]

3. The effectiveness of what will always be limited funds could be improved through a combination of:

    (a) reforming existing programs and policies in order to remove contradictory incentives and allow for funds now used to inadvertently promote the use of marginal crop lands to be used for habitat protection and environmental improvements in general, as long as these measures do not threaten food supplies;[28]

    (b) Promoting the use of private sector as well as public funds, using trusts, to purchase easements on farm properties and other contractual arrangements relating to environmental actions to be undertaken by the farmer.

4. From a legal perspective, a number of changes and additions to Canadian laws could be made in support of these changes:

---

26 Canada. Dept. of the Environment, Canadian Wildlife Service & United States. Dept. of the Interior, Fish and Wildlife Service, *supra*, note 3.

27 Canada. Dept. of the Environment, *Canada's Green Plan* (Ottawa: Environment Canada, 1990).

28 Girt, *supra*, note 6; John Girt, *Environmental Sustainability of Agriculture* (Paper presented at the Annual Meeting of the Canadian Federation of Agriculture, 27 February 1991) [unpublished].

(a) Property laws could be modified in possibly every province but P.E.I. to allow for the use of easements and other contractual agreements between a third party and the land owner. This would provide some measure of guaranteed performance by the land owner for his commitments to provide specified practices in exchange for assistance from public and private agencies for meeting environmental and wildlife objectives.[29] Some form of legal framework that provides a contractual base for financial and other payments to land owners with respect to publicly desired practices that would otherwise not be profitable must be available in Canada, as it is in parts of Europe and the United States. In most provinces, at present, zoning regulations, which are a more cumbersome and less comprehensive approach, or grants, which are ephemeral as well as being subject to political whims, are the closest available instruments.

(b) Crown agencies as well as government departments should be made accountable and responsible for the environmental impact of their operations. Without this legal responsibility it will be difficult to require that agencies fulfill their obligations and meet their mandate without contravening environmental objectives. One approach, long winded and cumbersome, to this problem would be to amend each Act that defines the responsibilities of Ministers, their Departments, and Crown agencies. The other would be to pass umbrella legislation requiring agencies, including Crown agencies which operate at arm's length from their governments, to conduct environmental impact assessments of their current and intended operations, publish the details of their findings, and adjust their operations to be consistent with the environmental rights of individuals and any goals for the environment that the government may set from time to time.

(c) It seems quite unrealistic to require that all negative environmental impacts be eliminated. On the other hand, governments should be able to identify and publicly announce environmental objectives for which their agencies will be accountable. Perhaps a Commissioner for the Environment could be created to provide annual assessments not only of the adequacy of the objectives that governments have chosen, but also of the progress being made in achieving them. As in the case of minority rights and public information, it is only when

---

29   See Oriana Trombetti & Kenneth W. Cox, *Land, Law and Wildlife Conservation: The Role and Use of Conservation Easements and Covenants in Canada* (Ottawa: Wildlife Habitat Canada, 1990).

such a legal framework is in place that agencies will operate in accordance with its requirements. Only then will the rapid adjustment of programs and policies so necessary to provide a supportive management and financial framework for sustainable development be accomplished.

(d) The concept of public trust should be introduced with the establishment of legal "environmental rights" in Canada. This would mirror and complement the goals and purpose of sustainable development as it has been defined by the World Commission on Environment and Development, and the various Round Tables on the Economy and Environment advising Canadian governments today. Generally, they have recognized that (i) plants and animals, land, air, and water are held in public trust by governments; (ii) governments should preserve and maintain them for present and future generations; and (iii) individuals should be provided with adequate remedies to protect and conserve natural resources, and to ensure their prevention from contamination and degradation as a result of the activities of individuals or the regulatory, fiscal, or proprietary controls exercised by governments.

Again, these moves are in conformity with the concept that humans are the alien rather than wildlife the exotic, though it must be pointed out that the environmental rights initiative originates within the environmental rather than wildlife community. As a consequence, discussions of the initiatives have tended to focus more on addressing the problems of environmental pollution and less on the viability of ecosystems, which also depend on the availability of soil, water, land, energy, and biological resources for their survival. This point will be considered further on in this paper.

It is interesting to note at this point that moves to reinforce environmental rights tend to assume both a public acceptance of the applicability of this concept, and the existence of a supportive action framework so that any legislation required would focus on regulations merely addressing recalcitrants. Neither seem to apply in the case of agriculture, and wildlife and the environment with the exception of farm chemicals. Farmers continue to demonstrate the independent spirit for which they are known, and the social contract binding them to society and vice versa is based more on public assistance and subsidies to provide well-organized markets for produce and stable farm incomes. Indeed, the contract is of such a form as to present barriers to effective environmental management that will benefit both the farmer and society as a whole.[30]

The situation of agriculture contrasts significantly with that of forestry. In the latter case, much of the land is held by the Crown and leased to the private sector. The arrangement provides far fewer rights to foresters than to farmers, who generally own their land or rent or lease it from the private sector. On the other hand, it seems that society is more willing to make the forestry sector more responsible for environmental impacts than farmers, and it seems that the forestry sector is also more prepared to assume responsibility for it. These inconsistencies need to be addressed, for they are in the best interests of neither these two sectors nor the public in general.

(e) Codes of accepted practice should be provided in legislation on environmental rights, and generally, work should progress towards a clearer definition of what constitutes a professional and acceptable level of performance by governments and farmers, focusing on the management of whole farms for other values in addition to the production of food commodities.

(f) Zoning and bylaws should be used to regulate land use sensitive to habitat management issues, and a Crown agency could be set up to act as the trustee for natural resource conservation initiatives. The agency would be responsible for two closely inter-related activities: (i) obtaining funds for conservation from private sources as well as governments (perhaps on the basis of a share of the saving accruing from making land ineligible for support from other programs); and (ii) providing funds for municipal and equivalent private organizations to develop multi-sector, comprehensive approaches to habitat protection and development, and the prevention of pollution.

(g) The necessary legal framework could be provided for agencies to offer "Conservation Bonds", and the specific uses for which earmarked public funds can be allocated could be identified legally. The public's willingness to provide money is closely linked to the use to which it is to be put. Environmental concerns figure high on the public agenda, and there appears to be a willingness to provide savings or allow taxes to be levied for environmental goals. At present, there is little or no legal accountability for the use of such funds by public agencies; government revenues generally go into general revenue accounts. The exercise of the public trust in the environment, just as with income support, should have clear legal,

---

30   Girt, *supra*, note 6.

financial accountability.

(h) Environmental issues and problems should be defined more clearly so as to move beyond a concern to minimize pollution, and requirements to avoid reducing the ecological integrity of areas should be included. This could mean, for example, the adoption of such principles as "no net loss of species diversity". This should be interpreted in terms of the ability of current levels of species diversity as well as numbers of individual members of species' to exist in the future, even with cumulative impacts. It would also mean that all six above-cited requirements should be implemented.

(i) Clearly, some institutional changes will be necessary to reflect the need to manage and support farms as more than simply suppliers of food products, and to recognize that an ecosystem approach to managing natural resources demands a geographical rather than the usual sectoral approach by private and public institutions. This would suggest a more active role for municipalities and conservation districts in farm and wildlife issues than in the past, as well as the need for private conservation organizations based on municipal or ecological areas, such as drainage basins.

A VISION FOR AN AGRICULTURAL LANDSCAPE

By way of conclusion, a vision of what agriculture would be like if our concerns for wildlife and the environment were addressed successfully is offered. It is drawn from a draft of the upcoming report on the status of wildlife habitat in Canada by Wildlife Habitat Canada:[31]

1. Farming systems that, in line with the recommendations of the Federal-provincial Agriculture Task Force on Environmental Sustainability:[32]

    *   produce food products profitably and efficiently by emphasizing the improved management of soil, water, energy, and biological resources, and

    *   reduce impacts harmful to the environment or the health of farmers and consumers.

2. Systems that:
    *   allow for habitat to support a wide range of native animal and plant species, and

---

31   Wildlife Habitat Canada, *The Status of Wildlife Habitat in Canada: Realities & Visions* (Ottawa: Wildlife Habitat Canada, 1991).

32   Federal-provincial Committee on Environmental Sustainability, *supra*, note 5.

- benefit from them through the improved productivity and protection to soil and water resources that they bring.

Such benefits will be realized through:

- species playing an enhanced role in integrated pest management,
- the maintenance and improvement of natural processes for nutrient recycling, and
- habitat providing alternative uses for land of limited production potential or for land that can actively contribute to the control of soil erosion and run-off from fields.

3. Systems that allow wildlife to maintain its biological vitality and avoid its isolation in pockets in a sea of intensive farm activity.

4. Systems that encourage farmers to think positively about wildlife as an economically important component in their operations, and that encourage the wildlife community to regard farmers as important partners in wildlife management.

The agricultural landscape that would emerge if these objectives were met would vary according to the region of the country and the commodities that farms specialize in. However, compared to the situation today, it would contain more numerous, well-connected areas of natural vegetation, including wetlands and surface water bodies on farms; and increased use of crop rotations, composting, and green manures in order to maintain and improve farm productivity, instead of chemical fertilizers and pesticides. Such systems, because of the increased availability of food sources, particularly for invertebrates which are themselves important agents for pest management and nutrient recycling, would provide a food chain for more diverse ecosystems than are now found on most farms in Canada. These ecosystems would create benefits extending beyond wildlife, and would form the foundation for the achievement of sustainable agricultural production in Canada.

RESOURCE EXPLOITATION vs. WILDERNESS PROTECTION: FUTURE SCENARIOS

Nikita Lopoukhine

"Wilderness" is an Anglo-Germanic word without an equivalent in other languages. The French/English dictionary equivalency for wilderness is either "desert" (a biblical connotation) or an "un lieu sauvage", a descriptive equivalent. Some of the literature associated with this conference translated wilderness as "conservation de la faune". In Russian the functionally equivalent word can also be used to describe emptiness. The etymology of "wilderness" is a "place (ness) with wild (will) animals (deer)".[1]

Roderick Nash,[2] during the Symposium on Wilderness Fire in Montana, spoke of the acceptable levels of intrusion into wilderness by civilization from two perspectives: from that of a resident of remote Alaska and that of a rancher in Montana. Their definitions of wilderness, he asserted, would no doubt vary in the acceptable amount of human intrusion. He produced a simple diagram of a rectangle split by a diagonal line, which created two triangles grading in content of wilderness and civilization qualities. Thus, each end of the rectangle represented all of one of these two qualities, and the middle of the rectangle represented an equal distribution. The Alaskan, he guessed, would prefer his or her wilderness with a minimum of civilization, while the rancher from Montana could put up with more intrusion.

The constituency of wilderness is clearly subjective and, as such, dependent on temporal or spatial concepts. Within the developed countries such areas are now designated, and the common thread among such designations is an element of non-control. In contrast, a citizen from the underdeveloped world, if asked the definition of wilderness, would not distinguish between such areas, preferring to treat all lands as humanity's habitat without distinction or degree of "wilderness".

Wilderness is a state of mind that has eluded definition. Personal views of wilderness were compared by Manning[3] to the tourism industry's

---

1   Roderick Nash, "Sorry Bambi, But Man Must Enter the Forest: Perspectives on the Old Wilderness and the New" *in* J.E. Lotan, B.M. Kilgore, W.C. Fischer & Robert Mutch, Proceedings of a Symposium and Workshop on Wilderness Fire (Missoula, Mo., 1983) U.S. For. Serv. Gen. Tech. Rep. INT-182 (Osten, Utah) at 264-269.

2   *Id.*

3   Robert Manning, "Free to be You and Me, or Some Random Thoughts about Wilderness" *in* D.N. Cole & R.C. Lucas, *Significant Wilderness Qualities: Can They Be Identified and Monitored?* (Lander, Wyoming: National Outdoor Leadership School, 1987).

classification "sense of place": a unique combination of qualities that defines the place. In combination, these qualities create a synergism that statisticians find difficult to explain.

It is appropriate to reconsider whether designating an area as wilderness addresses the objective of protection. There is considerable merit in the underdeveloped world's concept of wilderness. This context recognizes wilderness as our habitat and thus provides additional credence to the concern expressed by those already committed to the perhaps more conventional wildernesses, "the untrammelled", of the world.

The paradox of "the untrammelled wilderness" is that civilization created it, and now threatens its existence while setting up the conditions for its appreciation.[4] This kind of wilderness came about through the development of an agrarian society that went about separating the civilized from "uncontrolled" wild areas or, in the parlance of forestry, the unimproved. Civilization has in itself some value; in fact, it provides us with the means to appreciate this kind of wilderness.

This paper reviews Canadian and American wilderness attitudes over time. The reason for conflict over wildernesses and the current attitudes are presented as an opportunity for change. A future scenario for managing national parks for the objective of wilderness is offered. Concluding remarks bring these concepts to bear on the issue of conflicts over resource use.

A PERSPECTIVE ON CANADIAN/AMERICAN WILDERNESS ATTITUDES

Historically, Canadians have been indifferent to issues related to wilderness preservation. By contrast, the American wilderness movement can be traced to the creation of Yosemite National Park in 1892, which had the specific purpose of protecting wilderness. This park's purpose was in contrast to the earlier-established Yellowstone National Park, which was created simply as a public park and pleasuring ground.[5]

It was the 1913 debate over the damming of Yosemite's Hetch Hetchy Valley that in fact began to crystallize the wilderness preservation views of Americans. Interestingly, the debate was among the conservation (wise-use) lobby and the emerging preservation lobby. The former were concerned that the eastern-based decision makers were going to lock up land and take away westerners' ability to profit from the land.

---

4   *Supra*, note 1.

5   Marilyn Dubasak, *Wilderness Preservation: A Cross-Cultural Comparison of Canada and the United States* (Ann Arbor, Mich.: Case Western Reserve University, 1987) [unpublished].

In the United States, the formal wilderness protection movement began with the establishment of the Wilderness Society in 1935. This society, composed of a group of leading American conservationists, began promulgating the notion that wilderness had value. Initially, the value was that wilderness would serve as a benchmark, where an understanding of the natural world could be obtained and thus contribute to science.

These American debates and maturing views on the benefits of wilderness took some fifty years to reach Canada. It was not until the 1960s and 1970s, when Canadians went through the Lake Louise development debates, that there was a broader acceptance of national parks as more than recreational areas. However, the idea is still not broadly anchored, since in the 1980s and now in the 1990s, the debate continues over such proposals as the Sunshine Valley ski expansion in Banff National Park. One article in *The Globe and Mail* has even raised the same points as were debated in 1913 in the U.S.A.,[6] that eastern bureaucrats were deciding the disposition of park lands and affecting the potential tourist revenues in the West. The article did not mention the value of wilderness protection.

Canada has adopted wilderness protection in a typically Canadian fashion. The process was a reasoned and contained one whereby sustained yield (the precursor to sustainable development) dominated the allocation of resources. Parks were created, but primarily as recreation areas. In this light, we can begin to understand why the designation "wilderness" is in Canada assigned to areas not wanted for other uses.[7] It also serves to explain why this land-use designation has not been sacrosanct. The identification of more valuable uses for these areas has often made them available.

Canadian parks did not have a champion like the American Interior Secretary, Stephen T. Maher, who encouraged the creation of the National Parks Association. In 1918, Maher used his own fortune to pay the salary of the first director of the National Parks Association.[8] This bit of support launched a formidable lobby. It is true that in Canada the National Provincial Parks Association (predecessor to the Canadian Parks and Wilderness Society) was also initiated through a heavy subsidy. The Canadian government, at the time, was seeking to show the required support for park establishment and pro-wilderness decisions. The Canadian Parks and Wilderness Society continues to depend on an annual government contribution.

---

6   Al Strachan, "Sun Don't Shine on Sunshine", *The Globe and Mail* (29 March 1991) B4.

7   A.D. Crerar, "Comment" *in* Nigel Bankes & J. Owen Saunders, eds., *Public Disposition of Natural Resources: Essays From the First Banff Conference on Natural Resources Law* (Calgary: Canadian Institute of Resources Law, 1983) 355.

8   *Supra*, note 5.

The current legislative trends for wilderness protection in Canada are not any different from those described by McNamee in 1989.[9] Five Canadian statutes authorize the establishment of wilderness areas. The amended *National Parks Act* provides for the creation of wilderness areas within national parks,[10] and pilot studies are being contemplated at this time. Four provinces have enacted legislation the titles of which contain the word "wilderness" and all of which designate and protect limited areas as wilderness.[11] Zoning of wilderness rather than legislating seems to be the preferred approach to wilderness designation in Canada.

CONFLICTS OVER WILDERNESS

The subjectivity associated with wilderness designation has created the need for conflict resolution. The lack of standards for wilderness and the vulnerability of the isolated designated wildernesses to the inimical land uses outside and beyond such areas ensure a societal preoccupation with conflict resolution.

When views on an issue are hardened and etched in different languages, the amount of energy dedicated to resolution grows exponentially. To date, the debate over wilderness allocations versus the demands for resource exploitation is often mired in the same frame of reference and uses the same language. On both sides of the argument, and indeed within the wilderness lobby itself, the view is very often homocentric. Those arguing on behalf of exploiting resources or wilderness protection have a common denominator: humankind as the beneficiary.

The debate is often reduced to an economic argument. This indeed provides a common language for resolving conflicts. While perhaps attractive, however, it is in effect opening the door to the argument that the higher value wins access to the area in question. Furthermore, economic arguments do not capture the value of future utility, which can only be maximized through conservation.

In the final analysis, truncated wildernesses have been established. Inevitably, critical habitat is excluded or compromised either because of an oversight or because of local enterprises or national priorities. For the latter, a strong justification is the occurrence of a national crisis requiring an upgrade

---

9   Kevin McNamee, "Canada's Endangered Spaces: Preserving the Canadian Wilderness" *in Managing America's Wilderness Resource: A Conference* (Minneapolis: Tourism Centre, Minn. Ext. Serv. & Minn. Ag. Exp. St., U. of Minn., St. Paul, Minn., 1989) 111.

10   *National Parks Act*, R.S.C. 1985, c.N-14, s.5(8).

11   Ontario, Alberta, Newfoundland, and British Columbia have legislation with titles continuing the word "wilderness".

of transportation, access to oil, or even trees. The recently terminated logging in Wood Buffalo National Park was begun at a time of national crisis. The twinning of the Trans-Canada highway in Banff was a transportation upgrade, and access to oil is at the heart of the conflict in the northern slopes of Alaska.

It is clear from history that, wherever choices have to be made and the choice favours values other than wilderness, then the choice is irrevocable for wilderness. There are no examples of wilderness in the purest form having been reclaimed. Conservation is a defensive manoeuvre that invariably loses to other uses.

At the time of the establishment of wilderness areas, and after human needs are either discounted or taken into account, the announcements are often couched in homocentric terms. One of the more recent substantiations for wilderness creation is the associated gene pool values. To support this claim, as-yet undiscovered pharmaceutical wonders or other products for the benefit of humankind are invoked. Another common supporting argument is the usefulness of wilderness as a watershed protector, which provides a clean and steady supply of water to communities located downstream. The establishment of wildernesses in remote areas of a country is substantiated on the basis of national sovereignty. Political boundaries and, of course, recreational or spiritual values associated with wildernesses are obviously homocentric.

Even the suggestion that wilderness provides refuge for the vulnerable, threatened, or endangered has an homocentric spin. Humankind draws boundaries on a map and designates these areas as wilderness to absolve itself of the guilt associated with permitting other species to become vulnerable, threatened, or endangered. Ironically, humanity's demands created the dangerous situation and, to solve the problem, we choose a string of wilderness areas to serve as reservations where the endangered can linger before passing into oblivion.

In my view, the debate is likely to become more caustic, with arguments polarized on the benefits to humankind of exploitation in contrast to the benefits to deer or other species from protection through wilderness establishment. Wildlife rights groups and other single-issue lobby groups can provide clear examples of what lies ahead.

AN ALTERNATIVE LANGUAGE FOR CONFLICT RESOLUTION

Whether inanimate objects or living creatures other than *Homo sapiens* have rights is a question that in the past has been relegated to deep ecologists or ecosophists. The debate is slowly being taken up by others. My purpose here is not to engage in this debate. However, in decision making there are

distinct advantages to taking into consideration other elements of the
ecosystem than our own species. The first and foremost advantage is that this
broader approach provides a loftier platform for debating objectives.
Humankind is no longer the *direct* beneficiary in these debates. By extending
consideration to resources in all land-use decisions, we recognize the linkages
between beneficiaries; thus, we extend the range of beneficiaries and increase
the opportunity for reducing conflicts among humankind.

It can be argued that passing an endangered species act provides legal
rights to non-human species. Unfortunately, this gesture provides protection to
species only after human impact has in effect endangered the species. Quite
simply, there are no Acts that protect the ecosystem.[12]

Rowe,[13] an ecologist, reviewed the Law Reform Commission of
Canada's Working Paper No.44, *Crimes against the Environment*. His concern
was that the authors lacked a fundamental understanding of ecology. While
praising their efforts to deal with the issue, Rowe points out the
shortsightedness in placing people at the centre of the environment rather than
as a part of it. The authors missed the point that our species is but a lower
element of the hierarchy (atom to biosphere) that makes up our environment.
They failed to grasp the opportunity to confer values (the conferring of rights
is the recognition of value) on a higher level. In effect, had the ecosystem
frame of reference been accepted, the differing camps — the resource
exploiters and the wilderness lobbies — would have been offered a common
ground for realizing their objectives.

The ecosystem frame of reference provides the basis for resource
management. It is a method of management that transcends negotiating the
value of the environment. It also transcends disputing whether it is a
provincial or federal jurisdiction. It is dependent on recognizing the biological
underpinnings of most environmental problems and, finally, it recognizes that
all elements of the ecosystem have a value that is not based solely on utility
to humanity.[14]

Aldo Leoplold, the father of the American wilderness movement, was
influenced by the philosopher Ouspensky. The latter professed organicism: all
matter, from atom to whale, has consciousness. He also professed esotericism
as a means of looking at issues. His explanation was that this required a
complete view of not only the object, but its context in the world, which was

---

12   James R. Karr, "Biological Integrity and the Goal of Environmental Legislation: Lessons for
      Conservation Biology" (1990) 4:3 Conservation Biology at 244-250.

13   S. Rowe, *Home Place* (Edmonton: NeWest Publishing, 1990).

14   *Supra*, note 12.

without bounds. Ecosystems management is exactly that. The objective is not to define new boundaries but rather to remove boundaries: ideological, cultural, and certainly jurisdictional. When this objective is achieved, ecological consciousness will have become a part of everyday business and nature will no longer be an entity to be dominated.[15]

ENVIRONMENTAL CONSCIOUSNESS

The opportunity to alter the focus of objectives, and with it our language of conflict resolution, has never been better. The "cut and get out" mentality gripping resource exploiters of old is being replaced. Environmental considerations, genuine as well as publicity stunts, are enveloping resource managers. Calls for change have been heard on a global scale, most recently from the World Commission on Environment and Development,[16] better known as the Bruntland Commission. The national call has taken the form of the federal Green Plan.[17] At the local level, there are many examples, such as the City of Ottawa Master Plan. Contained in each of these guidelines is a commitment to "wilderness", that is, the protection of natural areas.

The Bruntland Report calls for the tripling of areas dedicated to the protection function on a world-wide scale. This has now become the 12 percent solution. The Green Plan has also declared a commitment to meet the 12 percent target. The Ottawa Master Plan does not opt for a percentage but delves right into protection issues. It sets out a "Greenway System", the objective of which is to sustain natural processes and maintain the integrity of the natural environment. While this objective may exceed realism, it does embrace the broader realization that the world is littered with the ruins of towns and cities.

These announcements have been politically astute. Based on personal observations of media coverage, few have raised a voice in opposition. In fact, there are clear examples of support from the traditional exploiters of resources. One example is the forestry sector's call to create forest reserves as a contribution to the 12 percent solution. More significant is the suggestion that the forestry profession alter its mission with a shift from wood production to the "preservation of life on earth".[18] Accordingly, the mission proposed

---

15   Douglas Torgerson, "The Paradox of Environmental Ethics" (1985) 12:2 Alternatives at 26.36.

16   World Commission on Environment and Development, *Our Common Future* (Oxford: Oxford University Press, 1987) (Chair: G.H. Brundtland).

17   Canada. Dept. of the Environment, *Canada's Green Plan* (Ottawa: Supply and Services, 1990).

18   Robert T. Perschel, "Pioneering a New Human/Nature Relationship: Report and

for the professional forester is stewardship of forests using principles of ecosystem management.

The evidence is mounting that our society's values are changing. Foresters and other traditional exploiters are beginning to alter their approach to resource extraction and management. I applaud this effort and leave it to them to describe their approach; I will instead review the direction wilderness managers are taking in applying ecosystem management.

ECOSYSTEM MANAGEMENT PRINCIPLES APPLIED IN WILDERNESS MANAGEMENT

The traditional process of establishing a wilderness area usually takes the area's potential for human enjoyment into account and ensures that resource-extraction opportunity loss is minimized. There is, of course, a deference to the notion of "protection". This word, in itself, seems to have been accepted as a panacea for ensuring biodiversity, ecological integrity, and the historical links that wilderness provides with the period of North American colonization.

Simply establishing wilderness areas does not automatically result in the sought-after protection. Such action only provides a milieu for the remnants of the past to drift into oblivion. To really protect a wilderness, we must in a sense also exploit it. However, the beneficiary must be, not the few who realize economic gain, but the ecosystem within which humankind is but an element. In this context, management becomes focused on providing compensation for truncated and altered natural processes and achieving objectives of representation within a system of reservations. On the edges of wilderness, objectives must be complementary. The self-sustaining ecosystem must be maintained and restored where necessary.

There is an inescapable need to *manage for wilderness*. This is as important as establishing wilderness areas. In fact, the two are inseparable if protection is truly the objective. One need only consider the following facts that a park manager must deal with in formulating strategies for resource management protection:

- Parks do not exist in isolation from neighbouring lands and the impacts thereon.

- Parks are multi-use areas, not strict protection zones. In-park use and development have always been within the scope of the governing legislation.

- Park areas are not, and never were, established strictly on the basis of

---

Recommendations to the New England SAF Concerning a New Mission Statement" (1991) 89:4 J. of Forestry 18.

functioning ecosystems.

- Management of most natural processes wholly within a park is impossible.

- Parks represent nodes or anchors for dynamic species and processes the ranges of which extend beyond the confines of a park area.

- Few, if any, parks contain unaltered ecosystems. All show signs of modification by modern humanity's activities. Vast areas of both land and water within even the largest of parks are profoundly altered by direct human intervention.

- Restoration of ecosystems to absolute pristine condition is impossible. Furthermore, an appropriate definition of "pristine" for the areas now occupied by parks is an unknown.

- Global changes preclude setting inherited ecosystems or vignettes of past landscapes as a goal of perpetuation.

With this kind of baggage, to expect designated areas to achieve protection in and of themselves is akin to dreaming in technicolour. Nevertheless, the *National Parks Act* was amended in 1988 to state: *"Maintenance of ecological integrity through the protection of natural resources shall be the first priority when considering park zoning and visitor use in a management plan."*[19] The Canadian Parks Service is now mandated to consider and maintain ecological integrity in a national park. A legal responsibility has been established. While a legal definition of "ecological integrity" may not be desirable, the term has avoided complete definition.

The simplest interpretation of the term is that there is now a requirement to protect and manage for "completeness or wholeness" in ecological terms, that is, a functioning ecosystem with all its parts, including processes. In the context of biological diversity, ecological integrity means the full complement of life and its processes, from genes to ecosystems. Maintaining ecological integrity is a mammoth task that Canadians have assigned to Environment Canada Parks Service. This assignment may in fact be unrealistic where predators, disease, or other ecosystem regulators have been tampered with or eliminated.

In a world without artificial boundaries, where landscapes would be unchanged and where climate would change slowly and gradually, maintaining ecological integrity would be simple. It would be a matter of not interfering. Now, with natural processes modified, and parks isolated by surrounding

---

19 *National Parks Act*, R.S.C. 1985, c.N-14, as am. by R.S.C. 1985 (4th Supp.), c.39, s.3 at s.5(1.2).

non-conforming land uses and bombarded by long-range transported pollutants, benign neglect cannot and does not equal ecological integrity.

An active management regime is the only recourse. Managers *"for wilderness"* will have to decide what kind of manipulation is acceptable. Objectives of ecological integrity/biodiversity will have to be clearly stated, and publicly debated. The results will need to be monitored, and changes to objectives will require adjustment according to newly gained knowledge. In effect, adaptive management[20] within the Canadian Parks Service will have been initiated.

It would be inadequate to provide adaptive managers with only an institutional framework within which to define appropriate management objectives. An ethical framework must also be provided.[21] *"Managing for wilderness"* must be governed by a framework of ecological integrity. We must strive for the most complete representation possible. As Torgerson[22] wrote:

> Even more fundamentally, however, ecological consciousness itself harbours internal tensions. In what is apparently its most advanced form — ecological sensibility — the "noninterference principle" is at odds with what ecology most clearly teaches us: we are connected. What we do or not do is part of a complex pattern of interdependence. Neutrality is not an option.

CONCLUSIONS

It is not the rights of resources that are at stake, but rather the legitimacy of considering their needs. Protecting resources for the sake of resources is but an indirect means of assuring human self-preservation. This argument, while admittedly homocentric, must be used, if only initially, to emphasize that we are part of the biosphere and that it, in turn, is the source of our life.

Those who argue that technology and cheap energy such as cold fusion will solve our problems fail to recognize a simple fact. Transgressing nature's regulatory powers through technology and cheap energy fixes can only be a temporary development. Further, the biosphere has a limited resource base. Once these resources are transformed, there are no other sources for them.

Our culture is in effect now associated with "cheap" energy and technology (the real costs are hidden). These means are now a part of the array of tools society is utilizing to erode our endowment. While legislating

---

20   Carl Walters, *Adaptive Management of Renewable Resources* (New York: Macmillan, 1986).

21   R. Serafin *et al.*, *Ecological Integrity and Management of Canada's National Parks* (Waterloo: University of Waterloo Heritage Resources Centre for Canada Parks Service) [unpublished].

22   *Supra*, note 15.

laws of nature is out of purview, we are nevertheless subject to corrective action whenever these natural laws are broken. The prediction of increased and more intense storms associated with climate change is but one indication of what to expect.[23]

As a result of the increasingly urban character of our society, only a minority now has direct experience of living off the land. The growing number of immigrants from countries with little knowledge of wilderness protection is reducing the general demand for the experience of nature, while indirectly placing higher demand on its exploitation. There is a likelihood that our current conflict over wilderness may be overtaken by new stakeholders with a completely different perspective.

The fundamental question to be asked of all Canadians is: What is to be protected within any fixed geographic area? Is it reasonable to expect the Canadian Parks Service to be responsible for protection as presently legislated?

In answering this question, we should consider whether or not national parks alone are to provide wilderness protection. The issue is simple: Do we pursue an approach of relegating "untrammelled wilderness" to parks, and exploit elsewhere with undue regard for all but humankind? If the answer is in the negative, then we must begin to join into a network all public and private lands dedicated to protection. This network would be assigned core protection for immigrating and emigrating communities and individual species.

The network must include more than the *status quo*. There is a requirement to scrupulously examine the barriers to the adjustment of ecosystems and devise mechanisms for overcoming these. These mechanisms could range from simple relocation to the more complex provision of additional (temporary and/or permanent) refuge areas along with corridors.

National parks have a leadership role to play. While one must recognize that the Canadian Parks Service is a politically accountable institution,[24] there is nevertheless room for leadership. The Canadian Parks Service must strive to demonstrate ecocentric values by ensuring that the country's biodiversity is afforded reasonable protection within national parks. This demonstration must at times be to the detriment of homocentric considerations. A policy revision should propose these guidelines rather than waiting for direction from society-at-large. There is also room for leadership in forging the needed national network. The issue is what the agency

---

23   T.M.L. Wigley, "Impact of Extreme Events" (1985) 316 Nature 106.

24   J. Freemuth, "The National Parks: Political versus Professional Determinants of Policy" (1989) 6:3 The George Wright Forum 26.

responsible for national parks can do for Canada and for the ecosystems that define and support Canadians.

Society, nevertheless, is responsible for determining the penultimate objective of national parks. Society must evaluate whether it is appropriate to relegate the responsibility of protecting our national heritage to reservations such as national parks. Complete protection in perpetuity is unachievable within a limited area. This is particularly true when an area has also been assigned other, often conflicting, objectives; when it was not chosen for these objectives in the first place; and when it is surrounded by influences inimical to these objectives.

Obviously, there is a much better chance of achieving a degree of protection when efforts are displayed on both sides of the often artificial park boundary. Regional management approaches must be instituted for a park to succeed in protection. This example is perhaps worth pursuing in that shared protection objectives must not be restricted to a focus on the role of a park, but must be applicable to the entire biosphere.

To avoid future conflicts over the best use of lands for humankind, ecosystem objectives must be the basis of determining best use of the land. Further, assignment of use should be, not in the context of traditional land use *per se*, but rather as a grade of wilderness, from the untrammelled to the patch of green in the inner city. In doing so we will not only have the attitude of the Third World citizen that wilderness is everywhere, as our habitat, but more importantly we will have agreed to this consciously as a society.

The challenge for us is to build on our wilderness heritage and to develop a language for the future with links to our environment. When we begin to evaluate the use of resources in the context of ecosystems and use language at this higher level of organization, there is a better likelihood that we will indeed have reached the wilderness phase of conservation. True conservation means caring for things other than ourselves.[25]

---

25   *Supra*, note 13.

3

LAND CLAIMS AGREEMENTS AS A MECHANISM FOR RESOLVING RESOURCE-USE CONFLICTS

THE POTENTIAL OF LAND CLAIMS NEGOTIATIONS FOR RESOLVING RESOURCE-USE CONFLICTS

Barry Stuart

Unquestionably, land claims negotiations have inordinate potential to develop proactive, comprehensive resource management regimes and to generate widely accepted methods for resolving resource-use conflicts. Why has this potential not been realized?

Based primarily on Yukon land claims negotiations from 1985 to 1990, this paper argues that the principal factors frustrating this potential are an irrepressible reliance on adversarial negotiations and a failure to design a negotiation process that considers the special circumstances of each negotiating environment.

The overwhelming pressure to immediately commence negotiations on substantive issues, arbitrarily set deadlines, long-standing adversarial relationships among the parties, their inexperience in multi-party cooperative bargaining, a lack of trust, and a failure to fully comprehend the significance of cultural differences among the parties, all contributed at the onset and throughout negotiations to the failure to design a process that maximizes the potential for negotiating lasting and fair agreements. Much of the widely held dissatisfaction with land claim negotiations stems from the abysmal process employed for negotiations.

Improving the process will not make the fundamental difficulties besetting land claim negotiations miraculously disappear. The source of such difficulties is too deeply rooted in history and too firmly entrenched in the structures of our institutions and legal systems to be eradicated by changing the process for negotiations, regardless of how profound such changes may be. Nor will land claims negotiations, even if ideally structured, ever replace the need for other means of dispute resolution such as litigation, arbitration, mediation, and various forms of political action. However, a much improved process for land claims negotiations can vastly improve the quality and acceptance of new management regimes and methods for resolving resource-use conflicts, foster a more productive dialogue to understand and resolve the fundamental difficulties imposed upon aboriginal people by our institutions and legal system, and significantly reduce the need to resort to other remedies to resolve conflicts over resource-use conflicts.

In this paper, some of the reasons why land claim negotiations offers so much potential to enhance effective resource-use management regimes will be canvassed and several of the techniques used to employ this potential in the Yukon land claim process will be described.

POTENTIAL OF LAND CLAIMS NEGOTIATIONS

The following factors exemplify the formidable potential of land claims negotiations to resolve resource-use conflicts.

Spans Jurisdictional Boundaries

Land claims negotiations in the North encompass all political jurisdictions. Municipal, territorial, and federal government resources and powers are brought within the realm of negotiations. No other process incorporates the same comprehensive array of government powers in designing new resource management regimes.

Interdepartmental Barriers Removed

The range of subjects addressed in land claims embraces the mandate of almost every line department. The ramifications of a land claims settlement are so pervasive that no department can afford to ignore the process. While the participation of many diverse departments has the potential to delay the process, their participation equally has the potential to invaluably enhance the breadth of powers and expertise used in the search for solutions. It is far better to include all departments in moulding solutions than to exclude them and risk their active opposition during implementation.

If, and this is a big if, significant political will for a settlement exists at the highest levels of government, then unnecessary delays can be avoided and the participation of numerous departments becomes a tremendous advantage in developing comprehensive solutions.

Private-sector Interest and Involvement

The impact of land claims settlements reaches into every sector of society. Everyone's interests are affected in some way. Business organizations, public interest groups, professional associations, and the general public are concerned and often insistent to know about land claims negotiations. With public interest aroused, a communication and participation strategy, if properly planned, can channel public interest into constructive public debate and input. The fundamental prerequisites of constructive public involvement are full knowledge and a meaningful opportunity to participate. An informed public, providing positive inputs, can generate the political will to settle and can contribute unique information and ideas that would otherwise be overlooked by the parties to negotiations.

Land claim negotiations attract the interest of all stakeholders, and if properly designed, the negotiation process can evolve the basis for extensive consensus among diverse interests.

Holistic Perspective

Land claims are not restricted to a narrow view of any single resource issue. The search for proper wildlife management tools is not limited to any particular species, nor concentrated on wildlife to the exclusion of habitat, nor narrowly focused on either traditional, recreational, or commercial uses of resources.

Land claims negotiations encompass all cultural, social, economic, and environmental issues that have an impact upon the use of resources. Such negotiations promote multi-faceted linkages across different resources (water, land, air, wildlife, forestry, and other renewable and non-renewable resources) and employ a broad range of techniques (planning, impact assessment, regulation, management schemes, and enforcement) in addressing conflicting demands on resources.

The comprehensive approach to resource issues afforded by land claims minimizes reliance upon the truncated solutions characteristic of uni-dimensional institutional responses and litigation. Land claims negotiations provide the best opportunity to overcome long-standing rules or policies that fail to reflect the interconnectedness of all resources, and fail to link a diverse range of strategies and techniques in managing resources.

Focus Government Attention

To reap any results from government, one must first attract its attention and secure priority among the numerous competing and exhausting demands upon its time and resources. The high public profile, intensity, and deadlines of land claims negotiations succeed in focusing government attention.

Litigation and public demonstrations are often heralded as the primary strategies for attracting government attention, but these techniques can provide an excuse for inaction: "can't comment or deal with that issue as the matter is before the courts", or "we will not bow to civil disobedience, and until they are prepared to negotiate without participating in illegal activities, nothing can be done."

Litigation or public demonstrations generally focus on single issues and engage only a few government departments. Land claims attract the attention of numerous departments in a much more positive fashion. If the elusive but essential political will to settle exists, and if the process for negotiation is designed to enhance the will of all parties to settle, then land claims can attract government attention in a very positive manner.

The case for the potential of land claims depends primarily upon the existence of a genuine will by all parties to settle. Without it, litigation and public demonstrations are unavoidable and the only useful recourse.

Advance Departmental Initiatives

Land claims, in calling for fundamental changes to resource management, can advance the timing and priority of departmental initiatives. Proposed changes that have been side-tracked by other business or are simply incapable of securing a commitment of resources or legislative time can be carried forward as a part of the settlement package. Conversely, an improperly designed land claim negotiation process may delay critical and long-overdue changes.

Cross-disciplinary Analysis

The negotiation process, if properly designed, creates the time, forum, and resources necessary for persons with diverse backgrounds, training, and experience to develop an understanding and respect for the value of their different contributions. Drawing solutions from a mix of expertise that includes scientific, local, and traditional knowledge fosters broadly based support for management practices among a diverse spectrum of resource users.

Consensual Problem Solving

More so than litigation or public protest, negotiations provide a greater potential to resolve differences through non-adversarial methods. To utilize this potential, the negotiation process must be carefully designed to generate trust among all parties. (Shifting away from adversarial methods often poses more difficulties for government than for aboriginal groups.)

Reduces Bias

Western values reflected in property rights, individual rights and responsibilities are deeply entrenched in the content of procedural and substantive laws governing courts and tribunals. In resolving disputes over renewable resources with aboriginal people, land claim negotiations, more so than other forums, are more malleable and can be structured to reflect a better balance between western and aboriginal values.

Cross-cultural education, adequate funding for effective aboriginal participation, community-based negotiations, and cooperative bargaining principles all assist in creating a better balance of understanding and mutual respect for the parties, different values and perspectives. Understanding and respecting differences is essential to achieve a fair settlement.

Summary

A negotiation process that takes full advantage of these factors has enormous potential to develop new approaches to resource management that will foster extensive public support. The successes and failures encountered in changing the process to take these factors into account in the Yukon illustrate the extent to which adversarial practices were entrenched, the lack of appreciation for the importance of the process, and the significant advantages even modest changes can achieve.

IMPORTANCE OF THE PROCESS

The first important task in multi-party, multi-faceted negotiations is to design a process specifically tailored to the interests, abilities, resources, and needs of the parties and to the political, cultural, geographic, and other special circumstances of the environment in which negotiations take place. While many common elements will be featured in all properly designed processes, the special circumstances of each negotiation will require unique procedures to ensure that the conditions fostering an agreement are maximized and those hindering an agreement are minimized. This is obvious, yet the lack of attention given by all parties to designing an appropriate process is convincing evidence that its importance flourishes only in theory, not in practice.

Once a process is properly designed, attention must be focused on ensuring that it is properly implemented. Too often, in the heat of negotiations, the parties fail to devote adequate attention to maintaining, adjusting, and improving the process. Short cuts, bypassing the steps carefully developed in designing the process, are often too tempting to resist. These short cuts can be costly, contributing to problems that may not emerge until attempts to ratify or implement agreements.

In complex resource-use negotiations, reaching an agreement about a proper process and employing that process are as crucial to achieving a settlement as any initial positions the parties develop for negotiations. Of all the mistakes plaguing the Yukon claim, none more profoundly hindered successful resolution than the failure to devote adequate time and resources to designing and developing an appropriate process for negotiations. Most crises confronted in negotiations were either caused or exacerbated by deficiencies in the process.

In any complex, multi-faceted negotiation, building trust among the parties must be a primary objective in designing the negotiations process.

Trust: An Essential Element of the Process

A land claim settlement has a direct or indirect impact upon the vested interests of all northerners, and reshapes their expectations and plans for the future.

The critical importance of a settlement for Yukon Indian People is unparalleled. Land negotiations are pivotal to the preservation of their culture and will dramatically determine the character if not the very survival of First Nation communities. Even delays in reaching a settlement can be measured in loss of life within First Nation communities, and certainly by the loss of vital opportunities to use resources to achieve their objectives. In the history of their culture, no other decisions will be as critical as those faced in land claims.

Far too much is at stake in land claims, and the scope far too complex, for a lasting, fair settlement maximizing the interests of all parties to be achieved without a foundation of trust among the parties.

Since 1985, the changes introduced to the process were designed primarily to enhance the level of trust among the parties. An environment of trust must encompass the immediate parties to the negotiations as well as all interests affected by a settlement.

After the recommencement of negotiations in 1985, several initial crises alerted all parties to the importance of examining and fundamentally changing the structures, principles, and practices shaping negotiations. Much was done, but not enough. What was done to change the process played an instrumental part in creating an environment conducive to reaching a settlement. But as the story of the process clearly and sadly illustrates, old habits, and particularly old bad habits, have a formidable tenacity. Tragically, mistrust between the parties may be too deeply entrenched to ever be removed. But much can be done to mitigate its destructive influence.

A failure to explore and appreciate the causes of mistrust, and to design changes to specifically redress these underlying causes, left the process constantly vulnerable to the destructive forces of mistrust.

The negative tensions endemic to government relations with aboriginal people, the predominantly adversarial nature of intergovernmental affairs, the legacy of suspicion generated by over a decade of adversarial negotiations, all contributed to the persistence of mistrust. This mistrust preserved attitudes and practices of adversarial negotiations.

The courage of the principals, Yukon Indian leaders, and numerous leaders of communities, businesses, and interest groups in experimenting with something new enabled implementation of a number of changes that began to build a foundation of trust. These changes reduced reliance upon adversarial strategies, facilitated more meaningful communication, and broadened the scope of input and understanding. Without the foundation of trust generated by these changes, any one of several crises confronting the process over the past six years could have terminated negotiations.

Focus on Interests, Not Positions

At the outset of negotiations, differences in the parties' positions on resource issues and other essential elements defied any prospect of settlement.

An adversarial process that focused on positions had little chance of producing a fair settlement. On many issues, compromises were not possible: the demands were too excessive and the differences too great for any hope of movement to a reasonable midpoint. The limited prospects for a settlement through adversarial negotiation, more than any understanding or appreciation of cooperative bargaining, began to open up the process to a number of changes designed to focus on the underlying interests of the parties.

A simple question posed by a First Nation negotiator made all parties recognize how different and much more demanding interest-based negotiations would be. Government had been pressing First Nation communities to explain their need for vast tracts of land, explanations First Nation communities were often hard pressed to reply. However, when government representatives were asked if they could justify *their* need to retain much bigger tracts of land, governmental silence, followed by incoherent mumbling, marked the beginning of their appreciation that interest-based negotiations required much more and quite different preparation.

Each position had to be justified by demonstrating how it advanced a specific interest. Each interest had to be explained and had to be consistent with the overall objective of each party. Facts began to replace rhetoric. As negotiations began to examine how the parties' negotiating positions served their interest, the absence of coherent connections between interests and positions was exposed. Examining the relationship between interests and positions revealed the degree to which all parties had relied on the school of thought that more (or, in some instances for government, less) is better.

As the negotiating process probed the respective interests of the parties in renewable resources, the revelations were both surprising and embarrassing. Careful assessment of party's interests and how those interests could be realized revealed that often parties had asked for too much, or too little, and in several instances had demanded the wrong things.

Some examples will illustrate how examining the underlying interests of each party shifts the search for solutions to a more creative and productive plane.

Once the First Nation position on the subject of harvesting was fully explored, it became clear that their central concern was not how much they could harvest in any given year, but how they could protect wildlife for future generations. This shifted the central point of wildlife negotiations from harvesting rights to management structures. The initial First Nation position on harvesting had demanded more than their current interests warranted, whereas their initial position on wildlife management had been inadequate to achieve their long-term interest in conservation.

As barriers to effective First Nation participation in impact assessment, wildlife management, land-use planning, and environmental protection were overcome, it became abundantly clear that their interests in resources were best served by creatively exploring opinions for shared responsibility in the management of water, wildlife, forestry, land, and culture. Effective and constitutionally protected First Nation management rights advanced their interests in resource use more effectively than simply acquiring vast tracts of land. While the differences between Indians and government over land quantum remained in issue, these differences became less disruptive to negotiations, as First Nation interests were increasingly addressed through changes to resource management agreements.

Similarly, the government's position on management regimes changed when an examination of their interests revealed extensive common ground between First Nation and government management objectives.

The Yukon government's desire to decentralize decision making and create meaningful opportunities for public participation in managing resources complemented First Nation interests in resource management, and served their interests more effectively than increasing settlement land holdings.

Government's adamant and inflexible opposition to any increases in the amount of settlement land was relaxed by focusing on the interests government sought to protect. Creating different categories of settlement land ownership and developing innovative regimes to govern public and private access to settlement lands secured government interests, and removed their inflexible opposition to additional settlement lands for First Nation communities whose particular needs and interests justified such increases.

Summary

As the process dug deeper into interest-based negotiations, especially through the various working groups, two important changes began to emerge.

First, as the parties began to understand and accept the legitimacy of each other's interests, each increasingly began to believe that a settlement was achievable. This in turn promoted a new commitment and creative energy.

Second, the parties increasingly developed a profound sense of the interconnectedness of all aspects of the emerging agreement. Accordingly, negotiators shifted from negotiating discrete parts of the agreement in isolation and began to develop methods of coordinating all elements of the settlement. Negotiations became less driven by simplistic battles over money, land, or harvesting rights, and began to focus on what was necessary to establish a viable social contract embracing all the elements necessary for Indian people to pursue their interests yet live and work in harmony with other residents of the North. This focus helped secure the support of many non-Indian interest groups, as negotiations began to reveal that First Nation communities sought solutions that reasonably accommodated competing interests.

An adversarial process, with its emphasis on winners and losers, on secret negotiations, on posturing, and on arbitrary compromises, would have prevented these two vital shifts in the kind and content of negotiations fostered by interest-based negotiation.

AN OPEN NEGOTIATION PROCESS

All the intensely divisive issues over the allocation and use of resources, all the hostility between diametrically opposed groups, between conservationists and industry, between conflicting commercial users fighting for priority, are caught up in land claims. Not a single resource issue or interest group escapes the reach of land claims. The resource-use issues raised in land claims generate acute interest among private, public, commercial, and non-commercial users of resources.

The resource-use questions that must be resolved by land claims negotiations are complex, are generally without appropriate precedent, and pose seemingly insurmountable obstacles to the achievement of broadly acceptable solutions.

Negotiations over resource issues, if exclusively restricted to a small group and conducted behind closed doors, will foster and have fostered fear, suspicion, and mistrust. Rumours fuelled by fear and mistrust spread quickly and become ardently believed. Even full disclosure is often incapable of dislodging assumptions moulded by fear and mistrust. A closed process whereby public awareness and opportunities for participation are minimal will generate opposition and mistrust to any proposed agreements from all quarters. Such negative public reaction can ultimately cause political leaders to hesitate in approving (and possibly to reject) proposed agreements.

Short cuts that minimize public participation usually produce disastrous consequences.

All parties knew there were significant risks in opening up the process. Thirteen years of unsuccessful negotiations had inflamed emotions on all sides. Every factor raised to argue for opening the process was countered by advocates of the *fait accompli* school of negotiations (keep the process primarily closed, out of public scrutiny, and deliver a final agreement that will then be sold to the public). Many argued that the complexities, extreme sensitivity of many issues, and rigid deadlines combined to deny the luxury of opening up the process. The proponents of an open process considered opening the process a precondition to achieving a fair agreement.

An open process was thought to impose the greatest risk to the Yukon parties, and particularly to Yukon First Nations. As one First Nation leader succinctly stated:

> We began negotiating against the Feds, then came the Yukon government, and now you want us to include every mining group, interest group, and everyone else in the Territory opposed to our claim. We've never had enough resources to fight the Feds, and now with even less resources you expect us to allow all these groups into negotiations. We'll be forever trying to fight our way to a settlement. After 13 years the Feds don't understand what we want; how can we expect in 18 months to make all these newcomers understand and accept a settlement. This is not a Yukon claim, it is a Yukon Indian claim — It is our business and our business alone — Keep them out and we'll get this thing done.

This powerful voice was joined by many government voices who feared an open process would foment racism and ignite public resentment.

While the process was not opened as far as it could have been, it was opened more than any other negotiating process involving comprehensive public issues. It was not opposition from the Yukon parties, but a lack of resources, time, and experience in how to meaningfully provide opportunities for public participation, that principally limited what could be done to open the process.

Yukon First Nations, with clearly the most to lose, often aggressively pursued strategies to open up the process to the public. The First Nation leader who once spoke eloquently against an open process eventually devoted time and energy to increasing public participation and awareness. The Indian people did not change their minds, but rather returned to their fundamental beliefs and primary objectives. They had always wanted a land claim that would be fair: fair to their long-standing moral and legal claims, and fair to other Yukon residents. They had nothing to hide. They were proud of their rights and heritage. Despite many past experiences that should have forever soured any prospect for a cooperative working relationship with the public and government, many of the Indian people supported opening the process, placing their trust in the public's ability to understand the legal and moral basis of their claim. Despite substantial grounds for scepticism, First Nation leaders at first cautiously and ultimately with greater zeal worked hard to facilitate public participation and to educate the public about their interests.

The Yukon Premier and his Cabinet from the outset supported an open process, but were sensitive to First Nation concerns and prudently worried about trade-offs between meeting negotiation deadlines and opening the process. A common front among the Yukon parties on opening up the process, supported by federal negotiators, neutralized pockets of persistent opposition from Ottawa. Numerous initiatives were tried to implement an open process; some failed and others were abandoned for lack of resources or time, but many became a permanent part of the process.

OPENING PROCESS TO INTEREST GROUPS

One early initiative almost killed the fledgling open negotiation process. A public forum on wildlife resources hosted by the Fish and Game Club drew a large crowd. A panel of negotiators representing all parties addressed a large audience of Indian and non-Indian people.

Interspersed among intelligent questions from the floor emerged the inflammatory passions that everyone feared. Hostile exchanges erupted. The racial undertone of the debate was regrettable and reprehensible. In the aftermath, accusations of a set-up flourished and the enthusiasm for an open process was severely threatened. Fortunately, some people viewed this unfortunate meeting not as evidence of the folly of an open process, but as an indication of how much more effort was required to remove the ignorance, suspicions, and fear surrounding resource-use negotiations and to build vital communication linkages among many parts of the community. The Indian people knew their families would always make the Yukon their home. They knew the racism exhibited at the meeting would render Yukon an unpleasant home for everyone. They set aside their anger and resentment and began anew to open the process.

Over the next three years, numerous meetings were held with the executive and members of the Fish and Game Club. These exchanges provided invaluable contributions that helped shape a fair settlement. Their support and acceptance of the Agreement in Principle and the participation of their President in a video explaining land claims helped plant the seeds of a positive relationship between aboriginal and non-aboriginal harvesters.

Much work lies ahead to maintain, develop, and utilize the potential of an emerging positive communication between aboriginal people and organizations such as the Fish and Game Club. The link built during the negotiations with such interest groups, with municipalities, and with other sectors of the public provided the basis for genuine attempts to search for solutions that earnestly sought to incorporate the interests of all resource users.

The following measures were taken to open up the process to interest groups.

Tri-party Briefings

Upon the request of any interest group, representatives of all three negotiating parties briefed members at plenary sessions or discussed the progress of negotiations on a more regular basis with the executive or a designated member of an interest group. These briefings were frank and constructive exchanges, dealing with issues currently under negotiation as well as those scheduled for future negotiations. As the walls of mistrust began to dissolve, the exchanges began to focus on seeking common ground and methods of working cooperatively towards solutions.

Invariably, the negotiating teams' inexperience in public relations, the persistent pressures of negotiation deadlines, and the weekly and often daily crises in negotiations sapped the time and resources needed to maintain the positive momentum generated by these exchanges.

The best relationships between interest groups and negotiating parties were created by the energy and commitment of key people within each interest group. These key people did much more than they realize (and more than most people realize) to help advance negotiations towards a settlement. Many of these interest group leaders experienced opposition and disapproval from their membership, but persisted in donating their time to enhancing awareness and providing constructive inputs.

Contact Persons

A member of the negotiating team was assigned as a contact person to each interest group. The responsibilities of the contact person were as follows:

- to schedule regular briefing sessions, especially before the negotiating agenda dealt with issues relevant to that interest group;
- to develop a counterpart contact person within the interest group to facilitate proactive communication;
- to answer all questions from the interest group (this was especially necessary to immediately dispel rumours or correct misunderstandings generated by media coverage);

- to keep track of inputs from interest groups to ensure they were properly considered in negotiations, and provide explanations for how their concerns were addressed; and

- to apprise interest groups of matters in negotiations relevant to their concerns.

This technique was in some instances an abject failure, in others a stunning success. Not all members of the negotiating team understood the importance of maintaining contact with interest groups. Most responded only to initiatives from the interest group. A proactive role by the contact person was clearly the most common element in the successful use of this technique.

To break down mistrust and to communicate a general desire to secure the involvement of interest groups, the negotiating process must pursue their involvement in an organized, regular, and proactive manner.

Problem-solving Session

When complex, technical questions were raised, sessions with experts from the interest group and from the negotiating process were arranged. The sessions provided opportunities to engage in detailed exchanges that immensely helped to create an understanding of the competing interests and to guide the search for common ground.

These sessions were invaluable; unfortunately, far too few of them were held. Once again a good initiative was lost in the pressure to meet deadlines, and was not accorded appropriate priority amidst the whirl of so many other distractions incessantly plaguing negotiations.

The following examples of the benefits gained from opening the process to interest groups barely begins to document the innumerable direct and indirect advantages of including all interests in some meaningful manner in negotiations.

Minimizes Misinformed Opposition

Aggressive and misinformed opposition from interest groups is the inevitable result of excluding meaningful interest group participation. In the past this opposition has caused costly delays in securing First Nation and government support for new positions on numerous resource-use issues that were essential to remove blockages in negotiations.

This opposition can delay government and First Nation ratification of agreements and undermine the will to ratify agreements previously endorsed in principle. Further, the persistent opposition of interest groups can over time dissipate government resolve to implement and carry out obligations in accord with the spirit and intent of the agreements.

No amount of publicity, no matter how extensive or clever, can offset the opposition of interest groups to an agreement developed without their input and foisted upon them.

Enhances Support

Meaningful rather than token participation from interest groups, especially when their contributions help shape final agreements, induces a sense of proprietorship in the agreement. This sense of proprietorship spawns a desire to make the agreement work, which is as important in securing the successful implementation of the agreement as any carefully drafted provision, and in some instances more important.

Improves Viability of Agreement

Inputs from interest groups on many occasions constructively changed the agreement. Without their unique perspective and input, many parts of the agreement would have been unworkable. Interest groups possess a knowledge and perspective distinct from that of both the government and First Nations. Their unique perspective is essential to gain a complete understanding of resource-use issues in order to design new resource management regimes that work.

Clarifies Government Concerns

Discussions with interest groups revealed that government had in several instances misunderstood the concerns of some of these groups, and had consequently erroneously developed positions to protect these concerns. A better understanding of interest groups assisted in building a better agreement, and in some instances removed the basis for government opposition to Indian interests in resource use.

Develops Common Ground between Interest Groups and First Nations

Exchanges with interest groups removed many of the unnecessary suspicions held by First Nations and interest groups about each other's motives and aspirations in land claims. These exchanges fostered understanding and trust, the essential ingredients in building regimes based upon shared responsibility for managing resources.

Many proposed management regimes were initially blocked by the inability of the parties to believe that their respective representatives could work cooperatively. As long as all parties were plagued by mistrust and misunderstanding, all proposed joint management regimes were subject to suspicion and opposition. The exchanges with interest groups significantly contributed to an awareness that Indian people and interest groups shared common interests.

Many important breakthroughs in land claims negotiations can be traced to the interaction of negotiating parties with interest groups.

Creates Positive Climate
for Experimentation

Negotiations were chronically stalled by the debate over the composition of joint management bodies. One side of the debate argued that First Nations and government representatives would blindly chant the special interests of their appointing authorities and never address resource issues on their merits. The other side of the debate, drawing more on faith in the ability of joint management bodies to generate cooperative working relationships, believed that, irrespective of past experiences, the deliberations would not be divided along the ethnic origins of the representatives. The representatives, it was argued, would develop a collective identity as a body responsible for managing resources; pride in their competence to deal with difficult issues would raise the quality of their deliberations, and surpass any blind adherence to the interests of the party that appointed them.

In developing new resource management initiatives, these theoretical debates over what would or would not happen are typical and produce an overabundance of pessimistic speculation. This speculation usually drives the search for solutions back to existing practices, limiting creativity and innovation. Pilot projects to test the practicality of new ideas immeasurably serve to replace speculation with fact. The pre-implementation of a Renewable Resource Council called for in the draft land claim agreement provided precisely this opportunity.

The agreement proposed establishing, within each First Nation Traditional Territory, a renewable resource council composed equally of representatives from the First Nation and government. The First Nation in Mayo wanted to establish this council before the agreement was ratified. It was a wonderful idea, advanced in part by the First Nation's enthusiasm to illustrate the degree of mutual trust and cooperation that had emerged in Mayo between Indian and non-Indian people.

During negotiations everyone had assumed that all representatives appointed by First Nations would be Indian people; this proved to be wrong. Equally, everyone had assumed that the initial meetings would be hampered by long-standing tensions and hostility between aboriginal and non-aboriginal harvesters: again, this proved to be wrong. Certainly problems will arise, but this bold pilot project marked a first step in demonstrating that most of the scepticism surrounding joint resource management bodies was ill founded. The pilot project was in part possible because of the positive exchanges with interest groups and within the Mayo community.

Fosters Perception of Fairness

To generate a widely based acceptance of land claims agreements, the agreement must not only be fair, but must be perceived to be fair. Since land claims agreements are long, complex, detailed, and overly legalistic documents, few people ever carefully scrutinize these agreements to assess the inherent fairness of the settlement. Further, since most parts of the agreement are interconnected, reading any one part of the agreement cannot afford a proper appreciation of whether the overall settlement fairly addresses all interests. Consequently, for the constituencies of all parties to believe the agreement will be fair, they must be able to believe the process creating it is fair. Widespread support for the process may be the only effective means of generating support for the agreement during its negotiation, ratification, and first years of implementation.

From the perspective of the interest groups, if the process is to be viewed as fair, it must benefit from the input of all competing interests. Providing an opportunity for interest groups to make constructive contributions, incorporating their input, or providing considered reasons for partial or whole rejection of their contributions was crucial in securing their understanding and acceptance of resource agreements. The interest groups that actively participated were more apt to believe the process was fair and consequently more inclined to believe in the overall fairness of the agreement. These interest groups were clearly the foremost supporters of the agreement and did more than other groups to exhort politicians and the public to support the settlement.

Generates New Ideas

Interest groups often injected new ideas that provoked fresh approaches to long-standing stalemates at the table. The value of including different perspectives was repeatedly proven by the constructive inputs of interest groups.

OPENING THE PROCESS TO THE MEDIA

The media possess a frightening power to influence and shape public opinion. In this case, they played a significant role in improving public understanding and perception of land claims. Over the course of five years of negotiations, some aspect of land claims was always "in the news" and was often the major news story of the day. During all of this coverage, only in a few isolated incidents did the media significantly create or exacerbate problems in negotiations. Most members of the media demonstrated a professional understanding of the potentially racial and explosive nature of negotiations.

In view of the lack of time and resources reporters have to research issues in depth, their penchant for controversy, conflict, or "bad news", and the inexperience of many Yukon reporters, much more trouble had been anticipated from the content and tone of media coverage. There are many possible reasons why the Yukon media performed significantly better in covering land claims in the Yukon than in other jurisdictions.

(a) Most of the media were aware that the best interests of the community would not be served by highlighting or heightening conflict in order to create a "story". They understood the fundamental importance of moving the public debate away from personalities, from irrational and potentially racist diatribes, and into constructive dialogues on the merits of the issues.

(b) The presence of some outstanding people in the media community set a level of professional conduct that discouraged superficial analysis and tawdry reporting. As unfortunately destructive and misinformed as some stories were, they were the rare exceptions, or the work of the same few people whose preference for sensationalism over facts prevailed from time to time.

(c) To promote constructive public debate on vital public issues, the public must be armed with accurate information. The media's contribution to such public debates can be enhanced by their in-depth understanding of issues. To this end, a full-day workshop with the media was held early in the process and shorter versions were repeated throughout negotiations. These workshops were organized by all the parties, and most of the media attended. Presentations by negotiators at these sessions concentrated on essential background information.

(d) After each major main table negotiation, negotiators held briefing sessions with the media to update them on progress in negotiations.

(e) On a daily basis, communication coordinators tried to ensure that any question from the media was quickly relayed to the negotiator with the expertise to provide a full answer.

One is tempted to conclude that the overall positive and professional coverage was derived from the time the media invested in understanding the context and background of issues in land claims, and from opening the process up to the media.

OPENING THE PROCESS TO THE PUBLIC

Ensuring that the public is properly informed and afforded reasonable opportunities for their input is a precondition to reaching and successfully implementing agreements that significantly influence the life of a community. This principle, enthusiastically and widely endorsed in theory, in the heat of negotiations is often readily ignored. Agreements, negotiated without the meaningful participation of persons whose interests are significantly affected, are destined to precipitate more problems than they resolve, and will soon be rejected or forced through further rounds of negotiations to accommodate the interests excluded in the first round.

All parties began negotiations in 1985 firmly committed to keeping the public informed and to developing reasonable opportunities for public input.

Despite some bad experiences, insufficient resources, and the pressure to conduct several negotiation sessions in Ottawa, the parties throughout negotiations strived to maintain their original commitment to open the process to the Yukon public.

Certainly more could have and should have been done, but the efforts by all parties to keep the public informed were remarkable given the limits on time and resources and the inexperience of both the public and the parties in an open negotiation process.

There were and still are few, if any, precedents to follow in Canada for successfully opening the negotiation process to the public. Of the numerous measures taken to open the process to the public, the following represent what best served to promote meaningful public input.

Communications Coordinator

Each party hired a communications coordinator to develop an overall approach to communicating with the public, interest groups, various government agencies, and the media. To avoid turning this position into that of a public relations officer, whose primary purpose was to serve as a buffer between the public and the process or simply as a supplier of highly edited and packaged information, the communications coordinator was assigned the following responsibilities:

(a) to discipline negotiators to include time in negotiations schedules for all activities designed for opening the process to the public;

(b) to plan and implement an aggressive, ambitious strategy to promote public input;

(c) to monitor public awareness and direct negotiations to invest time in any sector of the community where public information is deficient, and

(d) to ensure that any public question requiring a detailed answer is promptly assigned to a negotiator best able to respond directly and fully.

The communications coordinators were assigned responsibility for opening the process but were not accorded the status, priority, or resources necessary to fully succeed. Too often, the pressure of negotiations diminished the attention and resources needed by coordinators to maintain an open public process. Despite these problems, the coordinators miraculously kept the process open to the public and met all public inquiries for information about land claims.

Public Meetings

Each time that main table negotiations were held in a community, the parties attempted to arrange a tri-party public meeting hosted by the Chief and Mayor. Negotiators were always available to attend public meetings organized by interest groups. Some interest groups were very effective in taking the initiative to organize meetings.

Open Houses

In the beginning, two evenings a week were set aside for the public to attend an open house on land claims in Whitehorse. Negotiators were on hand with maps and other information to answer questions and informally discuss any public concerns.

Despite extensive publicity, the land claim staff usually outnumbered the public. On several occasions, when the media had given extensive exposure to particularly sensitive or controversial issues and several people had publically and vigorously criticized some aspect of the claim, a large crowd was expected. Sadly, this large crowd never materialized. In some cases, critics of land claims failed to use the opportunity to express their concerns directly or to invest time in ascertaining the facts. The open house evenings did provide an invaluable input for the public, and many public inquiries at the open house sessions were instrumental in improving the practicality of agreements.

Community Visits

The Yukon Premier, at critical times in the process, attended public and interest group meetings in every community throughout the Yukon. Similarly, the executive of the Council for Yukon Indians attended meetings within First Nation communities, as well as open public meetings and interest group sessions.

The commitment to an open process was made and enforced by both Yukon principals. The importance of engaging the principals directly in exchanges with the public during negotiations cannot be sufficiently stressed. Most of the anticipated disadvantages of directly engaging the principals in public consultation during negotiations never materialized, while many unanticipated advantages did occur. The positive change in public attitudes over the proposed agreements governing resource uses was significantly fostered by the active participation of Yukon principals in public meetings during negotiations.

Publications and Programs

A variety of innovative published material and radio and television programs were used to promote public awareness and input. It is difficult to know what did or did not work. Perhaps materials produced by communications experts that were simple, straightforward, and frank were more effective than the detailed, complex handiwork of negotiators and lawyers.

A video dramatization of life before and after claims, and several other creative publications by the Yukon Indians, were particularly effective. Resource issues provide ideal subject matters for plays, moots, and other participatory methods of public education.

School Programs

A course on land claims was developed for public schools, but unfortunately not fully implemented. Negotiators attended classes in community schools throughout the Yukon, and students were invited to attend negotiation sessions.

Despite numerous discussions about the importance of engaging schools and youth in the negotiation process, not enough was done to effectively involve them. As the full impact of changes introduced by land claims will not be felt for several years, land claims agreements are arguably just as, if not more, important to students than to others.

Summary

In a society that has grown increasingly dependent upon government to take responsibility for community issues, the desire and skills essential for participating in public issues have atrophied. It is not simply that the public has become apathetic, but rather that as the opportunities and challenges for public participation have gradually eroded over many years, so have the skills and habits of active, positive, and productive public participation.

Many lessons were learned from attempts to meaningfully engage public participation in land claims negotiations, but one lesson stands out. Once convinced that they are not merely being patronized or manipulated, but genuinely sought out for their input, members of the public will provide invaluably constructive inputs. But they have been manipulated so often that they are understandably suspicious of any attempt to engage their interest.

What ought to be remembered is not the sparsely attended public meetings, nor the few misinformed, irrational, and highly emotional outbursts, nor the anger, nor the racism, but the new linkages forged between Indian and non-Indian people, the emerging cooperative working relationship of First Nations with municipalities and with the business community, and the important, constructive inputs from numerous members of the public. Without an open process, most of these important gains would never have been realized.

The surprising public support for the process and for a fair settlement was generated primarily by the effort of all parties to open the process to the public. Whether or not the public actually participated, knowing they could did much to reduce suspicion and mistrust over land claims. Engaging the public may protract the negotiation process but immeasurably improves the longevity, viability, acceptance, and practicality of the settlement.

A closed process is forced to "sell" a massive agreement to a suspicious public that has not had an opportunity to appreciate what or why concessions were made. A closed process generates opposition to the agreement derived from criticism of the process, or arising simply from interest groups who feel their legitimate concerns were not "heard".

Including the public within the negotiation process removes most of the "surprises" within an agreement and thereby generates public understanding and acceptance of many parts of the agreement during negotiations.

OPENING PROCESS TO PUBLIC SERVANTS

Too often, too much reliance is placed upon "negotiators" from outside government, or upon "specialized public servants" to negotiate land claims agreements. In both cases the excessive reliance upon negotiators excludes departmental officials from any first-hand experience in negotiations. This exclusion builds several serious deficiencies into the process.

The minimal role departmental officials play in negotiations creates the "baton-passing" syndrome. Negotiators, after many strenuous years in far-away places, triumphantly return with an agreement to pass on to line departments for implementation. During implementation, the negotiators are usually long gone, perhaps negotiating yet another agreement to pass along to line departments. They are not available to ensure that the spirit and intent of the agreement are properly translated into implementation plans. No matter how much skill and time is invested in the language of agreements, there will always be room for different interpretations and for confusion.

By being intimately involved in constructing an agreement, a public servant acquires an understanding of what was intended and of which interests each party sought to protect or advance through the concessions that produced the agreement. More important, involvement in constructing the agreement instills the pride and responsibility of ownership. A determination to "make it work", and thereby demonstrate its inherent wisdom and practicality, is derived from personal involvement in shaping the agreement. The pride emanating from a sense of ownership promotes a commitment to explain and "sell" the agreement within government and to all interest groups. If the representatives of all parties responsible for the implementation of the agreement had a significant hand in negotiating the agreement, the prospects for a successful implementation would be significantly increased. "Hired gun" negotiators have a role, but too often they usurp the equally (and arguably more) important role of departmental officials in negotiations.

In Yukon negotiations, departmental officials were included through regular briefings and by participating both in caucuses and at the table. Contact persons were established within the negotiating team and within the department to maintain active communication.

Working Groups

The most significant and productive involvement of public servants occurred through the working groups established by the main negotiating table to work on specific issues. All resource-use and management agreements were produced by these working groups. Without them the innovative breakthroughs would never have occurred, and agreements on many key resource-use issues would not have been realized.

Working groups provided an opportunity to incorporate the unique circumstances of the Yukon into the process of building what became known as "made in Yukon" solutions. The principles of cooperative bargaining were reflected more in the practices of the working groups than in any other part of the negotiation process. Unquestionably, these principles were instrumental in establishing the basis for all agreements governing resource use.

In addition to their unparalleled contributions to the substantive work in building agreements, the working groups improved the overall negotiation process in the following ways.

Reduced Reliance upon Chief Negotiators

In light of the complexities and breadth of land claim negotiations, chief negotiators should function primarily as managers or supervisors of the process. Their negotiating role should be restricted to matters that cannot be resolved by persons with relevant expertise, to pulling the final pieces of major agreements together, and to resolving major process problems.

If the negotiating process revolves exclusively around chief negotiators, the process will be dependent upon the health of each negotiator, their availability, and the quality of relationships among chief negotiators. Consequently, such a process rests on very fragile foundations and cannot continually maintain progress in negotiations over extended periods.

Land claim negotiations impose far too much pressure and far too many demands to avoid disruptive confrontations among chief negotiators, or to avoid demands that divert the attention of one or more chief negotiators away from negotiations. Working groups reduce reliance upon chief negotiators and upon main table negotiations that can often dissolve into posturing and important but time-consuming outbursts of frustration and anger.

Expanded Sense of Ownership in Agreement

By spreading the workload into many different hands, working groups build a broadly based sense of pride and ownership in the agreement. This sense of proprietorship is crucial in securing support for agreement in many different quarters, and in successfully implementing the agreement.

Mutual Trust and Respect

A small group working diligently and continuously on matters within its expertise develops a collective pride in its work and generates mutual respect and trust. Without these personal factors, a frank and full exchange of what must be done to appease powerful dissent within their respective constituencies would not be possible.

The emergence of a positive working environment replaces partisan counterproductive debates with constructive and free-flowing exchanges directed to fearlessly exploring new ideas on their merits, irrespective of their authorship. It was exchanges of this calibre that produced the breakthroughs in the planning, water, wildlife, and impact assessment agreements.

Constant Source of Good News

Momentum in negotiations is indispensable to reaching agreements. To sustain positive momentum, all parties must feel that progress is being made and have tangible evidence to warrant an optimistic perspective. Since a dozen or more working groups were functioning at the same time, at least one was likely to report significant progress at each main table session. Riding on past successes or upon their collective dedication and determination to continue searching for answers, most groups, even when reporting no further progress, reflected a confident optimism that more hard work would likely produce progress.

By advancing the claim on so many fronts at the same time, working groups made sufficient progress in at least one area to prevent even major blockages in other areas from severely undermining the overall positive momentum in negotiations.

Bridge over Cultural Differences

The failure to fully appreciate the fundamental differences in perspective and values between white and aboriginal culture constantly hampers communication in land claims negotiations. Aboriginal people have a good understanding of the dominant white culture, but government understanding of aboriginal culture is significantly less. Aboriginal people painstakingly try to explain how many of their interests are based on their culture. A government's inability to accept or understand these connections builds resentment, anger, and frustration among aboriginal people.

The environment of the working group provided both the time and the intimacy for more meaningful cross-cultural exchanges. A much greater understanding of cultural differences and a better appreciation of linkages between culture and the interests pursued by aboriginal people in negotiations was gained through the working groups. This improved cross-cultural communication was particularly significant in resolving competing interests in resource use.

Mix of Expertise

The working groups provided an opportunity for mixing expertise based upon traditional, local, and scientific knowledge in order to work closely together in developing principles and structures to manage resources. The extended time working groups spent together facilitated a growing appreciation of the contribution such different sources of knowledge could make to moulding a fair and workable management regime.

The reputation of chief negotiators for distorting, confusing, and rendering complex what is regarded by others as simple information is legendary. Working groups enabled experts from all parties to avoid reliance upon chief negotiators as intermediaries to negotiate questions beyond the expertise of the negotiators.

The understanding and trust developed in working groups among the very persons most likely to be responsible for implementing the specific parts of agreements immensely benefits all parties.

Summary

Numerous problems were associated with working groups, but these did not offset the working groups' overwhelming contributions towards reaching agreements.

The single most serious deficiency of working groups was the inability of Yukon First Nations to fully staff and support their participation within those groups. This topic will not be discussed here, but significant deficiencies in the manner and amount of government funding for First Nations to carry on negotiations perpetuated adversarial attitudes and repeatedly drained the process of positive momentum.

Too often, the same First Nation resource people had to service numerous working groups. Their inability to afford adequate time to all working groups severely delayed the work of many groups, and the pressure of handling the onerous workload imposed by several working groups hindered their ability to carry out the in-depth analysis and creative thinking that is essential to the success of working groups.

On the government side, key resource people were often expected to maintain their full-time responsibilities within their departments in addition to the responsibilities imposed by the working groups. For many, an impossible situation emerged as their own Minister hounded them to attend to departmental priorities, while Ministers and other officials responsible solely for land claims hammered them with the pressing needs of negotiations. Many public servants, recognizing the historic importance of land claims, simply donated personal time and magically answered all demands of the land claim process. But resource issues are especially complex and demand more time and attention than can ever be squeezed from public servants forced to "moonlight" to participate.

Like the villagers who responded once too often to the false cry of "wolf" from the lonely shepherd, public servants had too many times over almost seventeen years heard the false "cry" for help from negotiators who had proclaimed that a settlement was imminent. Public servants could not continually postpone their internal departmental priorities to donate their time to the changing deadlines and intensity of land claim negotiations. The ebb and flow of negotiations caused by changes in government, in Ministers, and by incessant battles over federal funding for negotiations made it very difficult for public servants to maintain high levels of input or to retain their enthusiasm. Consequently, government participation in some working groups was often inconsistent in quality and intensity.

The working groups that focused on resource issues were blessed with excellent people dedicated to finding solutions that would work and generate broadly based support. These groups succeeded despite a lack of resources, and illustrated why the process should have invested more attention and resources in working groups. Unfortunately, the potential to open up working groups to public participation was not adequately explored.

Working groups, where cooperative bargaining principles were given the most prominent play, helped shift the process away from adversarial attitudes and practices.

CONCLUSION

Many adversarial elements in negotiations contributed to credibility gaps between First Nation communities and their negotiators. Doubts entertained about First Nation negotiators by their own people affected progress in the negotiations and pushed some leaders to quit or contemplate resigning at key stages in the process. None of this was necessary. The fault lay with the process, not with the First Nation negotiators.

Government, reliant upon senior bureaucrats with limited exposure to First Nation communities and to the dynamics of aboriginal negotiations, fails to appreciate that a process predominately designed to serve government interests and impose unnecessarily onerous difficulties on First Nation leaders undermines the overall objective of concluding a lasting and fair settlement.

The process for negotiations has an impact not only upon the ability to achieve a settlement, but also upon the acceptance, workability, and inherent fairness of that settlement. The process affects the readiness of all parties to ratify the agreement, and the good will the parties bring to its implementation. The mood, attitudes, and practices established by the negotiation process profoundly influence the ongoing relationships of the parties during the critical initial years of the agreement. If the negotiations instil resentment, suspicion, and mistrust, the early years of the agreement are bound to be crippled by these same forces.

Despite the phenomenal importance of the process, parties jump into negotiations with little attention paid to designing a process that minimizes the obstacles to reaching an agreement and maximizes the potential to develop a fair and lasting agreement.

The relative merits of cooperative versus adversarial negotiations, and the case for rejecting the notion that one overall approach fits all negotiations, cannot be properly addressed here. All negotiations must commence by addressing these issues, which fundamentally affect the negotiation process. Short-circuiting negotiations over these matters will ultimately protract negotiations on substantive issues, or altogether preclude the attainment of a workable settlement.

The modest investment of time and energy needed to shift the negotiating process from an adversarial to a cooperative process and to open the process to the public, interest groups, and media was instrumental in reaching an agreement that had eluded the Yukon for two decades.

THE INUVIALUIT FINAL AGREEMENT AND RESOURCE-USE CONFLICTS: CO-MANAGEMENT IN THE WESTERN ARCTIC AND FINAL DECISIONS IN OTTAWA

Michael Robinson and Lloyd Binder

The Inuvialuit Final Agreement (IFA), signed on 5 June 1984, contains the agreement between Canada and the Inuvialuit to settle the land claim of the Inuit of the Western Arctic of the Northwest Territories. Three goals of the Inuvialuit are outlined under the Principles of the IFA:[1]

1. to preserve Inuvialuit cultural identity and values within a changing northern society;

2. to enable Inuvialuit to be equal and meaningful participants in the northern and national economy and society; and

3. to protect and preserve the Arctic wildlife, environment, and biological productivity.

The origins of the Inuvialuit land claims can be traced back to the formation of the Committee for Original Peoples Entitlement (COPE), created in 1970 to articulate and communicate the concern of native people in the Northwest Territories over the style and pace of planned resource development projects. A single historic incident on Banks Island highlights the need for COPE's creation: a resource exploration firm undertook exploration on the island without any consultation with the Bankslanders. An eventual confrontation led to a threat to file an injunction against the resource company, but:

> the government lied to both them and the Canadian public about what was happening, and successfully manoeuvred the Bankslanders into dropping the injunction when it was clearly against their interests to do so. In a situation where there was neither the scientific basis for predicting the impact of exploration on the Banks Island environment, nor any attempt to establish this basis, industry and government blandly denied the possibility of any adverse consequences. Indeed, those officials who knew the least about environmental matters were the quickest to make these denials.
>
> In a situation of conflict between native people and resource developers over land use, what became evident was that the government offered inadequate research, inadequate regulations, inadequate enforcement, inadequate contingency plans, inadequate consultation

---

1   Canada. Dept. of Indian Affairs and Northern Development, *The Western Arctic Claim: The Inuvialuit Final Agreement* (Ottawa: Dept. of Indian Affairs and Northern Development, 1984) ss.11(27), (28) and (29).

and inadequate compensation. In short, native people were threatened with the loss of their land, their livelihood and their way of life with no assurance of any reasonable alternative.

The Banks Island incident was not isolated; it was only the most dramatic. Such conflicts over land use have probably been the single most important factor in mobilizing native people to seek a land claims settlement.[2]

The next major impetus to the process of claims settlement came from the split Supreme Court of Canada decision in the so-called *Nishga*[3] case in British Columbia, and the eventual political decision by the federal government to settle comprehensive land claims. But the critical turning point, from a northerner's point of view, came with the forum provided under the "Berger Hearings", the Mackenzie Valley Pipeline Inquiry, in 1973-75. In these community hearings, native northerners discovered the power of vocal, coordinated effort. Joint management of northern resources may be seen to have begun at that time.

INUVIALUIT STRUCTURES

The IFA is the legal document that describes how the Inuvialuit participate in the management of renewable and non-renewable resources in the western Arctic. The IFA created two major and parallel structures of Inuvialuit government: the Inuvialuit Game Council (IGC) and the Inuvialuit Regional Corporation (IRC). The former deals with renewable resources, the latter with financial and commercial issues.

The IGC is made up of Inuvialuit members from the Hunter and Trapper Committees of the six communities in the Inuvialuit Settlement Region (see Figure 1). It appoints the "Inuvialuit members for all joint government/ Inuvialuit bodies having an interest in wildlife."[4] The IGC represents the collective Inuvialuit interest in wildlife and, as such, advises government on policy, legislation, regulation, and administration dealing with wildlife conservation, research, management, and enforcement. It performs these functions through the different advisory councils, or directly. It also advises government on the Canadian position with respect to wildlife for international purposes.

The IGC should be seen as an "alter ego" to the more development-oriented Inuvialuit Regional Corporation. Interestingly, the relationship

---

2   Peter J. Usher & G. Noble, *New Directions in Northern Policy Making: Reality or Myth?* (Inuvik, N.W.T.: COPE, 1975).

3   *Calder* v. *A.G. of B.C.*, [1973] S.C.R. 313.

4   *Supra*, note 1, s.14(74)(a).

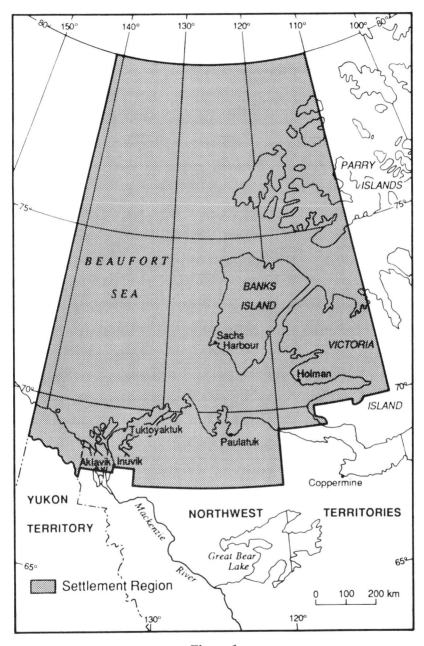

Figure 1

The Inuvialuit Settlement Region

between the two bodies is not specified within the IFA (see Figure 2). It might be said that the creation of the two bodies instituted a positive internal dichotomy or tension.

In addition to the IGC and the IRC, the IFA established five co-management boards and committees: the Fisheries Joint Management Committee, the Wildlife Management Advisory Council (Northwest Territories), the Wildlife Management Advisory Council (North Slope), the Environmental Impact Screening Committee, and the Environmental Impact Review Board. The Inuvialuit representation on each of these committees is 50 percent, with federal and territorial government representation comprising the other half. In each case, the chair is appointed by government but approved by the Inuvialuit. The only exception is the Fisheries Joint Management Committee, the chair of which is appointed by the members.

Wildlife Management Advisory Council
(Northwest Territories)

The Wildlife Management Advisory Council (Northwest Territories) (WMAC[NWT]) is responsible for all wildlife issues within the western Arctic region, advising both the territorial and federal governments with respect to wildlife harvest quotas. The total allowable harvests for game species are determined by the WMAC(NWT) "according to conservation criteria and such other factors as it considers appropriate."[5] The WMAC(NWT) "make[s] its recommendations to the appropriate minister, who shall, if he differs in opinion from the Council, set forth to the Council his reasons and afford the Council a further consideration of the matter."[6]

In setting of the total allowable harvest, "conservation shall be the only consideration" and "where the Inuvialuit have the exclusive right to harvest, they shall be entitled to harvest the total allowable harvest."[7] However, there is also a "greater certainty" provision for subsistence quotas to meet the needs of the Inuvialuit, within the total allowable game harvests. Provision is made to allow other native groups representation on the Council, especially those groups adjacent to the western Arctic region.[8]

An example of the role the Council has played was provided by Andy Carpenter of IGC at a recent conference:

---

5   *Supra*, note 1, s.14(36)(a).

6   *Supra*, note 1, s.14(36)(a).

7   *Supra*, note 1, s.14(36)(b).

8   *Supra*, note 1, ss.14(52) and (53).

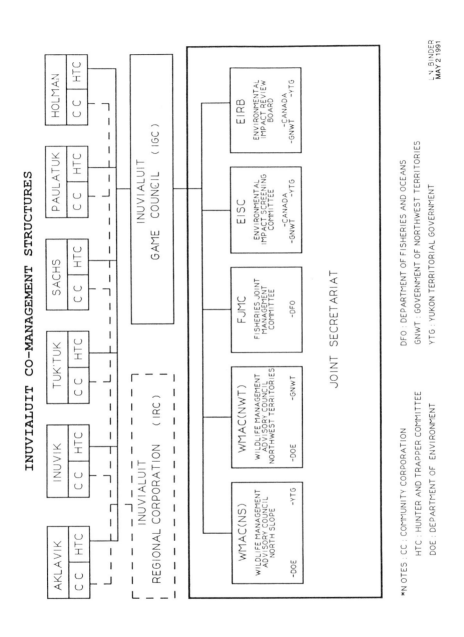

Figure 2

Inuvialuit Regional Corporation

In 1988 the establishment of a harvest quota for grizzly bear ... was initiated in the ISR, and for the first time in Canada, a native organization (and user group) enacted wildlife regulations under government Statutes ... With the WMAC(NWT) acting as a facilitator, consultations occurred between the government and the Inuvialuit until a consensus was reached ... At all times the WMAC(NWT) provided a forum for the government and the Inuvialuit to interact.[9]

Wildlife Management Advisory Council (North Slope)

The Wildlife Management Advisory Council (North Slope) (WMAC[NS]) is the Yukon counterpart to the NWT Council. The Inuvialuit and other native harvesting interests form one-half of the management membership.[10] The Yukon North Slope falls "under a special conservation regime whose dominant purpose is the conservation of wildlife, habitat and traditional native use."[11] Two parks were also created by the IFA: the Northern Yukon National Park and the Herschel Island Territorial Park.[12] The WMAC(NS) is involved in their management, and the Inuvialuit retain rights of harvest in both parks.[13]

An annual conference is held "to promote discussion among natives, governments, and the private sector with respect to management co-ordination for the Yukon North Slope."[14] It is something akin to a command performance for government, with industry and other special-interest representation as invited by the chairperson of the conference. The chair alternates between the Yukon and the Inuvialuit governments. The conference serves a very useful function as a forum for clarifying issues and interests of the different parties concerned with the North Slope of the Yukon.

Fisheries Joint Management Committee

The Fisheries Joint Management Committee (FJMC) is bipartite, composed equally of members of the federal and Inuvialuit governments, and, as noted earlier, its chairperson is appointed by the four committee members. The FJMC recommends subsistence and harvestable quotas for marine mammals and for sports or commercial fisheries. Any variations to or

---

9   Andy Carpenter, Bruce M.V. Hanbidge & Richard M. Binder, "Co-management of Wildlife in the Western Arctic: An Inuvialuit Perspective", Paper presented at Renewable Resources Colloquium (Calgary: Arctic Institute of North America, 1991).

10   *Supra*, note 1, s.12(50).

11   *Supra*, note 1, s.12(2).

12   *Supra*, note 1, ss.12(5)-(19).

13   *Supra*, note 1, s.12(24)(c).

14   *Supra*, note 1, s.12(57).

rejections of these recommendations by the Minister of Fisheries and Oceans must be communicated to the FJMC within thirty days, for its further recommendation. Research assessment and monitoring projects are also sponsored by the FJMC, using both scientific and traditional resource-user expertise in their undertaking. It is important that, under s.14(5) of the IFA, "[t]he relevant knowledge and experience of both the Inuvialuit and the scientific communities should be employed in order to achieve conservation." This is one mandate in the IFA for co-management in action.

A recent project under way at this time is the Beaufort Sea Beluga Management Plan,[15] which the FJMC is developing with the Hunter and Trapper Committees of Aklavik, Inuvik, and Tuktoyaktuk. Sustainable harvest levels, conservation guidelines, draft bylaws, and regulations are being established with an enforcement mechanism.

A joint management agreement is also being pursued with the Inupiat of Alaska. If the initiative is successful, this will be the second such international agreement with the Inupiat on wildlife: a Polar Bear Management Agreement was finalized in 1988 to protect and maintain the population while harvesting along sustainability criteria. The IGC and the North Slope Borough Fish and Game Management Committee were commended by the United States Fish and Wildlife Service and presented with an award for this work.[16]

Other Initiatives under the IGC and Related Boards and Councils

At the community level, a variety of initiatives are being pursued or have already been achieved:

- a voluntary quota has been established for char fishing in the Aklavik and Paulatuk communities of the ISR;

- a voluntary restriction has been set in Sachs Harbour for harvesting of Peary caribou on Banks Island;

- a community plan has been developed in Paulatuk for conservation and management of the renewable resources in the area; and

- community plans for the other five Inuvialuit communities are to be finalized over the next two years.

An appropriate conclusion to this section on renewable resources management is provided by the following:

---

15   Beaufort Sea Beluga Management Plan [draft].

16   Inuvialuit Game Council and North Slope Borough Fish and Game Management Committee, Polar Bear Management in the Southern Beaufort Sea [draft, 1988; xerox copy on file at Arctic Institute of North America, The University of Calgary].

It has been shown that co-management of renewable resources allows the Inuvialuit to play a meaningful role while still continuing to benefit from government management expertise. Co-management has been proven to be a system that works for the benefit of Inuvialuit, the land and its wildlife.[17]

Environmental Impact Screening Committee and Environmental Impact Review Board

The IFA establishes a two-stage mechanism and process for assessment and review of non-renewable resource development projects in the Inuvialuit Settlement Region (which includes the North Slope of the Yukon Territory). An Environmental Impact Screening Committee (EISC) determines "if the proposed development could have a significant negative environmental impact" and recommends one of the following: that it may proceed, that it has deficiencies that warrant a "termination of its consideration," or that it be assessed and reviewed.[18] Under "Wildlife Impact Assessment", s.13(7), projects are referred to the Screening Committee to determine whether there could be significant negative impacts on wildlife. The Inuvialuit may also, under s.11(1)(c), request environmental impact screening. Should the screening process indicate that further assessment is needed, projects are referred to the Environmental Impact Review Board (EIRB), which recommends whether or not the proposed development should proceed and under what constraints.[19]

The next section of the paper deals expressly with the review process, which "for greater certainty" does not restrict "the power or obligation of Government to carry out environmental impact assessment and review under the laws and policies of Canada."[20]

THE EIRB IN PRACTICE: KULLUK DRILLING PROGRAM CASE STUDY

Legislative Framework

The EIRB is the key co-management board in the cluster of committees and boards formed by the IFA and the subsequent *Western Arctic (Inuvaluit) Claims Settlement Act.*[21] Because the IFA is a land claims settlement pursuant to s.35 of the *Constitution Act, 1982*,[22] it is affirmed as an existing

---

17   *Supra*, note 9.

18   *Supra*, note 1, s.11(130).

19   *Supra*, note 1, s.11(18).

20   *Supra*, note 1, s.11(32).

21   *Western Arctic (Inuvialuit) Claims Settlement Act*, S.C. 1984, c.24.

22   *Constitution Act, 1982*, being Schedule B of the *Canada Act, 1982*, (U.K.) 1982, c.11.

aboriginal right and its terms are given preferential status over all federal and territorial laws applicable within the Inuvialuit Settlement Region.[23] The IFA thus empowers the EIRB to conduct its reviews and to make its recommendations to the government authority authorized to approve a given development. Section 11(24) of the IFA sets out the range of recommendation options available:

> The Review Board shall expeditiously review all projects referred to it and on the basis of the evidence and information before it shall recommend whether or not the development should proceed and, if it should, on what terms and conditions, including mitigative and remedial measures. The Review Board may also recommend that the development should be subject to further assessment and review and, if so, the data or information required.

Clearly the EIRB does not have the final say on development proposals in the Inuvialuit Settlement Region. The final decision always rests with the federal government authority competent to decide the issue, and ultimately the capacity to decide to develop or not to develop resides with the Minister of Indian Affairs and Northern Development (DIAND) or with the federal Cabinet.

If the recommendations of the EIRB to the appropriate competent government authority are unacceptable, or if the authority wishes to modify a recommendation, s.11(29) of the IFA prescribes that reasons must be made public in writing within thirty days of the EIRB decisions.

Given the above, an EIRB panel functions as a classic administrative tribunal constrained by the doctrine of natural justice, presumably guided by the original spirit and intent that underlay the negotiation of the IFA, and infused by the traditional wisdom and professional experience brought to bear by its members, who include a chairperson, two Inuvialuit Game Council appointees, and one nominee of either the Government of the Northwest Territories or the Government of the Yukon. The EIRB has recently stated its intention not to be "legalistic and rigid in its approach and in its practices and procedures."[24] Furthermore, it does not intend to be "restricted by a rigid application of the rules of evidence."[25]

Since its creation in 1985, the EIRB has heard only two referrals from the EISC: the 1989 ISSERK 1-15 Drilling Program proposed by Esso, Chevron, *et al.*; and the 1990-92 KULLUK Drilling Program proposed by Gulf Canada Resources Limited. The ISSERK proposal concerned a one-well winter oil exploration drilling program within the land-fast ice zone adjoining the

---

23   Environmental Impact Review Board, *Public Review of the Gulf Canada Resources Limited KULLUK Drilling Program* (Inuvik, N.W.T., 1990) at 1.

24   *Id.*, at 11.

25   *Id.*, at 12.

Tuktoyaktuk peninsula. The EIRB approved the ISSERK proposal because it was satisfied that should a blowout occur, a relief well could be drilled from the fixed-ice bench, and in such an eventuality damages to wildlife and hunter livelihood could be contained and managed. The costs of wildlife and loss-of-livelihood compensation were also assessed as being within acceptable limits, and Esso, Chevron, *et al.* were found to be financially able to bear these projected compensation costs.[26] The EIRB was especially impressed with the Wildlife Compensation Agreement negotiated between the IGC and Esso.

The KULLUK Drilling Program

Armed with the experience base of the ISSERK review, the EIRB was faced, in 1990, with its second referral from the EISC — the Gulf KULLUK Drilling Program Application (DPA). Unlike ISSERK, the KULLUK proposal contemplated a series of wells over a three-year period. Moreover, the proposed KULLUK DPA was to be based in the Amauligak structure in the offshore Beaufort, in a shear zone between the land-fast ice and pack ice where the potential oil release and damage from a blowout is much greater. In the language of the EIRB, "this Gulf application presents the Board with issues not previously considered by it — namely, the acceptability of blowout risks in cases where large quantities of spilled oil may enter open water and eventually reach shorelines."[27]

The Clash of Cultures

The KULLUK proposal is really the first strong test of the co-management philosophy enshrined in the IFA. It pits the best of the industrial economy's technology against shearing ice floes, extremes of temperature, and the risk of oiling the pristine, biologically sensitive environment of the Beaufort Sea. It also challenges the culture and traditional wisdom of the Inuvialuit, who for perhaps four thousand years[28] have harvested the resources of the Beaufort littoral zone. In KULLUK, we have a superb example of the perceived threats inherent in offshore Arctic drilling, which no doubt underlay the creation of the EIRB and which pose a direct challenge to the concept of co-management. Can the process effectively review without bias a worst-case scenario that, in the opinion of the EIRB's consultant, could yield "up to a volume four to six times that spilled from the Exxon Valdez"?[29]

---

26   Environmental Impact Review Board, *Public Review of the Esso, Chevron et al., ISSERK 1-15 Drilling Program* (Inuvik, N.W.T., 1989).

27   *Supra*, note 23, at 9.

28   Personal communication with Dr. Peter Schledermann, Arctic Institute of North America, Calgary, April 1991.

29   *Supra*, note 23, at 26 to 27.

The Inuvialuit Game Council appointees to the EIRB Review Panel for KULLUK were Calvin Pokiak and Albert Elias, both of whom are men of the land, competent guides and hunters. In addition, Mr. Pokiak had sat as a member in the ISSERK EIRB review. The Government of Canada's choice for the KULLUK panel was Ewan Cotterill, long-term public servant, once vice-president of Dome Petroleum, and currently a Yellowknife-based consultant. Mr. Cotterill was also a member of the ISSERK panel. The Government of the Yukon panel choice was Mike Stutter, the designated Yukon board member and a vice-chairman of the Yukon Territory Water Board. The chair of the KULLUK panel was James Livingstone, who also chaired the ISSERK panel. While currently president of a Calgary-based oil industry service company, he was for twelve years an employee of Gulf Canada Limited, the proponent of the KULLUK program.

It is hard to imagine a more Hegelian dialectic than that presented by the KULLUK panel, with the possible exception of Mr. Livingstone. Questions of perception of bias regarding the chair's previous employment with Gulf were raised just prior to the EIRB's commencement of public hearings, but were resolved to the satisfaction of all parties to the proceedings. Mr. Livingstone did chair the KULLUK review, and no other issues of bias were raised. As always, the EIRB was charged with the need to balance competing interests and seek a workable synthesis between development and conservation. For the Inuvialuit Game Council appointees this meant further exposure to the southern accoutrements of board process. It meant sitting for days in overheated rooms hearing lawyers and technical experts talk about possible impacts on the land and sea resource base. When industry and government tempers flared it meant that formal and essentially aggressive southern behaviours were exhibited rather than informal and conflict-reducing Inuvialuit behaviours. Much of the EIRB proceedings focused on cash, cost, and replacement value of country food rather than the non-pecuniary transactions of the land-based economy. For Messrs. Pokiak and Elias the EIRB hearings must have seemed as much about culture clash as they were about resource-use conflict.

All of this raises the issue of what co-management really seeks to accomplish. Is it aimed at forging a true synthesis of world views on resource use or is it simply another means in the long litany of southern acculturation processes? At face value the EIRB is a quasi-judicial administrative tribunal, rooted in the *Constitution Act, 1982*,[30] guided to a significant degree by legal counsel and expert southern consultants. It is interesting to note that the KULLUK panel saw no need to retain traditional knowledge experts (elders)

---

30   *Supra*, note 22.

to examine the material submitted by Gulf and that lawyers from Vancouver supplied the needed advice on conflict resolution. The authors of this paper are left to wonder how co-management can truly be cooperative, bicultural, informal, and conclusive when its formal appearance and process is so "southern"?

We now turn to an examination of the KULLUK panel decision and recommendations to try to evaluate the degree to which Inuvialuit concerns and values influenced the tribunal.

The KULLUK Decision and Recommendations

The KULLUK EIRB decision stands in stark contrast to the earlier ISSERK decision, which approved the one-well program without holding a full public hearing, subject to a five-page list of terms, conditions, and recommendations.[31] In KULLUK, the panel decided that "it has no responsible option but to recommend strongly against approval of the Gulf Drilling Program."[32] The EIRB stated that there were two principal reasons for its decision:

> Firstly, it is the conclusion of the Board, based on all the evidence and information it has heard and received, that there is a startling lack of preparedness evident on the part of government and on the part of Gulf to deal effectively with a major oil well blowout in the Beaufort Sea during the open water season.
>
> Secondly, nothing that the Board has heard enables it to make any sensible recommendation dealing substantively with Gulf's potential liability in the event of a worst case blowout, one of the obligations mandatorily imposed on the Board by the IFA.
>
> That such a situation exists after years of drilling in the Beaufort Sea is a sad reflection of a complacency which seems to have developed on the part of Gulf and the government authorities, driven by an ultimate belief that a blowout is so unlikely to occur that preparing to meet it is largely an academic exercise.[33]

These are harsh words, unequalled in their force in the short seven-year history of co-management of resource use in the Inuvialuit Settlement Region. They certainly put paid to any notions of pro-Gulf bias on the part of Mr. Livingstone, and they equally chastised government for its conspicuous failure to develop and test essential contingency planning measures. Neither industry nor government can complain of lack of notice either, as the ISSERK "General Observations"[34] highlighted the need for early planning and involvement of local people in oil spill response techniques. It seems that both

---

31   *Supra*, note 26, at 30 to 34.

32   *Supra*, note 23, at 16.

33   *Supra*, note 23, at 16.

34   *Supra*, note 26, at 32 to 34.

Gulf and government were caught off-guard by the KULLUK decision, and the authors suggest that this unpreparedness is astonishing in light of the immediately previous (March 1991) Exxon Valdez oil spill, which is often referred to in the body of the KULLUK report.

Further warning to Gulf and government should have arisen from the presentation of Nelson Green (himself an EIRB board member and panel member on the ISSERK review) to the EIRB on the topic of biological effects, delivered as vice-chair of the Inuvialuit Game Council:

> On the impacts of the project on wildlife, Mr. Chairman, the Inuvialuit depend on the whales, seals, fish, caribou and the migratory birds for their food. The existence of our traditional culture depends on the continuation of this subsistence economy. Short term employment opportunities or financial compensation as a result of a major oil spill or a blowout shouldn't be viewed as a means of offsetting the loss or decline of our wildlife food sources.[35]

Roger Gruben, chair of the Inuvialuit Regional Corporation, also provided evidence to the board based on a fact-finding tour of Valdez by the Inuvialuit Petroleum Corporation:

> The role of the scientific community has been negative. Most of the scientists worked either for Exxon or for the U.S. Government. Both parties have prohibited their scientists to release scientific data. Most of the scientific work is primarily done to protect Exxon and the U.S. Government from lawsuits, instead of constructively trying to contribute to the best and most active restoration of wildlife and environment.
>
> The collection of scientific data was badly organized. Essentially one needs three types of data:
>
> - base line data prior to the spill
> - intensive data collection during the spill
> - systematic data with respect to the longer term impacts of the spill.
>
> Essentially, the scientific data collection during the spill started generally too late to be of use. Prior base line data were largely non-existent. As a result most of the scientific work done on the oil spill is questionable.[36]

While the substantive contributions of the Green and Gruben reports are obvious, it is also important to note that this is the first time that Inuvialuit submitters (a term coined in the ISSERK report) are named in the body of an EIRB report, elevating them on paper to the same level as the regularly listed legal counsel and scientific consultants.[37] Nor should the cultural messages

---

35   Nelson Green, *Biological Effects* (presentation to Environmental Impact Review Board, 1990) (Inuvik, N.W.T.: Inuvialuit Game Council, 1990) at 30-40.

36   *Supra*, note 23, at 40.

37   Interestingly enough, neither the Environmental Impact Review Board's ISSERK report, *supra*, note 26, nor KULLUK report, *supra*, note 23, gives the names of the other participants/submitters; only organizational affiliation is listed.

be missed in these two presentations: clearly money and short-term industrial-economy employment is an unacceptable substitute for a healthy Inuvialuit resource base; and western science does not have all the answers. As the anthropologists would say, here we have a classic clash of epistemologies! We also find it fascinating that Messrs. Green and Gruben are on the same side of the fence in their presentations even though their respective organizations, the Inuvialuit Game Council and the Inuvialuit Regional Corporation, are charged with what in western industrialized societies are fundamentally opposite mandates: conservation and economic development. It seems that the Inuvialuit have culturally reconciled this gulf when it comes to high-risk offshore drilling.

The recommendations in the KULLUK[38] report address the deficiencies that multiplied to form the final decision. Of nine recommendations, only three[39] formally advocate Inuvialuit or "local involvement" in the process. The majority of the recommendations focus on institutional or agency fixes to the generic "complacency" identified in the board's decision.[40] Given that it was Gulf and the government that were found lacking by the board, it is perhaps not surprising that the bulk of the recommendations address their shortcomings. However, it should be remembered that the ISSERK report's "general observations"[41] focused heavily on the need to train more local people in oil spill clean-up, to utilize traditional Inuvialuit knowledge to map both onshore and offshore resource areas, and to involve the Inuvialuit in contingency planning from the earliest stages of project design. This same urgency of need for local participation is not reflected in the KULLUK recommendations. Where local people are mentioned (as participants in surprise exercises to test contingency plans, in the development of terms of reference for a study to define environmental assessments methodology, and in the organization of annual meetings with the Inupiat of Alaska to discuss current and future activities in the Beaufort Sea), their role is largely marginal.

On balance, in spite of the strange lack of focus on local and traditional expertise in the recommendations, the KULLUK decision stands as another Canadian tribunal landmark: once again a project has been stopped at the local level — at least as far as a recommendation to the competent government authority can go. Having rendered this co-management decision at the local

---

38   *Supra*, note 23.

39   See recommendations 3, 7 and 9.

40   *Supra*, note 23, at 16.

41   *Supra*, note 26, at 32 to 34.

level, the EIRB published its report and submitted it to the Minister of DIAND for his regulatory review.

*COGLA Delays and an Ad Hoc
Steering Committee is Born*

The Minister was duly notified of the EIRB's decision with respect to the KULLUK Drilling Program in late June 1990, and thirty days hence the Canadian Oil and Gas Lands Administration (COGLA),[42] the federal regulatory authority with the competence to issue the sought-after Drilling Program Approval, had not responded in any way. Section 11(29) of the IFA stipulates that the competent government authority, if unwilling or unable to accept the recommendations of the EIRB, or if it wishes to modify any of them, must declare so publicly in writing within thirty days of the decision. COGLA, almost a year later,[43] still has not announced a decision with respect to the sought-after Drilling Program Approval.

In the interim period, the EIRB has argued[44] that COGLA is obligated to respond within thirty days; and if it does not, it is prevented from approving the KULLUK Drilling Program under ss.11(27) and 11(29) of the IFA. COGLA's position is that it is still deliberating on the KULLUK report, and when it has reached its conclusion, the thirty-day time frame of s.11(29) will snap into place if the decision is either to modify or not to accept any recommendation of the board. Clearly there is ambiguity in the IFA wording of these key sections, and at least one legal commentator has recently argued that "the spirit of the IFA appears to be that all institutions created under it will deal with matters before them either expeditiously or on a strict timetable. It seems logical that other bodies ruling on these matters would deal with them on the same basis."[45]

In what is a classic bureaucratic response to this impasse, the Minister

---

42   The KULLUK report, *supra*, note 23, at 54 to 60, was especially critical of COGLA and held that it "had not adequately discharged [its] responsibility to protect the environment of the Beaufort Sea ...", *id.*, at 59. COGLA receives its mandate from the Minister of DIAND, who is empowered under the *Canada Petroleum Resources Act*, R.S.C. 1985 (2nd Supp.), c.36 and the *Oil and Gas Protection & Conservation Act*, R.S.C. 1985, c.O-7 to delegate certain powers, duties, and functions related to and exploration for and development and production of oil and gas on frontier lands to designated officials. The Administrator of COGLA is the recipient of these delegated powers, duties, and functions.

43   Interestingly enough, the Minister of Finance announced the disbanding of COGLA in the March 1991 federal budget.

44   Gordon Griffiths, "Environmental Review Under the Inuvialuit Final Agreement: The KULLUK Drilling Programme in Jeopardy" (1990) 31 Resources 1.

45   *Id.*, at 2.

has created the Beaufort Sea Steering Committee. As Griffiths has already noted, "the Steering Committee is not authorized under any legislation" and as such has no statutory or regulatory authority.[46] It is really a lateral arabesque to buy time for an *ad hoc* solution to the EIRB decision. Its mandate is basically to assess the nine recommendations made in the KULLUK report and to integrate them with the six recommendations on wildlife compensation that resulted from a workshop recently convened in response to a recommendation of the ISSERK report. We note that this mandate hangs heavily on two key words: "assess" and "integrate". Clearly, the *ad hoc* steering committee has no statutory or regulatory powers to decide or to recommend.

The steering committee membership is not indicative of the spirit of co-management otherwise reflected in the IFA structures. It is comprised of two Inuvialuit representatives, a representative from the oil and gas sector, one each from the governments of the Northwest Territories and the Yukon, two from the federal government (COGLA and DIAND, with the latter's representative being vice-chair), and one mutually acceptable nominee by the Minister of DIAND to serve as chair. Whereas the Inuvialuit form 50 percent of their IFA co-management boards' membership (not counting the chairpersons), on the steering committee their representation has fallen to less than 30 percent. One must ask what the legal implications are of Inuvialuit participation on the steering committee. Griffiths suggests that the Inuvialuit may be estopped from challenging the Minister's exercise of discretion if they participate. Obviously this potential estoppel should be of great concern to the EIRB and those who advocate the process of co-management.[47]

Conclusions on the EIRB Review of the KULLUK Drilling Program

From a distance it is tempting to conclude that co-management works when projects are recommended to proceed and that it is sidelined when recommendations are negative. However, the KULLUK report does provide cause for some celebration:

1. The EIRB review of the KULLUK Drilling Program proposal is thorough and interdisciplinary, and credits the Inuvialuit submitters for the provision of their traditional wisdom and their scepticism about the ends of western science.

2. The balance of Inuvialuit and government representation on the EIRB appears to check the domination of one cultural orientation by another.

---

46   *Id.*, at 2.

47   *Id.*, at 2.

We say "appears" because most of the visible trappings of EIRB process (presence of legal counsel, retained scientific consultants, maintenance of a hearing transcript, etc.) are formal and southern. They probably provide enough friendly visual and process cues to put industrial proponents at ease. One must hope that the Inuvik venue and the skilled back-up support of the Inuvialuit Game Council staff, and the joint management committees' and other resource people's expertise, is sufficient to place the Inuvialuit members similarly at ease.

3. The KULLUK report demonstrates that the EIRB has teeth. It names the complacent, provides good reasoning for its decision, and outlines practical recommendations to improve the prospects for future project applicants. Not since the publication of *Northern Frontier, Northern Homeland*[48] has a northern Canadian administrative tribunal been so direct in its castigation of government and industry shortcomings.

4. Industry and government for their part should not complain too loudly, for they have learned a great deal from the KULLUK process. It should now be clear that it is unfair to saddle one proponent with the extremely high costs of demonstrating the safety and workability of offshore drilling systems in the transition zone between the permanent pack ice and the land-fast ice. If the KULLUK report stands for anything, it is the principle that government and industry must team up to create contingency plans, test them regularly in real-time situations, and learn from the process. And this implies shared costs among all participants — rather shared costs in proving up a workable system than disputed costs in responding to a disaster.

5. The KULLUK process gives the currently negotiating land claims beneficiaries (such as the neighbouring Gwich'in Dene and the Tungavik Federation of Nunavut) a classic case study of how co-management regimes work in reality. Hopefully, they can learn from the EIRB experience and negotiate improvements in their final agreements.

THE QUESTION OF CO-MANAGEMENT ON INUVIALUIT LANDS

As we have seen in the KULLUK case study, a sophisticated regime of environmental screening and potential review is obligatory under the IFA for projects within or having an impact on the Inuvialuit Settlement Region. The KULLUK Drilling Project clearly fell within the region, and we have traced the due process of its local review. KULLUK did not, however, immediately

---

48 Thomas R. Berger, *Northern Frontier, Northern Homeland* (Ottawa: Supply and Services, 1977).

impinge upon Inuvialuit lands (see Figure 3); what would have been the case if it had? Developments planned for Inuvialuit private 7(1)(a) and 7(1)(b) lands require Inuvialuit authorization, generally via the negotiation of a participation agreement, access agreement, cooperation agreement, concession, or quarry concession. It is incumbent upon the developer to negotiate the above agreements and approvals. The first step in this process is generally application to the Inuvialuit Lands Administration Commission (ILAC). Direct proposals for participation and access agreements that are acceptable to the ILAC can be entered into without previous negotiations with the negotiating committee. However, any recommended negotiations aimed at concluding a cooperation agreement, participation agreement, access agreement, concession, or quarry concession must be carried out by the negotiating committee, comprising five members appointed by the Inuvialuit Lands Administration (ILA), the Inuvialuit Development Corporation (IDC), the IGC, an organization representing the Inuvialuit business community, and the IRC.[49]

When environmental problems or concerns arise in the above processes, a number of potential routes to the EISC exist. These include:[50]

1. a submission from a community corporation or the ILAC, through the IRC;

2. a direct submission from the IRC;

3. a submission from a community Hunters and Trappers Committee through the IGC; and

4. a submission from the IGC.

Should none of the above corporations, commissions, committees, or councils require EISC review, a proposed development is either approved, deferred, or rejected by the ILAC. It is at least theoretically possible in this system for an approval to be awarded to a linear development (e.g., a pipeline or multiple-array radar installations) on Inuvialuit lands that has at the same time been screened and referred to the EIRB because of potentially significant environmental impacts on public (Crown) lands in the Inuvialuit Settlement Region. We note that all projects proposed for the Inuvialuit Settlement Region are subject to screening by the EISC.

---

49   Inuvialuit Lands Administration 1991, at 2.

50   Canada. Minister of Indian Affairs and Northern Development, *Information and Procedures: Developing the Inuvialuit Settlement Region* (Ottawa: Dept. of Indian Affairs and Northern Development, 1988) at 7 to 8.

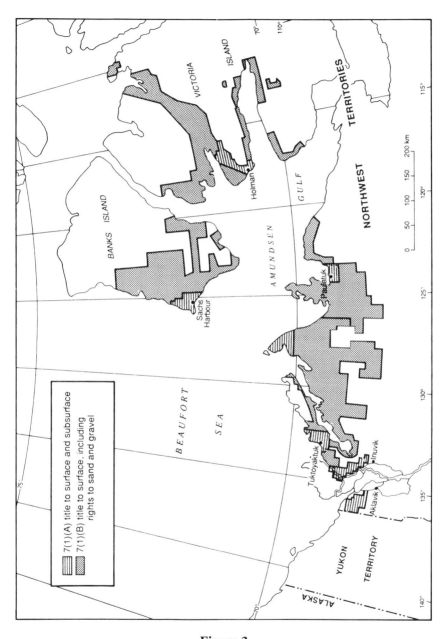

Figure 3

Inuvialuit Land

So what happens when the above hypothetical situation occurs? What happens especially if the EIRB recommends a KULLUK-like rejection of the project? Does the EIRB's decision take precedence over the silence of the review agencies on Inuvialuit ss.7(1)(a) and 7(1)(b) lands? How does the developer reconcile the situation?

It appears that this potential regulatory conflict would ultimately pit the IGC, which appoints the Inuvialuit members of both EISC and EIRB, against the IRC, which works to promote the development of economic opportunities for the Inuvialuit. As the keystone agency of the IFA — it received both title to the settlement lands and the cash portion of the land claim settlement — the IRC can apply a great deal of pressure to affect and influence development decisions on Inuvialuit lands. Conversely, the IGC represents the hunters and trappers of the six Inuvialuit communities, and is emblematic of the traditional cultural values of the Inuvialuit. We must remember in this context that the preservation of the Inuvialuit cultural identity is a prime goal of the IFA, and there can be little doubt that this is also the prime goal of the IGC. So which goal will triumph — development or conservation? The answer to this question is really at the core of co-management as an institution.

The KULLUK decision does more than suggest that the conservation side of the equation has teeth, but rumours abound about IRC's dissatisfaction with this particular EIRB review. Given that the IRC has both the land and the money, it has significant institutional advantages in a showdown. We think it would win and the hypothetical linear development would go ahead. Such a victory would not be without consequences, however, and one of those consequences could be the functional gutting of co-management. This could be accomplished by changing the EIRB's policies and procedures to ensure that pro-development Inuvialuit were appointed to the panels and, in time, to influence the choice of the chairperson. It may be the case that IRC would like to see the structural separation of IRC/IGC replaced with a system more directly under its control.

We hope and trust the above hypothetical scenario does not unfold. We think that the IFA co-management institutions and their workings to date have been open, direct, and fair. They provide the current generation of land claims negotiators with a growing body of precedent and a working example of how practical conservation values can be twinned with the need for regional economic development.

CONCLUSIONS AND RECOMMENDATIONS

General conclusions may be drawn from this review of the IFA's mechanisms for resource-use conflict resolution: co-management is working for the Inuvialuit, it is efficient in terms of both administrative cost and time expenditure, and it lives up to the basic goals of the IFA. It has democratized the development decision making process in the Inuvialuit Settlement Region, and it has injected traditional wisdom into debates that for too long have depended on the process services of lawyers and the transcripted testimony of southern scientists. To further enhance this process, we recommend the following:

1. an annual conference, open to Inuvialuit shareholders, between the IGC and the IRC to evaluate the past year's practice of co-management, to keep abreast of the evolving body of precedent, and to recommend needed changes in policies and procedures;

2. broader dissemination by the Joint Secretariat[51] and other joint-management committees supported by the Joint Secretariat of analysis of EISC and EIRB decisions in a variety of media, including explanatory videos, academic-peer-reviewed papers, pamphlets, and magazine articles;

3. the creation of an Inuvialuit scholarship trust fund to support beneficiaries in undergraduate and graduate programs of study that will lead to employment in some aspect of co-management practice;

4. the creation of a co-management research trust fund to enable ongoing research into administrative policy and practice issues, and feedback to the practitioners; and

5. the creation of an Inuvialuit elders' senate to act as a final arbiter in disputes between the IGC and the IRC. The elders' senate would utilize traditional conflict-resolution techniques and work to keep traditional knowledge embedded within the Inuvialuit government.

---

51   The Joint Secretariat provides administrative and technical support to the EISC, EIRB, and IGC.

THE JAMES BAY AND
NORTHERN QUEBEC AGREEMENT

Robert Mainville

This paper seeks to review concisely some of the provisions of the James Bay and Northern Quebec Agreement[1] as they pertain to resource development in northern Quebec. It also reviews some of the reasons why the JBNQA has not been a success in resolving conflicts between the native population of northern Quebec, particularly the Cree of James Bay, and resource developers operating in the territory contemplated by the Agreement, particularly Hydro-Québec. Though some provisions of the JBNQA have been partially implemented with success, those relating to control of future development through the environmental and social impact assessment and review process have met with mitigated success.

As a matter of introduction it appears appropriate to point out that the JBNQA was the first "modern" native lands claim agreement reached in Canada and has been hailed as a major step forward for the native populations covered by its provisions. This last assessment, which generally prevails in governmental circles, is a far cry from the reality faced by the concerned First Nations.

The JBNQA involves an immense territory of some 410,000 square miles covering all of northern Quebec. The principal aboriginal inhabitants of this territory are the Cree of James Bay and the Inuit of Quebec.

The Cree of Quebec are culturally and linguistically related to the larger Cree population of northern Ontario and western Canada, while the Inuit of Quebec form part of the larger linguistic group bearing the same name and inhabiting the most northern portions of Canada as well as parts of Greenland and Alaska. In Quebec, the Cree now number approximately ten thousand, while the Inuit number approximately seven thousand.

The Cree and Inuit inhabit and use most of the territory contemplated by the JBNQA. This territory is their traditional land in which they hunt, fish, and trap. They also use the coast, islands, and waters of Hudson Bay and James Bay for traditional purposes, though these areas are not covered by the provisions of the JBNQA. They depend on the land for their sustenance and harvest its resources. They consider this land their own.

The Quebec Cree are grouped in nine communities. One of these is located on the coast of the southern Hudson Bay along the Great Whale River (GWR) and is known as Whapmagoostui (a reference in the Cree language to

---

1 *The James Bay and Northern Quebec Agreement,* signed in November 1975, and approved by federal and provincial legislation, *infra,* notes 5 and 6.

the "White Whale"). Another four Cree communities are located along the coast of James Bay, and four more are located inland along the lakes and rivers of the eastern James Bay watershed. The Quebec Inuit are grouped in many communities all located along the Ungava and Hudson Bay coast. Being more familiar with the Quebec Cree, I will restrict my comments to this group.

The Cree territory is divided into various hunting territories, which are the object of traditional ownership rights and resource management traditions. For most of the year the trappers live off the land away from their communities in their respective territories. The Cree inhabitants are obviously largely dependent on the wildlife of the territory for the pursuit of their traditional ways. Until the early 1970s, the James Bay Cree were living in almost complete isolation, cut off from the rest of the world by hundreds of miles of taiga.

ORIGIN OF THE JAMES BAY AND NORTHERN QUEBEC AGREEMENT

In April 1971, the Premier of Quebec, Robert Bourassa, announced the construction of a hydroelectric megaproject of proportions unheard of in Quebec and Canada. This involved the damming of the La Grande River and the diversion of many important rivers into the La Grande to increase its flow and energy-producing capabilities. The La Grande project also involved very substantial flooding of prime hunting and trapping areas.

The Cree, who had inhabited the territory for thousand of years, had not even been consulted by the Quebec government on this project, which would entail the massive flooding of their lands and would substantially affect their way of life.[2] In fact the Cree had very little contact with the Quebec government, who had inherited these territories from Canada under the 1898 and 1912 boundary extension Acts. Quebec had never fully occupied these territories, nor had it maintained a substantial presence there until its decision to develop the hydroelectric potential located in the James Bay watershed.

The first James Bay project involved building a generating capacity of over 8,000 megawatts, the construction of four dams along the La Grande River, the creation of four huge reservoirs, the diversion of major rivers, and large increases and decreases in river flows. There was little doubt that the project would have major ecological and social impacts; however, it was designed and construction began without any meaningful ecological or social impact assessments or reviews.

The Cree of Northern Quebec organized themselves to oppose the project.

---

2   *Chief Max "One-Onti" Gros-Louis et al.* v. *James Bay Development Corp. et al.,* [1974] R.P. 38, 8 C.N.L.C. 188.

They, the Inuit, and other native groups started legal proceedings against Hydro-Québec and the Quebec government in order to stop James Bay I. In May of 1972, proceedings were initiated in the Superior Court of Quebec. It would be overly fastidious to summarize these proceedings; suffice it to say that after a lengthy hearing, Justice Malouf of the Superior Court (now of the Quebec Court of Appeal) issued an interlocutory injunction ordering a halt to all operations in relation to James Bay development on the basis of unsettled native claims applicable to the territory.[3]

One week later, the Quebec Court of Appeal suspended the injunction.[4] The Supreme Court of Canada refused permission to appeal the suspension, holding that suspension of an injunction was at the discretion of the Quebec Court of Appeal. The Cree therefore could not stop the James Bay project during its construction phase and had to rely on ineffective court proceedings.

The Quebec government made an offer of settlement to the Cree and Inuit who decided they had no choice but to negotiate, though they remained adamantly opposed to the project.

Some of the fundamental goals that the Cree sought to attain in these negotiations were the preservation of their traditional way of life; clear land rights; hunting, fishing, and trapping rights; control over public institutions operating in their lands; adequate protection for the environment; monetary compensation; and control of — and participation in — the development of the territory.

The negotiations were conducted hastily in a "boiler room" atmosphere, which, given the scope of the issues, was not conducive to thoughtful solutions to the problems at hand. The government and Hydro-Québec negotiators were pushing for a rapid deal that would insulate James Bay I development from further court actions. These hasty and difficult negotiations led to the James Bay and Northern Quebec Agreement, which was signed on 11 November 1975 and subsequently approved and declared valid by both Parliament[5] and the Assemblée Nationale du Québec.[6]

The Right Honourable Joe Clark, then Leader of the Opposition, qualified these negotiations as follows in the House of Commons debate concerning the *James Bay and Northern Quebec Native Claims Settlement Act*:

---

3   *Id.*

4   *Société de développement de la Baie James* v. *Kanatewat*, C.A.M. No.09-000890-73 (22 novembre 1973).

5   *James Bay and Northern Quebec Native Claims Settlement Act*, S.C. 1976-77, c.32.

6   *An Act Approving the Agreement Concerning James Bay and Northern Quebec*, S.Q. 1976, c.46.

It is not acceptable to me or to my colleagues ... that we approve of a process which has had the effect of forcing upon native people in a distant part of this land agreements which in all reasonable likelihood they would not have accepted had they been able to negotiate free of the constraints that were placed upon them.[7]

THE PROVISIONS OF THE JAMES BAY AND NORTHERN QUEBEC AGREEMENT RELATING TO RESOURCES AND THE ENVIRONMENT

The JBNQA is a complex legal document, ambiguous on many subjects. The principal provisions of this agreement relate to the surrender of native claims, rights, titles, and interests by the Cree and Inuit in and to land in the territory of Quebec and, in counterpart, the recognition in favour of the Cree and Inuit of the rights, privileges, and benefits specified in the agreement. The Agreement provides for land rights; guarantees dealing with future hydroelectric developments; local and regional governments; and health and education services and institutions. It also contains special provisions for justice and police matters; environmental and social impact assessment processes concerning future development; monetary compensation; economic and social development provisions and, finally, an income security program for Cree hunters and trappers.

The JBNQA provides for three categories of land. The legal regime applicable to each category is complex. However, the regimes can be characterized as follows: Category I lands are essentially set aside for the exclusive use and benefit of the Cree and Inuit; Category II lands are exclusive hunting, fishing, and trapping territories of the Cree and Inuit; and Category III lands include the rest of the territory in which the Cree and Inuit have some rights, and on which future development is subject to an environmental and social impact assessment and review process in which the Cree and Inuit are represented.

On Category I lands, Quebec remains the owner of mineral and subsurface rights; however, subject to acquired rights, extraction or mining activities can take place only with Cree consent and upon payment of agreed-upon compensation for the use of rights over such lands. The Cree also have the exclusive right to commercial exploitation of forest resources within Category I lands.

The Agreement provides for exclusive native hunting, fishing, and trapping rights over vast tracks of lands known as Category II lands. Outside Category II lands, the Cree can hunt, fish, and trap all species of animals, fish, and birds everywhere and at all times, with some limitations relating to conservation.

---

7   Hansard, *House of Commons Debates*, 14 December 1976 at 2002.

On Category III lands, development may be pursued subject to certain restrictions provided in the Agreement and subject to environmental and social impact assessment and review, which was intended to take into account the hunting, fishing, and trapping rights of the Cree. Moreover, the JBNQA includes special provisions relating to hydroelectric development.

Resource development is, for the most part, subject to the environmental and social impact and assessment processes provided in the JBNQA, which are summarily described below.

Two sections of the JBNQA relate to environment and future development. Section 22, applicable below the Fifty-fifth Parallel, and s.23, applicable to most of the territory above the Fifty-fifth Parallel. The choice of the Fifty-fifth Parallel was artificially imposed and bears no relationship to Cree hunting territories. My comments are limited to the s.22 process, which covers most, if not all, of the areas proposed for hydroelectric development, including the controversial Great Whale River and Nottaway-Broadback-Rupert rivers hydro projects.

Section 22 of the JBNQA provides for an environmental and social impact assessment and review process applicable to future developments in the territory. The Agreement lists certain major developments that are automatically subject to assessment, such as major mining operations, hydroelectric power plants and their associated works and forestry operations. These developments are to undergo what was foreseen to be a stringent impact assessment and review process.

In a nutshell, proponents must submit their development proposal to the "Administrator", who, in areas of provincial jurisdiction, is at the time of writing the Quebec Minister of the Environment and, in areas of federal jurisdiction, the head of the Federal Environmental Assessment Review Office. The Administrator must refer the development proposal to an "evaluating committee" on which Quebec, Canada, and the Cree are equally represented. This evaluating committee recommends whether a development should be submitted to assessment and review and, if so, it then acts as a scoping committee to determine the extent of impact assessment and studies to be carried out by the proponent. The tripartite nature of the committee reflects the recognition of the necessity to deal with issues of joint federal-provincial jurisdiction.

Once the proponent has completed an impact statement, that statement is reviewed by a review committee in matters of provincial jurisdiction and a review panel in matters of federal jurisdiction. The Cree are represented on each body. The review committee and the review panel make recommendations to the Administrators as to whether or not, on the basis of environmental and social impact considerations, the development should proceed and, if it should, upon what terms and conditions, including, if appropriate, preventive or remedial measures.

In deciding whether or not to authorize a development, including a resource development, the authorities must give due consideration to certain guiding principles stated in the JBNQA, including the protection of the hunting, fishing, and trapping rights of native people as well as their other rights; the protection of native people, societies, communities, and economies; and the involvement of the Cree people in the application of the regime.

The environmental and social impact and review process was intended to be the principal means of resource development control. One of the main resources now identified in the territory as presenting development potential is hydroelectricity. Indeed, the whole JBNQA was negotiated pursuant to a hydroelectric power project. Moreover, Hydro-Québec is itself a signatory to the JBNQA.

From 1975 onwards, the Cree have had extreme difficulties in ensuring that the provisions of the JBNQA were complied with. Bitter battles have been fought to ensure that a minimum of provisions are implemented. These problems were compounded by the absence of a dispute-settlement mechanism in the Agreement.

In a report entitled *James Bay and Northern Quebec Agreement Implementation Review*, the federal government recognized this problem as early as 1982: "The review team discovered several significant areas of implementation with regard to which there have been serious problems of implementation, unresolved disputes, and in some cases a failure to fully implement the Agreement in both its spirit and letter."[8] The report attributed much of this trouble to the pressure under which the Agreement had been negotiated.

> The Agreement had been negotiated under very severe constraints resulting from the Quebec position that the Hydroelectric Project had to go forward on an urgent basis, and from the resulting Crees' position that they would resume their court action to stop the project if a final agreement was not reached within one year of the signing of the Agreement ...
>
> The pressure under which the Agreement was negotiated, the inherent complexity of its provisions, and the fact that negotiating is by its nature a process of compromise, resulted in a document with many provisions which are vague, ambiguous and open to widely varying interpretations. It was generally understood during the negotiations that the precise details of the various programs, rights and benefits would be worked out over a lengthy process of implementation which would be carried out through the various entities established pursuant to the Agreement and through ongoing discussions involving all parties to the Agreement.[9]

---

8   Canada. Minister of Indian Affairs and Northern Development, *James Bay and Northern Quebec Agreement Implementation Review* (Ottawa: Supply and Services, 1982).

9   *Id.*, at 6.

Unfortunately, to this day many of the provisions of the Agreement still have not been implemented properly. An implementation review has yet to be undertaken by Quebec.

In the area of resource development, one of the principal control mechanisms provided in the JBNQA is the environmental and social assessment and review process. The application of this process has been a great disappointment. Neither the provincial nor the federal government appears to have respected the provisions of s.22 of the JBNQA. There is no adequate secretariat or personnel devoted to the application of this process, and both governments have shown a lack of interest in promoting the development of an adequate ecological database for northwestern Quebec.

The federal government has taken an exceedingly restrictive view of its responsibilities under the environmental and social impact assessment and review process and has, for all practical purposes, almost completely withdrawn from the process.

It is widely felt by the Cree that Quebec has not provided the committees operating under the process with adequate human and financial resources. As a result, these committees have become ineffectual and can no longer cope in any meaningful way with the projects submitted to them. For example, the committees responsible for the assessment of the Great Whale River and NBR megaprojects, involving between thirty to forty billion dollars of investments, are not even provided with a secretariat. The committee process is now close to becoming a simple rubber-stamping process. The Cree have repeatedly denounced this state of affairs.

The situation has become even more critical in the area of hydroelectric development. Hydro-Québec has now assumed almost full control of all environmental studies carried out in the James Bay territory and is creating a monopoly of base-line environmental information in the territory.

Moreover, ecological and social impacts unforeseen at the time of the signing of the JBNQA have resulted from the construction and operation of the Complexe La Grande (1975) and have confirmed that development schemes in a northern environment entail massive impacts often unpredicted at the onset of a project. One example is the methyl mercury contamination of the La Grande River system, which has been substantially increased by reservoir impoundments. The high mercury levels in fish have seriously curtailed fishing activities and fish consumption in the affected areas. This phenomenon was not known at the time of the signing of the Agreement.

Hydro-Québec has now announced plans to develop Phase II of the James Bay project and is attempting to have the new projects assessed in a piecemeal fashion, which undermining the protections and guarantees provided to the Cree under s.22 of the JBNQA.

THE CREE FIGHT AGAINST JAMES BAY II

Upon completion of the Complexe La Grande (1975) project, Hydro-Québec was faced with an energy surplus. All its other proposed projects, such as Great Whale River and Nottaway-Broadback-Rupert, were set aside in view of the surplus and the fact that the principal promoter of James Bay hydro development, Robert Bourassa, was no longer in control of the utility.

From 1978 to 1986, Hydro-Québec was operating in an energy-surplus position; it started to aggressively develop its domestic market by encouraging Quebec consumers to convert to electric heating. This policy was very successful, and, as a result, the present penetration of electricity in the domestic market is quite remarkable.

In 1985, Robert Bourassa returned to power with new visions of northern hydroelectric development. Hydro-Québec was still saddled with an electricity surplus, but it was instructed to embark on two new ambitious policies:

1. export electricity to the United States through major long-term export commitments with American utilities; this new policy had much to do with the support of the Quebec government for the Free Trade Agreement;

2. attract electricity-intensive industries such as aluminum and magnesium smelters with special advantageous electricity contracts.

The Cree consented in 1986 to the construction of additional Hydro-Québec production facilities on the La Grande River system, which they considered already greatly affected by the Complexe La Grande (1975) and its resulting flooding and mercury contamination. This would have allowed Hydro-Québec enough extra power to its system to meet most of Quebec's normal needs for many years had it not been for the two new above-mentioned energy policies relating to exports and the aluminum and magnesium smelting industries, risk-sharing contracts.

The Cree are particularly concerned about the proposed developments of the Great Whale and Nottaway-Broadback-Rupert projects. The proposed Great Whale River project would provide Hydro-Québec with over 3,000 megawatts of new power, while the Nottaway-Broadback-Rupert project would represent 8,000 megawatts of additional power. The Great Whale River project entails the diversion of several adjacent rivers and will result in an 85 percent reduction in the flow of the Great Whale River at the level of the community of Whapmagoostui. As with the original La Grande Project, both the Great Whale and Nottaway-Broadback-Rupert projects will entail massive flooding to create reservoirs managed for the sole purpose of electricity production.

The Cree are opposed to these projects, which are being built now essentially to service export commitments and multinational smelting corporations. Hydro-Québec plans to commit itself to export by the turn of the century 3,500 megawatts of power to the United States under long-term power and energy contracts. This would represent more than the full production capacity of Great Whale alone. In the past, Hydro-Québec for the most part exported its surplus electricity. Under its new policy, Hydro-Québec plans to commit Quebec for the first time to export electricity for which new production facilities will need to be built to service the export contracts.

To date, Hydro-Québec has signed four contracts under this new policy. The first, with Central Maine Power Company for 300 megawatts, was cancelled by the Maine authorities on environmental grounds. The other contracts, one for 450 megawatts with Vermont and another for 1,000 megawatts with New York, are the subject of bitter court battles in Canada and the United States. In this regard, although the National Energy Board has approved these exports, it has imposed on its licenses conditions relating to environmental assessment that Hydro-Québec and the Quebec government consider unacceptable. They have appealed the National Energy Board decision to the Federal Court of Appeal, and have announced that they may cancel the export contracts should the conditions relating to federal environmental standards and assessments be maintained by the Courts. The last export contract signed is for 800 megawatts of seasonal power with New York, and it has not yet been submitted for regulatory approval. The profitability of these export contracts has yet to be determined. Hydro-Québec has refused to disclose its profitability analysis of the contracts and is preventing public access to any meaningful information relating to the economics of these export commitments.

Under its new risk-sharing program, Hydro-Québec has committed itself to supply over 3,000 megawatts of power, almost the full production of the proposed Great Whale project, to multinational aluminum and magnesium smelting corporations. The electricity supply contracts between these smelting corporations and Hydro-Québec are being kept secret, even though utility supply contracts are, as a general rule, public throughout North America. There are serious reasons to believe that these contracts may provide for very low electricity rates.

Hydro-Québec has attempted to circumvent a full environmental assessment of the Great Whale River project by requiring the segmentation of the environmental and social assessment and review process provided for in the JBNQA. For nearly fifteen years, Hydro-Québec and the Government of

Quebec have stated that they would treat the Great Whale River project as a whole for purposes of environmental and social impact assessment. Now Hydro-Québec has advanced its construction schedules in order to meet its export commitments and its contracts with smelting multinationals, and it no longer deems it appropriate to proceed with a full environmental assessment of the complete project prior to obtaining building authorizations for the access infrastructure. This is, in our opinion, contrary to the JBNQA and is unjustified from an environmental point of view.

In these circumstances, the Cree have taken legal actions to prevent the development of the Great Whale River project by Hydro-Québec. First, they have requested the courts to order a full environmental assessment of the project, as provided under the JBNQA. The Cree argue that a full and impartial assessment of the proposal by an independent and expert panel will reveal the facts to the public and prevent this project from being built. They also insist that the secret aluminum and magnesium contracts be made public, and they are presently pursuing this before Quebec's Access to Information Commission.

The Cree maintain that the Great Whale River and the Nottaway-Broadback-Rupert projects make little economic sense, and that the secrecy surrounding many aspects of these projects does not allow the Quebec and Canadian public to openly and intelligently debate the facts about these projects.

Furthermore, the Cree have attempted and are still attempting through the courts and the regulatory agencies to prevent the export of electricity by Hydro-Québec to the United States. These export commitments are now being seriously questioned, and there is a distinct possibility that they will be cancelled.

Finally, the Cree are also pursuing in court a case relating to their interpretation of the JBNQA and other aboriginal rights issues, in which they argue that their consent is required for Hydro-Québec to proceed with the Great Whale River project.

Opposition to James Bay II is turning into the most controversial ecological, political, legal, and economic struggle relating to resource development in recent Canadian history.

CONCLUSIONS

The whole purpose of the JBNQA was to ensure the preservation of the traditional way of life of the Cree, notwithstanding the resource development of the territory. The partial failure of the JBNQA in this respect can be attributed in part to the lack of serious implementation by the concerned governments of the environmental and social impacts assessment and review process provided for in the Agreement. New developments were to be undertaken only after thorough investigation of their impacts on the native population, and only if they were compatible with traditional native activities.

This process has not been fully applied. This lack of concern for the native populations in developing northern Quebec has led to serious social tensions that could provoke a major crisis. The mechanisms put into place to ensure the joint use of the territory by the native and non-native populations have not operated properly.

This institutional problem must be resolved immediately. In particular, Hydro-Québec must accept its responsibility for having weakened the environmental and social impact assessment and review process in northern Quebec and, as a result, provoked a major confrontation with the native inhabitants of James Bay. A complete review of the James Bay and Northern Quebec Agreement is urgently required. This review will probably entail major amendments to the Agreement to ensure its effectiveness. It will also entail the full recognition by Hydro-Québec that it cannot proceed with future hydro development in the territory without the participation of the concerned native parties.

Notice

Since this talk was delivered (10 May 1991) many substantial developments have taken place. After many successful court decisions in their favour, the Cree signed with the federal and provincial governments a Memorandum of Understanding relating to the environmental assessment and review of the proposed GWR project.

This Memorandum of Understanding was executed on 23 January 1992 and provides for a global review of the GWR project (without segmentation of its access infrastructure) and the participation of the federal, provincial, Cree, and Inuit parties in the review. A joint secretariat is to be established to help carry out the review. Furthermore, the justification of the project is to be included in the review process, which will also provide for public meetings and hearings. Furthermore, a participant-funding scheme of five million dollars is also provided for.

Moreover, on 27 March 1992, New York Governor Mario Cuomo announced the cancellation of the 1,000 megawatts firm export contract with Hydro-Québec. Governor Cuomo indicated that, among other reasons, environmental and human rights considerations had motivated this decision.

4

INTERNATIONAL RESOURCE-USE CONFLICTS

TOWARDS A BIOREGIONAL PERSPECTIVE ON INTERNATIONAL RESOURCE-USE CONFLICTS: LESSONS FOR THE FUTURE

David McRobert and Paul Muldoon

Transboundary environmental relations are going to be one of, if not the, major bilateral concern(s) in Canadian-U.S. relations during the remaining decades of this century. It behooves citizens of both nations to see that they do not get out of control.[1]

Conflicts between Canada and the United States over resources and the environmental and social consequences of certain resource dispositions[2] have a long history. Indeed, it is probably fair to say that these disputes have always had some bearing on, and perhaps even have defined, the relationship between the two countries.

By the late 1960s, certain resource-use conflicts had gained a fairly high profile in Canada, but did not attain as high a profile in the United States. The rise in profile can be attributed in part to concerns about Canadian sovereignty posed by certain well-publicized incidents.[3] Further, resource use and

---

1   John E. Carroll, *Environmental Diplomacy: An Examination and a Prospective of Canadian-U.S. Transboundary Environmental Relations* (Ann Arbor: University of Michigan Press, 1983) at 305.

2   It is the subsequent resource development decisions made by those acquiring ownership rights that often spur the concerns expressed about international resource-use conflicts between the U.S. and Canada; see Andrew R. Thompson, "Legal Characteristics of Disposition Systems: An Overview" *in* Nigel Bankes & J. Owen Saunders, eds., *Public Disposition of Natural Resources* (Calgary: Canadian Institute of Resources Law, 1984) at 1.

3   A classic example was the ill-fated trip of the American oil tanker S.S. *Manhattan* into

allocation issues achieved greater priority on the Canadian public policy agenda owing to a revival in nationalism, and concurrent political pressures on provincial and federal governments to assert more control over development of those resources — especially minerals, oil and gas, and forestry products — that were seen to be controlled by foreign interests.[4]

Since the 1960s, bilateral resource use and allocation conflicts between the United States and Canada have maintained a high profile in Canada, with growing importance south of the border as well. Indeed, controversies over access to resources like fisheries and water, and debates over cross-border marketing of such resources as farm products and semi-manufactured forestry goods, became commonplace in the mid-1980s.[5] It would not be inaccurate to suggest that, as the 1980s drew to a close, a new epoch in transboundary resource conflicts had arisen in the wake of these often passionate disputes.[6]

While no one single factor can explain the emergence of this new epoch of transboundary relations, several trends are readily identifiable. First, historical problems identified and described much earlier in this century, such as transboundary air and water pollution in the Great Lakes region, remain largely unaddressed. Secondly, the continuing pressure by the United States to purchase "cheap" Canadian energy[7] and water supplies, and the Canadian government's willingness to consider marketing of fresh water in the United States,[8] have spawned outrage and sparked strong opposition from large

---

Canadian Arctic waters in 1968. This incident sparked a major diplomatic row between Canada and the United States. For background on this, see Edgar J. Dosman, *The National Interest: The Politics of Northern Development, 1968-75* (Toronto: McClelland & Stewart, 1975) at 15-26.

4   See Abraham Rotstein, "Foreign Control of the Economy: A Screening and Ownership Policy" *in* Abraham Rotstein & Gary Lax, eds., *Getting It Back: A Program for Canadian Independence* (Toronto: Clarke, Irwin, 1974) at 22.

5   A valuable collection of articles on the issues that were being debated in the mid-1980s is presented in J. Owen Saunders, ed., *Trading Canada's Natural Resources: Essays from the Third Banff Conference on Natural Resources Law* (Toronto: Carswell, 1987). See, in particular, the following essays in the volume: Bruce W. Wilkinson, "Canadian Resource Trade: An Economic Perspective" at 35; Christian Yoder, "United States Countervailing Duty Law and Canadian Natural Resources: The Evolution of Resources Protectionism in the United States" at 81; and Shirley A. Coffield, "United States-Canada Natural Resources Trade: Sources of Conflict/Prospects for Agreement" at 121.

6   There will always be a debate as to whether this is a new epoch or an intensification of traditional relations. Whatever the conclusion, the thesis is that there is need to develop new mechanisms to accommodate either the new epoch or this intensification.

7   For background on this issue, see David Poch, "Regulating the Export of Environmental Quality: The Case of Electricity Exports" *in* Saunders, *supra*, note 5, at 309.

8   On this subject, see two recent compilations of articles: W. Holm, ed., *Water and Free*

segments of the public in both nations, and prompted some critics to voice serious concerns about a loss of sovereignty over water exports.[9] Arguably, perceptions about the scarcity of certain resources (such as electricity) in the two countries and the relative abundance of other resources (such as fresh water in Canada) help explain this pattern of relations. However, new categories of issues that are more pervasive, complex, and interconnected are emerging in this epoch. No doubt, the conclusion of the Canada-U.S. Free Trade Agreement (FTA) on 2 January 1988, and its eventual implementation by both nations in 1989, symbolized the start of a new epoch in bilateral transboundary environmental relations, and in the structural economic relationship,[10] between the two countries.

Numerous books, articles, papers, and other comments have been written on the success of the U.S. and Canadian governments and their respective national and bilateral institutions in addressing and resolving certain resource-use conflicts.[11] The purpose of this paper is to examine the adequacy of current institutional arrangements to prevent, address, and/or resolve resource-use conflicts in this new epoch of transboundary relations. Having reviewed the adequacy of the institutional framework, we will propose some ways in

---

Trade (Toronto: Lorimer, 1988); and A.L.C. de Mestral & D.M. Leith, eds., *Canadian Water Exports and Free Trade* (Occasional Paper No.2) (Ottawa: Rawson Academy of Aquatic Science, 1989).

9   One of the most provocative analyses of the loss of sovereignty over water posed by the FTA is Mel Clarke & Don Gamble, "Water Exports and Free Trade" *in* de Mestral & Leith, *id.*, at 7-24.

10   For a discussion of some of the broader structural economic issues related to the Canada-U.S. Free Trade Agreement and trade in resources, see H.T. Wilson, *Retreat From Governance: Canada and the Continental International Challenge* (Hull: Voyageur, 1988).

11   Some of the important analyses on transboundary environmental relations in North America include: Carroll, *supra*, note 1; John E. Carroll & Newell B. Mack, "On Living Together in North America: Canada, the United States and International Environmental Relations" (1982) 12 Denver J. of Int. Law and Policy 35; Don Munton, "Dependence and Interdependence in Transboundary Environmental Relations" 36 Int. J. 139; Don Munton, "Paradoxes and Prospects" *in* R. Spencer *et al.*, eds., *The International Joint Commission Seventy Years On* (Toronto: Centre for International Studies, University of Toronto, 1981) at 60-105; and Peter S. Smedresman, "The International Joint Commission (United States-Canada) and the International Boundary and Water Commission (United States-Mexico): Potential for Environmental Control Along the Boundaries" (1973) 6 New York Univ. J. of Int. Law and Politics 499. Another important study on transboundary issues was conducted by the Standing Committee on Foreign Affairs of the U.S. Senate: see Standing Committee on Foreign Affairs, U.S. Senate, *Canada - United States Relations, Volume 1 — The Institutional Framework for the Relationship* (Washington, D.C.: U.S. Senate, 1975). For a more recent commentary related to the FTA, see J. Owen Saunders, "Legal Aspects of Trade and Sustainable Development" *in* J. Owen Saunders, ed., *The Legal Challenge of Sustainable Development* (Calgary: Canadian Institute of Resources Law, 1990) at 370.

which to enhance that framework to cope with the new bilateral challenges.

The paper is divided into three main sections. The first section reviews two disputes that are now complicating U.S.-Canada binational relations, and that are argued to be typical of this new epoch of transboundary resource-use conflicts. These issues are (1) the conflict between proponents and opponents of the James Bay II hydroelectric project; and (2) the environmental and trade implications of refillable quotas for beverages. The second section of the paper reviews three approaches to bilateral dispute resolution and analyzes their adequacy. The third section then provides some suggestions for institutional reform, and proposes the establishment of a new bilateral appellate tribunal. Finally, we summarize the discussion and offer some concluding comments related to a proposed trilateral North American Free Trade Agreement (NAFTA) between Canada, the United States, and Mexico.

THE POLICY CONTEXT: THE INHERENT CONFLICT BETWEEN TRADE LIBERALIZATION AND BIOREGIONALISM

Before turning to the case studies, it is important to set out two important assumptions in this paper:

1. that there is an inherent policy conflict between the long-term goal of environmental protection and extensive trade liberalization; and

2. that this policy conflict is the underlying reason why existing institutional frameworks have been unable to address transboundary environmental and resource-use conflicts adequately.

Indeed, it is argued here that one of the reasons why transboundary environmental conflicts have increased in the past few decades is that trade has expanded between nations, and that this trade has not been regulated so as to prevent certain environmental impacts and to promote the goal of resource conservation. While free trade is widely accepted as doctrine by most economists, the principles on which it is premised, such as comparative advantage, are flawed and do not take into account the ecological reality that there are resource and environmental limits to the planet.[12]

With this perspective in mind, it should not be surprising that increasing trade liberalization, and the implementation of the FTA, have not been enthusiastically supported by most environmentalists.[13] Environmentalists

---

12   On this theme, see Herman E. Daly & John B. Cobb, Jr., *For the Common Good: Redirecting the Economy toward Community, the Environment and a Sustainable Future* (Boston: Beacon, 1989) at 209-235.

13   For critical assessments of the FTA, see F. Tester, "Free Trading the Environment" *in* D.

who oppose the FTA argue that the trend towards liberalization of trade has demonstrated the divergent nature of two policy options.

The first option, free trade, or trade liberalization, is premised on the prospect of increased trade in certain resources and commodities between nations. Thus, the FTA was referred to by the federal government of Canada as "a commercial accord" between two large trading partners rather than "an environmental agreement" in public debates in 1988. On this basis, the Canadian federal government asserted that "[t]he environment was not, therefore, a subject for negotiations nor are environmental matters included in the text of the agreement."[14]

In this paper, it is argued that the trade liberalization approach to economic and social development is destined to create conflicts between those seeking to export resources and commodities to foreign markets by the removal of most, if not all, trade barriers, and those seeking to promote long-term, sustainable development. In the effort to promote exchange between nations and regions, supporters of trade liberalization downplay most of the negative externalities associated with long-distance trade and ignore some of the hidden costs of trade.[15] In contrast, those who are opposed to trade in certain resources like fresh water (because of its integral role in local or regional ecosystems), energy (because of the need to promote conservation, reduce pollution associated with energy consumption, and secure supplies for future generations), or wildlife (because of the need to protect wildlife populations) cannot accept downplaying of these costs. Finally, critics of trade liberalization also oppose most kinds of trade in resources because of legitimate concerns over the loss of political sovereignty that often results when resources are marketed in foreign jurisdictions.

Other concerns about the environmental implications of increased trade liberalization are highlighted by the following criticisms of the FTA. Critics of the FTA say that it will:

Cameron, ed., *The Free Trade Deal* (Toronto: Lorimer, 1988); M. Barlow, *Parcel of Rogues: How Free Trade is Failing Canada* (Toronto: Key Porter, 1990); Gatt Fly, "U.S. Companies Use FTA to Attack Regional and Environmental Aid", *Gatt Fly Newsletter*, September 1989.

14   Quotes are from a statement made by the federal Minister of Trade, John Crosbie, in response to questions posed in the House of Commons in the fall of 1987. They are cited in Tester, *id*.

15   Arguably, one of the most important environmental costs of trade is global warming caused by the consumption of fuel to transport goods over long distances. For a description of some of the hidden costs of trade, see David McRobert, "Questionable Faith: For Environmentalists, There Are Serious Problems with the Free Trade Agreement" (1988) 11:1 Probe Post 24.

• erode the already weak capacities of existing institutions to resolve certain types of disputes;

• further reinforce certain structural relationships between the United States and Canada, and encourage more exports of primary, unprocessed resources like minerals, trees, and fish from Canada to the United States; and

• harmonize environmental laws in both nations and reduce standards to a new, and lower, common denominator.[16]

Opposed to this free trade approach to economic development is an option sometimes referred to as bioregionalism, which is premised on the view that environmental problems almost always arise because of improper local environmental practices or consumptive life styles, even though the implications of those practices may be complex and even global in nature. This recognition has prompted many environmentalists to adopt the slogan "think globally, act locally" and to promote the view that problems that originate in a local environment must be solved locally.[17]

In contrast to the free trade approach, the bioregional approach stresses local production for local consumption.[18] It also does not separate economic, environmental, and political matters. Indeed, bioregionalism represents a convergence in thinking about ecology, politics, economics, and social justice.[19] It is based on the idea that political and ecological borders are not the same. Species migrate over political borders, and contaminants do not respect national, regional, or local boundaries in tracing their paths. More

---

16   The FTA (see S.C. 1988, c.65) is generally silent on the issue of environmental standards. However, two exceptions are technical standards at the federal level in Chapter 6 and pesticide and food safety standards in Chapter 7. Tester, *supra*, note 13, persuasively argues that standards in Canada will be lowered by the FTA.

17   An excellent example is provided by V. Shiva in her book *Staying Alive: Women, Ecology and Survival in India* (London: Zed, 1988). Shiva shows that the movement towards a sustainable society in India is being led by women, who maintain closer relationships to land and water resources and seem more willing to challenge the myth of "security-in-consumerism" that prevails in developed nations. Another recent work that attempts to employ a bioregional approach in a North American context is Royal Commission on the Future of the Toronto Waterfront, *Watershed: Second Interim Report of the Royal Commission on the Future of the Toronto Waterfront* (Toronto, 1990) (Commissioner: David Crombie). See also P.G. Sly, D.M. Leith & D.J. Waterson, eds., *Towards an Ecosystem Charter for the Great Lakes* (Ottawa: Rawson Academy of Aquatic Science, 1989).

18   This idea was first articulated by E.F. Schumacher in his path-breaking book, *Small is Beautiful: Economics as if People Mattered* (New York: Harper & Row, 1973).

19   One of the most important thinkers on bioregionalism is Kirkpatrick Sale, an American author who has produced two seminal books on bioregionalism, *Human Scale* (New York: Basic, 1980) and *Dwellers in the Land* (San Francisco: Sierra Club, 1985). Another important work in this area is David Morris, *Self-Reliant Cities: Energy and the Transformation of Urban America* (San Francisco: Sierra Club, 1982).

often, local or regional boundaries such as mountain ranges or rivers define ecologically relevant borders; thus, for the purposes of governance, geographical features such as valleys and watersheds should be important cornerstones of good environmental and economic planning.

Bioregionalists argue that there are numerous hidden costs associated with expanded international trade in many commodities, including excess consumption of energy resources for transportation of goods, and inappropriate patterns of economic development and land use in less developed countries (LDCs).[20] While certain kinds of trade can spur research and development and can aid the spread of environmentally sound technology, historical patterns tend to suggest that the environmental benefits of trade in technology have been far outweighed by the negative costs associated with this activity. Compelling arguments have been made that extending first-world development patterns to the LDCs has resulted in a cycle of debt accumulation and environmentally destructive land use activities.[21]

A more fundamental problem with international trade is posed by Daly and Cobb in the following passage:

> Given acceptance of the goal of sustainable development, there still remains the question of the level of community at which to seek this goal. International trade allows one country to draw on the ecological carrying capacity of another country and thus be unsustainable in isolation, even though sustainable as part of a larger trading bloc. The trade issue raises ... the question of complementarity versus substitutability of natural and humanly created capital.[22]

Daly and Cobb go on to make a persuasive argument that sustainable development is a process best carried out at the community level (although they do not precisely define appropriate size). While they recognize the need for the state as a political entity that supports the coordination of policies between communities, and as something that has cultural, historical, and social significance (a position which we also support), they show that much more emphasis must be placed on environmental protection and the conservation of

---

20 On this theme, see World Commission on Environment and Development, *Our Common Future* (London: Oxford University Press, 1987) (Chair: G.H. Brundtland); and Lloyd Timberlake, *Only One Earth: Living for the Future* (London: BBC Books & Earthscan, 1987).

21 One of the most influential books on this subject is S. George, *A Fate Worse than Debt* (London: Penguin, 1988). See also F. Lappe, J. Collins & D. Kinley, *Aid as Obstacle: Twenty Questions about our Foreign Aid and the Hungry* (San Francisco: Institute for Food and Development Policy, 1981); and H. Brookfield, *Interdependent Development* (London: Metheun, 1975).

22 Daly & Cobb, *supra*, note 12, at 75.

resources at the local level in establishing international and national economic development strategies.

From this perspective, freer trade between regions and continents can be viewed in environmentally negative terms. While free trade is premised on a "bigger and better" mentality, bioregionalism stresses the limits of growth based upon an ecological ethic. While free trade pushes towards expansion of trade in resources, with little focus on the environmental consequences of such action, bioregionalism supports self-sustaining economic systems that do not depend on massive infusions of imported energy and resources.

Just how this policy conflict between free trade and bioregionalism is played out in practice is reflected in the two case studies described below. The analysis also shows that because existing dispute-resolution mechanisms and institutions are unable to handle these policy conflicts, it may be necessary to develop new institutions or reform existing mechanisms.

INTERNATIONAL RESOURCE-USE CONFLICTS: TWO CASE STUDIES

In this section, two case studies of international resource-use conflicts, in the context of the bilateral U.S.-Canada relationship, are outlined. Both case studies provide important insights about the capacity of the current institutional frameworks and dispute-resolution mechanisms to resolve international resource-use conflicts and environmental problems.

James Bay II: The Failure of an Incrementalist Approach

The James Bay II hydroelectric development project is perhaps one of the most controversial and bitter disputes concerning resource use in Canada today. It is not a bilateral dispute *per se* since the conflict is primarily between those who support the project (such as the Quebec government, Hydro-Québec, labour unions in the province, and the provincial business community) and those who oppose the project (such as the Cree Indians of Northern Quebec, numerous Canadian and American environmental non-government organizations, and human rights advocates). The bi-national aspect to the dispute is that the undertaking is justified on the basis of lucrative U.S. export markets for Quebec's electricity. In a way, while U.S. demand for electricity is the driving force behind the project, sharp reductions in this demand could also provide the greatest impetus to scale down or cancel the project.

James Bay II is the second phase of a massive hydroelectric project in northern Quebec that was begun in the early 1970s.[23] On the scale of

---

23   For background on James Bay I and II, see A. Picard, "James Bay II", The Amicus Journal

megaprojects in Canada, James Bay II is in a class of its own. When complete, the project will flood at least seven thousand square kilometres of land. At least sixteen dams, ten reservoirs, and seventy dikes will be constructed. Up to eight rivers could be diverted. Thousands of trees will be cut down to prepare the areas before flooding. Recent estimates place the cost of the project in the range of tens of billions of dollars. The project will increase the hydroelectric generation capacity of the James Bay dams to over 25,000 megawatts from the current capacity of 10,000 megawatts.

Most of the power that is generated at James Bay II is already slated for distribution to U.S. markets in the state of Vermont and New York. In the past two years, Hydro-Québec has signed export contracts worth more than twenty-five billion dollars with New York State.[24] The deal, which is for the purchase of 1,000 megawatts of electricity year-round starting in 1995, renews a commitment for an additional 800 megawatts for six months of each year. A tentative deal between Hydro-Québec and Vermont worth more than eight billion dollars has also been negotiated.

While the physical size and costs of the undertaking are massive, so too are its environmental and social consequences. For example, according to some scientists, the project will:

- undermine the subsistence fishing, hunting and trapping activities that are fundamental to the lifestyle of many of the native people who live in the area;

- destroy natural habitats of terrestrial species such as moose and caribou, and migratory waterfowl such as geese, through massive flooding of the area; fisheries will also be severely altered by the project, as will be beluga whales that live in the local bays and estuaries;

- release mercury pollution into rivers and reservoirs, further exacerbating current mercury problems caused by James Bay I;[25]

(Fall 1990). See also F. Birkes, "Impacts of James Bay Development" in C.E. Delisle & M.A. Bouchard, eds., *Managing the Effects of Hydroelectric Development*, Proceedings of the Montreal Symposium of Canadian Society of Environmental Biologists (Montreal: Dept. of Geology, University of Montreal, 1990) at 623-626; Earthroots Coalition, *Amazon North: Assault on James Bay* (Toronto, 1991); and Sierra Club of Canada, *James Bay 2: The Monster Mega-project that must be Stopped* (Ottawa, 1991).

24   The contract for 1,000 megawatts of power should run from 1995 to 2016 and is worth at least seventeen billion dollars while the six-month 800-megawatt contract is estimated to be worth around eight billion dollars in revenues.

25   Mercury pollution resulting from the first phase of this project and the poisoning of fish and other species in the food chain in the area are well documented. It has been estimated that over 60 percent of Cree Indians living in Chisasibi at the mouth of the La Grande River have unsafe levels of mercury in their bodies, and some people are estimated to have more than twenty times the acceptable level as established by the federal government. Scientific studies suggest that it could take between ten and twenty years before these mercury-

- ruin or despoil wilderness areas and forests for roads and transmission lines (the Cree Indians living in the area estimate that over the past twenty years wilderness spaces have been destroyed at a rate nearly ten times that in British Columbia and nearly twice that of Ontario);

- produce numerous global impacts (some scientists have provided compelling evidence that vast quantities of methane gas, one of the most powerful greenhouse gases contributing to global warming, will be released as vegetation trapped in the flooded reservoirs decays).

In view of these potential impacts, it seems imperative to conduct an environmental review of the James Bay II project before construction is begun. Numerous aboriginal and environmental groups in Canada and the U.S. have asked that a single hearing be undertaken because this would allow aboriginal groups and third-party intervenors to participate in a review of the project and its infrastructure in its entirety before any licences for construction are granted. They have also demanded that all construction on James Bay II be stopped until such a single review of the project, including infrastructure such as roads and airports to service the project, deems the project to be environmentally sound.

Three issues now cloud the debate over the project:

1. Demand for a Single Hearing: Demands for a single hearing have not met with much enthusiasm from the Quebec government.[26] Quebec Minister of Energy Lise Bacon had contended up until the summer of 1991 that the environmental assessment of the project should be divided into two parts: one for the project's infrastructure, such as access roads, an airport, and work camps, and another for the project's dams, dikes, and reservoirs. It has been estimated that at least $755 million will be spent on building 575 kilometres of roads and three airports associated with the Great Whale project, the first phase of James Bay II. In November 1990, the Federal Environmental Assessment Review Office (FEARO) accepted this two-stage environmental assessment process.

    By July 1991, the then-newly appointed federal Environment

---

contaminated fish are safe for humans to eat. In any case, the entire ecosystem will be adversely affected by this mercury for decades to come. For more background on this subject, see Peter Gorrie, "The James Bay Power Project: The Environmental Cost of Reshaping the Geography of Northern Quebec" (1990) 110:1 Canadian Geographic 20. See also J. Rosenthal & J. Belyea, *Long-term Threats to Canada's James Bay from Human Development: Environmental Policy Analysis Development Report No.29* (New York: National Audubon Society, 1989).

26 In the summer of 1991, the Quebec government agreed to split the environmental assessment of James Bay II into two parts: see Robert McKenzie, "Great Whale Plunged into Depths of Secrecy", *Toronto Star* (24 August 1991) at D4.

Minister, Jean Charest, began to send out signals in media interviews that he was willing to consider a full, integrated federal public review of the project by FEARO. However, in response to pressure from the Quebec government, Charest agreed to allow the provincial government to conduct its own integrated review. Work on the provincial review began in the fall of 1991 and continued in 1992. At hearings on the project held in the spring of 1992, Quebec business leaders and unionists expressed strong support for proceeding immediately with work on the first phase of the project as a way to kick-start Quebec's ailing economy. Thus, it is possible that some construction of the project's infrastructure will commence before the provincial review panel has completed its work.

2. Federal-provincial Division of Powers: The Quebec government continues to reject the proposition that the federal government has jurisdiction on environmental issues such as those raised by James Bay II.

3. Future Electricity Demand: Another controversial issue is whether there is even a need for the project. It is estimated that electricity conservation measures using available technology could reduce energy demand in the United States by up to 75 percent over the next twenty to thirty years.

These three issues have provided a focus for extensive advocacy work by opponents of James Bay II. For reasons of space, we focus our analysis on the advocacy work of two of the key opponents: the Cree of northern Quebec and U.S. environmental groups.

In order to fight the project, the Cree Indians have launched several court challenges in the Canadian courts. Beginning in 1990, the Cree challenged a ruling made by the National Energy Board (NEB) in 1990 that approved the export licences for sales contracts between Hydro-Québec and its U.S. customers in New York and Vermont subject to the condition that an environmental screening of the project be conducted before construction commenced.[27] Thus far, they have had some success with this challenge,[28]

---

27   The Quebec government quickly filed an application in the Quebec Court of Appeal challenging the authority of the NEB to impose this environmental screening condition. See *Le Procureur General Du Quebec -et- L'office National de L'energie*, Application filed in the Quebec Court of Appeal by the Province of Quebec, 26 October 1990.

28   In September 1991, Federal Court of Canada Judge Paul Rouleau ruled that the James Bay and Northern Quebec Agreement negotiated between the federal government, the Province of Quebec, and native groups in 1974 and 1975 is a federal law, not just a contract between the federal government and the Cree and Inuit, as argued by the federal government, the Province of Quebec, and Hydro-Québec. On this basis, the Cree have contended that a full federal review of the James Bay II project must be carried out before the project is begun (*Cree Regional Authority* v. *Robinson* (10 September 1991), Montreal T-451-91 (T.D.)). See Sandro Contenta, "Quebec Project Blocked: Dams Need Federal Approval, Court Says",

and have managed to convince a federal court judge to overturn the NEB regulatory decision to approve the project without a full federal environmental assessment under the James Bay and Northern Quebec Agreement (1975). However, it is unclear if their argument can ultimately succeed in the Supreme Court of Canada given the usually restrictive mandates of the courts in reviewing tribunal decisions, and the narrow mandates of the regulatory tribunals whose actions have been challenged.

Probably the most important development in the conflict over James Bay II has been the growth of public interest in the United States about the environmental and social consequences of the project.[29] For several years, U.S. public interest groups and the Cree have been putting pressure on local power authorities in several states not to purchase electricity from Hydro-Québec.

One of the first jurisdictions to respond to this pressure was the State of Maine. In the early fall of 1990, the State cancelled a four-billion-dollar export contract with Hydro-Québec. In late August 1990, a coalition of groups including the Sierra Club and the Cree Indians of northern Quebec filed a writ in the New York Supreme Court seeking a stiff review of James Bay II before the contracts are allowed. The New York Power Authority filed a response contending that the state government could not act unilaterally on a matter of international trade. They also contended that New York's environmental assessment laws did not apply, and that Canadian laws were sufficiently strong to make sure the project was fully assessed.[30] Partially because of the publicity attracted by the Supreme Court challenge, New York City Council adopted a motion calling on the state power authority to reduce purchases from the province in the fall of 1990. With public pressure still mounting,[31] New York Mayor David Dinkins wrote a letter to the New York Power Authority in August 1991 asking it to reconsider the deal and urging

---

Toronto Star (11 September 1991) A1.

29   In part, some of this activism was inspired by the Cree themselves, who travelled through the eastern United States by canoe in summer 1990 to help alert U.S. citizens, groups and environmentalists to the James Bay II project. See Pegi Dover, "U.S. Groups Fight James Bay II" (1991) 14:2 Probe Post 6.

30   For its part, officials in the consulate-general office in New York argued that a ruling in favour of the environmentalists would be discriminatory against Canada and was banned under the FTA.

31   On 6 January 1991, more than 250 New Yorkers crowded a sidewalk outside the Canadian consulate to protest development of James Bay II, chanting and singing folk songs and comparing the project with similar projects in South American rainforests. This protest went on for several days and was the source of great embarrassment to the federal government of Canada.

that an extension on the withdrawal deadline be sought.[32] It is thought that the public pressure and Dinkins' letter may have been key factors in the recent announcement that Hydro-Québec intends to delay the James Bay II project.[33]

Activists in other U.S. states have also put pressure on the Quebec and Canadian governments. In March 1991, a referendum was held in Vermont asking residents whether or not they were willing to buy power from Quebec if the lands of Cree Indians had to be flooded and vast wilderness areas destroyed. While environmentalists narrowly lost the Vermont referendum, they did demonstrate that a remarkable degree of concern about the James Bay II project exists in that state.

Pressure has also been growing in several U.S. and Canadian jurisdictions to implement a new approach to analyzing energy demand based on energy conservation. For example, the Public Service Board of Vermont issued an order in April 1990 that established that the "least-cost demand" option should be the guiding principle behind all energy decisions in the state. This option would require the Board to take into account environmental damage as well as energy conservation when hydroelectric power purchases are contemplated. It is expected that these kinds of institutional reforms will reduce demand for hydroelectric power substantially in the next decade. Similar kinds of reforms are being urged in Ontario.[34]

Despite all of these activities, it is likely that this project will be undertaken without the blessing of a full review that would take into account its long-term implications for the environment. In sum, this international resource-use conflict is rooted in the policies of the federal and Quebec governments, which have been promoting electricity exports without fully reckoning with the social and environmental impacts associated with such large dam projects. The key failure identified by this example is that existing institutions in both nations appear incapable of examining the broad context in which sound energy planning and management must take place.

Refillable Beverage Containers and International Trade

A future conflict is almost certain to develop under the General

---

32 Associated Press, "Demonstrators Oppose Hydro Deal", *The Globe and Mail* (13 August 1991) at B2; Canadian Press, "New York City Mayor Urges Delay in $13 Billion Quebec Hydro Deal", *Toronto Star* (6 August 1991) at B2.

33 See McKenzie, *supra*, note 26.

34 Hearings on the use of least-cost energy planning in Ontario (with a focus on the natural gas sector) are scheduled to be held in the summer of 1992 by the Ontario Energy Board.

Agreement on Tariffs and Trade (GATT), the FTA, or a future NAFTA because of the expressed intention of some governments in North America and other industrialized nations to implement or maintain systems of deposits that promote refillable containers, and/or quotas requiring refillable containers for domestic beer, wine, wine coolers, and soft drinks sold in their jurisdictions. These systems, while enhancing environmental protection goals, conflict with one of the key goals of liberalized trade — to encourage expansion of efficient producers into foreign markets — because they often either require producers and distributors to transport their empty containers back to the point of origin for refilling or necessitate the establishment of depots and bottling plants for local refilling. This case study illustrates most clearly the policy conflict between free trade and bioregionalism.

The backdrop to this environmental and resource-use conflict is the garbage crisis in most industrialized nations. Problems have become acute in many parts of North America, and political pressure on legislators to develop new regulations to encourage waste reduction, and to promote reuse and recycling of used materials, has grown steadily in many jurisdictions.[35] Meanwhile, recent estimates suggest that Canadians produce about one ton per person each year of solid waste and that more than 85 percent of this waste is landfilled, 10 percent is incinerated, and approximately 5 percent is recycled.[36]

A great deal of this solid waste is packaging waste, which does not add a great deal to the quality of life experienced by most urban-industrial people.[37] In order to reduce packaging waste produced in North America,

---

35   By the end of the 1980s, approximately three thousand landfills were operating in the United States, and it is widely expected that many U.S. communities will run out of landfill space to bury their garbage before the turn of the century. A similar situation has developed in Ontario. Whether this presents a "crisis" or not is debatable. Environmental groups see the looming landfill crunch as an opportunity to promote the 3Rs. For example, "It's Not Garbage", an Ontario coalition of environmental groups formed in late 1989, argues that what are called domestic and industrial solid wastes and exported out of large cities to landfills, or to incinerators for burning, are used resources that can and should be recycled and reused. Environmentalists also oppose incineration because of concerns about toxic emissions. For further discussion on these themes, see Paul Connett, *Waste Management as if the Future Mattered* (New York: Work on Waste, 1989).

36   Friends of the Earth Canada, Pollution Probe & World Wildlife Fund, *The Summit Environmental Accountability Project — Report on Canada* (Ottawa: FOE, 1991) at 19-22.

37   In fact, even though North Americans use about twice as much packaging as most Europeans, it could be argued that Canadians and Americans do not really benefit from use of this additional material. Moreover, making the packaging, especially plastic and paper packaging, causes considerable damage to the environment. On this subject, see Canadian Institute for Environmental Law and Policy, *A Regulatory Agenda for Solid Waste Reduction*

environmentalists have advocated a shift back to refillable beverage containers. Studies of waste composition suggest that 4 to 8 percent of the domestic solid waste by volume (before compaction) being landfilled in developed nations is used beverage containers for beer, milk, soft drinks, mineral water, fruit drinks, wine, and spirits.[38]

Advocates of refillables argue that this is a terrible waste of valuable materials such as glass metal, and plastic. Thus, political pressure to increase refilling rates for used containers has grown enormously; the aim is both to conserve landfill and to encourage people to make life-style changes to protect the environment. To a great extent, this advocacy has been prompted by the recognition that:

1. recycling rates for used beverage containers are often low, even where voluntary and mandatory curbside collection programs (such as the Blue Box program in Ontario) are in place;[39] and

2. reuse of bottles and other products is an important principle to incorporate into solid waste laws and policies.

While a debate persists as to the relative merits and efficiency of reusing refillable beverage containers rather than recycling them, there are several life-cycle studies which show that reusing bottles in a decentralized manner produces enormous benefits for the environment.[40] The exact level of environmental benefits from refillables is tied to "trippage rates" for the specific container,[41] the weight and design of the empty container, and the

---

(Report Prepared for the Solid Waste Environmental Assessment Plan [SWEAP], Metropolitan Toronto Works Department) (Toronto: SWEAP, 1989).

38 Returpack, "Beverage Containers — An Environmental Issue" in *Synopsis of the Swedish and Norwegian Industry-organized Deposit and Recycling Concept* (Stockholm, 1990) at 1.

39 For example, the number of used soft drink containers collected in Blue Box programs is in the order of 10 to 20 percent of those sold in Ontario: see D. McRobert *et al.*, *Five Years of Failure: A Documentation of the Failure of the Ontario Government to Reduce Solid and Hazardous Waste Quantities* (Toronto: Pollution Probe, 1990).

40 For example, a 1989 life-cycle study prepared for the U.S. plastics industry showed that reusing a refillable glass bottle more than eight times (rather than making a new one) will produce lower levels of air and water pollution emissions, and will save energy because the amount of energy required to make a new container is substantially more than that required to wash and redistribute a refillable container. See V. Sellers & J. Sellers, *Comparative Energy and Environmental Impacts of Soft Drink Delivery Systems* (Report prepared for National Association of Plastic Container Recovery) (Prairie Village, Kans.: Franklin Associates, 1989). For a review of this study, and other life-cycle studies on refillables, see U. Valiante & P. Vopni, *Environmental Options for Wine and Spirits Bottles* (Toronto: Pollution Probe, 1991).

41 "Trippage rate" is the term used to describe the average number of trips the container can

distance from bottlers to markets. Plastic refillable containers now being used in Europe for soft drinks offer additional benefits such as lightness and increased safety and durability, and have produced massive energy savings there as well. In any case, when the used containers are collected, refilled, and washed close to where the product is marketed, this creates local jobs and ensures that spin-off benefits are largely retained by the community consuming the beverage product rather than exported to adjacent or foreign jurisdictions.

To establish and maintain refillable systems for distribution of beverage containers, deposit/refund systems are almost always used to ensure that the containers are returned for reuse. Deposit/refund systems have proven very effective in diverting used containers from landfill sites and incinerators. Where deposit/refund systems are employed with depots and are well promoted, container redemption rates can reach up to 95 percent.[42] Deposits also have a proven track record in reducing litter, and for this reason are supported by numerous people, including naturalists and cottagers.

Despite all these advantages, small and large retailers of beverages in many developed nations dislike deposit/refund systems because they create more work for employees handling the bottles or cans,[43] the cans and bottles are unsightly and dirty, the glass bottles sometimes break, and deposit systems are awkward to maintain. This opposition of grocers to deposit systems has contributed significantly to the decline in the use of refillable containers in many developed nations. However, other factors contribute to the decline, including growing consumer interest in convenience, concerns about product safety (because glass containers break and plastic containers can absorb toxics

---

make before it is recycled by the bottler, broken by the consumer (and thus, is not returned for deposit), or inadvertently landfilled. In the 1950s, the eye-glass-thick Coke bottles were washed and reused up to forty-five times. In fact, compared to disposable aluminum cans often used to distribute beer and soft drinks, which require staggering amounts of electricity to produce and are often carelessly landfilled, this was a phenomenal rate of resource conservation. In some sectors, these high rates of bottle reuse, or trippage, lasted into the 1980s. For example, beer bottles in Ontario were reused an average of twenty-two times before the switch to "tall neck" bottles. Even today, beer bottles in Ontario are reused between twelve and fifteen times.

42   In Ontario's beer industry, the container redemption rate for beer bottles with a ten cent deposit exceeds 98 percent: see D. McRobert & A. Imada, *Doing More For Less: The Role of An Expanded Deposit/Refund System for Recovery of Ontario's Used Beverage Containers* (Brief Submitted by Pollution Probe to the Ontario Government) (Toronto: Pollution Probe, 1991) at 18. See also Valiante & Vopni, *supra*, note 40.

43   Handling fees are usually paid to store owners to compensate for storage and handling costs. However, most store owners contend that these fees are inadequate.

and become contaminated),[44] and the corporate goals of the beverage industry to maximize profits.[45]

In order to force bottlers and other beverage producers to reuse beverage containers in the wake of this resistance to refillables and deposit systems, many governments have enacted and enforced quotas requiring that a certain percentage of beverage product be sold in refillable containers. Some have gone so far as to ban the sale of non-refillable containers such as cans, tetra briks ("juice boxes"), and plastic bottles for certain beverages. Some advocates of refillables have proposed as a further step the standardization of bottles to simplify their collection and reuse.

Among governments the most popular of these measures is refillable quotas. In the past two years, there has been a resurgence of interest in the use of quotas to promote the use of refillable beverage containers,[46] which will no doubt pose this issue in stark terms to trade tribunals. For example, the German government has established ambitious targets for refillable container use.[47] These targets will certainly raise concerns on the part of those who want to export beverage products to Germany. Nevertheless, the German government defends these targets because they will contribute to energy conservation and reduce the threat of global warming.

The issue of refillable quotas has also been gaining attention in Canada. During the 1990 election campaign in Ontario, a plan by the then-Liberal government to scrap a quota of 30 percent refillables for the soft drink industry became an intense political issue. In the heat of the election campaign, Bob Rae, leader of the New Democratic Party (NDP), promised to implement a fully refillable system for the domestic beer, wine, wine coolers, and soft drink industries, in order to reduce the amount of beverage container waste going to Ontario landfills.

---

44   These contaminated containers can pose health risks if not screened out for recycling instead of reuse. Fortunately, new technology now being used in Europe allows for detection and screening of contaminated plastic refillable containers.

45   For example, these goals include increasing market share (this has been true of the soft drink industry's push for one-way containers); reducing labour costs associated with refilling operations and transportation of bottles; squeezing out local bottlers in small communities and centralizing bottling operations in major urban centres; and externalizing the environmental and social costs associated with beverage container disposal and/or recycling onto society as a whole.

46   S. Chaplin, "The Return of Refillable Bottles", Resource Recycling: North America's Recycling Journal 9:3 at 130-135.

47   Targets for refillables established in Germany, which are to be implemented in the next two years, include the following: 90 percent for beer and mineral water; 80 percent for soft drinks; 50 percent for wine; and 35 percent for fruit drinks. See Chaplin, id.

Since the election of the NDP as the government of Ontario, its passion for refillables seems to have cooled somewhat, partially because of growing pressure from industry. In October 1990, the soft drink industry threatened to commence a legal challenge on enforcement of the current 30 percent refillable quota, on the grounds that the province does not require bottlers and distributors of other beverages to sell their product in refillable containers and, consequently, that this could violate the FTA and even certain sections of the Charter of Rights and Freedoms.[48] If successful, a challenge under the FTA or the Charter could undermine Ontario's current regulatory regime. Meanwhile, the Ontario distilleries warned the Ontario government in late April that they will probably move their operations to the United States if the provincial government requires them to use refillable containers. They were able to do this, to a large degree, because the FTA allows them to produce and bottle their product in the United States even though it is marketed in Canada.

Pressure to break down interprovincial and bilateral barriers to trade in beer is also growing.[49] If the barriers to trade in beer are partially removed, or completely broken down, then it will be much more difficult to ensure refillables are used for beer in Canada: American companies, who are seeking entry into the Canadian market, use non-refillable cans for export markets almost exclusively, because this container is cheaper to produce, market, and transport over longer distances.

Finally, it should be noted that the New Brunswick government has implemented a system of deposits that favours refillables.[50] Under the

---

48   It could be argued that there are dozens of court decisions that would hold that this type of regulation would not violate the Charter (*Canadian Charter of Rights and Freedoms*, Part I of the *Constitution Act, 1982*, being Schedule B of the *Canada Act, 1982* (U.K.), 1982, c.11). However, the argument that there should be a certain degree of equality in the treatment of all domestic beverage industries does have some merit, and might find a sympathetic audience, particularly in the lower courts.

49   Canadian Press, "Tentative Deal May Spell End to Provincial Beer Barriers", *Toronto Star* (16 February 1991) at C2. As this article went to press, two GATT rulings on beer trade between Canada and the U.S. (one handed down in late 1991 which ruled that provincial governments in Canada discriminated against American beer distributors, and another handed down in March 1992 which ruled that American governments discriminated against Canadian beer companies) had forced provincial governments in Canada to allow beer to flow between provinces more readily. In addition, the federal government of Canada was in the process of completing negotiations on an agreement with the U.S. Office of the Trade Representative on compliance with the requirements of the two GATT decisions.

50   *Beverage Container Act*, S.N.B. 1991, c.B-2.2. For a summary, see Government of New Brunswick, "Beverage Container Legislation: Summary", Spring 1991. As this article went to press, the Ontario government announced a 10 cent per container environmental tax on all

legislation, all containers are returned for deposit. However, half of the deposit is forfeited to a fund in support of container recycling when a non-refillable container is returned to a depot or store. It could be argued that the New Brunswick system violates the FTA to the extent that it promotes refillables and discriminates against American imports, which are all non-refillable.

These proposed measures raise important trade issues, and it has been argued that such requirements, if ever implemented, would be construed by tribunals as non-tariff barriers to trade. The only international case on refillables quotas and bans on non-refillable containers was decided by the European Court of Justice in September 1988.[51] In that case, the Danish government was challenging Directive 85/339, which had been issued by the European Economic Commission (EEC) in 1985. This directive was intended to encourage the goal of recycling of beverage containers in the European Community (EC), but did not specify that member states of the EC were to employ refillable systems and deposit/refund systems in order to achieve this goal.

Prior to the issuing of the EEC directive, Denmark had banned the sale of metal cans and other non-refillable containers for soft drinks and beer in Denmark, and had severely restricted the sale of non-refillable containers by setting an annual limit on sales and requiring that the containers be returned to the retailer from which they had been purchased to obtain the refund.[52] However, Denmark allowed Danish companies to export non-returnable, non-

---

non-refillable alcohol beverage containers sold in the province as part of its 1992 Budget Statement. It is expected that the new tax will raise $85 million and help to preserve the extensive refillable beer system in Ontario for domestic beer distribution. However, federal Trade Minister Michael Wilson stated in early June 1992 that the new tax could undermine a trade deal he had negotiated with the U.S. government to avoid a "brewing" beer trade war between the U.S. and Canada: see "Beer Can Levy Undermines U.S. Trade Deal, Wilson Says", *Toronto Star* (4 June 1992) at B3. In addition, the B.C. government introduced legislation in May 1992 similar to New Brunswick's into its legislature and the Ontario government had made clear that it was considering applying the approach to soft drinks as well.

51   *Re Disposable Cans — Commission of the European Communities* v. *Denmark*, Case 320/86, [1989] C.M.L.R. 619 (European Court of Justice). For an analysis and critique of this decision, see P. Kromarek, "Environmental Protection and the Free Movement of Goods: The Danish Bottle Case" (1990) 2:1 J. of Environmental Law 89.

52   To make the system work, the Danish government imposed a deposit on all beverage containers and limited the number of approved container types that could be sold and returned to retailers to thirty types. This latter measure was intended to reduce handling and storage costs to retailers. The Danish government also put into place regulations and penalties to ensure that the system would function effectively.

refillable containers to other markets in Europe. In part, these ban and quota measures were intended as an environmental measure to maximize container reuse and substantially reduce beverage container litter. However, the ban was also embraced by the Danish brewing industry with enthusiasm because the extra costs associated with transportation of empty bottles back to other nations made it uneconomic for German breweries to export bottled beer to Denmark.

After several years of operation, Denmark's ban was challenged in 1986 by the EEC under Article 30 of the Treaty of Rome. Under the Treaty provision, any non-tariff barrier to trade must balance the protection of the environment and the freedom to market a product in the European community.

In its decision the Court examined numerous precedents dealing with the extent to which a member state in the EC can develop laws and regulations in order to accomplish certain environmental goals. Since protection of the environment had been held to be one of the essential objectives of the European Community, the Court recognized that it might well circumscribe the application of Article 30 in the Treaty of Rome. At the same time, the Court held that the proposed initiatives intended to protect the environment must not "go beyond the inevitable restrictions which are justified by the pursuit of the objective of environmental protection."[53]

In applying this generalized test, the Court upheld the use of deposit/refund systems for beverage containers in Denmark. Indeed, it recognized that deposit/refund systems are an essential measure to ensure that the EEC directive is implemented and that such systems can be justified as a legitimate restriction on the movement of goods. At the same time, the Court ruled that the refillable quota restricting the sale of beverages in non-approved, refillable glass bottles was not a legitimate restriction.[54]

There are several interesting points about this case. First, as may be anticipated, the German brewers were not deterred by the requirement to

---

53   *Re Disposable Beer Cans — Commission of the European Communities* v. *Denmark, supra,* note 51, at 630.

54   The Court ruled that the following considerations must be taken into account in formulating its ruling:

1.   a deposit/refund system, while far from the ideal system, would still divert substantial waste from landfills;

2.   the producers of the beverages sold in non-approved containers had set up a system for reuse of the non-approved collected containers; and

3.   the non-approved sales constituted only a small portion of the overall quantity of beverages consumed in Denmark.

establish refillable systems in Denmark. In fact, even before the case was brought to the Court they had established efficient systems for operating with refillable bottles. Second, the ban on use of metal cans for beer and soft drinks sold in Denmark was not struck down by the European Court of Justice; rather, the EEC amended its complaint so that the challenge to these provisions in the law was deleted from the original complaint.[55]

In the result, the key message of this case is that member states of the EEC do have a degree of latitude in shaping environmental protection laws, but these laws will be struck down if they are construed by the European Court as an unjustifiable barrier to trade in goods and services. Since the level of environmental protection that is justifiable and the kinds of measures that will be rescinded on trade grounds were not really clarified by this decision, this issue will be explored further by the EEC in the future.

The case has received mixed reviews. Some European environmentalists contend that the case upheld important facets of the Danish law and do not think the result is a problem. In contrast, one Canadian environmentalist lambasted the Court.[56]

In sum, refillables quotas pose important issues about the trade-offs between environmental protection and free trade. The Danish case suggests that the goals of waste reduction and increased freedom in the marketplace, including freedom to concentrate and centralize operations, will not be easily reconciled. While it can be argued that a deposit/refund system for all beverage containers probably can be rationalized as an appropriate environmental measure within the context of current trade agreements, refillable quotas and product bans for non-refillable containers will probably be subject to challenge, and it is likely that they would be struck down under current international trade laws if they appeared to restrict trade between nations.

---

55   In doing so, the EEC appears to have recognized that a challenge to this provision would probably not have succeeded, because the restriction applied to both foreign and domestic producers wishing to sell cans in the Danish market. In addition, this amendment appeared to recognize that member states should retain some power to restrict the kinds of packaging used to distribute products sold in their countries.

56   In an article published in July 1990, Steve Shrybman wrote:

It is difficult to imagine a situation in which an environmental regulation could be on a stronger footing. Yet despite the absence of any demonstrable impediment to trade, the European Court of Justice had no reservation about finding Denmark's container legislation inconsistent with the principle of freer trade. By characterizing national environmental laws as non-tariff barriers to trade, opponents of strong regulation have a potent new weapon with which to assail these important initiatives.

For further discussion, see Steven Shrybman, "International Trade and the Environment: An Environmental Assessment of Present GATT Negotiations" (1990) 17:2 Alternatives 20.

The problem with the European Court decision is that it appears to reject the principle of local production for local consumption. Meanwhile, economies of scale are driving corporations towards non-refillable, single-use containers that are often disposed of in scarce landfill space, cause increased pollution, and waste energy. The diversity of laws in different jurisdictions in Europe and North America also poses problems and militates against development of more stringent refillable quotas. Finally, there are no institutional means to put pressure on corporations and governments in North America to consider the issue of refillables quotas in the context of a bioregional approach to trade and economic development. If this issue is to be addressed in a systematic way, then a new approach to resolving this kind of international resource conflict must be established.

ARE CURRENT DISPUTE-RESOLUTION MECHANISMS WORKING?

The two case studies discussed above represent two types of transboundary resource issues that are likely to become more commonplace in North America in the next decade. It is argued here that such issues are symptomatic of the expanding scope and complexity of bilateral and trilateral relations on the continent during the past thirty years. Some commentators have argued that, despite this expansion in the scope and complexity of bilateral and trilateral relations, institutional development has remained stymied.[57] With respect to environmental matters, transboundary accords, agreements, memos of understandings, and other such instruments have proliferated in recent years. However, it could be argued that these new agreements and instruments have not strengthened current bilateral relations or improved dispute-resolution mechanisms. Rather, it appears that some binational institutions are being weakened by incrementalism and devolution of authority to other bodies or subnational authorities.

What then are the mechanisms available to resolve the James Bay II dispute and a possible conflict over refillable quotas as described above? Are these existing mechanisms sufficient to ensure the appropriate allocation of resources and the effective settlement of disputes about those resources? Both issues are discussed below. Three types of approaches to dispute resolution are examined and discussed: (1) the "*ad hoc*" approach; (2) a more structured binational mechanism, as illustrated by the International Joint Commission; and (3) the dispute-resolution mechanism relied on in the FTA. We argue that current institutional mechanisms are desperately inadequate, and, as a result,

---

57   For example, see D.G. LeMarquand & A. Scott, "Canada's International Environmental Relations" *in* O. Dwevidwi, ed., *Resources and Environment: Policy Perspectives for Canada* (Toronto: McClelland & Steward, 1980) at 79.

gaps in institutional mandates are causing inappropriate resource allocations and exacerbating certain environmental conflicts.

The Ad Hoc Approach: An Overload of Crisis Management

The machinery that exists to deal with bilateral conflicts is in many respects as complex and varied as the relationship itself. While a comprehensive review of these institutions cannot be provided here,[58] it is important to note that well-developed diplomatic networks continue to manage the bulk of Canada-U.S. relations with particular regard to the settlement of binational conflicts. In addition, a great many common institutional linkages exist between the two nations. These institutional networks, which have evolved over the course of Canada-U.S. relations, vary greatly in their nature and functions. Some of the joint institutions range from essentially consultative ones that provide only for casual or incidental coordination of policies, to others that are purely technical and administrative in nature (such as the International Boundary Commission).

Two commentators have characterized this incremental or *"ad hoc"* approach to dispute resolution in this way:

> In the past the two nations have handled environmental problems by reaching temporary accommodations; they have not agreed on rules of behavior. Their environmental relationship is thus founded on a series of ad hoc arrangements, in contrast with a problem-solving approach based upon commonly shared principles and guiding rules. This ad hoc approach is the key problem in the environmental relationship.[59]

To put it simply, the *ad hoc* approach is not working, and appears to be overburdened, because of the nature and diversity of disputes now on the public policy agenda. Issues such as the transboundary movement of hazardous and solid waste, transboundary air pollution, fisheries allocations and quotas, and potential water diversion projects (which could affect numerous rivers and lakes[60]) are complicated and cannot be adequately handled using the *ad hoc* approach.

Continuing reliance on the *ad hoc* approach was demonstrated in the

---

58   For reviews on this subject, see Standing Senate Committee on Foreign Affairs, U.S. Senate, *supra*, note 11; Kal J. Holsti & Thomas Allen Levy, "Bilateral Institutions and Transgovernmental Relations Between Canada and the United States" *in* Annette Baker Fox, Alfred O. Hero, Jr. & Joseph S. Nye, Jr., eds., *Canada and the United States: Transnational and Transgovernmental Relations* (New York: Columbia University Press, 1976) 283; and William R. Willoughby, *The Joint Organizations of Canada and the United States* (Toronto: University of Toronto Press, 1979).

59   Carroll & Mack, *supra*, note 11, at 36.

60   On this subject, see the case studies presented in de Mestral & Leith, *supra*, note 8.

negotiation of the Acid Rain Accord signed by Canada and the United States in 1990 and released in February 1991. While the specific provisions of the Accord should reduce acid rain emissions in both nations, the process employed to develop the Accord was secretive and unsatisfactory. For this reason, it should not be surprising that the Accord does not provide for independent reviews of progress towards goal achievement and does not provide for public consultation prior to preparation of government reports on compliance with the Accord.[61]

The International Joint Commission: Still in Search of a Mandate

Perhaps the best known, and most analyzed, bilateral Canada-U.S. dispute-settlement body is the International Joint Commission (IJC). In recent times, the Commission has gained considerable profile owing to its work in the Great Lakes region, although its mandate extends "along the common frontier." Almost any discussion of institutional reform leads to a discussion of possible reform of the IJC.[62] When one examines the IJC's mandate, it is easy to understand this tendency.

The IJC was established under the Boundary Waters Treaty of 1909. The Treaty vests the Commission with a number of capacities, including quasi-judicial, investigative, and arbitral powers. In its quasi-judicial role,[63] the Commission is empowered to investigate and pass judgment on all cases involving the use, obstruction, or diversion of boundary and transboundary water when the result is to alter the flow of boundary waters or to "raise" the natural level of transboundary waters.

As to its investigative function, the IJC has jurisdiction under Article IX to examine and report on "any questions or matters of differences arising ... involving the rights, obligations, or interest of either ... along the common frontier." As long as the matter pertains to the "common frontier", there are no limitations on the Commission's power to investigate questions of fact or law involved in any dispute or problem. Rather than make decisions, however, the Commission can only apply its investigative machinery to the issue posed and provide governments with a report that may serve as a basis for policy reform.

---

61   Jean Hennessey & Don Munton, "Background Statement on Canada-U.S. Acid Rain Agreement" 13 March 1991.

62   The most comprehensive review of these reform proposals is Munton, *supra*, note 11.

63   *Treaty Between the United States and Great Britain Relating to Boundary Waters, and Questions Arising between the United States and Canada*, 11 January 1909, T.S. 548, reproduced in R.S.C. 1985, c.I-17, Schedule, Articles III, IV, and VIII.

Finally, under Article X of the Treaty, the IJC is empowered to arbitrate "any question or matter of difference" in Canada-U.S. relations, whether arising along the common frontier or not. However, such jurisdiction will rest only with the "advice and consent of the Governor-in-Council" in Canada, and of the Senate in the United States. Once jurisdiction is established, a majority of the IJC is given the authority to render a binding decision on any matter so referred. Perhaps the most interesting aspect of the Commission's arbitral power is that it has never been exercised. It has been suggested that the requirement of U.S. Senate approval, especially "in light of the political history of the exercise of the 'advise and consent' powers of the Senate", would set a significant precedent, and this may be why the Commission has never been vested with this arbitral jurisdiction.[64]

Despite the IJC's potentially broad mandate, most commentators doubt there will ever be sufficient political will to give the Commission the power to exercise its arbitral powers or to expand its role. On the contrary, current trends suggest that the IJC is being marginalized and its importance is being reduced because of diminished resource allocations to it, the reorganization of some of its boards, and a decrease in work delegated to it by both national governments. In view of this pattern of marginalization, some commentators believe that the IJC will be lucky to maintain its present stature. It seems ironic that this is the case. It could be argued that, if the IJC's role were expanded in such a way that it could undertake bioregional assessments of activities along the U.S.-Canada border — and along the Atlantic, Pacific, and Arctic Ocean border regions and in the Great Lakes Basin in particular — then it would be able to play a very important role in fostering more appropriate environmental practices in both nations.

Dispute-resolution Provisions in the FTA: An Inadequate Response

Under the Canada-U.S. Free Trade Agreement, a panel may be established to resolve conflicts that arise under the Agreement when a matter is referred by either the U.S. or Canadian government. While few cases have been decided to date, it is argued here that the ability of these panels to deal with transboundary resource-use conflicts and environmental problems is seriously limited.

The first decision made by a panel under the FTA illustrates this thesis. In this case, it was found that the Canadian requirement that all salmon and herring caught in British Columbia waters be landed in Canada for

---

64   Maxwell Cohen, "The Régime of Boundary Waters: The Canadian-United States Experience", [1975] 3 Recueil des Cours 219 at 258-259.

conservation and fisheries management purposes was an unfair trade restriction (disguised as a conservation measure).[65] While a compromise was eventually reached between the governments involved in this dispute, it is unclear whether the goal of species conservation is protected by it.[66] The fact that the precedent favours trade over environmental objectives can be seen as a rationale for apparently conflicting policy objectives. As Saunders has noted in commenting on this decision, "it is unlikely that GATT or other trade-related institutions will be significant forums for initiating measures aimed at the environmental consequences of trade."[67]

In sum, existing dispute-resolution mechanisms are problematic for two main reasons. First, the *ad hoc* approach that now characterizes bilateral institutions creates a number of gaps and limits to the effective resolution of binational resource conflicts. Second, the institutions created to deal with trade disputes do not have a sufficient mandate to protect the environment.

SUGGESTIONS FOR A NEW POLICY AND INSTITUTIONAL FRAMEWORK

If the trends in international resource-use conflicts identified above are not addressed in a more systematic manner, environmental problems seem likely to continue to grow, and conflicts may escalate. In order to address this situation, and ensure that long-term environmental impacts of current development patterns are taken into account by existing institutions, the *ad hoc* approach to dispute resolution must give way to a new approach. This new approach must, at the very least, provide a means to accommodate or resolve the policy conflict between the bioregionalist perspective for governance and the trend towards trade liberalization.

In this section, two options are explored. The first option deals with improving existing mechanisms by incorporating an environmental mandate into those institutions. The second option is to establish a new institution.

Incorporating or Expanding Environmental Mandates in Existing Institutions

It could be argued that the problem of FTA panels to date is not a lack of bilateral and multilateral institutions. Instead, it is the inability of panels established under the FTA, owing to either a lack of desire or a perceived

---

65   *In the Matter of Canada's Landing Requirement for Pacific Coast Salmon and Herring.* Canada-United States Trade Commission Panel, 16 October 1989, 2 TCT 7162.

66   See Madelaine Drohan, "Canada Agrees to Allow Fish to be Sold Directly for Export", *The Globe and Mail* (7 November 1989) at B1; J. Lewington, "Trade Mechanism Little Help in U.S. Fish Dispute", *The Globe and Mail* (10 November 1989) at B1.

67   Saunders, *supra*, note 11, at 386.

lack of mandate, to deal effectively with transboundary environmental relations. Certainly an argument could be made that it would be inappropriate for a tribunal to resolve environmental and resource disputes under the FTA because it would lack the authority and the mandate to deal comprehensively with trade-related environmental issues. Meanwhile, it has been argued that the capacity of some existing domestic tribunals, such as the NEB, to resolve disputes has been substantially eroded by the FTA.[68]

The failures of other institutions and dispute-resolution mechanisms are more difficult to understand. In part, a lack of political desire on the part of national governments may have contributed to these failures. However, the lack of a clear environmental mandate to plan or examine issues on a bioregional basis has probably played a more important role in many cases. For example, one of the interesting trends evident in the work of the IJC is that, even though bilateral problems have been increasing, the number of references going to the IJC compared to two decades ago is decreasing. Areas where work should have been delegated to the IJC include toxic chemicals, air pollution, and spills.

Whatever the source of deficiencies in existing dispute-resolution mechanisms, it is important that the problem be remedied as quickly as possible, especially in view of the "new epoch" of environmental concerns described in the first section of this paper. One approach would be to supplement the mandate of all institutions to include an environmental mandate, and thus perhaps enlarge the scope of their adjudication. For some institutions, such as the panels under the FTA, this may require some delicate negotiations, since the mandate of the institution may indeed conflict with the goals and objectives of the agreement under which it is established. For other tribunals, especially those that have some experience with environmental matters, the task may be less onerous. With respect to the IJC, for example, the challenge might be simply to make explicit that it be able to begin treating the Great Lakes Basin as a bioregion.

The weakness of this approach, of course, is that it assumes that bilateral or multilateral institutions cover a broad range of transboundary environmental issues. As the case studies suggest, some of the multi-faceted issues that are likely to arise in certain conflicts will not be easily delegated to a single tribunal or institution. The approach further assumes that existing institutions can in fact be modified without affecting their capacities to carry out their primary mandates, which in some cases may not be compatible with the goals of environmental protection and bioregional sustainable development.

---

68   For a discussion of this issue, see J. Dillon, "Continental Energy Policy" *in* D. Cameron, ed., *The Free Trade Deal* (Toronto: Lorimer, 1988).

A Call for a New Appellate Tribunal

Enhancing existing institutions so that they must take bioregional concerns into account in making decisions is one way of addressing bilateral environmental and resource-use conflicts. Another approach would be to create a new appellate tribunal to cope with the multiplicity of environmental issues that might require expert adjudication.[69] This institution could review decisions made under the FTA, a future NAFTA, or even under the GATT, to ensure that environmental factors have been considered appropriately by panels or tribunals under trade agreements. The basis for, and the mandate of, this new appellate tribunal would have to be carefully studied before it could be established. However, based on this preliminary analysis, the following mandate for a tribunal adjudicating disputes arising in North America is proposed:

- It would able to adjudicate any dispute pertaining to an environmental or natural resources use, unless another institution (including a court or tribunal in Canada, Mexico, or the United States) was already dealing with that dispute,

- It would be accessible to all aggrieved parties, including affected public and private interest groups in any affected nations, and would seek to ensure an efficient and timely response to a matter raised,

- Each country would make adequate financial resources available to its environmental groups to launch actions,

- Its decisions would be binding on the parties,

- It would have investigatory and reporting powers similar to those now possessed by the IJC.

Admittedly, this institutional response to resolving very fundamental policy conflicts is incomplete. However, this approach would allow the public and environmental non-governmental organizations to raise important issues about the implications of trade agreements or disputes in an organized forum that has a mandate to deal with such concerns. At least there will be some public confidence that someone is "minding the environmental store". It seems appropriate that this kind of institutional reform be undertaken immediately in the context of the free trade negotiations.

CONCLUSIONS

In the long term, we believe that the most practical way to resolve

---

69   There are a number of other proposals for new institutions that we are aware of. For example, see L.K. Caldwell, "Emerging Boundary Environmental Challenges and Institutional Issues: Canada and the United States" (Paper presented at The Tri-national Conference on the North American Experience on Managing International Transboundary Water Resources: The Boundary Commissions of Canada, the United States and Mexico, 13-19 April 1991) [unpublished].

growing international resource-use conflicts is to establish a new appellate body where those concerned can raise issues in a systematic manner. There are disadvantages to this approach, including the risk that this tribunal will be undermined by the appointment of insensitive panel members. However, there are numerous advantages, and there would be an opportunity to raise interconnected issues, such as energy use and resource conservation.

In the short term, integration of broader environmental protection goals into the mandates of existing tribunals and regulatory bodies such as the NEB, the IJC, and the various panels established under the FTA or the NAFTA would provide a preliminary basis for actions by environmentalists. Accomplishing this integration will be complex, and enormous pressure will need to be brought to bear on the U.S., Canadian, and Mexican governments as part of the trilateral discussions now underway, to ensure that the integration process is started in the next few years.

INTERNATIONAL REGULATION OF DRIFTNET FISHING ACTIVITIES

Judith Swan

Driftnet fishing activities have, in a dramatically short time, attracted global attention and action in international law and organizations. The stand-off between the driftnet fleets of Japan, Taiwan, and Korea[1] carrying out economically efficient fishing methods and other countries promoting conservation and management of living marine resources is happily being resolved in favour of the resources.

Many factors have contributed to resolution of the situation. An emerging awareness that the planet's resources are finite and need careful management has encouraged political and diplomatic responsiveness.[2] A changing legal order acknowledging the interdependence of resources has promoted international measures for their conservation.[3] Economic realities that were previously related only to the cost of an efficient fishing operation now include trade sanctions against countries that do not take adequate conservation and management measures.[4] Where international law does not explicitly provide for sanctions against refusal to adopt conservation measures, international organizations have promoted such measures through resolutions[5]

---

1 France also carries out driftnet fishing, but with shorter nets than the Asian countries.

2 The issue of what the response is to — the planet or political pressure groups (which may or may not have the planet as a primary interest) is discussed in the text, *infra*.

3 For example, the 1982 United Nations *Law of the Sea Convention* promotes agreement between countries on the conservation and management of fish stocks subject to different jurisdictions and in the high seas. A range of other relevant international conventions (e.g., on highly migratory and endangered species, the atmosphere, and water environmental quality) have been concluded in the past few decades as international cooperation strengthens. A focus for these developments will be the 1992 United Nations Conference on Environment and Development.

4 Article XX(g) of the *General Agreement on Tariffs and Trade* permits trade restrictions for the purposes of conservation, but its application to a range of situations protecting national industry rather than resources has been the subject of dispute resolution within GATT. The United States effectively uses trade as a lever to secure extraterritorial compliance, discussed in text, *infra*. This is in happy contrast to using withdrawal of foreign aid to promote its "highly migratory species" policy, which has encouraged U.S. tuna-boats to disregard exclusive economic zones, and has penalized countries enforcing their own laws by reduction of foreign aid under the *Fishermen's Protective Act*, 22 U.S.C. §§1971-1980 (1982 & Supp. V 1987).

5 The following organizations have taken action: The United Nations Environment Programme, in sponsoring workshops; the South Pacific Forum, in adopting the Tarawa Declaration in July 1989 aimed at banning driftnet fishing in the region; the Joint Assembly

and countries have developed a network of bilateral sanctions.[6] And on a non-governmental level, organizations, special-interest groups, and some sectors of industry work to promote their objectives through legal, institutional, or other means.

On the other side of the issue, driftnet fleets represent an investment in time and money for the fishermen. Cultural factors can inhibit early acquiescence to restricted fishing activities. Scientific data are claimed to be inadequate for taking early conservation measures.[7] Politically and diplomatically, driftnetting countries may find leverage by linking their cooperation (or absence of it) in other areas[8] to the issue.

---

of the African Caribbean and Pacific States and the European Economic Community (ACP/EEC) in adopting a resolution in September 1989 urging members to take measures in relation to driftnets; the Commonwealth Heads of Government in adopting the Langkawi Declaration on Environment in October 1989, supporting the Tarawa Declaration and agreeing to seek to ban driftnet fishing; the Food and Agriculture Organization Conference in November 1989 in agreeing that the issue should continue to receive FAO's closest attention (opinion was divided on how much scientific evidence was needed to ban driftnet fishing); the Organization of Eastern Caribbean States in the Castries Declaration in November 1989, resolving to establish a regime that would outlaw the use of driftnets; the United Nations General Assembly in December 1989, in adopting Resolution 44/225 entitled *Large-scale Pelagic Driftnet Fishing and its Impact on the Living Marine Resources of the World's Oceans and Seas*, discussed in text, *infra*; the North Atlantic Salmon Conservation Organization in June 1990, in adopting a resolution endorsing General Assembly Resolution 44/225; the International Whaling Commission in July 1990, in adopting a resolution supporting General Assembly Resolution 44/225; the South Pacific Forum in August 1990, in reiterating its commitment to the elimination of driftnet fishing; the Preparatory Committee for the United Nations Conference on Environment and Development, in requesting a report on, in effect, the impact of driftnet fishing and conservation measures needed on the high seas; and the Fisheries Committee of the Organization for Economic Cooperation and Development in September 1990, in supporting the implementation of General Assembly Resolution 44/225. See *Large-Scale Pelagic Driftnet Fishing and its Impact on the Living Marine Resources of the World's Oceans and Seas: Report of the Secretary General*, 45 U.N. Doc. A/45/663 (1990) [hereinafter *Report of the Secretary General*].

6   Although many such sanctions have extraterritorial effects, they usually operate within the principles of international law and are consistent with sovereignty. For example, refusal to allow landing or transshipment of driftnet-caught fish within the territorial sea or exclusive economic zone is intended to discourage driftnet fishing activities on the high seas. However, some countries reject the prohibition of driftnet vessels from transiting the two-hundred-mile zone, regarding it as contrary to freedom of navigation.

7   This argument is frequently used by countries that wish to continue to fish and, so their reasoning goes, collect more data on the fishery in order that proper conservation measures can be developed. This overlooks the possibility that the resource could be fished out before an adequate database is assembled.

8   Such as trade or aid.

Underlying the issue of driftnet fishing are the technical components of science and law, and the tools of politics, trade, and diplomacy. These are discussed below. The bigger picture of how driftnet fishing relates to conservation and management of high seas fisheries is also considered. Can the successes of the driftnet issue be transposed to the other areas?

BACKGROUND

General

Large-scale indiscriminate fishing practices that have emerged in the last half-century have been market driven. Especially before the use of the two-hundred-mile zone, developments in fisheries technology preceded the perceived need to gather adequate scientific information about the resource. Because of the focus on the industry rather than the resource, it followed that management and legal measures regarding the resource took second place to the profit margin.[9]

Large-scale driftnet fishing followed this pattern. Although driftnet fishing is a variation of gillnet fishing, which has long been used for subsistence in the developing and developed world, it was not until the 1950s that use of lightweight synthetic fibres allowed the technology of very long nets, extending to fifty to sixty kilometres and approximately ten metres deep.

The nets are deployed by vessels for several hours, often overnight, to allow fish to become enmeshed. While this means a large amount of fish can be caught in a relatively short time, the disadvantages of this method are legion: many species of living marine resources other than the targeted fish, including other species of fish, turtles, cetaceans, and seabirds, are caught in the nets; some nets are lost or discarded, becoming "ghost nets" and causing "ghost fishing", environmental degradation, and threats to navigation;[10] or if a net is retrieved in heavy seas, as much as 40 percent of the targeted fish caught can be lost through drop-out. In the North Pacific, it is estimated that at the 1990 level, squid driftnet fisheries annual take 40,000 to 60,000 marine mammals, 750,000 seabirds, and large quantities of pomfret, tuna, and other fish species.[11]

A significant increase in the high seas driftnet fishing effort occurred at

---

9   The need for fish as food should not be overlooked.

10   For a report on the differences between Japanese scientists who claim that lost nets lose their length and turn into a solid mass, and Canadian scientists who claim that this research is inconclusive, see *Report of the Secretary General, supra,* note 5.

11   See Canada's Submission to the United Nations Office of Ocean Affairs and the Law of the Sea, Large-Scale Pelagic Driftnets, 31 August 1990.

about the same time the two-hundred-mile exclusive economic zones (EEZs)[12] were being declared in the 1970s and negotiations were underway for the *Law of the Sea Convention*, which would agree on terms for high seas fisheries conservation and management. However, these terms are only guidelines and need further definition. Much of the driftnet activity now takes place on the high seas, but some occurs illegally within EEZs of coastal states in the hope of avoiding detection.

The surge in high seas driftnet fishing in the 1970s reflected the economic viability of the times — productivity was high and costs were low. This caused many vessels outfitted for other types of fishing, such as longlining, to convert to driftnets. On the whole, the international driftnet fleets use older vessels that underwent conversion some years ago. It is estimated that of a total global fleet of over one thousand vessels, about one hundred to two hundred driftnet vessels are reasonably "modern".[13]

There is no hard scientific evidence on the effect of driftnet fishing on the sustainability of the resources in areas where scientific cooperation has not existed, because the driftnet fleets either do not keep careful records or do not share the details with an independent scientific body.[14] Even in the North Pacific where a form of scientific cooperation on salmon has existed,[15] there is thought to be insufficient information on the amount and origin of salmonoids, marine mammals, and birds intercepted, and uncertainties regarding enforcement.[16]

The United Nations Report of the Secretary General on driftnet fishing[17] refers to the present state of world fisheries, and concludes that, in general, the yields of most preferred fish have reached or are approaching levels of full exploitation while the demand for fish continues to rise. It calls for a high priority to be given the monitoring and prevention of environmental

---

12   Some countries declared two-hundred-mile fishing zones.

13   In June 1989, at the consultation held in Suva, Fiji, between Pacific Island countries and driftnetting countries, Korea announced that it would discontinue driftnet fishing in the South Pacific. Japan and Taiwan protested that they would continue. Korea's announcement, however, was not made as a result of conservation practices; only two of its vessels, both of them very old, had participated in the fishery, and it was economically more practical to either retire them or send them to fishing grounds closer to home.

14   Although scientists from driftnet fishing countries are represented on the South Pacific Albacore Research Group, the information has been provided through government-industry sources rather than directly by the fishing fleet, and is summarized rather than detailed.

15   Through the International North Pacific Fisheries Commission, established in 1953.

16   *Supra*, note 5, at paras.89, 90, 99.

17   *Supra*, note 5, at paras.50-54.

degradation in recognition of the importance of sustainability in the use of living resources.

North Pacific-South Pacific

The driftnet issue has been focused in the North Pacific and the South Pacific,[18] where different conditions have fostered different approaches by concerned countries.[19] The North Pacific driftnet fishery target species are salmon, squid, and albacore, with a salmon by-catch in the squid fishery. The South Pacific driftnet fishery takes juvenile southern albacore.

Resource-use conflicts in these regions are different. In the South Pacific, the driftnets, which intercept juvenile southern albacore, affect the longline and troll fishery, for mature species. The North Pacific conflict is characterized as by-catches in the squid fishery and catches and by-catches by Asian fleets of salmon originating in North America.

The North Pacific

Salmon

Japan developed the North Pacific high seas salmon driftnet fishery in the 1950s. The fishery is regulated in area by agreement of members of the International North Pacific Fisheries Commission (INPFC) — Canada, Japan, and the United States. Japan negotiates separately with the Soviet Union, also a state of origin for this anadromous species. The fishery has declined in recent years, with the fleet size in 1989 at about 56 motherships and 156 land-based boats. Taiwan carries out high seas salmon driftnet fisheries that are considered unacceptable by countries of origin under the Law of the Sea,[20] and although import prohibitions were adopted in 1985 by these countries,[21] it is estimated that illegal trade in salmon from all countries of origin (which is usually laundered by marketing through third countries) is over ten thousand tons annually.

Squid

The North Pacific driftnet fishery for squid is relatively new, developed in the late 1970s by Japan and prosecuted by the Republic of Korea and

---

18   Japan claims that, with respect to the high seas outside the Pacific Ocean, Japanese law prohibits Japanese fishing vessels from using driftnet gear in the Atlantic and Indian Oceans. See K. Kagawa, First Secretary, Fisheries, Embassy of Japan, Washington, D.C., "In Defense of Japanese Driftnet Fisheries", *The Washington Times* (28 September 1990).

19   For detailed descriptions of the driftnet fisheries in the North and South Pacific, see the *Report of the Secretary General, supra*, note 5.

20   See discussion in text, *infra*.

21   Canada, Japan, and the United States.

Taiwan. Massive increases in squid driftnetting took place in the late 1970s and early 1980s. Japan increased its squid driftnet fishery, after its salmon quotas were reduced in 1978 as a result of negotiations with the U.S.S.R. and the INPFC. As a result, about 170 salmon driftnet vessels entered the squid fishery. The total level of driftnet fishing reached about 770 vessels in 1988,[22] with the Koreans and Taiwanese having fished over a wider ocean area than Japan. It is easier to harvest North Pacific squid (flying squid), which do not group together, by using driftnets.

There is concern about the levels of by-catch of salmon of North American origin in this fishery. In particular, the wider the area fished the greater the likelihood of salmon interceptions, whether deliberate or accidental. Canada has protested the unilateral decision taken by Japan, Korea, and Taiwan to establish the northern limits for their squid driftnet fishery because they do not provide sufficient distance from the migration routes of North American salmon.[23]

Albacore Tuna

The North Pacific high seas albacore driftnet fishery was also developed by Japan in the mid-1970s, and is also fished by the Taiwanese fleet. Vessel levels reached about 460 in 1988. Many of these vessels are believed to have participated in the South Pacific albacore driftnet fishery in the late 1988-89 season.

The South Pacific

The South Pacific high seas albacore driftnet fishery presented different problems, owing to the dependence of the developing island countries on the resource and the dramatic increase in the number of vessels — Japanese, Taiwanese, and Korean — in just one season. The fleet mushroomed from about 20 vessels in the mid-1980s to at least 130, but as many as 180, vessels in 1988-89.

The island countries, with few other resources, were in various stages of developing a longline fishery for the albacore resource, both under access arrangements and by developing their own fleets. Because the driftnet fishery captures juveniles that swim near the surface and the longline fishery targets the deeper-swimming mature albacore, the South Pacific Albacore Research Group (SPAR)[24] predicted in preliminary estimates before the 1988-89

---

22   *Supra*, note 5, at para.78.

23   Notes for an Opening Address by Dr. V. Rabinovitch on behalf of The Hon. B. Valcourt, Minister of Fisheries and Oceans (International North Pacific Fisheries Commission Annual Meeting, 7 November 1990) [unpublished].

24   SPAR is an informally constituted group of resourcers from various countries who are

season that continued fishing at the dramatically increased levels would seriously deplete the entire stock in two years, time. In other words, there would be very few juveniles left to grow into adults for Pacific Island countries to harvest.

This affected the troll fishery for southern albacore — also a surface fishery — prosecuted primarily by New Zealand and American vessels. Troll fishermen reported that it was necessary to carry divers aboard during the 1988-89 season because of the frequency with which driftnets would foul the propellers of the vessels.

In October 1990, SPAR reports indicated that the driftnet fleet prosecuting southern albacore was reduced to about 30 vessels in 1989-90, and would be further reduced to 11 vessels in 1990-91. The troll, on the other hand, continued to increase at a moderate rate. However, abundance analyses suggest that the stock is responding to the reduced trend of exploitation.

Other Regions

Taiwanese vessels conduct a high seas driftnet fishery for albacore tuna in the Indian Ocean, which fishery was developed by the Japanese and Korean longline fleets from the 1950s. Many countries also prosecute artisanal and semi-industrial driftnet fisheries in the areas. Incidental catches of billfishes and small cetaceans are reported, and it is estimated that about 130 vessels participated in the high seas driftnet fishery in 1988.[25]

The Indian Ocean Fishery Commission has recently reviewed the status of the stocks of Indian Ocean tuna and concluded that there is no special cause for concern over stocks within national jurisdiction.[26] Although the Commission sees a need for further investigation of by-catches, an evaluation of the effect of driftnet fishing on stocks outside national jurisdiction would be very useful if data and relevant information could be obtained.

The Atlantic Ocean supports various driftnet fisheries within national jurisdiction, and French vessels conduct a high seas albacore driftnet fishery in the Bay of Biscay. The length of the driftnets used in this fishery ranges from only two to six kilometres, rather than the fifty to sixty kilometres used by other fleets. To distinguish its own driftnetting practices and possibly give them a sense of legitimacy, the French delegation insisted on including the word "long" in the title of the 1989 Wellington Convention on the prohibition

---

interested in South Pacific albacore; it meets at intervals, usually in response to changes, or likely changes, in the fishery.

25   *Supra*, note 5, at para.120.

26   *Supra*, note 5, at para.129.

of the use of long driftnets.[27]

Summary

Although worldwide opinion has resulted in unprecedented global institutional measures against driftnet fishing, the practice, while somewhat diminished owing to the political, diplomatic, and legal measures described below, still continues. There is concern that the regional measures taken in the North and South Pacific result only in many of the vessels relocating to the Caribbean or Indian Ocean.

In reviewing management measures to regulate or prohibit driftnet fishing, I will consider the following: public awareness and political process; regional/institutional measures; distinguishing features of driftnet fishing activities that could set it apart from other resource management; and lessons that could be applied to management of other high seas resources.

PUBLIC AWARENESS AND POLITICAL PROCESS

There is no doubt that the planet is the beneficiary of activities undertaken by "eco-organizations", which have raised public consciousness about conservation and management of its living and non-living resources. These organizations range from reactionary to radical in their philosophy and activities, and of course include those with responsible policies and strategies.[28] Some of these non-governmental organizations (NGOs) use confrontational tactics, and there is no doubt that successful fundraising is carried by "emotional" presentations,[29] often at the expense of careful management or indigenous peoples.[30] Others take a more responsible attitude in their work and international lobbying, and base their work and priorities on honest scientific grounds.

Well-known marine resource-related issues espoused by these organizations have included whaling and sealing. In the case of whaling, a resolution on a moratorium for commercial whaling was agreed to at the 1982 meeting of the International Whaling Commission (IWC). It was without doubt a triumph for some of these NGOs, which secured representation at the

---

27   Discussed in text, *infra*.

28   For detailed consideration of philosophies and tactics of many of the eco-organizations, see Janice Scott Henke, *Seal Wars! An American Viewpoint* (St. John's: Breakwater, 1985); and Alan Herscovici, *Second Nature: The Animal-Rights Controversy* (Montreal: CBC Enterprises, 1985).

29   Such as the anthropomorphism attributed to seals (use of terms "baby", "mother", soulful eyes) and characterizations of harvesters as "slaughterers"; *id.*

30   *Id.*

IWC in three different capacities: within delegations of member countries, by persuading countries to join IWC and providing delegates with appropriate expertise and viewpoints, and as observers at the meeting.[31]

In the case of sealing, international campaigns were waged using expensive public relations materials. Some elements of the tactics were massive public campaigns, including direct mail packages (with preprinted cards for boycotting, lobbying purposes, and donation envelopes); public relations/education campaigns; lobbying of European and American politicians; and lobbying at international fora.[32]

In each case, these NGOs, for better or worse, succeeded in changing public opinion and strongly influencing the national and international diplomatic and political decision-making systems. A common element of the above campaigns was political attractiveness. Particularly in EEC countries, where few voters were involved in the whaling or sealing industries, and in parts of Canada and the United States that are not home to fishermen, any politician favouring closing down these industries would likely benefit at the polls.

Emotional issues, or issues cast in that light, bring emotional responses, and attempts to respond with "science" do not usually succeed. On the other hand, overfishing has been carried out in the name of "science" — we must continue to collect information on the fishery, and the only way to do that is to continue to fish until we have enough information.

The driftnet fishing issue was a natural one for the NGOs to espouse. It has the recipe for a prominent public relations, and fundraising, campaign — high seas adventure, marine mammals, seabirds, threats to navigation, potentially wasteful drop-out rates, and environmental degradation. In considering the global action taken to date in relation to driftnet fishing,[33] the NGOs' role and contribution to the results could be used as a bellwether

---

31 It was owing in large part to the changed composition of the IWC (whose constitutive mandate is to promote the orderly development of commercial whaling), and consequent lack of attention to scientific advice, that Canada withdrew its membership that year. It continues to cooperate in the scientific work. Unofficially, it cannot be overlooked that Canada and other countries were targets in an international campaign to stop whaling (Canada had closed down its operations in 1972) and non-governmental organizations were encouraging voluminous mailing campaigns to politicians and Cabinet Ministers.

32 Such as the *Convention on International Trade in Endangered Species of Wild Fauna and Flora*, 3 March 1973. These groups lobbied unsuccessfully for many years to include various proposals for listing seals on endangered species lists, when facts to the contrary — that they were copiously abundant and increasing — were clear. Such listing could have assisted in the credibility of fundraising campaigns.

33 See *supra*, note 5.

when considering progress in other sectors of resource management.

The basis of the defence for continued driftnet fishing has been the scientific argument that because we don't yet know enough about this fishing method, we should continue to fish and in the process carry out scientific research and observations to permit rational management.[34] At the other end of the spectrum is the view that it should be stopped completely. Proponents of this view rely on an opposed scientific argument: Because we know that this fishing method is wasteful and destructive, it should be stopped for lack of clear scientific justification.

It is this line-drawing exercise that is common to other resource management issues — at what point must the quest for scientific evidence be abandoned in favour of conservation practices? Or, put another way, how much scientific evidence is enough to put conservation and management measures in place?

In the case of driftnet fishing activities, while the legal, political, and diplomatic debate has been taking place, NGOs have moved effectively at all levels from grass-roots campaigns to confrontational tactics[35] and political lobbying.[36] They have generated consumer action that has depressed the market for driftnet-caught fish, an appropriate response to the fisher's market-driven incentive.[37]

Public opinion, which was mobilized to a great extent by the NGOs, has contributed to the global action,[38] culminating in the 1989 General Assembly Resolution setting a deadline for a moratorium on, or interim cessation of, driftnet fishing activities unless joint scientific analyses can provide the basis

---

34   For example, when requested by Pacific Island countries in June 1989 to cease its driftnet operations in the South Pacific, Japan responded that there was not enough scientific information to justify such a decision, and research vessels — with an observer representing Pacific Island nations — would return with a reduced number of vessels the following year. The "reduced number", while lower than that reported for the previous season, was still an increase over the number of vessels fishing in the 1987-88 season.

35   *Rainbow Warrior II* was sent to the South Pacific in the 1989-90 season.

36   Although at least one such organization was successful in developing firm relations at the level of the Prime Minister's Office in the South Pacific, its personnel used continuous disruptive tactics to try to gain entrance into regional governmental meetings dealing with sensitive policy matters. Confrontation in such circumstances does not necessarily advance the mutual objective.

37   However, it is difficult to trace with great accuracy whether a fish in a can was actually caught in a driftnet. Some processors of tuna have announced that they do not buy driftnet-caught fish; this is a good marketing strategy. However, this leaves salmon (see discussion in text, *infra*, about salmon laundering) and squid.

38   See *supra*, note 5.

for conservation and management measures.[39] While this can be seen as a precedent for other line-drawing exercises, there are already many countries[40] that prefer to rely on a combination of minimal (but sufficient) science and perhaps public opinion, and believe the only option is complete cessation.

Is resource management, previously undertaken on the basis of the best scientific advice with socio-economic and other considerations included, now moving towards an emotional campaign-driven system with the NGOs setting the agenda? If so, is this a welcome development or is there a middle ground? To what extent does it introduce "ethics" into resource management? Is it likely to affect other sectors, and if so, which ones? These are all key questions, the answers to which may take some time to emerge. Perhaps the most positive result is a heightened consciousness about the finite resources of the planet and the need for international cooperation and an integrated approach towards their management.

REGIONAL APPROACHES TO DRIFTNET FISHING

Regional measures on driftnet fishing have been focused in the North and South Pacific. In the North Pacific, agreement under the International North Pacific Fisheries Commission (INPFC) and other bilateral or unilateral initiatives have been taken to control driftnet fishing. In the South Pacific, where (as noted above) a completely different type of driftnet fishery than exists in the North Pacific suddenly developed in 1988, existing regional cooperation led by the South Pacific Forum Fisheries Agency[41] handled the crisis.[42]

The United Nations has given priority to this recently emerged issue, especially in the General Assembly and through its agencies, including the Food and Agriculture Organization. I will review its measures, adopted with the agreement of member driftnetting countries, after setting out the approaches in the North and South Pacific to driftnet fishing.

---

39   UN General Assembly Resolution 44/225 entitled *Large-scale Pelagic Driftnet Fishing and its Impact on the Living Marine Resources of the World's Oceans and Seas.* See *supra*, note 5, and discussion in text, *infra*.

40   Including the United States.

41   Established by the *South Pacific Forum Fisheries Agency Convention*, 1979 with headquarters at Honiara, Solomon Islands.

42   Other regional organizations or groups participating in meetings and/or contributing to the procedures were the South Pacific Commission (SPC) and the South Pacific Albacore Research Group (both of which provided scientific analyses), and the Forum Secretariat as observers.

Regulation of High Seas Driftnet Fishing in the North Pacific

Canada, Japan, and the United States are members of the International North Pacific Fisheries Commission, established in 1953.[43] Its main objective is to minimize high seas interception of salmon of North American origin. Japan is the only member country whose fleets undertake directed high seas salmon fishing, and this fishery is also regulated by quotas set under a bilateral agreement with the U.S.S.R. Non-member countries that have engaged in high-seas driftnet fisheries affecting salmon of North American origin are Taiwan and Korea.

Key considerations in addressing the effectiveness of regulation within INPFC are the cooperation available within INPFC, the applicability of the INPFC Convention to current circumstances, and the debate on how much science is "enough" for agreement on regulatory measures. Focal concerns include regulating fishing by non-members, international cooperation to prohibit trade in driftnet-caught fish, and surveillance-enforcement. These concerns are discussed below.

Regulation of High Seas Driftnet Fisheries within INPFC

The annual INPFC meetings regulate the Japanese high seas fishery and exchange scientific information.[44] During its existence, and particularly after declaration of the two-hundred-mile zones and consistent with the 1982 United Nations *Law of the Sea Convention* provision that coastal states of anadromous species have primary interest in and responsibility for such stocks, the INPFC has required the Japanese salmon fleets to shift westward

---

43   Under the *International Convention for the High Seas Fisheries of the North Pacific Ocean*, June 1953.

44   According to Department of Fisheries and Oceans, *Backgrounder*, 7 November 1990, HQ-B-90-14-1, the annual INPFC meetings:

   1.   adopt measures to limit interceptions of North American-origin salmon in Japan's directed high seas salmon fisheries and in other fisheries;

   2.   monitor the phase-out of the Japanese salmon fishery in the Bering sea;

   3.   review progress on research programs identifying continent of origin of salmonoids in the high seas of the North Pacific, particularly within the Japanese salmon fishing areas;

   4.   review data on incidental capture of marine mammals in the salmon fisheries and the results of experiments aimed at eliminating this by-catch; and

   5.   review and exchange scientific information on species exploited in the North Pacific and Bering Sea fisheries.

in order to avoid intercepting salmon of North American origin.

The Canadian Department of Fisheries and Oceans reports that:[45]

> In recent years the INPFC has focused its attention on the impacts of driftnet fisheries on
> marine species and seabirds. The effects of lost and discarded marine debris in the North
> Pacific and Bering Sea have been examined. At Canada's initiative, a special working group
> was formed in 1989 to examine alternatives to driftnet fishing. The INPFC has also
> discussed joint efforts to halt the international commerce in high seas salmon caught by
> non-INPFC members such as Taiwan.

The work of the special working group is being carried forward by Canada in the United Nations Food and Agriculture Organization (FAO). Although this is the logical next step, immediate results are unlikely,[46] owing in part to Japan's influence in the FAO at diplomatic and financial levels[47] and its standard reluctance to heed international trends and demands in fisheries matters.

It appears that 1989 was a watershed year in building a focus on driftnet fishing, and not only because of the formation of the INPFC special working group described above. Although measures against non-members had been agreed upon in 1985 (these measures are described below), and while 1987 marked the intensification of efforts by Canada and the United States to control driftnet fishing,[48] it was not until May 1989 that Japan agreed to

---

45   *Id.*

46   At the meeting of the FAO Committee on Fisheries (COFI) held 8-12 April 1991,
      delegations discussed the use of more selective fishing gear and methods in the context of
      the sustainability issue and reducing by-catch. Some delegations proposed that FAO
      organize an international meeting to examine the fish by-catch issue. Such a meeting would
      analyze, on a scientific basis, the situation of incidental catches and contribute to reducing
      catches of non-target species and sustainable development of fisheries, thereby augmenting
      economic and nutritional benefits from the utilization of fishery resources. In the case of
      driftnet fishing, it is apparent that driftnet fishing countries that are members of COFI could
      seek to prolong the scientific by-catch arguments so fishing could continue, without
      addressing the other environmental consequences. See text, *infra*, for further discussion.

47   For example, when Japan was resisting entering into a multilateral tuna fisheries access
      arrangement with Pacific Island countries (in which it perceived it could lose valued
      leverage), it announced financial grants to the FAO towards the apparent end of securing
      that body's endorsement, in some form, of management authority by a distant water fleet
      over tuna.

48   In 1987 the Canadian government announced a new policy to ban the use of large-scale
      squid driftnets inside the two-hundred-mile zone, and Canada and the United States
      demanded that Japan, the Republic of Korea, and Taiwan implement more stringent
      regulation of their driftnet fleets. As a result of the latter, domestic regulations have since
      been enforced to prohibit incidental taking of salmon, control the discarding of marine
      debris, and place fishery boundary limitations on their squid fleets. See Canada. Department

comply with Canadian and U.S. demands that North American scientific observers be allowed on Japanese squid vessels. An expanded agreement was concluded for 1990, allowing ninety-eight scientific observers (ten Canadians, forty-seven Americans, and forty-one Japanese) to be placed onboard Japanese squid and large mesh tuna driftnet vessels.[49] The value of placing Japanese observers on Japanese vessels, leaving an opportunity for some collaboration, is open to question. However, it could be considered a breakthrough that fifty-seven vessels carried non-Japanese observers for high seas fisheries under INPFC.

In July 1989, a meeting on North Pacific high seas driftnet fishing was called by the Pacific States and British Columbia, and co-sponsored by both federal governments. It resulted in a Proclamation on the High Seas Driftnet Fisheries of the North Pacific Ocean, which was accomplished at the regional level[50] and which recommends approaches to deal with the problem.[51] The fact that neither federal government participated in the Proclamation could reflect their international responsibilities, relations, and negotiations with the driftnetting countries.[52]

At the 1990 INPFC meeting, with approximately one hundred administrators, scientists, and advisers participating in discussions, considerable attention was focused on driftnet fisheries, as indicated by the official news release.[53] After exchanging views on the operation of high seas driftnet fisheries in the Convention Area by INPFC members and non-members, and discussing the 1989 UN General Assembly Resolution on Large-Scale Pelagic Driftnet Fishing, the Commission "endorsed the full implementation of this Resolution".[54]

---

of Fisheries and Oceans, "North Pacific Conservation", *Backgrounder*, 7 November 1991, HQ-B-90-14-5.

49   *Id.* The agreement also requires satellite transmitters on all Japanese vessels, clear vessel and gear markings, and submission to enforcement boardings.

50   Signed at a subsequent meeting in 1989 by Alaska, British Columbia, California, Hawaii, Idaho, Oregon, and Washington.

51   These include recommendations of decreasing individual catch quotas, establishing multinational research organizations, increasing resources for monitoring and enforcing international agreements, and establishing international agreements to limit illegal salmon harvesting.

52   In particular, agreement on the ninety-eight observers had just been reached and it could have affected this form of cooperation. The Proclamation has been carried forward by the federal government in the United Nations.

53   INPFC News Release (8 November 1990).

54   *Id.*

Because a vital element of the Resolution was its support by the driftnetting countries, this result would be expected in the context of the INPFC. Their support was attracted by allowing a moratorium not to be imposed (or if imposed, lifted) if effective conservation measures are taken based on "statistically sound" joint analysis by interested parties.

Consistent with the cooperative spirit of the Resolution, Canada invited representatives of Japan and the United States to participate in a scientific review of North Pacific large-scale pelagic driftnet fishing.[55] In addition, an INPFC-sponsored scientific symposium was held 4-6 November 1991 in Tokyo.

In evaluating of the work of INPFC at arm's length, it appears that a major advantage of its establishment is its formalization of cooperation in the regulation of high seas fisheries. The Commission was formed in an era that marked the beginning of international cooperation on high seas fisheries, preceded the development of modern driftnet technology, and lacked a strong agreed body of scientific evidence showing immediate need for high seas management. Given the absence of these elements, it can be regarded as a visionary first step towards high seas fisheries conservation and management. It serves as a precedent in other regions for regulation of driftnet fisheries.

Although INPFC remains successful in providing a meaningful forum for members, collecting and analyzing scientific data, managing high seas fisheries, and cooperating to prevent unacceptable high seas fishing by non-members, current realities show that by itself, it does not go the distance in meeting all needs in North Pacific high seas fisheries management, including driftnet fishing. A range of actions, discussed below, have been taken outside INPFC to accomplish effective management, which indicates the need for stronger action in or by INPFC or a new organization. The critical trade-off is building an organization, with driftnetting countries as members, that could achieve sound management, including enforcement and a possible phase-out of this fishing method, on a cooperative basis. Because this does not appear likely to materialize in the short term, other cooperative action is needed.

Underlining the need for broader cooperative action at a regional level is the Canadian initiative to replace the INPFC under the terms of a new convention. In October 1990, a quadrilateral meeting was held in Ottawa to discuss the principles that could form the basis of a new convention for the conservation of North Pacific salmon, with Canada, Japan, the United States, and the U.S.S.R. participating. The proposed convention would seek to prohibit high seas fisheries for anadromous stocks in the North Pacific.[56]

---

55   Tentatively scheduled for June 1991 in Canada.

56   This initiative is consistent with the 1989 Proclamation, discussed in text *supra*. In the

In addition, Canada hosted a multilateral meeting in December 1990 to promote agreement on a North Pacific Marine Science Organization (PICES).[57] It is envisioned that membership would be broader, and could include Canada, China, Japan, the United States, and the U.S.S.R. Research would cover oceanography and pollution, as well as marine biology, and the impacts of driftnet fishing would be included in the terms of reference.

These initiatives, which seem to relate to each other in terms of membership, do not invite all driftnetting countries to participate, and can be considered as part of the international drive to control or prohibit the practice through collective pressure. They could be based on the assumption that because of the collective pressure from these initiatives and globally through, *inter alia*, the United Nations, driftnetting will cease completely in the short term.[58] This is highly desirable, and, one hopes realistic. But if not, what measures could be considered within the context of the initiatives?[59]

Without detailed knowledge of either initiative, it appears that a "replacement" organization to INPFC would be binding only on parties. If non-member salmon-fishing countries are not invited to participate, terms of membership could include undertakings to implement domestic laws and measures having extraterritorial effect[60] aimed at prohibiting high seas salmon fishing by any non-member country. Non-member salmon-fishing countries or organizations could be invited to participate in some capacity, but this would no doubt require a comprehensive and agreed diplomatic strategy. Given the success of the United States in requiring transponders to be placed on driftnetting vessels,[61] inviting all driftnetting countries to participate in

---

opening address by Mr. Robert Rochon, Chairman, the issue was described as:

> not only the acceptable conduct, on the basis of currently agreed principles, of the North Pacific Salmon fishery, which we all have been conducting for many years to our considerable benefit. What matters just as much if not more, I believe, is to arrive at an overall comprehensive salmon conservation regime which would secure, on the basis of advanced management, technology and science, the optimal, sustainable benefits for all and every one of us in the future.

57   This initiative appears to be consistent with the 1989 Proclamation, discussed in text, *supra*.

58   It has already ceased in the South Pacific, and there is hope that the UN General Assembly Resolution 44/225, *supra*, note 5, will have the same effect elsewhere. However, some driftnetting countries are giving indications that they may wish to find ways to circumvent a complete ban.

59   For measures outside the context of INPFC and these initiatives, see the discussion in the following section.

60   Such as trade prohibitions or denial of related fisheries or other benefits.

61   In August 1989, Taiwan and the United States signed an agreement that required Taiwanese driftnetting vessels to carry transponders by 1990. The agreement also gave U.S. Coast

some form is a possibility. The overriding consideration in securing their membership would be to avoid situations in which the management of the resource could be compromised.[62]

The scientific organization would provide independent advice on a range of inter-related areas, including driftnet fishing, that would be useful in developing international management policy. Again, without details, the forte of this initiative seems to be establishment of a formal collaborative mechanism that could be used in shaping international policy. The integration of marine resources, pollution, and oceanography shows the vision that will be needed for resource management in future, but by itself the organization would appear not to have a decision-making power. One hopes that at the least it would have a recommendatory function, in addition to performing information collection and analysis.

It would be premature to speculate on the relationship between the scientific organization and the INPFC or any successor, but it is expected that this would be a major consideration in consultations on the organization's establishment. As noted above, while INPFC provides a starting point and offers a useful forum in which to develop action in respect of non-member driftnetting countries, it does not offer a complete solution and, at its worst, could stall agreement on the ground of lack of scientific data. With Japan as a member the organization provides a forum for compromise, but is compromise the most appropriate basis for effective resource management, or just a reasonable starting point? Supplementary action is reviewed below.

Regulation of North Pacific High Seas Driftnet Fisheries outside INPFC

There has been a clear need for measures that control or prohibit driftnet fishing in the North Pacific to be taken outside INPFC. The basic problem in attracting such measures to date has been the high seas by-catch of salmon by non-members not countries of origin. Possible legal actions and diplomatic options cover all traditional bases,[63] but successful implementation of these measures depends on the impact of the type of measure taken[64] against the

---

Guard personnel the right to board Taiwanese fishing vessels in high seas areas of the North Pacific and monitor vessels suspected of illegal driftnetting for salmon. Similar agreements have been signed with Japan and Korea. See discussion in text, *infra*.

62   For example, by the decision-making process, in giving objection or veto power to driftnetting countries.

63   These are thoroughly considered by D.M. Johnston in "The Driftnetting Problem in the Pacific Ocean: Legal Considerations and Diplomatic Options" (1990) 21:1 Ocean Development and Int. Law 5.

64   E.g., direct sanctions such as bilateral trade restrictions would be more immediately effective

driftnetting country, and on the strength of the collective effort of other countries. Such measures have included domestic policy and legislation, bilateral agreements, threatened trade sanctions, diplomatic initiatives, and increased surveillance and enforcement. Underlying these measures is the policy of the two major players, the United States and Canada. The respective policies of course also apply in the INPFC context, but it is important in considering broad-based action to review these underpinnings.

U.S. Policy

U.S. policy is clear on driftnet fishing involving salmon by-catch:[65]

The acceptability of impacts of incidental taking of stocks of anadromous species shall be determined by the states of origin, which have the authority to establish total allowable catches for stocks originating in their rivers. High seas harvest of salmonoid species is wasteful and any significant by-catch of these species not sanctioned by the nations of origin is unacceptable.

While the same policy statement acknowledges the conditions regarding a joint scientific assessment called for in the United Nations General Assembly Resolution, a hard line is taken in warning that unless the conditions are met, pelagic high seas driftnet fisheries cannot operate. Further, "even when" they are met, a driftnet fishery "should only be conducted pursuant to adequate monitoring and enforcement agreements between interested members of the international community." This extra condition likely exceeds any "home free" expectation of driftnetting countries should the first hurdle — agreed scientific analyzes — be cleared. In effect, U.S. policy as stated[66] appears to recognize that joint scientific agreement allowing driftnet fishing to take place is a very remote possibility, and even if it happened, further monitoring-enforcement controls would need to be agreed upon by any country expressing an interest; to say that such agreement is highly unlikely would be to understate the case.

Canadian Policy

The Canadian submission to the United Nations Office of Ocean Affairs and the Law of the Sea on Large-scale Pelagic Driftnets[67] contains the following policy statement:

---

than indirect actions such as institutional resolutions, but the latter have an important role in the overall process.

65   United States. Department of State, "U.S. Policy Concerning Large-scale Pelagic Driftnets" (submitted to the United Nations Office of Ocean Affairs and the Law of the Sea, July 1990).

66   *Id.* However, it is understood that this policy is changing towards prohibiting driftnet fishing whether or not agreed scientific analyzes can be reached.

67   Dated 31 August 1990.

[Canada notes in respect of UN General Assembly Resolution 44/225] that by adversely affecting migratory and interdependent species critical to the integrity of the marine ecosystem within adjacent exclusive economic zones, large-scale pelagic driftnet fishing can undermine the ability of coastal States to fulfil their responsibilities for the effective conservation and management of living marine resources within their jurisdictions. Canada considers therefore that while the provisions of UNCLOS provide a framework for adoption by States of effective conservation measures for high seas fishing, and for cooperation between them in establishing such measures, there is an urgent need for prevention of injurious consequences of high seas fishing and the development of international standards to this end, including the prohibition of indiscriminate and wasteful fishing and the overexploitation of high seas resources ....

The incidental and, in particular, the targeted interception to salmonoids in high seas squid driftnet operations, has led to a public outcry in Canada, in particular in the Canadian fishing industry. While prohibited from catching and retaining salmon by domestic regulations, many Asian vessels have been harvesting and marketing through South-East Asia large quantities of high seas salmon from the North Pacific, causing considerable losses to the Canadian fishing industry. Canada views such fishing activities as contrary to specific provisions of UNCLOS which, *inter alia*, recognize the coastal States' primary interest in and responsibility for anadromous stocks originating in their rivers.

Other Action Taken in the North Pacific Region

International

In addition to general cooperation in the United Nations and other international organizations,[68] and North Pacific initiatives described above to establish two new international organizations to replace INPFC and to promote scientific research, international cooperative action has been taken to curtail unregulated driftnet fishing and prevent "salmon laundering" — trade of driftnet-caught salmon through third countries — as follows:

(a) INPFC members adopted import restrictions in 1985 on high seas salmon caught by non-members, and there has been subsequent cooperation between Canada and the United States to prevent the "laundering" of fish through North American ports and third countries.

(b) Japan and the U.S.S.R. established a Joint Fishery Commission in 1985[69] to regulate high seas salmonoid fisheries in the Northwest Pacific. The Commission agreed not to use driftnets exceeding ten to fifteen kilometres in length for the 1990 seasons, and adopted regulations on the minimum distance between nets, maximum mesh size, and total allowable catch.

(c) Canada and the United States in 1987 demanded that Japan, the Republic

---

68   See *supra*, note 5, and discussion of UN Resolution 44/225 in text, *infra*.

69   By the *Agreement on Fishery Cooperation*.

of Korea, and Taiwan implement more stringent regulation of their driftnet fleets. As a result, they have since enforced domestic regulations to prohibit incidental taking of salmon, control the discarding of marine debris, and place fishing boundary limitations on their squid fleets.

(d) The U.S.-Taiwan driftnet monitoring agreement signed in August 1989 allows U.S. observers on some Taiwanese vessels and requires transmitters on all Taiwanese vessels, and a similar agreement was signed with Korea in October 1989.

(e) Efforts have been made by Canada and the United States to persuade other governments to prevent their industries from participating in the salmon trade (as part of this process, Thailand has agreed to ensure that its canning industry withdraws from purchases of fish caught by driftnets on the high seas).[70]

These actions are complementary and cover all bases adequately, but the most dramatic is the agreement of Taiwan to high seas monitoring and enforcement. Threats of trade sanctions and denial of fisheries access were used by the United States as an incentive for agreement, but this type of agreement could be the forerunner of new developments in high seas fisheries management.[71] It is expected that the results of the observers' reports will be considered by the United Nations General Assembly in the context of Resolution 44/225. As a further enforcement tool, "sting" operations involving laundered high seas salmon have successfully been conducted by the United States.[72]

Unilateral

In 1987, the Canadian government announced a new policy to ban the use of large-scale pelagic driftnets inside the Canadian two-hundred-mile zone. This ban does not go as far as the measures taken by some other countries,[73] which also prohibit nationals or national vessels from undertaking or assisting in driftnet activities (defined to include transshipment and supply). Perhaps there is scope for further development along these lines.

The Canadian Department of National Defence has undertaken air

---

70   Canada. Department of Fisheries and Oceans, "North Pacific Conservation", *Backgrounder*, 7 November 1990, HQ-B-90-14-3.

71   Some countries have included provisions in fisheries acts relating to transponders on foreign fishing vessels even though they are not yet in use. See, for example, Cook Islands, *Marine Resources Act*, 1989.

72   See Johnston, *supra*, note 63.

73   For example, Australia, Cook Islands, New Zealand, and Marshall Islands.

surveillance flights north of the high seas squid driftnet fishing boundary so that photographic evidence can be obtained of vessels carrying out illegal salmon driftnet fishing operations. Another national measure in this respect is the gathering of data on high seas squid driftnet fisheries during the summer of 1990 by a team of Department of Fisheries and Oceans scientific researchers on the departmental research vessel *W.E. Ricker.*

On the trade side, the United States has enacted the strongest legislation with extraterritorial effects, which acts as a major disincentive to high seas driftnet fishing.[74] The *Driftnet Impact Monitoring Assessment and Control Act of 1987*[75] requires that the Secretary of State negotiate agreements with countries undertaking driftnet fishing in the North Pacific Ocean, with the objectives of cooperative monitoring of the fishing activity, assessment of its impact on marine resources, and arranging for the enforcement of regulations and laws governing such fishing. If the foreign country does not negotiate an arrangement with the United States, consideration of economic and trade sanctions is required — for example, the prohibition on importing fish products from the offending country. Precedents for linking trade sanctions with fishery-related action in more general terms are found in the *Magnuson Fishery Conservation and Management Act*[76] and the Pelly Amendment to the *Fishermens Protective Act of 1967*,[77] which link high seas action and compliance with international fishery conservation programs, respectively, to allocations within the U.S. zone.[78]

Regulation of Driftnet Fishing in the South Pacific

The South Pacific presents a different set of circumstances, both in the logistics of the fishery as described above and in the institutional arrangements. The number of vessels prosecuting the relatively newly developed high seas driftnet fishery in the South Pacific — targeting southern albacore — increased exponentially in the 1988-89 season. There was no history or tradition of developing the fishery through an organization

---

74   See R. Eisenbud, "Problems and Prospects for the Pelagic Driftnet" (1985) 12 Boston College Environmental Affairs Law Rev. 473, and Johnston, *supra*, note 63, at 79.

75   *Driftnet Impact Monitoring Assessment and Control Act of 1987*, 16 U.S.C. §1822 (1982), as amended by Pub. L. No.98-623, §404, 98 Stat. 3408 (1984).

76   *Magnuson Fishery Conservation and Management Act*, 16 U.S.C. §§1801-1882 (1982 & Supp. V 1987) [hereinafter the *Magnuson Act*].

77   *Fishermens Protect Act of 1967*, 22 U.S.C. §§1971-1980 (1982 & Supp. V 1987).

78   Other relevant legislation includes the *Lacey Act Amendments of 1981*, Pub. L. No.97-79, 95 Stat. 1073, and the *Marine Mammal Protection Act of 1972*, 16 U.S.C. §§1361-1407 (1982 & Supp. V 1987).

equivalent to the INPFC, and two regional organizations and a research group existed that were well placed to deal with the urgent situation.

The South Pacific Forum Fisheries Agency (FFA) was established in 1979[79] to maximize benefits of the recently acquired fisheries resource[80] for the newly independent member countries. It serves primarily as a management body, while the South Pacific Commission, a technical organization, provides general scientific coordination for fisheries. The South Pacific Albacore Research Group, an informal group of scientists from interested countries, including the South Pacific and driftnetting countries, had been convened to review and analyze the southern albacore fishery.

The FFA reports to the South Pacific Forum,[81] an annual meeting of heads of government of states in the region. The Forum provides policy direction to its member countries, which is usually implemented through the FFA (for fisheries matters) or the Forum Secretariat.[82] The Forum is unique in international policy making: as an annual meeting at the highest level, its directions are followed throughout the year by member countries. Its "combined agenda" approach results in strong regional cohesiveness.

The rapid mobilization of FFA members and other interested parties in the South Pacific is testimony to the responsiveness of the FFA Secretariat. The first information that the driftnet fishery, already estimated by SPAR to be fishing at about the maximum sustainable yield level, would likely increase sharply[83] was received towards the end of 1988. A meeting among concerned countries was quickly convened by FFA in November 1988 to address the matter. For purposes of comparison with action taken in the North Pacific, it should be noted that there was very little scientific information on the fishery at this stage, and no regularized mechanism was in place for scientific data collection, analysis, or consultation.

Swift and decisive action was taken at the November 1988 meeting and subsequently. Within a year a convention to prohibit driftnet fishing activities — the Wellington Convention[84] — was concluded, and discussions for high

---

79   By the *South Pacific Forum Fisheries Agency Convention.* The FFA has sixteen member countries, all independent states in the region and excluding distant water-fishing nations; it is headquartered in Honiara, Solomon Islands. Its members are Australia, Cook Islands, Federated States of Micronesia, Fiji, Kiribati, Marshall Islands, Nauru, New Zealand, Niue, Palau, Papua New Guinea, Solomon Islands, Tonga, Tuvalu, Vanuatu, and Western Samoa.

80   Most countries had declared a two-hundred-mile zone within a few years prior to 1979.

81   Forum membership is the same as that the FFA, except that Palau is not yet a member.

82   As a fifteen-member bloc, the Forum is also influenced on the international level.

83   The fleet increased from about 16 vessels to as many as 197.

84   *Convention for the Prohibition of Fishing with Long Driftnets in the South Pacific,* 29

seas management were initiated. Why has the South Pacific been able to move faster than the North Pacific, what were the motivations for concluding the Convention, and how effective has it been?

Meetings to Consider the Driftnet Fishery

Key to the rapid action of the South Pacific was the high degree of responsiveness to all situations[85] developed by a strong FFA Secretariat.

Three important meetings were held to consider and take measures on the sudden escalation in driftnet fishing during the 1988-89 season. The first, in November 1988, included all South Pacific countries affected by the activity. The meeting concluded that, *inter alia*, the current southern albacore longline fishery was already at maximum sustainable levels, the entire southern albacore fishery would probably collapse if the driftnet fishery expanded as foreseen, and the expected arrival of between sixty and eighty driftnet vessels would spell disaster to established troll and longline fisheries.

The meeting also agreed on a plan of action, including giving priority to the collection of relevant data during the 1988-89 season; instituting bans on landing, transshipment, and use of port facilities for driftnet vessels and driftnet-caught fish; strengthening regional legislation; providing extraregional support; taking specified diplomatic action; and seeking information from relevant international organizations.

In March 1989, after the fishing season, FFA convened another meeting with affected South Pacific countries to review the results of the fishing season. It was concluded that collective action must be continued and that wider support needed to be developed. As a result, a third meeting was called for June 1989, to consult with the driftnetting countries; in the meantime, a regional legal consultation took place. The consultation considered all relevant law[86] and concluded that high seas driftnet operations are not consistent with

---

November 1989 (the Convention was signed by thirteen countries and territories and has received one of four required ratifications).

85   For example, illegal fishing by U.S. tuna boats was replaced by a strong multilateral access treaty between member countries and the United States, with the FFA coordinating negotiations.

86   In particular, *United Nations Conference on the Law of the Sea*, U.N. Doc. A/Conf. 62/122 (1982) [hereinafter UNCLOS], Part V, and Articles 87 (freedom of fishing on the high seas); 116 (right to fish on the high seas); 117 (duty of states to adopt with respect to their national measures for the conservation of the living resources of the high seas); 118 (cooperation of states in the conservation and management of living resources); 119 (conservation of the living resources of the high seas); and 300 (abuse of right). The doctrine of preferential rights and precedents for international management of fishing on the high seas were also reviewed.

international legal requirements regarding rights and obligations of high seas fisheries conservation and management and environmental principles. The consultation also considered the possibility of designating the southern albacore fishery as a driftnet-free area, and the practical impact this could have.

In June 1989 the consultation was held in Suva, Fiji, with all major players present, including FFA member countries, distant water countries engaged in the southern albacore troll fishery,[87] driftnetting countries, and scientists from SPC-SPAR. It was reported that a SPAR meeting held immediately before the consultation agreed on a conservative estimate that the surface fishery would exceed the maximum sustainable yield available to longline fisheries by a factor of two. The sustainability of the present stock was considered "a concern".

The press release issued by the meeting reports, "The participants were unable to arrive at a common position on future driftnet fishing activity in the South Pacific, and the views of the South Pacific nations and the distant water fishers of Japan and China [Taiwan] remain markedly divergent." This reflects the call by the Pacific Island countries that the distant water fishers join in a public commitment to cease driftnet fishing in the region until a satisfactory management regime is established.

Korea agreed to this, possibly because only two very old vessels had prosecuted the fishery. However, balanced against that was the collective spirit engendered by the trilateral meetings held among Japan, Taiwan, and Korea regarding their approach to the driftnet fishery for squid in the North Pacific; any agreement to stop driftnet fishing in the South Pacific was likely seen by Japan and Taiwan as breaking ranks.

The refusal of the driftnetting countries to agree to stop driftnetting activities was based on lack of governmental authorization to do so at the meeting and on scientific evidence.[88] However, the driftnetters did not have long to wait for the repercussion — the Tarawa Declaration adopted by the 1989 South Pacific Forum, an event that coalesced regional and international[89] action.

---

87   The United States participated and Canada, which had only a minor interest in the fishery, attended as observer.

88   The position that the call for an immediate cessation without scientific evidence is totally irrelevant and unacceptable did not seem to take into account the conclusions of the SPAR group, or implicitly dismissed them.

89   The subsequent resolutions and so on of other international organizations set out in *supra*, note 5, expressed support for the Tarawa Declaration, adopted by the South Pacific Forum meeting at Tarawa, Kiribat, 10-11 July 1989.

In the Tarawa Declaration, The Forum:

resolve[d] for the sake of [future] generations of Pacific peoples, to seek the establishment of a regime for the management of albacore tuna in the South Pacific that would ban driftnet fishing from their region; *such a ban might then be a first step to a comprehensive ban on such fishing.*[90]

The Declaration also expressed determination to convene an urgent meeting to develop a convention creating a driftnet-free zone, and resolved to take supplementary action nationally and through international organizations.[91] It became an urgent priority at the regional level to ban driftnet fishing, which is a strong and immediate action. Scientific evidence was available, but certainly not finely tuned after only one year's effort.

Non-governmental organizations, which lobbied vigorously at national levels, especially in Australia and New Zealand, were not permitted to participate in regional meetings despite strong campaigns to do so.[92] Perhaps their main contribution to the process was to advertise the issue in the political arena.

The Declaration, therefore, was a policy-political decision and strategy, generated by strong regional infrastructure and collectivism. It reflected South Pacific priorities of sound ecosystems and peoples' welfare over a debate about scientific evidence. And the rest of the world agreed.[93]

The Wellington Convention

The Wellington Convention[94] was an exercise in speedwriting. Signed

---

90   *Id.* [emphasis added].

91   South Pacific countries, including New Zealand, carried this forward in the United Nations. On 2 October 1989, the Prime Minister of New Zealand, the Rt. Hon. Geoffrey Palmer, addressed the General Assembly; opposition to driftnet fishing was the main theme of his speech. He said, "Freedom of the high seas cannot be invoked to protect what is in effect a systematic assault on the regional marine ecosystem."

92   It was believed that although activists had succeeded in raising global consciousness about the issue, their confrontational tactics would be unlikely to achieve results in a diplomatic setting.

93   General Assembly resolutions, discussed in text, *infra*, and the various other resolutions and actions (*supra*, note 5) indicate international agreement. Although the resolutions negotiated with the objective of securing the driftnetters' agreement refer to scientific evidence, the political realities are the deadlines and pressure that will likely be exercised against the driftnetters should there be non-compliance with the majority interpretation of the resolution.

94   The then-Prime Minister of Australia, the Rt. Hon. Bob Hawke, proposed the Tarawa Declaration at The Forum; aides reported it was drafted on the back of an envelope in the Hercules aircraft en route to Tarawa. The Prime Minister of New Zealand, the Rt. Hon. Geoffrey Palmer, responded by inviting member countries to Wellington to conclude the convention required by the Declaration.

approximately four months after it was called for in the Tarawa Declaration, it was only considered informally by member countries at the regional level once before the Wellington meeting. The context for regional consideration was one of convenience — the FFA hosted a regional meeting on other issues, and space/time during that meeting was used by regional legal experts to agree on a draft convention, which was then circulated to countries for their internal consideration. Commentary was also distributed for their information, in accordance with FFA standard practice.

The Meeting on a Convention to Prohibit Driftnet Fishing in the South Pacific took place 21-24 November, with countries in the region reviewing and finalizing the text; the extraregional "sympathetic countries" and Japan and Korea were invited to join the meeting. Taiwan had been invited and arrived in Wellington, but did not participate owing to a misunderstanding about the use of its name, given rise to issues of non-recognition.

The objective of the Convention is to prohibit driftnet fishing on the high seas and in EEZs of countries or territories lying within a defined area. To do this in a manner consistent with international law, in the most effective way possible and with the maximum agreement, the following principal features of the Convention were agreed upon:

(a) The Convention relates to "driftnet fishing activities" rather than simply the act of fishing. The definition of activities includes supply, trans-shipping, and processing operations.

(b) Parties, or countries signing a protocol, are required to take specified measures in relation to areas within the territorial or EEZ jurisdiction (in certain classes of action there is a discretion), or extraterritorial measures affecting their nationals and vessels.

(c) Collaboration on surveillance and enforcement is encouraged, but there is no general high seas enforcement authority.

(d) Consultation with non-parties is encouraged.

(e) Institutional arrangements, particularly with respect to data collection and analysis, are provided.

The value of this Convention lies in its political and diplomatic usefulness rather than its legal effect. It helped to energize world action, even though has not yet entered into force. Its legal merit is the precedent it provides for adopting an encompassing approach towards a fishery, reflected in its various components — from the references to fishing "activities", to collaborative surveillance and enforcement, and to cooperation through international organizations. Its concern with fishing on the high seas adds to the growing world concern about the need for regulating these fisheries.

A Management Regime for Southern Albacore

The component of the Tarawa Declaration that has yet to be concluded is a management regime for southern albacore. It envisions a regime covering the high seas and coastal state EEZs, and includes distant-water fishing nations (DWFNs) and coastal states. Although driftnet fishing will hopefully have terminated when arrangements are agreed upon, it provided a catalyst for taking these steps.

The main challenge is to construct a regime recognizing continued absolute coastal state sovereign rights over the resource in the face of the traditional Japanese position that DWFNs must have a say in the management of highly migratory species, even in EEZs of other countries.[95] There is also concern that DWFNs may regard a regime for southern albacore as a precedent for other species. In such a case, any softening by Pacific Island countries on the highly migratory species issue could be used as a precedent in subsequent arrangements. However, regional collective-spirit and determination to date have been strong, with the result that countries in the South Pacific region enjoy superior bargaining power, management expertise, and, consequently, control over their resources, even extending as appropriate to the high seas.[96]

Some central issues in the process of negotiating management arrangements are agreement that all interested parties (i.e., coastal states and states participating in the southern albacore fishery) have a legitimate interest in participating in the management arrangements; the role existing regional organizations have to play; agreement on provision of relevant scientific data in a timely fashion; the principle of flag state responsibility; the driftnet issue; a fair balance between the rights of coastal states and distant-water fishing nations; decision-making procedures; scope and membership of the management arrangement; functions of a management body; a high seas observation and inspection scheme; a dispute-settlement mechanism; and the legal form of the arrangement.

---

95   Japan bases its argument on a distorted interpretation of Article 64 of UNCLOS, which rests on the premise that because highly migratory species survive, countries (over a very great area, all interested distant-water fishing nations and coastal states) have an equal say in management. The United States and Japan are the only two countries to invoke this interpretation, and tuna industries in both countries have (or have had) a great stake in the implementation of this interpretation. The United States, having recently amended the *Magnuson Act, supra*, note 76, no longer subscribes to this interpretation.

96   For example, the multilateral *Treaty on Fisheries* between FFA member countries and the United States requires U.S. tuna-boats to report on high seas catches.

THE INTERNATIONAL PROCESS
IN THE UNITED NATIONS

The international process has been quick to respond to the driftnet controversy in the South Pacific, and the North Pacific has been a benefactor. Although many international fora have concerned themselves about driftnet fishing, the culmination of the process has been continuing work (described below) in the United Nations, especially in the United Nations General Assembly, the FAO Committee on Fisheries, and the Office of Ocean Affairs and the Law of the Sea.[97] It is expected that this issue will be part of the broader concern of management of high seas fisheries and large-scale harvesting to be considered at the 1992 United Nations Conference on Environment and Development.[98]

The issue of driftnet fishing in this process is one element of much larger related issues — high seas fishing, oceans ecosystems, and sustainable development. Management of ocean resources and uses can differ within EEZs from country to country. The overlay is the high seas regime, which some countries treat as a free-for-all and others as an area where careful and cooperative management of resources needs to be implemented on an urgent basis.

A brief look at the driftnet issue in the context of the United Nations may assist in analyzing the progress of resource, and planet, protection internationally. Initiatives in the General Assembly, the FAO Committee on Fisheries, and the Office of Ocean Affairs and Law of the Sea are outlined. Preparations for the 1992 UN Conference on Environment and Development are underway and include relevant issues,[99] but it is hoped that driftnet fishing will have ceased by the time of the conference.

United Nations General Assembly

The United Nations General Assembly has adopted its two well-known resolutions on driftnet fishing. In 1989, Resolution 44/225 called for moratoria in the North Pacific by 30 June 1992 and cessation of activities in the South Pacific by 1 July 1991. Because, as noted above, the Resolution needed the support of driftnetting nations, language is vague with respect to whether a moratorium can be lifted or the cessation is an interim measure.[100] And

---

97   See *supra*, note 5, for other international action. Within the United Nations, other agencies such as the United Nations Environment Programme (UNEP) have also been involved.

98   See note 102, *infra*.

99   See note 102, *infra*.

100 Following is the language of the resolution:

there is also the ubiquitous reference to scientific evidence. In 1990, Resolution 45/197 on "large-scale pelagic driftnet fishing and its impact on the living marine resources of the world's oceans and seas"[101] was adopted by the General Assembly. The Resolution commended unilateral, regional, and international efforts undertaken by countries and international organizations to implement and support the objectives of Resolution 44/225.[102] It also reaffirmed Resolution 44/225 and called for its full implementation by all members of the international community.[103] Both resolutions are testimony to the continuing spotlight on the driftnet issue at the United Nations.

FAO Committee on Fisheries

The FAO Committee on Fisheries (COFI) recently[104] concerned itself with several high seas fisheries issues that affect driftnet fishing. A key concern was high seas data collection. The system now in place does not permit FAO to report globally on high seas catches, and COFI requested FAO to plan a decisive role in the standardization of improved methods for data

---

a) Moratoria on all large-scale pelagic driftnet fishing on the high seas by 30 June 1992, with the understanding that such a measure will not be imposed in a region or, if implemented, can be lifted, should effective conservation and management measures be taken based upon statistically sound analysis to be jointly made by concerned parties of the international community with an interest in the fishery resources of the region, to prevent the unacceptable impact of such fishing practices on that region and to ensure the conservation of the living marine resources of that region;

b) Immediate action to reduce progressively large-scale pelagic driftnet fishing activities in the South Pacific region leading to the cessation of such activities by 1 July 1991, as an interim measure, until appropriate conservation and management arrangements for South Pacific albacore tuna resources are entered into by the parties concerned.

101   U.N. Doc. A/C-2/45/6.77, 10 December 1990.

102   Following are some developments noted: the 1990 Forum reaffirmed opposition to large-scale pelagic driftnet fishing; SPC adopted a resolution on same; one member state decided to suspend driftnet fishing operations in the South Pacific a year early, and other member states decided to cease or suspend driftnet fishing; the organization for Eastern Caribbean states resolved to establish a regional fisheries regime that would outlaw the use of driftnets; developments on the issue occurred in the Mediterranean; the INPFC has concerned itself with the need to accumulate scientific knowledge on driftnet fishing and has given support to Resolution 44/225; the IWC endorsed Resolution 44/225; the Preparatory Committee for the United Nations Conference on Environment and Development required a comprehensive report on the impact of large-scale harvesting, new fishing technologies, and fishing technologies in accordance with sustainable management, taking into account Resolution 44/225.

103   Other elements include requesting the UN system and other global, regional, and subregional fishery organizations to continue urgently to study large-scale pelagic driftnets fishing and its impact on living marine resources, bearing in mind moratoria/cessation dates.

104   At its meeting in Rome, 8-12 April 1991.

collection and reporting.[105]

Regarding high seas management, COFI emphasized that action was required to improve the long-term sustainability of fisheries and to reduce waste, especially giving attention to ecological consequences in the high seas. It called for management of multispecies assemblages, taking into account the need for conservation of biodiversity.

Another practical aspect of the sustainability issue was identified as the application of more selective fishing gear and methods.[106] This may result in a meeting on the by-catch issue. However, it could also provide another "stalling" mechanism until further scientific information is gathered on by-catch.[107]

The controversial optimum level for scientific advice was discussed, reflecting a range of views, including the position that the absence of scientific advice should not be taken as a reason for delaying action. This is probably the most critical issue in resource management, and inconclusiveness within COFI illustrates the depth of the dilemma. However, continued attempts to legitimize economic rather than resource needs, through a sliding scientific scale, could result in increased international determination to seek an end to wasteful practices.

Office of Ocean Affairs and Law of the Sea

The UN Office of Oceans Affairs and the Law of the Sea draws together the various initiatives and is responsible for maintaining and preparing reports on all oceans activities, including driftnet fishing. It scheduled a meeting to consider conservation and management of high seas fisheries in July 1991 in New York. This meeting followed a similar meeting held in St. John's, Newfoundland, in September 1990, which agreed on high seas fisheries conservation and management, including driftnet fishing.[108] Both of these initiatives may be able to build on the UNCLOS provisions to give greater definition to existing requirements.

---

105 High seas reporting is a regionally accepted non-negotiable condition of fisheries access among FFA member countries; standardized measures for data collection and reporting are a first step towards responsible high seas management.

106 See *supra*, note 46.

107 It would also provide driftnetting countries with a forum to promote the view that driftnet fishing is more selective than other forms of fishing.

108 The meeting, attended by participants from fifteen countries, the United Nations, provinces, and by international legal and scientific experts, concluded that there must be full, timely, and effective implementation of Resolution 44/225.

CONCLUSIONS

In a perfect world there would be no need for pressure tactics. Resource management would be carried out by consensus in a harmonious manner. It would take into account the well-being of the resource and the present and future needs of humanity, rather than the economic viability of relatively small (but politically forceful) industries.

Coordinated integrated resource management would alienate inter-zonal management variances and protect high seas resources.[109] It could even lead to the emergence of new international norms and jurisdictions. If the "common heritage" notion underlying UNCLOS III was extended to all high seas resources, and to the oceans themselves, global sustainable development could assume better definition. Political and institutional systems would respond to the increasing need for global vision in a new age of communication and consciousness of finite resources. How close are we to a perfect world? Is our direction on course, and on time? If not, what lessons can be learned from the driftnet issue?

Considering high seas fisheries management generally, much has been done over the past four decades in terms of building institutional, fisheries-specific arrangements and in terms of the emergence of international legal norms.[110] Exclusive economic zones have been in place for only about fifteen years. International coordination and integrated management approaches are in the early stages of development, and there is recognition that this must accelerate.[111] Because of the inter-relationship of the resources, high seas regimes should be consciously developed in lock-step with action at the EEZ level.

High seas fisheries resource management needs, in addition to gear-type regulation required for driftnet fishing, include cooperative straddling stocks an immediate renegotiation or replacement of the institutional infrastructure of the various fisheries commissions and research institutions regulation of by-catch, and regulation of related environmental factors.[112] An effective universal database, and global monitoring and enforcement measures, are necessary components of any action to meet these needs.[113]

---

109 Such integrated management should take into account non-fisheries areas, such as land- or ship-based pollution.

110 Legal norms have emerged from the four 1958 Geneva Conventions on the Law of the Sea, UNCLOS III, treaties, judicial precedents, and state practice.

111 This is one theme of UNCED.

112 Such as discharge from supply ships, derelict ships, and gear.

113 Uniform data collection could be processed through regional organizations using, for

Given the breadth of these resource management needs and the need for an integrated approach towards resource management, why does the driftnet issue stand alone in achieving relatively rapid and conclusive universal action? Like the whaling and sealing campaigns, which closed down those industries, anti-driftnet campaigns raised voters' consciousness on an emotional level. With emotions and science at opposite ends of the management spectrum, the reluctance to deviate from rational scientific bases for decisions is both understandable and justifiable. The challenge remains to find an appropriate balance.

In the driftnet controversy, the balance was markedly different between the North and South Pacific. In the former case, public campaigns and progress on scientific cooperation through INPFC seemed to be deadlocked and unable to resolve the situation.[114] The South Pacific responded immediately and effectively, without a similar opportunity for thorough scientific analysis, through existing regional institutions.

The action taken at the political level by the Forum — the pioneering Tarawa Declaration — flowed from two balanced sources: the results of technical meetings and consultations within an existing regional framework; and anti-driftnet campaigns spearheaded by NGOs in some of the major countries, which in this case followed rather than led the original intergovernmental initiatives.

In addition to the spur provided by NGOs, the high seas driftnet activity was ripe for international political and diplomatic action: driftnetting countries had earned international reputations as oceanic opportunists, and their generally arrogant attitude towards sincere management efforts by other countries evoked sentiments comparable to those generated by oil tycoons in popular television dramas; the high seas are beyond the jurisdiction of any politician, and voters are unlikely to engage in driftnet fishing practices; there is some scientific basis for halting the fishery; the fishing methods can be

---

example, a standardized logsheet for high seas and EEZ catches. As noted in text, *supra*, some progress has been made in requiring high seas reporting. With respect to monitoring and a form of enforcement, the model provided by FFA member countries could provide the basis for a worldwide Register of Foreign Fishing Vessels. Information regarding the vessel and its owners-operators would be submitted to a central authority, and "good standing" on the Register would automatically be given. If the vessel was involved in designated circumstances (relating to a serious offence, for example), "good standing" would be withdrawn and the vessel would not be permitted to fish in the waters of any participating coastal state.

114 It is to be remembered that in the North Pacific, unlike the South Pacific, a legitimate focus for campaigns was the by-catch of marine mammals. In the South Pacific, the major problem was, of course, the threat of stock depletion.

replaced with others, so there is no threat to world food supply; and driftnet fishing causes environmental hazards. Other considerations are increasing international attention to the environment and the need for hands-on regulation of a previously less regulated area.

The driftnet issue is not yet over. Representations will be made and pressures applied at the highest levels until it is. However, it has become a model for concerted international action at the diplomatic-political level. Key to its development is the collective consciousness of individuals. Although many of the outstanding high seas resource uses are not as easily "marketable" as the driftnet issue, responsible NGOs should initiate or renew efforts to raise that collective consciousness.

Identification of resource uses that are incompatible with sustainable development, environmental protection, and the ecosystem approach should be made on responsible grounds, taking into account all the standard scientific, socio-economic, cultural, and other considerations. National and international measures should then be taken as appropriate.

The driftnet issue has reinforced the lesson that part of this equation must be public knowledge engendered by responsible communications and campaigns. The time for confrontational NGO tactics is over, and the time has come for responsible organizations to serve environmental needs by being effective communicators between government and the public.[115] In that context, governments' agendas could be influenced by reasonable, rather than predominantly emotional, arguments. This approach is consistent with emerging state practice, which is to seek a balanced public input, and with the international process, which is to involve non-governmental organizations and institutes in preparatory work. The United Nations Conference on Environment and Development is an example of such a process.

The way of the future is to avoid resource-use conflicts through responsible national, regional, and international action based on an integrated approach to management of our common heritage.

---

115 It is recognized that special-interest groups representing industry may not always agree with needed measures, but the important task is educating and involving the public as a whole in these issues.

THE NORTH AMERICAN WATERFOWL MANAGEMENT PLAN: AN EXAMPLE OF NATIONAL AND INTERNATIONAL COOPERATION IN RESOURCE MANAGEMENT

Gerald McKeating

In an attempt to reverse a serious trend in the decline of waterfowl populations and associated nesting habitat, the North American Waterfowl Management Plan (NAWMP)[1] was developed by agency partners in Canada and the United States. Signed in 1986 by the Canadian federal Minister of the Environment and the U.S. Secretary of the Interior, the NAWMP is a multi-agency effort to restore waterfowl populations and habitat to the levels of the mid-1970s. It is a fifteen-year blueprint for cooperative management initiatives and defines population and waterfowl habitat objectives in both countries. Although it focuses specifically on waterfowl, I would much prefer the plan to be called the North American Wetland Management Plan, as in my view it is a land-use program, given that the decline in waterfowl populations is symptomatic of problems in land use throughout prairie Canada and elsewhere.

The NAWMP itself provides for a strategic and policy framework for cooperative waterfowl conservation initiatives. It clarifies priority habitat areas and identifies the financial resources and actions required to resolve land-use problems. Thirty-four areas of concern have been identified throughout North America. The plan calls for a full partnership of all governments, the private sector, other government departments, and, in particular, agricultural interests.

It also calls for an expenditure of one billion dollars in Canada, oriented primarily to habitat restoration activities, with a further five hundred million dollars to be spent in the United States. As with many programs, however, this one is dynamic in nature, with changes being made as more needs are identified/clarified and as additional partners participate and new joint ventures are formed.

With respect to prairie Canada, 75 percent of the funds for the Prairie Habitat Joint Venture will, generally speaking, be raised in the United States but spent in Canada. Of the remaining 25 percent of program cost, 10 percent

---

1   Canada. Department of the Environment, *North American Waterfowl Management Plan: A Strategy for Cooperation* (Ottawa: Supply and Services, 1986).

will come from federal sources, 10 percent from provincial governments, and a further 5 percent from non-government organizations.

HOW DOES IT WORK?

In order to implement a plan of such magnitude it was necessary to break it down into smaller, manageable segments. To achieve this, thirteen joint ventures were formed throughout North America. In the United States, the joint ventures are the Prairie Pothole Joint Venture, which encompasses parts of Montana, North and South Dakota, Minnesota, and Iowa; the Playa Lakes Joint Venture; the Lower Mississippi Valley Joint Venture; the Lower Great Lakes/St. Lawrence Basin Joint Venture; the Central Valley Joint Venture, which encompasses California's San Joaquin and Sacramento Valleys; the Upper Mississippi River/Great Lakes and Rainwater Basin Joint Venture; the Atlantic Coast Joint Venture, which extends from Maine to South Carolina; and the Gulf Coast Joint Venture, which spans the Gulf states from Alabama to Texas.

In Canada, there are five joint ventures: the Eastern Habitat Joint Venture, which includes Ontario, Quebec, and the Atlantic provinces; the Prairie Habitat Joint Venture, which includes the major waterfowl areas in the three prairie provinces; the newly formed Pacific Coast Joint Venture; the Arctic Goose Joint Venture; and the Black Duck Joint Venture. The last two are more population-monitoring and research-oriented endeavours, while the others have a strong land-use-based program. To provide an example of how these joint ventures are structured, I will review two in Canada: a land-use venture and one dealing primarily with population monitoring and research.

Prairie Habitat Joint Venture

The Prairie Habitat Joint Venture (PHJV), which is the largest in North America, seeks to enhance and restore wetland and upland habitat on 3.6 million acres of land in the southern Canadian prairies and parkland belt. Through individual provincial plans, a variety of programs have been identified for field implementation. These are considered to be the most suitable for the geographic region involved. These are undertaken by the participating agencies in the province, necessitating a full cooperative approach between provincial, non-governmental, and federal agencies. It is with respect to the actual program implementation that I cannot overstress the need for a cooperative approach among all parties who have an interest in how the land is managed.

The prairie delivery agents formally structured a joint venture by an agreement amongst the parties that sets up the process for doing business as well as establishes the structure for coordinating the activity of the partners. Within each province, a coordinating body has been established to facilitate the partner's planning, delivery of, and reporting on programs. Regional coordination is achieved through an eight-person PHJV Advisory Board, composed of representatives from each of the major Canadian delivery agents. This advisory board represents the joint venture nationally in dealing with the North American Wetlands Conservation Council (Canada).

The PHJV acts as the overall coordinating agency in prairie Canada and endorses the program plans that are presented to it by the provincial implementation groups, as well as setting the policy for overall program approach within the venture. The chairperson of the PHJV is the key liaison person with the North American Wetlands Conservation Council (Canada) and represents the venture when necessary at meetings in the United States. PHJV staff consists of a coordinator, a secretary, and a biological evaluation coordinator, whose responsibility is to ensure that the biological programs put in place will produce the desired results. Provincial implementation bodies have both administrative and biological staff.

From this prairie-wide coordination, there is an implementation group in each of the three provinces. Alberta has formed an Alberta NAWMP Centre comprising a variety of agencies in that province, while in Saskatchewan and Manitoba the implementation of the plan is under the direction of Crown corporations specifically structured for that purpose. The most far-ranging membership is found in the Saskatchewan Wetlands Conservation Corporation, which includes not only the traditional federal and provincial groups but also the Saskatchewan Water Corporation, the Association of Rural Municipalities, the Saskatchewan Natural History Society, the Saskatchewan Wildlife Federation, Ducks Unlimited, the Saskatchewan Rural Development, Saskatchewan Environment and Public Safety, and Wildlife Habitat Canada. The Manitoba Habitat Heritage Corporation does not have as large a membership, but its membership is broadly based and reflective of agricultural and wildlife interests. Figure 1 schematically illustrates the information-flow structure of the PHJV.

Each implementation group has various subcommittees that are appropriate for the specific needs within that jurisdiction. All have technical committees whose membership consists of those individuals in agencies who must themselves deliver the program on the ground. These groups provide the technical recommendations after much deliberation and consultation with agriculture and wildlife groups. For example, joint programs are planned with the cooperation of regional agricultural representatives. All the technical issues are generally resolved at this level, with their recommendations then forwarded to the corporate board for endorsement. The provincial technical committees have developed provincial plans that have identified the nature of

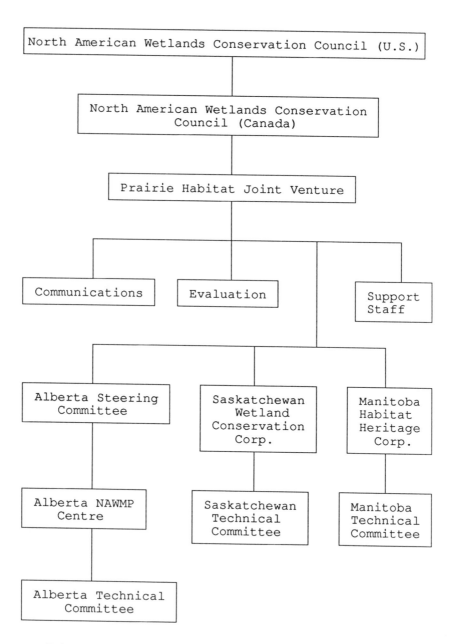

Information-flow Structure of the Prairie Habitat Joint Venture

Figure 1

the programs as well as the more specific priority areas within the provincial jurisdiction. In endorsing these project plans and specific project proposals, the policy group must ensure that it conforms with the approved provincial plan and with the overall thrust of the North American plan program.

Project work plans are developed annually and include a number of program elements, for example, land securement through acquisition or lease; conversion of marginal farmland to permanent vegetation cover; modification of grazing practices; implementation of various conservation farming practices; and policy review processes.

In summary, there is a wide variety of participants involved in these implementation groups and technical committees, including provincial agricultural agencies, municipal governments, irrigation districts, agriculture service boards, environmental non-government agencies, naturalists, fish and game groups, and, most of all, cooperating land owners. However, we still need to involve others, such as First Nation federations. The structures are complicated, since we must provide a forum that allows for the participation of all interest groups. The achievement of PHJV goals will not be reached without the participation of everyone having an interest in the land base. To date, land-owner response has been very positive. The prospectus of the PHJV outlines in more detail the structure and program objectives of the Venture.

In addition to the foregoing, NAWMP programs are integrated into programs being undertaken by other agencies, particularly the permanent cover program of the Prairie Farm Rehabilitation Administration. We link wildlife programs to other existing programs wherever feasible. A number of the American joint ventures are centred on the wintering grounds and are therefore complementary to Canadian work on the breeding grounds.

Arctic Goose Joint Venture

Another example of a joint venture structure is the Arctic Goose Joint Venture. This program is international in scope and represents interests in the United States and Canada. The difference in this approach is that the work is directed to those goose populations regarding which there is concern, rather than to issues based on a geographic jurisdictional level. There is an international steering committee with two chairpeople, of which I am the Canadian Co-chair and a representative of the U.S. Fish and Wildlife Service is the American Co-chair. A management board has been formed, comprising six members from each country, and a technical committee having a similar membership. The representation reflects federal, state, and provincial interests and the various waterfowl committees and flyway councils.

Project proposals are reviewed by the technical committee and are forwarded to the management board for endorsement. The program is, however, fairly young, and it is only in the past few months that we have begun to put a structured process in place. At the same time, four hundred thousand dollars were spent in 1991 on various projects throughout Canada, from the St. Lawrence to Queen Maud Gulf and Brant wintering grounds in Georgia Strait.

FUNDING

Funding is a complicated process, as a variety of agencies and governments must in one way or another contribute to this program. I will attempt to simplify this process for the PHJV. The five-year program for the PHJV calls for an expenditure of $229 million between 1991 and 1995. The plan, which has been adopted by the North American Wetlands Conservation Council, projects the securement of 650,000 acres of upland nesting habitat, with the improvement — either directly or indirectly as a result of the programs — to a total of 2.2 million acres. In addition, it is planned that 181,000 acres of wetland habitat will be secured. During 1991, the program will be implemented on sixteen project areas throughout the prairie parkland.

Actual expenditures for 1991 in the PHJV are projected to be approximately 33.8 million dollars, with the majority of the funds distributed between Alberta and Saskatchewan, where the greatest numbers of high-quality waterfowl habitat are located. Where does the money come from? Are the dollars real or just sleight of hand? I suggest that they are real. I previously indicated that the U.S. share is approximately 75 percent, with the Canadian share comprising 10 percent federal, 10 percent provincial, and 5 percent environmental non-government organizations.

To meet the federal share, the Treasury Board allocated 30 million dollars over five years for NAWMP implementation, with that money to be matched by provincial agencies. Funding requests are then made through the appropriate Canadian body for endorsement and submission to U.S. sources. There, the U.S. *Wetland Conservation Act* has a legislated budget of 15 million U.S. dollars, with provision for a further 15 million to be allocated through the congressional budget process. Those federal dollars must be matched by state or environmental non-government organizations. For 1991, over 6 million Canadian dollars has been allocated to the PHJV and over 2.3 million dollars to the Eastern Habitat Joint Venture. Since the program's inception in 1990, over 28.3 million dollars Canadian has been allocated for work in Canada by American sources.

The foregoing has attempted to simplify the complex workings of NAWMP. Given the vast array of agencies, political jurisdictions, and personalities who have been involved, the results that we now are beginning to see are encouraging. Dollars are translated into actual projects on the ground, ones that can only help provide us with a healthier environment for the benefit of all wildlife. It is worth the effort.

5
ALTERNATIVE ROUTES FOR DISPUTE RESOLUTION

CO-MANAGEMENT ISSUES IN THE FOREST WILDERNESS: A STEWARDSHIP COUNCIL FOR TEMAGAMI

Jamie Benidickson

This paper offers an overview of general institutional issues in co-management with particular reference to recent experience in the Temagami area of northeastern Ontario where, in the aftermath of an increasingly intense debate over resource use, aboriginal rights, and the environment, an arrangement for joint management has recently been implemented.

Of the general issues in co-management, perhaps the most basic yet also the most complex are the problems of objectives and definition. In the absence of a firm understanding of co-management,[1] definition by comparison can serve to place the co-management concept in context; that is, in attempting to understand co-management, it is often helpful to compare it with alternative institutional arrangements for making decisions about the use of resources.

To a considerable extent, experience with co-management has involved so-called common property resources. Commentators have indicated that such resources are characterized by excludability and subtractability problems: access to the resource is difficult if not impossible to control, and competing

---

1   For a valuable exploration of a working definition of co-management, see Evelyn Pinkerton, "Introduction: Attaining Better Fisheries Management through Co-Management — Prospects, Problems, and Propositions" *in* Evelyn Pinkerton, ed., *Co-operative Management of Fisheries: New Directions for Improved Management & Community Development* (Vancouver: University of British Columbia Press, 1989) 3.

users will diminish each other's potential to utilize or enjoy the resource.[2]

Although there are examples of co-management arrangements dealing comprehensively with a range of resource uses within a designated territory, these appear to be less common than agreements that attempt to regulate a single sector — fisheries and wildlife, for example.

Co-management agreements have emerged from a variety of background circumstances, generally involving jurisdictional disputes, shared jurisdiction that is acknowledged, multiple-use conflicts, or significant externalities.[3] The institutional arrangements frequently emphasize the relationship between two parties: on the one hand a primary user group or local community (often an aboriginal community), and on the other hand a primary regulator whose authority includes responsibility in the locality but is also much broader. Participants will view the initial implementation of co-management as an advance on an unpromising *status quo*, though it is not always evident at the outset that they propose to advance in the same direction.

By no means all of the co-management experience has been confined to native communities, but co-management agreements involving native users have been fairly common. These have several distinctive features, the most noteworthy of which is the challenge of reconciling divergent philosophical perspectives in decision-making structures.[4] Observers are frequently pessimistic that this reconciliation can in fact be accomplished. Peter Usher, for example, having contrasted indigenous management with the technocratic approach of the state model, describes the goal of co-management as the promotion of devolution and decentralization of the management system through increased local participation and creation of user advisory boards. Ultimately, though, he suggests that co-management may be aimed at "encouraging Native people to become qualified to work as technicians and managers in the state system."[5]

Parties to co-management arrangements have sought a variety of objectives, but as summarized by Evelyn Pinkerton in the fisheries context, "the benefits sought by one or all of the actors through ... co-management are

---

2   David Feeny *et al.*, "The Tragedy of the Commons: Twenty-Two Years Later" (1990) 19:1 Human Ecology 1 at 3.

3   See Pinkerton, *supra*, note 1, for essays on a series of co-management experiments in the fisheries sector involving native and non-native resource users.

4   Marilyn Kansky, *Native Indian and Inuit Views on the Federal Environmental Assessment and Review Process* (Edmonton: Environmental Law Centre, 1988), deals with the differing perspectives in the environmental assessment context.

5   Peter J. Usher, "Indigenous Management Systems and the Conservation of Wildlife in the Canadian North" 14:1 Alternatives 3.

more appropriate, more efficient, and more equitable management."[6] In addition, there are secondary goals — also benefits in their own way. Community-based development, decentralization of decision making, and mobilization of local consent through the processes of participatory democracy have all been considered as advantages of co-management regimes. Benefits accrue both to government and to local resource users, with the former buttressing itself against challenges to the legitimacy of its authority while the community gains from increased involvement and influence. Yet attempts to rank and assess the apparent attractions of co-management are fraught with difficulty: "Whether one thinks of community development, decentralized decision-making, and participatory democracy as secondary goals equally as important as the primary management goals of equity, efficiency, and appropriate management depends on who one is .... Ultimately the goals could be seen as processes for achieving other goals, as well as ends in themselves."[7] Not surprisingly, then, the search for standards against which to evaluate the performance of co-management arrangements remains an uncertain quest.

THE TEMAGAMI EXPERIENCE AND THE CREATION OF THE STEWARDSHIP AUTHORITY

The renowned Temagami country of northeastern Ontario has been the subject of a prolonged dispute over aboriginal rights and the setting for recurring conflicts about resource management.[8] Although the local aboriginal community, the Teme-augama Anishnabai (hereafter the TAA), had not participated in treaty arrangements relating to the area of their homeland (N'Daki Menan), the Ontario government designated much of Temagami as a provincial forest reserve in 1901, ostensibly to provide long-term management of a valuable pine forest. Historically, local interests, including the native community, the mineral and forest resource industries, and members of a diverse recreational constituency have clashed over matters such as water level regulation, forest access roads, mineral development, shoreline protection, and timber-cutting practices, with local officials of the Ministry of Natural Resources asserting an ultimate authority.

In the past decade or so several factors combined to increase the intensity and visibility of the Temagami conflict:[9] in the context of growing popular

---

6   Pinkerton, *supra*, note 1, at 5.

7   *Id.*

8   Bruce W. Hodgins & Jamie Benidickson, *The Temagami Experience: Recreation, Resources and Aboriginal Rights in the Northern Ontario Wilderness* (Toronto: University of Toronto Press, 1989).

9   The area has in fact been described as "the pre-eminent example of resource conflict in

understanding of the basis of native claims, the aboriginal community has asserted its legal interests with increasing vigour; the media and province-wide environmental organizations have helped to focus attention on the issues at stake in areas such as Temagami, with forest management practices and "old growth" emerging as the central battleground; and economic conditions prompted the forest industry to expand capacity with the encouragement of government officials who have been moving towards increased production levels. Confrontations and lumber road blockades, litigation that eventually reached the Supreme Court of Canada,[10] and critical national television coverage of the old growth forest and aboriginal conflicts at Temagami aroused strong public interest and created the circumstances for a major institutional adjustment in the spring of 1990.

In a Memorandum of Understanding (MOU), the TAA and the Province of Ontario agreed to the formation of a stewardship council that would assume responsibility for the four townships most closely associated with the intensifying controversy surrounding old-growth pine forest.[11] The council, comprising equal numbers of TAA appointees and persons named by Ontario, and presided over by a mutually agreed chair, was initially to exercise authority over timber licences in the four townships of Delhi, Acadia, Shelburne, and Canton. In addition, the MOU provided for a bilateral process of consultation between the TAA and Ontario's Ministry of Natural Resources concerning the Ministry's timber management plans for other parts of the aboriginal homeland. The TAA's recommended modifications of the plan were to be incorporated by the ministry "where feasible".

The proposal for a stewardship council offered a much-beleaguered government some respite from severe public criticism of its land management practices in a controversial situation. The arrangement offers the TAA recognition of the native community's status in the region and an acceptable level of involvement and control in land management for the small area of the council's initial jurisdiction. Both principals get an opportunity to test an experimental institution, with the future possibility of applying the lessons learned from the stewardship council in a broader context.[12] Beyond this,

---

Ontario, if not Canada." See Crandall A. Benson *et al.*, *The Need for a Land Stewardship, Holistic Resource Management for N'Daki Menan* (report for the Teme-augama Anishnabai, July 1989) [unpublished].

10   *Bear Island Foundation* v. *A.G. Ontario*, [1991] 2 S.C.R. 570 (appeal dismissed).

11   The Memorandum of Understanding was signed on 23 April 1990 by Chiefs Gary Potts and Rita O'Sullivan on behalf of the Teme-augama Anishnabai and by the Honourable Lyn McLeod and the Hon. Ian Scott on behalf of the Province of Ontario.

12   The MOU, *id.*, calls for the creation of an evaluation process and joint review of the results

Ontario and the TAA agreed to pursue a Treaty of Co-existence to deal with the underlying question of relations between the native community and the province.

As finally constituted in May 1991, the stewardship council, whose structure and responsibilities are described below, was named the Wendaban Stewardship Authority.[13] The initiative, though interim and provisional, certainly falls within the general category of co-management.

PUBLIC PARTICIPATION AND ENVIRONMENTAL STANDARDS

General

A phrase used in the title of this volume, "Growing Demands on a Shrinking Heritage", presents a dilemma arising from the clash of two perspectives on the future use of resources. The notion of growing demands serves as a surrogate for claims about use and access and for claims about entitlements to participation, including community involvement in decision making. The shrinking heritage, on the other hand, represents some sense of ultimate threshold, natural constraint, or substantial limit on the environment's capacity to satisfy claims made upon it.[14]

To the extent that co-management is about the resolution of disputes when these two competing perspectives conflict, we need to examine how co-management might serve to resolve the dilemma or to promote a reconciliation. How does co-management influence the demand end, that is, peoples' claims on and access to resources? And how does it affect the heritage end, that is, resource conservation, sustainability, and environmental protection? The Wendaban Stewardship Authority will shortly be analyzed for its potential contribution to the reconciliation process, but I will first comment on participation and environmental standards in their own terms, for each of these concepts reflects considerations that are relevant to the challenge of managing resource-use conflicts.

Participation can be expected to serve a variety of objectives. It can, for example, increase the "intelligence" of the decision in the sense that better

---

as a basis for considering expansion of the concept of shared stewardship.

13   At an earlier stage of negotiations the council was referred to as the Wakimika Stewardship Council. Creation of the Wendaban Stewardship Authority was announced on 23 May 1991. The WSA's terms of reference are set out in an Addendum to the MOU, *id.*, signed one year earlier between the TAA and the previous Ontario government.

14   See Feeny *et al.*, *supra*, note 2, for discussion of the importance of separating the control regime from the nature of the resource and for a summary of recent findings calling in question the link between successful management and particular ownership arrangements.

information derived from the involvement of those affected by anticipated outcomes may demonstrably improve the quality of results. Fairness, too, may be enhanced by the participation of those who are concerned with the impacts of decisions. And fair process can contribute to the acceptability of outcomes that might otherwise be suspect or vulnerable to criticism. It has also been suggested that there are inherent values in participation, such as the reinforcement of citizenship and its attendant features — debate and deliberation, for example.[15]

There are significant variations in the mechanisms available to foster participation, and the point requires little elaboration here. Public and community involvement in decision making about resource use can range from informal and clearly non-binding consultation in a variety of forms to more influential types of involvement. In certain circumstances participation may be a legal requirement[16] and may result in various control measures, veto power, or ultimately self-determination. The latter, though, moves the mechanism off the spectrum of co-management.[17]

One variation on participation that is of particular interest in the present context is the resource management agreement or equivalent. The model is essentially that of a contract, through which the provincial authority as owner and the licensee as operator contract with regard to resource access and management. Terms may include periodic performance reviews, means to accommodate the interests of other resource users, and conditions concerning environmental matters.[18]

---

15 Carolyn Tuohy, "Bureaucracy and Democracy" (1990) 40 U. of T. Law J. 598; Alastair R. Lucas, "Legal Foundations for Public Participation in Environmental Decisionmaking" (1976) 16 Natural Resources J. 73 at 74; Bruce R. Rettig, Fikret Berkes & Evelyn Pinkerton, "The Future of Fisheries Co-Management: A Multi-Disciplinary Assessment" *in* Pinkerton, *supra*, note 1, at 273.

16 Lucas, *supra*, note 15.

17 For illustration of different forms of participation in decision making for fisheries resources, see John F. Kearney, "Co-Management or Co-Optation? The Ambiguities of Lobster Fishery Management in Southwest Nova Scotia" *in* Pinkerton, *supra*, note 1, at 88 ; Lucas, *id.*, at 75.

18 Frank Cassidy & Norman Dale, *After Native Claims? The Implications of Comprehensive Claims Settlements for Natural Resources in British Columbia* (Lantzville, B.C.: Oolichan Books & Institute for Research on Public Policy, 1988) 107. For descriptions of forest management agreements or equivalent arrangements, see Julian A. Dunster & Robert B. Gibson, *Forestry and Assessment: Development of the Class Environmental Assessment for Timber Management in Ontario* (Toronto: Canadian Institute for Environment Law and Policy, 1989) 96-99; Andrea B. Moen, *Demystifying Forestry Law: An Alberta Analysis* (Edmonton: Environmental Law Centre, 1990) at 31.

When we turn to consider the environmental or heritage dimension of potential conflicts over resource use, we are confronted with the realization that although the general importance of environmental values has risen significantly in recent years, knowledge often remains limited and little agreement has been reached on the applicable standards. For example, although "sustainable development" is a widely accepted principle, it is not always possible to specify the level of development that might be sustainable in any particular setting. Similarly, in the context of pollution there may be agreement on "clean" as the objective, but there is little certainty about "how clean is clean enough."[19] Furthermore, even while agencies such as Law Reform Commissions insist that compensation rules for injury to natural resources must encompass losses for "intrinsic" values as well as "use" values, they acknowledge the limitations of methodologies for determining those intrinsic values.[20]

The absence of practical agreement on environmental and resource-use standards may have encouraged reliance on process-based solutions. Fox, commenting on the interaction of interest groups and institutions in the process of managing water resources, noted that "[t]he influence of each entity on the final decision will depend on a number of factors including the rules which govern what it can do, its capability to generate information, and its ability to impose burdens or provide benefits to other entities concerned with the decision. The product of this set of interactions should be the preference of society."[21] The concluding assumption is an important one: accommodation or consensus amongst the participants substitutes for an externally recognized standard against which outcomes could be measured.[22]

Participation and Resource Management Standards in Temagami

The difficulties of measuring environmental and resource values have been evident in the Temagami situation. The work of several prominent forest researchers demonstrates that divergent perspectives are deeply embedded in

---

19   Dianne Saxe, *Contaminated Land: Protection of Life Series* (Working Paper prepared for the Law Reform Commission of Canada, 1990) at 149-155 [unpublished].

20   Ontario Law Reform Commission, *Report on Damages for Environmental Harm* (Toronto, 1990).

21   Irving K. Fox, "Institutions for Water Management in a Changing World" (1976) 16 Natural Resources J. 743 at 745.

22   For a discussion of the relationship between various environmental viewpoints — popular, technocratic, and deep ecological — and perspectives on institutional arrangements, see Stephanie Pollack, "Reimagining NEPA: Choices for Environmentalists" (1985) 9 Harvard Environmental Law Rev. 359.

the methodological emphases and priorities of the scientific community. Timber resource production, forest ecology (especially the nature of old-growth regeneration), and the challenges of evaluating and integrating alternative forest uses into an evolving framework for holistic stewardship have each been the focus of recent work on the Temagami region.[23]

Benson, a respected advisor to the TAA, explained his position in a consultant study:

> The many resources of N'Daki Menan with their multiple values and potential uses require careful holistic planning and management so that the public can appreciate the integral value of the area and other associated uses. Wherever possible, multiple-uses should be planned for in each area, but in specific locations, certain uses must be given priority or even exclusive use and as a result, incompatible uses would be assigned to other places within the planning area.[24]

For their own part, the TAA have declared their homeland to be "an experimental outdoor laboratory for four hundred years" and resolved "that the management plan for our motherland for thousands of years to come, be finalized in the year 2387."[25] This apparently rhetorical proposition in fact reflects the native community's appreciation of its ancestors' four-century occupation of N'Daki Menan, as well as a deep commitment to a future that is at least as long as the past.

The Ministry of Natural Resources planning objectives have broadened over the years, moving away from a preoccupation with timber production to encompass other concerns in what is now described as a comprehensive planning process intended to produce a plan dealing simultaneously with all resource uses and incorporating the perspectives of other provincial departments.[26] The Temagami experience over the past twenty years

---

23 Robert Day, "The Dynamic Nature of Ontario's Forests from Post-Glacial Times to the Present Day" in *Old Growth Forests ... What are They? How do They Work?* (Symposium materials, 20 January 1990) (Toronto: Faculty of Forestry, University of Toronto, 1990); Peter A. Quinby, "Old Growth Forest Survey in Temagami's Wakimika Triangle" (1989) Research Report 2, Temagami Wilderness Society's Tall Pines Project; and Peter A. Quinby, "Self-Replacement in Old Growth White Pine Forests" (1990) Research Report 3, Temagami Wilderness Society's Tall Pines Project [unpublished research reports]; Benson, *supra,* note 9.

24 Benson *et al., supra,* note 9, at 105.

25 Chief Gary Potts to Ontario Premier David Peterson, 19 May 1987, quoted in Hodgins & Benidickson, *supra,* note 8, at 297.

26 Comprehensive planning appears to be a broader concept than the Ministry of Natural Resources' previous objective of integrated resource management (IRM), which was defined as "the coordination of resource management programs and activities so that long-term benefits are optimized and conflicts between programs are minimized." See Ontario.

illustrates a range of participatory structures relating to land management and forest resource use. These reflect the expansion of ministry objectives to encompass non-timber uses and to permit some involvement by non-timber interests in the decision-making processes. In addition to the use of purely consultative or opinion-gathering exercises in the early 1970s, some *ad hoc* institutions were created; these were advisory in nature, reporting with non-binding recommendations either to district officials of the Ministry or to the Minister. Additional bodies have more closely resembled municipal government structures and local planning boards. The latest creation, a Comprehensive Planning Council, has advisory powers related to land use and resource management in the Temagami area exclusive of the territory administered by the WSA.[27]

Utilization of provincial decision-making processes of general application throughout Ontario, such as the procedures of the *Environmental Assessment Act*, has offered still further opportunities for the participation of different groups in the management of Temagami lands, but with no guarantees of satisfaction. Indeed, litigation efforts by frustrated observers of a narrowly crafted environmental assessment process in the Temagami forest essentially confirmed that the substantive requirements of the process may be extremely modest.[28]

Generally absent from all these proceedings and institutions, however, was the native community. The TAA chose as part of its fundamental challenge to the jurisdiction of the province not to accept membership on decision-making institutions that were inconsistent with its claim to continued ownership of Crown/public lands within the boundaries of its ancestral homeland.[29]

With these considerations as background, I now describe the WSA in more detail and examine its contribution to participation and resource-use standards.

Ministry of Natural Resources & Policy and Planning Secretariat, *A Framework for Resource Management Planning In MNR* (Toronto, 1986).

27   The Comprehensive Planning Council was created at the same time as the WSA's composition was announced in the spring of 1991. Its membership emphasizes the involvement of local non-native interests in natural resource management.

28   Richard D. Lindgren "The Temagami E.A. Decision: The Legal Perspective" (Summer 1989) Seasons 46.

29   The Temagami Indians have asserted an aboriginal rights claim over public lands within the territory of their homeland. They are not seeking to displace private owners living within the territory, but have requested government compensation for the loss of such previously patented lands.

THE WENDABAN STEWARDSHIP AUTHORITY

Structure and Composition

With the implicit understanding that bilateral structures combining representation by government as the primary regulator with participation of the primary resource user might well be the norm, most designers of co-management institutions would emphasize the importance of getting the right parties to the table. Bu. outside the co-management field there has been a broader stakeholder movement in public decision making, with stakeholders included, at least for purposes of consultation, because they are in some way interested in or affected by the decisions relating to the resource. The WSA's composition reflects the influence of the stakeholder movement on bilateralism as a co-management norm.

Commenting recently on the formation of the Stewardship Authority, the Ontario Minister of Natural Resources indicated a preference for increasing the council's size from the announced plan of four plus four with a neutral chair to six plus six with a neutral chair. In explanation, the Minister stated simply that "we feel we need representation from the municipalities, industry, labour, tourism, the cottagers and the environmentalists."[30] Assuming one member per category on the government side of the bilateral structure for co-management, this would suggest that the Province of Ontario has no seat at the table.

Perhaps it has been determined that the public interest in Ontario is fully represented by the sectors selected for participation. In British Columbia, on the other hand, provincial concerns about losing jurisdiction over major tracts of forest lands in the context of comprehensive land claims have been summarized as follows:

> [U]nder native control forest resources would be less efficiently and completely utilized; the net economic and social benefits to British Columbia would be diminished; multiple-use management and the coordination of forest activities with other government responsibilities would become complicated and ineffective; native-controlled forest enterprises would not be able to cope with the increasingly difficult world timber market; both a loss of provincial revenues and inequitable levels of rent collection might result.[31]

Many will regard these concerns as exaggerated, or subject to reasonable resolution through negotiations. However, the apparent absence of comparable concerns in the Wendaban arrangement is noteworthy.

It is not immediately apparent how Ontario's representatives on the new

---

30   Amie Hakala, "Joint Stewardship Council May Decide Fate of Temagami", *North Bay Nugget* (23 January 1991) A8.

31   Cassidy & Dale, *supra*, note 18, at 90.

stewardship authority would perceive these issues. But unless one takes the view that future expansion of the WSA's geographic jurisdiction is not a serious possibility, and that the other management body — the Comprehensive Planning Council (eventually with more significant participation from the TAA) — will be the real influence on decision making in the broader Temagami district over the longer term, the apparent exclusion of state interests is quite striking.[32]

What is the nature of participation by the new provincial appointees? They serve as provincial representatives, yet it appears that they are also intended to represent concerned interest groups. But in the second sense are they to be seen as representatives by virtue of having been selected by or through consultation with organizations to which they are accountable, or are they interest group representatives only in the sense that they are considered to be typical spokespersons for various perspectives on forest management? In whatever respect they may be representatives of a point of view, is it their function to articulate or advocate that view in the deliberations of the WSA?[33] And how, assuming their one-year terms are renewed, are they expected to interact over a period of time? No simple answer to these questions will emerge from a scrutiny of the Temagami appointment process, although ministerial statements and other factors provide some indications.

In a text prepared for delivery before the annual conference of the Ontario Forestry Association, 2 February 1991, the Minister reflected upon the implications of public participation and environmental awareness for forest management. Adopting the now-fashionable argument that we "have been managing timber, not forests", Mr. Wildman urged commitment to "sustainable forestry", a principle that "will evolve over time" but that he defined as "the practice that ensures the long-term health of forest ecosystems, which contribute to global environmental benefits while providing an array of social, cultural and economic opportunities now and in the future." He anticipated a process that will lead to "a broad social consensus for forest management policy" supported by all the stakeholders, a group that, in this context, the Minister thought needed redefinition to include "aboriginal groups, municipalities, small business, unions, educators — in short, a broad spectrum of citizens from all walks of life."[34]

---

32   The Comprehensive Planning Council was announced by the Ontario Minister of Natural Resources, 23 May 1991, to replace an existing organization known as the Temagami Advisory Council.

33   Tuohy, *supra*, note 15, at 602; Norman Wengert, "Citizen Participation: Practice in Search of a Theory" (1976) 16 Natural Resources J. 23 at 32-33.

34   Bud Wildman, "Notes for Remarks" (Address to Annual Conference of the Ontario Forestry

The TAA, incidentally, is not without internal constituencies that may need to be accommodated within the native-appointed membership on the council. Thus, it is also relevant to ask whether the TAA appointees will act as a bloc with a predetermined position, or as individuals with authority to make flexible independent judgments.

One avenue of inquiry would be to consider in the abstract the possible content of a native forest management policy. Operational practices might differ from conventional approaches to forest use in a variety of respects. Some would anticipate a greater degree of concern to promote regeneration or to undertake reforestation measures. There is also the possibility that wildlife habitat and culturally significant sites might receive a higher priority, or that more ecologically sensitive harvesting systems would be favoured over clear-cutting. In addition, the economic stability of local communities and linkages between timber production and other forms of local economic activity, such as construction and manufacturing, might receive more serious consideration.

These and related possibilities ought not to be dismissed, but it could be equally misguided to assume a complete transformation of forest management procedures as the natural and inevitable outcome of native influence on resource use. In a study of the implications of comprehensive claims settlements for natural resources in British Columbia, Cassidy and Dale reported that "[n]o blanket opposition to forest operations on the part of native peoples was encountered ...."[35] They emphasize that "bands and tribal councils have made it clear through plans and actions that logging, or more broadly modern forestry, has an important place in community economic development."[36]

General preferences and preliminary observations from British Columbia tell us little, of course, about what to expect in the Temagami area. Chief Potts has vigorously opposed clearcutting and permanent timber access roads. He has also clearly indicated a willingness to permit extractive resource activity to continue in parts of the Temagami homeland, emphasizing the potential well-being of the native and non-native residents of the region. I do not question the sincerity of these preferences, or in any way suggest they are questionable choices, in observing that some exercise of judgment will still be needed to determine whether a particular tract of the forest will be reserved or used for timber purposes, and if used for timber, under what conditions and procedures.

Association, 2 February 1991) [unpublished].

35   Cassidy & Dale, *supra*, note 18, at 91.

36   *Id.*, at 99.

Making specific choices about such matters for the four townships it now administers is the challenge facing the WSA, a body purposefully composed of individuals representing different interests who are charged with making decisions by consensus.[37] In light of the fact that none of the participants in Temagami's new stewardship council can be considered as the embodiment of some universal norm for the use of forest resources, it is of particular interest that the stewardship agreement itself incorporates a management standard.

The Management Standard

The agreement establishing the WSA sets out fundamental principles to which the authority is expected to adhere in fulfilling its mandate:

(a)   the primary goal of land stewardship is Sustained Life wherein the natural integrity of the land and of all life forms therein and thereon are maintained;

(b)   use of and activities on the land will follow the principle of Sustainable Development ....[38]

The agreement adopts the Brundtland explanation of sustainable development,[39] while "sustained life" is defined in the agreement as follows:

The enduring cycle whereby currently living organisms live, then must die, fall to the earth, become decomposed, be combined with elements from earth, air, and water to give continuing life to the land, including all biological life forms within it. Sustained life emphasizes the self-renewal of the land through the life, death and recycling of current life to provide nutrients in combination with earth, air, and water that will support continuous life.[40]

These principles circumscribe the range of permissable land-use decisions and provide guidance on substantive standards applicable to management of the stewardship area.

By implication, adherence to the principles may define the concept of stewardship, for the purposes of the agreement. Some reinforcement of that view may be found in Benson's discussion of forest stewardship. "The

---

37   "Consensus" is defined in the Addendum, *supra*, note 11, as "agreement by no less than two-thirds of the membership of the Authority, excluding the chairperson."

38   *Supra*, note 11.

39   The World Commission on Environment and Development, *Our Common Future* (Oxford: Oxford University Press, 1987) (Chair: G.H. Brundtland).

40   The concept of "sustained life" also appears in Benson *et al.*, *supra*, note 9, at 6, where it is similarly defined with the additional observation that "sustained life" means:

protecting and maintaining the quality of the earth, air, and water which give life to the forest, which in turn protects and replenishes the earth, air and water, and creates an independent home for all biological life forms within it. Designated trees and/or forest areas must be allowed to die and fall to the earth, thus giving life to earth, which can then support the growth of a new forest for future generations, forever.

responsibilities of the managers and users of the forest", Benson explains, "are to recognize and respect the capacities and needs of the forested area." "Forest stewardship", he continues, "goes beyond simple management, it is a commitment to care for the resources. It includes responsibilities to meet not a monetary end, but an end determined by the capacities and needs of the resource to be managed. Forest stewardship means being entrusted with administration of the forest in ways that will provide sustained development and ensure sustained life."[41]

The principles and management objective agreed to by the TAA and the Ontario government, however imprecise, represent a performance standard that differs quite substantially from resource-use objectives current in the surrounding area, and constitute a significant limitation on the otherwise largely unfettered scope of local compromise.[42]

The Mandate and the Nature of the Decisions

Within the four townships that constitute its geographic jurisdiction the WSA has several responsibilities. Specifically, the WSA "shall monitor, undertake studies of, and plan for, all uses of and activities on the land within its area of jurisdiction"; findings are to be reported from time to time to the TAA and to the Province of Ontario. The mandate further provides that the TAA and Ontario intend "to assign responsibility to the Wendaban Stewardship Authority to plan, decide, implement, enforce, regulate, and monitor all uses of and activities on the land within its area of jurisdiction."[43] This is a notable expansion of the authority over timber licenses originally conferred by the MOU.

Resource-use decisions are often understood as the outcome of a series of phases or procedures, including policy formulation, planning, and — where applicable — environmental assessment applied to projects put forward for consideration and approval. By way of illustration, Pinkerton identifies the general components of fisheries management: data gathering and analysis, operational decisions such as licensing and controls on access and technology, allocation decisions amongst primary users, habitat protection or regulation of impacts by other users, enforcement, enhancement and long-term planning of

---

41 *Id.*, at 5.

42 Arguably, the principle of sustained life represents the kind of "fundamental reconsideration between ourselves and the world" that "deep ecology" has called for. See Cynthia Giagnocavo & Howard Goldstein, "Law Reform or World Reform: The Problem of Environmental Rights" (1990) 35 McGill Law J. 345.

43 Wendaban Stewardship Authority, "Terms of Reference", *supra*, note 11, paras.1.1 and 1.2.

priorities, and broad policy decision making.[44]

The WSA's responsibilities, from planning to monitoring and enforcement, appear to constitute a comprehensive management process. In so far as all interests accept that range of authority, and so long as competing claims to governmental exclusivity (public or aboriginal) are not finally resolved, then the stewardship authority can operate as a special case based on local circumstances and will not necessarily serve as an example for broader application.[45] But the nature of the authority's decisions is a question of some interest and importance, for it raises fundamental issues from the perspective of institutional design. Thus, it is worth reflecting on the relationship between the scope of co-management as illustrated in the WSA arrangements and various phases of resource-use decision making.

The WSA's mandate clearly confers decision-making responsibility, making the new institution something quite different from an advisory body. One might still ask whether the WSA's decisions will serve primarily to implement or "operationalize" policies whose basic content has been determined in other forums, or whether it is in fact responsible for determining policy. To put the problem in the traditional — and not entirely satisfactory — framework of classification of functions, should the Authority be regarded as engaged in legislative, adjudicative, or administrative action? There are significant difficulties in characterization, particularly in light of both the range of issues that might come before the Authority and the conflicting views of native and non-native people regarding the proper approach to resource use. The characterization process is further complicated by such features of the agreement as decision making by consensus, the prospect of an appeal procedure, and the short terms of office for the initial appointees.[46]

Setting aside the problem of classifying the nature of the WSA as a decision maker, we are left at least with the idea that it is responsible in some sense for management in accordance with the principles of sustainable development and sustained life, again acknowledging their imprecision. To whom and on what basis might the WSA be accountable for the satisfactory performance of its responsibilities?

---

44   Pinkerton, *supra*, note 1, at 6.

45   As the provincial government pursues discussions of self-government with other native communities in Ontario, however, it will certainly be thought by some that the Temagami model may be a suitable prototype for further refinement.

46   All initial appointments to the WSA are for a one-year term.

Accountability

The "broad social consensus" on forest management hoped for by the Minister of Natural Resources is unlikely to emerge in the short term. Nor will the divergent perspectives pre-dating the creation of a decision maker such as the WSA be eliminated simply by the implementation of institutions of co-management. This is true even though decision makers may agree amongst themselves through compromise or consensus, on a local operational understanding of their governing principles.

Compromise outcomes in the context of resource management conflicts have had their defenders: "Who is to say that the benefits from the compromise do not exceed the costs stemming from the inefficiencies involved?"[47] On the other hand, numerous examples of attempts to facilitate agreement by narrowing the initial agenda demonstrate that excluding the big issues does not make them disappear. One commentator has recently suggested that this strategy for reaching agreement "virtually guaranteed that the unresolved larger questions would jeopardize the political integrity of the decision."[48]

Some external observers — excluded from the WSA by the localist preferences of the designers — may express concern that the internal accommodations made by those involved in co-management are something other than "more appropriate", "more efficient", or "more equitable". Questions of accountability to this constituency arise, for insofar as co-management is to be viewed as an exercise of public decision making or governmental functions, there will be considerable apprehension about a process that essentially operates as a device to reduce participation or obstruct scrutiny of the manner and substance of decision making.

Individual decisions by the WSA may not always be readily susceptible to precise or self-sufficient explanations.[49] This (as well as continuing jurisdictional concerns) may complicate the development of an appeal process as contemplated, but not described, in the agreement. However, the more

---

47 Fox, *supra*, note 21, at 748.

48 Stark Ackerman, "Observations on the Transformation of the Forest Service: The Effects of the National Environmental Policy Act on U.S. Forest Service Decision Making" (1990) 20 Environmental Law 703 at 715.

49 See Roderick A. Macdonald & David Lametti, "Reasons for Decision in Administrative Law" 3 Canadian J. of Administrative Law and Practice 123. Catherine Shapcott argues that the Haida bring to resource decision making "the wisdom of life experience accumulated over centuries." See Catherine Shapcott, "Environmental Impact Assessment and Resource Management, a Haida Case Study: Implications for Native People of the North" (1989) 9 Canadian J. of Native Studies 55 at 75.

general challenge for the WSA will be to render itself adequately accountable for the substantive performance of its stewardship where the rationale for particular decisions cannot readily be explained to non-participants. Numerous mechanisms, from reports and policy statements through to some form of external scrutiny or review of the stewardship decisions, can be imagined. Or, even in advance of decisions, we might expect the institutions of co-management to engage in consultation with outside interests who might be affected. The same arguments that call for the participation of local users in co-management might also apply to the proceedings of the co-management council. For example, if the decision maker requires knowledge, where is it to be obtained? How are others to be assured that the necessary information was available, especially in circumstances where some element of that information concerns the preferences of those who may not be at the table?

A shared vision and a new appreciation of the implications of human demands on the provincial resource base and the environment are likely to emerge only from an open and acceptable process. Thus, if it is to succeed as a transitional institution — and perhaps even as a prototype — the WSA will have to deal responsibly with the wider public audience of those concerned about Ontario's resources in general and the Temagami forest in particular. Adding this challenge to the task of local and internal consensus building certainly will not make the WSA's difficult assignment any easier, but it will make that assignment ultimately more worthwhile.

COMMENTARY AND CONCLUSIONS

There are several indications that the participation of native people in decisions concerning resource use in Ontario can only increase. First, a series of Supreme Court of Canada decisions has confirmed the obligation of governments to take native interests into account and has recognized the legitimacy and constitutional status of aboriginal rights concerning resource use.[50] Moreover, following the commitment of Ontario Premier Rae to self-government negotiations in the fall of 1990, the Minister of Natural Resources indicated that co-management agreements on resources will be pursued as part of the self-government negotiation process.[51] Indeed, the authors of a

---

50   *Guerin* v. *R.*, [1984] 2 S.C.R. 335; *R.* v. *Sioui* (1990), 70 D.L.R. (4th) 427; and *R.* v. *Sparrow*, [1990] 1 S.C.R. 1075. For recent commentary on the implications of *Sparrow*, see W.I.C. Binney, "The *Sparrow* Doctrine: Beginning of the End or End of the Beginning?" (1990) 15:2 Queen's Law J. 217; Patrick Macklem, "First Nations Self-Government and the Borders of the Canadian Legal Imagination" (1991) 36:2 McGill Law J. 382 at 445.

51   Ontario Native Affairs Secretariat, "Transcript of Remarks by Premier Bob Rae to the Assembly of First Nations Banquet" (2 October 1990); Ontario Ministry of Natural Resources Release, "Ontario Ready to Begin Discussions on Land Claim with Algonquins of Golden Lake" (28 March 1991).

thoughtful recent synthesis of co-management studies in the fisheries field argue that "co-management is not only a logical development of trends set into motion in North American ... management of the 1970s, but also a necessary development in confronting management problems that loom before us in the 1990s and beyond."[52]

If something like co-management is indeed both logical and necessary — a proposition there is no immediate need to question — we may well inquire, Who are the cheerleaders, and where is the bandwagon? These questions about co-management are of interest in comparison with the status of another and more fashionable contemporary slogan, sustainable development.

The advocates of sustainable development are ubiquitous, although the content of their message continues to elude precise definition. Much of the Canadian literature on sustainable development, however, urges vigorous government action rather than collaborative decision-making procedures. One recent example aggressively advocates federal initiatives: "The Committee is of the view that federal government has an obligation to assume a stronger leadership role in environmental protection, scientific research and public education in support of the concept of sustainable development."[53] The rationale for this preference was located in the background circumstances of the present age: "Underlying the concepts of environment and sustainable development is the even broader realization of global interdependence, which suggests a need for strong national leadership, direction and control."[54]

Against this backdrop it is worth asking about the relationship of co-management to the sustainable development movement, particularly in light of significant similarities between the two concepts.

Sustainable development is a result-oriented or "outcome" concept offered as a response to a series of resource constraints, and its procedural implications have generally been secondary. In contrast, co-management appears generically to be a process-type solution to conflicts over resource allocation, and its substantive implications have been assumed or generalized into projections of "more appropriate, more efficient and more equitable" management. Few would in principle disagree with this selection of objectives, but they could equally serve to describe the nature of sustainable development. The real difficulties for both co-management and sustainable

---

52   Rettig, Berkes & Pinkerton, *supra*, note 15, at 278.

53   Canadian Bar Association, *Sustainable Development in Canada: Options for Law Reform* (Committee Report) (Ottawa, 1990) at 5.

54   *Id.*, at 4V. The recommendations are marked by a notable insistence on stricter measures, including enforcement and compliance strategies.

development lie in the realization that equity may not be efficient and efficiency may not be appropriate. Once it is accepted that trade-offs have to be made — often in the context of a declining and deteriorating resource base — the questions then become, How and by whom?[55] Co-management and sustainable development face these challenges together.

There has been another and more extended debate about the most effective social and institutional arrangements to provide for the long-term conservation of resources, whether or not the concept of stewardship is directly involved. Much of the discussion and related research has been responsive to Hardin's "tragedy of the commons",[56] with advocates of private ownership, communal governance, or state regulation each endeavouring to identify the circumstances in which these particular forms of management are most likely to promote conservation of the resource base. The authors of a recent assessment of this literature conclude that none of these approaches demonstrates unqualified superiority. "Success in the regulation of uses and users is not universally associated with any particular type of property-rights regime. Communal property, private property, and government property have all been associated with success and failure."[57]

The institutional debate persists in the Temagami forest, with Benson posing the question, "[C]an we really expect sustained management unless the management of N'Daki Menan has its policies determined by those most closely associated and dependent upon it?"[58] Yet he acknowledges that the past failures of provincial resource managers are at least in part attributable to bureaucratic constraints rather than purposeful mismanagement.[59] However, his assessment is sharply critical of lumber companies operating in the area, and quite optimistic about the potential influence of the broader public on certain issues: "If the public were truly informed of what was happening to the forests of N'Daki Menan, would they want the old growth eliminated?"[60]

Of some significance is Benson's implicit acceptance of the idea that the resolve of local interests to maintain the quality of an environment such as

---

55   These dilemmas are by no means new. For a historical examination of the continuing tension between competing public values over access to common resources, see Christopher Armstrong & H.V. Nelles, *Monopoly's Moment: The Organization and Regulation of Canadian Utilities, 1830-1930* (Philadelphia: Temple University Press, 1986).

56   Garrett Hardin, "The Tragedy of the Commons" (1968) 162 Science 1243.

57   Feeny *et al.*, *supra*, note 2, at 12.

58   Benson *et al.*, *supra*, note 9, at 40.

59   *Id.*, at 41.

60   *Id.*, at 54.

that of the Temagami forest may usefully be reinforced by the scrutiny of a wider community. Other researchers have explained the attractions of hybrid systems combining increased community influence with continuing involvement by regulatory authorities. The attractions of involving local users are consistent with what has been said above, but Feeny *et al.* continue:

> Communities of resource users are ... no longer relatively isolated and resources often have multiple uses. Therefore, complete devolution may not be appropriate; it makes sense for the state to continue to play a role in resources conservation and allocation among communities of users. Shared governance or state regulation jointly with user self-management can capitalize on the local knowledge and long-term self-interest of users, while providing for coordination with relevant uses and users over a wide geographic scope at potentially lower transaction (rule-enforcement) cost.[61]

Co-management, like its alternatives, is probably not an ideal form of resource management, but in certain circumstances it offers strong attractions. In the new Wendaban Stewardship Authority, the co-management idea has provided the first real opportunity in a long time to develop a reasonable working relationship among the native community, the provincial government, and other users of the resources and environment of the area. Despite the limitations and uncertainties in the current design, we should hope that the new agency can learn to operate effectively to provide a foundation for stable co-existence over the long term.

---

61   Feeny *et al.*, *supra*, note 2, at 14.

OVERCOMING BARRIERS TO THE EXERCISE OF CO-MANAGEMENT RIGHTS

Evelyn W. Pinkerton

North American Indian rights to co-manage fisheries and to protect fisheries habitat have seldom, if ever, received greater recognition and protection than under the landmark case of *U.S.* v. *Washington* in its 1974 Phase I[1] and its 1980 Phase II[2] decisions. The "Boldt decision", as it is popularly called, interpreted the language of 1850s treaties that the U.S. government had made with western Washington tribes as providing a guarantee that the tribes could manage their own fisheries, subject to certain conservation restrictions and to joint planning with state managers.[3] However, there can be an enormous distance between legal decisions and their application to the practice of resource management, especially when legal rights run counter to prevailing power relationships. This paper contrasts Phase I and Phase II of *U.S.* v. *Washington*, first, with regard to how easily and quickly rights were translated into co-management agreements, and second, with regard to how quickly and completely these agreements have been implemented.

These two phases are used in part to illustrate best-case and worst-case scenarios in demonstrating how barriers to co-management are successfully

---

*   The initial part of this research was supported by a grant from the Social Sciences and Humanities Research Council of Canada and conducted in collaboration with the Nuu-chah-nulth Tribal Council, August-December 1988, as part of a larger study of institutions for cooperative fisheries management. I extend thanks to Nelson Keitlah, Al McCarthy, Bill Green, the Barkley Sound Tribal Fisheries Committee, and the Point No Point Treaty Council. Follow-up research was conducted during 1989-91. Thanks go also to Westwater Research Centre, University of British Columbia, for logistical support, and to Neal Gilbertsen, Marcy Golde, Jim Lichatowich, Tim Hennessy, Bjorn Sagahl, Terry Williams, Jim Hatten, Katherine Baril, John Miles, Fay Cohen, Ray Travers, Judy Turpin, Mike Reed, Cindy Halbert, and Michael Fraidenburg for helpful comments or discussion of concepts in earlier versions of this paper. The greatest thanks is owed to the dozens of interviewees whose dedication to sound public policy led them to spend hours answering questions and discussing issues with me over the last three years.

1   *U.S.* v. *Washington*, 384 F.Supp. 312 (Phase I) (1974).

2   *U.S.* v. *Washington*, 506 F.Supp. 187 (Phase II) (1980).

3   See Fay G. Cohen, *Treaties On Trial: The Continuing Controversy over Northwest Indian Fishing Rights* (A Report prepared for the American Friends Service Committee) (Seattle: University of Washington Press, 1986); Fay Cohen, "Treaty Indian Tribes and Washington State: The Evolution of Tribal Involvement in Fisheries Management in the U.S. Pacific Northwest" *in* E. Pinkerton, ed., *Co-operative Management and Community Development* (Vancouver: University of British Columbia Press, 1989) 37.

overcome. In addition, the comparison of these phases generates new middle-range theoretical propositions about the conditions under which the development and implementation of co-management of renewable natural resources is possible. These extend propositions already advanced about conditions for the development of successful fisheries co-management[4] and about a variety of successful "common pool" or "common property" resource management regimes that avoid the "tragedy of the commons".[5] Work in this subfield of cultural ecology and institutional analysis has been using empirical case studies to predict inductively the conditions most favourable to the development of self-management and co-management, and to generalize about how co-management arrangements alter relationships between manager and managed so that sustainable management of resources can occur and the "tragedy" can be avoided. This discussion focuses specifically on favourable conditions in the latter stages of the development of co-management: the stages between the legal recognition of rights and the achievement of agreements, and the stage between agreements and full implementation. Work in this area is still rare.

DEFINING CO-MANAGEMENT: A RANGE OF FUNCTIONS, PARTIES AND SCOPE

Co-management can be generally defined as power-sharing in the exercise of resource management between a government agency and a community or organization of stakeholders — in this case Indian tribes with treaty rights.[6]

---

4   See E. Pinkerton, "Co-operative Management of Local Fisheries: A Route to Development" *in* John Bennett & John Bowen, eds., *Production and Autonomy: Anthropological Studies and Critiques of Development* (Landham, MD: University Press of America, 1988) 257; E. Pinkerton, "Attaining Better Fisheries Management Through Co-Management — Prospects, Problems and Propositions" *in* E. Pinkerton, ed., *Co-operative Management of Local Fisheries: New Directions For Improved Management and Community Development* (Vancouver: University of British Columbia Press, 1989) 3.

5   See Fikret Berkes, ed., *Common Property Resources, Ecology and Community Based Sustainable Development* (London: Belhaven, 1989); Bonnie McCay & James Acheson, eds., *The Question of the Commons: The Culture and Ecology of Communal Resources* (Tucson: University of Arizona Press, 1987); D. Feeny, Fikret Berkes, Bonnie McCay & James Acheson, "The Tragedy of the Commons: Twenty-two Years Later" (1990) 18:1 Human Ecology 1; and Elinor Ostrom, *Governing the Commons: The Evolution of Institutions for Collective Action* (New York: Cambridge University Press, 1990).

6   Some twenty tribes in western Washington had signed treaties with the U.S. government in the 1850s. The treaties stated that the tribes had exclusive rights to on-reservation fisheries and that off-reservation "the right of taking fish at usual and accustomed grounds and stations is further secured to said Indians in common with all citizens of the United States." The treaties had the force of law because of the Commerce Clause and the Supremacy Clause of the U.S. Constitution: see Cohen, "Treaty Indian Tribes and Washington State", *supra*, note 3, 37 at 38.

Co-management arrangements are not confined to aboriginal groups with special management rights,[7] although they may occur more frequently among such groups, especially where management rights have been clearly delineated in court decisions.

Co-management agreements may be more or less comprehensive, covering one or all aspects of management activity. The co-management agreement resulting from the Phase I decision covered shared data collection and analysis, allocation, and shared planning of the salmon harvest between treaty tribes and the Washington Department of Fisheries. In contrast, the co-management agreement resulting from the Phase II decision is more complex and multi-party. It covers the management function of habitat protection for fish and wildlife, and includes — in addition to the tribes and environmental umbrella groups — the Washington Departments of Fisheries, Wildlife, Ecology, and Natural Resources, and the logging industry's Washington Forest Protection Association. This is because the Phase II decision recognized a tribal right to protect fish habitat; the judge reasoned that the right to an allocation of fish would be meaningless if habitat, and hence fish, could be destroyed. Environmentalists had no such legal right to protect wildlife habitat, but made common cause with the tribes in order to associate wildlife and fisheries issues.

In such a multi-party agreement, the performing of the management function (habitat protection) may not be the goal of all participants. The criterion for inclusion in the agreement is not necessarily agreement on the goals, but rather the power to further *or to frustrate* the management function. Industrial parties whose activities can potentially destroy habitat seek different trade-offs in co-management agreements than do government agencies charged with habitat protection. They thus have a fundamentally different definition of the purpose of the agreement, and continue to seek to impose this definition. The struggle to reach and implement agreements in such situations inevitably involves different types of barriers and different dynamics in overcoming them. The analysis of types and degrees of resistance to implementing the Phase II decision begins with an outline of the same issues in Phase I.

---

7   See Donald F. Amend, "Alaska's Regional Aquaculture Associations Co-Management of Salmon in Southern Southeast Alaska" *in* Pinkerton, *Co-operative Management of Local Fisheries, supra,* note 4, at 125; Svein Jentoft & Trond Kristoffersen, "Fishermen's Co-management: The Case of the Lofoten Fishery" (1989) 48:4 Human Organization 355; and Svein Jentoft, "Fishermen's Comanagement: Delegating Government Responsibility to Fishermen's Organizations" (1989) 13:2 Marine Policy 137.

FIVE STAGES OF TRANSLATING RIGHTS
INTO CO-MANAGEMENT PRACTICE

Seeing how long it takes for co-management to progress through five stages can help us better understand the different points of resistance in the two situations. The five stages are (1) adopting a negotiating posture, (2) conducting negotiations, (3) producing an agreement, (4) fully implementing the agreement, and (5) institutionalizing procedures.

In Phase I, resistance was confined mostly to stage one, with a residual spill-over into stage two. It took seven years of court battles and civil disobedience after the 1974 decision before the state government decided to adopt a negotiating posture with the tribes. During most of these seven years the state government had championed court appeals and resistance to the 1974 decision as it and related cases made their way to the U.S. Supreme Court and were upheld in 1979.[8] Even after that, citizens' initiatives still strove to abrogate treaty rights, and state policy did not change. As the judicial system approached overload, new court officials were appointed to help, but the system was still cumbersome, slow, and in many cases non-binding. Often the state would simply appeal decisions and take them back to court.[9] At various points federal enforcement officers were sent in to carry out court orders, and the federal court had to take over fisheries management for several years. Despite this, the state was able to exercise mechanisms to drag out every disputed management decision. State managers today claim that this situation could have lasted almost indefinitely.[10]

The federal political climate in this decade, however, included not only the U.S. Supreme Court, but also a nation-wide and local civil rights movement in support of southern blacks and Indian tribes. This contributed to the eventual defeat of local resistance both in the south and in Washington state. In 1981 a new Washington state governor, Spellman, decided that the costly court battles were unproductive and a waste of money: the tribes were winning almost all of the cases, even if they were not getting the management action they wanted. He appointed a new head of the Washington Department of Fisheries, who agreed to negotiate with the tribes.

It still took three more years and the replacement of six of the eight senior people in the agency to reverse the war mentality that had permeated

---

8   See Cohen, *Treaties on Trial, supra*, note 3, at c.6 and 7.

9   Rolly Schmitten, "Co-operative Management" (Speech to Pacific Northwest/British Columbia Tribal Cooperative Fisheries Management Conference, Four Seasons Hotel, Seattle, WA, 27 May 1987) [unpublished].

10 See Cohen, *Treaties on Trial, supra*, note 3, for a detailed analysis and the role of federal inertia in this process.

not only the fisheries management agency and the fishing industry, but even the legislature. In summary, it took seven years to reach a negotiating posture (stage one), and then three more years to start the actual negotiation of a co-management agreement (stage two). Phase I is a "best-case scenario" only after the first stage, unless one considers the 1979 final Supreme Court decision the beginning of stage one.

After stage two, everything progressed smoothly and rapidly to stage five. The Puget Sound Salmon Management Plan Agreement was signed and adopted by the court in 1985 (stage three); court cases over implementation were rare after this. The Agreement laid out a schedule of all the procedures the tribes and state would go through in jointly planning the harvest. It included such activities as sharing of data; agreement on run-size estimates; agreement on levels of harvest and alternatives, should the run be larger or smaller; hatchery production goals; and eggs sources. It also included conflict-resolution mechanisms, although there has been little need for these. Instead, the process of harvest management has been immediately and smoothly implemented (stage four), and the process of joint planning and problem solving has been institutionalized in bi-annual retreats between tribes and the state (stage five). Although management problems and disagreements remain, the tribes and state jointly now give workshops to other agencies looking at co-management, to illustrate how the process works. Their travelling road show, a day-long workshop of nine presentations containing spirited and good-willed debate has all the hallmarks of an institutionalized co-management process. The Phase I co-management agreement and implementation process is thus a best-case scenario in the sense that it progressed smoothly and completely through the five stages once initial resistance was overcome.

PHASE II: DIFFERENT PARTIES, FUNCTIONS AND ISSUES

Negotiating and implementing Phase I rights regarding shared harvest management involved changing the expectations of relatively powerless stakeholders, commercial and recreational fishermen, and the decision-making procedures of a relatively powerless government agency, the Washington Department of Fisheries. In contrast, the Phase II decision regarding tribal rights to protect fish habitat affected actors and agencies with far more political and financial power. The multinational timber companies "controlled" the state legislature,[11] and the Department of Natural Resources was an

---

11   See James Waldo, "Redefining Winning: The TFW Process" (1988) 4:3 Forest Planning Canada 14. In recent years such control was possible only through alliances with business and agriculture.

agency "captured"[12] in its regulatory function by its other mandate to log the state timberlands it held in trust to raise funds for public school construction and its own budget. As such, its relations with major logging companies had tended to be as much collegial as regulatory. In response to court challenges by environmental groups, a new agency head in 1980 began a gradual reorientation of the DNR towards its mandate to regulate forest practices (mostly logging) for the protection of fish and wildlife. The progress in this direction was extremely slow, however: DNR did not have a separate Forest Practices Division until 1990.

Not surprisingly, the points of resistance to progression through the five stages described above were therefore quite different. Deciding to negotiate happened quickly; actually negotiating happened under duress and took longer; and implementation of the agreement has been exceedingly difficult and is still only partial.

ADOPTING A NEGOTIATION
POSTURE ON PHASE II

Following the Phase II 1980 decision, it took only one year for the major industrial water resource users (logging companies, hydroelectric companies, factories discharging waste, etc.) to analyze the situation and adopt a negotiating and mitigating stance.[13] In 1982, three years before the salmon co-management agreement was signed by the tribes and state, key industrial leaders had formed the Northwest Water Resources Committee to work with tribes in rehabilitating damaged salmon habitat and carrying out joint projects for rehabilitation and enhancement. By 1984 they had institutionalized this relationship as the Northwest Renewable Resources Center, which organized conferences and workshops to discuss resource conflicts and press for their resolution through mediation — another service provided by the Center.

Of course, one reason that business responded more quickly than government to court rulings is that it had learned from previous history that court appeals had a very low success rate. In addition, however, businesspeople tend to be pragmatists: they have little tolerance for the threat

---

12   See Theodore Lowi, *The End of Liberalism: Ideology, Policy and the Crisis of Public Authority* (New York: Norton, 1969, rev. ed. 1979) for the most influential analysis of agency capture by economic producers. In this case, the capture might be considered ideological, since the DNR itself, as well as the timber companies, considered the legal requirement to protect fish and wildlife under the 1974 *Forest Practices Act* as almost trivial compared to the importance of timber production.

13   See James Waldo, *U.S. v. Washington, Phase II: Analysis and Recommendations* (MSS, 1981) (prepared for the Northwest Water Resources Committee) for the analysis that was the basis of the decision to follow this path.

of disruptions or delays to normal operations, and will consider all options to avoid them. While the income of government officials usually does not depend on the outcome of court rulings or policy decisions, businesspeople's standard of living, or their stockholders' profits, often depend completely on such matters. Hence they are quicker to seek out-of-court solutions, but also likely to continually seek to postpone costly effects and to search for ways to recapture the institutions they are losing through court battles.

DECIDING TO NEGOTIATE AN AGREEMENT ON PHASE II

Despite industry's ease of adopting a negotiating posture (stage one), beginning to actually negotiate an agreement (stage two) took five more years. It may be argued that the negotiating stance of industry in 1981 did not necessarily indicate a willingness to reach an agreement involving significant power sharing, but rather involved appeasement: an attempt to stay out of court and to forestall or prevent the formation of a coalition strong enough to force a real power-sharing agreement. The analysis that persuaded industry to be conciliatory towards the tribes rather than to depend on the courts predicted that a coalition of tribes, environmentalists, and non-Indian commercial fishermen could be a political threat to industry and that industry/tribal negotiations could reduce this threat.[14]

Eventually industry was brought to the negotiating table and recalled to the table several years later because the tribes and their allies used a successful combination of five strategies, involving five separate sources of power: (1) coalitions and issue networks, (2) new legislation and the threat of legislative amendments, (3) the threat of greater regulation and public review through the citizens' Forest Practices Board, (4) court actions to reform legislation and to amend regulation, and (5) a citizens' initiative to stop conversion of forests to real estate. The tactical use of these five strategies eventually enabled the tribes and their allies to overcome the resistance of industry and the Department of Natural Resources to negotiating a co-management agreement, and later to implementing the agreement. The first four strategies are discussed below, first in summary overview and then in historical narrative, while the fifth is discussed later.

Strategy 1: Coalitions and Issue Networks

The coalition that eventually formed and was instrumental in forcing real negotiations included not only tribes and environmental groups, but also the three relevant state agencies: Fisheries, Wildlife, and Ecology. The addition of

14   *Id.*

the latter three agencies was possible only because of the Phase I co-management agreement, which allowed the tribes and agencies to overcome their differences and to express their common interest in protecting fish habitat.[15]

Tribes, environmentalists, and state agencies brought complementary resources to the coalition. Environmental groups had experience in lobbying the legislature and the Forest Practices Board and using the courts on these issues, but had narrowly defined rights and little access to field data. The tribes had been largely isolated from mainstream political processes, but now had field biologists and habitat analysts on staff, and the clearest legal rights to protect habitat. The agencies had paid staff, access to technical information, and an interest in developing more rationally defined (rather than politically influenced) decision-making procedures. As they were brought into working committees with tribes and environmentalists (see below), they were able to further the discussion of alternative models and standards for measuring habitat protection. The combination of resources available to this coalition, and its ability to form an active issue network[16] to generate and discuss new models and standards, was key to its success. As is discussed below, issue networks have been identified as a potent force for change, because they unify diverse policy actors across governmental and non-governmental sectors in sharing information and exploring alternative possibilities; they thus support and legitimize the attempt to institute practices believed to be superior to the *status quo.*

Strategy 2: Legislation and Legislative Amendments

Some parties in the coalition were also active in seeking reform of forest practices (including both logging and silviculture), through new legislation and the continued threat of legislative amendments. Despite the strength of the timber lobby in the legislature, the public interest in legislating environmental protection for water, wildlife, and fish had become well organized and powerful by the late 1960s. Public interest groups were successful in passing the *State Environmental Policy Act* (SEPA) in 1971,[17] which set up the Department of Ecology and an environmental impact review process for

---

15   Curt Smitch, former assistant director of the Department of Fisheries, was appointed head of the new Department of Wildlife (formerly Department of Game) with a mandate to "bring in" co-management. Smith has survived this controversial posting, and became a highly respected member of the Phase II negotiating team.

16   Hugh Heclo, "Issue Networks and the Executive Establishment" *in* Anthony King, ed., *The New American Political System* (Washington, D.C.: American Enterprise Institute for Public Policy Research, 1978) 87.

17   *State Environmental Policy Act*, 1971, chapter 43.21C RCW.

agencies that regulate industrial activities. SEPA required that a range of impacts be analyzed, including direct, indirect, and cumulative ones. Measuring cumulative impacts of forest practices was to become a key issue in fish and wildlife habitat protection.

Partially to avoid SEPA review of forest practices, as well as review under the federal *Clean Water Act*,[18] the logging industry allowed passage of the *Forest Practices Act* in 1974.[19] This Act was intended to provide the scope of regulation that could adequately protect forest-related resources: fish, wildlife, and water. It was amended in 1975 to restrict potential SEPA review to a narrow list of activities "which have a potential for substantial impact on the environment."[20] A large part of the struggle to protect fish and wildlife habitat has centred on the tribes' and their allies' effort to enlarge the definition of logging activities that have to be reviewed by a SEPA process as potentially harmful.

Strategy 3: Threat of Greater Regulation and Public Review

The definition of forest practices considered potentially harmful comes from the Forest Practices Board, a citizens' board appointed by the governor, which is empowered by the *Forest Practices Act* to commission studies, hold public hearings, and make protective regulation. Regulations are adopted under a public review process as part of the Washington Administrative Code, and carry the force of law.

Even though the industry held several seats on this body, and at first dominated it, it eventually provided a forum for citizens' action. As the state urbanized in the 1980s, the Board had to give more consideration to the concerns of citizens from beyond the resource sector. It was indeed actions around the Forest Practices Board that finally brought the industry seriously to the negotiating table in 1986 and began to force serious discussion of cumulative effects standards in 1991.

Strategy 4: Court Action to Reform Legislation and Amend Regulation

The impetus for the Forest Practices Board to adopt stricter forest practice regulations came in several stages, however. The first stage resulted from the 1977 *Noel* v. *Cole* case[21] on Whidbey Island, in which an environmental

---

18   *Clean Water Act*, 33 U.S.C.A., s.1251 (West 1986).

19   *Forest Practices Act*, 1974, chapter 76.09 RCW.

20   Current RCW 76.09.050 was added as an amendment to the Act.

21   *Noel* v. *Cole*, No.98 Wn2d 375, 655 P.2d 245 (1980) in Snohomish County Superior Court.

group won a ruling that the definition of what activities were potentially harmful to the environment was too narrow and restrictive to fulfill the purposes of the *Forest Practices Act* (to protect other public resources). The Forest Practices Board was required by the court to review the regulations. The Board then identified cumulative effects as one of fourteen issues that should be considered for inclusion in the definition of environmental sensitivity and started a three-year review of its regulations on this matter. Court actions and threatened court action in 1989 would finally force the Forest Practices Board to make regulations requiring further consideration of cumulative effects.

Historical Narrative: Strategic Use of the Four Sources of Power in Stage Two

After the Phase II decision in 1980, tribes and environmental groups began more actively to use the Forest Practices Board to affect regulation. For example, they stopped an industry initiative to freeze stream typing, because they knew inventories were inadequate and many streams were unclassified or improperly typed in terms of their importance as fish habitat.

The environmental groups and tribes also began using the public hearing process of the Forest Practices Board to identify key issues, and to organize and focus a strong public demand for regulations on cumulative effects and protection of the riparian zone (the wetted zone alongside stream banks). The Forest Practices Board was forced to commission a study of options for dealing with cumulative effects and riparian zone protection. A tribal and an environmental representative were appointed to the committee overseeing the study, somewhat counterbalancing the industry's domination of the process. After the Timber/Fish/Wildlife Agreement (see next section), tribes and environmentalists both got seats on the Forest Practices Board, because they had been recognized as part of the policy community.

The environmentalist/tribal coalition also worked through the legislature in 1985 to change the composition of the Forest Practices Board by an amendment to the *Forest Practices Act*. The coalition attempted to replace the board positions for the Department of Trade and Economic Development and the Department of Agriculture with positions for the Department of Fisheries and the Department of Wildlife. Although unsuccessful, this effort demonstrated the degree of legislative support for the concept, and showed industry and political leaders they could not ignore strong public concern for protection of public resources.

Industry was finally brought to the negotiating table when the completed Forest Practices Board study recommended stricter regulations for cumulative effects and riparian zone protection, and a coalition of tribes, environmentalists, and Departments of Ecology (on the Board), Fisheries, and Wildlife supported strong regulation. Although industry managed to alter the proposed regulatory package, they were horrified by the proposals.

NEGOTIATING AN AGREEMENT ON PHASE II (STAGE THREE)

In the face of these unacceptable regulations, which it believed would be adopted by the Forest Practices Board in 1986, the timber industry agreed to enter into negotiations with the tribes, the environmental umbrella groups, and four state agencies (Fisheries, Wildlife, Ecology, and Natural Resources). In six months these parties had agreed on interim compromise regulations and on a process by which they would implement the regulations and resolve future disputes over issues that would have been "agreement breakers" during the first negotiations. Initial implementation of this Timber/Fish/Wildlife (TFW) co-management agreement began about a year later, after funding was acquired and staff hired. Funds were successfully solicited from the state legislature for the agencies ($4.5 million for 1987-88), from the federal government for the tribes ($2 million), and from private foundations for environmental groups on a three-year pilot basis ($750,000). The umbrella Washington Environmental Council also contributed significant volunteer staff time. The TFW Agreement was implemented most importantly and directly through a review by the representatives of all these parties of "sensitive" forest practices applications. In the spirit of negotiation and cooperation, parties met to review or even pay field visits to such sites and to decide whether more than the minimum protection was needed, and how to mitigate or avoid potential impacts.

At this stage, the tribes were willing to compromise because immediate regulatory action and inclusion in the policy process were more attractive to them than continued litigation. However, because of tribal concern to keep open the possibility of eventually relitigating the Phase II decision,[22] the co-management agreement was never officially signed. It still carried the force of official policy, however, and the court asked for regular progress reports during negotiations. The court could potentially view a failure of the agreement as cause to reopen litigation.

Environmentalists were willing to compromise because wildlife concerns were included in the agreement, and their own inclusion in the policy and implementation process was an unprecedented opportunity. They hoped that improvements in industry performance would justify the implied three-year moratorium on new regulation in the agreement. They also believed, at least

---

22   Which by this time had been vacated by the court. See Cohen, *Treaties on Trial, supra,* note 3.

at the outset, that the agreement would be a tool far superior to use of the courts and the press for bringing about reform of logging practices. On the theory that incentives to negotiate would evaporate if courts or the press were used, there was an implicit understanding that neither of these tools would be used in the first three years.

For their part, the timber companies (who were the industry leaders of the negotiations) did not necessarily think of the agreement as having a substantial impact on their activities. At worst, it cost them far less to live with the agreement (one million dollars in administration, seven to eight million dollars in uncut trees, five million dollars in improved logging roads and deferred logging in 1988) than the cost of litigation (fifty to sixty million dollars a year)[23] and the proposed stricter regulations. At best, it would buy them several years' freedom from court cases *and* increased regulation, enhance their stature as responsible corporate citizens, and transfer most of the cost of conflict resolution to taxpayers. Furthermore, the tribes and their allies had to accept the maintenance of a lucrative timber industry as one of the goals of the agreement, because they feared conversion of private forest land to real estate even more than they feared poor logging practices. The industry could thus continue to use the threat of becoming less profitable than real estate as an indirect threat to habitat. In other words, the benefits of the agreement were widely shared by all parties, but the costs of the agreement were disproportionately borne by tribes, environmentalists, and taxpayers.

In addition, the regulatory history of the forest industry in Washington gave the timber companies reason to believe that they would be able to continue as the major influence on implementation of policy and agreements. The Department of Natural Resources, the state agency that issues logging and other forest practice permits, was in the mid-1980s still an agency "captured"[24] by its own and its clients' timber interests and whose past operations and regulatory practices had been little affected by forest practice regulations to protect fish, wildlife, and water quality. In addition, the timber industry still held a commanding position in the legislature and the state power structure.[25]

---

23   Cindy Halbert & Kai Lee, "The Timber, Fish and Wildlife Agreement: Implementing Alternative Dispute Resolution in Washington State" (1990) 6 Northwest Environmental Journal 139.

24   See Lowi, *supra*, note 12; George J. Stigler, *The Citizen and the State: Essays on Regulation* (Chicago: University of Chicago Press, 1975).

25   See Michael F. Fraidenburg, "The New Politics of Natural Resources: Negotiating a Shift Toward Privatization of Natural Resource Policymaking in Washington State" (1989) 5 Northwest Environmental Journal 211; Waldo, *supra*, note 11.

The rest of this discussion deals with stage four, the first four years of attempts to implement the Phase II TFW Agreement, from mid-1987 to mid-1991. Implementation is still incomplete, and from this vantage point, three substages of implementation appear significant:

1. partially failed early attempts at consensus on site-specific action: mid-1987 to mid-1989;

2. partially failed enlargement of the issue to cumulative effects in watersheds and the inclusion of counties and new environmental groups in TFW through the Sustainable Forestry Roundtable: mid-1989 to 1990;

3. successful attempts to propose the idea of implementing threshold mechanisms on a watershed basis to measure cumulative effects and establish criteria for when logging restraints are necessary, through an evolved Forest Practices Board: 1991.

The progression of implementation through these three substages illustrates both the nature of resistance and how the five strategies were used effectively to begin putting the principles of the agreement into practice.

THE TIMBER/FISH/WILDLIFE AGREEMENT: STAGE A IMPLEMENTATION

The final negotiated draft of the TFW Agreement in January 1987 looked workable at first. The agreement covered a range of issues (e.g., old-growth preservation, road building and maintenance, two pilot watershed plans), but for the purposes of this discussion I focus on those most critical to long-range habitat protection. Industry accepted mandatory riparian zones of twenty-five feet alongside most streams, half of the zone required by the proposed Forest Practices Board regulations. On most other issues, especially regarding a larger riparian zone or upland wildlife habitat areas, site-specific review by field representatives of all the cooperators was to replace mandatory regulation. The industry knew that site-specific negotiations would be less constraining than across-the-board restrictions, which, it believed, were often overly rigid and unnecessary.

Field review was done by regional "interdisciplinary" teams: technical representatives of all the TFW cooperators (tribes, environmentalists, state agencies, logging companies) of proposed logging on sites classified as sensitive. The idea was that, by looking at site-specific problems, the cooperators would be able to reach consensus about compromises that were in the spirit of the agreement. Since decisions by the lead agency, the Department of Natural Resources (DNR), could be appealed to the Forest Practices Appeal Board by any of the cooperators, it was assumed that all cooperators would work hard to reach consensus and make the agreement work. In addition, the cooperators agreed to abide by the results of the scientific evaluation and research program (CMER), which would indicate what final standards of protection for public resources were necessary.

The initial hopefulness of the tribes and their allies was put to the test by problems that emerged even in the first year, but that were thoroughly confirmed by the third annual review of the process in October 1990. One major problem was the too-narrow definition of sensitive sites: only 0.05 percent of all applications qualified for SEPA review before 1986, and by 1989 this had risen to only 0.2 percent. Combined with "regionally sensitive" applications that DNR had made a commitment to identify, only 9 percent of all logging applications were sent to the cooperators for their review in 1989.[26] The other related major problem, which is really a more comprehensive restatement of the first problem, is that site-by-site review of logging permits does not permit cumulative effects to be judged. Even though the TFW process allowed an annual pre-harvest review and identification by DNR of "priority issues" of concern in each region, this was not comprehensive enough to identify threats to public resources that would appear in a watershed-wide consideration of cumulative impacts of logging. The size of a continuous clearcut and the rate of logging in one area over a five-to-twenty-five-year period would produce effects that might not be detectable from looking at any one permit in isolation. The cooperators' interdisciplinary field teams could exhaust themselves looking at individual permits and never have an opportunity to identify the more fundamental problems. Comprehensive, integrated, long-range planning was required to protect public resources, but industry had resisted more than a vague espousal of this principle in the original negotiations.

A third problem was that DNR, as the agency that decided whether or not to put conditions on the logging permit, would often override the consensus of all the cooperators but industry. There were at least three reasons why this happened:

1. DNR in many cases still saw the timber industry as its major concern and client and felt much less obligation to the other cooperators, who were not viewed as significant constituents.

2. Of the 11.5 million acres of non-federal forest land regulated by DNR, the agency is itself a landowner in trust for some 2.1 million acres of state land, which it logs to raise money, principally for public schools and counties. Twenty-five percent of some timber trust sales goes directly into DNR's budget. Although the TFW agreement reorganized the DNR to

---

26   Washington. Department of Natural Resources, *Forest Practices Program: 1989 Report* (Olympia, Wash.: Dept. of Natural Resources, 1990).

more clearly reflect the two separate functions — regulatory and proprietary — the same personnel and mentality tended to remain; new attitudes toward public resources and other constituents developed very slowly.

3. Most DNR foresters were not trained in fish and wildlife biology, forest ecology, or hydrology, and often had difficulty accepting the technical advice of the other cooperators' field personnel as valid.

As a fourth problem, the voluntary provisions of the agreement were seldom followed: more often, only the minimum regulatory requirements were met. Riparian zones rarely exceeded twenty-five feet on private lands. Much less upland wildlife territory was set aside than suggested in the agreement (2 acres per 160 logged) and the set-asides were sometimes temporary. Although some landowners made a conscientious effort to protect public resources, many did not, and were essentially free-riders. TFW did not truly constitute a move from a regulation-based system to one based on managing towards certain goals, as had been hoped.

Fifth, the agreement did not provide for monitoring or enforcement of site-specific agreements. Although tribal staff conducted some monitoring, tribal reporting of violations had little impact on DNR and usually resulted in tribes threatening court cases against DNR for not enforcing regulations or agreements made among TFW cooperators.[27]

Finally, the research process has been extremely slow to produce usable results for field managers. Tribal staff and academics at the University of Washington have criticized the fact that many research questions have not been conceptualized so as to produce results or techniques that could be used in the field in the short term.[28] While these problems may result simply from lack of coordinated leadership at the technical level, they tend to reinforce industry's position that "we don't have enough data yet to indicate how we should change the *status quo.*"

In this first substage of implementation, all parties had recognized that issues such as cumulative effects would be postponed; the scope of this issue and the time when it would receive high priority were left vague in the agreement. While the TFW cooperators grappled with all the above problems in the first two years, mid-1987 to mid-1989, few of them realized how much they had raised public expectations for improvements in protection of public

---

27   See TFW Field Implementation Committee, *1991 Forest Practice Compliance Survey* (Olympia, Wash.: DNR) and *Forest Practices Program, 1990 Calender Year Report* (Olympia, Wash.: DNR) for violations and enforcement efforts.

28   For an example see Halbert & Lee, *supra*, note 23.

resources. The first substage of implementation failed to produce the results expected by the allies, but was a necessary stage for raising public awareness, expectations, and eventually outrage that there was little apparent improvement in management. Ironically, industry's attempts in the press to emphasize their responsible corporate action through the agreement merely made more glaring the discrepancy between rhetoric and management actions. The second substage of implementation was propelled chiefly by public perception that nothing had changed in the damage to fish and wildlife habitat.

TFW IMPLEMENTATION, STAGE B:
SUSTAINABLE FORESTRY ROUNDTABLE

The two major issues of cumulative effects and the definition of environmental sensitivity, not adequately addressed in the original TFW process, eventually forced themselves onto the agenda through pressure from groups outside the TFW policy community. In this second substage of implementation, political activism and court cases against the Department of Natural Resources by counties and new environmental groups forced it to react. DNR seized the initiative by attempting to forge a new corporatist compromise (discussed below) that included the outside agitators in a new process, but did not define habitat protection as the major objective. The struggle in this stage centred on DNR's attempts to convince the public through the press that public resources would be protected in a new agreement and that industry would make major sacrifices. The allies got bad press during this stage for attempting to assert their own definition of the goals of the agreement, but furthered their struggle through the courts, through extending the issue network to Forest Practices Board members, and through a second attempt at legislative reform. These uses of power and their results are briefly described below.

The most important new challengers that forced DNR to take action were the political activists in Kittitas and Snohomish Counties. The RIDGE group in Kittitas County on the east side of the Cascade range was effective in bringing press attention to the rate-of-cut/community-stability issue. The Burlington Northern Railway, which had received substantial land grants from the U.S. government to construct the railhead to the west coast in the nineteenth century, had turned first to mining and then to logging. The small towns in Kittitas County had a history of boom-and-bust employment, but those who stayed were unwilling to tolerate another cycle of it. As the Plum Creek Timber Company (recycled from Burlington Northern) began clearcutting some five thousand acres annually in this area in the 1980s, in response to a booming Japanese market for raw logs, outrage mounted in the communities that the much-touted TFW process did nothing to affect the rate of cut. The communities argued that a gift from the nation should not give a logging company the right to make windfall profits and wipe out their communities for the next generation. They put forth their own plan for a slower and sustainable rate of cut, a one-hundred-year cycle in which only 10 percent of the area could be cut in ten years, with preference given to local contractors.[29] (Plum Creek was logging at the rate of 40 percent in ten years, leading to a non-sustainable twenty-five-year rotation cycle.) Although RIDGE was composed of retired coal miners and younger, more left-wing activists, its issues won sympathy from the local right-wing county commissioner, who was also deeply concerned over a sustainable rate of cut and community survival.[30]

While Kittitas County activists attacked DNR forest management from the perspective of the non-sustainable rate of cut, Snohomish County took the DNR, the Forest Practices Board, and the logging companies to court in summer 1989 for ignoring cumulative effects and public opposition to the logging of a large wildlife corridor around Lake Roesiger, north of Seattle.[31] This largely suburban county, whose homeowners valued their proximity to forests and wildlife, resented the rapid and seemingly uncontrollable clearcutting of forests, much of which ended up being converted to real estate, removing wildlife habitat permanently. Outraged that the celebrated TFW process was doing nothing to prevent this loss of habitat, they won a ruling from the Forest Practices Appeal Board, and eventually the court, that it was impossible to assess the potential environmental harm of one logging permit without putting it in the context of the cumulative impact of other adjacent logging. The court ordered the Forest Practices Board to find a process for considering the cumulative impact of logging on watersheds. The court also suggested that the TFW process be used to develop the new procedures for judging cumulative impacts. (The TFW policy committee, composed of the chief representatives of the cooperators, could do this simply by agreeing on the new procedures.)

Although DNR appealed the ruling (and lost at the next level), the combination of RIDGE, Snohomish County, political pressure from the Whidbey Island group that had launched *Noel* v. *Cole*, and a general rise in environmental activism over logging practices and conversions to real estate convinced DNR that it had to respond to a sizeable and growing constituency that would no longer accept business as usual. As one DNR official put it

29   John G. Mitchell, "War in the Woods II: West Side Story" (1990) 1 Audubon 82.

30   Board of Kittitas County Commissioners, *Economic Impact Study of the Forests Lands of Kittitas County* (Kittitas County, Wash., 1990).

31   *Snohomish County* v. *State of Washington et al.*, No.89-2-06923-5 in Snohomish County Superior Court.

during an interview:

> There is a big difference in public involvement in the last 10 years, and membership in
> environmental groups has skyrocketed in the last five years. Some of our congressional
> delegates talk about the "environmental industry" as better funded and better organized than
> the timber industry. There are about a zillion groups out there that want more protection of
> fish and wildlife [referring to SUSTAIN, a new environmental coalition]. The Sierra Club
> Legal Defense Fund and the Wilderness Society both now have permanent offices in Seattle.
> In California, the Forests Forever initiative is trying to ban clearcutting. Initiative 547[32] in
> this state is trying to prevent conversion of forest land to real estate. We have to respond to
> all this.

In other words, DNR began to respond to its perception of countervailing
power in other constituencies, and to free itself somewhat from agency
capture.[33]

The head of DNR took the initiative in responding to both the court order
and his interpretation of public sentiment by convening the Sustainable
Forestry Roundtable in the fall of 1989. It included the TFW cooperators, the
counties, and the new environmental groups. Its mandate was to extend the
TFW process to the new issues. DNR's head had been elected with the
support of environmentalists, and his ambition was to bring about a peaceable
agreement with industry. At a series of Sustainable Forestry Roundtable
meetings during 1990 in which the parties attempted to reach agreement on a
package of issues, the tribes played a mediating role. Sensing the process's
vulnerability to changes in political climate, they tried to persuade the new
environmental groups to reach agreement by compromise. The tribes were
successful in keeping the negotiations going for a time, but the environmental
caucus was divided on where to compromise.

For the environmental groups new to the process, the rate of harvest was
the key issue. However, industry would not agree to a rate of harvest lower
than 4 percent in ten years (a non-sustainable rate), which made agreement
impossible for the new environmental groups. The Washington Environmental
Council, an older environmental umbrella organization that had participated in
TFW, believed that a more important issue than rate of harvest was getting
agreement to apply cumulative-effects thresholds that would shut down
logging if exceeded. TFW research[34] was beginning to develop some

---

32   Citizens' initiative 547 proposed to create local-control mechanisms to limit the conversion
     of forested land to real estate. It gathered the necessary number of signatures to be placed
     on the ballot in record time, but was defeated in the fall 1990 election. Much of the
     opposition to the initiative focused on the mechanism's red tape rather than the conversion
     issue itself, and public concern about conversion did not die.

33   James Q. Wilson, ed., *The Politics of Regulation* (New York: Basic, 1980).

34   Based partly on Canadian models; for example, see D.J. Wilford, *Watershed Workbook*.

mechanisms based on degree of tree canopy closure and hydrological flow in a watershed, sediment levels in streams, and water temperature that could be used to measure damage to public resources from logging. The "older" environmentalists and the tribes reasoned that use of these measures would prevent damage to public resources as well as, or better than, the rate of harvest. Protection of public resources was in fact a more secure foundation for their arguments than rate of harvest, given the private nature of forest landholdings. This had been recognized by the court, which had ordered the Forest Practices Board to find ways to consider cumulative effects in logging applications. Negotiators for the Washington Environmental Council maintained the position that DNR's mandate was to protect the public interest in protection of these resources. Ironically, the DNR's urgency in bringing the "newer" environmental groups into the policy process and sticking to a timetable for their agreement paved the way for the agreement's failure. As newcomers to this policy arena, these groups would have required more time to view state-wide issues from more than a local perspective. Just as important, the development of federal proposals to protect the old growth habitat of the endangered northern spotted owl — which occurred during the SFR negotiations — reduced industry's willingness to compromise on other issues.

The Sustainable Forestry Roundtable did not reach agreement, but in debating numerous options for the protection of public resources it did air the concept of using cumulative-effects thresholds based on TFW research. In particular, Forest Practices Board members who attended were exposed to this option and were pulled into the issue network. Because of this, the Round Table furthered the process of finding a political and technical solution that would garner wide support and be difficult for industry to reject.

STAGE C IMPLEMENTATION: THE FOREST PRACTICES BOARD

During most of 1990, the Sustainable Forestry Roundtable had been the forum of action. The hope had been that an agreement could be sent to the legislature for enactment into law. After the legislature rejected three attempts in early 1991 to pass compromise packages that had not received the support of all parties, the ball was thrown back into the court of the Forest Practices Board, which now was required to produce measures for calculating and avoiding negative consequences of cumulative effects of logging on public resources.

Forest Hydrology Sensitivity Analysis for Coastal British Columbia Watersheds: Interim Edition (Smithers, B.C.: B.C. Ministry of Forests and Lands, 1987).

What the Board did at this point must be viewed not only in terms of the requirements of *Snohomish County* v. *State of Washington et al.* that it produce action on cumulative effects, but also in terms of its reaction to TFW and the Sustainable Forestry Roundtable process. In the past the Board had relied on DNR to provide the major direction; now public members of the Board became far more active in looking for solutions themselves, because the processes they were watching suggested that there were solutions to be had. They became part of the issue network of TFW and made direct contact with the TFW research effort. They formed six different subcommittees, working on developing solutions to issues with different agency personnel, tribes, environmental groups, and academics. Heclo[35] and McFarland[36] link the existence of lively and diverse issue networks, which communicate criticisms of policy and generate ideas for new policy initiatives, to the breaking of agency capture. As one Board member put it in an interview, "When you come up with a solution that all these people have worked on, it is far more likely to fly, get public support." The cumulative-effects committee of the Forest Practices Board studied the preliminary TFW research and was convinced that it was possible to find some reliable and politically acceptable measures of cumulative effects. At this point, the failure of the TFW cooperators to reach agreement on a cumulative-effects policy package (because industry vetoed agreement by the other cooperators) merely had the effect of passing the initiative to the Forest Practices Board. In its May 1991 meeting this body resolved to begin considering proposals to implement cumulative-effects measures that would result in rule making.

WILL FULL IMPLEMENTATION AND INSTITUTIONALIZATION OCCUR?

Is the TFW process, as it has evolved from the initial agreement through the Sustainable Forestry Roundtable and the more active role of the Forest Practices Board, merely a temporary policy reform that will never produce a fully implemented and institutionalized co-management process for habitat protection? How can we best conceptualize what TFW does and the basic conditions that make it possible?

The most sophisticated analysis so far of the TFW process[37] uses the pluralist paradigm to view TFW as a reform cycle in policy making that has only temporarily broken the agency capture situation by which industrial

---

35   Heclo, *supra*, note 16.

36   Andrew S. McFarland, "Interest Groups and Theories of Power in America" (1987) 17 British J. of Political Science 129.

37   Halbert & Lee, *supra*, note 23.

interests dominate policy. In this model, tribal interests are considered minor and environmentalists are merely another special interest group, while the general public is seen as still largely excluded from access to information and from participation in the process (see also Fraidenburg,[38] who viewed TFW as a conspiracy among special-interest groups, which exclude the public from participation). The *National Environmental Policy Act*'s[39] environmental impact statement process is seen as a preferable model of public review or public input into policy. Although some elements of this argument seemed reasonable enough at the time, subsequent developments have shown that important fundamentals of this interpretation can now be questioned. Each is discussed below.

Is the TFW process merely a temporary reform? This question can be linked to the question of whether TFW is an example of temporarily successful pluralist pressure-group politics. The most recent and interesting version of pluralist politics cited by Halbert and Lee is the "triadic power" model of McFarland.[40] This model pictures an ebb and flow between the "agency capture" situation (in which the major economic producers dominate agency policy) and a triangle of power in which "countervailing forces" (such as tribes and environmental groups) exert enough pressure to break agency capture by the economic producers. In the triangle or "triadic power" situation, other groups are presumed to have equal power with economic producers, and this is presumed to give the agency more ability to act according to professionalized standards of decision making, independent of both groups. However, the power triad is only a temporary reform: as countervailing power ebbs with the lessened activity of countervailing groups, agency capture is reasserted by the economic producers. In other words, reforms are not institutionalized, but can be eliminated.

The environmentalists and tribes were included in the policy community because they had the resources to take the logging companies to court and to draw public attention to the destruction of *public* resources. As an alliance, they do not act as a private-interest group, or as simply one of a plurality of interests. Because of their stance on the protection of public resources, as well as the legal position of both groups, it is more appropriate to view the tribal/environmental alliance as an associative-corporatist rather than a pluralist body. Associative-corporatist bodies are characterized by the identification of their own interests with the larger public interest.[41] In this

---

38   Fraidenburg, *supra*, note 25.

39   *National Environmental Policy Act*, 42 U.S.C.A., s.4321 (West 1977).

40   McFarland, *supra*, note 36.

41   W. Streeck & P. Schmitter, "Community Market, State — and Associations? The

they are fundamentally different from the logging companies, which have only a private interest. The logging companies' inability to identify their interests with the public interest was clearly shown in their inability to accept a sustainable rate of cut. The influence of the tribes and environmentalists on public opinion, and their ability to identify themselves with the protection of the public interest, must also be seen in the context of a substantial drop in public confidence in governmental decision making, and an equally substantial rise in awareness and concern about irreversible destruction of public natural resources, particularly in the last five years. The associative-corporatist or "micro-corporatist" mode of policy making in this situation appears more likely to be associated with a paradigm shift or basic transformation in policy than with a reform cycle.

Is the general public excluded from the policy-making process in TFW? This issue is a genuine problem for corporatism, because the level of knowledge of the issues and the level of debate is such that it is indeed difficult for the general public to participate. Negotiating the TFW agreement took by some counts about one hundred meetings, many of which were technical discussions among staff of the various parties.

When judged against these difficulties, the TFW process has shown a remarkable ability to expand to include new issues and new actors when there was significant public pressure from these actors or about these issues. Groups or parties have been excluded, if at all, because of limited resources. They (the counties, some of the environmental groups) have dropped out voluntarily when they did not have the time and energy to continue participation in the extensive, in-depth debates that characterized the Sustainable Forestry Roundtable and the continuing TFW process. Furthermore, it is unlikely that the new environmental groups and the counties would have had any opportunity at all to act in this policy-making fashion without the pre-existing TFW process.

Although opportunities for the general public to participate in policy debate and to set the TFW agenda are limited, there are significant opportunities for the public to participate with site-specific comments on proposed logging practices. The interdisciplinary team process can and does include observers who have a specific concern about a particular site. In some regions, the environmental participant on the interdisciplinary teams has been particularly effective in informing the public about proposed logging and soliciting public input about particular concerns. Some environmental

Prospective Contributions of Interest Governance to Social Order" *in* W. Streeck & P. Schmitter, eds., *Private Interest Government: Beyond Market and State* (London: Sage, 1985) at 1.

representatives have become highly visible public contact people, who become depositories of public concern and are effective in communicating these to DNR. In other regions, organized environmental groups that were not party to TFW have developed good working relations with the DNR district manager and make regular comments on proposed logging.

Of course, any member of the public has always been able to make submissions to the Forest Practices Board and to make comments on proposed regulations at public hearings. This process existed before TFW. However, the TFW process has energized the Board and made it more interested in agenda setting and independent activity. The Board has incorporated TFW research and independently communicates with the TFW research team. General public members of the Forest Practices Board attended both the Sustainable Forestry Roundtable and the Third Annual Review of TFW. Curiously, when Board members requested to become part of TFW, the TFW policy group expressed concern that this might be seen by the public as too much privatization of policy making. TFW invited Board members to attend all their meetings as observers, but felt it was important for the Board to maintain a separate process and be perceived by the public as separate. As we have seen, when TFW cooperators did not reach agreement on policy for implementing cumulative-effects research, the debate was passed on to the Forest Practices Board. This should be seen as a sign that the TFW process has been successful not only at more in-depth issue debating and policy making than would be possible in environmental impact review processes, but also at passing on unresolved issues to other forums.

What was the role of the tribes and the courts in creating the process? It is important to remember that the Phase II decision about tribal rights to protect habitat was the original catalyst for the TFW process. Although the decision had been appealed and vacated by the court,[42] the court gave instructions to the parties to negotiate and requested regular reports during the TFW original negotiations. At critical later points, environmental groups and counties secured court decisions that propelled the process into dealing with more fundamental issues. Tribal appeals of violations of forest practice regulations, and of agreements made under the TFW process, also maintained pressure on DNR to implement the agreement.

Clearly, the environmentalists alone would have had far more limited success in protecting wildlife or fisheries habitat. Their legal position was much weaker than that of the tribes, because they had to chip away at the definition of public rights, while the tribes could use proprietary rights to defend resources. Environmentalists had talented and experienced volunteers

---

42   See Cohen, *Treaties On Trial, supra,* note 3.

who could organize effective lobbies, letter-writing campaigns, and public testimony, but they were also spread thin and had periodic fund-raising crises. Without the support of tribal rights, access to tribal research, and especially the TFW research, they would not now be in a position to press for mechanisms such as thresholds to measure cumulative impacts on public resources.

What the tribes could have accomplished alone is also limited. As Scheingold notes, "[W]hen legal rights run counter to prevailing power relationships, it surely cannot be taken for granted that these rights will be redeemed on demand."[43] The tribes alone would have had more difficulty convincing the public that they were protecting public resources, because of their economic use of the fishery. Acting with the environmentalists, however, they were able to make the linkage that protecting tribal resources is the same as protecting public resources, and to use far more forcefully the arguments about protecting the spiritual values associated with natural resources. Although the tribes had critical political expertise in their leaders, and excellent technical and political expertise on staff, these were both spread very thin. The issue network they could form with the environmentalists and agencies was far more powerful than would have been the case given reliance solely on their resources. In short, the tribes were almost certainly necessary to the process, but probably could not have done it alone. The courts, as used both by the tribes and by other challengers, were very important in pushing the process along at key points, and *may* also have been a necessary condition to implementing habitat protection.

What is the linkage between co-management and the corporatist policy-making sought by government during the Sustainable Forestry Roundtable? What elements of either or both are present in the TFW process? This discussion began by comparing the co-management agreement emerging from the Phase I decision with the difficulty of achieving and then implementing an agreement to protect habitat. From the tribal perspective, TFW was another co-management agreement, covering another management function — fish habitat protection. For environmental groups, the same could be said for wildlife. However, for government's lead agency, DNR, the Phase II agreement and process was quite different, because powerful and influential interests were fundamentally in opposition to measures that the tribes and environmentalists believed were barely adequate. (As one tribal habitat biologist put it in an interview, we cannot afford to treat habitat protection as an area of continual political compromise. If we keep accepting even small

---

43   As quoted in Rita Bruun, "The Boldt Decision: Legal Victory, Political Defeat" (1982) 4:3 Law and Policy Quarterly 271 at 273.

habitat losses, eventually there will be no habitat and no species left. Critical thresholds below which some species cannot survive may be closer than we think.) For DNR, as evidenced in the Sustainable Forestry Roundtable, keeping peace — within its own dual roles as well as between industry and environmentalists — was the goal, not habitat protection.

While co-management agreements are usually initiated from the bottom to solve the problems or concerns of communities or groups dependent on resources, corporatist decision making is often initiated by government to solve the problems they encounter with expanded power and the high costs of running an orderly process. The Sustainable Forestry Roundtable was an attempt by government to make the parties reach an agreement outside the courts.

The unresolved tension in the TFW process comes partially from the difference between (a) the goal of the allies to define the process as habitat protection co-management and (b) the goal of DNR to define the process as a conflict between two stakeholders in public resources who have equally legitimate demands and must each compromise. During the Sustainable Forestry Roundtable, the tribal/environmentalist allies tried to work within the government's corporatist framework by attempting to define themselves as the more legitimate policy-making partner with government, representing the public interest. A significant portion of the Forest Practices Board, and at least some of the public, do not believe that the logging companies have the right to destroy public resources in their pursuit of private wealth. However, as the lead agency, DNR has only recently appeared to lean toward this position. A great deal of the struggle around the Roundtable, and the repeated use of the courts, results from the fact that DNR as a captured agency is apparently only now beginning to free itself from its old relationship with the logging companies and from domination by its own role as logger of public trust lands. As far as the allies are concerned, the companies are involved in corporatist policy making in order to reduce and mitigate the economic impact of increased regulation and to improve compliance with rising public standards of protection if possible. In Washington state, some of the leading logging companies are locally based and thus especially responsive to public opinion.

In summary, the TFW process contains a struggle between two opposing but overlapping ways of defining that process. The allies seek co-management, and measure the success of the process by whether habitat is in fact protected. DNR seeks corporatist agreement, and measures success by whether it is able to escape court challenges. It appears that the process of achieving genuine co-management will be slow, but not impossible. Along the way, would-be co-managers such as the allies may have to participate in corporatist policy-making forums in order to convince government and the public that they are protecting the public interest, and in order to achieve their more specific goals.

CONCLUSION

This discussion has shown five strategies that tribes and environmentalists used and continue to use effectively to work towards translating the legal promise of *U.S.* v. *Washington*, Phase II,[44] into management practices to protect fish and wildlife habitat. Issue networks/alliances, legislation and threatened legislative amendments, threat of greater regulation and public review, court action and threat of court action to reform legislation and amend regulations, and initiatives to prevent conversion of forest land to real estate were used to bring the logging industry to the negotiating table and to push forward implementation at various stages. The allies' adoption of a corporatist-associative mode of policy making may in itself be considered another strategy.

The sources of power used by the allies were not simultaneously available. The stages of development of implementation therefore reflected what they could achieve in any one period. Mobilizing the interest and support of more players, such as counties, radical environmental groups, and the Forest Practices Board, was possible only as these players observed the distance between the rhetoric of agreements and the reality of management practice. One source of power was used to raise public awareness in order to mobilize another source of power.

In the beginning, the allies were able only to effect some minimal standards of habitat protection and to become involved in some implementation and in research. While the TFW agreement won the industry a temporary reprieve from public pressure, new court cases and negative press reappeared when the limitations of the agreement became obvious. The negative press and court challenges were more virulent in response to exaggerated claims by industry and DNR of the agreement's accomplishments. The aroused public awareness led DNR to try to duplicate the original credibility and popularity of the TFW agreement through convening the Sustainable Forestry Roundtable. To do this, DNR had to put more difficult long-range issues such as cumulative effects on the table, and include counties and radical environmental groups. This process placed pressure on the TFW research effort to produce technical measures of cumulative effects that would be usable in the field. Discussion of such technical measures in an active issue network of agencies, tribes, environmentalists, counties, and Forest Practices Board members was fruitful enough in this second stage that the board

---

44   *Supra*, note 2.

became proactive in seeking a solution itself when the Sustainable Forestry Roundtable negotiations did not produce one. At this point, the issue network had become more important than press coverage or what anyone imagined public opinion to be.

During the Sustainable Forestry Roundtable, the allies consistently fought on the ground of protection of public resources from damage by private interests. The allies resisted DNR's attempt to redefine the issue as corporatist decision making between big industry and other groups, but insisted that the public interest in fish, wildlife, and water quality protection was its own priority. Together with the technical hope of measuring damage to public resources, the allies' position convinced members of the Forest Practices Board that they were obligated to move to protect these resources.

The successful use of these strategies and the comparative strength of the barriers to translating rights into practice in Phase I and Phase II suggest several new middle-range theoretical propositions about permitting conditions for co-management that can be added to the existing list:[45]

1. Previous co-management agreements may facilitate reaching a negotiating posture, but may not facilitate negotiation or implementation of new agreements.

2. Barriers to negotiating and implementing co-management agreements are greater in proportion to the power of other parties affected and the extent to which they have captured a government agency.

3. Barriers to implementing co-management are more easily overcome through alliances of stakeholders, non-governmental organizations, and agencies with complementary resources, especially when these parties form issue networks that generate new technical information and alternative models.

4. Barriers are more easily overcome through the use of multiple sources of power, such as courts, legislature, public boards, and citizens' initiatives at strategic times, creating a spill-over effect from one to another.

5. In situations of substantial power differential between parties, implementation of co-management agreements may be furthered by an appeal to the general public interest through the use of corporatist-associative-style policy-making forums. This strategy may be most successful in more developed regions with diversified economies and stakeholder groups.

---

45   Pinkerton, *Co-operative Management of Local Fisheries, supra*, note 4.

6. The composition of courts and the political climate in any particular decade may influence the degree to which court action is preferred over political action. The changing composition of the U.S. Supreme Court between 1970 and 1990 (to more conservative), as well as the changing political climate in the state of Washington (to more supportive of tribal rights), is likely to affect the mix of strategies that can effectively overcome barriers to co-management in a particular historical period.

The TFW agreement is still only partially implemented, and there may be further points of resistance to putting cumulative-effects measures into specific rules. This discussion has shown the general nature of barriers to implementing co-management, and strategies for overcoming them.

RESPONDING TO LAND-USE AND ENVIRONMENTAL CONFLICT: ENVIRONMENTAL ASSESSMENT AND LAND-USE PLANNING IN SOUTHERN ONTARIO

*Robert B. Gibson**

We tend to view environmental conflicts as clashes of competing interests, as the immediate and continuing struggles of various parties wanting to use or protect resources and other environmental values. Accordingly, we respond with conflict-resolution mechanisms. And when these fail, we seek better conflict-resolution mechanisms.

This approach is reasonable, even necessary, but it is fire-fighting in a city of arsonists. Most of the environmental conflicts we face today are the product of growing demands on a limited and already extensively degraded environmental legacy. So long as these demands increase, environmental conflicts will proliferate. Under such conditions, the reactive approach is eventually futile.

Efforts to anticipate and avoid environmental conflicts offer more hope, but also more interference with business as usual. They require recognition that each conflict has a history as well as a present; that these histories feature failures of sensitivity, understanding, and vision; and that correction will entail adoption of approaches to planning and decision making that are much better integrated, informed, and far-sighted than those that prevail today.

The nature of this challenge could probably be illustrated through examination of any current set of environmental conflicts. But one particularly illuminating area is that of land-use planning conflicts in southern Ontario, which have begun to reveal serious inadequacies not only in prevailing land-use planning practices under the provincial *Planning Act*,[1] but also in the more demanding environmental planning and evaluation requirements of Ontario's *Environmental Assessment Act*.[2]

---

* The author is a member of the Ontario Ministry of the Environment's Environmental Assessment Committee, which advises on matters related to the province's *Environmental Assessment Act* and its implementation, usually after holding informal public hearings. Several of the cases addressed by the Committee in recent years have centred on land-use planning controversies and are discussed in this paper.

1 *Planning Act*, S.O. 1983, c.1.

2 *Environmental Assessment Act*, R.S.O. 1980, c.140.

ENVIRONMENTAL ASSESSMENT
IN ONTARIO

The *Environmental Assessment Act* is the province's premier vehicle for imposing environmental responsibility in the planning of a wide range of undertakings. In design, if not always in implementation, the Act is model environmental assessment legislation. Passed in 1975, it established the first formally legislated environmental assessment process in Canada and one of the first in the world. But it was also extraordinarily innovative for its times and set a standard for environmentally responsible planning that is not yet met in many jurisdictions.[3]

The central aim of the *Environmental Assessment Act* is to force careful consideration of environmental factors, along with conventional economic and technical concerns, throughout the planning of undertakings.[4] It defines "environment" broadly to include social, economic, and cultural as well as biophysical effects,[5] and it requires proponents to consider these matters not just in the design of new undertakings, but also earlier, in the initial stages of planning. Proponents must show how environmental considerations have been addressed in the examination of purposes, in the identification of alternative responses to these purposes, and in the evaluation of these alternatives, as well as in the selection and elaboration of one alternative as the proposed undertaking.

Before proponents can receive approval to proceed with an undertaking, they must first submit an environmental assessment document reporting on their planning efforts. This document, which is subject to government and public review, must set out the purposes of the undertaking, show how the environmental implications of alternative ways of meeting this purpose have been identified and evaluated, and provide an environmental justification for the selection and design of the proposed undertaking.[6] Where the government and/or public reviewers have significant objections, the case must usually go to an independent tribunal, the Environmental Assessment Board, for formal

---

3   Robert B. Gibson & Beth Savan, "Lessons of a Legislated Process: Twelve Years of Experience with Ontario's Environmental Assessment Act" (1990) 8:3 Impact Assessment Bulletin 63.

4   According to s.1(o) of the *Environmental Assessment Act, supra*, note 3, "undertakings" are defined to include "an enterprise or activity or a proposal, plan or program in respect of an enterprise or activity ..." for public-sector proponents, and "'major commercial or business enterprises or activity ...'" for private-sector proponents.

5   *Supra*, note 2, s.1(c).

6   *Id.*, s.5(3).

public hearing and decision.[7]

Because the Act is focused on early planning as well as detailed design, because a broad definition of "environment" is adopted, and because the public as well as government reviewers assess proponents' work before approval is given, Ontario's environmental assessment process is remarkably well suited to encouraging effective integration of environmental considerations into conventional (largely economic) decision making. Such integration of environmental and economic considerations is now widely accepted as a crucial means of reducing and preventing environmental abuses and the human tragedies and conflicts that accompany these abuses.

Despite the significance of its strengths, Ontario's environmental assessment process also has important weaknesses, especially in application and administration. The requirements set out in the *Environmental Assessment Act* can be applied broadly. The Act defines "undertakings" to include not just projects but also plans with respect to projects, and provides for assessment of private-sector as well as public-sector activities. In practice, however, assessment requirements have been imposed mostly on provincial and municipal public-sector authorities planning capital projects; assessments of other kinds of public-sector undertakings and most private-sector undertakings have been rare.[8]

To some extent, reluctance to apply the Act more broadly has reflected the limited environmental commitment of governments and their deeper concerns about adding to regulatory burdens. But a history of inefficient administration also plagues the process and has provided a further incentive for avoiding assessment requirements. Because it is designed to force new considerations into the planning of undertakings, Ontario's environmental assessment process is burdensome for proponents. These inevitable burdens have, however, been exacerbated, especially in recent years, by delays and other inefficiencies in the administration of the process, especially in the review and hearing phases.

The province has recognized these problems and is moving to correct them. A governmental task force has prepared a report addressing a wide range of major and minor complaints about the application and administration

---

7   *Id.*, ss.12-13.

8   Only public-sector undertakings are automatically subject to assessment requirements (unless specifically exempted). Application to private-sector activities is achieved only through specific designation orders, which successive governments have proved most hesitant to issue. As a result, assessments of public-sector activities (other than waste-disposal projects) have been rare. See *id.*, s.3 and the accompanying *General Regulation*, O.Reg. 205/87, which sets out exemptions.

of the Act,[9] and the Minister's Environmental Assessment Advisory Committee is currently conducting a public review of the task force's recommendations. The new Minister of the Environment has also announced plans to establish a further task force to provide specific recommendations on how the Act should be applied to the private sector.[10]

In seeking solutions to the application, administration, and other problems with the current process, both the present and previous governments presumed that the Act was fundamentally sound. The authors of the task force report stated that their work was based:

> on the premise that the Act, and its underlying principles of public consultation, broad definition of the environment, analysis of alternatives and consideration of environmental effects provides for a comprehensive, effective and environmentally sensitive decision-making tool.[11]

This assumption was largely reasonable. It recognized the major advances in assessment law that had made the Act innovative and exemplary in 1975, and it implicitly defended these advances against the critics who had, over the years, argued that Ontario's environmental assessment requirements were too broad, too open, and too demanding.

At the same time, the assumption of fundamental soundness has overlooked a set of rising concerns that have brought the adequacy of Ontario's environmental assessment process into question. These concerns centre on the evident inability of the *Environmental Assessment Act* — even if applied more broadly and with greater efficiency — to ensure appropriate attention to the overall environmental effects of individually "acceptable" undertakings. This limitation has been revealed most clearly in recent controversies about the immediate and cumulative effects of various "development" projects conventionally handled under Ontario's land-use planning and approvals process.

LAND-USE CONFLICTS AND DEMANDS FOR APPLICATION OF THE ENVIRONMENTAL ASSESSMENT ACT

Private-sector land "development" undertakings and broader land-use planning activities of regional and municipal authorities have not been subject to environmental assessment requirements in Ontario. Decisions on regional

---

9   Ontario Ministry of the Environment, Environmental Assessment Task Force, *Toward Improving the Environmental Assessment Program in Ontario* (Toronto, 1990).

10   Hon. Ruth Grier, Minister of the Environment, p.2 of the covering letter accompanying the task force report, *id.*

11   *Supra*, note 9, at 1.

and municipal plans, amendments to accommodate land-use changes, and approvals for specific land "development" applications are generally made without formal assessment of the environmental merits of alternatives or the potential overall environmental effects of proposed plans and activities.

There are several reasons why land-use decision making has generally escaped environmental assessment requirements. A major factor has been desire to avoid duplication of process. Wherever there are organized municipal authorities in Ontario, land-use decisions fall under the *Planning Act*, which, like the *Environmental Assessment Act*, sets out formal procedures for decision making, including public notice and provision for independent, quasi-judicial, public reviews of controversial decisions.

Because the *Planning Act* requires decision makers to "have regard for" environmental considerations,[12] there is some basis for arguing that environmental responsibility can be encouraged, if not ensured, in the existing planning process, without imposing the additional burdens and duplicative procedures of environmental assessment law. In practice, however, the story is different. There is now growing recognition, among regional and municipal officials and independent observers as well as citizens' groups and environmental professionals, that those responsible for land-use planning decisions have generally not had satisfactory information about potential environmental implications, have not given adequate attention to environmental considerations, and have not been successful in protecting environmental values.

One response to this has been increasing pressure on the Minister of the Environment to apply the *Environmental Assessment Act* to land-use planning and project approvals.

Over the past few years, individuals and groups dissatisfied with the consideration given to environmental concerns in land-use planning decisions have begun to lobby Ontario's Minister of the Environment to require environmental assessments of disputed undertakings. Under the *Environmental Assessment Act*, the Lieutenant Governor in Council may, by regulation, designate any "major commercial or business enterprise or activity" subject to environmental assessment requirements.[13] If a designation is made, the proponent is required to prepare and submit an environmental assessment document for formal review and approval.

In the two years from 1 April 1988 to 31 March 1990, the Minister received designation requests related to sixty-eight different undertakings.

---

12   *Supra*, note 1, s.2(a).

13   *Supra*, note 2, s.40(d).

Most of these involved land-use conflicts of various kinds (concerning forest management options, aggregate extraction proposals, parks plans, waste treatment/disposal facilities, etc.), and at least a third involved land development activities normally addressed through land-use decision making under the *Planning Act*. The disputed undertakings included both private-sector proposals (especially proposed subdivisions and other major residential, resort, and infrastructural projects) and municipal planning activities (especially proposed official plan amendments to allow intensification of land uses).[14] In many cases, designation requests were submitted by hundreds of individuals and organizations representing many individuals.

As noted above, the designation power has rarely been used in Ontario. Less than 10 percent of designation requests have led to designations, and most of these have been private-sector waste management undertakings (chiefly landfill proposals) that would have been subject to assessment requirements automatically if proposed by municipalities.

In this light, it is significant that special attention is now being given to requests for designation of land-use activities. This attention is reflected in decisions by the Minister of the Environment to refer a series of land-use conflict designation requests to the Environmental Assessment Advisory Committee (EAAC) for public review. EAAC is an independent body composed of three private citizens appointed to advise the Minister on matters relating to the application of the *Environmental Assessment Act*. The Committee has some continuing responsibilities, but its major role is holding informal public reviews on matters referred to the Committee by the Minister. Most of these referrals have concerned controversial exemption and designation requests.

In the past three years, a majority of the cases referred to the Committee have centred on land-use planning issues. While many of these have been sparked by concerns about specific proposals, especially private-sector land "development" undertakings, the concerns have typically broadened to include more comprehensive dissatisfaction with the handling of environmental considerations in municipal and regional land-use planning.

LAND-USE CONFLICT CASES REFERRED TO ONTARIO'S ENVIRONMENTAL ASSESSMENT ADVISORY COMMITTEE

The land-use cases referred to the Committee have included controversies about roads, subdivisions, lakeshore redevelopments, wetland elimination,

---

14   See Ontario Environmental Assessment Advisory Committee, *6th and 7th Annual Reports 1988-89/1989-90* (Toronto, 1990) at 31.

wells, and agricultural land severances. They have also raised a fundamentally consistent but expanding set of issues pointing to inadequacies in the established planning and environmental assessment processes. Four of the most significant cases are summarized here.

Referral #33 — Redevelopment of the Motel Strip Lands in the City of Etobicoke — involved a request for designation of a proposed Official Plan Amendment by the City of Etobicoke that would facilitate a set of largely private sector projects, including high-density commercial and residential buildings, marinas, and shoreline roads, on about twenty hectares of land on the Lake Ontario waterfront.

Opponents of the Official Plan Amendment and the associated projects expressed concerns about a variety of potential environmental effects, especially those resulting from proposed lakefilling and dredging given the extent of existing contamination. They advocated careful examination of alternative development options and integrated evaluation of cumulative impacts, and wanted designation under the *Environmental Assessment Act* because they did not believe their concerns would be addressed in conventional decision making under the *Planning Act*. Representatives of the municipality and the developers argued that environmental considerations would be given proper attention without application of environmental assessment requirements.

EAAC, in this case, recommended designation of the shoreline and nearshore components of the redevelopment plans. It also identified a need for more comprehensive efforts to integrate planning and assessment of other waterfront redevelopments in the area, to allow for recognition and evaluation of cumulative environmental and planning effects. Finally, the Committee recognized that application of the *Environmental Assessment Act* alone would not be enough in this and similar cases, and recommended review of the *Planning Act* and its ability to ensure proper attention to cumulative effects.

Referral #37 — Development on the Creditview Wetland, City of Mississauga — centred on requests for designation of two developers' plans for filling and constructing a residential subdivision on the Creditview wetland. The developers owned the lands in question, had already received draft plan of subdivision approval from the municipality, and were unwilling to preserve the wetland without compensation. Opponents of the developers' plans argued that the 11.5-hectare wetland was unique and valuable, that it should have been identified for permanent protection, and that it should not be destroyed.

EAAC recommended efforts to reach a mediated settlement. It also observed that the case revealed needs to improve environmental data collection in the planning process, particularly concerning the identification and evaluation of natural areas, and to strengthen tools and incentives for preservation.

Referral #38 — The Adequacy of the Existing Environmental Planning and Approvals Process for the Ganaraska Watershed — was the first of two cases where the Minister requested comment on land-use planning practices covering an area of dispute, rather than a single project. In this first case, concern focused on a part of the Oak Ridges Moraine that provided the headwaters of the Ganaraska River. The area had been rehabilitated after serious degradation earlier in the century and now provided extensive greenspace as well as ground and surface water recharge and other environmental values. However, because of its attractiveness and location on the fringe of the Greater Toronto area, the upper Ganaraska and the Oak Ridges Moraine generally were increasingly subject to "development" pressures.

The Minister had rejected several requests for designation of certain rural residential subdivision proposals, on the ground that these projects by themselves did not pose significant threats to the environment. But the problem of cumulative effects remained, and the Minister asked the Committee to consider the adequacy of the existing planning and approvals process and options for improving the process, including application of the *Environmental Assessment Act.*

In the course of its review the Committee heard from provincial and municipal officials as well as from environmental groups and members of the public about the environmental deficiencies of the existing planning and approvals process, especially in the identification of environmental protection objectives and in protection against negative cumulative effects.

In its report, EAAC recommended a variety of measures to improve planning and to strengthen environmental protection in planning approvals for land-use changes in the Ganaraska area. However, its overall conclusion was that "the existing land-use planning and approvals process in Ontario is inadequate to the task of maintaining social and ecological quality in the face of 'development' pressures."[15]

The Committee's analysis was based on four basic requirements of "an environmentally enlightened land-use planning process":

- it must ensure collection of adequate baseline information on environmental resources, their importance and vulnerability;

---

15   Ontario Environmental Assessment Advisory Committee, *The Adequacy of the Existing Environmental Planning and Approvals Process for the Ganaraska Watershed,* Report No.38 to the Minister (Toronto, 1989) at 37.

- it must ensure that land-use plans and planning policies recognize resource preservation and environmental protection goals and needs, identify the cumulative as well as specific impacts to be avoided, and set appropriate development objectives and limitations;

- it must ensure consistent and effective adherence to the identified goals, requirements and limitations, in all decision making on plan amendments and on individual development proposals; and

- it must be sufficiently broad, or at least well coordinated, to ensure that inter-regional environmental resources (e.g., watersheds, extensive natural features such as the Oak Ridges Moraine, etc.) are recognized and given comprehensive and consistent protection.[16]

The Committee found that the current planning and approvals process met none of these prerequisites.

While the Committee recognized that, in theory, environmental values and cumulative effects could be recognized in the preparation of official plans, it observed that this was discouraged in practice by ecologically inappropriate administrative boundaries, by narrow environmental protection agency mandates, and by the absence of legal or economic incentives for attention to long-term environmental responsibility.

The Committee also observed that where official plan protections were put in place, they were "vulnerable to incremental erosion"[17] through plan amendments and approvals for individually acceptable "development" projects. Indeed, it found that the established process under the *Planning Act* was "structurally inclined to favour incremental elimination of land use restrictions":

> The current process expects and permits amendments and approvals, which are almost invariably for more intensive land uses, and the proposals are evaluated and granted on a case by case basis. Comments are sought from authorities in a variety of agencies, including ones with environmental responsibilities, but the commentators focus on technical matters and specific concerns according to their agency mandates. Consideration of cumulative effects is apparently rare and unwelcome. Individuals and groups advocating or merely seeking to retain land use restrictions that protect against cumulative environmental damages generally have fewer resources than developers applying to intensify land uses. Moreover, once a decision has been made to dedicate lands to more intensive uses, the results are virtually irreversible, while decisions to maintain limitations are always subject to change.[18]

The Committee considered a variety of possible responses, including

---

16   *Id.*, at 35.

17   *Id.*

18   *Id.*, at 36-37.

application of the *Environmental Assessment Act*. It concluded that imposition of environmental assessment requirements could be beneficial for some specific development controversies, but would not provide an effective vehicle for addressing cumulative environmental effects. It also considered application of the Act to the preparation of official plans as a means of encouraging evaluation of alternative development options in light of their potential environmental effects, but judged that application of assessment requirements on top of *Planning Act* requirements would be excessively awkward and inefficient.

Instead, EAAC recommended a major new initiative to "green" the planning and approvals process, and the institutional arrangements supporting it. This greening would, in the Committee's view, seek to meet the four basic requirements for an environmentally enlightened land-use planning process by incorporating the desirable qualities of the environmental assessment process, establishing an ecosystem basis for land-use data gathering and planning, and requiring attention to cumulative effects.

Shortly after EAAC's Ganaraska report was released in late 1989, its main findings were supported by the findings of other inquiries examining related land-use planning and environmental protection issues affecting the Greater Toronto area and the Oak Ridges Moraine. These included the work on the Toronto waterfront of the Crombie Commission, which had adopted a comprehensive watershed approach,[19] and the Kanter study, examining provision and preservation of green space in the Greater Toronto area.[20] Like the Committee, these other studies urged significant improvement in the collection and consideration of information on environmental values in land-use decision making, and they recommended adoption of an integrated, ecosystemic approach to land-use planning with particular attention to the protection of natural landscapes and water resources.

Referral #41a and b — Sydenham Mills Subdivision in the Township of Sydenham, Grey County, and the Adequacy of Environmental Planning and Approvals in Grey County — was sent to the Committee shortly after the Ganaraska report had been completed, and posed a similar challenge. The Committee was asked for advice on the appropriateness of requiring environmental assessment of a rural subdivision proposal that raised concerns about loss of a woodlot, effects on surface and ground water, and implications for future municipal servicing. But the Committee was again also assigned the

---

19   Royal Commission on the Future of the Toronto Waterfront, *Watershed*, interim report (Toronto, 1990) (Commissioner: Hon. David Crombie).

20   Ron Kanter, *Space for All: Options for the Greater Toronto Greenlands Strategy* (Toronto: Government of Ontario, 1990).

task of examining the existing land-use planning and approvals process, in this case applied within an entire county.

Owing to the initiative of a local resident, the subdivision issue was already slated to be addressed in a formal hearing before the Ontario Municipal Board. The Committee therefore recommended extraordinary steps by provincial agencies to ensure effective presentation of environmental concerns before this Board, rather than requiring an environmental assessment. However, the Committee also observed that the conventional process for such individual cases was not designed to address cumulative effects, relied heavily on review agencies that had insufficient resources for the task, and put an unfair burden on volunteer private intervenors to make the case for environmental protection.

The larger question of planning practice in Grey County was considered in detail in a separate report by the Committee. Since this report has yet to be released by the Minister, its contents cannot be discussed here.[21] However, it is no secret that the findings confirmed those of the Ganaraska report.

ENVIRONMENTAL ASSESSMENT AND LAND-USE PLANNING — PROBLEMS AND LESSONS

No doubt the land-use conflict cases examined by Ontario's Environmental Assessment Advisory Committee are in some ways exceptional. However, the consistency of the Committee's findings in diverse cases and the similarity of conclusions arrived at by other inquiries (e.g., Crombie and Kanter) indicate that a package of confirmed lessons can be drawn from these experiences. The main lessons are as follows.

Environmental assessment is not enough. Assessment processes that define "environment" broadly and demand examination of needs and alternatives can force attention to ecological and community factors in the early planning of environmentally significant projects and other specific undertakings. But this does not ensure adequate attention to the cumulative, collective effects of many undertakings, existing and new.

Nor will improvement in the practice of land-use planning be enough. The identified barriers to environmentally sensitive planning reflect fundamental problems that cannot be resolved through tinkering with implementation procedures. These problems include:

• absence of overall environmental objectives, defining ecological and

---

21 Ontario Environmental Assessment Advisory Committee, *Environmental Planning and Approvals in Grey County*, Report No.41b to the Minister (Toronto, 1990). The report was released after this paper was presented. It is available from the Committee.

community sustainability goals and setting indicators for monitoring of successes and failures;

- failure to use planning boundaries that recognize ecosystem realities;

- lack of a comprehensive base of environmental information for evaluation of cumulative effects;

- lack of cooperation and integration among environmental protection agencies with narrow mandates, differing philosophies, and uneven powers;

- excessive burdens on objectors to reveal the environmental deficiencies of proposed plans and projects;

- weakness of legal and other means of protecting existing natural areas and other components of environmental quality;

- vulnerability of environmental resources to incremental degradation through project-specific decisions;

- primacy given to short-term economic priorities in planning decisions; and

- difficulties in reconciling environmental protection requirements for the overall public good with established rights and expectations of land owners.

Few of these problems are peculiar to land-use planning. A similar set of concerns could easily be identified in deliberations on pollution control, resource management (e.g., regarding forests), and sectoral policies and practices (e.g., regarding energy and health). But even the lessons from land-use conflict cases alone provide reasonably clear implications for the reform of environmental assessment processes and the larger framework of planning and environmental regulation.

BROADER EFFORTS TO ANTICIPATE
AND ADDRESS LAND-USE AND
ENVIRONMENTAL CONFLICTS

Like most other review and approval processes, environmental assessment in Ontario proceeds case by case without much attention to the overall context or cumulative effects of individual decisions. This approach rests on the increasingly fragile assumption that the world is generally unfolding as it should and attention to the specifics of particular problems and proposals is sufficient. As overall declines in environmental quality become more widely recognized regionally and globally, confidence in the case-by-case approach is undermined.

At the global level, deliberations have focused on how to achieve ecological as well as socio-economic sustainability in the face of expanding poverty and environmental abuse.[22] In Ontario, the most evident controversies have focused on cumulative effects of land-use changes resulting from approval and implementation of many individual undertakings. But here, too, the basic concern is that of sustainability, and the worries about cumulative effects reflect perceptions that the path of conventional "development" — the continuing spread of more intense land uses — is a path of incremental environmental sacrifices leading sooner or later to intolerable effects on ecosystems and communities.

It is, as usual, easier to describe the problem than to identify appropriate solutions. But the immediate implications are clear enough. If the case-by-case approach is insufficient, and if the basic concern is to ensure that the combination of individual decisions leads toward sustainable ecological and socio-economic well-being, then what is needed is a more comprehensive and integrated regime for environmental planning and decision making covering the vast set of undertakings, existing and new, that together determine whether we move closer to, or further away from, the objective of sustainability.

There is an important lesson here for the several jurisdictions in Canada that are now establishing or reforming environmental assessment processes. It is that the recognized models for assessment process design are no longer appropriate, and a new generation of initiatives, extending well beyond the current scope of environmental assessment, is needed.

Expectations for environmental assessment legislation evolved through at least two identifiable stages over the past twenty years. The first stage was impact assessment. It responded to the inadequacies of the reactive regulatory tradition, which concentrated on correcting environmental abuses, by introducing a preventative approach. But it aimed only at identifying and mitigating the potential effects of proposed projects; it focused narrowly on biophysical concerns and treated decision making as a largely technical matter to be handled by experts.

The second stage, represented by the current Ontario process, involves more ambitious and more open environmental assessment efforts. The objective is not just mitigation of pre-selected projects, but good planning that identifies environmentally preferred responses to recognized problems or opportunities. To accomplish this, environmental assessment processes demand integration of broader environmental considerations from the outset of planning. They require examination of purposes, needs, and alternatives, and

---

22   See especially World Commission on Environment and Development, *Our Common Future* (Oxford: Oxford University Press, 1987) (Chair: G.H. Brundtland).

address socio-economic as well as biophysical effects. They also recognize the importance of choices about values and risks, and therefore emphasize effective involvement of public interests as well as experts.

Experiences with land-use planning conflicts in Ontario — and experiences with other conflicts in other places where the cumulative effects and overall sustainability of activities have been questioned — has revealed that this second generation of environmental assessment processes is itself now insufficient, and a third stage of environmental assessment evolution is due.

Stage three would integrate environmental assessment requirements and decision making into a comprehensive regime devoted to achieving community and ecological sustainability. Such a regime could be designed in a variety of ways, but it would have to include means of:

- clarifying the implications of a commitment to sustainability and determining what the standards for "acceptability" should be;

- integrating planning, assessment, and regulatory requirements for all undertakings that affect sustainability, including policies, plans, and programs as well as projects, and existing as well as new activities;

- gathering information on ecosystems and their vulnerabilities as well as on individual resources, and ensuring that decision making respects ecosystemic considerations;

- recognizing areas of ignorance and uncertainty as well as identifying likely effects;

- covering cumulative and global concerns as well as the more immediate implications of individual activities;

- maintaining attention to large-scale issues while empowering the public to participate effectively in decision making; and

- ensuring efficiency.

The changes required would be sweeping, substantial, and difficult. But there is no reason to suppose they are not possible. Indeed, many relevant initiatives have already begun. Several governments are beginning to seek sustainability indicators; steps towards adoption of ecosystem approaches to research and planning have been taken in response to the Great Lakes environmental problems; the otherwise unfortunate federal environmental assessment bill requires attention to cumulative effects;[23] and the draft

---

23   See Bill C-13, *Canadian Environmental Assessment Act*, 3rd Sess., 34th Parl., 1991, ss.11(1)(A) and 14(4).

Yukon *Environment Act* introduced in 1991 outlines a comprehensive regime built on the principles listed above.[24]

The difficulties here must also be weighed against the need. It is certainly a long jump from land-use planning controversies in southern Ontario to a claim that a whole new planning, assessment, and regulatory regime is required in most Canadian jurisdictions. And the conclusion may have to remain tentative until there is better documentation of evidence from elsewhere to confirm the lessons from the Ontario land-use conflicts. But it is evident without much study that concerns about the long-term if not immediate sustainability of resource uses and ecological demands are present and proliferating in most of this country, and that the existing processes for environmentally significant decision making have not been designed to address such concerns. We can hope that many fears of environmental loss are exaggerated and that the existing processes can, with modest adjustments, minimize the larger abuses. But the strength of such hopes seems a weak rationale for risking further losses of environmental quality. For its part, Ontario's Environmental Assessment Advisory Committee favoured environmental prudence and political courage. Summarizing its findings after advising the Minister on several land-use conflict cases, the Committee concluded:

> A major, coordinated effort is required to meet the challenge of establishing mechanisms to ensure overall, long-term protection of the environment without creating costly delays in decision making. This will undoubtedly require a new vision, with major changes in legislation and administration; tinkering is not enough.[25]

---

24   *Environment Act*, S.Y.T. 1991, c.5.

25   *Supra*, note 14, at 33.

APPENDIX 1
Environmental Assessment Advisory
Committee Conclusions About the
Environmental Adequacy of Land-use
Planning and Approvals in Ontario

(excerpt from the Ganaraska report, at 35-37)

The basic principles are simple enough. An environmentally enlightened land-use planning process must meet four basic requirements:

- it must ensure collection of adequate baseline information on environmental resources, their importance and vulnerability;

- it must ensure that land-use plans and planning policies recognize resource preservation and environmental protection goals and needs, identify the cumulative as well as specific impacts to be avoided, and set appropriate development objectives and limitations;

- it must ensure consistent and effective adherence to the identified goals, requirements and limitations, in all decision making on plan amendments and on individual development proposals; and

- it must be sufficiently broad, or at least well-coordinated, to ensure that inter-regional environmental resources (e.g., Watersheds, extensive natural features such as the Oak Ridges Moraine, etc.) are recognized and given comprehensive and consistent protection.

The evidence presented to the Committee in this review of a single, but reasonably representative case, suggests that none of these prerequisites is now met in planning in Ontario, at least not in planning affecting the Ganaraska headwaters, the Oak Ridges Moraine, and the south-central part of the Province subject to urban/suburban expansion pressures:

- Basic environmental information, particularly concerning resources and values potentially threatened by the cumulative effects of more intense land use, is often unavailable. The existing process does not require efforts to collect such information and the prevailing nature of budgetary constraints and spending priorities for municipalities and relevant provincial agencies means that there is little practical likelihood that the information will be collected voluntarily.

- In part because of the inadequacy of the information base, environmental protection needs and appropriate limitations on development are not adequately identified and incorporated in official plans. Regional and municipal authorities responsible for land-use planning are under no effective burden to show how environmental quality will be compromised by the intensity of land use already permitted in official plans or proposed in official plan amendments and project approvals.

- In theory, the preparation of official plans for guiding land use under the

Planning Act, could anticipate and address the problems of cumulative environmental impacts, and other larger environmental planning concerns, at least within the individual planning regions, if a reasonably complete information base were available. But in practice this doesn't happen and the limited protection afforded by official plan designations is vulnerable to incremental erosion. Simply put, the current planning process is not capable of ensuring permanent protection for environmentally important areas.

- Procedures for amending official plans and approving individual projects do not ensure effective recognition of environmental protection needs, especially where cumulative effects may be involved. On the contrary, the current process is structurally inclined to favour incremental elimination of land use restrictions. The current process expects and permits amendments and approvals, which are almost invariably for more intensive land uses, and the proposals are evaluated and granted on a case by case basis. Comments are sought from authorities in a variety of agencies, including ones with environmental responsibilities, but the commentators focus on technical matters and specific concerns according to their agency mandates. Consideration of cumulative effects is apparently rare and unwelcome. Individuals and groups advocating or merely seeking to retain land use restrictions that protect against cumulative environmental damages generally have fewer resources than developers applying to intensify land uses. Moreover, once a decision has been made to dedicate lands to more intensive uses, the results are virtually irreversible, while decisions to maintain limitations are always subject to change.

- Finally, there is little coordination, and consequently little consistency, in the environmental protection efforts of planning authorities even in adjacent regions with important shared resources. Except for the laudable but limited work of the conservation authorities (and that of the Niagara Escarpment Commission regarding one of Ontario's major environmental features), there are few significant efforts to address inter-regional environmental protection needs, and the existing planning process does not provide a mechanism for encouraging inter-regional cooperation on such matters.

As a consequence, the Committee heard that the only reasonably reliable means of ensuring preservation of extensive environmentally important areas is through acquisition. Others suggested, with somewhat less confidence, that preservation prospects for certain specially identified features could be enhanced through creation of further bodies like the Niagara Escarpment Commission. The reality is, however, that funding for land acquisitions by the public sector for environmental protection purposes is not now, nor likely to become, nearly adequate to the task. And while it is conceivable, and perhaps desirable, that special planning commissions be created to protect a few extraordinary inter-regional resources, e.g., the Oak Ridges Moraine, these are not vehicles for general application. In the usual case, neither significant acquisition nor creation of a special planning commission will be feasible.

In sum, the existing land-use planning and approvals process in Ontario is inadequate to the task of maintaining social and ecological quality in the face of "development" pressures.

AN EVALUATION OF JOINT ENVIRONMENTAL IMPACT ASSESSMENTS

Monique Ross*

The years 1989-90 have witnessed extensive development in the use of the environmental impact assessment (EIA) process as a tool in the decision-making process. Fuelled by ever-increasing public concern over environmental deterioration and the endorsement by government of internationally recognized principles of conservation and sustainable development,[1] both the environmental movement and native groups have been lobbying for the consideration of environmental as well as economic factors in the governmental decision-making process. The EIA procedure, which aims at early identification and evaluation in the planning process of the environmental and socio-economic consequences of a project, is generally considered to be an essential element in the "balancing" of various factors affecting a decision. Further, in its public review phase, the EIA process provides a forum in which the public is able to voice their concerns with respect to specific proposals, and thus become involved in the decision-making process. By enabling all concerned parties to exchange their views as to the costs and benefits associated with a proposal, public hearings assist decision makers in defining all the issues at stake, as a result of exposure to perspectives broader than those of the proponent and of government.

The power to conduct environmental impact assessments is inherently linked to the power to legislate over matters of an environmental nature. In the Canadian constitutional context, however, responsibility for environmental matters is not unequivocally attributed to either of the two levels of government. Rather, under the *Constitution Act, 1867*, jurisdiction over certain aspects of environmental concern is inferred from varying heads of power, and there has been and continues to be disagreement as to the exact limits of federal and provincial environmental jurisdiction.[2]

---

*   This essay reflects the law as of June 1991.

1   See, for example, *Report of the National Task Force on Environment and Economy* (Canadian Council of Resources and Environment Ministers, 24 September 1987) (Chair: Gerard Lecayer).

2   See, for example, Dale Gibson, "Constitutional Jurisdiction over Environmental Management in Canada" (1973) 23 U. of T. L.J. at 54; J.W. MacNeill, *Environmental Management* (Ottawa: Information Canada, 1971); A.R. Lucas, "Natural Resources and Environmental Management: A Jurisdictional Primer" *in* Donna Tingley, ed., *Environmental Protection and the Canadian Constitution* (Edmonton: Environmental Law Centre, 1987) at 31.

This shared environmental jurisdiction has resulted in each level of government enacting its own EIA legislation, to ensure the review of projects coming under its authority. In cases in which the federal government assumes the role of proponent of a project, when it has clear proprietary or legislative rights over the lands affected by a proposal (i.e., national parks, Indian reserves), or when it is providing funds for a project pursuant to its spending power, the federal government's authority to conduct an EIA is clear and unlikely to be challenged by provincial governments. Complications arise when a proposal concerns the use of provincial lands, when it is initiated by a provincial government, or when it deals with a provincial resource (constituting what I will later refer to as a "provincial" project), therefore coming under the prime responsibility of the province. In such situations, even though a proposal may have impacts on areas of federal jurisdiction and thereby justify the federal government's scrutiny, federal intervention by means of an EIA of the proposal is more likely to be resisted by the concerned provincial government.

Ever since the development in 1973 of a federal environmental impact assessment process,[3] only a limited number of proposals have undergone a full public review. In recent years environmentalists, native groups, and a concerned public have exerted increasing pressure on the federal government to subject a wider range of proposals to the federal review process. Further, the courts have become involved in the interpretation and analysis of the federal *Environmental Assessment and Review Process Guidelines* (EARP), and a direct result of these judicial decisions has been a sharp increase in the number of proposals now being submitted to public review under the EARP process. From 1974 to 1989, thirty-five proposals were referred to public review at the federal level, with thirty-three of these being completed (averaging two a year), whereas in the years 1989-90 the number of referrals suddenly increased to twenty-four.[4]

However, the federal government appears to be reluctant to become involved in the assessment of projects that have traditionally been viewed as primarily within the constitutional jurisdiction of the provinces.[5] Predictably, most provincial governments strongly oppose what they perceive as an "intrusion" of the federal government into provincial constitutional

---

3   As established in December 1973 by a federal Cabinet directive, which was amended in February 1977 and replaced in 1984 by the *Environmental Assessment and Review Process Guidelines Order*, SOR/84-467, 22 June 1984.

4   Federal Environmental Assessment Review Office, *Bulletin of Initial Assessment Decisions and Panel Reviews* (Editions 6 to 9) at 3 (Panel Reviews).

5   See the discussion in section entitled "Decision to Establish a Joint Review Process".

jurisdiction. The recent intervention in the *Oldman River Dam* case, heard in the Supreme Court of Canada on 19-20 February 1991, of six provinces in support of the Alberta government position[6] provides ample evidence of the standpoint of the provinces in this regard. In that case, all six provinces essentially argued that the application of the federal review process to "provincial" undertakings was unconstitutional.[7]

In an attempt to avoid confrontation and overlaps, the federal government, rather than unilaterally imposing its own review process on projects that are also subject to a provincial review process, has chosen in a number of cases to negotiate with provincial governments the application of a joint review process. At the present time, this appears to be the solution preferred by both levels of government, as reflected in the rapid increase in joint reviews in the past two years.[8] However, questions arise as to the validity, both legal and practical, of cooperative assessments as opposed to the unilateral application by each level of government of its own assessment procedure.

The purpose of this study is, firstly, to discuss the legislative basis of the joint review process; secondly, to examine how joint reviews have functioned in the past; and finally, to assess the success that has been achieved in reaching certain defined objectives. The effectiveness of the joint review process in resolving jurisdictional disputes over environmental management will be assessed, and certain requirements for sound environmental assessments and reviews across jurisdictional boundaries will be defined. The joint review of the proposed Alberta-Pacific pulp mill (Al-Pac) in northern Alberta, which was completed in March 1990, and the joint review of the proposed expansion of the Celgar pulp mill in British Columbia, completed in January 1991, provide major points of reference for this study, since both are examples of federal participation in the assessment of distinctly "provincial" projects.

---

6   These were British Columbia, Manitoba, Newfoundland, New Brunswick, Quebec, and Saskatchewan. Manitoba was, however, more moderate, suggesting that the constitutional conflict could be resolved through joint federal-provincial reviews.

7   A similar argument was made by the Quebec government in an appeal to the Federal Court of Appeal of a National Energy Board decision to issue to Hydro-Québec electricity export licences subject to conditions relating to the environmental assessment and review of the production facilities (*A.G. Que.* v. *National Energy Board*, [1991] 3 F.C. 443, 83 D.L.R. (4th) 146 (F.C.A.)). In deciding in favour of the appellant, Marceau J did not consider this argument.

8   Until 1989, only five joint reviews had been undertaken (four of which were completed); fourteen further joint reviews were either announced or completed in 1989-90. See *supra*, note 4.

LEGISLATIVE BASIS OF THE
JOINT ASSESSMENT PROCESS

The federal *Environmental Assessment and Review Process Guidelines Order* (hereinafter Guidelines Order), while it anticipates the occurrence of federal-provincial reviews, provides minimum guidance as to the form such reviews may take. Section 5(1) sets out the general principle that "where a proposal is subject to environmental regulation, independently of the Process, duplication in terms of public review is to be avoided." Paragraph 2 of the same section further provides that in order to avoid duplication, a public review the results of which must be "available for use in any regulatory deliberations respecting the proposal", must be used in the early stages of development of the proposal. This reflects a concern that repetitive procedures be avoided by communicating the results of the public review to the appropriate regulators in the preliminary phase of the decision-making process. The Guidelines Order contains two other sections that refer to potential federal-provincial cooperation. Section 35(c) provides that it is the responsibility of the Federal Environmental Assessment Review Office (FEARO), "where appropriate, to negotiate provincial or territorial participation in a public review, federal participation in a provincial review, or any other participation in any other cooperative mechanisms." Section 32 states that "any of the requirements or procedures set out in ss.21 to 31 may be varied by the Office in the case of any federal-provincial review or any review that involves special circumstances." The first three of these sections (ss.21-23) define the process by which the Minister of the Environment appoints the members of federal panels established to conduct public reviews. The remaining sections (ss.24-31) contain procedural rules applicable to the conduct of the reviews. The assumption can therefore be made that, if and when federal-provincial reviews occur, not only the rules and procedures but also the manner in which panel members are appointed under the Guidelines Order can be varied. Although there is no explicit authorization in the Guidelines Order to establish joint panels, arguably both ss.32 and 35 may be interpreted as allowing the creation of such panels.

However, much uncertainty surrounds the conduct of joint reviews. In view of the courts' increasing scrutiny of the Guidelines Order, and of the strict adherence to these guidelines that the Federal Court has imposed on the federal government, it is debatable, in the context of a joint review, whether the federal government is empowered to modify the substance of the EARP process. In his judgment in the *Oldman River Dam* case, Justice Stone identified two unique features of the federal review process when he noted, firstly, that the provincial legislation under which environmental impact studies were carried out "places much less emphasis on the role of the public in addressing the environmental implications than does the *Guidelines Order*", and secondly, that "nothing in those laws guarantees the independence of the review panel in any discernible measure, and certainly not in a measure quite like that provided for in s.22 of the *Guidelines Order*."[9] It can be inferred from this ruling that, should a joint panel procedure fail to provide a degree of independence of the panel members and public participation equivalent to that guaranteed by the EARP process, such a procedure could be successfully challenged in court.

The Federal Court decision in the *Oldman River Dam* case has been appealed to the Supreme Court of Canada, which, it is anticipated, will render its judgment within the next few months and will provide insights into the legal nature of the Guidelines Order and the extent of its reach over "provincial undertakings". The Supreme Court decision may prove to be of assistance to FEARO in its attempts to establish cooperative reviews with the provinces. However, a debate regarding the legislative basis of joint reviews under the Guidelines Order would be short-lived, since Bill C-13, the proposed *Canadian Environmental Assessment Act*,[10] is designed to replace the EARP Guidelines and provides a sound legislative basis for joint review processes. Section 37(2) of the proposed Act specifically authorizes the Minister of the Environment to establish a review panel jointly with other jurisdictions, including a provincial government or any provincial body or agency having the power, duty, or function to assess the environmental effects of a project. In addition, in an attempt to limit potential court challenges of the legality of federal-provincial reviews, Bill C-13 stipulates that the assessment conducted by a joint review panel "shall be deemed to satisfy any requirements" of the Act and regulations thereunder (s.39). Nevertheless, as discussed below, Bill C-13 provides insufficient particulars as to the functioning of the joint review process.

At the provincial level, statutes establishing EIA procedures do not, for the most part, provide for any form of joint assessment with the federal government. It is only in recently enacted statutes, such as Alberta's *Natural*

---

9   *Friends of the Oldman River Society* v. *R.* (1990), 5 C.E.L.R. (N.S.) 1 at 33, [1990] 2 F.C. 18 at 50, [1991] 1 W.W.R. 352 at 378, reversing (1989), 4 C.E.L.R. (N.S.) 137, [1990] 2 W.W.R. 150 (F.C.T.D.).

10   The bill was originally introduced as Bill C-78, *An Act to Establish a Federal Environmental Assessment Process*, and received first reading on 18 June 1990. Bill C-78 died on paper on 9 May 1991 and was reintroduced (without changes) as Bill C-13 on 29 May 1991. The discussion of Bill C-13 is based on the Bill as it was originally introduced in the legislature on 29 May 1991. Bill C-13 has since been amended and some of the deficiencies of the joint review process identified in this paper have now been remedied. Bill C-13 received Royal Assent on 13 June 1992 (and awaits proclamation).

Resources Conservation Board Act[11] and Manitoba's *Environment Amendment Act*,[12] that provisions for joint assessments are now to be found.[13]

THE JOINT REVIEW PROCESS

As a result of the almost total absence in both federal and provincial statutes of unambiguous legislative provisions relating to the conduct of joint assessments, decisions pertaining to the establishment of joint panels, the selection of panel members, the definition of terms of reference, and the review process itself have in the past been made at the discretion of the federal and provincial Ministers of the Environment. As indicated previously, proposed or newly enacted EIA statutes or amendments to existing statutes reflect a concern on the part of the federal and some provincial governments to provide specifically for cooperative reviews with other jurisdictions. However, with the exception of Manitoba's, such provisions in regard to the initiation and conduct of joint reviews remain imprecise and continue to grant broad discretionary powers to the concerned Ministers.

Decision to Establish a Joint Review Process

The fact that until 1989 only five joint federal-provincial reviews had ever been established reflects a long-standing tradition of Environment Canada to refrain from involvement in provincial regulatory matters under the primary responsibility of the provinces. Of the four reviews that were completed, three were to assess offshore exploration or development of oil and gas resources,[14] and the fourth was to assess the construction of a nuclear reactor.[15] In all four instances, federal jurisdiction over the projects was clearly established. The fifth review, involving the assessment of a proposed airport expansion, has not yet been completed.[16]

Even though primarily provincial projects had potential impacts on areas

---

11 *Natural Resources Conservation Board Act*, S.A. 1990, c.N-5.5, s.20.

12 *Environment Amendment Act*, S.M. 1990-91, c.15, amending the *Environment Act*, S.M. 1987-88, c.26, s.13.1.

13 See also British Columbia, Ministry of the Environment, *Major Project Review Process — Guidelines* (Victoria, 1991), which guidelines involve federal representatives in the review process and, in the event a review panel is established, provide for the participation of federal appointees in a joint panel.

14 These were the Venture Development Project, Hibernia Development Project, and West Coast Offshore Hydrocarbon Exploration.

15 Second Nuclear Reactor, Point Lepreau.

16 The review concerns the proposed expansion of St-Jean-sur-Richelieu airport. A panel was appointed in May 1987.

of federal responsibility, the federal government relied on the application of provincial processes and endeavoured to ensure that federal concerns were addressed. This position developed as a result of the assumption that the Guidelines Order was merely discretionary in nature and did not impose a binding obligation on federal departments to apply the federal review process.

The 1986 *Agreement Concerning Environmental Impact Assessments of Projects in Alberta with Implications for Canada and Alberta*[17] between the federal and Alberta governments, which has now expired, exemplifies the kind of arrangement, whether tacit or express, that prevailed until recently between the two levels of government. The agreement stipulates that "the environmental assessment procedures of the party within whose constitutional jurisdiction lies the prime responsibility for approval of a development initiative will apply" (s.1). Further, it stipulates that this party will "ensure that the relevant interests and concerns of the other party are included and addressed in the environmental impact assessment procedures" (s.2). Only when "the question of primary responsibility is not self-evident", or in special circumstances, is it provided that both parties may agree to implement a procedure such as "joint or cooperative reviews" (s.3).

The federal government, in the *Rafferty-Alameda*[18] and the *Oldman River Dam*[19] cases, maintained this same position. Although repeatedly requested by individuals and public groups to apply the Guidelines Order to the proposed construction of the dams, the concerned federal departments declined to intervene on the grounds that the projects were primarily provincial undertakings and federal concerns were being adequately taken into consideration. In both cases, the Federal Court rejected arguments by the provincial and federal governments, firstly, that application of the provincial EIA processes and internal referral to the federal Ministers fully satisfied the requirements of the EARP process, and secondly, that provincial procedures were comparable to the federal process. The court held that the Guidelines Order imposed a statutory duty on the federal government and that the latter could not delegate its responsibility to conduct an assessment to a provincial body. A direct result was that the federal government felt compelled to reconsider and revise its previous policy.[20] However, the recent attempt by

---

17   This agreement, dated 15 May 1986, is a subsidiary agreement under the *Canada-Alberta Accord for the Protection and Enhancement of Environmental Quality*, dated 8 October 1975.

18   *Canadian Wildlife Federation v. R.*, [1989] 3 F.C. 309; [1989] 3 C.E.L.R. (N.S.) 287; [1989] 4 W.W.R. 526; aff'd (1990), 4 C.E.L.R. (N.S.) 1 (F.C.A.D.).

19   See *supra*, note 9.

20   See Federal Environmental Assessment and Review Office, *Post-Rafferty Environ-*

the federal government to exclude Alcan's Kemano hydroelectric project in British Columbia from a federal assessment under EARP (which was struck down by the Federal Court on 14 May 1991)[21] attests to the continued reluctance of the federal government to apply the Guidelines Order to certain provincial undertakings.

The proposed construction of the Alberta-Pacific pulp mill can be cited as the first example of federal participation in the assessment of a primarily "provincial" project, scheduled to be built on provincial lands without a commitment of federal funds. Other than the size of the project, the precise reasons for the singling out of this particular pulp mill for a joint review process are unclear, since other proposed major pulp mill development projects in Alberta, such as the Daishowa Peace River pulp mill, announced at the same time, were not subjected to a public review process. It would appear that, initially, the federal government was undecided as to its responsibilities in the application of the Guidelines Order.[22] The decision to review the proposed pulp mill jointly with the provincial government was taken at a late stage, after the initial announcement by the Alberta government that a Review Board would be established to assess the proposal, and the federal decision was certainly influenced both by the Federal Court's decisions and by public concern over the size of the proposed mill.[23]

The Ministerial Order issued by the provincial Minister of the Environment that established the Review Board specifically refers to s.32 of the federal Guidelines Order. However, the requirements of the Guidelines Order with respect to an initial assessment to be performed by the initiating department, and the subsequent referral of the proposal to the federal Minister of the Environment for public review, were not followed in this particular case. The federal Department of the Environment was *post facto* designated as the initiating department.[24]

---

mental Assessment and Review Process (EARP) Implementation Guidelines (Ottawa: Environment Canada, 1989). Item 8(b) of this document reads: "The EARP Guidelines Order does not permit delegation or deferral to the results of provincial processes but it does recognize the possibility of 'federal-provincial' public reviews and it permits FEARO in those circumstances to vary the procedures somewhat from those usually followed in purely federal public reviews. Such variations must however be limited if court challenges to the legitimacy of joint reviews are to be avoided or overcome ...."

21   *Carrier-Sekani Tribal Council* v. *R.* (1992), 6 C.E.L.R. (N.S.) 265 (Fed. T.D.), [1991] 48 Adm. L.R. 102 (Fed. T.D.).

22   Paul Edwards, *The Al-Pac Review Hearings: A Case Study* (Edmonton: Environmental Law Centre, 1990) at 40.

23   *Id.*, at 21 and 38-39.

24   *Id.*, at 40.

In the absence of specific directions in both the Guidelines Order and relevant provincial legislation as to when and on what basis federal-provincial reviews may be undertaken, ministerial discretion with respect to the undertaking of such reviews remains absolute, and the uncertainty and secrecy characterizing the negotiation process are viewed with suspicion by the public.

Under the proposed *Canadian Environmental Assessment Act*, the decision-making process leading to the establishment of joint panels continues to be entirely discretionary. Section 37(2) of Bill C-13 merely provides that the Minister "may" establish a joint review panel when a project is to be assessed by both a federal panel and another jurisdiction.

By comparison, Manitoba's newly enacted *Environment Amendment Act* restrains ministerial discretion to some degree. Firstly, the Act prohibits the Minister from entering into an agreement for the purpose of establishing a joint review process unless he is satisfied that the assessment will be "at least equivalent to the assessment that would otherwise be required under this Act." The Act further specifies the basic requirements to be included in any such agreement with another jurisdiction (s.2). The Manitoba statute also authorizes the Minister, with the approval of the Lieutenant Governor in Council, to enter into an agreement with another jurisdiction "to provide for the use of that jurisdiction's assessment process." In an unprecedented effort to include the public in the negotiation of federal-provincial reviews, Manitoba Environment has circulated for public comments three draft agreements with the federal government for the joint review of three major projects.[25]

Selection of Panel Members

The announcement of a joint public review is generally accompanied or shortly followed by the publication of the names of panel members, comprising federal and provincial representatives, with the chairperson of the panel being jointly appointed or each level of government appointing a co-chairperson.

The size and composition of panels vary. The Al-Pac Review Board, with eight members, was exceptionally large, and in its final report it recommended to the Ministers that they consider reducing the size of future boards.[26] On

---

25   The three projects are: (a) the Conawapa Project, involving the construction and development of the Conawapa generating station on the Nelson River, transmission lines, and access road; (b) the proposed Repap Mill Development and Forestry Plan; and (c) the proposed construction of the North Central Transmission Line (a project cost-shared by Indian and Northern Affairs Canada, Manitoba Hydro, and the Province of Manitoba). As of June 1991, the agreement for a joint review of the Conawapa project had been signed (on 29 May 1991) and the other two agreements were awaiting signature.

26   Alberta-Pacific Environmental Impact Assessment Review Board, *The Proposed*

the other hand, the three-member panel appointed to review the proposed expansion of the Celgar pulp mill in British Columbia acknowledged that it "felt small at times".[27]

With respect to the qualifications of panel members, an imbalance between federal and provincial standards appears to exist. Section 22 of the Guidelines Order requires that panel members be free of conflict of interest and political influence, and further, be knowledgeable and experienced in the subject under review. These requirements are non-existent in most provincial EIA statutes. In certain provinces, the Boards that are responsible for conducting EIAs and holding public hearings are permanent and their members develop a certain degree of expertise that facilitates the conduct of reviews.[28] Further, certain provincial statutes, for example, the Ontario *Environmental Assessment Act*,[29] provide for the appointment of special experts who can assist the Board in respect of any matter before it. However, with the sole exception of Manitoba, the federal requirements that ensure the impartiality as well as the independence of the Boards are unmatched at the provincial level.[30]

The selection of panel members under a joint process, being the result of negotiation between two jurisdictions, does not guarantee the same standard of independence as that provided under the Guidelines Order. Further, the position held by both levels of government, that the number of appointees of each government should reflect the percentage of their responsibility for the project, is arbitrary and, as such, vulnerable to challenge by frustrated parties.

Although the proposed *Canadian Environmental Assessment Act* establishes a legislative basis for the appointment of joint panels, it fails to provide guidance with respect to their composition. Section 38(a) permits the

---

Alberta-Pacific Pulp Mill: Report of the EIA Review Board (Edmonton: Alberta Environment, 1990) at 79.

27   Celgar Expansion Review Panel, *Celgar Expansion Review Panel — Final Report*, submitted under the Federal Environmental Assessment and Review Process and British Columbia Major Project Review Process, February 1991, at 78.

28   The Environmental Assessment Board in Ontario, the Energy Resources Conservation Board (ERCB) in Alberta, or the Bureau d'audiences publiques sur l'environnement in Quebec are examples of such permanent Boards.

29   *Environmental Assessment Act*, R.S.O 1990, c.E.18, s.18(10).

30   Section 13.1(2) of Manitoba's *Environment Act, supra*, note 12, stipulates that, in the event of a joint assessment, the Minister must be satisfied that each panel member is "unbiased and free of any conflict of interest relative to the proposal" and, further, "has special knowledge or experience relevant to the anticipated environmental effects of the proposal."

Minister to "appoint or approve the appointment of a chairperson or co-chairperson and one or more members of a joint panel", without imposing any further requirements. Of greater concern is the fact that the former requirements of the Guidelines Order with respect to independence and impartiality of panel members no longer apply under the proposed Act.[31]

Scope of Joint Reviews

The scope of joint reviews is the most contentious and most critical issue in the joint review process. If indeed the objective of joint reviews is to avoid duplication and overlap, a jointly appointed review panel should be given comprehensive terms of reference and required to assess potential environmental impacts on areas of both federal and provincial jurisdiction. In addition, in order to be meaningful, a joint assessment necessitates consideration not only of narrowly defined environmental effects, but also of the social and economic effects of a proposal.

However, constitutional and political issues arise with respect to the definition of the scope of federal reviews (whether or not they are joint reviews). For example, when a federal public review is triggered under the EARP Guidelines Order, is the federally appointed panel authorized to assess environmental impacts on areas of provincial as well as federal jurisdiction? Further, should the panel be empowered to consider issues such as alternatives to or the need for a project, and to assess economic as well as environmental effects?[32] Does delegation of jurisdiction on the part of both levels of government occur in a joint review process? Some of these questions have been raised before the Supreme Court of Canada in the above-mentioned *Oldman River Dam* case, and by providing answers to some of the queries the court will assist government bodies in defining more clearly the scope of future joint reviews.

In the absence of decisive legislative authority and guidance in either the Guidelines Order or provincial EIA statutes with respect to cooperative reviews, and until scrutinized by the courts, these questions remain unanswered. In practice, two factors have operated against comprehensive assessments. Firstly, the scope of a joint review results from political negotiations between the two levels of government and, as such, reflects a compromise. Despite the fact that the federal and most provincial EIA processes in Canada are only consultative in nature and do not infringe upon

---

31   Under s.30(a) of Bill C-13, only knowledge and experience are required of panel members.

32   The relevance of an "ecological approach" to federal environmental impact assessments is analyzed in J.B. Hanebury, "Environmental Impact Assessment in the Canadian Federal System" 36 McGill L.J., October 1991, at 987-990.

the decision-making power of the respective jurisdictions, provincial governments, when they do agree to cooperate with the federal government in assessing primarily "provincial" projects, tend to be reluctant to permit a comprehensive review for fear of federal interference with their constitutional rights. Secondly, a joint review is, to a certain extent, delineated by existing provincial EIA procedures. Factors such as the statutory definition of "environment" or "environmental impacts", the types of activities subject to assessment, or the requirements with respect to the contents of a proponent's environmental impact statement or report, all contribute to expand or restrict the scope of the assessment conducted under provincial statutes. These factors, which vary considerably with each province, will influence the type of assessment conducted jointly with the federal government. For example, it is unlikely that proposed activities that are not identified in provincial enabling statutes and regulations as requiring an EIA will be assessed under a joint review process.

The joint review of the Alberta-Pacific pulp mill provides an illustration of both of these limitations. One of the criticisms expressed at public hearings with respect to the mandate of the Al-Pac Review Board was the fact that the environmental effects of forest-harvesting activities to be carried out to feed the mill were excluded from the environmental review.[33] The federal government favoured the inclusion of timber-harvesting practices in the review, but met with strong resistance from the provincial government.[34] The latter viewed forest management matters as being within exclusive provincial jurisdiction, and did not favour the application of its own EIA process to such matters.[35] As a result, the Board was required to assess the environmental impacts of timber harvesting only as they relate to Indian reserve lands.

Similar obstacles were encountered by the federal government in the course of its negotiations with the Quebec government for the joint assessment of Phase II of the James Bay Development (the Great Whale Complex). After prolonged delays, the Quebec government finally agreed to combine the federal and provincial processes for the purpose of a public review of the complex, with the exclusion, however, of all access infrastructures and camps, which were to be assessed separately by the provincial government.[36] The intergovernmental agreement reached by the

---

33   *Supra*, note 26, at 5 and in Appendix A.

34   *Supra*, note 22, at 79.

35   Rather, the provincial Department of Forestry, Lands and Wildlife has recently established a public consultation process that is to take place at the time Forest Management Plans are developed by companies holding Forest Management Agreements. This process cannot be compared to an EIA process.

36   The *Federal-Provincial Agreement for the Joint Environmental Assessment of the*

parties has since been struck down by the Federal Court of Canada as an unlawful substitution by the federal government of the EARP Guidelines for its obligations under the JBNQ Agreement.[37] Nevertheless, the fact that the federal government had agreed, against the wishes of the James Bay Crees and various environmental groups, to a separate assessment of important components of the project demonstrates that political barriers can prevent a truly "holistic" joint assessment from occurring.

The proposed *Canadian Environmental Assessment Act* fails to provide sufficient detail with respect to the potential range of cooperative reviews. The only requirement imposed on the Minister with respect to the definition of the scope of a joint review is that "the Minister may fix or approve the terms of reference for the panel" (s.38(b)). Further, Bill C-13 has been criticized in general as narrowing the scope of federal reviews as compared to the Guidelines Order,[38] and entrusting the Minister with broad discretionary powers. If such is the case, and unless Bill C-13 is amended, the "bargaining power" of the federal government in the negotiation of joint reviews with the provinces will be restricted, and the scope of such reviews will continue to be dictated by "political" rather than "ecological" imperatives.

Joint Assessment Procedure

Ministerial announcements that a joint panel has been established to review a proposal usually define the mandate and terms of reference of the panel as well as the general procedure it will follow in the conduct of a public review. Joint reviews typically follow the same pattern as any other federal public review: (a) preparation by the proponent of an environmental impact statement,[39] (b) public distribution of this statement and all relevant information, (c) conduct of public hearings and presentation of written and oral submissions to the panel, (d) preparation by the panel of a written report containing conclusions and recommendations, and submission of the report to the appropriate provincial and federal Ministers, and (e) publication of the report.

Great Whale Project was signed by the Quebec government on 25 November 1990 and by the federal government on 12 February 1991.

37   *Cree Regional Authority* v. *Robinson* (1991), 84 D.L.R. (4th) 51 (Fed. T.D.).

38   The definitions of "environment" and "environmental effect" are thought to be overly restrictive.

39   In virtually all instances, public consultations are held in regard to the development of guidelines for the environmental impact statement (these are known as "scoping" sessions). At this stage, the public identifies priority issues and concerns; however, issues that the panel considers to be beyond its terms of reference, as defined by the Ministers, will not be included in the guidelines.

Within these broad parameters, panels are empowered to adopt their own rules of procedure for the conduct of the hearings. The only restrictions are that the hearings are to be held in a non-judicial and informal manner[40] and that, in certain cases, panels are given a deadline.

The broad flexibility that characterizes informal public hearings has had the advantage of enabling panels to adjust procedures according to the nature of the review being conducted. Further, in the case of public reviews, flexibility is essential to deal with various locations and peoples, and procedures may even be modified for certain sessions of the same review. On the other hand, the informal nature of public hearings has had disadvantages. For example, access by panel members as well as the public to all necessary information in the course of a review is of vital importance. Under the Guidelines Order, government departments that have special knowledge or responsibilities relevant to a proposal are expected to provide a panel with "any available data, information or advice that is requested from them" and with "experts at public hearings ... to make presentations or to respond to questions" (s.36). This provision, however, applies only to federal departments, and joint panels are unable to impose similar obligations on recalcitrant provincial departments. Informal and non-judicial panels lack the power to compel parties or to subpoena them to attend hearings and produce pertinent information. In the case of the Al-Pac review, the provincial Department of Forestry, Lands and Wildlife refused to provide the Board with relevant information in regard to forestry, fish, and wildlife matters and also declined to participate in the hearings.[41] The panel was powerless to constrain the department to provide the necessary information.

EVALUATION OF THE JOINT REVIEW PROCESS

The success achieved by the joint review process can be measured only against certain defined goals that underlie the purpose of the cooperative review, and are thus specific to the joint process itself. In addition, a cooperative review, however modified in form, must nevertheless meet the principal requirements of the public review process as stated by Mr. Justice Stone in the *Oldman River Dam* case: independence and impartiality of the panel, and a wholly public review.

As noted previously, with the main purpose of a cooperative review being to avoid duplication and overlap of assessment procedures, and thus

---

40   Section 27(1) of the Guidelines Order.

41   In the case of the review of the Celgar mill expansion in B.C., the terms of reference of the appointed joint panel did specify that "at its discretion, the Panel may also direct specific information requests to federal and provincial agencies." See *supra*, note 27, at 81.

unnecessary costs and delays, the process should be comprehensive and include an assessment of *all* potential significant impacts, be they environmental, social, or economic, on both federal and provincial areas of responsibility.[42] A further implicit goal of a cooperative review is to enhance the political acceptability of the results of the process (i.e., the final recommendations of the panel), within both levels of government as well as the public, thereby maximizing chances of their implementation. Credibility of the process is a key factor that can be established only if the following requirements are met: (a) complete independence and impartiality of the panel, (b) fairness and openness of the process, and (c) a commitment by both levels of government to seriously consider the final recommendations of the joint panel *prior to* making a decision about the proposal.

The above observations indicate that the level of success achieved by joint reviews can be measured against four main criteria: the comprehensive nature of the assessment undertaken, the qualities of independence and expertise of the selected panel members, the extent and quality of public involvement, and the influence of the panel's recommendations on the final decision with respect to the proposal. I will discuss each of the criteria briefly, drawing general conclusions in regard to the joint review process.

To attempt to analyze the merits of the joint review panels established in 1989-90 would be premature, since the work of most of these panels is ongoing. The joint review agreements that are being negotiated between the federal government and the Manitoba government with respect to three major projects appear to be more comprehensive and provide for greater public involvement than previous joint reviews.[43] In a radical departure from the way in which governments have in the past undertaken cooperative reviews, the Government of Manitoba has circulated for public comments the three draft federal-provincial agreements defining the terms of reference of the reviews to be conducted. This developing concept of cooperative reviews is still at a preliminary stage and, as such, is beyond the scope of this paper.

My evaluation will focus on two fully completed joint reviews in which the federal government participated in the assessment of typically "provincial" projects. These are the construction of the Al-Pac pulp mill in Alberta and the expansion of the Celgar pulp mill in British Columbia.

Comprehensiveness of the Assessment

The comprehensive nature of an assessment can be evaluated by referring

---

42   See the section entitled "Scope of Joint Reviews".

43   See *supra*, note 25.

to the terms of reference as defined jointly by the federal and provincial ministers.

In the case of the Al-Pac review, the terms of reference specifically directed "examination of the potential environmental impacts that relate to areas of the Government of Canada's responsibilities ...."[44] As well, overall impacts of effluent discharges on the river system (a provincial as well as a federal responsibility), including cumulative impacts of discharges from existing and proposed mills on the Peace-Athabasca river system, were to be assessed. The Board was also required to address local concerns. Specifically excluded from the Board's mandate were the environmental impacts relating to timber harvesting for the Al-Pac mill (except as these impacts affected Indian reserve lands), which, according to the terms of reference dated August 1989, were to be "dealt with through the Timber Management Planning Process of the Alberta Department of Forestry, Lands and Wildlife."[45] In its final report, the Board commented that "the suggestion that such a review can be done separately — at a later time by a separate agency — seems ... to violate the principles of good environmental impact assessment and of good management."[46]

A similar comment was included in the final report submitted by the Celgar Expansion Review Panel.[47] The mandate of the panel extended to the assessment of the effects of the proposed expansion of a bleached kraft pulp mill located on the Columbia River. Included in the terms of reference was the availability of surplus wood chips to supply the proposed expansion. However, the company claimed that the mill expansion proposal was not contingent upon the company's securing new sources of fibre supply requiring new timber-harvesting agreements, and, as a result, the impact of the proposal upon the management of provincial forests was excluded from the mandate of the Panel. The Panel found this limitation to be "frustrating to participants and to the Panel, because the excluded issues were so closely interrelated with those the Panel was required to consider."[48] Accordingly, two of the Panel's recommendations with respect to the issue of wood chip supplies deal with forest management concerns. In particular, the Panel recommended to the British Columbia Forest Resources Commission that the public be involved in

---

44   Alberta, Department of the Environment, Ministerial Order No.08/89 (Edmonton: 11 July 1989) at 4.

45   See *supra*, note 26, Appendix A.

46   *Id.*, at 77.

47   See *supra*, note 27.

48   *Id.*, at 79.

the selection of land-use options and forest management practices.[49]

Public interest groups have frequently protested that the terms of reference for EARP reviews are too restrictive and that substantive issues of concern to the public are often omitted.[50] In both of the above-mentioned joint reviews, members of the review panels concurred with these observations. Although not unique to this form of cooperative assessment, the problem of restrictions in regard to terms of reference assumes greater dimensions in the case of joint reviews. Even though both levels of government may feel justified in limiting the scope of a cooperative review, the credibility of the entire joint review process would be increased if the public was involved, at an early stage, in the definition or review of the terms of reference of appointed panels. In this respect, the experience in Manitoba will likely provide an insightful precedent for both the federal and provincial governments.

Independence and Expertise of Panel Members

As noted previously,[51] unlike the EARP Guidelines, and with the exception of Manitoba's provisions, provincial statutes do not guarantee the impartiality and expertise of Review Board members. In the case of the Al-Pac Review Board, the absence of statutory criteria governing the selection of Board members resulted in two of the original provincial appointees withdrawing from the Board on grounds of bias. The final composition of the Review Board, although criticized by some participants, was "reasonably" satisfactory in terms of its expertise and independence.[52] The Review Panel established to assess the proposed expansion of the Celgar pulp mill was composed of only three members, all of whom had the necessary expertise, although the panel commented in its final report that it "could have benefited from a still wider range of knowledge, experience and personal values", and that "this could be accomplished by one or two more members."[53]

---

49   *Id.*, at 14.

50   This issue is discussed in Federal Environmental Assessment and Review Office, *Public Review: Neither Judicial Nor Political, But an Essential Forum for the Future of the Environment*, A Report Concerning the Reform of Public Hearing Procedures for Federal Environmental Assessment Reviews (Ottawa: Supply and Services, 1988) at 23.

51   See the section entitled "Selection of Panel Members".

52   In a self-evaluation of its own composition, the Al-Pac Review Board concluded that, although oversized, it presented a strong combination of expertise. As well, conditions relating to lack of vested interest and availability "were reasonably met". See *supra*, note 26, at 79.

53   *Supra*, note 27, at 78.

In federal-provincial reviews of controversial proposals, the composition of the panel selected is inevitably subject to scrutiny and criticism. In view of the lack of guarantees of impartiality in most provincial processes, it is essential, in future joint reviews, that selection criteria such as those included in the federal Guidelines Order and Manitoba's *Environment Act* not only be maintained, but also be adopted by provincial governments. Unfortunately, the proposed *Canadian Environmental Assessment Act* eliminates previous requirements to ensure impartiality and fails to provide criteria for the appointment of joint panel members.

Extent and Quality of Public Involvement

The credibility and success of public reviews depend largely on the extent and quality of involvement of the citizens affected by the project under review. Public hearings provide a forum for citizens' participation in the decision-making process. Further, their purpose is "to assist decision makers in their traditional roles by identifying the issues at stake, determining the problem areas of a proposal, its justification and other upstream questions from a different angle than that of the initiator."[54]

In the case of the Al-Pac review, the Ministerial Order establishing the Board prescribed that public hearings be held within four weeks of the distribution by Alberta Environment of the deficiency review. The Review Board went to great lengths to attempt to accommodate as many participants as possible, but the quality of the public hearings suffered from the demanding schedule under which the Board was operating. A large number of deficiencies in Al-Pac's environmental impact statement were identified by both levels of government, and the company continued to respond to the deficiencies and to provide new information after the commencement of the hearings. As a result, the participants often had insufficient time to familiarize themselves with the documentation provided and to prepare adequately for the hearings. Several participants expressed concern that the hearings were conducted too rapidly; the Board concurred that the complaints were partly justified and that "a somewhat greater review time should be provided".[55]

Other objections were raised with respect to the provincial funding of participants. Although participant funding is now generally recognized as a prerequisite for the effective participation of citizens affected by a project, it becomes meaningful only if provided early enough in a review to allow individuals or groups to prepare for the hearings. In the case of the Al-Pac review, the late date on which the provincial government finally announced

---

54   *Supra*, note 50, at 1.

55   *Supra*, note 26, at 76.

that funds would be awarded was heavily criticized. Also criticized was the fact that funding was channelled through local authorities, an unusual procedure that led to further delays in the awarding of funds and that was unjustifiable in view of the fact that several of the authorities had expressed opinions favourable to construction of the mill.

The Celgar Expansion Review Panel shared the concerns of the Al-Pac Review Board with respect to the timing of the review. While acknowledging that panels must proceed expeditiously, the Review Panel expressed the view that "governments, proponents and affected communities must expect that competent, thorough, independent reviews need the freedom from externally imposed deadlines", and cautioned against setting unrealistic deadlines.[56] However, the deadlines imposed on the Celgar Panel were not as stringent as in the Al-Pac case. Interested parties were allowed forty-five days from the date of distribution of the company's submission to submit their written comments to the Panel. The Panel was able to schedule its hearings as soon as it was satisfied that an adequate information base had been established. No participant funding was provided for the Celgar review.

Influence of Panel's Recommendations

The influence of a panel's conclusions and recommendations on governmental decisions with respect to a proposal constitutes a test of the effectiveness of the review process. In Canada, with the exception of Ontario,[57] the EIA process is consultative in nature, since federal and provincial Ministers, acting in a discretionary capacity, are entitled to disregard the recommendations of an appointed panel.

In the case of the Al-Pac review, the recommendations of the Board were only partially adhered to. Despite the provincial Minister of the Environment's public declaration that the provincial government would accept the Board's recommendations, the Premier of Alberta later criticized the Board for failing to assess adequately the information presented. Al-Pac submitted a revised proposal that was re-evaluated by a scientific panel and subsequently approved by the provincial government. Although the joint review has been viewed by many as a failure because the construction of the mill, albeit in a modified form, was approved against the recommendations of the Board, the process did compel the company to adopt state-of-the-art in-mill technology, resulting in a much less polluting plant than would otherwise

---

56 *Supra*, note 27, at 79.

57 Similar to the Ontario Board, Alberta's Natural Resources Conservation Board is, further to a review of a project, empowered to grant (with the prior authorization of the Lieutenant Governor in Council) or refuse approvals (*Natural Resources Conservation Board Act*, S.A. 1990, c.N-5.5, s.9).

have been built. In addition, the Board's recommendations in regard to the conduct of extensive river studies were adopted by both levels of government and led to a joint announcement that a series of major river studies would be undertaken in northern Alberta, by the federal, Alberta, and Northwest Territories governments. The federal government, while endorsing the final report of the Board, did not dissociate itself from the provincial position, since it agreed to a further scientific and technical review of Al-Pac's revised proposal. With respect to the issue of a public review of the Forest Management Agreement being negotiated between Al-Pac and Alberta Forestry, Lands and Wildlife, the federal government declared that it "would welcome the opportunity to participate in these reviews" and that, should a public review under EARP be required, "a mechanism for a joint review with Alberta" would be sought.[58]

The Celgar review achieved more striking success; after the Panel's final recommendations were released, the federal and provincial Ministers announced that the project could proceed on condition that the Panel's recommendations to the company be met. It remains to be seen whether specific recommendations the Panel addressed to the federal and provincial governments concerning the undertaking of air and water quality studies and programs, and to British Columbia's Forest Resources Commission concerning issues of forest management, will also be followed.

CONCLUSIONS

The joint review process has, to date, produced mixed results. One of the fundamental weaknesses of the joint review process is the fact that it has no defined legislative basis in either the Guidelines Order or most provincial EIA statutes. The practice of conducting joint reviews has evolved as a policy and taken the form of *ad hoc*, informal agreements between federal and provincial governments. It is noteworthy that since the Federal Court decisions in the *Rafferty-Alameda* and *Oldman River Dam* cases, Environment Canada has played a more active role in the assessment of an increasing number of provincial projects that have potential impacts on areas of federal responsibility. However, the extent and nature of federal-provincial cooperation is highly dependent on the willingness of provincial governments to participate in joint assessments with the federal government, and complex issues as to exclusive constitutional jurisdiction and federal intrusion into

---

58   The "Federal Government Response to the Alpac Review Board Final Report", issued by Environment Canada and dated 12 July 1990, states that "since forest harvesting activities may affect fish and fish habitat, the Department of Fisheries and Oceans has a decision-making authority under the *Fisheries Act*, and will be screening such activities under EARP." As of June 1991, the Department of Fisheries and Oceans is conducting an internal review of the Forest Management Agreement.

provincial matters tend to weaken the entire cooperative process. Further, the lack of legislative guidelines for the conduct of joint reviews has hampered the effectiveness of the reviews.

Legal challenges to federal and provincial applications of EIA processes have multiplied in recent years, resulting in increased uncertainty within government departments, industry, and the public as to the exact role of federal and provincial EIAs in the decision-making process. The Federal Court's interpretation of the Guidelines Order, which is the driving force behind the federal government's increasing involvement in assessment of provincial projects, is being contested by several provincial governments. It is anticipated that the Supreme Court of Canada's decision in the *Oldman River Dam* case will provide responses to some of the legal issues raised concerning the nature and scope of the federal process. Up to the present time, the joint review process has not been disputed in court; nevertheless, the situation may soon change, given the increasing use and uncertain legal foundations of this process.

The recent court actions have induced federal and provincial governments to legislatively strengthen and better define their EIA processes.[59] As noted earlier, cooperative mechanisms tend to be specifically included in new statutes. However, Manitoba is, as yet, the only province to have established detailed legislative provisions for the conduct of joint reviews, which guarantee extensive public participation and the conduct of an assessment at least equivalent to that required by the provincial statute.

At the federal level, the proposed *Canadian Environmental Assessment Act*, while providing a legislative basis for the joint review process, falls short of establishing complete and precise guidelines for the implementation of cooperative reviews that would preserve the integrity of the federal process. Under the proposed Act, the joint review process remains substantially discretionary in nature and fails to provide sufficient guarantees of comprehensiveness, independence, and openness of the process. While it is desirable for federal and provincial Ministers to retain a certain degree of discretion and authority in the negotiation of joint reviews, the lack of explicit federal standards with respect to such issues as the appointment of panel members, the scope of the review to be undertaken, or the nature of public involvement, can only foster inconsistencies and discrepancies in the conduct

---

59   Mention has already been made of Alberta's and Manitoba's statutes (*supra*, notes 11 and 12). In addition, Alberta has tabled Bill C-53, the *Environmental Protection and Enhancement Act*, 3rd Sess., 22nd Leg. Alta., 1991, and the provinces of British Columbia, Ontario, Quebec, and Saskatchewan are in the process of revising their EIA legislation.

of joint reviews across Canada. Further, the failure to involve all concerned parties at an early stage in the review process may undermine the credibility of the entire process. In Justice Muldoon's words, the public review should be "the antithesis of secret and unpublicized arrangements in these matters of quintessentially public interest."[60]

The public as well as legal experts tend to view constitutional disputes over environmental matters, and more specifically the conduct of environmental impact assessments, as having to be resolved through cooperative processes that preserve a strong role for the federal government. The challenge facing the federal and provincial governments is to promulgate legislation establishing high standards of environmental impact assessment and guaranteeing that these standards will be upheld in cooperative reviews undertaken with other jurisdictions. In the absence of such guarantees, it is unlikely that the joint review process will successfully resolve jurisdictional conflicts over environmental impact assessments, nor will its credibility in the eyes of the public be established.

---

60 *Canadian Wildlife Federation* v. *R., supra*, note 18.

RESOURCE-USE CONFLICTS: THE ROLE OF THE COMMON LAW

Adrian J. Bradbrook

In Canada and other western industrialized nations, the traditional choice of power generation is between coal, oil, gas, and nuclear fission. Until now, power generation has been a highly centralized function where the choice of fuels is made by the relevant power companies with little or no public involvement in the decision-making process.[1] In the case of fossil fuels and nuclear energy, the exploitation, production, and allocation of the various energy resources have been controlled for many decades by comprehensive statutory management regimes.[2] For these reasons, in the area of energy supplies there is seldom (if ever) any resource-use conflict that results in litigation and little (if any) scope for the involvement of the common law.

In future, we are likely to see a steady change in the sources of power generation. There are several reasons for this. First, as recent events in the Middle East have shown, the price stability and availability of oil on the world trading markets cannot be assured. Canada and most other industrialized nations are not self-sufficient in oil, and unless alternative sources of energy are found, increasing imports will be required. Secondly, there is the greenhouse effect. If the Toronto conference target of a 20 percent reduction in the emission of greenhouse gases from 1988 levels by the year 2005 is to be achieved, drastic curtailment of the use of fossil fuels and increased use of alternative fuels will be required. Thirdly, the costs of building large-scale fossil-fuel-fired or nuclear power stations have become colossal, and significantly aggravate the problem of foreign indebtedness. Finally, there is the environmental factor. Fossil-fuel-fired power generation is a significant contributor to acid rain and smog,[3] and was a subject of concern to the World Commission on Environment and Development (the Brundtland Report).[4] The

---

1 In North America, the only public involvement is the power to challenge investment decisions by public utilities as being imprudent and so to exclude such expenditures from the rate base. See, for example, *Utilities Commission Act*, S.B.C. 1980, c.60; *Public Utilities Board Act*, R.S.A. 1980, c.P-37.

2 Nuclear energy: *Atomic Energy Control Act*, R.S.C. 1985, c.A-16; Oil and gas: *Petroleum Resources Act*, R.S.O. 1980, c.377; *Mines and Minerals Act*, R.S.A. 1980, c.M-15; *Petroleum and Natural Gas Act*, R.S.B.C. 1979, c.323; *Mines Act*, R.S.M. 1987, c.M-160; *Petroleum and Natural Gas Regulations*, Sask. Reg. 8/69; *Crown Minerals Act*, S.S. 1984-85-86, c.C-50.2.

3 See, for example, J. Brunnée, *Acid Rain and Ozone Layer Depletion: International Law and Regulation* (New York: Transnational, 1988).

4 World Commission on Environment and Development, *Our Common Future* (Oxford:

Commission strongly urged the adoption of energy efficiency and conservation measures and recommended that the use of fossil fuels should not unnecessarily and unreasonably deplete the resources available to future generations.[5]

For these reasons, the 1990s and the early part of the next century are likely to produce a silent revolution in energy usage. We may witness a dramatic increase in the use of non-fossil-fuel sources of energy such as hydro-power, solar energy, wind energy, geothermal energy, and ocean energy. The exact mix of the energy sources will vary from country to country based on climatic, geographic, and geological factors. This change will be accompanied by an emphasis on energy conservation in all sectors of the economy — transport, industry, buildings, and appliances. Indeed, as energy conservation offers the greatest potential for financial savings to both power generators and consumers,[6] it is likely to become the major issue of energy policy and planning in the near future. Because of the nature and characteristics of most forms of renewable energy, the envisaged changes will result in power generation becoming more decentralized. For example, individuals can install various kinds of solar and wind energy equipment on their own properties and can become partially or totally independent of the local power companies. The anticipated revolution will also likely increase the number of private electricity generators and the scope for independent power production. All these changes will have legal implications for both power generators and power consumers.

In general, renewable energy, energy conservation, and independent power production are largely uncontrolled by legislation in most countries. In Canada, there is no legislation at all regarding solar and wind energy, and very little governing energy conservation. As for independent power production, only the Province of Alberta has intervened to ensure that this source of power generation is encouraged.[7] Even in Australia, which has a very high incidence of solar radiation, solar access controls exist only in a few municipalities in three states — New South Wales, South Australia, and Western Australia.[8] Amongst common law countries, the United States is the

---

Oxford University Press, 1987) (Chair: G.H. Brundtland). See also J. Owen Saunders, ed., *The Legal Challenge of Sustainable Development: Essays from the Fourth Institute Conference on Natural Resources Law* (Calgary: Canadian Institute of Resources Law, 1990).

5   World Commission on Environment and Development, *id.*, at 213.

6   See generally, C. Flavin & N. Lenssen, *Beyond the Petroleum Age: Designing a Solar Economy* (Worldwatch Paper 100) (Washington, D.C.: Worldwatch Institute, 1990).

7   *Small Power Research and Development Act*, S.A. 1988, c.S-13.75.

8   The current Australian solar access controls are discussed in Adrian J. Bradbrook,

only country that has taken significant legislative action in these areas, although there is still considerable scope for further reforms.[9]

Numerous reports on renewable energy and energy conservation have urged the need for new legislation governing these resources.[10] In the absence of such legislation, however, the common law has a role to play in resolving disputes between independent power producers and utility companies and ensuring access to the various resources. This paper will discuss the role of the common law in this area.

If the common law is to be effective in this area, three factors must exist: appropriate and effective common law remedies must be available; the judiciary must be sympathetic to the relevant policy issues; and the subject matter of the disputes must be compatible with the common law process. Unfortunately, as we will see below, there are problems with all three factors. Appropriate and effective common law remedies only partially exist; the judiciary's past track record in dealing with the policy issues regarding independent power production is patchy; and the subject matter of the disputes in this area appears to be largely incompatible with the common law process.

"Australian and American Perspectives on the Protection of Solar and Wind Access" (1988) 28 Natural Res. J. 229 at 254-259.

9   The U.S. writings in this area are voluminous. See, for example, Steven B. Plass, "A Look at Federal and State Cogeneration and Small Power Production Regulations" (1983) 3 J. Energy L. and Policy 329; Linda Elizabeth Buck & Lee M. Goodwin, eds., *Alternative Energy — The Federal Role* (Colorado: McGraw-Hill, 1982); Sandy F. Kraemer, *Solar Law* (Colorado Springs: Shepard's, 1978); John H. Minan & William H. Lawrence, eds., *Legal Aspects of Solar Energy* (Lexington, Mass.: Lexington Books, 1981) at 179-196; Tamara C. Sampson & R. Alta Charo, "Access to Sunlight: Resolving Legal Issues to Encourage the Use of Solar Energy" (1986) 11 Columbia J. Env. L. 417; L. Coit, *Wind Energy: Legal Issues and Institutional Barriers* (Solar Energy Research Institute) (Colorado: U.S. Dept. of Energy, 1979); Steven D. Naumann, "Form Over Function: The Law of Hot Water" (1983) 4 J. Energy L. and Policy 205; Owen Olpin & Barton H. Thompson, "Water Law and the Development of Geothermal Resources" (1982) 14 Nat. Res. Lawyer 635.

10   See, for example, National Energy Research, Development and Demonstration Council, *Legal Aspects of the Practical Application of Solar Energy Technology in Australia* (Report No.452) (Canberra, 1985); Ontario. Dept. of Energy, *Perspectives on Access to Sunlight* (Toronto: 1986); U.S. Solar Energy Research Institute, *Solar Envelope Zoning: Application to the City Planning Process* (Report SERI/SP-281-1651) (1980); California Energy Commission, *California's Appliance Standards: An Historical Review, Analysis, and Recommendations* (Report P400-83-020) (1983); Environmental Law Institute, *Legal Barriers to Solar Heating and Cooling of Buildings* (Washington: Books for Business, 1981); R.J. Noun, *Product Liability and Small Wind Energy Conversion Systems: An Analysis of Selected Issues and Policy Alternatives* (Report SERI/TR-354-365) (Washington, D.C.: U.S. Dept. of Energy, 1979); N.Z. Ministry of Energy, *Geothermal Resources: A Policy and Management Framework* (Wellington: 1986).

The inadequacies of the common law will be discussed separately in the context of each of the energy technologies under review.

SOLAR ENERGY

The rapid development in recent years of solar energy technology has outstripped the law's ability to guarantee access to the direct rays of the sun for solar collector panels. The nub of the problem is that in Canada and other non-tropical regions of the world the sun is never overhead: sunlight reaching a solar device or the solar user's land must pass through the skyspace of one or more neighbouring properties. During this passage through the neighbour's skyspace, the sunlight may be blocked by vegetation or a building, shading the solar collector panels.[11] There is little incentive for a private landowner or an industry to install a solar appliance if the efficiency of the appliance can be ruined at any time by the erection of a building or the planting of vegetation on neighbouring land. Some form of legal protection for the solar user must be found.

In the absence of legislation, it appears that the relevant common law remedies for the protection of solar access are easements, restrictive covenants, and the law of nuisance. It is instructive to examine each of these remedies in order to determine their effectiveness in the present context.

Easements

One possible method for a solar user to safeguard his right of solar access is to obtain an express easement. Is such an easement enforceable?[12] An easement of solar access may be treated by the courts as an extension of the easement of light or may be regarded as a separate, novel type of easement. Its classification will affect the enforceability of such an agreement. For this reason its enforceability as an easement of light and as a novel type of easement must be considered separately.

Enforceability as an
Express Easement of Light

Although express easements of light are recognized at common law,[13]

---

11   For a fuller discussion of this point, see A.J. Bradbrook, *Solar Energy and the Law* (Sydney: Law Book, 1984) c.2; S.F. Kraemer, *Solar Law* (Colorado Springs: Shepard's, 1978).

12   For a more detailed discussion of this issue, see Marie-Ann Bowden, "Protecting Solar Access in Canada: The Common Law Approach" (1985) 9 Dalhousie L.J. 261; A.J. Bradbrook, "The Development of an Easement of Solar Access" (1982) 5 U. New South Wales L.J. 229; Kraemer, *id.*, c.4; John William Gergacz, "Legal Aspects of Solar Energy: Easements for Sunlight and Individual Solar Energy Use" (1980) 18 American Business L.J. 414.

13   See, for example, *Commonwealth* v. *Registrar of Titles for Victoria* (1918), 24 C.L.R. 348 (H.C.).

this may not assist the solar user, as there is still some doubt as to the correct test for determining when an action for nuisance for breach of the easement of light will lie. The established authorities on the quantum of light to which the dominant owner is entitled have suggested that nuisance will not lie for interference with the light as long as sufficient light remains for the purposes of illumination.[14] The amount of light required by a solar user is far in excess of this standard. The classic statement of the law is that of Lord Lindley, who stated in Colls v. Home and Colonial Stores Ltd.:

> [G]enerally speaking an owner of ancient lights is entitled to sufficient light according to the ordinary notions of mankind for the comfortable use and enjoyment of his house as a dwelling-house, if it is a dwelling-house, or for the beneficial use and occupation of the house if it is a warehouse, a shop, or other place of business. The expressions "the ordinary notions of mankind", "comfortable use and enjoyment", and "beneficial use and occupation" introduce elements of uncertainty; but similar uncertainty has always existed and exists still in all cases of nuisance.[15]

Other cases, however, have suggested that nuisance may lie in certain circumstances even if the amount of light remaining is suitable for illumination. In Ough v. King[16] the Court of Appeal held that there was no fixed standard of lighting that can be used as a yardstick by which to assess whether the diminution of light by shading is an actionable nuisance. Lord Denning stated that the notions of mankind on the subject of light have changed and are changing; a judge is entitled to have regard for the locality and the higher standards expected for comfort as the years go by.[17]

The most recent and significant case on this point is Allen v. Greenwood.[18] In this case, the plaintiffs and the defendants were neighbours. The plaintiffs had constructed a greenhouse alongside the boundary over twenty years ago. The defendants later parked a caravan alongside the greenhouse on their side of the boundary and erected a fence only six inches from the greenhouse. The combined effect of the fence and caravan was to deprive half of the greenhouse of direct sunlight and to make it unsuitable for the growing of tomatoes and potted plants. The plaintiffs sought by injunction the removal of the fence and the caravan, arguing that they had a prescriptive right to sufficient light to enable the greenhouse to be used for the cultivation

---

14   *Charles Semon and Co.* v. *Bradford Corporation*, [1922] 2 Ch. 737; *Horton's Estate Ltd.* v. *James Beattie Ltd.*, [1927] 1 Ch. 75.

15   *Colls* v. *Home and Colonial Stores*, [1904] A.C. 179 at 208.

16   *Ough* v. *King*, [1967] 3 All E.R. 859 (C.A.). See also *Lazarus* v. *Artistic Photographic Co.*, [1897] 2 Ch. 214.

17   *Ough* v. *King*, *id.*, at 861.

18   *Allen* v. *Greenwood*, [1979] 1 All E.R. 819 (C.A.).

of plants and vegetables. To achieve this purpose the direct rays of the sun were required. At first instance, Blackett-Ord V.C. dismissed the action on the ground that a greenhouse requires a special amount of light and that the amount of light reaching the greenhouse was still sufficient to enable it to be used for the ordinary purposes of a room in a house. On appeal, however, this decision was reversed by the Court of Appeal on the basis that the plaintiffs had acquired by prescription the right to that degree of light, including the sun's direct rays, necessary for the growth of plants in the greenhouse. The court held that the correct test of the quantum of light that must remain in order to avoid liability for nuisance differs according to the nature of the building. If the building is a dwelling-house, the measure of light must be sufficient to maintain reasonable standards of comfort as a dwelling-house. Similarly, if the building is a greenhouse, the measure must be related to the reasonably satisfactory use of the building as a greenhouse. Goff LJ stated:

> I confess for my own part that I do not wholly understand the conception of an ordinary amount of light in the abstract. It seems that what is ordinary must depend on the nature of the building and to what it is ordinarily adapted. If, therefore, the building be, as it is in this case, a greenhouse, the normal use of which required a high degree of light, then it seems to me that that degree is ordinary light.[19]

Based on this dictum, a solar user could argue that as the normal use of a solar collector requires a very high degree of light, that degree is ordinary light.

Although the matter is still not free from doubt, based on these recent authorities it seems that the old fixed standard of illumination has been discarded and that where an express easement of light exists, the degree of protection from shading will depend on the use to which the building is put.

On one analysis, the case of *Allen* v. *Greenwood* can be construed as being favourable to the recognition of an easement of solar access as an extension of the easement of light. The fact that the old fixed standard of illumination appears to have given way to a more flexible standard of quantum of light is highly significant. The solar user could argue that under the easement of light he would be entitled to the degree of protection necessary to ensure the efficient operation of a solar appliance (i.e., direct access to the sunlight for several hours every day). The other significant factor in *Allen* v. *Greenwood* is that under the easement of light the dominant owner was held to be entitled to receive the direct rays of the sun where there is proof that this is necessary for the use of the building on the dominant land.

Despite these factors, however, parts of the same judgment strongly suggest that the court did not intend its decision to apply in the solar energy

---

19   *Id.*, at 825.

context. In two separate passages there are dicta to the effect that a distinction must be drawn between the heat and other properties of the sun and the light that emanates from it. Goff LJ, with whom Orr LJ agreed, stated, "On other facts, particularly where one has solar heating ... it may be possible and right to separate the heat, or some property of the sun, from its light, and in such a case a different result might be reached."[20]

Goff LJ referred to this issue again in another part of his judgment when dealing with a hypothetical argument made by counsel for the defendants that an owner of a swimming pool, part of which is fortuitously warmed by sunlight coming through a window, could have no cause of action based on an easement of light if the sunlight were blocked and the benefit of the heat or radiant properties of the sun were lost. Goff LJ agreed that in these circumstances the owners of the swimming pool would have no cause of action for the removal of the chance warmth provided that fully adequate light for the enjoyment of the swimming pool remained.[21]

Based on these dicta, it is highly doubtful whether the express easement of light is sufficiently broad to include solar access for solar energy purposes.

Enforceability as a
Separate Novel Easement

The dicta of Goff LJ in *Allen* v. *Greenwood* strongly suggest that an easement of solar access for solar energy purposes, if it exists at all, will be regarded by the courts as a novel type of easement. This issue was not settled in that case, however. Both Goff and Orr LJJ expressly stated that they were leaving open the question whether solar heating would be appropriate for the creation of a new type of easement.[22]

If the right of solar access is to be regarded as a separate easement, it must satisfy the essential characteristics of an easement at common law. Based on the decision in *Re Ellenborough Park*,[23] the essential characteristics are as follows:

1. there must be a dominant and a servient tenement;

2. an easement must "accommodate" the dominant tenement;

---

20   *Id.*, at 828.

21   *Id.*, at 827.

22   See *supra*, note 18 and accompanying text.

23   *Re Ellenborough Park*, [1956] 1 Ch. 131. See also *Vannini* v. *Public Utilities Commission of Sault Ste. Marie*, [1973] 2 O.R. 11 (Ont. H.C.), 32 D.L.R. (3d) 661.

3. the dominant and servient owners must be different persons; and

4. the right must be capable of forming the subject matter of a grant.[24]

Other cases have added the further requirement that the right must not amount to exclusive use of the servient tenement.[25] I submit that these requirements are satisfied by the right of solar access. The only possible doubt relates to the fourth requirement, the meaning of which, in essence, is that the right claimed as an easement must not be phrased widely or vaguely. In light of the decision in *Commonwealth* v. *Registrar of Titles for Victoria*[26] that a right to an undefined flow of air can constitute an easement if created by express grant or reservation, *a fortiori* a right to solar access in favour of specified solar collector panels should have no difficulty in overcoming this requirement.

Even though the right of solar access satisfies these essential characteristics, such a right may still not constitute an easement at common law. The issue is whether novel easements of a negative nature (which, if recognized, is how the easement of solar access would be classified) can be recognized at common law. It is clear that the class of possible easements is not closed altogether. Authority for this proposition is *Attorney-General of Southern Nigeria* v. *John Holt & Co. Ltd.*, where Lord Shaw of Dunfermline, delivering judgment of the Privy Council, stated:

> The law must adapt itself to the conditions of modern society and trade, and there is nothing in the purposes for which the easement is claimed inconsistent in principle with the right of easement as such. This principle is of general application, and was so treated in the House of Lords in *Dyce* v. *Hay* [(1852) 1 Macq. 305] by Lord St. Leanords L.C., who observed: "The category of servitudes and easements must alter and expand with the changes that take place in the circumstances of mankind."[27]

There is, however, some authority for the proposition that although the categories of positive easements are unrestricted, no new negative easements can be created. The major case in point is *Phipps* v. *Pears*.[28] In this case, a house had been built in 1930 with its flank wall so close to the wall of the adjoining house that it did not need to be completely weatherproofed. In 1962 the defendant, the owner of the adjoining property, demolished his building,

---

24   The meaning of this requirement is discussed in *Dukart* v. *District of Surrey* (1978), 86 D.L.R. (3d) 609 (S.C.C.).

25   *Thorpe* v. *Brumfitt* (1873), L.R. 8 Ch. App. 650; *Thomas W. Ward Ltd.* v. *Alexander Bruce (Grays) Ltd.*, [1959] 2 Lloyd's Rep. 472 (C.A.).

26   *Commonwealth* v. *Registrar of Titles for Victoria* (1918), 24 C.L.R. 348 (H.C.).

27   *A.G. of Southern Nigeria* v. *John Holt Co.*, [1915] A.C. 599 at 617.

28   *Phipps* v. *Pears*, [1965] 1 Q.B. 76.

causing the unprotected wall to become exposed to the elements. The Court of Appeal unanimously rejected the claim for a prescriptive easement on the basis that an easement to be protected from the weather did not exist at law. Lord Denning M.R. stated: "seeing that it is a negative easement, it must be looked at with caution. Because the law has been very chary of creating any new negative easements."[29]

This possible rule that no new negative easements can be created was justified by Lord Denning on the ground that if the law were otherwise it would restrict the development of property. However, this is also true of some positive easements, such as a right of way, and restrictive covenants. In this latter respect, it is noteworthy that Lord Denning himself pointed out that a restrictive covenant might have been used in the context of the facts in *Phipps* v. *Pears* to produce the desired result. While the restriction of the redevelopment of property is a legitimate concern, it can be argued that the necessary protection could be achieved more appropriately by a judicious use of the procedures established for the discharge and modification of existing easements than by the establishment of a blanket prohibition against all negative easements.

It is still unclear whether novel easements of a negative character may be created in Canada. The more likely position is that novel easements can be created, in the absence of any Canadian authority to the contrary, despite the decision in *Phipps* v. *Pears*. This conclusion avoids the creation of unnecessary divisions in the law and is consistent with the following dictum of Griffith CJ of the High Court of Australia in *Commonwealth* v. *Registrar of Titles for Victoria*:

> In the course of argument I referred to several possible easements novel in kind. For instance, an easement or servitude for the passage of aeroplanes through the super adjacent air of the servient tenement to a landing place, for the passage of an electric current through suspended wires passing through that air, for the free passage of the flash from a heliograph station. *Why not also the sun's rays?*[30]

Summary

Based on the above analysis, it appears probable, although by no means certain, that express easements of solar access will be recognized as valid by the courts. Unfortunately, the issue has not yet been litigated. In many American states legislation has been enacted that specifically affirms the validity of such an easement.[31] It is significant that among common law

---

29   *Id.*, at 82-83.

30   *Commonwealth* v. *Registrar of Land Titles for Victoria* (1918), 24 C.L.R. 348 at 354 (H.C.) [emphasis added].

31   The states with legislation authorizing express solar easements are Alaska: Alaska Stats.

jurisdictions it is only in these states that easements of solar access are known to exist. Thus, in the absence of legislative recognition, the public and the legal profession appear to be reluctant to rely on the uncertainties of the common law.

Perhaps the greatest difficulty here is practical rather than theoretical. Even if an express easement of solar access is recognized at common law it may be difficult to obtain, as a neighbour may be unsure of the consequences of relinquishing rights to a portion of the airspace over his land. The possibility exists that one landowner, realizing that his consent is essential for the solar user, may hold out for an unreasonable sum of money as the price for granting a solar access easement. This could lead to a huge windfall gain for a landowner who may never have had any intention of developing his property to the extent that the access of sunlight to neighbouring property would be infringed.

Restrictive Covenants

Like easements, restrictive covenants are a consensual transaction and may be negotiated between adjoining landowners or between a developer of a subdivision and the purchasers of individual blocks of land.[32]

Like any other covenant, a solar covenant entered into by negotiations between two neighbours will be enforceable between the original contracting parties under normal contractual principles. If either party assigns his interest to a third party, the covenant may be enforceable under the doctrine in *Tulk* v.

---

§34.15.145 (1985); California: Cal. Civ. Code §801.5 (West 1982); Colorado: Colo. Rev. Stat. §§38-32.5-100.3 to 38-32.5-103 (1982); Florida: Fla. Stat. Ann. §704.07 (West 1979); Georgia: Ga. Code Ann. §§44-9-20 to 44-9-23 (1987); Idaho: Idaho Code §55-615 (1979); Illinois: Ill. Ann. Stat. ch.96 §7303(f) (Smith-Hurd Supp. 1987); Indiana: Ind. Code Ann. §§32-5-2:5-1 to 3 (Burns 1980); Iowa: Iowa Code Ann. §§93.22 to 93.25 (West Supp. 1987); Kentucky: Ky. Rev. Stat. §381.200 (Baldwin Supp. 1987); Minnesota: Minn. Stat. Ann. §500.30 (West Supp. 1988); Missouri: Mo. Ann. Stat. §442.012 (Vernon 1986); Montana: Mont. Code. Ann. §§70-17-301 to 70-17-302 (1987); Nebraska: Neb. Rev. Stat. §§66-901 to 66-914 (1986); Nevada: Nev. Rev. Stat. §§111.370 to 111.380 (1986); New Jersey: N.J. Stat. Ann. §§46:3-24 to 46:3-26 (West Supp. 1987); North Dakota: N.D. Cent Code §§47-05-01.1 to 47-05-01.2 (1978); Ohio: Ohio Rev. Code. Ann. §5301.63 (Page 1981); Oregon: Or. Rev. Stat. §§105.880 to 105.895 (1984); Rhode Island: R.I. Gen. Laws §§34-40-1 to 34-40-2 (1984); Tennessee: Tenn. Code Ann. §§66-9-201 to 66-9-206 (Supp. 1987); Utah: Utah Code Ann. §§57-13-1 to 2 (1986); Virginia: Va. Code Ann. §§55-352 to 55-354 (1986); Washington: Wash. Rev. Code Ann. §§64.04.140 to 64.04.170 (Supp. 1987).

32   For a more detailed discussion of this issue, see A.J. Bradbrook, "The Role of Restrictive Covenants in Furthering the Application of Solar Technology" (1983) 8 Adel. L.R. 286; Comment, "Solar Rights and Restrictive Covenants: A Microeconomic Analysis" (1978-79) 7 Forham Urban L.J. 283.

Moxhay[33] if the following conditions are satisfied:

1. The covenant must be restrictive in nature.[34] Provided that the solar covenant is drafted carefully, the rule should present no difficulties in this context.

2. Both the covenantor and the covenantee must own land.[35] By the very nature of the problem this will always be the case in a dispute over access to direct sunlight.

3. The covenant must "touch and concern" the land.[36] By analogy with various reported decisions construing other forms of covenant, it seems clear that a solar covenant, however drafted, will satisfy this third requirement.

If these requirements are satisfied, the benefit of the solar covenant will pass to the successor-in-title of the covenantee if the covenant is expressly annexed to the land. If the three requirements are satisfied, the burden of the solar covenant will pass to the successor-in-title of the covenantor provided that the burden of the covenant was intended by the original contracting parties to pass to successors-in-title when the covenant was originally entered into.[37]

If the solar covenant is drafted by a developer and forms one of a series of restrictions imposed on the use of each block of land in a new housing development, the covenant may be enforceable under the doctrine of the scheme of development.[38] This doctrine was devised to enable earlier purchasers of blocks covered by the scheme to enforce covenants entered into by later purchasers, and to enable the benefit of a covenant to pass to a successor-in-title of the covenantee where it has been neither expressly annexed nor expressly assigned. The requirements of a valid scheme of development were stipulated by Parker J in the seminal case of *Elliston* v. *Reacher*:

---

33   *Tulk* v. *Moxhay* (1848), 2 Ph. 774, 41 E.R. 1143 (Ch.).

34   See, for example, *Shepherd Homes Ltd.* v. *Sandham (No. 2)*, [1971] 2 All E.R. 1267 (Ch. Div.); *Parkinson* v. *Reid* (1966), 56 D.L.R. (2d) 315 (S.C.C.).

35   See, for example, *Re Mack and the Conveyancing Act*, [1975] 2 N.S.W.L.R. 623 (Eq. Div.); *Re British United Automobiles Ltd. and Volvo Canada Ltd.* (1980), 114 D.L.R. (3d) 488 (Ont. H.C.J.).

36   See, for example, *Rogers* v. *Hosegood*, [1900] 2 Ch. 388; *Ricketts* v. *Churchwardens of the Parish Enfield*, [1909] 1 Ch. 544; *Lorne Ritchie Enterprises Ltd.* v. *Canada Life Assurance Co.*, [1976] 5 W.W.R. 130 (Man. Q.B.).

37   See *Re Royal Victoria Pavilion, Ramsgate*, [1961] Ch. 581.

38   Sometimes referred to as the doctrine of building schemes.

In my judgment, in order to [prove the existence of the doctrine] it must be proved (1) that both the plaintiffs and defendants derive title under a common vendor; (2) that previously to selling the lands to which the plaintiffs and defendants are respectively entitled the vendor laid out his estate, or a defined portion thereof (including the lands purchased by the plaintiffs and defendants respectively), for sale in lots subject to restrictions intended to be imposed on all the lots, and which, though varying in details as to particular lots, are consistent and consistent only with some general scheme of development; (3) that these restrictions were intended by the common vendor to be and were for the benefit of all the lots intended to be sold, whether or not they were also intended to be and were for the benefit of other land retained by the vendor; and (4) that both the plaintiffs and the defendants, or their predecessors in title, purchased their lots from the common vendor upon the footing that the restrictions subject to which the purchases were made were to enure for the benefit of the other lots included in the general scheme whether or not they were also to enure for the benefit of other lands retained by the vendors.[39]

The more relaxed requirements for a scheme of development will increase the number of cases in which a scheme is upheld. This is a positive move for the development of solar technology, as a solar covenant imposed in a scheme of development, which satisfies the legal requirements for a scheme, can automatically be enforced by any purchasers of any of the blocks of land in the scheme or their successors-in-title.

Summary

Although in this context restrictive covenants suffer from the fact that they are consensual transactions, like express easements, and cannot be imposed on unwilling parties, where agreement is reached the covenant is capable of providing adequate protection for solar access.

Nuisance

In this section I will consider the legal right of solar users lacking an easement or covenant to prevent neighbours under the common law of nuisance from developing their properties so as to shade solar collector panels. If successful, this action may result in the remedy of an injunction and/or damages. Other tortious remedies are not sufficiently broad to assist solar users in protecting the right of solar access.

Public Nuisance

Public nuisance has been defined as "[S]ome act or omission likely to affect the comfort or safety of people generally which is such as to amount to a criminal offence punishable at common law or by statute and which causes

---

39   *Elliston* v. *Reacher*, [1908] 2 Ch. 374 at 384 to 385; *Re Wheeler* (1926), 59 O.L.R. 223 at 231 (C.A.); *Moir* v. *Chong and Boyle (Intervenor)* (1979), 34 N.S.R. (2d) 33 (S.C.T.D.). The English Court of Appeal added in *Reid* v. *Bickerstaff*, [1909] 2 Ch. 305, that the area subject to the scheme of development must be clearly defined.

greater damage or inconvenience to the plaintiff than to the generality of the public."[40]

Despite the fact that the breach of the duty to the public is a criminal offence, in certain circumstances an individual can bring a civil action against the wrongdoer. For this to occur, the individual must be able to prove that he has suffered particular or special damage in excess of that likely to be suffered by the general public as a result of the defendant's activities.[41] A further requirement is that the defendant's activities must have inconvenienced or annoyed a considerable number of people or an entire community or neighbourhood.[42]

In the solar context, the requirement that the plaintiff prove that he has suffered "particular" or "special" damage in excess of that likely to be suffered by the general public, could be overcome if the solar user proves that the shading caused by buildings or vegetation on the neighbour's land cause him or her direct economic loss by virtue of the need to rely on alternative non-renewable energy supplies. The shading of the solar energy system would thus cause the solar user to suffer "particular" damage not experienced by the public at large.

Despite this factor, there is a major shortcoming associated with the public nature of the remedy, which is likely to inhibit solar users' reliance on public nuisance as a cause of action. It will be very difficult, if not impossible, for the solar user to satisfy the requirement that the defendant's activities must have affected a segment of the public that comes within the sphere or neighbourhood of the alleged nuisance. This may occur when a multi-storey building substantially shades the land of numerous nearby landowners at certain seasons during certain times of the day, but would probably not occur in the usual situation where a large tree or a two-storey house shades the immediately adjoining land. While a decision must be made by the courts on the facts of each case, it is extremely doubtful whether the shading of one or more solar collectors by a large building or tree would constitute an injury sufficiently widespread as to be an injury to the public at large.[43] Similarly, it is doubtful whether the Canadian courts would declare

---

40   H. Luntz, D. Hambly & R. Hayes, *Torts: Cases and Commentary* (Sydney: Butterworths, 1980) at 826.

41   See, for example, *Harper v. G.N. Haden & Sons*, [1933] Ch. 298; *Canada Paper Co. v. Brown* (1922), 63 S.C.R. 243; *Fillion v. New Brunswick International Paper Co.*, [1934] 3 D.L.R. 22 (N.B.C.A.).

42   See, for example, *A.G. v. P.Y.A. Quarries Ltd.*, [1957] 2 Q.B. 169 (C.A.); *Southport Corporation v. Esso Petroleum Co. Ltd.*, [1954] 2 Q.B. 182 (C.A.); *A.G. B.C. ex rel. Eaton v. Haney Speedways Ltd.* (1963), 39 D.L.R. (2d) 48 (B.C.S.C.).

43   This conclusion is reinforced by the decision in *R. v. Lloyd* (1802), 4 Esp. 200, 170 E.R.

the blocking of access of direct sunlight to be of "public" concern even in cases where the energy collected by a solar collector system is shared by a number of persons owning separate blocks of land.

It might be argued that any amount of interference with the collection of solar energy caused by shading increases the present reliance on fossil fuels, affects the energy supplies of the community, and is thus of public concern. This argument may become of increasing force in the years to come, especially when it is linked with the future depletion and shortage of non-renewable energy resources. Without any significant relaxation by the courts of the requirements for an action for public nuisance, however, this argument will in all probability be regarded by the courts as irrelevant. The impact on the public interest of the blocking of solar access of individual property owners is far more indirect than that in past cases where the action for public nuisance has been successful. Although situations where oil has been discharged from a ship into harbour waters[44] and a stationary vehicle has been left on the highway for a long period with no lights showing[45] have been held to ground action for public nuisance where private individuals have suffered loss as a consequence, these cases are easily distinguishable from the shading of solar collector panels.

In summary, on the present authorities the action for public nuisance must be discarded as an effective possible cause of action for the enforcement of the right of solar access.

Private Nuisance

The major obstacle a solar user faces in an action for nuisance is proving that the blocking of solar access from the solar collector panels constitutes an interference with the reasonable use and enjoyment of the land. As the blocking of solar access is an "intangible interference" with the land, it is also necessary to prove that the interference is "substantial".[46]

Is the Right of Solar Access a Protected Interest?

Not every advantage enjoyed by landowners is protected by the law of nuisance. Some advantages are not protected even though interference with

---

691. Cf. R. v. Webb (1848), 2 Car. & K. 933, 175 E.R. 391; R. v. Madden [1975] 1 W.L.R. 1379 (C.A.).

44 Overseas Tankship (U.K.) Ltd. v. The Miller Steamship Co. Pty. Ltd., [1967] 1 A.C. 617.

45 Ware v. Garston Haulage Co., [1944] K.B. 30 (C.A.). Cf. Maitland v. Raisbeck, [1944] K.B. 689 (C.A.).

46 Halsey v. Esso Petroleum Co., [1961] 2 All E.R. 145 (Q.B.).

them may cause an economic loss to the landowner. Three well-recognized illustrations of unprotected advantages are the enjoyment of a view,[47] freedom from spying or observation,[48] and the enjoyment of water percolating through undefined channels.[49] The issue of whether the blocking of solar access will be regarded as an unprotected interest arises.

To determine this issue in the absence of direct authority, it is necessary to examine the nature of the right claimed. The basic point that has yet to be resolved is the question of whether the claimed right of solar access is an extension of the traditional right to light or whether it is a distinct right of its own. As has been shown earlier,[50] it is highly doubtful whether the easement of light is sufficiently broad to include the right of access for solar energy purposes; in all probability, the right of solar access would be accepted at common law as a separate easement. If this conclusion is correct, the courts will examine the issue of whether the right of solar access should be regarded as a protected or an unprotected interest in land quite separately from considerations relating to the traditional right to light.

In the absence of any direct authorities, the courts will turn to analogies to determine whether the right of solar access should be regarded as a protected interest. Perhaps the closest analogy would be the traditional right to light, which may be applied by analogy even if it is held to have no direct application in the solar context by virtue of the fact that the right to light and the right to solar access are quite distinct. The right to solar access may also be likened to a claim for privacy. In this event, it appears that the right will be regarded as unprotected. Courts in Canadian and other Commonwealth jurisdictions have been reluctant to recognize a legal right to privacy,[51] although privacy has been recognized in recent years by the American judiciary.[52] Finally, the right of solar access may possibly be likened to a claim for an uninterrupted view. Such an analogy would be similarly

---

47   See *infra*, note 53. *Shepperd* v. *Municipality of Ryde* (1952), 85 C.L.R. 1 (H.C.), held that the enjoyment of a view may be protected by contract.

48   *Victoria Park Racing and Recreation Grounds Co. Ltd.* v. *Taylor* (1937), 58 C.L.R. 479 (H.C.). *Cf. Poole* v. *Ragen*, [1958] O.W.N. 77 (H.C.).

49   *Chasemore* v. *Richards* (1859), 7 H.L. Cas. 349, 11 E.R. 140.

50   See *supra*, notes 13-21 and accompanying text.

51   See, for example, *Victoria Park Racing and Recreation Grounds Co. Ltd.* v. *Taylor* (1937), 58 C.L.R. 479 (H.C.); *Re X*, [1975] 1 All E.R. 697 (Fam. Div. & C.A.). *Cf. Saccone* v. *Orr* (1981), 34 O.R. (2d) 317 (Co. Ct.); *Motherwell* v. *Motherwell* (1977), 73 D.L.R. (3d) 62 (Alta C.A.). On this issue, see Allen M. Linden, *Canadian Tort Law*, 4th ed. (Toronto: Butterworths, 1988) at 52.

52   *Nader* v. *General Motors Corp.*, 307 N.Y.S. 2d 647 (C.A. 1970).

unhelpful for the solar user, as English, Canadian, and Australian courts have consistently held that a view is an unprotected interest.[53]

The application of these possible analogies does not bode well for the solar user. However, possible assistance for the solar user comes from the line of cases on the application of the law of nuisance, which draws a distinction between alleged nuisance that produces material injury to the property and other types of alleged nuisance. Lord Westbury LC stated in *St. Helen's Smelting Co.* v. *Tipping*:

> [I]t is a very desirable thing to mark the difference between an action brought for a nuisance upon the ground that the alleged nuisance produces material injury to the property, and an action brought for a nuisance on the ground that the thing alleged to be a nuisance is productive of sensible personal discomfort. With regard to the latter, namely, the personal inconvenience and interference with one's enjoyment, one's quiet, one's personal freedom, anything that discomposes or injuriously affects the senses or the nerves, whether that may or may not be denominated a nuisance, must undoubtedly depend greatly on the circumstances of the place where the thing complained of actually occurs. If a man lives in a town, it is necessary that he should subject himself to the consequences of those operations of trade which may be carried on in his immediate locality, which are actually necessary for trade and commerce, and also for the enjoyment of property, and for the benefit of the inhabitants of the town and of the public at large. If a man lives in a street where there are numerous shops, and a shop is opened next door to him, which is carried on in a fair and reasonable way, he has no ground for complaint, because to himself individually there may arise much discomfort from the trade carried on in that shop. But when an occupation is carried on by one person in the neighbourhood of another, and the result of that trade, or occupation, or business, is a material injury to property, then there unquestionably arises a very different consideration. I think ... that in a case of that description, the submission which is required from persons living in society to that amount of discomfort which may be necessary for the legitimate and free exercise of the trade of their neighbours, would not apply to circumstances the immediate result of which is sensible injury to the value of the property.[54]

The distinction between nuisances causing "material injury to the property" and those causing "sensible personal discomfort" appears to reflect the importance granted by the courts to proprietary rights and the fact that it is easier for the courts to assess property damage than to compensate the plaintiff in respect of personal discomfort.[55]

---

53   *Aldred's* case (1610), 9 Co. Rep. 57b, 77 E.R. 816; *Harris* v. *De Pinna* (1885), 33 Ch. D. 238; *Chastey* v. *Ackland* (1895), 11 T.L.R. 460 (C.A.). Cf. *Freeman* v. *Shoalhaven Shire Council*, [1980] 2 N.S.W.L.R. 826 (Eq. Div.), in which Kearney J awarded damages to the plaintiff, whose commanding view of the ocean had been blocked, based on "loss of amenity" in addition to damages for reduction in the value of the land.

54   *St. Helen's Smelting Co.* v. *Tipping* (1865), 11 H.L. Cas. 642 at 650, 11 E.R. 1483 at 1486. See also *Scarborough Golf & Country Club* v. *City of Scarborough* (1986), 55 O.R. (2d) 193 at 232 (H.C.); *Russell Transport Ltd.* v. *Ontario Malleable Iron Co.* [1952] O.R. 621 (H.C.).

55   See B.S. Markesinis & A.M. Tettenborn, "Cricket, Power Boat Racing and Nuisance"

On Lord Westbury's analysis, it seems that the blocking of solar access should be regarded as a case of material injury to the property rather than a case of sensible personal discomfort. If this conclusion is correct, then the courts will be more likely to treat the right of solar access as a protected interest. However, the issue is contentious. The exact meaning of "material injury to property" was not explained by Lord Westbury and has not been considered by any subsequent court. At least three possible interpretations of "material injury to property" can be advanced:

1. any activity done on neighbouring land that reduces the value of the plaintiff's land;[56]

2. any activity done on neighbouring land that has physical consequences on the plaintiff's land that reduce the value of that land; or

3. injury caused by actual physical deposits on the plaintiff's land.

The first interpretation would probably be rejected as too wide because any form of nuisance (for example, by smell or noise) would satisfy a test of this nature. The same objection could not be made of the second (the broad) or the third (the narrow) possible interpretations, and the effective choice is between these two alternatives. The blocking of solar access would fall within the broad interpretation in that the solar energy appliance, once installed, forms part of the real estate by the doctrine of fixtures and would normally enhance the value of the property; the blocking of solar access would have physical consequences on the plaintiff's land and would undoubtedly reduce the value of the property. On the other hand, the blocking of solar access would not fall within the narrow construction of "material injury to property" as the obstruction of sunlight does not cause any actual deposits on the plaintiff's land. From the standpoint of the public interest in furthering the application of solar energy technology, it is to be hoped that the broad construction prevails.

Do Solar Appliances Constitute a Sensitive or Unusual Use of the Land?

Even if the right of solar access overcomes this threshold difficulty and is regarded as a protected interest, nuisance will not necessarily lie for a

---

(1981) 131 New L.J. 108.

56   There is still some doubt as to whether a cause of action will lie in private nuisance for economic loss, but the better view appears to be that it does. See *Dunton* v. *District Council* (1977), 76 L.G.R. 87 at 93 *per* Griffiths J; *British Celanese Ltd.* v. *A.H. Hunt (Capacitors) Ltd.*, [1969] 1 W.L.R. 959 at 969 *per* Lawton J. Damages for economic loss can definitely be claimed in an action for public nuisance: see, for example, *Harper* v. *G.N. Haden & Sons*, [1933] Ch. 298; *Smith* v. *Warringah Shire Council*, [1962] N.S.W.R. 944 (S.C.).

substantial breach of the right. The reason for this is that the solar user who sues his neighbour in nuisance for blocking the direct rays of the sun may be met by the defence that he is making an especially sensitive or unusual use of the land.[57]

There is no case law in any common law jurisdiction determining whether solar appliances fall within the rule relating to sensitive or unusual use of land. Although solar collector panels are sensitive in that they require the direct rays of the sun for their efficient operation and cannot operate effectively on diffuse light, it could be argued that they are not unduly sensitive in that they do not require access to the sun during all the daylight hours. Solar collectors can operate efficiently with as little as four hours' direct access to sunlight, provided that this four-hour period is centred on the zenith position of the sun.[58] Thus, solar collector panels can be blocked for more than 50 percent of daylight hours without damage to the solar user. This fact reduces the strength of the argument that solar energy collection is an especially sensitive use of land.

When determining this issue, the court is also likely to be concerned with the incidence of the use of solar appliances in Canada. The greater the incidence of use, the less likely it is that the courts will allow the defence under discussion to prevail. While the situation may change dramatically in the years to come, in light of current low incidence of use of solar appliances in Canada, it is likely that the courts will hold that the defence to an action for nuisance of sensitive or unusual use of the land will prevail in the solar context. This is not necessarily conclusive, however, as the following discussion shows.

Malicious Obstructions of Solar Access

So far, in this discussion, no mention has been made of the motive of the neighbouring landowner who interferes with the solar user's right of access to the direct rays of the sun by erecting a building or other obstruction or permitting vegetation to grow until it shades the collector panels. What is the situation if the neighbour blocks the right of solar access purely out of malice?

Although, as a general proposition of the law of torts, motive is irrelevant,[59] there are authorities that state that damages may be awarded

---

57   See, for example, *Robinson* v. *Kilvert* (1889), 41 Ch. D. 88; *Grandel* v. *Mason*, [1953] 3 D.L.R. 65 (S.C.C.); *Hoare & Co.* v. *McAlpine*, [1923] 1 Ch. 167; *Rattray* v. *Daniels* (1959), 17 D.L.R. (2d) 134 (Alta. C.A.).

58   See Gail Hayes, *Solar Access Law: Protecting Access to Sunlight for Solar Energy Systems* (Washington, D.C.: U.S. Dept. of Commerce, 1979) at 22-24.

59   *Borough of Bradford* v. *Pickles*, [1895] A.C. 587 at 601. See also *Allen* v. *Flood*, [1898]

even where the plaintiff is making an especially sensitive use of his land if the defendant's acts, which cause the damage, are motivated by malice.[60] This principle may allow the solar user to obtain a remedy in nuisance for the blocking of solar access in the limited circumstances in which the "malice" principle applies.

As already discussed in detail,[61] it is still not certain whether a right of solar access is a legally protected interest. If the conclusion tentatively reached above (that such a right is a protected interest) is correct, then depending on whether or not the right of solar access is regarded as an especially sensitive or unusual use of land, nuisance will lie for a substantial interference with the right of solar access either in all cases (if the land use is held not to be sensitive) or in cases where the blocking of access is caused by a malicious act of the defendant (if the land use is held to be sensitive). In the event that the right of solar access is held to be an unprotected interest, it seems that nuisance will not lie in any circumstances.

Even though the rule in relation to malice appears to offer some encouragement to the solar user, it will have only a very limited application. Although there are no English or Canadian authorities directly on point, it appears likely that the rule will apply only where it can be shown that the building or tree shading the solar collector panels has no utility value to the defendant who erected or planted it.[62] There is case law in the United States to this effect.[63] In the vast majority of cases, the defendant will be able to prove benefit from the tree or building even if he erects or plants it partially out of malice.[64]

The Position in the United States

This rather depressing account of the assistance likely to be given to the

---

A.C. 1 at 124 *per* Lord Herschell.

60   See, for example, *Christie* v. *Davey*, [1893] 1 Ch. 316; *Motherwell* v. *Motherwell* (1977), 73 D.L.R. (3d) 62 (Alta. C.A.); *Hollywood Silver Fox Farm* v. *Emmett*, [1936] 1 All E.R. 825 (K.B.).

61   See *supra*, notes 54-56 and accompanying text.

62   See G.H.L. Fridman, "Motive in the English Law of Nuisance" (1954) 40 Virginia L. Rev. 583 at 585.

63   See, for example, *D'Inzillo* v. *Basile*, 180 Misc. 237, 40 N.Y.S. 2d 293 (S.C. 1943), affd. 266 App. Div. 875, 43 N.Y.S. 2d 638; *Green* v. *Shick*, 194 Okla. 491, 153 P. 2d. 821 (S.C. 1944).

64   It has been suggested that a finding of malice by a court is most unlikely in cases where a building has been erected in conformity with the relevant local planning and zoning regulation. See Ralph E. Becker, "Common Law Sun Rights: An Obstacle to Solar Heating and Cooling?" (1976) 3 J. Contemp. L. 19 at 29.

solar user under the current Anglo-Canadian law of private nuisance should be compared with the situation in the United States. In that country, two conflicting decisions have been handed down.

In *Prah* v. *Maretti*,[65] the plaintiff, the owner of a solar-heated residence, sued for an injunction to restrain his neighbour, the defendant, from constructing a residence on the defendant's property in a position that would interfere with the plaintiff's access to unobstructed direct sunlight to his solar panels. The plaintiff's residence was the first constructed in the subdivision and had been erected close to the defendant's boundary line. This maximized the likelihood of shading problems arising from any building erected on the neighbouring property. The defendant had received the necessary planning and building approval from the Planning Commission. The plaintiff endeavoured by negotiation to persuade the defendant to relocate his proposed residence further away from the boundary line, but the defendant refused to do so because the residence would not then receive a view of the nearby lake.

The major argument advanced by the plaintiff was that the defendant's residence constituted a private nuisance by virtue of the shading problems. At first instance, the nuisance claim was rejected by the Circuit Court of Waukesha County, Wisconsin.[66] This decision was reversed by a two-to-one decision of the Supreme Court of Wisconsin. Judge Abrahamson, for the majority, noted that the defendant's argument — that he has a right to develop his property in compliance with existing legislation and private covenants, regardless of the effect that this has on the plaintiff's solar access — amounts to an assertion that the private nuisance doctrine is not applicable in the present case. In other words, the defendant's right of development is *per se* superior to his neighbour's interest in access to sunlight.[67] Such an assertion is based on the maxim *cujus est solum, ejus est usque ad coelum et ad inferos*.[68] However, this maxim has not been interpreted by the courts as vesting unlimited rights in the landowner.[69] The argument that the plaintiff can have no property interest in sunlight was accordingly rejected.[70]

Judge Abrahamson went on to identify three policy considerations that

---

65   *Prah* v. *Maretti*, 108 Wis. 2d 223, 321 N.W. 2d 182 (S.C. 1982).

66   *Prah* v. *Maretti*, the circuit court decision, is reported in (1981) 2 Solar L. Rep. 1013.

67   *Supra*, note 65, at 188.

68   Loosely translated, this means, "Whoever owns the land surface also owns the airspace above the land as far as the outer limits of the atmosphere and the subsoil beneath the land as far as the centre of the earth."

69   This maxim is discussed in detail at *infra*, notes 137-143 and accompanying text.

70   *Supra*, note 65, at 188.

account for the court's earlier reluctance to provide legal protection for access to sunlight. The first factor was the jealous protection given to the right of landowners to use their property as they wish, provided that they do not cause physical damage to a neighbour. Second, the only value given to sunlight is for illumination or for aesthetic enjoyment. As artificial light could be used for illumination, this factor was considered trivial. Third, land development should not be impeded or restricted, and a right to sunlight hinders such development.

The court held that these three policies are no longer fully accepted or applicable, as they reflect outmoded factual circumstances and social priorities.[71] In relation to the right of landowners to develop their property as they wish, Judge Abrahamson noted that society has increasingly regulated, for the general welfare, the use of land by the landowner.[72] As to the value of sunlight, the court stated that access to sunlight as an energy source is significant both to the landowner who invests in solar collectors and to a society that has an interest in developing alternative energy sources.[73] Finally, the court noted that the policy of favouring unhindered private development in an expanding economy is no longer in harmony with the realities of modern society.[74]

The court concluded that common law private nuisance rules must adapt to changing social values and conditions, and that what is legally regarded as a nuisance in modern times would undoubtedly have been tolerated without question in former times.[75] The court added that the fact that the defendant complied with the relevant zoning and building laws does not automatically bar a nuisance claim, although this fact is entitled to some weight.[76]

This landmark decision was not followed by the California Sixth District Court of Appeals in *Sher* v. *Leiderman*.[77] In this case, the plaintiffs constructed a passive solar home,[78] designed and built to take advantage of

---

71   *Id.*, at 189-190. The court quoted with approval the following dictum of Chief Justice Rosenberry of the Supreme Court of Wisconsin in *Ballstadt* v. *Pagel*, 202 Wis. 484 at 489, 232 N.W. 862 at 864 (1930): "What is regarded in law as constituting a nuisance in modern times would no doubt have been tolerated without question in former times."

72   *Village of Euclid* v. *Ambler Realty Co.*, 272 U.S. 365 (C.A. 1926); *Just* v. *Marinette County*, 56 Wis. 2d 7, 201 N.W. 2d 761 (S.C. 1972).

73   *Supra*, note 65, at 189.

74   *Id.*, at 190, citing *State* v. *Deetz*, 66 Wis. 2d 1, 224 N.W. 2d 407 (S.C. 1974).

75   *Id.*, citing *Ballstadt* v. *Pagel*, 202 Wis. 484, 232 N.W. 862 (1930).

76   *Id.*, at 192, citing *Bie* v. *Ingersoll*, 27 Wis. 2d 490, 135 N.W. 2d 250 (S.C. 1965).

77   *Sher* v. *Leiderman*, 181 Cal. App. 3d 645, 226 Cal. Rptr. 698 (C.A. 1986).

78   A passive solar device does not employ any solar collector panels or mechanical devices,

the winter sun for heat and light. Trees planted by their neighbour on adjoining land eventually grew sufficiently tall to block the sun to the plaintiff's house for most of the day during the winter months. The court found that in order to restore the sunlight it would be necessary to trim certain trees on the neighbouring property, to top some trees, and to remove others. The defendant refused to carry out this work. The plaintiff argued, *inter alia*, that the shading constituted a private nuisance.

The court emphasized that sunlight is important in modern society not only for its aesthetic value, but also as an important alternative energy source, and stated that promoting the use of solar energy is of paramount public interest.[79] Despite this, the court held in favour of the defendant for the following reasons:

1. The existing law on private nuisance states that the obstruction of light to a neighbour's property, except in cases where malice is the overriding motive, does not constitute actionable nuisance, regardless of the impact on the injured person's property or person.

2. It is solely within the province of the legislature to assess the relative importance of social priorities and decide whether to change the law.

3. California legislation relating to the application of nuisance law to the blockage of sunlight already exists.[80] A court should not intrude into the precise area of the law where legislative action is being taken.

4. Although we may now be in the solar age, it does not follow that individual property rights are no longer important policy considerations. The expanded use of police power and eminent domain only support the conclusion that society is increasingly prepared to regulate private land use for the *public* health, safety, morals, or welfare. It offers no support for a *private* benefit, as in the present case.

5. The expansion of the nuisance law in this area would have the undesired effect of fostering ill will and a proliferation of litigation between neighbours.

6. It is more appropriate to protect solar access by zoning and other local ordinances than by the law of nuisance.

---

but seeks to control temperature by the architectural features of the building itself. Critical features of passive solar-designed buildings are the size and placement of windows, the type of materials of which the walls and ceilings are constructed, and the orientation of the building towards the sun. See Bradbrook, *supra*, note 11, at para.118.

79   *Sher* v. *Leiderman*, 181 Cal. App. 3d 645, 226 Cal. Rptr. 698 at 702 (C.A. 1986).

80   California: Cal. Pub. Res. Code §§25980 to 25986 (West 1986 & Supp. 1988).

Summary

Under a traditional legal analysis, the obstruction of solar access will not constitute a nuisance unless it is protected by an express easement. Only rights that have been held to constitute "protected interests" can receive the benefit of nuisance law. The only reason that the solar user was successful in *Prah* v. *Maretti* was that, unlike other courts, the majority of the Supreme Court of Wisconsin was willing to disregard established principles of nuisance law and to decide the case on the basis of public policy. Based on their past track record in torts law, Anglo-Canadian courts are unlikely to take such a bold initiative.

Other Legal Difficulties

The Use of the Injunctive Remedy

If a solar user is granted a judgment for a breach of solar access, the issue of an appropriate remedy becomes important. The solar user has a special interest in ensuring that an injunction is granted requiring the removal of offending trees or buildings or preventing the erection of future buildings or planting trees. A damage award is unsatisfactory from the standpoint of the solar user.[81] While monetary compensation would allow the solar user to recover the cost of the solar appliance and the increased cost of substitute fuel, this is only a minor consequence. Denying an injunction would leave the solar user with a solar energy system incapable of functioning. Many solar users install their solar appliances for reasons other than to save fuel, and these interests cannot be quantified when awarding monetary damages. Prime factors motivating conversion to solar energy, in many cases, are the control it gives individual persons over their energy source, the reduction of pollution, and the preservation of the community's supply of fossil fuels. Awarding damages would not advance either the solar user's purpose or society's interest in the development of solar energy.

The discretionary nature of the remedies makes it impossible to predict with certainty when the court will award damages rather than an injunction. This uncertainty is itself a problem in the present context, as it deters potential purchasers from investing in solar devices. Some courts appear to regard an injunction as the normal remedy for nuisance because they are concerned that a damages award effectively licenses the defendant to commit unlawful acts in the future, subject to the payment of compensation.[82] This effectively

---

81   The issue of the nature of the remedy in the solar context is discussed in Becker, *supra*, note 64, at 30-31; Hayes, *supra*, note 58, at 99-100; Carol Polis, "Obtaining Access to Solar Energy: Nuisance, Water Rights and Zoning Administration" (1979) 45 Brooklyn L. Rev. 357 at 366.

82   This is the rule in English law. See, for example, *Sefton* v. *Tophams Ltd.*, [1965] Ch. 1140

amounts to a form of compulsory acquisition. In many jurisdictions, the courts balance the convenience to the parties when determining the appropriate remedy and refuse to grant an injunction that would cause damage to the defendant greatly disproportionate to the plaintiff's injury,[83] or where substantial redress can be afforded by the payment of money. Under the "balance of convenience" test, there is a significant likelihood that the solar user will be awarded damages rather than an injunction. The basis for this outcome is either that substantial redress can be afforded by the payment of money or that an injunction can cause damage to the defendant greatly disproportionate to the injury suffered by the solar user.

This is another area where the court possesses wide discretion. There is the danger that the court will take a narrow view of the injury suffered by the solar user and conclude that justice will be done if compensation is awarded for increased fuel bills incurred because of the shading of solar collector panels. However, it is submitted that the courts should adopt a wider view of the nature of the injury caused by shading. As discussed in the preceding section, they should bring into consideration the various public policy arguments in favour of advancing the use of solar energy. I do not suggest that an injunction should be granted as a matter of course in all cases. For example, in all but the most exceptional circumstances, it is clearly inappropriate for the court to order the demolition of a high-rise building in order to preserve access to sunlight for a neighbouring solar device. What I do suggest is that the "balance of convenience" should be tilted in favour of the injunctive remedy by taking into account the relevant public policy considerations. Here again, however, the past track record of the courts gives no confidence that this will occur.

Restrictive Covenants Impeding Solar Devices

Covenants can be used to enhance the use of solar devices; for example, one might enter into a covenant to protect solar access.[84] However, restrictive covenants are a two-edged sword since they can also be used to inhibit the use of solar devices. Although restrictive covenants that specifically outlaw solar devices are rare, there are numerous restrictive covenants that, although not aimed directly at solar devices, have the effect of excluding any

---

at 1169 (Stamp J); *Kennaway* v. *Thompson*, [1981] Q.B. 88 at 92 to 93 (C.A.) (Lawton LJ).

83   See, for example, *De Cecco* v. *Beach*, 174 Conn. 29, 381 A. 2d 543 at 547 (S.C. 1977). See also *Boomer* v. *Atlantic Cement Co.*, 26 N.Y. 2d 217, 257 N.E. 2d 870 (C.A. 1970), where the court awarded damages in lieu of an injunction to persons living in an area suffering from heavy pollution caused by the defendant company.

84   See *supra*, notes 32-39 and accompanying text.

such installations that are visible to neighbours.[85] For example, covenants that preclude "appliances and installations on roofs", "the construction of a roof containing any reflective material," "extensions to existing buildings", or "exterior change or addition" make it difficult, if not impossible, for the covenantor to install a solar device. Covenants that impose height requirements or setback requirements from the front or side property boundary lines, may also interfere with the most efficient placement of solar collectors.

The issue for consideration is whether the courts will be prepared to declare void restrictive covenants prohibiting or impeding the installation of solar devices in the absence of specific legislation. The common law doctrine voiding contracts contrary to public policy is relevant in this context. This doctrine justifies the court in striking down any agreement that is against the public interest.[86] The argument put by the solar user would be that there is a public policy in favour of promoting reliance on renewable energy resources and that any restrictive covenant that impedes the installation of solar devices should be declared void.

To date, this issue has not been considered by the Anglo-Canadian judiciary. Arguments of this nature have been made before American courts, but have failed in the absence of a legislative declaration of public policy. In *Kraye* v. *Old Orchard Association*,[87] a prospective solar user advanced an argument, based on public policy, to persuade the Superior Court of California to overturn a covenant that prohibited placing on roof-tops any installations or appliances visible from neighbouring properties or adjacent streets. This argument was ultimately successful, but only on the basis of state legislation enacted while the case was in progress, which barred the enforcement of a covenant that would effectively impede the use of solar energy. Prior to the introduction of the legislation, Judge Cardenas had delivered an oral statement indicating that he was unwilling to find that there was a public policy in favour of solar energy development. In *Nicholas* v. *Gurtler*,[88] the Arizona Superior Court for Maricopa County considered a challenge by a prospective solar user against a restrictive covenant prohibiting a structure of any type from unreasonably obstructing the view from other lots in the subdivision. Under the covenant, plans of existing houses in a subdivision could not be varied without the approval of the subdivision's review board. The defendant

---

85   See J. Wiley, "Private Land Use Controls as Barriers to Solar Development: The Need for State Legislation" (1979) 1 Solar L. Rep. 281 at 283.

86   This doctrine is explained in G.H. Treitel, *The Law of Contract*, 7th ed. (London: Stevens & Son, 1987) at c.11.

87   Case No. C-209453, Civ., 1 Solar L. Rep. 503 (1979).

88   Case No. C-384239, Civ., 1 Solar L. Rep. 251 (1979).

argued that, as a matter of public policy, this covenant should not be applied to solar collector panels. The court rejected this argument and prevented the defendant from varying the plans of his home to include solar collector panels without the approval of the subdivision's review board.

It thus appears that in the absence of legislation declaring that solar energy research and development is in the public interest, the likelihood of a court's striking down on common law principles a restrictive covenant inhibiting the application of solar collector panels is remote. The probable attitude of the Anglo-Canadian courts is that in the absence of legislation, any government policy in favour of renewable energy and energy conservation is not sufficiently intense or enduring to justify overriding privately negotiated covenants.

WIND ENERGY

Canada has very significant wind resource potential, particularly on the west and east coasts and in the Rocky Mountains. As in the case of solar energy, however, little (if any) consideration has been given to the actual and potential roles of the common law in assisting in the exploitation of wind energy. The major legal issue is access to the wind.[89] Even if a wind generator is ideally situated at a windy location it may be rendered ineffective or inefficient if a building development, the growth of trees, or the erection of another wind generator upwind[90] on neighbouring land restricts the natural flow of wind.

The adverse effect on the operation of wind generators of physical objects located on neighbouring property upwind is far more significant than is commonly realized. The power obtained from the wind varies as the cube of its velocity. For example, the power available almost doubles if the wind velocity increases from twelve to sixteen kilometres per hour, and increases by a factor of eight if the wind velocity increases from sixteen to thirty-two kilometres per hour. Again, a wind generator designed to produce two kilowatts at thirty-five kilometres per hour will generate only five hundred watts at twenty-two kilometres per hour. Thus, since relatively minor

---

89 For further discussion of this issue, see A.J. Bradbrook, "The Access of Wind to Wind Generators" (1984) A.M.P.L.A. Yearbook 433.

90 Wind generators significantly reduce the wind energy potential in the immediately surrounding area for a distance of approximately ten times the diameter of the generator's blades depthwise and three times the diameter of the blades perpendicular to the wind. For this reason, a large wind generator could adversely affect the performance of another large wind generator located on neighbouring property downwind. See R.W. Baker & S.N. Walker, *Wake Studies at the Goodnoe Hill Mod-2 Site* (Report prepared for the Bonneville Power Administration) (Portland, Oregon, October 1982).

obstructions to the wind are capable of causing a large reduction in the production capacity of a wind generator, the need for a wind generator to be guaranteed access to the unobstructed flow of the wind is critical.[91]

In the absence of any provincial legislation in Canada guaranteeing access to the wind for a wind generator, the most effective avenue open to a wind user is to purchase title to, or a long-term lease over, a sufficient tract of land upwind to ensure that no obstructions will impede wind access. Unfortunately, for economic reasons, this will be unrealistic in most situations. The only other avenue is to place reliance on easements, covenants, and nuisance, as in the case of solar access.

Restrictive Covenants

At any time, a wind user may negotiate with his neighbours upwind for the grant of a suitably worded restrictive covenant designed to protect access of the natural flow of the wind to the wind generator. Covenants of the type that are commonly used to preserve property values (for example, covenants limiting the height of buildings and preventing the removal of vegetation) could, if suitably drafted, be similarly used to guarantee access to the wind.

Once a wind access covenant is executed and registered, it will be enforced in the same manner as other forms of covenant. The issues raised here are identical to those that arise in respect of a restrictive covenant designed to safeguard solar access.[92] Thus, although a restrictive covenant is a consensual transaction, and therefore cannot be imposed on unwilling parties, where agreement is reached the covenant is capable of providing adequate protection for wind access.

Easements

The legal position of a wind user who wishes to protect wind access by means of an express easement is more problematic.

Although it has long been held that landowners have, as against their neighbours, no natural rights to the uninterrupted flow of air in respect of their property,[93] common law recognizes that a right to the natural flow of air can be created by easement.[94] A wind user may argue that he may protect

---

91   R. Lomell & D.A. Schaller, *Small Power Production and Wind Energy: Regulatory Actions Under PURPA* (Report SERI/SP-635-794) (Washington, D.C.: U.S. Dept. of Commerce, 1982) at 3-4; *Legal-Institutional Implications of Wind Energy Conversion Systems* (Report NSF/RA-770203) (Washington, D.C.: National Science Foundation, 1977) at 35.

92   See *supra*, notes 32-39 and accompanying text.

93   *Byrant* v. *Lefever* (1879), 4 C.P.D. 172 at 180 *per* Cotton LJ.

94   For example, *Commonwealth* v. *Registrar of Titles for Victoria* (1918), 24 C.L.R. 348 (H.C.); *Tuckett* v. *Brice*, [1917] V.L.R. 36 (S.C.); *Bryant* v. *Lefever, id.*

the access of wind to a wind generator by negotiating an easement of air with his neighbour upwind.

In this context, the major issue is whether the right of wind access to a wind generator is encompassed by the easement of air, or whether it is outside the scope of that easement. There appears to be no direct authority on this issue. All the cases in the present century on the easement of air are concerned with the issue of the need to ensure adequate ventilation to buildings on the dominant tenement and are irrelevant to the point under discussion.

The only exception is *Webb* v. *Bird*,[95] which concerned the access of air to a windmill erected by the plaintiff on his land. Thirty-one years after the windmill was built, the owner of neighbouring land upwind built a schoolhouse on his land, which substantially obstructed the passage of air to the windmill. The plaintiff claimed that he had acquired a prescriptive easement to air after twenty years' continuous use of the mill. This claim was rejected by the Court of Exchequer Chamber on the basis that the owner of the servient land could not have prevented the acquisition of the easement.

Considerable confusion surrounds the effect of this decision. According to *Gale on Easements*,[96] the case decides that there can be no right to the passage of air over an unlimited surface. With respect, however, it is submitted that this analysis is erroneous, as the decision in *Webb* v. *Bird* merely dealt with the scope of a prescriptive claim to air, and did not purport to determine the question of whether a right of air to a windmill could be acquired by express grant. Thus, unfortunately, the case is unhelpful in determining whether the right of wind access is encompassed by the easement of air.

Given the present state of authorities, an argument can be made that the easement of air is limited in scope to the purpose of ventilation and thus cannot encompass the need for wind access to a wind generator. This argument can be supported by a useful analogy with the issue of whether the scope of the easement of light is sufficiently broad to include the right of access to the direct rays of the sun to solar collector panels employed in solar energy devices.[97] As we have seen, the established authorities, by insisting that nuisance will not lie for interference with the right of light as long as sufficient light remains for the purposes of illumination (a standard clearly

---

95   *Webb* v. *Bird* (1861), 10 C.B. (N.S.) 268, 142 E.R. 455 (C.P.); aff'd. (1863) 13 C.B. (N.S.) 841, 143 E.R. 332 (C.P.).

96   *Gale on Easements*, 15th ed. (London: Sweet and Maxwell, 1986) at 280-281.

97   See *supra*, notes 13-21 and accompanying text.

inadequate in the solar energy context), strongly suggest that a right of access to the sun's rays must be regarded as a novel form of easement separate from the easement of light. This analogy may be regarded as particularly close since, until the early twentieth century, it was thought that light and air constituted the same easement rather than two separate easements.[98]

The argument is also supported by a dictum of Griffith CJ of the High Court of Australia in *Commonwealth* v. *Registrar of Titles for Victoria,*[99] where His Honour referred to several possible easements novel in kind and concluded that "[i]n the light of modern knowledge ... there is no difference in principle between a right to the free passage of moving air to my windmill and the free passage of running water to my watermill."[100] The most logical interpretation of this statement is that the right of wind access to a windmill (and by inference to a wind generator) is not encompassed by the easement of air but can exist as a separate, novel easement.

It is submitted that the only valid conclusion is that, in the absence of direct authorities, it is uncertain whether the right of wind access is encompassed by the easement of air. In light of this uncertainty, the enforceability of an express grant of a right of wind access will be discussed on the alternative assumptions that the right is a separate, novel easement and that it is an extension of the easement of air.

If the right of wind access is regarded as an extension of the easement of air, it appears to be clear that the right can be created by express grant.[101] The only doubt that arises is based on the distinction drawn by certain English cases between a right to a defined flow of air and the right to the general flow of air. The phrase "defined flow of air" has been used to encompass access of air enjoyed both through a defined aperture on the dominant tenement (for example, a door or a window)[102] and through a defined channel over adjoining property.[103] The reason for the distinction is that, in some instances, the availability of the various methods of creation of easements is

---

98 *Atkinson* v. *Long* (1885), 2 Q.L.J. 99 (T.D.); *Harris* v. *De Pinna* (1885), 33 Ch.D. 238 at 250; *Thwaites* v. *Brahe* (1895), 21 V.L.R. 192 (S.C.). The issue was not finally settled until the decision in *Commonwealth* v. *Registrar of Titles for Victoria* (1918), 24 C.L.R. 348 (H.C.).

99 *Commonwealth* v. *Registrar of Titles for Victoria, id.*

100 *Id.,* at 354.

101 For example, *Bryant* v. *Lefever* (1879), 4 C.P.D. 172; *Tuckett* v. *Brice,* [1917] V.L.R. 36 (S.C.); *Commonwealth* v. *Registrar of Titles for Victoria, supra,* note 98.

102 For example, *Cable* v. *Bryant,* [1908] 1 Ch. 259.

103 For example, *Bass* v. *Gregory* (1890), 25 Q.B.D. 481.

restricted in the case of a claimed right to the general flow of air. For example, it has been consistently held that the right to the general flow of air across the servient tenement cannot be claimed by prescription.[104] It is unclear whether wind access to a wind generator would be classified as a defined or a general flow of air. As only a certain portion of the servient tenement is subject to the claimed easement of wind access, it could be argued that this is sufficient to constitute a defined channel; on the other hand, the tract of land would in most instances be sufficiently broad that it is arguably not a "defined channel".[105]

If the right of wind access is regarded as a separate easement, it must satisfy the essential characteristics of an easement at common law. I suggest that these characteristics, discussed earlier in the context of solar access,[106] are satisfied by the right of wind access. The only possible doubt relates to the requirement that the right must be capable of forming the subject matter of a grant. In light of the decision in *Commonwealth* v. *Registrar of Titles for Victoria*[107] that a right to an undefined flow of air can constitute an easement if created by express grant, it seems clear that the natural flow of wind to a wind generator satisfies this requirement.

Even though the right of wind access satisfies these essential characteristics, as is the case with the right of solar use discussed earlier,[108] such a right may still not constitute an easement at common law. Based on reasons set out above, the probable position is that novel easements can be created in the absence of any Canadian authority to the contrary.

In summary, it seems that an easement of wind access can be created by express grant, either as a part of the established easement of air or as a separate, novel easement. However, as in the case of solar access,[109] the availability of an express easement should not be seen as a total solution to the problem of wind access, as neighbouring landowners may refuse to grant

---

104 *Webb* v. *Bird* (1861), 10 C.B. (N.S.) 268, 142 E.R. 455 (C.P.); affd. (1863) 13 C.B. (N.S.) 841, 143 E.R. 332 (C.P.); *Harris* v. *De Pinna* (1885), 33 Ch.D. 238; *Bryant* v. *Lefever* (1879), 4 C.P.D. 172; *Chasemore* v. *Richards* (1859), 7 H.L. Cas. 349; 11 E.R. 140.

105 On this point the decision in *Webb* v. *Bird* (1861), 10 C.B. (N.S.) 268, 142 E.R. 455 is irrelevant, as in that case the plaintiff claimed a right of air over the whole rather than a certain portion of the plaintiff's land.

106 See *supra*, note 23, and accompanying text.

107 *Commonwealth* v. *Registrar of Titles for Victoria, supra,* note 98.

108 See *supra*, notes 28-30 and accompanying text.

109 See *supra*, note 13.

such an easement. There is no mechanism at common law to force the creation of easements.

Nuisance

If a wind user is unable to acquire fee simple title, or a suitable express easement or covenant from his neighbour, the final possible avenue of protection available to the wind user at common law is the law of nuisance. The wind user may claim that any physical object situated on neighbouring land obstructing the free flow of wind to a wind generator constitutes a public or private nuisance, the remedy for which would be damages and/or an injunction.

To date, there have been no cases on the application of the law of nuisance to protect wind access in any common law jurisdiction. Because of the similarity, from a legal perspective, of the positions of a solar user and a wind user in relation to the availability of the law of nuisance to protect access to the relevant resource, the legal analysis provided earlier would apply.[110] Thus, public nuisance appears to have no application here, and private nuisance will only protect wind access in the unlikely event that the neighbour erected the wind obstruction purely out of malice.

The Use of the Injunctive Remedy

Once again, the wind user is in the same position as the solar user. For reasons discussed earlier,[111] an award of damages is unsatisfactory in this context, yet it appears to be the most likely remedy to be granted to a wind user under the current common law position. This position is unlikely to change unless the courts adopt more radical conceptions of their role as the arbiters of public policy considerations, and there is no indication from the Canadian courts that such is likely to occur in the near future.

GEOTHERMAL ENERGY

The management of geothermal energy resources raises legal issues that are quite distinct from those of solar and wind energy. In recent years, geological research has shown that geothermal energy is far more widespread than was at once thought. The existence of geothermal resources in areas of volcanic activity and geological instability is well known. Such areas usually occur on or close to the border of the tectonic plates into which the earth's crust is divided.[112] Iceland and New Zealand are perhaps the most

---

110 See *supra*, notes 40-64 and accompanying text.

111 See *supra*, notes 81-83 and accompanying text.

112 See generally D.H. Tarling & M.P. Tarling, *Continental Drift: A Study of the Earth's Moving Surface* (London: Bell & Sons, 1971).

spectacular illustrations of these areas, and considerable reserves of geothermal resources exist in both countries.[113] Less well known is the fact that geothermal resources exist in commercial quantities in many parts of the world that are geologically stable, such as Canada, the United States, and Australia.

The reason for the availability of geothermal resources in geologically stable areas is that volcanic or magmatic reserves and vapour-dominated systems, which are associated with instability in the earth's crust, are only two of five identified types of the resource.[114] Geopressured systems are frequently found in subsiding basins containing young sedimentary rock, while hot groundwater is found in a variety of different underground terrains. The other type of geothermal resource is hot dry rocks. This resource is exploited by injecting cold water into the earth through drilled holes; the water becomes superheated on contact with underground heated rock and is discharged at the surface in the form of steam.[115]

In the common law world, legislation specific to geothermal resources has been enacted in British Columbia, New Zealand, and several western states of the United States.[116] Although there is no unanimity of approach between the jurisdictions as to the most appropriate system of structuring geothermal legislation, each Act establishes a management regime and resolves the issue of ownership of the resource. In the majority of jurisdictions that have not yet

---

113 See Ministry of Works and Development, *Power from the Earth* (Wellington: Government Printer, 1984); Ministry of Energy, *Report of the Electricity Sector Planning Committee* (Document No. ISSN 0111-7947) (Wellington: Government Printer, 1985).

114 For a discussion of the various types of geothermal resources, see Sho Sato & Thomas D. Crocker, "Property Rights to Geothermal Resources" (1977) 6 Ecology L.Q. 250 at 255-262: Kenneth R. Bjorge, "The Development of Geothermal Resources and the 1970 Geothermal Steam Act — Law in Search of Definition" (1974) 46 U. Colorado L. Rev. 1 at 2-3.

115 For a detailed discussion of the hot dry rocks resource, see Morton Smith *et al.*, "Induction and Growth of Fractures in Hot Rock" *in* Paul Kruger & Carel Otte, eds., *Geothermal Energy: Resources, Petroleum, Stimulation* (Stanford: Stanford University Press, 1973) at 251 *et seq.*

116 New Zealand: *Geothermal Energy Act 1953*; British Columbia: *Geothermal Resources Act*, S.B.C. 1982, c.14; Alaska: Ala. Stats. Ann. §38.05.181; Arizona: Ariz. Rev. Stat. Ann. §§27-651 to 27-677; California: Cal. Pub. Res. Code §§3700 to 3776 and §§6902 to 6925; Hawaii: Ha. Rev. Stats. §§182-1 to 182-15; Idaho: Id. Code §§42-4001 to 42-4015; Montana: Mont. Rev. Codes Ann. §§81-2601 to 81-2613; Nevada: Nev. Rev. Stat. §§534A.010 to 524A.010; New Mexico: N.M. Stat. Ann. §§65-11-1 to 65-11-24; Oregon: Ore. Rev. Stats. §§522.005 to 522.990; Washington: Wash. Rev. Code Ann. §79.76.010.990. In addition, there is U.S. Federal legislation regulating geothermal development on federal lands: see 30 U.S.C. §§1001 to 1027.

introduced geothermal legislation, these issues have to be resolved at common law.

The most pressing issue is that of ownership.[117] This is not an issue where geothermal resources are developed on public lands, as on any analysis the ownership rights will vest in the Crown. However, the issue arises in respect of private lands, where claims to ownership may be lodged by both the surface landowner, by virtue of his fee simple estate; by the developer, if the resource is *res nullius*; or by the Crown, by virtue of its rights to minerals and to groundwater. What are the possible alternative approaches at common law to resolving the ownership issue? One possibility is for the courts to declare the resource to be a "mineral", and therefore subject to the relevant minerals allocative regime; a second approach is to deem it to be a "gas", in order to subject it to the relevant oil and gas allocative regime; a third approach is to declare the resource to be "water", and therefore subject to the local groundwater allocative regime; and the final alternative is to declare the resource to be *sui generis*. In the absence of legislation, any one of these approaches could be taken. A further complication is that the result at common law may differ according to the type of geothermal resource.

Geothermal Resources as a Mineral

Because of the lack of an exhaustive definition of "minerals" at common law, it is possible to argue that geothermal resources are encompassed within the scope of that term. The scope of "minerals" is left unclear even by the existing statutory minerals-allocative regimes. Thus, while the statutory definition differs significantly between jurisdictions, most jurisdictions include vague catch-all phrases such as "all naturally occurring substances" or give an inclusive rather than an exhaustive definition.[118]

What is the effect of declaring geothermal resources to be minerals? The common law rule is that the surface landowner owns all the minerals except precious metal (i.e., gold and silver)[119] beneath the land.[120] However, this

---

117 For a more detailed discussion of this issue, see A.J. Bradbrook, "The Ownership of Geothermal Resources" (1987) A.M.P.L.A. Yearbook 353; Joseph W. Aidlin, "Representing the Geothermal Resources Client: The Nature and Character of Geothermal Resources" (1974) 19 Rocky Mt. M.L. Inst. 27.

118 See, for example, *Mines and Minerals Act*, R.S.A. 1980, c.M-15, s.1; *Mining Act*, R.S.O. 1980, c.268, s.1; *Mineral Resources Act*, S.S. 1984-85-86, c.M-16.1, s.2.

119 See *Case of Mines* (1568), 1 Plow. 310, 75 E.R. 472 (K.B.); *Woolley* v. *Attorney-General of Victoria* (1877), 2 App. Cas. 163; *A.G.* v. *Great Cobar Copper Mining Co.* (1900), 21 N.S.W.R. 351 (C.A.).

120 *Wade* v. *N.S.W. Rutile Mining Co. Pty. Ltd.* (1969), 121 C.L.R. 177 (C.A.); *Wilkinson* v. *Proud* (1843), 11 M. & W. 33, 152 E.R. 704 (Ex.).

common law position is subject to express reservation.[121] Thus, in order to determine whether the owner of the land surface also owns the minerals beneath the land, it is necessary at common law to examine the terms of the original Crown grant and also any subsequent conveyance to determine whether the right to minerals has been reserved in favour of the Crown or any other party.[122]

Geothermal Resources as a Gas

If geothermal steam is held to be a gas, the relevant oil and gas allocative regimes will be applicable. Many jurisdictions outside Canada have legislated to ensure complete Crown ownership over oil and gas under private land regardless of when the relevant Crown grant was made.[123] In these jurisdictions, any geothermal resource will be automatically vested in the Crown. In Canada private rights over oil and gas still remain. There, common law principles concerning the ownership of petroleum *in situ* will apply to geothermal resources.

At first glance, it may appear to be unlikely that geothermal resources would be held to constitute a gas. However, this conclusion was reached by the United States Court of Appeal, Ninth Circuit, in *Reich* v. *Commissioner of Internal Revenue*.[124] This case examined the issue for the purpose of determining whether geothermal stream was a gas within the meaning of the U.S. Internal Revenue Code provisions for percentage depletion deduction for intangible costs of drilling and developing oil and gas wells. The court decided the issue in the affirmative after reviewing extensive documentary evidence and hearing expert testimony from geologists and engineers.[125]

Geothermal Resources as Groundwater

A finding that geothermal resources classify as groundwater would give rise to a detailed consideration of ownership rights in groundwater, both at common law and pursuant to legislation. Geothermally heated water beneath

---

121 *Williamson* v. *Wootton* (1855), 3 Drew. 210, 61 E.R. 883 (V.C.). Common law has always recognized the possibility of separate ownership in the subsoil and/or any minerals beneath the surface: *Cox* v. *Glue* (1848), 5 C.B. 533, 136 E.R. 987 (C.P.); *Re Haven Gold Mining Co.* (1882), 20 Ch.D. 151.

122 Some minerals are vested in the Crown by legislation: see, for example, *Law of Property Act*, R.S.A. 1980, c.L-8, s.52.

123 For example, Australia: *Petroleum Act 1955* (N.S.W.), s.6; *Petroleum Act 1923* (Qld.), ss.5, 6; *Petroleum Act 1940* (S.A.), s.4; *Mining Act 1929* (Tas.), s.28; *Petroleum Act 1958* (Vic.), s.5; *Petroleum Act 1967* No.72 (W.A.), s.9.

124 *Reich* v. *Commissioner of Internal Revenue*, 454 F.2d 1157 (9th Cir. 1972).

125 *Id.*, at 1158.

the earth's surface is likely to be regarded at common law as percolating groundwater,[126] although the other types of geothermal resources would presumably fall outside this classification.

In many Canadian provinces, the ownership of groundwater is vested in the Crown pursuant to legislation.[127] The legislation prohibits the person who owns or occupies land under which groundwater exists from using the water except for domestic purposes without a licence issued under the Act. A breach of this legislation constitutes an offence. A system of this nature operates in Alberta, British Columbia, Saskatchewan, Manitoba, Nova Scotia, and the Territories. In Ontario and the Maritime provinces (except Nova Scotia) a different system operates. There, the relevant groundwater statutes do not vest title in water in the Crown,[128] and prior common law rights as to ownership remain in existence.

What is the common law position as to ownership of groundwater? The major authority is *Acton* v. *Blundell*,[129] where Tindal CJ refused to apply by analogy to groundwater the common law rule established earlier that a riparian owner must allow water to flow without sensible diminution.[130] The judge stated:

> The person who owns the surface may dig therein, and apply all that is there found to his own purposes at his free will and pleasure; and that if, in the exercise of such right, he intercepts or drains off the water collected from underground springs in his neighbour's well, this inconvenience to his neighbour falls within the description of *damnum absque injuria*, which cannot become the ground of an action.[131]

Thus, the effect of the decision is to allow the overlying landowner the right of unlimited exploitation of any percolating groundwater beneath his

---

126 For a discussion of common law rights to groundwater, see Australia. Dept. of National Development & Australian Water Resources Council & Sandford D. Clark, *Groundwater Law and Administration in Australia* (Canberra: Australian Government Publications Services, 1979); Alastair R. Lucas, *Security of Title in Canadian Water Rights* (Calgary: Canadian Institute of Resources Law, 1990) c.2-3; D.R. Percy, *The Regulation of Ground Water in Alberta* (Edmonton: Environmental Law Centre, 1987).

127 *Water Act*, R.S.B.C. 1979 c.429 and B.C. Reg. 393/83; *Water Resources Act*, R.S.A. 1980, c.W-5, s.2; *Water Rights Act*, R.S.M. 1988, c.W80, s.2; *Water Corporation Act*, S.S. 1983-84, c.W-4.1, s.41; *Water Act*, R.S.N.S. 1989, c.500, s.3(1); *Northern Inland Waters Act*, R.S.C. 1985, c.N-25, s.4.

128 *Ontario Water Resources Act*, R.S.O. 1980, c.361, s.20. See *Johnson* v. *Anderson*, [1937] 1 W.W.R. 245 (B.C.S.C.). The *Clean Water Act*, S.N.B. 1989, c.C-6.1, s.9 vests "control" of all water in the Crown.

129 *Acton* v. *Blundell* (1843), 12 M. & W. 324, 152 E.R. 1223.

130 *Mason* v. *Hill* (1833), 5 B. & Ad. 1, 110 E.R. 692 (K.B.).

131 *Acton* v. *Blundell* (1843), 12 M. & W. 324 at 354, 152 E.R. 1223 at 1235.

land, regardless of its effect on adjoining landowners. Whether this right is fettered in any way by a requirement that the use of the water be reasonable was litigated before the House of Lords in *Chasemore v. Richards*,[132] which held in the negative. Later cases even went so far as to hold that the use made by an overlying landowner of percolating groundwater cannot be restrained even if the landowner's motive is improper or malicious.[133]

In light of the extent of the overlying landowner's rights, the question arises whether these rights amount to ownership. The judgment of Tindal CJ in *Acton v. Blundell* arguably supports the view that the right does amount to ownership, but the prevailing view is to the contrary. Lord Wensleydale in *Chasemore v. Richards* stated that it is the use of the percolating groundwater, rather than the property in it, that belongs to the overlying landowner.[134] This proposition was affirmed by the English Court of Appeal in *Ballard v. Tomlinson*.[135]

Clark summarizes the common law position regarding the property rights of the overlying landowner in respect of groundwater as follows:

> The right to appropriate and use groundwater is said to be a natural incident of the ownership of land. As the overlying landowner has no proprietary interest in the unappropriated water beneath his land, it follows that such water cannot be the subject of easement or grant; nor is it possible for a neighbour to obtain an adverse prescriptive right to have the water flow on from under one's land. Such proprietary interest as does exist in percolating groundwater is thus measured in terms of a right to appropriate that water. Once water is appropriated by the overlying owner, by seeping to his well or being pumped to the surface, it does become his property. Until that time, however, he has but a right of appropriation.[136]

Geothermal Resources as Sui Generis

If geothermal resources are found to be neither minerals, nor gas, nor groundwater, they will be classified as *sui generis*. What would be the effect of such a determination on ownership rights in the resource?

The ancient maxim *cujus est solum ejus est usque ad coelum et ad inferos* is the starting point for determining this question. Applied in the present context, the maxim suggests that geothermal resources should belong to the overlying landowner merely by virtue of their location beneath his land.

There is considerable doubt whether the wide application of the maxim

---

132 *Chasemore v. Richards* (1859), 7 H.L. Cas. 349, 11 E.R. 140.

133 See, for example, *Mayor of Bradford v. Pickles*, [1895] A.C. 587.

134 *Chasemore v. Richards* (1859), 7 H.L. Cas. 349 at 385, 11 E.R. 140 at 154.

135 *Ballard v. Tomlinson* (1884), 26 Ch.D. 194 (first instance) (1885), 29 Ch. D. 115 (C.A.).

136 *Groundwater Law and Administration in Australia, supra*, note 126, at 28.

represents the current position at common law. Unfortunately, very few cases relevant to the maxim are concerned with the ownership of subsoil and substances beneath the earth's surface. Such authority that does exist suggests that the maxim is of only limited application. The Privy Council, for example, stated in *Commissioner of Railways* v. *Valuer-General*[137] that in no previous case is there an authoritative pronouncement that "land" means the whole of the space from the centre of the earth upwards; so sweeping, unscientific, and unpractical a doctrine was unlikely to appeal to the common law mind. The present position appears to be that the landowner has limited rights over the subsoil close to the earth's surface.[138] This proposition is supported by cases declaring entry into the subsoil to exploit a coal-seam and an underground cave to be a trespass against the owner of the overlying land.[139] These cases, however, concern subsoil within two hundred metres of the surface, and even these decisions have been disputed.[140] It would appear difficult for a landowner to use these authorities to justify a claim to geothermal resources located much deeper in the earth.

As the authorities on the operation of the maxim in respect of subsoil are sparse, in the present context a court might examine the application of the maxim to the ownership of airspace and apply the relevant authorities to the issue under discussion by analogy.

The major case in recent times supporting a wide application of the maxim in the context of airspace is *Kelsen* v. *Imperial Tobacco Co. (of Great Britian and Ireland) Ltd.*[141] In this case, the plaintiff sought an injunction based on a claim of trespass to airspace to require the defendant to remove an advertising sign which projected into the airspace above the plaintiff's shop. McNair J held that the plaintiff, as tenant, had the right to use the airspace and that the interference by the sign constituted a trespass.

Other authorities, however, suggest a different result. The best-known case limiting the scope of the maxim is *Lord Bernstein of Leigh* v. *Skyviews and General Ltd.*,[142] where the defendants had flown over the plaintiff's

---

137 *Commissioner of Railways* v. *Valuer-General*, [1974] A.C. 328 at 351 to 352 (P.C.).

138 See *Corbett* v. *Hill* (1870), L.R. 9 Eq. 671.

139 *Bulli Coal Mining Co.* v. *Osborne*, [1899] A.C. 351 (P.C.); *Edwards* v. *Sims*, 24 S.W. 2d 619 (C.A. 1929). See also *Elwes* v. *Brigg Gas Co.* (1886), 33 Ch. D. 562.

140 See, for example, *Boehringer* v. *Montalto*, 254 N.Y.S. 276 (1931).

141 *Kelsen* v. *Imperial Tobacco Co.*, [1957] 2 Q.B. 334. See also *Gifford* v. *Dent*, [1926] W.N. 336 (Ch. Div.). Cf. *Woollerton and Wilson Ltd.* v. *Richard Costain Ltd.*, [1970] 1 W.L.R. 411 (Ch. Div.).

142 *Lord Bernstein of Leigh* v. *Skyviews & General Ltd.*, [1978] Q.B. 479.

land and taken an aerial photograph of it with the intention of selling it to him. The plaintiff unsuccessfully sued the defendants in trespass on the basis of his alleged unrestricted ownership of the airspace above his land. Griffith J distinguished the earlier cases in favour of the broad application of the maxim on the ground that they concerned rights in the airspace immediately adjacent to the surface of the land. His Honour rejected the claim that a landowner's rights extend to an unlimited height, and stated that the rights of a landowner in the airspace above his land should be restricted to such height as is necessary for the ordinary use and enjoyment of his land and the structures upon it.[143]

This latter approach supports the proposition that private ownership of the airspace does not extend to a height beyond that which can reasonably be held to be within the control of the occupier, which appears to represent the current law. This conclusion, which is conjunctive with the earlier discussion concerning the application of the maxim to the ownership of subsoil, suggests that the maxim operates only to a very limited distance above and below the land. The significance of this conclusion for the present discussion is that it is unlikely that the maxim would operate to give ownership of geothermal resources, all of which lie deep within the earth's crust, to the surface owner.

If the conclusion is correct, it follows that the geothermal resources are *res nullius* and will become the property of the first person to reduce them into possession.[144] In the absence of any statutory management regime for geothermal resources, the rule of capture would operate to allow the surface owner to exploit the resource to the maximum extent possible on his land regardless of whether his operations cause the resource to be drained from underneath neighbouring land.

It thus appears that there are two possible alternative conclusions as to ownership of the resource if the resource is regarded as *sui generis*: first, the *cujus est solum* maxim will vest the resource in the overlying landowner; second, the resource will be *res nullius* and will be subject to ownership only when it is reduced into possession. As a practical matter, however, it appears that the effective result in both cases will usually be the same. Even if the resource is *res nullius*, access to it can be obtained only by the overlying landowner or by developers allowed entry onto the overlying land with the

---

143 *Id.*, at 488. See also *Graham* v. *K.D. Morris & Sons Pty. Ltd.*, [1974] Qd. R. 1 (S.C.).

144 This conclusion is based on an analogy with the qualified ownership theory relating to petroleum in the United States. Under this theory, the surface owner has the exclusive right on his own land to seek to acquire petroleum, but it does not become private property until the petroleum has been reduced into actual possession. See M. Crommelin, "The U.S. Rule of Capture: Its Place in Australia" (1986) A.M.P.L.A. Yearbook 422.

landowner's consent. Thus, exclusive control over access to the resource is effectively, if not legally, the equivalent of ownership.

Summary

The significance of this analysis for the purpose of the present discussion is that common law appears incapable of providing a definitive answer to the fundamental issue of ownership of geothermal resources in the absence of legislation. Such indecision and uncertainty militates against private development and exploitation of the resource and acts contrary to the public interest in developing alternative energy resources.

ENERGY CONSERVATION

Energy conservation has a number of different aspects and applications. One of its major applications is in domestic and commercial building, where the implementation of a variety of conservation measures, such as passive solar devices[145] and insulation, can have a dramatic impact on the amount of energy consumed for heating and cooling purposes.[146] A second application of energy conservation relates to the overall energy efficiency of typical industrial plant. Such efficiency may be increased significantly by the use of cogeneration[147] and improved motor drives and combustion processes. The other applications of energy conservation are the efficiency of domestic appliances[148] and the curtailment of waste in transportation fuels.[149]

What is the actual and potential role of the common law in the area of

---

145 See *supra*, note 78.

146 For a discussion of legal aspects of energy conservation in buildings, see, for example, Grant P. Thompson, *Building to Save Energy: Legal and Regulatory Approaches* (Cambridge, Mass.: Ballinger, 1980); William D. Kopper, "Energy Building Regulations: The Effect of the Federal Performance Standards on Building Code Administration and the Conservation of Energy in New Buildings" (1980) 13 U.C.D. Law Rev. 330; Brenda M. Wood, "Energy Conservation: Government Mandated Utility Programs for Residential and Commercial Buildings — An Expensive Way to Save" (1981) 24 Howard L.J. 183; California Energy Commission, *Building Energy Efficiency Standards* (Report P400-88-001) (Sacramento, 1988).

147 Cogeneration is sometimes referred to as "combined heat and power" or "total energy plant". For a discussion of cogeneration technology, see Frank B. Cross, "Cogeneration: Its Potential and Incentives for Development" (1979) 3 Harvard Environmental L. Rev. 236; Duane A. Siler, "Cogeneration and Small Power Production" *in* Linda Elizabeth Buck & Lee M. Goodwin, eds., *Alternative Energy: The Federal Role* (Colorado: McGraw-Hill, 1982) ch.7.

148 See, for example, Adrian J. Bradbrook, "The Development of Energy Efficiency Laws for Domestic Appliances" (1990) 12 Adelaide L. Rev. 306.

149 See, for example, Robert W. Crandall & John D. Graham, "The Effect of Fuel Economy Standards on Automobile Safety" (1989) 32 J. Law and Economics 97.

energy conservation in the absence of any statutory framework? Sadly, the role appears to be virtually non-existent. There has been no reported litigation to date in relation to energy conservation in any common law jurisdiction.

There seem to be only two situations where the common law may be of assistance in the drive towards energy conservation:

1. In certain limited circumstances, it may be possible to argue that a person who unnecessarily wastes energy is guilty of public nuisance. However, as can be seen from the definition of public nuisance cited earlier,[150] it is only in exceptional circumstances that public nuisance would be held to exist. It would be difficult to argue that the wastage of energy affects the "comfort and safety" of the public, unless a severe energy shortage arises in the future.

2. The common law may have some application in the case of the installation of energy conservation measures in rented commercial buildings. Unlike in the case of residential tenancies, where the law in Canada[151] and most other common law countries[152] is now codified by statute, the common law of landlord and tenant continues to apply to commercial tenancies. Which principles of tenancy law might have some application to the issue of energy conservation? One important question is whether either party has the duty to install conservation measures in the building. The answer appears to be in the negative. There is a common law duty on a landlord to ensure that premises are fit for habitation at the commencement of a tenancy.[153] However, this duty has been limited narrowly so as to apply only to situations that make living conditions intolerable. There is also an implied covenant on the tenant at common law to use the premises in a tenant-like manner.[154] Once again,

---

150 See *supra*, note 40 and accompanying text.

151 *Landlord and Tenant Act*, R.S.A. 1980, c.L-6; *Residential Tenancy Act*, S.B.C. 1984, c.15; *Landlord and Tenant Act*, R.S.M. 1987, c.L-70, Part V; *Residential Tenancies Act*, S.N.B. 1975, c.R-10.2; *Residential Tenancies Act*, S.N. 1988, c.44; *Residential Tenancies Act*, S.N.W.T. 1987(1), c.28; *Residential Tenancies Act*, S.N.S. 1970, c.13; *Landlord and Tenant Act*, 1980, c.232, Part V; *Residential Tenancies Act*, R.S.S. 1978, c.R-22; *Landlord and Tenant Act*, R.S.Y.T. 1986, c.98, Part 4.

152 Australia: *Residential Tenancies Act 1987* No.26 (N.S.W.); *Residential Tenancies Act 1975* No.61 (Qld.); *Residential Tenancies Act 1978* (S.A.); *Residential Tenancies Act 1980* No.9514 (Vic.); *Residential Tenancies Act 1987* No.128 (W.A.); New Zealand: *Residential Tenancies Act 1986* No.120.

153 *Smith* v. *Marrable* (1843), 11 M. & W. 5, 152 E.R. 693; *Collins* v. *Hopkins*, [1923] 2 K.B. 617. This duty may be restricted to furnished premises: *Hart* v. *Windsor* (1843), 12 M.& W. 68, 152 E.R. 1114 (Ex.).

154 *Marsden* v. *Edward Heyes Ltd.*, [1927] 2 K.B. 1; *Wellington Square Holdings Ltd.* v.

however, the possible installation of energy conservation measures appears to be beyond the scope of this covenant. The covenant has traditionally been limited in its scope to small repair jobs,[155] and without a revolution in judicial thinking cannot realistically be argued to include an obligation to install any energy conservation measures.

Ironically, the common law is not only ineffective in this area, but is even counterproductive. In regard to the installation of energy conservation measures in rented buildings, the fundamental problem from the tenant's perspective is that, since tenants do not own the premises, they are very reluctant to make capital investments in the landlord's property by installing energy conservation measures.[156] This problem could be partially overcome if tenants were allowed to remove certain conservation measures at the end of the tenancy, if this were possible without damaging the building. Unfortunately, the common law rules on this issue are otherwise. Any energy conservation measures installed by a tenant in the rented premises will become fixtures under traditional common law rules, and legal title will vest in the landlord.[157] The landlord is under no obligation to compensate the tenant for the value of the improvements in the absence of express agreement. Although tenants are given certain rights at common law to remove fixtures prior to the termination of the tenancy agreement, such right of removal is limited to trade, ornamental, and domestic fixtures.[158] In light of the existing case law as to what falls within the scope of these exemptions, it appears most unlikely that a tenant would be legally permitted to remove any energy conservation measures.

INDEPENDENT POWER PRODUCTION

The encouragement of independent power production[159] is closely allied

---

Chinook Appliances Ltd. (1977), 17 N.R. 52, 5 A.R. 389 (S.C.C.); *Warren* v. *Winterburn* (1907), 6 W.L.R. 498 (B.C. Co. Ct.); *Dickie* v. *Methot* (1958), 25 W.W.R. 446 (B.C. Co. Ct.).

155 *Warren* v. *Keen*, [1954] 1 Q.B. 15 at 20 (C.A.) *per* Denning LJ.

156 See Richard H. Counihan & David Nemtzow, "Energy Conservation and the Rental Housing Market" (1981) 2 Solar Law Reporter 1103 at 1105.

157 For a discussion of the common law rules relating to fixtures, see Robert Megarry & H.W.R. Wade, *The Law of Real Property*, 5th ed. (London: Stevens & Sons, 1984) at 730 to 738; *Cheshire and Burn's Modern Law of Real Property*, 13th ed. (London: Butterworths, 1982) at 136 to 141.

158 See, for example, *Smith* v. *City Petroleum Co. Ltd.*, [1940] 1 All E.R. 260; *Spyer* v. *Phillipson*, [1931] 2 Ch 183; *Concepts Projects Ltd.* v. *McKay*, [1984] 1 N.Z.L.R. 560 (H.C.); *New Zealand Government Property Corporation* v. *H.M. & S. Ltd.*, [1982] Q.B. 1145 (C.A.); *D'Arcy* v. *Burelli Investments Pty. Ltd.* (1987), 8 N.S.W.L.R. 317 (Eq. Div.).

159 For further discussion of this issue, see S. Ferrey, *The Law of Independent Power* (New

to the drive to foster renewable energy and energy conservation. Renewable energy, energy conservation, and independent power production all constitute demand-management techniques, and all assist in the drive to reduce reliance on fossil fuels. Traditionally, electric utilities have had a monopoly over electricity generation in their physical area of jurisdiction. In many countries, this monopoly is protected by legislation that makes it an offence for any person to sell or supply electricity to third parties without the approval of the relevant electric utility, and prohibits any other person from erecting transmission lines outside the confines of his property.[160]

While every electric utility may legitimately require a monopoly over power supply and distribution in order to be economically viable, this argument does not extend to power generation. Many utilities are now recognizing that, in light of the soaring cost of building new power stations, any viable means of reducing demand or increasing supply should be adopted in preference.[161] One such means is independent power production. Many landowners and industries have traditionally generated their own power supplies on their own premises. If there is any excess electricity generated, why should this not be fed into the local electric transmission system and sold to the relevant electric utility?

In the present context, the issue is whether the common law is able to provide any assistance in the move towards increasing independent power production. Once again, the answer appears to be in the negative. The only jurisdiction in which there has been any reported litigation to date in relation to independent power production is the United States.[162] However, this litigation concerned the constitutional validity of U.S. federal legislation[163] rather than common law remedies designed to enhance the incidence of independent power production.

None of the existing common law concepts appears to be capable of

---

York: Clark Broadman, 1989); Bradford S. Gentry, "Public Utility Participation in Decentralized Power Production" (1981) 5 Harvard Environmental L. Rev. 297; L.A. Gregoris, J. Lang & L. Moore, *Canadian Utility Policies on Private Generation* (Toronto: Ontario Ministry of Energy, 1988).

160 See, for example, Australia: *Electricity Act 1943* (S.A.), ss.16, 17; *Electric Light and Power Act 1958* No.6241 (Vic.), s.6; *Electricity Act 1945* (W.A.), s.7.

161 See generally, Canada. Dept. of Energy, Mines and Resources, *Demand Side Management in Canada* (Ottawa, 1988).

162 *F.E.R.C.* v. *Mississippi*, 456 U.S. 742 (C.A. 1982); *American Paper Institute Inc.* v. *American Electric Power Service Corp.*, 461 U.S. 402 (C.A. 1983).

163 *Public Utility Regulatory Policies Act* 16 U.S.C., c.46, §§791-796, 824-825, 2601-2645 (1982).

being moulded into an effective option in relation to the issue under discussion. Legislation will be required to promote the increased use of independent power production. Encouragingly, such legislation has been introduced in the United States,[164] the Province of Alberta,[165] and several other common law jurisdictions[166] in recent years. The role of the courts will be restricted to giving a favourable interpretation to the scope of the relevant statutes.

CONCLUSION

The analysis in this paper shows that in the areas of energy use and planning, the role of the common law is extremely limited. As we have seen, it appears (although not without some doubt) that solar energy and wind energy use may be protected by consensual agreements between neighbours in the form of easements or restrictive covenants. However, in the absence of such agreements and in the absence of legislation, these forms of energy use can be protected only by the law of nuisance, and then only in the most limited circumstances. To compound the problem, even where the law of nuisance might operate in the solar user's or wind user's favour, it is probable that the courts will award damages rather than an injunction, which militates against the future use of resources. The position regarding other sources of energy is even worse. In the case of geothermal energy, common law has been unable to provide a consistent approach to a determination of the central legal issue, that of ownership of the resource, while in the case of energy conservation and independent power production, common law is too inflexible to adapt its rules to new situations.

What is required of common law is bold new initiatives extending

---

164 *Id.* In addition to the federal statute, the following U.S. state legislation exists: Alabama: Ala Code, §37-12-3 (1987); California: Cal. Pub. Util. Code, §2801-2831 (West 1987); Connecticut: Conn. Gen. Stat. Ann., §16-243a (West 1987); Georgia: Ga. Code Ann, §§46-3-50 to 46-3-53 (1982); Hawaii: Haw. Rev. Stat. §269-27.2 (1985); Indiana: Ind. Code Ann. §8-1-2.4 (West 1982); Iowa Code, §476.41-476.45 (1987); Kansas: Kan. Stat. Ann., §66.1, §§184-185 (1986); Louisiana: La. Rev. Stat. Ann., §§121, 1161, 1164 (West 1982); Maine: Me. Rev. Stat. Ann. tit. 35-A, §3301-3308 (1984); Minnesota: Minn. Stat. Ann., §216B.164 (West 1988); Montana: Mont. Code Ann., §§69-3-601 to 69-3-604 (1987); New Hampshire: N.H. Rev. Stat. Ann., §362-A (1984 & Supp. 1987); New York: N.Y. Pub. Serv. Law., §66-c (Consol. 1983); North Carolina: N.C. Gen. Stat., §62-156 (1982); Oregon: Or. Rev. Stat., §§758.505 to 555 (1989); Pennsylvania: Pa. Cons. Stat. Ann., §527 (Purdon 1988); Texas: Tex. Rev. Civ. Stat. Ann., art.1446c(41A) (Vernon 1988); Utah Code Ann., §54-12-1 (1986); Vermont: Vt. Stat. Ann. tit. 30, §209(a)(8)(1986); Virginia: Va. Code Ann., §56-232 (1986).

165 *Small Power Research and Development Act*, S.A. 1988, c.S-13.75.

166 See, for example, *Energy Act 1983* c.25 (U.K.), ss.5 to 7, 9, 10 and 19; *State Electricity Commission Act 1958* No.6377 (Vic.), ss.12(2), 20(2).

established concepts beyond their traditional confines. This has occurred at crucial stages in the past in other areas of resource-use conflicts. One example is *Rylands* v. *Fletcher*,[167] which was common law's answer to the problems of urban pollution that first arose during the Industrial Revolution. Another case in point is *Tulk* v. *Moxhay*,[168] which established the first system of land-use planning at the time of rapid urbanization of society. The only case in the area of energy is *Prah* v. *Maretti*,[169] in which, as already discussed,[170] the Supreme Court of Wisconsin was prepared to radically alter the established principles of the law of private nuisance in order to encourage the use of solar energy. Unfortunately, there is no indication that the Anglo-Canadian courts would be prepared to adopt such a maverick approach, and indeed, no indication even in the United States that *Prah* v. *Maretti* is any more than an isolated exception. The basic problem appears to be that the subject matter of the disputes in the energy field is largely incompatible with common law concepts. Legislation seems to be required in all cases if the use of new forms of energy technology is to be encouraged.

In the absence of any dramatic changes, the courts appear to have restricted their role in the energy area to their traditional one as guardians of the constitution and interpreters of legislation.[171] By construing such legislation favourably, the judiciary will be able to make a limited contribution towards the increased utilization in society of new sources of energy. However, this disguises the greater tragedy that the courts, by refusing to reconsider the traditional common law concepts, have voluntarily abandoned the opportunity to assume a far greater role in this area.

The issue of the development of energy law, and the relevance of the common law to this process, should not be viewed in isolation. There are numerous areas of resource and land use where the common law has proved too inflexible and has been forced to vacate the field in favour of statute law. Planning and building laws are two obvious illustrations. As Lord Scarman once stated, "Tied to concepts of property, possession and fault, the judges have been unable by their own strength to break out of the cabin of the

---

167 *Rylands* v. *Fletcher* (1868), L.R. 3 H.L. 330.

168 *Tulk* v. *Moxhay* (1848), 2 Ph. 774, 41 E.R. 1143 (Ch.).

169 *Prah* v. *Maretti*, 108 Wis. 2d 223, 321 N.W. 2d 182 (S.C. 1982).

170 See *supra*, notes 65-76 and accompanying text.

171 See *F.E.R.C.* v. *Mississippi*, 456 U.S. 742 (C.A. 1982); *American Paper Institute Inc.* v. *American Electric Power Service Corp.*, 461 U.S. 402 (C.A. 1983); *Governor's Ranch Homeowner's Association, Inc.* v. *Gunther*, 705 P. 2d 1011 (Colo. App. 1985); *Sher* v. *Leiderman*, 181 Cal. App. 3d. 645, 226 Cal. Rptr. 698 (1986).

common law and tackle the broad problems of land use in an industrial and urbanised society."[172]

For advocates of the common law system, this will be viewed as a seemingly inexorable and depressing trend.

---

172 Leslie Scarman, *English Law — The New Dimension* (London: Stevens & Sons, 1974) at 53.

L'UTILITÉ JURIDIQUE D'UNE CHARTE DES DROITS À UN ENVIRONNEMENT DE QUALITÉ

*Michel Bélanger**

D'aucuns prétendent que le droit est l'institution par laquelle l'être humain harmonise ses rapports avec ses semblables pour assurer le respect du fameux contrat social de Jean-Jacques Rousseau. Mais voilà qu'un nouveau sujet de droit est apparu il y a à peine deux décennies. L'environnement, pour ce qu'il représente en soi, doit être protégé contre les abus que l'espèce humaine en a fait. Le philosophe Michel Serres va plus loin, concluant qu'au contrat exclusivement social, devrait s'ajouter la passation d'un contrat naturel de symbiose et de réciprocité entre l'homme et la nature devenu sujet de droit; un contrat où chacun des partenaires devrait, de droit, à l'autre, la vie sous peine de mort.[1]

L'être humain devra donc réapprendre à intégrer à ses rapports une réalité oubliée au siècle dernier: son interdépendance avec la nature. Dès lors que ce dernier a envisagé de "maîtriser" la nature, il s'est, en effet, engagé dans un combat perdu à l'avance, puisqu'il a tenté d'asservir l'essence même de sa propre existence.

Le droit, comme institution impliquée au coeur même de l'élaboration et de l'application des normes et politiques, a un rôle important à jouer afin de retrouver un certain équilibre écologique essentiel à la survie des espèces dont fait partie l'être humain.

Le droit a toujours été le reflet des valeurs d'une société. Il est vrai qu'à ce titre, le droit ne pourrait, en principe, servir à influer des changements de valeur sociale, en imposant à la collectivité une ligne de conduite que chacun de ses membres, individuellement, ne serait pas prêt à suivre. Mais voilà précisément le rôle que l'on souhaiterait ou espérerait lui voir jouer dans le domaine de l'environnement. Existerait-il seulement d'autres avenues possibles dans nos sociétés? Quelle institution pourrait permettre d'imposer, assez rapidement, des comportements écologiquement viables, à une collectivité qui se soucie d'abord d'atteindre une qualité de vie matérielle reposant sur l'insatisfaction de l'acquis et le désir de l'inaccessible? Une

---

*   Le présent exposé est partiellement tiré d'un ouvrage du même auteur, intitulé *La reconnaissance d'un droit à un environnment de qualité* (Montréal: Éditions Thémis, Université de Montréal, 1990).

1   Michel Serres, *Le contrat naturel* (Paris: Éditions François Bourin, 1990) à la p.69.

société qui, de la nécessité est passée au confort, et du confort au luxe. Le "luxe" qui, par définition, est la qualité de ce qu'on ne peut s'offrir. C'est précisément ce que nous avons fait et faisons en ignorant le coût environnemental de notre mode de vie. Ainsi que devait le conclure la Commission mondiale sur l'environnement et le développement, "nous empruntons un capital écologique aux générations à venir, en sachant pertinemment, que nous ne pourrons jamais le leur rembourser".[2]

Nous avons fait ressortir, dans le cadre de la présente étude, qu'il fallait ramener le débat aux motivations profondes qui ont entraîné notre crise environnementale actuelle et qui sont, fondamentalement, le reflet de nos priorités économiques et sociales. En fait, "la protection de l'environnement n'est pas une fin en soi; elle répond plutôt à un besoin social. Ainsi, une compréhension du problème exige d'abord une compréhension des perceptions, des valeurs et des institutions sociales du point de vue de leur relation avec l'environnement".[3] La dimension environnementale devrait, en fait, comme le faisait remarquer Alexandre Kiss, être "la toile de fond" de toutes les politiques tant économiques que sociales.[4]

Au rythme où se succèdent les déclarations des groupes écologistes dans différents forums régionaux ou nationaux, les articles de journaux et revues vantant les mérites d'une Charte de l'environnement, il devient important de tenter de rapprocher cette affirmation de principe à la réalité juridique. Inscrite au programme politique de presque tous les partis, cette idée trouve des appuis jusqu'au Vatican où le Pape Jean-Paul II a demandé, le 5 décembre 1989, dans le cadre de la journée mondiale de la paix, que le droit à la sécurité de l'environnement soit inscrit dans une Charte des droits de l'homme, mise à jour.

---

2   Commission mondiale sur l'environnement et le développement, *Notre avenir à tous* (Montréal: Éditions du Fleuve, 1988) à la p.9.

3   Paul D. Emond, "La politique et le droit de l'environnement: un examen de l'expérience canadienne" dans Ivan Bernier & Andrée Lajoie, éd., *La protection des consommateurs, le droit de l'environnement et le pouvoir des sociétés*, Commission royale sur l'union économique et les perspectives de développement du Canada, vol. 50 (Ottawa: Approvisionnements et Services Canada, 1985) 105 à la p.108; voir également: J. Bockrath, "Environment, Development and the National Interest: Problems in Definition and Prerogatives" (1975) 8 Natural Resources Lawyer 29 aux pp.39-40; et Kathleen W. Marcel, "The Role of the Courts in a Legislative and Administrative Legal System — The Use of Hard Look Review in Federal Environmental Litigation" (1983) 62 Oregon L.R. 403 à la p.410, qui précise que chaque décision en droit de l'environnement requiert un changement fondamental des valeurs sociales, économiques, politiques et du rôle du système juridique.

4   Alexandre-Charles Kiss, "Interventions des rapporteurs" *dans* Alexandre-Charles Kiss, éd., *La protection de l'environnement et le droit international*, Colloque 1973 (Leiden: Sijthoff, 1975) 466.

Il faudrait d'abord s'entendre sur ce que l'on veut dire par "Charte". Est-ce une affirmation d'intention politique, une déclaration législative ou, comme on semble le laisser entendre, l'enchâssement d'un nouveau droit parmi ceux déjà reconnus dans les chartes canadienne et québécoise des droits de la personne?

UNE DÉCLARATION D'INTENTION POLITIQUE

La consécration, au plan politique, d'une telle affirmation de principe apparaît une évidence. À la lumière des discours électoraux, qui cachent mal un certain opportunisme et laissent peu de place au véritable courage politique nécessaire dans les circonstances, une telle déclaration semble déjà dépassée.

Une reconnaissance prioritaire de la dimension environnementale au plan politique devrait se refléter tant au niveau de la législation que des décisions administratives émanant de tous les ministères susceptibles de porter atteinte à cette réalité. Pareille déclaration politique devrait favoriser, notamment, l'harmonisation des politiques et normes qui est censée en découler.

Toutefois, considérant les dispositions législatives existantes au Québec, qui reconnaissent expressément, de façon générale, un tel principe,[5] il y aurait lieu de s'interroger sur la pertinence d'une reconnaissance politique si l'affirmation, même balisée, d'un tel droit dans une législation, n'a pas contribué à améliorer suffisamment notre situation environnementale? Permettons-nous donc de croire qu'une telle déclaration politique devrait aller beaucoup plus loin que l'affirmation législative de principe énoncée ci-haut.

DÉFINIR UN DROIT À UN ENVIRONNEMENT DE QUALITÉ

Ainsi, la simple déclaration politique qui énonce un tel principe n'a d'utilité que proportionnellement aux mesures concrètes qu'elle génère. Au nombre de ces mesures, nous estimons, dans le contexte de notre étude, qu'une reconnaissance législative ou supra-législative d'un droit à un environnement de qualité est, sans doute, l'affirmation la plus tangible de cette volonté politique et également, dans le dernier cas, la plus coûteuse au plan de la suprématie parlementaire.

En fait, les moyens utilisés par les autorités politiques, de qui relève cette ultime décision, ont une importance capitale pour le juriste. Accorder ou non une portée juridique à la reconnaissance de ce principe reflétera, d'une certaine manière, cette volonté politique et l'objectif poursuivi.

Une première question fondamentale ayant des conséquences importantes

---

5   En l'occurrence les articles 19.1 et 20 de la *Loi sur la qualité de l'environnement*, L.R.Q. 1977, c.Q-2 mod. par L.Q. 1978, c.64, s.4.

au plan de la conceptualisation juridique d'un tel droit, a trait à la définition même des termes: "Droit à un environnement de qualité".

Bien qu'il ait paru attrayant de consacrer des droits à la nature en elle-même, la protection juridique de l'environnement ne semblerait se définir aujourd'hui, selon une majorité d'auteurs, sans tenir compte de ceux et celles qui en exigent le respect. C'est-à-dire que l'environnement, comme valeur en soi, ne pourrait être protégé que pour ce qu'il représente essentiellement et il semble irréaliste, tant sur le plan juridique que philosophique, d'assigner des droits à des entités non humaines, alors qu'il est reconnu depuis toujours que seuls les êtres humains peuvent être sujets de droit.[6]

Il semblerait que ce droit, qualifié de collectif, appartienne à la catégorie de droits dits "socio-économiques", c'est-à-dire qui ne peuvent s'entendre sans mesures concrètes de mise en oeuvre. Ces mesures permettant concrètement

---

6   Commission de réforme du droit du Canada, *Les crimes contre l'environnement* (Ottawa: Approvisionnements et Services Canada, 1985) à la p.18. Sur l'aspect anthropocentrique du droit de l'environnement, voir notamment Jean-Pierre Levy qui rappelle qu'"Il n'y aurait pas de droit de l'environnement s'il n'y avait pas d'homme et l'homme a un rapport direct avec les phénomènes de pollution et partant avec le droit que nous devrions être en train de créer." Jean-Pierre Levy, "Discussion" *dans* Kiss, *supra*, note 5, à la p.426; voir également à ce propos Jean-Claude Deschesnes, "La détermination des priorités en environnement" *dans* Association des biologistes du québec, *Vers une gestion globale de l'environnement du Québec* (Montréal: Bibliothèque Nationale du Québec et du Canada, 1987) 66; Michael Bothe, "La relation entre le droit international de la santé et le droit international de l'environnement" (1985) 2 R.Q.D.I. 125 à la p.135; Jehan de Malafosse, *Le droit de l'environnement — le droit à la nature — aménagement et protection* (Paris: Éditions Montchrestien, 1973) à la p.250; Commission de réforme du droit du Canada, *Pour une nouvelle codification du droit pénal* (Ottawa: Approvisionnements et Services Canada, 1987) à la p.106; Michel Yergeau, "Le droit civil du Québec et la protection de l'environnement" *dans Droit de l'environnement — Le droit, les problèmes et conseils pratiques* (Toronto: Canadian Institute, 1988) à la p.B-13, où ce dernier précise que "nous ne sommes pas à un stade d'évolution qui favorise la protection de l'environnement et de la nature en eux-mêmes et pour eux-mêmes. Il s'agit plutôt de la protection du bien collectif *comme ressource exploitable ou utilisable*" (nous soulignons). Enfin, Kiss, tentant de concilier les deux positions, esquisse une synthèse possible: "En effet, si un droit créé par les humains ne peut s'entendre dans sa conception et dans sa mise en oeuvre en-dehors d'eux-mêmes, sa finalité dépasse le cercle des humains — on en sait maintenant assez sur la biosphère pour penser que, si l'on ne conserve pas ses ressources, si l'on ne respecte pas ses grands équilibres, les humains ne survivront pas plus que beaucoup d'autres êtres vivants. Ainsi, la protection de la biosphère en tant que telle mène indirectement, mais nécessairement, à celle des humains. L'essentiel est de comprendre la place, le rôle et les effets des êtres humains et de leurs oeuvres dans l'univers pour les protéger au coeur de l'ensemble au besoin contre eux-mêmes." Alexandre Kiss, "Définition et nature juridique d'un droit de l'homme à l'environnement" *dans* Pascale Kromarek, éd., *Environnement et droit de l'Homme* (Paris: Organisation des Nations Unies pour l'éducation, la science et la culture (UNESCO), 1987) 13 aux pp. 16-17.

de réaliser les objectifs qui sous-tendent la reconnaissance d'un droit à un environnement de qualité ont été bien identifiées par les juristes spécialistes en cette matière.

Pour en résumer l'essentiel, mentionnons notamment: la nécessité de promouvoir une participation publique accrue au niveau des prises de décisions fondamentales (l'action gouvernementale risquerait ainsi de sembler moins anachronique et favoriserait l'acceptation et le respect des normes), la nécessité de favoriser l'accès aux informations sur lesquelles le citoyen pourra se baser pour apporter une participation utile et nécessaire au processus décisionnel, la nécessité de faciliter l'accès du public à la justice, en allégeant le fardeau financier qu'entraîne ce genre de procédures judiciaires, en assouplissant les règles relatives à l'intérêt à poursuivre et en renversant le fardeau de la preuve de l'innocuité d'une substance en faveur de la victime potentielle. Également, la nomination d'un médiateur des conflits environnementaux et l'imposition d'études d'impacts obligatoires pour tout projet susceptible d'entraîner des répercussions environnementales permettraient d'éviter le recours systématique au processus judiciaire.

Il y a lieu toutefois d'être prudent dans l'élaboration de telles modalités d'application nécessaires à la réalisation de ce droit collectif visant à sauvegarder notre environnement. En raison du caractère particulier de ce nouvel objet de droit, en l'occurrence l'environnement, ces mécanismes de mise en oeuvre risqueraient d'entrer en conflit avec certains droits ou libertés déjà garantis constitutionnellement; mise en garde qui pourrait également s'étendre à des dispositions actuelles de la loi.

Certains droits individuels souffriraient inévitablement d'une atteinte, dont l'étendue dépendrait de l'évaluation judiciaire des divers intérêts en cause. Ainsi, pourrions-nous opposer aux droits d'accès aux informations environnementales, la liberté d'expression de celui qui les détient ou encore, aux mesures facilitant l'accès du public à la justice, la présomption d'innocence de l'accusé. En fait, dès l'application des mesures destinées à affirmer un tel droit à un environnement de qualité viendraient s'opposer, paradoxalement, les autres droits humains reconnus fondamentaux.

En somme, la *Charte canadienne*[7] pourrait être invoquée pour tenter de stériliser les effets des mesures d'application suggérées, incompatibles avec la réalisation de certains droits individuels. De l'avis de la Commission de réforme du droit du Canada, cela reviendrait à se demander si "l'institution chargée d'élaborer des politiques (le gouvernement) devrait avoir le pouvoir

---

7   Partie I de la *Loi constitutionelle de 1982*, constituant l'annexe B de la *Loi de 1982 sur le Canada* [R.-U.], 1982, c.11.

de restreindre la capacité d'un autre ensemble d'institutions (les sociétés commerciales) d'exposer les citoyens à certains risques ou, en d'autres termes, de 'réglementer' par le biais de politiques imposant une situation de fait. Il est facile d'invoquer [poursuit-elle] la liberté individuelle, seulement, pour faire correspondre l'absence d'intervention gouvernementale à un accroissement de la liberté, il faut présupposer que seules les politiques établies par les gouvernements sont susceptibles de porter atteinte à la liberté. Or, cette hypothèse est indéfendable: ce qui est en cause, habituellement, c'est 'la liberté de devenir riche' en faisant supporter à des tiers certains effets externes."[8]

Après réflexion, il peut sembler pour le moins paradoxal de reconnaître l'importance de droits et libertés individuels nécessaires à l'épanouissement de l'être humain en société, alors que la nature, dont cette même société dépend étroitement, imminemment menacée, ne bénéficierait pas d'une reconnaissance équivalente. Dans la mesure où les chartes des droits humains n'ont pas eu simplement pour but d'assurer la qualité de vie de ceux qui les ont vues naître, il faut d'abord se soucier de redonner un monde à ceux qui désireront également profiter de ces acquis, au prix d'un nouvel équilibre des valeurs imposé par la prépondérance du poids de cette nouvelle dimension écologique. Plusieurs auteurs ont d'ailleurs reconnu le caractère éphémère de nos droits humains si la nature ne trouve pas une reconnaissance équivalente. Ainsi, à l'instar de la liberté d'expression, de la liberté de religion et des autres droits fondamentaux, la qualité de l'environnement devrait être reconnue par la loi comme un droit inaliénable, car sans un environnement propre à subvenir aux besoins de la race humaine, tous les autres droits sont illusoires.[9]

LA RECONNAISSANCE LÉGISLATIVE D'UN DROIT À UN ENVIRONNEMENT DE QUALITÉ

Indépendamment de l'incompatibilité possible avec les chartes des droits

---

8   Commission de réforme du droit du Canada, *L'élaboration des politiques en matière d'environnement* (Ottawa: Approvisionnement et Services Canada, 1984) à la p.83.

9   David Estrin et John Swaigen, *Environment on Trial*, édition révisée (Toronto: Mary-Anne Carswell and John Swaigen, 1978) à la p.459, traduit par la Commission de réforme du droit du Canada, *supra*, note 7, n.19 en bas de la p.16. "Dans ces conditions, le droit à l'environnement fera en outre figure de préalable indispensable, à défaut duquel la plupart des droits de l'homme demeureraient de simples voeux pieux"; Mohamed Ali Mekouar, "Le droit à l'environnement dans ses rapports avec les autres droits de l'homme" *dans* Kromarek, *supra*, note 7, 91 à la p.103; également Richard O. Brooks, "Coercion to Environmental Virtue: Can and Should Law Mandate Environmentally Sensitive Life Style?" (1986) 31 American J. of Jurisprudence 21 aux pp.63-64; et William D. Kirchick, "The Continuing Search for a Constitutionally Protected Environment" (1975) 4 Env. Affairs 515 à la p.531.

et libertés de la personne, les propositions invoquées pour qualifier un droit à un environnement de qualité ont été mises de l'avant dans l'optique d'une réforme globale du droit environnemental et des institutions chargées de son application.

De la démocratisation du processus de prise de décision garantie par une information suffisante, à l'accès à la justice environnementale, une législation spécifique ou un amendement à la législation actuelle devra pourvoir à l'exercice de ces modalités d'application nécessaires à la réalisation des objectifs poursuivis par la reconnaissance de ce droit fondamental. Les mécanismes procéduraux favoriseraient, en quelque sorte, l'atteinte de l'idéal de justice environnementale, le rétablissement de l'équilibre entre l'épanouissement des "besoins" humains et l'environnement naturel, en conscientisant et responsabilisant directement le public, victime de sa propre consommation.

Pour ne s'en tenir, toutefois, qu'à la simple affirmation d'un droit à un environnement de qualité ou, du moins, du droit de se prémunir contre toute agression environnementale, la législation québécoise, malgré ses lacunes, établit, par les articles 19.1 et 20 de la *Loi sur la qualité de l'environnement*, les bases d'une telle reconnaissance de principe, énonçant que:

> Toute personne a droit à la qualité de l'environnement, à sa protection et à la sauvegarde des espèces vivantes qui y habitent, dans la mesure prévue par la loi, les règlements, les ordonnances, les approbations et les autorisations délivrées en vertu de cette même loi". (Article 19.1)

Cette reconnaissance est, bien entendu, limitée dans son application. Au risque de déplaire aux tenants de la thèse contraire, il nous paraît utopique de croire qu'un tel droit pourrait être "absolu" dans une société comme la nôtre. Les limites imposées par l'État sont nécessaires à la réalisation progressive des objectifs environnementaux, sans risquer de débalancer une certaine stabilité économique et sociale. Même une reconnaissance au niveau supra-législatif serait appelée à souffrir certaines atteintes, dans la mesure de ce que notre société jugerait justifié et raisonnable.

Nous n'écartons pas pour autant l'utilité d'une telle reconnaissance de principe au niveau supra-législatif. Au contraire, puisque la législation environnementale octroie un pouvoir discrétionnaire à l'autorité gouvernementale de limiter la portée de ce droit par règlement, autorisation ou permis, une telle reconnaissance supra-législative instituant un pouvoir de contrôle sur l'intervention gouvernementale, irrespectueuse des objectifs environnementaux consacrés, imposerait le respect de ces valeurs et de ces droits enchâssés.

LA RECONNAISSANCE SUPRA-LÉGISLATIVE
D'UN DROIT À UN ENVIRONNEMENT DE QUALITÉ

C'est précisément en raison des limites prévues par la loi, accentuées par un certain laxisme des autorités gouvernementales à imposer le respect des dispositions législatives et réglementaires au-delà de telles limites, que l'opinion populaire s'est tournée vers nos instruments supra-législatifs, c'est-à-dire, les chartes des droits et libertés de la personne.

Aucune des chartes des droits et libertés, canadienne ou québécoise, ne garantit expressément un droit à un environnement de qualité, ce qu'il ne faudrait pas interpréter comme un oubli ou l'effet du hasard. Lors de l'élaboration de la *Charte canadienne*, aucune recommandation ne fut adoptée à cette fin par le comité spécial mixte sur la constitution, en dépit des pressions exercées par certaines associations telles l'Association du Barreau canadien ou l'Association canadienne du droit de l'environnement (C.E.L.A.).[10]

Néanmoins, comme le faisait remarquer la Commission de réforme du droit du Canada, "bien qu'aucune des propositions n'ait été couronnée de succès ..., leur existence et l'appui non négligeable qui leur a été donné sont, à tout le moins, un signe irréfutable de l'importance qu'un grand nombre de personnes attachent de nos jours à la qualité de l'environnement."[11]

En raison de la portée de sa terminologie et de l'absence de disposition plus spécifique à cette fin, l'article 7, l'une des dispositions les plus fondamentales de notre *Charte canadienne*, devrait, à notre avis, se prêter à une interprétation extensive afin d'en déduire la reconnaissance implicite d'un droit à un environnement de qualité.[12] Comme le concluait Colin P.

---

10   L'Association du Barreau canadien avait alors proposé d'inclure à l'article 7 une protection à la jouissance de la propriété. Et, à son avis, cela ne pouvait se faire sans garantit également un droit à un environnement sain afin de pouvoir se prémunir contre l'abus de ce premier droit aux dépends de l'autre. Voir à ce sujet Environmental Law Centre, "Charter of Rights" (1985) 3:3 *NewsLetter* 6; Colin P. Stevenson, "A New Perspective on Environmental Rights After the Charter" (1983) 21 O.H.L.J. 390 à la p.402; et John Swaigen et Richard E. Woods, "A Substantive Right to Environmental Quality" *dans* John Swaigen, éd., *Environmental Rights in Canada* (Toronto: Butterworths, 1989) 195 à la p.207. Quant à la Charte québécoise, selon Me Jean Piette, directeur des relations intergouvernementales au ministère de l'Environnement du Québec, on a également refusé l'enchâssement d'un tel droit qui avait été proposé par la Société pour vaincre la pollution (S.V.P.), en raison de l'ingérence qu'aurait eue la Commission des droits de la personne dans des décisions relevant strictement du ministère de l'Environnement: Conseil consultatif de l'environnement du Québec, *Charte de la qualité du milieu de vie*, notes de travail (5e version), tome 1, non-publié, mai 1988, annexe 4, 3.

11   Commission de réforme du droit du Canada, *supra*, note 7, à la p.16.

12   Soulignons également l'hypothèse avancée pour reconnaître en l'article 35 de la *Loi*

Stevenson: "If section 7 purports to protect rights to life, liberty and security of person, surely this must also be taken to include a right to a clean environment."[13]

Néanmoins, une telle reconnaissance de principe enchâssée explicitement dans la *Charte canadienne* ou déduite des dispositions actuelles, en l'occurrence de l'article 7 de la *Charte canadienne* garantissant le droit à la vie et à la sécurité de la personne, n'aurait d'utilité qu'en regard des abus dans l'exercice des pouvoirs étatiques. La *Charte québécoise*, garantissant également un droit à la vie, à la sécurité et à l'intégrité de la personne, serait plus avantageuse si l'on en déduisait ou si on y enchâssait expressément un pareil droit, permettant d'être invoqué directement contre toute intervention étatique ou privée qui irait à son encontre. Soulignons toutefois que ce droit, s'il était enchâssé dans la *Charte québécoise* au chapitre des droits collectifs et sociaux, ne saurait forcer davantage le gouvernement à les mettre en oeuvre, l'article 52 de la *Charte québécoise* ne faisant pas prévaloir ce type de droit reconnu aux articles 39 à 48 sur la législation.

Ainsi, la reconnaissance constitutionnelle ou quasi constitutionnelle d'un droit à un environnement de qualité serait souhaitable dans la mesure où elle a pour effet d'inciter les gouvernements à avoir le courage politique de mettre en oeuvre les mesures permettant la réalisation de cet objectif. Ce faisant, la

---

constitutionelle de 1982, relatif à la reconnaissance des droits autochtones, une interprétation extensive en ce sens. John U. Bayly, "Section 35 of the Constitution Act 1982, and Collective Aboriginal Rights to Environmental Quality" *dans* Nicole Duplé, éd., *Le droit à la qualité de l'environnement: un droit en devenir, un droit à découvrir* (Montréal: Quebec-Amérique, 1988) 251 à la p.256. En ce qui a trait à la *Charte québécoise*, son article premier garantit à tout être humain un droit équivalent à la vie, à la sûreté et à l'intégrité de sa personne, et l'article 6 garantit le "droit à la jouissance paisible de ses biens". Ce dernier article pourrait trouver application advenant, entre autres, atteinte à la jouissance de la propriété par l'intrusion d'une source de contamination. Rappelons-nous toutefois que ce "droit à la jouissance des biens" est limité aux mesures prévues par la loi. Nous aurions ainsi tendance à favoriser plutôt l'interprétation, en ce sens, de l'article premier, dont le libellé s'apparente à celui de l'article 7 de la *Charte canadienne*, permettant à l'une ou l'autre de ces dispositions de bénéficier réciproquement de l'interprétation judiciaire qui en sera faite. Voir André Morel, "La coexistence des Chartes canadienne et québécoise: problèmes d'interaction" (1986) 17 R.D.U.S. 49.

13   Stevenson, *supra*, note 11, 413. Soulignons que le Comité des droits de l'homme des Nations-Unies, alors qu'il était saisi d'une consultation d'un groupe environnemental de "Port Hope Environmental Group" d'Ontario, alléguant violation du droit à la vie garanti par l'article 6 du *Pacte international relatif aux droits civils et politiques* ((1976) 999 R.T.N.U. 187) devait rejeter la demande sur la prétention que l'organisme n'avait pas épuisé les recours internes disponibles au Canada, concluant: "the Committee notes that the author could now also invoke the Canadian Charter of human rights and freedoms which explicitly (section 7) protects the right to life"; voir l'affaire *Pereira c. Canada* (1984-85) 2 A.C.D.P. 351 (Comité des droits de l'homme, 17ième session, le 27 octobre 1982, Doc. NU R/16/67).

justesse du jugement politique apparaîtrait à la lumière du processus d'analyse de l'article premier de la *Charte canadienne*, et de l'article 9.1 de la *Charte québécoise*, permettant à l'instance politique d'en retirer autant de crédibilité *vis-à-vis* du public, dans la mesure où elle agit en conformité avec les objectifs d'un tel droit.

La procédure d'application d'un droit constitutionnel à un environnement de qualité

Pour bien comprendre les enjeux au plan juridique de la reconnaissance d'un tel droit au niveau supra-législatif, nous devons rappeler le processus d'application des droits et libertés garantis constitutionnellement. Se référant aux garanties offertes par la *Charte canadienne* en son article 7, nous devons, dans un premier temps, établir que la *Charte* reconnaît un droit à un environnement de qualité auquel il ne peut être porté atteinte que conformément au principe de justice fondamentale. Après avoir interprété l'article 7 de la sorte, les tribunaux doivent qualifier, sur la base de preuves scientifiques, sociologiques ou autres, ce qu'ils conçoivent être un "environnement de qualité" suffisant à assurer la sécurité de la personne humaine. Il s'agit ensuite de démontrer que la mesure attaquée en l'espèce porte atteinte à cette évaluation environnementale, et qu'en conséquence elle doit être déclarée inconstitutionnelle.

Il faut reconnaître que plus les tribunaux élargiront la portée du terme "sécurité", plus l'autorité publique verra augmenter les risques de porter atteinte au bien-être physique, mental et social des individus, sujets à la protection constitutionnelle. Ainsi en serait-il par exemple d'"une décision administrative dont l'effet est de mettre en danger ce bien-être, comme l'octroi de permis de construire une usine polluante ou l'autorisation de mettre sur le marché ou de transporter un produit dangereux, l'autorisation de construire ou de détruire un ouvrage public à certains endroits."[14]

Pour ne donner que quelques exemples d'application pratique de cette mécanique constitutionnelle, référons-nous à la *Loi sur la qualité de l'environnement* qui limite, comme nous l'avons vu, dans une certaine mesure, le droit à un environnement de qualité. Puisque la législation environnementale octroie un pouvoir discrétionnaire à l'autorité gouvernementale de limiter la portée de ce droit par règlements, autorisations ou permis, une telle reconnaissance supra-législative instituant un pouvoir de contrôle sur l'intervention gouvernementale, rendrait inconstitutionnelle une telle limite dans la mesure où le tribunal serait d'avis qu'elle ne respecte pas

---

14   Patrice Garant, "Droits fondamentaux et justice fondamentale" *dans* Gérald A. Beaudoin & Edward Ratushny, *Charte canadienne des droits et libertés* (Montréal: Wilson et Lafleur, 1989) 381 à la p.416.

les objectifs environnementaux consacrés. Une norme réglementaire pourrait également être déclarée inapplicable dans la mesure où elle serait par ailleurs susceptible de porter atteinte à la qualité de l'environnement. Enfin, la balance des intérêts en cause en matière d'accès à l'information, risquerait de pencher en faveur d'une plus grande ouverture aux citoyens, sans laquelle la reconnaissance d'un droit à un environnement de qualité serait illusoire.

Au chapitre de l'intérêt à poursuivre dans ce type de litige, nous estimons, à cette étape des procédures, que l'absence de préjudice distinct de celui de la collectivité ne devrait pas entraîner le rejet des allégations de celui ou celle qui se prétend victime d'une atteinte à ces droits environnementaux ainsi garantis. Que d'autres individus, voire même la collectivité en entier, souffrent d'une atteinte semblable à leur droit, cela ne devrait, à notre avis, que confirmer davantage la nécessité pour le tribunal d'intervenir. Si la collectivisation de l'atteinte au droit a pour effet de discréditer les prétentions de celui qui l'allègue, le tribunal va au-delà de la simple appréciation objective de l'existence de la violation, pour y conjuguer des facteurs qui relèveront davantage de l'analyse de l'article premier de la *Charte*.

Ainsi, quoiqu'une disposition puisse être déclarée inconstitutionnelle, les tribunaux devraient, dans une dernière étape, évaluer la pertinence d'une telle atteinte aux droits garantis, selon son caractère raisonnable et justifiable dans le cadre d'une société libre et démocratique. Car, ne nous berçons pas d'illusions, si les droits reconnus fondamentaux actuellement sont sujets à pareille évaluation judiciaire permettant d'en justifier certaines atteintes, une éventuelle garantie de droits à un environnement de qualité ne saurait être plus absolue. Cette dernière étape risquerait de limiter grandement l'utilité d'une reconnaissance supra-législative d'un droit à un environnement de qualité. Parmi les motifs pouvant justifier une atteinte à pareil droit, se retrouveraient inévitablement les impératifs économiques d'un marché concurrentiel et leurs répercussions au plan social.

Cette dernière étape de l'analyse judiciaire ne devrait pas nous faire craindre de voir un droit aussi fondamental limité dans sa portée. En fait, il est rationnellement impossible de tenir quelque discours que ce soit, justifiant la dégradation progressive du milieu de vie dont on dépend. Toutefois, la réalité témoigne de pressions sociales différentes appelant des choix de valeurs qui, dans le contexte de l'article premier de la *Charte canadienne*, relèveront des tribunaux (nous retrouvons le pendant provincial de cette disposition à l'article 9.1 de la *Charte québécoise*).

Comme l'exprimait Pearson: "the public interest in preserving environment integrity is not only one of degree, but it also competes with the public interest in maintaining material progress ... courts could accomodate necessary concessions to individual liberty and societal progress, at the same time, however, once a court determined that a particular instance of degradation was unreasonable, relief would be available unless a compelling state interest in continuing the degradation were shown."[15]

À la lumière de la jurisprudence actuelle, peut-on se permettre de croire que les tribunaux préféreraient la sauvegarde du patrimoine naturel à un développement économique anarchique? La Cour Suprême a effleuré la question lorsqu'elle eut à se prononcer sur le caractère raisonnable de certaines infractions de responsabilité absolue entraînant une peine d'emprisonnement obligatoire, en l'occurrence l'infraction d'avoir conduit une automobile avec permis suspendu. Dans le *Renvoi sur la "Motor Vehicule Act" (C.-B.)*, le juge Lamer rappelait l'hypothèse qu'une personne morale puisse prétendre, dans un cas donné, bénéficier d'une liberté de commerce garantie en vertu de l'article 7, laquelle se verrait alors violée par une disposition législative instituant une responsabilité absolue pour une infraction de pollution. Ce dernier précisait alors:

> Je comprends bien sûr l'inquiétude de plusieurs quant aux infractions commises par des personnes morales, spécialement, comme le mentionne la Cour d'appel, dans certains secteurs délicats comme la préservation du milieu où nous vivons et de nos ressources naturelles. Cette inquiétude pourrait bien être dissipée si l'on devait décider, dans une affaire appropriée, que l'article 7 protège les personnes physiques seulement et qu'il ne s'étend pas aux personnes morales.
>
> Même si l'on décidait que l'article 7 s'applique aux personnes morales, *je crois que l'équilibre à réaliser, en vertu de l'article premier, entre l'intérêt public et les intérêts financiers d'une société donnerait des résultats très différents de ceux de l'équilibre à réaliser entre l'intérêt public et la liberté ou la sécurité d'une personne physique*. [Et de conclure ...] l'intérêt public concernant les infractions relatives à la pollution de l'air et de l'eau exige que le coupable soit traité avec fermeté, mais à mon avis la gravité de l'infraction ne permet pas d'affirmer qu'un être humain innocent peut être déclaré coupable, bien au contraire.[16]

Dans cet *obiter*, la Cour analyse l'article 7 dans l'hypothèse d'une garantie constitutionnelle des droits économiques et précise qu'une analyse en vertu de l'article premier pourrait tendre à favoriser des intérêts plus fondamentaux tels la préservation des milieux de vie.[17]

---

15   J.Y. Pearson, "Notes: Toward a Constitutionally Protected Environment" (1970) 56 Virginia L.R. 458 à la p.473. En somme, ajoute ce dernier, la décision ultime reviendrait à déterminer si le bien-être public est mieux servi en protégeant l'environnement ou en maintenant une prospérité matérielle et un certain confort, id. 479; voir également James L. Oakes, "The Judicial Role in Environmental Law" (1977) 52 N.Y.U.L.R. 498 à la p.504.

16   *Renvoi relatif à la Motor Vehicule Act (C.-B.)*, [1985] 2 R.C.S. 487 à la p.518 (nous avons souligné).

17   Ce qui rejoint l'opinion qu'avait émise le juge Dickson dans un autre contexte, alors qu'il avait à statuer sur le caractère particulier des différents types d'infraction pénale, qui

Cette décision est d'autant plus intéressante que l'intérêt public de préserver les milieux et les ressources y fut invoqué à titre de mesure raisonnable justifiant une atteinte à des intérêts d'ordre financier supposément garantis en vertu de l'article 7 de la *Charte canadienne*.

Nous estimons qu'un tel intérêt, cette fois garanti implicitement aux termes de cette même disposition devrait, de surcroit, avoir priorité sur des valeurs d'ordre économique que l'on invoquerait au soutien d'une atteinte raisonnable à ce droit, au sens de l'article premier de la *Charte*. Toutefois, bien que fondamentaux, ces mêmes intérêts ne sauraient justifier une atteinte à d'autres droits individuels également garantis constitutionnellement, comme nous l'avons déjà souligné. On pourrait donc en déduire que, selon la tendance jurisprudentielle actuelle, les intérêts financiers devraient céder devant l'intérêt public de sauvegarder notre environnement, dans la mesure où les autres droits et libertés garantis constitutionnellement ne seraient pas également en jeu.[18]

Enfin, il serait fort douteux qu'une telle affirmation de principe ne soit pas sujette à une fameuse clause "nonobstant" qui permettrait aux législatures de s'en dispenser dans des cas donnés.

Conséquence possible de la reconnaissance constitutionnelle de ce droit: le risque d'une super-législature judiciaire

Placer le droit à un environnement de qualité au rang des droits garantis constitutionnellement entraîne l'inévitable critique quant au rôle et à la capacité des tribunaux de mesurer le poids des valeurs sociales en cause dans toute prise de décision environnementale. Le pouvoir ainsi conféré aux tribunaux, que ce soit par l'interprétation de dispositions telles que "les principes de justice fondamentale" ou le caractère "raisonnable et justifiable dans le cadre d'une société libre et démocratique", a fait craindre l'élimination du principe de la souveraineté parlementaire et l'émergence d'une super-législature judiciaire.

On a mentionné, avec raison, que le fait d'enchâsser certains droits ou libertés dans une charte constitutionnelle avait comme effet de judiciariser le

---

précisait que "les infractions contre le bien-être public impliquent que la protection des intérêts publics et sociaux passe avant celle des intérêts individuels", *R. c. Sault Ste-Marie*, [1978] 2 R.C.S. 1299 à la p.1310-1312. Cette dernière décision rendue avant l'enchâssement de la Charte laisse entrevoir, à tout le moins, une certaines constante dans la conscientisation des tribunaux à ce type de problème.

18   Cette dernière affirmation doit être reconsidéré à la lumière de la récente décision de la cour suprême du Canada, *The Wholesale Travel Group Inc. c. R.*, [1992] 3 R.C.S. 154.

politique et de "politiser" le judiciaire.[19] D'une certaine façon, la souveraineté parlementaire cède la place au "gouvernement des juges", où les cours de justice jouent le rôle d'arbitres appelés à mesurer les lois et les politiques en fonction de critères matériels posés par la *Charte*.

Néanmoins, comme l'a rappelé l'honorable juge Lamer de la Cour suprême du Canada, "les tribunaux ont le pouvoir et même le devoir d'apprécier le contenu de la loi en fonction des garanties accordées par la Constitution .... Il ne faut pas oublier que la décision historique d'enchâsser la Charte dans notre constitution a été prise non pas par les tribunaux, mais par les représenants élus de la population canadienne. Ce sont ces représentants qui ont étendu la portée des décisions constitutionnelles et confié aux tribunaux cette responsabilité à la fois nouvelle et lourde".[20]

En définitive, la question revient à se demander si l'on préfère voir dans nos tribunaux l'arbitre ultime des conflits entre les intérêts respectifs de la société ou faire confiance au système démocratique en laissant au peuple, par l'entremise de ses représentants élus, la responsabilité de faire les choix qui s'imposent.

Si un droit à un environnement de qualité doit être entendu comme le corollaire d'un droit à la vie et à la sécurité de sa personne au sens de l'article 7 de la *Charte canadienne* ou de l'article 1 de la *Charte québécoise*, ou être spécifiquement enchâssé, toute atteinte portée à ce droit entraînera l'intervention judiciaire pour en imposer le respect. Si, pour ce faire, la Cour doit évaluer les politiques qui ont motivé pareille atteinte, elle ne saurait se désister sous prétexte d'usurper le pouvoir de l'organe politique en défaut de respecter ces dispositions impératives.

Bien qu'approuvant le partage des pouvoirs entre les divers organes décisionnels et l'exclusivité de principe des fonctions des uns par rapports aux autres, nous estimons que le rôle du judiciaire s'impose comme mesure de contrôle et de réévaluation des choix sociaux incompatibles avec les valeurs environnementales nécessaires à la jouissance des droits garantis constitutionnellement.

---

19   Pour reprendre les termes de Peter H. Russel, "The Political Purpose of the Canadian Charter of Rights and Freedoms" (1983) 61 R. du B. Can. 30 aux pp.51-52. "Le moins que l'on puisse dire, [de rappeler Gélinas], c'est que l'appareil judiciaire est en meilleure posture pour s'approprier le pouvoir législatif que ne l'est le Parlement pour s'arroger le pouvoir judiciaire"; Fabien Gélinas, "La primauté du droit et les effets d'une loi inconstitutionnelle" (1988) 67 R. du B. Can. 454 à la p.467. De l'avis du professeur Gold, "la Cour remet en question la sagesse d'un texte législatif chaque fois qu'il y a contrôle judiciaire"; Marc Gold, "La rhétorique des droits constitutionnels" (1988) 22 R.J.T. 3 à la p.18.

20   *Renvoi relatif à la Motor Vehicule Act (C.-B.)*, *supra*, note 17, aux pp.496-497.

En fait, le but n'est pas de réécrire le droit de l'environnement, mais plutôt de s'assurer que les mesures existantes garantissent suffisamment la réalisation des objectifs que doit poursuivre la société par l'intermédiaire de ses élus. Si, en définitive, cette reconnaissance de droit constitutionnel suggère, comme résultat, une réforme ou une remise en question complète du droit en la matière, l'on pourra s'enorgueillir d'avoir atteint les objectifs visés par sa consécration. Peut-être assisterons-nous, inversement, à la confirmation de l'exécution du mandat politique de nos élus, qui auront parfaitement mesuré le poids des valeurs qu'attachent leurs mandants à la qualité de leur environnement. Ainsi, une législation ou des politiques respectueuses d'un droit fondamental à un environnement de qualité ne sauraient craindre de souffrir quelques revers décisionnels des instances judiciaires, advenant la reconnaissance constitutionnelle de ce droit.

Toutefois, d'importantes réserves et certaines mises en garde s'imposent. Les citoyens et l'environnement en général devront être prêts à défrayer les coûts qu'entraîneront une telle judiciarisation. Le citoyen, par l'obligation de porter devant les instances judiciaires toute mésentente sur l'évaluation politique d'un environnement d'une qualité suffisante, impliquant des frais judiciaires et d'experts importants. Certes, la Commission des droits de la personne du Québec pourrait éventuellement, en élargissant son mandat, prendre fait et cause au nom des citoyens dans certaines causes type, mais cette intervention demeurerait sporadique.

Au niveau de l'environnement, les délais qu'entraîneront de telles procédures, durant lesquelles aucune action ne saurait légitimement être prise, méritent la plus sérieuse réflexion. Dans la perspective où l'on nous exhorte à prendre des mesures énergiques et drastiques pour modifier nos comportements d'ici dix (10) à quinze (15) ans, il est fort douteux qu'une telle reconnaissance de principe au niveau supra-législatif puisse même avoir jamais porté de fruits.

Ne serait-il pas préférable de mettre à la disposition des citoyens des moyens techniques et financiers leur permettant d'assurer le respect des lois et règlements existants qui, à bien des égards, auraient pu répondre adéquatement à plusieurs problèmes vécus jusqu'à ce jour? À tout le moins, de tels moyens auraient permis de faire ressortir les lacunes du droit, évitant de leurrer leurs bénéficiaires inconsciemment satisfaits par des textes vidés de leur sens et de leur portée juridique.

Se reposer essentiellement sur les tribunaux pour y chercher le réconfort d'une oreille attentive à nos besoins nous paraît, malgré tout, idéaliste, puisque c'est ignorer le caractère purement subjectif du jugement humain. Que l'on reconnaisse au judiciaire une certaine indépendance de jugement cela confirme, bien entendu, le rôle primordial qu'il est appelé à jouer dans notre société. Toutefois, les attentes publiques peuvent se heurter à l'opinion divergente de cet arbitre final appelé à interpréter la loi et à trancher entre les divers intérêts en cause. L'intransigeance des uns peut causer plus de tort que de bien dans la recherche d'un objectif déterminé, en s'imposant selon la règle du "stare decisis". Comme le rappelle la Commission de réforme du droit du Canada, cela dépend, en définitive, "de la conscience écologique du juge".

> La conscience écologique, c'est une capacité de faire abstraction d'intérêts contradictoires manifestes et immédiats comme, par exemple, le droit d'exploiter une entreprise en toute liberté et le droit de jouir d'un bien sans être troublé dans sa jouissance. Elle suppose également une intelligence de l'interdépendance de tous les éléments qui composent l'environnement et la conviction que toute atteinte à l'un de ces éléments, si insignifiante ou si étrangère aux intérêts de l'homme qu'elle puisse sembler, est susceptible de s'aggraver et, à la longue, de réduire la diversité et la vitalité de l'écosystème"[21]

Une conscience écologique doit non seulement être l'attribut des tribunaux appelés à trancher en définitive des grandes questions de l'heure, mais également de nos politiciens responsables de l'élaboration des grandes politiques et, si l'on remonte à l'essence même de ces processus de prise de décisions, de chacun de nous, reflet de ce que notre société décide d'être. L'on constate, après ce long cheminement, que le choix entre le politique ou le judiciaire, que ramène tout le débat sur la reconnaissance d'un droit fondamental à un environnement de qualité, n'est finalement que le choix du porte-parole de nos propres valeurs. Ainsi, le judiciaire ne fera rien de plus que confirmer ce que le politique, en mal de pouvoir, tente de laisser paraître et qui correspond, trop souvent, à ce que la société considère prioritaire sans se l'avouer.

CONCLUSION

En définitive, la question revient à déterminer qui est le mieux placé pour faire des choix qui risqueront d'hypothéquer la collectivité présente et future. Ainsi exposés, les risques sont grands de voir s'éterniser, en longs débats stériles, une proposition visant à reconnaître un droit à un environnement de qualité qui, initialement, se voulait plus efficace pour régir un problème imminent et complexe.

Il faut toutefois demeurer prudent face à cette propension, devant un péril imminent, à vouloir faciliter ou faire avancer les choses en retirant des pouvoirs à une entité à qui la responsabilité incombe avant tout, pour les redonner à une autre entité qui nous semblerait plus efficace, en terme d'indépendance de jugement.

---

21   Commission de réforme du droit du Canada, *La détermination de la peine en droit de l'environnement* (Ottawa: 1985) 20.

À l'instar de Paul Émond, nous croyons que la loi a certes "un rôle à jouer dans la résolution de la crise environnementale", mais un "rôle plus modeste que les législateurs ou le public ne veulent bien l'admettre."[22] Bien que la législation québécoise tende à vouloir jouer un rôle préventif, le processus judiciaire intervient, de façon générale, pour corriger une situation de fait et, en ce sens, joue un rôle plus curatif que préventif. D'aucuns prétendent que le droit, normalement invoqué après que le préjudice ait été subi, institutionnalise l'inefficacité.

Le droit s'exprimant par un instrument supra-législatif, mesure la valeur d'une disposition législative, réglementaire ou autre règle de droit. L'approche est, en ce sens, plus préventive puisqu'elle n'exige pas la démonstration d'un dommage actuel, comme c'est le cas généralement des dispositions d'ordre pénal ou civil. Toutefois, quoique d'application plus préventive, les dispositions de la Charte ne pourraient aller, à notre avis, jusqu'à promouvoir l'orientation d'un développement social. Elles devraient plutôt servir à énoncer les objectifs généraux d'un tel développement, en précisant une ligne de conduite ou des paramètres pour le législatif ou l'exécutif.

Nous faisons nôtres les craintes évoquées par Mohamed Ali Mekouar:

> La revendication du droit à l'environnement devrait, avant tout, éviter de tomber dans le piège de l'idéalisme juridique. En effet, confinée par la sphère juridique, cette revendication ne risque-t-elle pas, tout en apaisant les consciences tourmentées, de n'être rien de plus qu'une nouvelle célébration pharisienne du culte des déclarations des droits de l'homme? Il s'ensuit que la défense de l'environnement implique d'abord la désacralisation du rôle du droit comme facteur de changement. Démystifié de la sorte, le droit pourra alors s'imbriquer réellement dans les rouages des transformations sociales. Ainsi, le droit cessera de servir d'alibi — quand il ne s'en fait pas le complice — à une société qui, tout en claironnant ses préoccupations environnementales, refuse de consentir les sacrifices indispensables.
>
> Dans cet esprit, le droit à l'environnement, droit de la globalité et des profondeurs, ne saurait se contenter de réajustements circonstanciels. Il lui appartiendra plutôt de s'insérer dans la mouvance d'une stratégie de mutation radicale vers une société écologique à imaginer. Dans l'adhésion à ce projet se trouve peut-être la survie des droits de l'homme.[23]

Loin de vouloir écarter le judiciaire du processus décisionnel en matière de politique environnementale, nous favorisons l'implication de tous les intervenants susceptibles d'exprimer des choix collectifs et d'imposer leur respect, dont nos élus, par l'entremise du pouvoir exécutif ou législatif. Ainsi, le droit lorsqu'il intervient, est l'expression d'une volonté politique initiale qui dicte, pour l'avenir, une ligne de conduite à laquelle a choisi de se lier le politique.[24]

---

22   Emond, *supra*, note 4, à la p.109.

23   Mekouar, *supra*, note 10, à la p.105.

24   Voir R.J. Dupuy, "Discussions" *dans* Kiss, *supra*, note 5, 420 à la p.430. Comme le

Ainsi, le politique a le devoir de rechercher et d'imposer sa perception des intérêts sociaux majoritaires, tout comme devrait le faire le judiciaire appelé à trancher un litige invoquant un droit constitutionnel à un environnement de qualité, si l'on favorisait l'enchâssement d'un tel droit. Ce choix de société dépend donc de la priorité des valeurs de chacun de ses membres.

En somme, chacun de nous est partie du problème et de sa solution. Conclusion évidente sans doute, mais non moins véridique, car la mesure de notre volonté de rendre aux générations futures ce dont nous avons eu le privilège de profiter, dépend essentiellement de cette prise de conscience de notre responsabilité personnelle à cet égard, et des actions concrètes que nous serons appelés à poser. Dans un deuxième temps, il est tout aussi important de pourvoir au moyen d'exprimer et de voir appliqués dans toute leur rigueur les choix de sociétés qui s'imposeront.

Le temps nous est compté, il n'y a plus de place pour l'oisiveté, l'inefficacité ou l'erreur.[25] C'est pourquoi nous souhaiterions qu'une telle reconnaissance de principe lie à la fois le politique et le judiciaire de manière à assurer la primauté de ce concept dans les prises de décisions à tous les niveaux.

À l'Alpha, le politique, comme moteur d'une nouvelle éthique environnementale, sur lequel reposerait l'élaboration des mesures destinées à conserver et surtout à améliorer la qualité des milieux de vie. À l'Oméga, le droit, marquant la limite au-delà de laquelle une intervention législative, réglementaire ou administrative deviendrait abusive, c'est-à-dire l'affirmation au dernier échelon de la hiérarchie décisionnelle, de la primauté d'une telle valeur.[26] Le caractère d'objectivité et d'indépendance de ce dernier bastion de la confiance publique, que représentent les tribunaux, favorise leur intervention, en dernier recours, pour rappeler les seuils au-delà desquels nos

---

précisait également John Cole: "It appears environmental law provides the framework in which environmental politics can take place ... thus outside of the role of the judiciary, most of the responsibility for decisions relating to the environment under existing environmental laws is, in this sense, political", John Cole, "Environmental Law and Politics" (1981) 4 U.N.S.W.L.J. 55, 67.

25   Voir C.G. Morley, "Pollution as a Crime: The Federal Response" (1973) 5 Man. L.J. 297 à la p.311.

26   "Laws alone cannot transform our relationship to our environment from rape to caress, but they can describe the intended relationship with a degree of clarity and prescribe its consequences. Whether we have an environmental bill of rights or a patchwork quilt of symbolic gestures will determine whether our laws are intended to protect the environment or pay lip service to it." John Swaigen, "Introduction: the Emergence of the Public in Environmental Decision-Making" dans Swaigen, supra, note 10, 1 à la p.8.

actions défavoriseraient les générations futures; en somme, ils pourraient jouer le rôle de curateur aux biens des générations futures.

Si le droit devait participer à l'élaboration d'une éthique environnementale, c'est principalement par des lois et règlements assurant la transparence et la démocratisation dans les décisions ayant un impact sur l'environnement, qu'apparaîtrait toute son efficacité.

6

SUSTAINABILITY — NEW ZEALAND'S RESOURCE MANAGEMENT LEGISLATION

*The Right Hon. Sir Geoffrey Palmer**

Ever since Garrett Hardin introduced us to the "tragedy of the commons" we have known that we are imperilled.[1] Population growth and use of the stocks of the planet's resources created a problem to which there was no technical solution. "Ruin is the destination toward which all men rush, each pursuing his own best interest in a society that believes in the freedom of the commons. Freedom in a commons brings ruin to all."[2] The problem Hardin poses is how to legislate for temperance. He makes the point that prohibitions are easy to legislate but temperance is much more difficult. The cure lies in mutual coercion, and coercion requires legislation.

The World Commission on Environment and Development in its 1987 report entitled *Our Common Future* provided a new analysis of the world's resource and environmental problems that linked two key ideas: economic growth and sustainability.[3] The report did not predict increasing decay, poverty, and environmental degradation. It saw instead "the possibility for a new era of economic growth, one that must be based on policies that sustain and expand the environmental resource base. And we believe such growth to be absolutely essential to relieve the great poverty that is deepening in much of the developing world."[4] That vision is highly attractive politically, even if

---

*   As Minister for the Environment (1987-90), Geoffrey Palmer was responsible for the reform project dealt with in this paper.

1.   Garrett Hardin, "The Tragedy of the Commons" (1968) 162 Science 1243 (reprinted *in* Herman E. Daly, ed., *Economics, Ecology and Ethics* [San Francisco: W.H. Freeman, 1973] 100).

2.   *Id.*, at 104.

3.   World Commission on Environment and Development, *Our Common Future* (Oxford: Oxford University Press, 1987) (Chair: G.H. Brundtland).

4.   *Id.*, at 1.

the contradictions inherent in it are not fully resolved in the document. Indeed, my experience in politics makes me sceptical about the ability to achieve unremitting economic growth for all of the world's people all of the time. It is time we faced up to this point.

With the environmental side of the Commission's equation it is hard to disagree. Profligacy is out. Thought must be given to the options for future generations who may feel the impact of developmental decisions taken now. Growth in the world's population is a serious problem. It cannot be sustained by the existing environmental resources. The problems, in the view of the Commission, could all be encompassed within one overarching principle — sustainability. That principle was articulated as follows:

> Humanity has the ability to make development sustainable — to ensure that it meets the needs of the present without compromising the ability of future generations to meet their own needs. The concept of sustainable development does imply limits — not absolute limits but limitations imposed by the present state of technology and social organisation on environmental resources and by the ability of the biosphere to absorb the effects of human activities.[5]

In developing the idea of sustainability the Commission asserted that all countries and all types of economies will need to form a consensus on the basic concept of sustainable development, and on a broad strategic framework for achieving it. The Commission wrote an elegant essay on the idea but stopped short of detailing how it would work in practice. It did say, however, that there was a need to merge environment and economics in decision making.[6] Indeed, the common theme of the strategy for sustainable development "is the need to integrate economic and ecological considerations in decision making."[7]

The principles developed by the Commission were the subject of a drafting exercise by a group of experts on environmental law.[8] Twenty-two principles were stated in terms of broad legal propositions. The statement addresses such matters as the right to an environment adequate for health and well-being; the principle of inter-generational equity; the maintenance of ecosystems and biological diversity; the setting and monitoring of environmental standards; obligations to cooperate internationally, to exchange information, and to consult; and transboundary obligations.[9] In terms of advancing the specifics of sustainability, two of the legal statements, Articles 3 and 7, stand out:

---

5. *Id.*, at 8.

6. *Id.*, at 62.

7. *Id.*

8. *Id.*, at Annex 1, 348.

9. *Id.*, at Annex 1, 348-349.

3. States shall maintain ecosystems and ecological processes essential for the functioning of the biosphere, shall preserve biological diversity, and shall observe the principle of optimum sustainable yield in the use of natural living resources and ecosystems.

7. States shall ensure that conservation is treated as an integral part of the planning and implementation of development activities and provide assistance to other States, especially to developing countries, in support of environmental protection and sustainable development.

Over the next few years these principles will make themselves felt in domestic efforts to change natural resources and environmental law. What may not be appreciated is the extent to which the concept of sustainability requires a fundamental shift in approach. Remaking the law of any state to conform to the idea of sustainable development is an enormous undertaking. Just what is involved and how difficult it is can be understood from examining the recent New Zealand experience. There may be some lessons in it for others. Many of those lessons will not emerge until the new legislation in New Zealand is up and running, but the policy formation stage in Zealand was itself fascinating and is worthy of study for its own sake. To that reform process I now turn.

New Zealand's resource-use laws, like the laws of most countries, had over the years grown up statute by statute. They bore the marks of the country's history — gold mining, soil erosion owing to clearing of too much land for pastoral farming, harbour development, zoning laws for urban development, and a whole host of one-off regimes for regulating particular problems such as noise, air pollution, petroleum exploration, and geothermal energy.[10] A number of observations can be made about this large collection of separate laws. They contained no unifying principle or approach. Permission to do things was usually required but there was no golden thread running through the statutes of the standards to be applied or the outcomes to be achieved. The mechanisms for settling disputes contained no uniformity. The institutional structures for dealing with the issues were almost infinitely various. It would be fair to characterize New Zealand's resource management laws as an uncoordinated, unintegrated hotch potch involving more than fifty statutes passed at different times in response to different problems.

But for a series of political developments it is very doubtful that anything very comprehensive would have been attempted in relation to New Zealand's resource management laws. Having won the 1978 election quite narrowly, the National government set about developing a political strategy in 1979 to boost New Zealand's economic development and provide employment. It began with the idea that New Zealand should be self-sufficient in energy. A number of large development projects sponsored or guaranteed by the government were

10.   New Zealand Parliament, *Resource Management Bill 1989*, as reported by the Select Committee, 1990, 4th Schedule. See also *Resource Management Act 1991*, 4th Schedule.

to be undertaken to develop New Zealand's natural resources. At various times a number of such projects were contemplated or undertaken, including a large hydroelectricity dam in the South Island, an aluminium smelter, a synthetic gasoline plant using natural gas, and the expansion of New Zealand's steel plant using ironsand. This developmental strategy became known as the "Think Big" program. The projects were very expensive and generated much government debt.[11]

The developers and the government discovered another problem that posed an obstacle to the achievement of their goal — the myriad of laws under which consents of one sort or another were required before any development could proceed. The government decided to overcome these problems by passing a piece of legislation that would provide a fast track through all these laws. Normal procedures would be suspended. For designated developments there were to be one set of hearings before a tribunal, with recommendations made to the government, and an order-in-council by the government granting the necessary consents. When the National Development Bill was introduced into the House of Representatives in October 1979 there was widespread opposition. Environmentalists argued that it was a recipe for environmental disaster and that all the usual protections would be thrown out the window. Constitutionalists argued that this method of suspending the laws was inherently undesirable and was dictatorial.[12] Public meetings were held up and down New Zealand. The hearings on the Bill in front of the Select Committee of Parliament were extensively covered, and there were hundreds of submissions. The Bill changed as a result of the protests but was eventually passed, although it was actually used only once.

The Labour Opposition had something of a field day with this issue, vigorously opposing the Bill. If the resource-use laws were as defective as the government said why did they not reform those laws properly? The streamlined legislation was characterized as repressive. The Opposition pledged to repeal the *National Development Act 1979* and also promised to reform the planning laws upon gaining the Treasury benches. These promises were ultimately carried out in a much more elaborate manner than was contemplated at the time they were made.

The fourth Labour government was too busy with other issues in its first three-year term 1984-1987 to do a great deal on the resource law reform front. A report from a leading lawyer on the *Town and Country Planning Act*

---

11. Geoffrey Palmer, *Environmental Politics — A Greenprint for New Zealand* (Dunedin: John McIndoe, 1990) at 123-128.

12. See generally Geoffrey Palmer, *Unbridled Power: An Interpretation of New Zealand's Constitution and Government*, 2nd ed. (Auckland: Oxford University Press, 1987).

was commissioned,[13] and the *National Development Act 1979* was repealed. But the real work did not begin until after the 1987 election when a number of developments made it possible to engage in a massive law reform project. In 1987 I became Minister for the Environment. The Ministry was a policy department set up in Labour's first term with wide-ranging responsibilities to tender advice on all aspects of environmental policy.

One of the old line departments in New Zealand at that time was called the Ministry of Works and Development. It had been a prime mover over the years in carrying out construction for the government, and it was expert in planning and building dams for the generation of hydroelectricity. In short, it was old and big and good at defending its bureaucratic territory. The Ministry was often involved in both building big projects and providing advice and carrying out regulatory functions in relation to the construction industry. Given this range of functions performed by the Ministry, serious conflicts of interest had grown up. The government, involved in a massive program of corporatization and privatization of its functions, decided that the answer to its problems was to abolish the Ministry as a department of state. Its construction and some other functions went to a commercially oriented state-owned enterprise that would compete on equal terms with firms from the private sector.[14] Some of its functions that were of a non-contestable public nature were transferred to other government departments. The Ministry had contained two divisions dealing with resource law: the Town and Country Planning Division and the Water and Soil Division. These were downsized and their functions transferred to the Ministry for the Environment.

Considerable bureaucratic upheaval was involved in these changes. One consequence of this was to free up funds. At the time the changes were being processed through the decision-making structures of the government, I procured enough money to carry out a properly funded law reform project on New Zealand's resource laws. The reform was driven by myself as Minister for the Environment and by the Ministry for the Environment. Between early 1988, when the project began, and October 1990 the exercise cost five and one-half million dollars.[15] By the time it was finished it cost more than eight million dollars, an unprecedented sum for a law reform project in New Zealand.

---

13.   A. Hearn, *Review of the Town and Country Planning Act 1977* (Wellington: Dept. of Trade and Industry, 1987).

14.   See generally, M. Clark & E. Sinclair, eds., *Purpose, Performance and Profit: Redefining the Public Sector* (Studies in Public Administration No.32) (Wellington: New Zealand Institute of Public Administration, 1986); and M. Palmer, "The State-Owned Enterprise Act 1986: Accountability?" (1988) 18 V.U.W.L.R. 169.

15.   Palmer, *supra*, note 11, at 91.

With so many different statutes administered by different government departments involved in the review, it was necessary to guard against the jealous defence of bureaucratic territory and a plethora of conflicting advice that would bog down the project. This was accomplished by devising an unusual decision-making structure and advisory machinery. Rather than an interdepartmental committee, a Core Group of four officials was established. The Director of the project came from the Ministry of the Environment, another official from that Ministry had the responsibility for developing and coordinating the advice on Maori issues, a Treasury official was involved to provide the economic analysis, and an expert environmental lawyer in private practice completed the Core Group. When the project was advanced, an experienced parliamentary draftsman in private practice was also retained to draft the Bill.

The advantages of this process were substantial. While it did not eliminate "end runs" by Departments going to their own Ministers when they lost, it did minimize that behaviour. It also ensured that there was a rigorous filter on advice before it was tendered to Ministers for decisions, which made decision making more orderly.

To make the decisions and supervise the work of the Core Group, a special Cabinet Committee was established. The reform of the resource laws was closely allied to a parallel reform of the structure of New Zealand's local government. Both topics were dealt with by the same Cabinet Committee, which I chaired. Papers were tendered to the Cabinet Committee through the Core Group, and Ministers asked questions of officials concerning various recommendations. I met weekly with the Core Group to discuss progress, and my Associate Minister, who later became Minister of Conservation, dealt with a great many of the difficult political issues. The entire project became known, in the inevitable acronyms of government, as RMLR — Resource Management Law Reform.

The objectives I established for the project at the beginning were as follows:

(1) The Primary goal for Government involvement in resource allocation and management is to produce an enhanced quality of life, both for individuals and the community as a whole, through the allocation and management of natural and physical resources.

(2) Resource Management legislation should have regard to the following, sometimes conflicting objectives:

    (a) to distribute rights to resources in a just manner, taking into account the rights of existing rightholders and the obligations of the Crown. The legislation should also give practical effect to the principles of the Treaty of Waitangi;

    (b) to ensure that resources provide the greatest benefit to society. This requires that rights to use resources are able to move over time to uses which are valued most highly, and that the least costly way is adopted to achieve this transfer;

(c)   to ensure good environmental management (as specified in the World Conservation Strategy) which includes considering issues related to the needs of future generations, the intrinsic value of ecosystems, and sustainability;

(d)   to be practical.[16]

The method by which the policy was developed involved massive and prolonged public consultation. The first part of the process analyzed the purposes, objectives, and priorities of the reform. It asked hard questions, such as to what extent, if any, natural and physical resources should be managed through public processes. The approach taken was to think through the issues from scratch and take nothing for granted.

Throughout the process of policy generation the Ministry for the Environment published *Viewfinder*, a professionally produced newsletter containing information and discussion about the reform process and providing opportunities for participation in that process. Details of the numerous working papers developed were also publicized by this medium, and interested people were given the opportunity to secure these documents. During the life of the project, thirty-two substantial working papers were published and made available.[17] At the beginning a freephone was organized for the public from all over New Zealand to express their views on the content of the reform. Advertisements were placed in newspapers, providing a means to distribute RMLR information kits. Commercials on radio also drew attention to the project.

The first phase of the process ended in August 1988 with the publication of a discussion paper entitled *Directions for Change*,[18] which covered the following issues:

---

16.   *Id.*, at 91-92.

17.   E.g., *Fundamental Issues in Resource Management* (Resource Management Law Reform Working Paper No.2) (Wellington: Ministry for the Environment, July 1988); and *Public Submissions in Response to People, Environment and Decision Making* (Resource Management Law Reform Working Paper No.32) (Wellington: Ministry of the Environment, April 1989). Included in the topics dealt with by these working papers were analysis of existing statutes; the treaty of Waitangi; implementing the sustainability objective; coastal legislation; geothermal energy; Maori value systems and perspectives; enforcement and compliance issues; national policy matters; public participation; compensation; objectives; users-group working papers; town and country planning legislation and procedures; the role of local and regional government; the management of pollution and hazardous substances; the *Clean Air Act*; the *Petroleum Act*; the *Mining Act*; Waitangi tribal findings; the various roles of the Crown; the role of information in resource management; natural hazards; decision-making processes and structures; public participation in policy formation and development consents; impact assessment in resource management; resource management disputes (Part A — the role of the courts and tribunals; Part B — mediation).

18.   New Zealand. Ministry for the Environment, *Directions for Change: A Discussion Paper* (Wellington: Resource Management Law Reform, August 1988).

- Why reform was needed
- What the objectives and purposes of the reform should be
- The role of government
- The form the laws should take (should there be a single Act?)
- The integration of consents (a "one-stop shop" approach)
- Treaty of Waitangi and Maori issues
- The decision-making processes, including appeals
- Instruments and mechanisms

The paper developed four reform models, and submissions were invited to choose between them. The first involved a single *Resource Management Act* operated principally by regional government, although some matters could be delegated to territorial government. Resource allocation decisions under this approach would then be dealt with by a different Act administered by central government. The second model also envisaged a single act, but anticipated territorial local government having direct responsibility for land-related resources management. The third model involved a single Act with split functions as in model 2, but with coastal management dealt with centrally by the Department of Conservation and minerals dealt with centrally by the Ministry of Energy. The fourth model envisaged four separate pieces of legislation: water, soil, and air resource management administered by regional government; land use and noise management administered by territorial local government; coastal legislation administered by the Department of Conservation; and minerals legislation administered by the Ministry of Energy.

Extensive consultation proceeded on this document, and public meetings were held all over New Zealand, together with extensive working meetings with interested and affected groups. Seminars were provided for the media. Despite the fact that the process was so open and the consultation so extensive, RMLR never took off as a political issue. It was a holistic reform that concerned matters of considerable complexity, often dealt with by professionals but not widely known by the general public. Planners, lawyers, local government staff, environmentalists, engineers, mining companies, Maori groups, and public servants were the main ones to show an interest. And while that interest was intense and tended to be expert, it was limited in extent. RMLR lacked the essential ingredients of political sex appeal. This was no bad thing. Big changes could be made, and the defence of adequate notice and public consultation was available and could be relied upon.

In December 1988, after Cabinet consideration, the government's proposals were published. The paper set out the framework for the new law.

My preface stated: "Resource management must protect the needs of future generations by recognizing the concept of sustainable development. We need laws to help us to enjoy and use what we have without endangering or compromising quality of life for ourselves or future generations."[19] For a third time submissions from the public were called for. The paper summarized an approach to twenty-five of the more important issues and in the course of more than seventy pages indicated the possible shape of the legislation. A total of 1,256 written submissions were received on this paper, and a working paper summarizing the submission was published.[20] The extensive public consultation did allow the Cabinet Committee to avoid serious political traps that could have emerged. Indeed, in no law reform exercise I have been involved with has the consultation and public participation been greater. Even before the Bill was introduced, 3,500 submissions had been received. I have no doubt that this project set new records for public participation in the process of decision making in New Zealand.

The next step — Phase 3 — was the legislation itself, and things were now getting much harder. It was difficult to complete all the work. Deadlines had to be put back, as the process ground out the decisions and they were drafted. In my experience this process almost always takes longer than expected, and the process of repairing the Bill after preliminary exposure drafts is always difficult and time consuming. The Bill was finally introduced into the New Zealand Parliament in December 1989.

The Bill was massive — 314 pages. As befitted a project of this complexity, it was accompanied by an unusually detailed explanatory note and an extensive information kit, but it was written in plain English and attempted to eschew the complexity and prolixity that often accompanies legal drafting. A specially enlarged Select Committee of Parliament was set up to hear submissions on it. The Bill set out to rectify a number of problems:

- there was no consistent set of resource management objectives;

- there were arbitrary differences in management of land, air, and water;

- there were too many agencies involved, with overlapping responsibilities and insufficient accountability;

- consent procedures were unnecessarily costly and there were undue delays;

---

19. New Zealand. Ministry for the Environment, *People, Environment, and Decision Making: The Government's Proposals for Resource Management Law Reform* (Wellington: Resource Management Law Reform, December 1988) at 3.

20. *Public Submissions in Response to People, Environment and Decision Making, supra,* note 17.

- pollution laws were *ad hoc* and did not recognize the physical connections between land, air, and water;
- in some respects there was insufficient flexibility and too much prescription with a focus on activities rather than results;
- Maori interests and the Treaty of Waitangi were frequently overlooked;
- monitoring of existing law was uneven and enforcement difficult.

The explanatory note to the Bill said this about its purposes:

> The objective of this Bill is to integrate the laws relating to resource management, and to set up a resource management system that promotes sustainable management of natural and physical resources. This Bill integrates existing laws by bringing together the management of land, including land subdivision, water and soil, minerals and energy resources, the coast, air, and pollution control including noise control. It sets out the rights and responsibilities of individuals, and territorial, regional and central government. The central concept of sustainable management in this Bill encompasses the themes of use, development and protection. The Bill sets up a system of policy and plan preparation and administration which allows the balancing of a wide range of interests and values. The Bill allows the needs of the present generation to be met without compromising the ability of future generations to meet their own needs.[21]

The analysis of the Bill as introduced was as follows:

Part I — Interpretation and Application

Part II — Purpose and Principles

Part III — Duties and Restrictions under this Act

Part IV — Functions, Powers and Duties of Central and Local Government

Part V — Policy Statements and Plans

Part VI — Resource Consents

Part VII — Designations, Heritage Orders and Water Conservation Orders

Part VIII — Subdivision

Part IX — Crown-owned Minerals

Part X — Planning Tribunal

Part XI — Declarations, Enforcement and Ancillary Powers

Part XII — Miscellaneous Provisions

Part XIII — Transitional Provisions

---

21. *Resource Management Bill 1989*, *supra*, note 10, explanatory note at i.

Part XIV — Transitional Provisions relating to Minerals

Part XV — Hazards Control Commission[22]

The Select Committee was inundated with submissions from the public and interest groups; more than fourteen hundred were received. Many of them were heard; the hearings took months. The Bill was not reported back to the House by the Select Committee until August 1990, and a general election was due in October. There simply was not time to pass the Bill before Parliament stopped in September. But the Bill was well advanced; the Select Committee had made extensive amendments to it as a result of submissions. The Bill was read a second time and had reached the Committee of the Whole stage before Parliament went into recess. There was some political manoeuvring about which party should bear the responsibility for not having passed the Bill. The National Party Opposition was not prepared to cooperate in its passage by keeping the parliamentary time taken to reasonable proportions. It said that the Bill needed change. The government sought to blame the Opposition for holding up a carefully worked out and much needed reform. The Bill was held over by resolution of Parliament prior to the election and remained in front of the House of Representatives.

In the general election the Labour government was defeated and the National Party formed the government. The new Minister for the Environment, the Hon. Simon Upton, was a supporter of the general thrust of the RMLR project. He quickly appointed a group of five people chosen for their expertise to review the Bill and make recommendations relating to it, as the National Party's election pledge had stated would occur.

The group published a 62-page discussion paper and received 160 submissions.[23] Its 186-page review was published in February 1991 and came to the conclusion that "[i]n general terms, the changes are regarded as worthwhile although a number of areas have been identified for amendment."[24] Quite a number of detailed drafting amendments were recommended, together with some policy changes. The report was basically a vote of confidence in the Bill, which is hardly surprising given the extensive process by which the policy was developed. There can be few views on the questions involved that remain uncanvassed in New Zealand. The development of policy through an open-textured process of public consultation

---

22. *Id.*, at 1.

23. Review Group on the Resource Management Bill, *Discussion Paper on the Resource Management Bill* (Wellington, December 1990) (Chairperson: A.P. Randerson).

24. Review Group on the Resource Management Bill, *Report of the Review Group on the Resource Management Bill* (Wellington, 11 February 1991) at 2 (Chairperson: A.P. Randerson).

can provide robust proposals that will survive not only because they have been thought through, but also because interested groups and experts see their advantages and constitute a body of opinion in favour of the changes.

On 2 May 1991 the government announced its decisions on the Resource Management Bill in more than thirty pages of press release and explanatory material. On 9 May the minister introduced into the House of Representatives a supplementary order paper containing the government's proposed amendments to the Bill, which was debated and referred to a parliamentary Select Committee for submissions. The Committee heard submissions and produced a lengthy report with recommendations. A new supplementary order paper was produced incorporating the recommendations, and after a short debate the Bill was finally enacted in July 1991, with a commencement date of 1 October 1991.

The most critical feature of the Resource Management Bill lies in the provisions describing its purposes and principles. This part sets the standards upon which the entire integrated decision-making system must rest. The key concept is sustainability. In providing an underlying philosophy of sustainable management, the New Zealand legislation breaks new ground. As developed in the reform process, sustainable management is a broad concept that reflects aspects of use, development, and protection. It is on these aspects that the National Party government's review concentrated.

The structure of the Bill as introduced was not greatly altered by the Select Committee, in relation to the purpose of sustainable management. As reported back from the Select Committee, clause 4 provided as follows:

4. Purpose

(1) The purpose of this Act is to promote the sustainable management of natural and physical resources.

(2) In this Act, "sustainable management" means managing the use, development, and protection of natural and physical resources in a way, or at a rate, which enables people to meet their own needs and includes the following considerations:

    (a) The maintenance and enhancement of the quality of the environment, including the life supporting capacity of the environment and its intrinsic values:

    (b) The use, development, or protection of natural and physical resources in a way which provides for the social, economic, and cultural needs and opportunities of people and communities:

    (c) Where the environment is modified by human action, the adverse effects of irreversible change are fully recognized and avoided or mitigated to the extent practicable:

    (d) The use, development, or protection of renewable natural and physical resources so that their ability to yield long term benefits is not endangered:

    (e) The use or development of non-renewable natural and physical resources in a way that sees an orderly and practical transition to adequate substitutes including renewable resources:

(f)   The exercise of kaitiakitanga which includes an ethic of stewardship.

This definition had been based on extensive work by the Core Group, including lengthy published paper entitled *Ecological Principles for Resource Management*.[25] Clause 5 established a number of principles to be observed by those exercising functions and powers under the Bill. These included such matters as maintenance and enhancement of the quality of the environment, the effects of activity on ecosystems, and the economic, cultural, and social well-being of people and communities. The relationship between clauses 4 and 5 had become a matter of some debate, and the Review Committee established by the National government was invited to examine it. They found a number of difficulties:[26]

- the problem of applying the purposes and principles in practice;
- the failure of the purpose and principles clauses to recognize the built environment;
- a lack of balance between preservation principles and reasonable opportunities for economic growth and development;
- the failure to indicate priorities among the various matters to be taken into account;
- the uncertainty of the relationship between clauses 4 and 5;
- the absence of a positive planning obligation.

While not accepting all these criticisms, the Review Committee was of the view that sustainable management should remain the cornerstone of the Bill.[27] But the Committee was not attracted to the broad concept developed by the World Commission on Environment and Development, which included social inequities and global redistribution of wealth. It did recommend a second purpose that would reflect the Bill's intention to place less emphasis on existing statutory requirements and instead move to control the adverse effects of activities on the environment. The aim was to secure a high

---

25. Karen Cronin, *Ecological Principles for Resource Management* (Wellington: Ministry for the Environment, July 1988). In addition, the following working papers dealt with sustainability: Ministry for the Environment, *Resource Values* (Working Paper No.10) (Wellington, 1988); Ministry for the Environment, *Sustainability, Intrinsic Values and the Needs of Future Generations* (Working Paper No.24) (1989); and Ministry for the Environment, *Implementing the Sustainability Objective in Resource Management Law* (Working Paper No.25) (1988).

26. *Report of the Review Group on the Resource Management Bill, supra,* note 24, at 5.

27. *Id.,* at 6.

standard of environmental outcomes while at the same time encouraging the use of alternative methods to achieve the goals.

The Review Committee approached the matter by referring to the simple purpose of promoting the sustainable management of natural and physical resources. This would be followed by a definition of sustainable management that refers to managing the use, development, and protection of natural and physical resources in a way that will provide for current social, economic, and cultural well-being, as well as health and safety. The definition would be subject to two parameters, in the view of the Committee: the need to safeguard the ability of future generations to meet their needs, and the need to avoid, remedy, or mitigate any adverse effects of activities on the environment.

The Review Committee's recommended draft of clause 4 was:

4. Purpose

(1)   The purpose of this Act is to promote the sustainable management of natural and physical resources.

(2)   In this Act, "sustainable management" means managing the use, development and protection of natural and physical resources in a way or at a rate which enables people and communities to provide for their health and safety, and their social, economic and cultural wellbeing while —

    (a)   Safeguarding, to the extent reasonably foreseeable, the ability of future generations to meet their needs in relation to natural and physical resources; and

    (b)   Avoiding, remedying or mitigating any adverse effects of activities on the environment.[28]

There follows a new clause 5(a), which sets out matters of national importance that should be recognized, and then clause 5, which states principles to which all persons exercising functions and powers under the Act shall have particular regard. A number of the factors mentioned in the previous version of clause 4 are included here.

These tests were designed to apply to a whole range of resource management decisions — town and country planning, the granting of water rights, subdivision of land, resource consents, coastline decisions. The review recommended, and the government accepted, that a separate Crown minerals bill would govern minerals, which was accomplished by splitting the minerals provisions out of the Bill at the third reading stage. Sustainability will not apply to decisions about the use of minerals. The Review Committee recommended, however, that minerals activity still require consents under the Resource Management Bill. This recommendation was combined with a

---

28. *Id.*, at 145-146.

retention of the landowner veto over access to privately owned land, which would have ensured that mining is subject to a more level playing field than the preferred position it occupied under the previous law.[29] In its supplementary order paper the government did not accept this recommendation in full. It instead provided that a refusal of access by the landowner can be overridden by the government's issuing an order-in-council. In practice, however, this change may not amount to much. The political costs of interfering with the rights of landowners in New Zealand are high, and the power is likely to be exercised very sparingly indeed. The overall balance of the Bill is not much affected. The Bill, as introduced, allowed the Planning Tribunal to override a landowner's refusal.

The purpose and principles were the focus of further adjustment in the government's supplementary order paper, and by the Select Committee considering it after hearing further submissions. As it was finally enacted, the purpose clause is as follows:

5. Purpose

(1) The purpose of this Act is to promote the sustainable management of natural and physical resources.

(2) In this Act, "sustainable management" means managing the use, and development, and protection of natural and physical resources in a way, or at a rate, which enables people and communities to provide for their social, economic, and cultural wellbeing and for their health and safety while —

    (a) Sustaining the potential of natural and physical resources (excluding minerals) to meet the reasonably foreseeable needs of future generations; and

    (b) Safeguarding the life-supporting capacity of future generations; and

    (c) Avoiding, remedying, or mitigating any adverse effects of activities on the environment.

How this brave new world of sustainability will work in practice remains to be seen. How far the decisions will bite in favour of future generations and against immediate exploitation will be the key issue. In this respect the new formulation has weakened sustainability a little. Nonetheless, how the various tests play out against each other will be a fascinating legal exercise with substantial economic consequences. There is no doubt that the result will be a new legal baseline that is friendlier to the environment and offers some protection for those who are to come after us.

The ultimate arbiter will be the Planning Tribunal, which is a court. It will have the benefit of decisions from local and regional government. It will be able to draw upon policy statements and management plans constructed

---

29. *Id.*, at 72.

under the legislation and required by it. Questions of law can go on appeal to the High Court.[30] It should also be noted that the Planning Tribunal can ask for a dispute to be mediated or conciliated at any time before or during a hearing.

It might be argued that questions of this sort cannot be made justiciable, that the Planning Tribunal judges and their assessors are being handed a task with such sweeping social and political consequences that it is impossible. Certainly it is ambitious, but there are a number of reasons to think the exercise will succeed. The first is that the Planning Tribunal and the courts in New Zealand have built up a degree of expertise and sensitivity in dealing with issues of considerable breadth under the existing town and country planning legislation.[31] The extension should not trouble them unduly. Secondly, the regime of decision making below the Tribunal provides for policy input of a political character through national policy statements on "matters of national significance that are relevant to achieving the purpose of this Act."[32] The Review Committee recommended that they be renamed "statements of Government policy." There should be a prescribed process of public inquiry before they are issued and they should be issued by order-in-council. All this was accepted by the government. Thirdly, there is sufficient flexibility in the approach of the legislation to avoid detailed prescription in favour of securing optimal outcomes.

There is some irony in the fact that New Zealand, a relatively rich country in terms of resources and one with a small population, will be one of the first countries to adopt sustainability as the key to its resource management laws. It could not have occurred but for the way in which the reform exercise was put together. The fact that the reform was able to survive a change of government is significant: bipartisan commitment will help the changes to endure. Despite the vigour of party politics in New Zealand, sometimes quite big changes can secure this sort of support.

In a paper of this character it is possible to deal only briefly with what was a massive reform project with many facets. I have highlighted the issue of sustainability, and it is vital. But there were many other formidable policy issues that had to be faced in the course of the project. Many were technical, such as esplanade reserves and the application of the Bill to conservation estate land. Some were political — for example, the landowner veto over access for mining was controversial.

---

30. *Resource Management Bill 1989*, New Zealand Parliament, 1989, cl.334.

31. *Town and Country Planning Act 1977* R.S.N.Z. Vol.16; *Water and Soil Conservation Act 1967* R.S.N.Z. Vol.17; *Soil Conservation and Rivers Control Act 1941* R.S.N.Z. Vol.17.

32. *Resource Management Bill 1989*, *supra*, note 30, cl.41.

Always it was a question of securing a solution that advanced the policy of the reform project and maintained a balance between environmental protection and development. Both sides criticized the reforms at various points, which suggests that the policy was about right.

The issues that gave the most difficulty in the policy generation process may be worth summarizing, although there is no space to analyze them in detail. The issue of how to handle mining and minerals was one of the most difficult issues from a technical point of view, and one of the most controversial politically. The pattern of New Zealand mining legislation historically gave mining a preferred position. How to overcome that and yet treat the industry fairly was not a simple issue. As indicated above, the Review Group recommended a different approach from that which emerged from the Select Committee, and the former found favour with the government.

Coastal management also gave rise to problems over a long period. This was another area in which there were divergent views and some special interests. Local authorities thought they should be the controlling authority, while the Department of Conservation thought it should be the principal manager of the coastline. The coastline and territorial sea in New Zealand have never been subject to such close control as has existed for land through land-use planning, so there were no established systems that could easily be adapted to the new purposes. The Bill as it emerged from the Select Committee split the control but the Department of Conservation had both regulatory and allocation functions — a conflict that caused criticism. The Bill also contained a provision calling for the preservation of the natural character of the coastal environment without precluding appropriate use and development. The Review Group did not like the balance struck in the Bill but acknowledged the difficulties, and the majority recommended that the Bill remain as it is for the present. The decisions of the government alter details only.

From the beginning of the reform project special efforts were made to build in proper consideration of resource allocation decisions from a Maori perspective. In recent years the Maori renaissance in New Zealand has seen increasing weight given to the principles of the Treaty of Waitangi as a means of addressing Maori grievances.[33] Many of those grievances centre on resource use, especially land. This issue caused the Labour government quite a few headaches. Several progressive pieces of legislation had given real

---

33. *Treaty of Waitangi Act 1975* R.S.N.Z. Vol.8; *Treaty of Waitangi Amendment Act 1985* S.N.Z. No.148; *State-owned Enterprises Act 1986* S.N.Z. No.124, s.9; *New Zealand Maori Council* v. *A.G.*, [1987] 1 N.Z.L.R. 641; *Treaty of Waitangi (State Enterprises) Act 1988* S.N.Z. No. 105.

rights to Maori, which was beginning to cause political backlash from the pakeha majority. Maori had prevailed against the government in several landmark judicial decisions. (Maori constitute 12.5 percent of the New Zealand population.)

Clause 6 of the Bill as introduced provided: "In achieving the purpose of this Act, all persons who exercise functions and powers under this Act have a duty to consider the Treaty of Waitangi." The Bill was careful not to deal with issues relating to ownership of resources. A fundamental decision was taken early in the life of the project not to resolve such questions, since that would, among other things, require resolution of a number of difficult Treaty of Waitangi issues. The Review Group recommended that clause 6 should provide: "In achieving the purpose of this Act all persons who exercise functions and powers under it shall take into account the principles of the Treaty of Waitangi Te Tiriti O Waitangi."[34] The Bill should be further amended, they recommended, to allow the Planning Tribunal to make declarations as to the nature and extent of the duty. The government accepted the former recommendation but does not appear to have actioned the latter.

The functions of territorial and local government were a big feature of the reform. A new tier of local government, called regional government, was formed around water catchments for the express purpose of dealing with resource management. Under the reorganization of local government that has already been legislated and is in effect, Catchment Boards and Regional Water Boards were replaced by directly elected Regional Councils.[35] The new National Party Minister of Local Government had threatened to abolish Regional Councils, but the Review Group considered it would "be unwise to attempt to unravel regional government."[36] Certainly the logic of the resource management legislation would be seriously affected if the tier of regional government was abolished. It will be interesting to see how this issue is resolved in the government's decisions on local government. There are no changes in this respect in the supplementary order paper, but one would expect some tinkering with local government structures for political reasons. Indeed, in 1991 a Bill was introduced to downsize the Regional Councils but not to tamper with their functions under the *Resource Management Act.* It is beyond doubt that some regional organization is necessary for the resource management legislation to function effectively.

The National government was particularly concerned to see that the new legislation included economic instruments or mechanisms in the allocation and

---

34. See Annex 1 to this paper.

35. *Local Government Amendment Act 1990.*

36. *Report of the Review Group on the Resource Management Bill, supra,* note 24, at 115.

management of resources. The Committee found that the Bill "in its current form does not provide a suitable framework for the large scale introduction of national level instruments such as carbon taxes or tradeable emission rights at a national level."[37] The issues would have to be developed at a future date. But the Committee did recommend that regulation be constrained by enactment of a new clause requiring consideration of all the alternatives available, including doing nothing, weighing the costs and benefits of using different instruments at the margin, and being under a duty to adopt the most efficient instrument to achieve the objectives.[38] No doubt more work will be done on this — the Minister is particularly keen on it. I am sceptical that anything significant can be achieved by such instruments despite the opinions of the OECD and the New Zealand Treasury.

New Zealand has completed a massive effort to reform its resource management law. The *Resource Management Act 1991* enacted in July came into effect on 1 October 1991. The result is major change with the replacement of some seventy-five statutes. Both main political parties have been involved in the changes and the result enjoys broadly bipartisan support. No doubt there will be a number of unexpected results in the initial stages of the operation of the new resource management program, but it is certainly a scheme that is likely to attract much overseas interest.

---

37. *Id.*, at 97.

38. *Id.*, at 79-98.

Resource Management Act 1991

Part II

Purpose and Principles

5. Purpose —

(1) The purpose of this Act is to promote the sustainable management of natural and physical resources.

(2) In this Act, "sustainable management" means managing the use, development, and protection of natural and physical resources in a way, or at a rate, which enables people and communities to provide for their social, economic, and cultural wellbeing and for their health and safety while —

    (a) Sustaining the potential of natural and physical resources (excluding minerals) to meet the reasonably foreseeable needs of future generations; and

    (b) Safeguarding the life-supporting capacity of air, water, soil, and ecosystems; and

    (c) Avoiding, remedying, or mitigating any adverse effects of activities on the environment.

6. Matters of national importance — In achieving the purpose of this Act, all persons exercising functions and powers under it, in relation to managing the use, development, and protection of natural and physical resources, shall recognise and provide for the following matters of national importance:

    (a) The preservation of the natural character of the coastal environment (including the coastal marine area), wetlands, and lakes and rivers and their margins, and the protection of them from inappropriate subdivision, use, and development;

    (b) The protection of outstanding natural features and landscapes from inappropriate subdivision, use, and development;

    (c) The protection of areas of significant indigenous vegetation and significant habitats of indigenous fauna;

    (d) The maintenance and enhancement of public access to and along the coastal marine area, lakes, and rivers;

    (e) The relationship of Maori and their culture and traditions with their ancestral lands, water, sites, waahi tapu, and other taonga.

7. Other matters — In achieving the purpose of this Act, all persons exercising functions and powers under it, in relation to managing the use, development, and protection of natural and physical resources, shall have particular regard to —

(a) Kaitiakitanga;

(b) The efficient use and development of natural and physical resources;

(c) The maintenance and enhancement of amenity values;

(d) Intrinsic values of ecosystems;

(e) Recognition and protection of the heritage values of sites, buildings, places, or areas;

(f) Maintenance and enhancement of the quality of the environment;

(g) Any finite characteristics of natural and physical resources;

(h) The protection of the habitat of trout and salmon.

8. Treaty of Waitangi — In achieving the purpose of this Act, all persons exercising functions and powers under it, in relation to managing the use, development, and protection of natural and physical resources, shall take into account the principles of the Treaty of Waitangi (Te Tiriti o Waitangi).

INSTITUTE PUBLICATIONS

Following is a complete list of CIRL publications currently available:

Resource Development and Aboriginal Land Rights, by Richard H. Bartlett. 1991. ISBN 0-919269-33-8. 122 p. $25.00

Managing Interjurisdictional Waters in Canada: A Constitutional Analysis, by Steven Alexander Kennett. 1991. ISBN 0-919269-31-1. 238 p. $26.00

Security of Title in Canadian Water Rights, by Alastair R. Lucas. 1990. ISBN 0-919269-22-2. 102 p. $22.00

The Offshore Petroleum Regimes of Canada and Australia, by Constance D. Hunt. 1989. ISBN 0-919269-29-X. 169 p. $14.40

The Inuvialuit Final Agreement, by Janet M. Keeping. 1989. ISBN 0-919269-28-1. 160 p. $14.40

Toxic Water Pollution in Canada: Regulatory Principles for Reduction and Elimination with Emphasis on Canadian Federal and Ontario Law, by Paul Muldoon and Marcia Valiante. 1989. ISBN 0-919269-26-5. 120 p. $22.00

Interjurisdictional Issues in Canadian Water Management, by J. Owen Saunders. 1988. ISBN 0-919269-27-3. 130 p. $22.00

The Framework of Water Rights Legislation in Canada, by David R. Percy. 1988. ISBN 0-919269-21-4. 103 p. $20.00

Maritime Boundaries and Resource Development: Options for the Beaufort Sea, by Donald R. Rothwell. 1988. ISBN 0-919269-24-9. 61 p. $9.00

A Reference Guide to Mining Legislation in Canada (Second Edition), by Barry Barton, Barbara Roulston and Nancy Strantz. 1988. ISBN 0-919269-25-7. 123 p. $18.00

Liability for Drilling- and Production-Source Oil Pollution in the Canadian Offshore, by Christian G. Yoder. Working Paper 12. 1986. ISBN 0-919269-20-6. 84 p. $10.20

A Guide to Appearing Before the Surface Rights Board of Alberta (Second Edition), by Barry Barton and Barbara Roulston. Working Paper 11. 1986. ISBN 0-919269-19-2. 124 p. $10.20

Crown Timber Rights in Alberta, by N.D. Bankes. Working Paper 10. 1986. ISBN 0-919269-17-6. 128 p. $10.20

The Canadian Regulation of Offshore Installations, by Christian G. Yoder. Working Paper 9. 1985. ISBN 0-919269-18-4. 116 p. $10.20

The Assignment and Registration of Crown Mineral Interests, by N.D. Bankes. Working Paper 5. 1985. ISBN 0-919269-11-7. 126 p. $10.20

Oil and Gas Conservation on Canada Lands, by Owen L. Anderson. Working Paper 7. 1985. ISBN 0-919269-16-8. 122 p. $10.20

Canadian Electricity Exports: Legal and Regulatory Issues, by Alastair R. Lucas and J. Owen Saunders. Working Paper 3. 1983. ISBN 0-919269-09-5. 40 p. $5.70

The International Legal Context of Petroleum Operations in Canadian Arctic Waters, by Ian Townsend Gault. Canadian Continental Shelf Law 2; Working Paper 4. 1983. ISBN 0-919269-10-9. 76 p. $5.40

Acid Precipitation in North America: The Case for Transboundary Cooperation, by Douglas M. Johnston and Peter Finkle. 1983. ISBN 0-919269-05-2. 75 p. $6.00

Resources: The Newsletter of the Canadian Institute of Resources Law. ISSN 0714-5918. Quarterly. Free

Annual Report. Free

ESSAYS FROM THE INSTITUTE'S CONFERENCES ON NATURAL RESOURCES LAW

The Legal Challenge of Sustainable Development, Essays from the Fourth Institute Conference on Natural Resources Law, Ottawa, Ontario, May 10-12, 1989. J. Owen Saunders, ed. ISBN 0-919269-32-X. 401 p. (hardcover) $75.00

Trading Canada's Natural Resources, Essays from the Third Institute Conference on Natural Resources Law, Banff, Alberta, May 6-9, 1987. J. Owen Saunders, ed. 367 p. (hardcover) $75.00*

Managing Natural Resources in a Federal State, Essays from the Second Institute Conference on Natural Resources Law, Banff, Alberta, April 17-20, 1985. J. Owen Saunders, ed. 372 p. (hardcover) $70.00*

Public Disposition of Natural Resources, Essays from the First Institute Conference on Natural Resources Law, April 12-15, 1983. Nigel Bankes and J. Owen Saunders, eds. ISBN 0-919269-14-1. 366 p. (hardcover) $28.20

*20% off if you order two or more volumes of Essays from the Institute's Conferences on Natural Resources Law from Carswell. See "Other Publications" section for ordering information.

DISCUSSION PAPERS

Successor Liability for Environmental Damage, by Terry R. Davis. 1989. 46 p. $10.00

Surrounding Circumstances and Custom: Extrinsic Evidence in the Interpretation of Oil and Gas Industry Agreements in Alberta, by David E. Hardy. 1989. 38 p. $10.00

Views on Surface Rights in Alberta, Papers and materials from the Workshop on Surface Rights, Drumheller, 20-21 April 1988. Barry Barton, ed. 77 p. $10.00

Classifying Non-operating Interests in Oil and Gas, by Eugene Kuntz; Presented at a seminar sponsored by the Faculty of Law and the Canadian Institute of Resources Law, The University of Calgary, 7 April 1988. 31 p. $10.00

Publications are available from: Canadian Institute of Resources Law, 430 BioSciences Building, Faculty of Law, The University of Calgary, Calgary, Alberta, Canada T2N 1N4. Telephone (403) 220-3200. Facsimile (403) 282-6182. Telex 03-821545.

Orders from within Canada please add 7% GST. Orders from outside Canada please add $2.00 per book for postage and handling.

OTHER PUBLICATIONS

Canada Energy Law Services.
Canada Energy Law Service: Federal, 2 vols.
Canada Energy Law Service: Alberta, 1 vol.
ISBN 0-88820-108-7.

Available from: Carswell
Thomson Professional Publishing
Corporate Plaza
2075 Kennedy Road
Scarborough, Ontario, Canada
M1T 3V4

For more information call:
Toronto: (416) 609-8000
Ontario and Quebec: 1-800-387-0142
Other provinces: 1-800-387-5164
Fax: (416) 298-5094